Anonymous

Cassell's Illustrated Family Paper Exhibitor

Anonymous

Cassell's Illustrated Family Paper Exhibitor

ISBN/EAN: 9783337321017

Printed in Europe, USA, Canada, Australia, Japan

Cover: Foto ©Thomas Meinert / pixelio.de

More available books at **www.hansebooks.com**

CASSELL'S
ILLUSTRATED EXHIBITOR;

CONTAINING

ABOUT THREE HUNDRED ILLUSTRATIONS,

WITH LETTER-PRESS DESCRIPTIONS

OF

ALL THE PRINCIPAL OBJECTS

IN

THE INTERNATIONAL EXHIBITION
OF 1862.

PREFACE.

—

The Illustrated Exhibitor aims to be a permanent and valuable record of the International Exhibition of 1862. It contains pictures of all the principal objects of interest in the building, many of them taken from photographs, or from drawings furnished by the exhibitors themselves. We have thus, we trust, secured the greatest amount of accuracy in detail combined with general beauty of effect.

The Illustrated Exhibitor will be found both useful and ornamental—a volume sufficiently elegant in appearance to adorn the drawing-room table, and of a character not unfitting it to take its place, among works of reference, in the bookcase or on the shelves of the library. No pains have been spared to render it as complete, and at the same time as interesting, as possible. Irrespective of its engravings—no small or unimportant element of its success—it contains a descriptive account of the rise, progress, and completion of the Exhibition, with views and plans of the building itself, and such remarks as seemed necessary to a fair understanding of the great scheme enunciated in 1850 by the late Prince Consort, and carried forward in 1862 by the Royal Commissioners. We have done our best to produce a book that will pleasantly remind visitors of the glories of the World's Fair at South Kensington, while at the same time it will give to many who were not fortunate enough to witness those glories for themselves, a good notion of the general aspect of the structure and its unequalled contents.

As regards the influence for good attending periodical exhibitions of the world's progress in arts and manufactures there can be no cavil; of the immense social and political importance of these gatherings of the peoples there is no longer any question; of the improvements, inventions, and discoveries that result from the inquiry and competition awakened in the breasts of scholars, manufacturers, and artisans there remains, we believe, no manner of doubt. These questions admitted, there can be no hesitation in also conceding that the publication of a volume like this must result in a large amount of positive benefit to its readers.

LIST OF ILLUSTRATIONS.

INTERNATIONAL EXHIBITION OF 1862.

PRIZE MEDALS TO BRITISH EXHIBITORS

(AWARDED BY THE INTERNATIONAL JURIES.)

CLASS I.—MINING, QUARRYING, METALLURGY, AND MINERAL PRODUCTS.

JURORS WHO WERE EXHIBITORS.

C. Overweg (Dr. Wedding, proxy for Mr. Overweg), Landowner, Zollverein. | Thomas Sopwith, F.R.S., F.G.S., Mining Engineer, Newcastle.
Nicholas Wood, F.G.S., Pres. of Northern Institute of Mining Engineers, Newcastle.

"If Exhibitors accept the office of Jurors, or Associate Jurors or Experts, they cease to be competitors for prizes in the Class to which they are appointed, and these cannot be awarded either to them individually, or to the firms to which they may be partners."—*Decisions regarding Juries, Section 5.*

OFFICIAL AWARDS OF THE JURIES.

The number which precedes the name is that which each Exhibitor occupies in the Official Catalogue. After the name is given a brief description of the articles to which the Prizes have been awarded.

9 Aberdare Iron Co., model of a blast furnace.
14 Bell Brothers, p ocess of aluminium.
28 Bickford, Smith, & Co., safety fuse.
79 Berkey* R., application of minerals to ornament.
79 Blaenavon Iron and Coal Co., iron.
81 Belchow and Vaughan, economy of production.
83 Bowling Iron Co., malleability of ore-iron.
40 Brown and Jeffcock, map of coal in South Yorkshire.
36 Brown, J., and Co., large rolled armour plates.
6 Featherby and Co., smooth iron.
30 Cheesewring Granite Co., granite.
6 Coal Owners of North America and Durham, maps and sections of the Northern coal-field.
68 Courage, A., and Co., process of extracting zinc.
76 Crawshay, H., and Co., flinking shaft of large
Lamorna.
90 Doulton, J., increasing the ventilating power of colliery furnace.
90 Dowlais Iron Co., rolled girders and rails.
91 Easton and Sons, iron.
91 Ebbw Vale and Pontypool Coal, iron of superior
quality.
102 Evans and Askin, nickel and German silver.
101 Farnley Iron Co., iron bent red t.
104 Filgus, G., and Sons, plans of mines.
110 Freeman, W. and J., granulation of Pen y s and
Lamorna.
114 Geological Survey of the United Kingdom, published explanations and descriptions.
127 Governor and Co. of Copper Miners, copper, tin
plate, and iron.
171 Gowean, J., galvanic blasting to quarries.
172 Grant Bro, Karl, fine s echo-ers of minerals.
177 Greaves, J. W., slate-dressing machine.
179 & 190 Greenwell, G. C., specimens and sections of
Somersetshire coal-field.
148 Henderson, J., maps of Cornish mines.
151 Hewlett, A., section of sinkings to bed of tunnel.
157 Higes, R., and Sons, plans of mines.
154 Hird, Dawson, and Hardy, excellence of quality.
156 Holland, S., and Co., quality and skill.
156 Howard, J., monument of fine grained sandstone.
159 Howard, J., illustrative collection of minerals
of Forest of Dean.

160 Howard, Ravenhill, and Co., novelty in the manufacture of bridge links.
171 Johnson, Matthey, & Co., manufacture of platinum.
189 Kirkstall Forge Co., iron of excellent quality.
201 Littlehall Iron C., cold blast-stroke pig iron.
203 Lizard Serpentine Co., Lizar serpentine.
219 Llangollen Slab and Slate Co., largest slab in the
Exhibition.
207 Londonderry, Marchioness of, instructive model
showing arrangements of a coal-shipping harbour.
210 Low y, J W., arrangement of fossils in strata.
214 Martineah J., opening out new quarries of granite
in Aberdeenshire.
216 Merg in The P ate Co., high quality of tin plates.
235 Mercy Br s I i n Co., heavy forgings and taper
toll of iron.
226 Michell, D., model and specimens of tin smelting.
251 Mena Mine Co., copper specimens, illustrating processes of copper smelting.
292 Monk Bridge Iron Co., iron.
236 Mote, Rev T. F., model of lead-mining district in
the Lower Silurian Rocks, Shropshire.
245 Museum of Practical Geology, model showing the
workings in mineral veins.
246 Myles, R., map of the water supply basins of Paris
and London.
248 Newcastle, Duke of, perseverance in opening out a
new coal district.
265 Parkside Mining Co., sections of mines, and specimens.
705 Patent Plumbago Crucible Co., black-lead and fireclay crucible.
267 Pearce, W., Jun., specimens of serpentine.
266 Price, Dr. J. S., collection illustrating manufacture of iron.
296 Quali Iron, T., stones and marbles of Isle of Man.
10 Raw son, Barker, and Co., decomposited lead and slag
of iron.
299 Rhydgyfdir Slate Co., examples of cleavage.
303 Robinson, W., and Co., tin plate and galvanised
sheet iron.

306 Rogers, Ebr., for his native share in developing,
since 1851, the iron ores of the Brendon Hills.
311 Sub Chamber of Commerce, industry conducted on
an extensive scale.
316 S inniclair and H ney, specimens illustrating the
very large works of I on ore furnace.
313 Scottish Ironmasters, iron ores and coal, and pig
iron of Scotland.
322 Sh I ion Bar Iron r e, iron, smelting products, &c.
326 ... W., obelisk of silver grey granite.
340 Smith, r, f r East ridge, coal.
341 Sozeren and L cal t ventures, model of a harbour
and rail ways.
346 Sm ss a Local Comm te, metallurg al products.
350 Taylor Bro bars and t a, wrough, iron.
354 Thomson, Hut n, and Co., tin plate.
378 Turner, Casso s, and Co., excellence of quality.
384 Vivi. G., and Brothers, obelisk of coal measure
sandstone.
383 Vivian and Clogau Copper Mining Co., working of
a gold-bearing vein.
394 Westdale Iron Co., pig iron.
393 Welsh Slate Co., extra cut-on of slates.
410 Winshaven's Patent Metal Foil Co., cut lead.
412 Wombwell Main Coal Co., coal and Lincolnshire
iron ore.
423 Woo league and Jeffcock, model showing long-wall
mode of working.
444 Wright, S., green slate from Borrowdale.
431 Varigless Iron Co., or beauty of production of
an hematite iron and tin plate.

In this Class there were also awarded the following
number of medals to Exhibitors f om the several places
mentioned:—Cornda, 17; India, 8; Jamaica, 1; Natal,
1; New Brunswick, 1; Newfound and, 1; New South
Wales, 0; New Zealand, 4; Nova Scotia, 4; South
Australia, 4; Tasmania, 4; Trinidad, 1; Vancouver, 1;
Victoria, 34; Austria, 3; Bavaria, 3; Belgium, 18;
Brazil, 1; Denmark, 1; France, 34; Greece, 2; Hanover, 1; Rome, Grand Duchy, 1; Italy, 21; Nassau, 2;
Netherlands, 1; Portugal, 6; Prussia, 36;
Russia, 14; Spain, 7; Sweden, 20; Switzerland, 1;
United States, 1.

CLASS II.—CHEMICAL SUBSTANCES AND PRODUCTS, AND PHARMACEUTICAL PROCESSES.

JURORS WHO WERE EXHIBITORS.

M. Kuhehn, Ph.D., Manufacturer, Berlin, Zollverein.
James Young, F.R.S.E., F.C.S., Chemical Manufacturer, Edinburgh.

G. J. Mesier, Chemical Manufacturer, France.

Daniel Hanbury, F.L.S., Sec., Pharmaceutical Chemist, London.
T. N. R. Morson, F.L.S., Pharmaceutical Chemist, London.

SECTION A.—CHEMICAL PRODUCTS.

460 Albright and Wilson, amorphous phosphorus.
461 Allhusen, C. and Sons, manufacturer of soda.
462 Allen, F., production of aniline.
464 Bailey, J., colours for porcelain and glass.
465 Bailey, W., and Son, specimens of chemicals.
473 Bell, I. L., sodium, aluminium, & exhibitorale of lead.
471 Berger, S., and Co., rice starch.
473 Blundell, Spence, and Co., pigments for painting.
482 Bowditch, Rev. W. R., invention for removing bisulphide of carbon from coal gas.
484 Bramwell & Co., red and yellow prussiate of potash.
480 Brodie, B. C., disintegrating and purifying graphite.
487 Broomhall, J., starch.
483 Bryant & May, lucifer matches without phosphorus.
485 Chance Brothers and Co., soda products, &c.
490 Colman, J. and J., starch.
500 Coudy, H. B., manganates and permanganates.
502 Cox and Gould, substances obtained by distillation of wool.
— Crookes, W., discovery of a new element (thallium).
510 Direck, R. O., collection of aniline colours.
518 Foot, C., and Co., acetic and nitric acids.
520 Gaskel, Deacon, and Co., soda compounds.
523 Hallett, G., and Co., antimony white, for painting in place of white lead.
524 Hare, J., and Co., pure colours.
520 Holliday, R., derivatives of benzol and tar products.
550 Hopkin and Williams, chemical products.
555 Hurlet and Campsie Alum Co., manufacture of alum from alum-schist, and red and yellow prussiate of potash.
557 Hutchinson and Davie, raw materials used in manufacture of soda.
539 James, E., starch from rice, and bleached.
540 Jarrow Chemical Co., manufacture of soda.
511 Johnson and Sons, lunar caustic.
542 Johnson, W. W. and R., and Sons, Dutch process for manufacturing white lead.
545 Jones, O., and Co., rice starch.
548 Kane, W. J., chemical products.
565 Marshall, J., Sons and Co., dyes from lichens.

466 Mellners then Chemical Co., acetates.
567 Metropolitan Alum Works, ammonia alum in manufacture of gas.
563 Miller, G., and Co., products obtained by distillation of coal.
671 Muspratt Brothers & Huntley, manufacture of soda.
— Muspratt, James, and Sons, manufacture of soda.
— Muspratt, Fred., manufacture of soda.
573 Newman, J., artists' colours.
578 Patent Plumbago Crucible Co., articles exhibited
581 Perkin and Sons, aniline for the purposes of dyeing
592 Pincoff and Co., extracting the colouring principle from madder root.
584 Rea, J., varnishes.
581 Reckitt, J., and Son, starch.
580 Reeves and Son, pigments used by artists.
585 Roberts, Dale, and Co., caustic soda.
591 Rowney and Co., artists' colours.
592 Rumney, R., dyeing and printing.
587 Sands, G., bone-oil fit for burning.
598 Shanks, J., process for generating chlorine.
600 Simpson, Maule, and Nicholson, aniline, rosaniline, chrysaniline, and compounds for transformation of coal into aniline colours.
601 Smith, R., and Sons, acetic and sugar of lead, with the lichens used.
2963 Smith, J.L., apparatus for absorbing carbonic acid from expired air.
605 Spence, P., manufacture of alum.
607 Stanford, K. C. C., products from seaweed.
605 Stenhouse, J., organic substances chiefly in combination.
602 Still and Fry, starch from rice and wheat.
612 Tudor, E., and W., manufacture of white lead by the Dutch method.
613 Vennables, F., tungstate of soda, for rendering fabrics uninflammable.
611 Vincent, C. W., composition employed for machine printing of chromo-lithographs.
613 Walker, Alkali Co., carbonate and hyposul, bite of soda.
616 Wallis, G. and T., resins, oils, varnishes, &c.

639 Ward, J., and Co., iodine and salts from kelp.
613 Ward, E. O., separating vegetable and animal in gredients from fibrous tissue.
620 Whistle, H., elastic vehicle for printing tissue.
621 Wylie, J. and J., preparation of potash.
624 Wilkinson, Heywood, and Clarke, oxydised oil.
672 Wilson, J., and Sons, alum from alum schist.
627 Winsor and Newton, artists' colours.
6,8 Wood and Bedford, oil and dyes from lichens.
630 Wotherspoon, W., starch from sago flour.

SECTION B.—MEDICAL AND PHARMACEUTICAL PRODUCTS AND PROCESSES.

CLASS III.—SUBSTANCES USED FOR FOOD.

JURORS WHO WERE EXHIBITORS.

Elsner Von Gronow, of the Royal Board of Agriculture, Kalinowitz, Zollverein.
Ch. Woollton, Joint Secretary, Hop Merchant, London.

A. Campbell, M.D., Superintendent at Darjeeling, India.
Robert Schlumberger, Member of the Chamber of Commerce, Vienna, Austria.

SECTION A.—AGRICULTURAL PRODUCE.

737 Abbot and Thomas Taylor, hops.
700 Addiss, T. K., flour made by Callard's process.
705 Butler and M'Culloch, dried culinary herbs.
707 Carter and Co., seeds, flowers, and floral designs.
708 Chambers, W. T., cereals.
710 Christie, W., wheaten flour.
709 Darnley, Earl, hops.
711 Davis, E. J., hay and other forage.
718 Kitchen, J., pocket of Golding hops.
719 Liverpool Committee, imports and their appliances.
722 Paine, Caroline, pocket of Farnham hops.
735 Raynbird, Caldecott, and Bawtree, seed corn.
726 Robinson, Bellville, and Co., patent barley and groats.
726 Wellsman, J., oats.

In this Section there were also awarded the following number of medals to Exhibitors from the several places mentioned:—Barbadoes 3; British Honduras, 1; Canada, 17; Ceylon, 1; India, 2; Jamaica, 1; Malta, 1; Natal, 1; New Brunswick, 1; Newfoundland, 1; New South Wales, 5; Nova Scotia, 1; New Zealand, 1; Prince Edward's Island, 1; South Australia, 6; Queensland, 1; Tasmania, 6; Trinidad, 1; Vancouver, 1; Victoria, 26; Western Australia, 9; Austria, 20; Baden, 1; Bavaria, 3; Belgium, 12; Brazil, 3; Bremen, 1; China, 1; Cochin China, 1; Denmark, 8; Egypt, 1; France, 87; Algeria, 31; French Guiana, 2; French Indies, 1; Guadaloupe, 1; La Réunion, 2; Martinique, 1; Greece, 9; Hesse, Grand Duchy, 1; Italy, 17; Netherlands, 4; Norway, 8; Portugal, 31; Prussia, 19; Russia, 89; Spain, 27; Sweden, 8; Turkey, 6; United States, 2; Uruguay, 1; Venezuela, 1; West Coast of Africa, 2; Würtemberg, 1.

SECTION B—DISTILLERY, GROCERY, AND PREPARATIONS OF FOOD AS SOLD FOR CONSUMPTION.

793 Anderson, Orr, and Co., sugar.
798 Bailey, Morgan, and Co., jams and bottled fruits.
794 Batty and Co., pickles and preserved fruits.

763 Heli, Duncan, and Scott, sugar.
763 Blair, Reed, and Steele, sugar.
706 Colman, J. and J., mustard.
773 Duncan, A., M. E., and Co., preserved oysters and other foods.
782 Fortnum, Mason, and Co., preserved fruits.
786 Fry, J. S., and Sons, cocoa.
783 Garrard, J. T., hams and bacon.
763 Greenock Sugar Refining Co., sugar.
810 Nall and Boyd, sugar.
798 Huntley and Palmer, biscuits.
791 Jones, R., and Trethkink, P. M., canned raw meat.
796 Keiller, J., and Son, marmalade and confectionery.
810 Marchment, D., and Sons, sugar refining.
801 M'Call and Stephen, biscuits.
802 M'Call, J., and Co., preserved provisions.
806 Mackie, J. W., biscuits.
807 Makepeace, J., preserved meats.
815 Morris, J. T., preserved provisions.
816 Partridge, E., pickles.
817 Peek, Frean, and Co., biscuits.
821 Schweling and Co., confectionery.
810 Smith, G., and Co., ditto and telegram.
837 Stance, J., coffee.
810 Swanshorough, W., and Co., sugar.
828 Thomas, E., flowers in sugar.
830 Tobler, J., nougats.
897 Wotherspoon, J., and Co., confectionery and jams.
858 Wotherspoon, R., and Co., confectionery.

In this Section there were also awarded the following number of medals to Exhibitors from the several places mentioned:— Barbadoes, 1; Bremen, 1; British Guiana, 5; Canada, 7; Cape, 1; India, 55; Jamaica, 4; Malta, 1; Mauritius, 3; Natal, 1; New Brunswick, 1; Newfoundland, 2; New South Wales, 4; Nova Scotia, 1; Prince Edward's Island, 2; Queensland, 1; St. Vincent, 3; Tasmania, 3; Trinidad, 1; Victoria, 3; Austria, 85; Baden, 1; Bavaria, 3; Belgium, 15; Denmark, 6; France, 47; Algeria, 14; Nova Scotia, 1; Greece, 9; Hanover, 1; Hesse, Grand Duchy, 1; Italy, 27; Nassau, 1; Netherlands, 4; Norway, 2; Portugal, 31; Prussia, 9; Russia, 18; Saxony, 1; Spain, 12; Sweden, 2; Turkey, 8; Würtemberg, 4.

CLASS IV.—ANIMAL AND VEGETABLE SUBSTANCES USED IN MANUFACTURE.

JURORS WHO WERE EXHIBITORS.

W. W. Williams, Soap Maker, London.
L. A. Godchey, Chemical Manufacturer, France.
Robert Guichard, Landowner, Austria.
J. Jowitt, Wool Merchant, Queensland.

Robert Fanshawe, Hard Wood Merchant, London.
Soza, Peter, Purifier of Perfumes, France.
Eugene Rimmel, Perfumer, London.

SECTION A.—OILS, FATS, AND WAX, AND THEIR PRODUCTS.

910 Barclay and Sons, wax and wax candles.
916 Cook, E. C., and Co., soaps.

917 Cowan and Sons, soaps.
918 Field, J. C., and Co., paraffine candles.
920 Gossage, W., and Sons, silicated soaps.
923 Knevett and Austin, orchids and creepers.

924 Knight, J., and Sons, yellow soap.
925 Lambert, E. B., bath of wild flowers.
926 Langton, Bicknell, and Sons, spermaceti.
920 Mackwan, W., yellow and curd soaps.

916 Oglesby, C., and Co., paraffine and stearine candles.
928 Pierson, J., group of roses.
942 Rose, W. A., lubricating oils and compounds.
947 Rowe, T. H., and Co. soaps.
946 Symons, Mrs., roses, lilies, &c.
947 Taylor, W., and Co., composite candles.
948 Trewolla, Mrs. B., modelling of flowers.
949 Tucker, E., and Co., wax and church candles.
950 West of England Soap Co., brown oil soaps.

In this Section there were also awarded the following number of medals to Exhibit rs from the several places mentioned:—Barbadoes, 1; British Guiana, 2; Nova Scotia, 1; Queensland, 2; Victoria, 1; Austria, 10; Belgium, 5; Brazil, 2; Denmark, 2; France, 22; New Caledonia, 1; Western Africa, 1; Greece, 2. Hesse, Grand Duchy, 1; Ionian Islands, 1; Italy, 9; Liberia, 1; Netherlands, 5; Portugal, 8; Prussia, 9; Rome, 1; Russia, 3; S. ain, 8; Sweden, 7; Turkey, 1; United States, 7; Württemberg, 1.

SECTION B.—OTHER ANIMAL SUBSTANCES USED IN MANUFACTURES.

872 Cantor and Co., Turkey sponges.
875 Darney, J., and Sons, glues.
1020 Famili-rov, R., and Sons, rare ivories.
970 Fenton, M., work in ivory.
989 Heinrich, J., tortoise-shell combs.
989 Jaques, J., and Son, inlaid balls and chessmen.
990 Jewesbury, H. W., and Co., cochineal.
999 Moore, W. S., stained brush handles.
1004 Prockter and Bevington, glues.
1005 Puckridge, F., gold-beaters' skin.
1007 Royal Agricultural Society:—
— Carrol, wool.
— Dennt, Joseph, Oxford down fleeces.
— Finlay, Alexander, M.P., South Down fleeces
— Garne, Robert, Cotswold fleeces.
— Greetham, Thomas, Lincoln fleeces.
— Harris, T., Leicester fleeces.
— Harris, T., cross bred fleeces.
— Heyzate, Mr F., quality of wool.
— Hope, George, Cheviot washed fleece
— Hunter, James W., South Down and Leicester cross fleeces.
— Meve, O., Kent fleeces.
— Radnor, Lord, South Down fleeces
— Rintoul, A., Cheviot and Leicester cross fleeces.
— Rodwell, Down and Leicester fleeces.
— Sandbach, H. B., Shropshire Down fleeces.
— Sturgeon, Charles, merino fleeces
— Tweeddale, Marquis of, Highland washed fleeces
1015 Stewart, R. S., and Co., real and imitation tortoise-shell.

In this Section there were also awarded the following number of medals to Exhibitors from the several places mentioned:—Bahamas, 2; Friendly Islands, 1; India, 1; Natal, 2; New South Wales, 12; New Zealand, 4; Queensland, 3; South Australia, 4; Tasmania, 5; Victoria, 26; Austria, 19; Belgium, 2; Brazil, 1; China, 1; Denmark, 1; Dutch Colonies, 1; France, 29; Algeria, 27; French Colonies, 1; French Guiana, 1; New Caledonia, 1; Frankfort, 1; Greece, 2; Hamburg, 1; Hesse Grand Duchy, 2; Ionian Islands, 1; Netherlands, 2; Peru, 1; Portugal, 8; Prussia, 11; Russia, 10; Saxony, 1; Spain, 3; Sweden, 3; Tahiti, 1; United States, 1; Uruguay, 2.

SECTION C.—VEGETABLE SUBSTANCES USED IN MANUFACTURES, &C.

1071 Azava Patent Hair Co., imitation horse hair.
1036 Aldred, T., bows and arrows (archery)
1057 Anderson, R., salmon flies.
5642 Baylis, W. M., artistic carvings in wood.
1989 Bazin, Q., artificial bait.
1049 Beke, W. L., trout flies and rods.
1041 Bernard, J., fishing tackle.
5674 Bryer, W., artistic carvings in wool.
914 Cattell, Dr., gutta percha purified and decolourised.
1047 Chevalier, Downes, and Son, fishing tackle.
1024 Coles, W. F., cork lining of boots and shoes.
1035 Collyer, Dr., half stuff for paper.
1154 Creasy, T. S., corks made by machinery.
1061 Duffield, J., dairy utensils.
1067 Farlow, C., fishing rods and tackle.
1070 Fauntleroy, R., and Sons, hard woods.
1077 Gowland and Co., rods and tackle.
1028 Gutta Percha Co., articles in gutta percha
1060 Hawes, J., plants, &c., anatomised.
1068 Howard, A., blocks for making ladies' hats and bonnets.
1092 Jones and Co., salmon rods, flies, and other tackle.
5763 Kendall, T. H., artistic wood carvings.
— Liverpool Committee (to Mr. Chas. Spence), gutta percha purified and decolourised.
1101 Meersham, C., and Co., air and waterproof textures.
1103 Mackay, A., fancy wicker work.
1104 Mason, G., flax and silk cultivated at Yately, Hants.
1103 Meyers, B., canes and walking-sticks.
1106 North British Rubber Co., vulcanised India rubber.
1112 Parkes, A., "parkesine."
1926 Perreaux and Co., rubber pump valves.
6796 Perry, W., artistic carvings in wool.
1119 Robertson, A., turned packages of wood.
5692 Ragers, J. A., artistic carvings in wood.
1121 Scottish Vulcanite Co., manufactures in vulcanite.
1128 Silver, S. W., and Co., ebonite.

1130 Smith, W., and A., Scottish fancy wood work.
1151 Spill, G., and Co., vegetable leather.
1186 Taylor, Harry, and Co., hemptallcon.
1127 Taylor, R., vegetable ivory.
1130 Treloar, T., coir matting and application of coir fibre.
5843 Tudsbury, R. J., carvings in lime wood.
1011 Walker and Steambridge, guns and resins.
5649 Wallis, T. W., carvings in wood from nature.
1146 Warne, W., and Co., ferruginous caoutchouc.
1157 Wright, Joseph, tying of salmon and trout flies.

In this Section there were also awarded the following number of medals to Exhibitors from the several places mentioned:—Bahamas, 1; Barbadoes, 1; Bermuda 4; British Columbia, 1; British Guiana, 17; Canada, 14; Cape of Good Hope, 1; Ceylon, 7; Dominica, 1; India, 65; Jamaica, 7; Malta, 2; Mauritius, 3; Natal, 7; New Brunswick, 4; New South Wales, 21; New Zealand, 22; Nova Scotia, 5; Prince Edward's Island, 1; Queensland, 10; South Australia, 2; St. Helena, 1; Tasmania, 11; Trinidad, 4; Vancouver's Island, 1; Victoria, 19; Western Australia, 10; Austria, 84; Bavaria, 3; Belgium, 11; Brazil, 13; Bremen, 1; China, 2; Costa Rica, 1; Denmark, 10; Egypt, 1; France, 36; Algeria, 45; French Guiana, 8; French Indies, 4; Guadeloupe, 7; La Réunion, 4; Martinique, 2; Mayotte and Nossi-Bé, 1; New Caledonia, 3; Ste. Marie de Madagascar, 1; West Africa, 3; Baden, 2; Greece, 16; Hanover, 3; Hamburg, 6; Hayti, 3; Hesse, Grand Duchy, 3; Ionian Islands, 2; Italy, 42; Liberia, 1; Madagascar, 1; Netherlands, 7; Norway, 8; Oldenburg, 1; Peru, 1; Portugal, 19; Prussia, 9; Russia, 30; Saxony, 4; Spain, 13; Sweden, 8; Switzerland, 5; Tahiti, 2; Turkey, 27; United States, 2; Uruguay, 2; Venezuela, 1; Würtemberg, 1.

SECTION D.—PERFUMERY.

1163 Atkinson, J., and E., perfumery.
1164 Bayley and Co., essence bouquet.
1165 Bemhow and Son, toilet soap.
1168 Cleaver, F. S., toilet soaps.
1162 Low, J., purified fat
635 Holland, W., essential oils.
1177 Lewis, J., perfumery.
1179 Low, R., Son and Co., toilet soaps.
1181 Pears, A. and F., transparent soap.
1193 Yardley and Statham, toilet soap.

In this Section there were also awarded the following number of medals to Exhibitors from the several places mentioned:—India, 4; New South Wales, 1; Victoria, 1; Belgium, 2; Brazil, 1; France, 11; Algeria, 2; La Réunion, 4; Frankfort, 1; Italy, 3; Portugal, 1; Prussia, 5; Saxony, 1; Spain, 1; Sweden, 2; Turkey, 2; United States, 1; Würtemberg, 1.

CLASS V.—RAILWAY PLANT, INCLUDING LOCOMOTIVE ENGINES AND CARRIAGES.

JUROR WHO WAS AN EXHIBITOR.

J. E. M'Connell, late Locomotive Superintendent of the London and North Western Railway Company.

1221 Ashbury, J., construction of a railway goods wagon.
1236 Bateman, F. S., preventing the spheroidal action of heated water in a tube.
— Beattie J., economy of water on railway wheels.
1238 Bruyer, Peacock, and Co., engine and tender.
1240 Brown, G., and J., and Co., solid wrought iron tires.
1252 Fay, C., break on railway carriages.

— Gibson, J., securing tires on railway wheels.
1241 Kitchin, R., weighing machines.
1274 Manning, Wardle, and Co., colliery locomotive engine.
— Maxwell, securing tires on wheels.
6118 Naylor, Vickers, and Co., cast steel tires and wheels.
1241 Newall, J., breaks on railway carriages.
1296 Pooley, H., and Son, weighing machines.

1239 Ramsbottom, J., locomotive engine, apparatus for supplying water to tenders, and a duplex safety valve.
1203 Sharp, Stewart, and Co., locomotive engine.
1110 Wright, J., and Sons, tram-car carriage.
In this Class there were also awarded the following number of medals to Exhibitors from the several places mentioned:—Canada, 1; Austria, 3; Belgium, 3; France, 6; Italy, 1; Prussia, 5; Saxony, 1; Sweden, 1.

CLASS VI.—CARRIAGES NOT CONNECTED WITH RAIL OR TRAM ROADS.

JURORS WHO WERE EXHIBITORS.

H. Holmes, Coach Builder, Derby.
J. W. Peters, Coach Builder, London.
George N. Hooper, Sec., Coach Builder, London.

1386 Adams, J., light landau
1363 Booker and Sons, sociable.
1366 Braby, J., and Son, wagon.
1366 Hopps, G. and B., double brougham.
1364 Corben and J. Parlour.
1364 Cole, W., double brougham.
1366 Cook and Holloway, light landau.
1904 Edwards, Son, and Churchill, landau.
1374 Hall and Sons, barouche.
1878 Haseldine, G., road van.

1387 Holroyd, Nolde, and Collier, wheels and fancy carriage panels.
1394 Hutton, J., and Sons, brougham.
1997 M'Naught and Smith, waggonette, with inclosure.
1400 Mason, W. H., waggonette, with inclosure.
1415 Rigby and Robinson, landau.
1420 Rock and Son, dormphia, with inclosure.
1436 Shanks, H. H. and F., landau.
1431 Silk and Sons, landau.
1443 Thrupp and Maberly, light coach.

1414 Turrill, H. L., private Hansom cab.
1448 Ward, J., invalid chair.
1452 Woodall and Son, coach of good form.
1461 Wyburn and Co., landau.

In this Class there were also awarded the following number of medals to Exhibitors from the several places mentioned:—Belgium, 1; France, 3; Hesse, Grand Duchy, 1; Netherlands, 1; Prussia, 1; Russia, 2; United States, 1.

CLASS VII.—MANUFACTURING MACHINES AND TOOLS.

JUROR WHO WAS AN EXHIBITOR.

J. Whitworth, F.R.S., Engineer, Manchester.

SECTION A.—MACHINERY EMPLOYED IN SPINNING AND WEAVING, &C.

1443 Anderston Foundry Co., fancy looms.
1467 Apperly, J., and Co., feeding apparatus for woollen carding machines.
1491 Combe, J., and Co., expanding reed.
1497 Dickenson, W., and Sons, application to their loom of Taylor's patent crank arm.
1499 Dobson and Barlow, carding engines.

1502 Ferrabee, J., and Co., apparatus for forming bats of fleece and for fulling cloth.
1709 Hattersley, C., and Son, looms for fancy goods.
1511 Hetherington and Sons, carding machine.
1513 Higgin, W., and Sons, roving and slubbing frames.
1515 Hodgson, G., looms.
1522 Mason, J., self-acting woollen mule.
1526 Parker, C., and Sons, self cloth loom.

1528 Platt, Brothers, cotton gins.
1531 Rowan, J., and Sons, flax scutching machine.
1532 Sharp, Stewart, and Co., self-acting reel winding machine.
1535 Smith, W., and Brothers, woollen loom for weaving cloth two yards wide.
1537 Tuer and Hall, cotton loom.
In this Section there were also awarded the following number of medals to Exhibitors from the several places

b

mentioned; Belgium, 3; France, 10; Italy, 2; Saxony, 1. Switzerland, 1; United States, 3.

SECTION B.—MACHINES AND TOOLS EMPLOYED IN THE MANUFACTURE OF WOOD AND METAL.

1790 Bernoll, 3., aërated water apparatus.
1656 Bertram, G. paper-making machine.
1657 Beyer, Peacock, and Co. machines for working metal.
1341 Bradley and Craven, brick-making machine.
1370 Clayton, H. and Co., brick machinery.
1384 De Bergue, C., and Co., riveting and punching machine.
1585 Donkin, B., paper machine.
1594 Fairbairn, P., and Co., series of machines for working metals.
1855 Forrester, G., and Co., sugar pan apparatus.
1699 Garside, H., electric engraving machine.
1610 Greenwood and Batley, ingenious machines.
1874 Handyside, A., and Co., hop machinery.
1421 Holtzapffel, L., and Co., turning lathes.
1425 Hulse, J. S., machines for cutting metal

1632 Johnson and Atkinson, apparatus for type-casting and finishing.
1649 Lockett, J., Sons, and Leake, engraving machine.
1924 Mulore, Abbott, and Co., sugar and laundry machinery.
1057 Mathieson, A., and Son, hand tools.
1921 M'Onie, W. and A., sugar mill
1982 Mirrlees and Tait, sugar-cane crushing apparatus.
1682 Mitchell, W. H., type composing and distributing machines.

1670 Naesmyth and Co., dividing apparatus.
1946 Normandy and Co., apparatus for the distillation of salt-water.
1688 Powis, James, and Co., machinery for working wood, and a steam engine.
1695 Robinson, T., and Son, wood-working machines.
1979 Samuelson, M. and Co., linseed-oil making machine.

1705 Shepherd, Hill, and Co., machinery for cutting metal.
1784 Slate, D., lee-making machine.
1707 Siemens, Halske, and Co., telegraph-wire covering
1715 Smith, Beacock, and Tannett, machinery for working metals.
1792 Smith, J., and Son, wire cylinder.
1732 Vicars, T. and T., and Co., bread and biscuit machinery.
1784 Waterlow and Sons, railway ticket printing and numbering machine.
2204 Whitehead, brick machinery.
1745 Worssam and Co., wood-working machines.
1714 Yates, W. S., hinotic suting machine.
1731 Youngman, C. T., paper bag-making machine.

CLASS VIII.—MACHINERY IN GENERAL.
JURORS WHO WERE EXHIBITORS.

L. R. Bodmer, Consulting Engineer, Switzerland.

1782 Allen, Harrison, and Co., fittings for steam-engine.
1753 Armstrong, Sir W. G., and Co., water pressure engine, crane, &c.
1266 Ashton, J. P., steam-engine and hoist.
1772 Beattie, J. U., chain pump.
18 3 Bowser and Cameron, Derrick crane.
1805 Bray's Traction Engine Co., traction engine.
1806 Broughton Copper Co., copper and brass work.
1815 Curratt, Marshall, and Co., steam-engines, steam-pump, cranes, &c.
1610 Chaplin and Co., steam crane.
1820 Chudgey, J., grass rollers, pumps, pipes, &c.
1829 Clark, H. E., smoke consumer and feed-water heater.
7296 Clarke, E., fire-escape.
1824 Clayton, Shuttleworth, and Co., steam-engine.
1613 Eadie and Spencer, iron tubes.
1844 Easton, Amos, and Sons, turbine, Appold's centrifugal pump.
1845 Edwards, C. J., and Son, leather bands, hose, and fire-buckets.
1800 Fawcett, Preston, and Co., steam-engine and sugar-mill.
1854 Forrest and Barr, Derrick crane.
2046 Fowke, Capt. F., R.E., fire-engine adapted for military purposes.
1857 Falcoke and Thercolo, salinometers, telegraphs, indicators, &c.
6492 Greaves and Bailey, and Co., machine for testing strength of steel.
1870 Gwynne and Co., double acting centrifugal pump.
1877 Harrison, J., cast-iron boiler.
1990 Harvey and Co., model of pumping engine.

John Penn, C.E., Mechanical Engineer, London.

1591 Humphreys and Tennant, marine engines.
1894 Imperial Iron Tube Co., metal tubes.
1902 Laird, J., Sons, and Co., marine engines.
1933 Lambert, T. and Son, Jo.tlog's water-meter, sluice valves &c.
1910 Lilleshall Co., blast engines.
1815 Lloyd, G., blowing fan.
1933 Manchester Water Meter Co., water meters.
1923 Manistey, Son, and Field, marine engines.
1921 M'Onie, W. and A., 30-horse power steam-engine and sugar-mill in motion.
1923 Merryweather and Son, fire-engines.
1930 Middleton, T., Murray's chain pump.
1932 Mirrlees and Tait, steam-engine and sugar-mill in motion.
1936 Morrison, R., and Co., inverted cylinder vertical engines.
1935 Napier, D., and Son, centrifugal machine for curing sugar, automaton mine-weighing machine.
1909 Napier, R., and Sons, marine engines.
1944 Newton, Keates and Co., copper and brass articles.
1946 Normandy and Co., apparatus for obtaining distilled fresh water from sea water.
1947 North British Rubber Co., driving belts.
1948 North Moor Foundry Co., turbines, steam fans.
1934 Peel, Williams, and Peel, pumps.
1969 Prefier, C. A., antennae of leather driving belts.
1961 Ransomes and Sims, portable steam-engine.
1961 Re-ason, G., and Sons, marine engines.
1969 Roberts, W., fire engines.
1970 Robinson, W., machine for cleaning casks without unheading.

1972 Routledge and Greenway, engines, pumps, boiler feeder, expansion joint for separating iron and brass turn cocks.
1975 Russell, J., and Sons, tubes and fittings.
1978 Salter, G., and Co., spring balances, dynamometers, pressure gauges.
1919 Samuelson, M., and Co., oil mill.
1961 Shand and Mason, fire engines.
1995 Simmon, C. W., register for gas engine, register fire furnace, water meter.
1921 Stephenson Tube Co., seamless metal tubes and rollers.
2041 Taylor, J., and Co., traction engine.
2024 Tangye, James, water-works, fans, pumps.
2347 Thornewill and Warham, winding engines.
1230 Tod and M'Gregor, tire t te engines.
2191 Taxford and Son, traction engine.
2317 Webb and Son, leather driving belts, buckets, hose, &c.
2119 Wenham, J. H., thermo-expansive engine.
2046 Weston, F. A., differential pulley, &c.
2341 Whitmore and Binyon, horizontal steam engine driving corn mill.
2927 Wilson, J. C., steam sugar-cane mill.
2926 Williamson, Brothers, turbine.

In this Class there were also awarded the following number of medals to Exhibitors from the several countries mentioned:—Victoria, 2 ; Austria, 3 ; Baden, 1 ; Germany, 8 ; Hansen, 1 ; France, 39 ; Norway, 3 ; Prussia, 1 ; Saxony, 1 ; Switzerland, 2 ; United States, 25.

CLASS IX.—AGRICULTURAL AND HORTICULTURAL MACHINES AND IMPLEMENTS.
JUROR WHO WAS AN EXHIBITOR.

J. Pintus, Manufacturer, Berlin, Zollverein.

2073 Aveling, J., agricultural locomotive engine.
2074 Bamlett, A., and Co., manual delivery reaper.
2076 Barrett, Exall, and Andrews, thrashing machines and ice-th engines.
— Bell, Reverend P., original reaper.
2079 Burrell, F. H., cattle food machines and root pulpers.
3082 Boby, H., machine for cleaning and separating grain.
1805 Bray's Traction Engine Co., traction engine.
2082 Burgess and Key, reaping and mowing machines.
2092 Childs and Owen, grain separators.
2501 Clayton, Shuttleworth, and Co., steam engines and thrashing machines.
2095 Coleman and Son, cultivator.
2097 Corues, J., chaff-cutters.
2102 Croskill, W. (Trustees of), reaping machines, carts, and bone-crusher.
2115 Fowler J., jun., steam plough and steam cultivator, apparatus generally for applying steam.
2117 Garrett and Son, steam engines and thrashing machines.
2191 Gray, L., and Co., tillage implements.
2122 Green, T., lawn mowing machine.

2124 Hancock, J. and F., and Co., pulverising plough and barrow machine.
2181 Howard, J. and F., ploughs, harrows, rakes, haymaking machines, and a cultivator.
2127 Herson, H., a yeast cart.
2129 Hingman's S ns, thrashing and mowing machines.
2195 Hornsby and Sons, steam engines, thrashing machines, winnowing machines, and ploughs.
2132 Hughes and Son, corn mills.
2137 Hunter, P., chains and dairy utensils.
2147 Kemp, Murray, and Nicholson, reaping and mowing machines.
2141 Kennan and Sons, lawn mowing machines.
2150 Musgrave, Brothers, iron stalls for cattle and horses.
2160 Ormson, H., hot-water tubular boilers.
2165 Priest and Woolnough, turnip, manure, and corn drills.
2168 Ransomes and Sims, steam engines, thrashing machines, corn screens, mills, and ploughs.
2171 Richmond and Chandler, chaff cutters.
2172 Robey and Co., farm engine and thrashing machine.
2173 Ruston, Proctor, and Co., portable steam engine.
2181 Smith, J., and Son, ploughs.

2147 Samks and Sons, lawn mowers.
2193 Smith, W., horse-hoe.
2198 Savory and Sons, draining and sowing machines.
2167 Smyth, W., parsnip machine.
2191 Taylor, J., condensatory and implements.
2201 Turner, E. R. and F., steam engines, thrashing machines, and corn grinders.
2195 Tuxford and Sons, steam engine and corn grinding machines.
2196 Underwood, W. S., improved corn sheller.
2199 Wallis and Haslam, thrashing machines.
2241 Work, J., milk cans, butter-working machines.
2294 Whitehead, J., pipe and tile making machine.
2253 Whitehead, J., drain ware mills.
2257 Yeung, J. and F., drill for mangold worzel and turnip seed.

In this Class there were also awarded the following number of medals to Exhibitors from the several countries mentioned:—Canada, 6 ; New Brunswick, 1 ; East Australia, 1 ; Victoria, 1 ; Austria, 4 ; Belgium, 3 ; Denmark, 1 ; France, 11 ; Italy, 6 ; Norway, 6 ; Switzerland, 1 ; United States, 9 ; Württemberg, 1.

CLASS X.—CIVIL ENGINEERING, ARCHITECTURAL, AND BUILDING CONTRIVANCES.
JURORS WHO WERE EXHIBITORS.

Cesare Valerio, Member of Italian Parliament, Italy.

SECTION A.—CIVIL ENGINEERING AND BUILDING CONTRIVANCES.
2256 Barrett, H., fireproof floor.
2240 Bushell, J., creosoted wood.
2245 Brunel, I., representative of his father, the late I. K. Brunel, F.R.S., models of two bridges.

2255 Clark, E., hydraulic graving dock.
2258 Cowen, J., dome scaffold and traveller.
2268 Cowen, J., and Co., gas mixers, firebricks, &c.
2268 Doulton, H., and Co., stoneware pipes, &c.
2280 Gibson and Turner, station roof.
2290 Gilkes, Wilson, and Co., railway viaduct.

J. W. Bazalgette, C.E., Engineer to Metropolitan Board of Works, London.

2307 Kennedy, Lieut.-Colonel, screw pile for bridges great extent in India.
2316 Macneill, Sir J., F.R.S., bridge over the Boyne.
341 Murray, John, Spadelined docks.
2321 Norman, R. and N., ornamental bricks and tiles.
1361 Ransome, F., block of artificial stone.

:351 Salter, S., model exhibited by C. Vignoles.
:331 Soott, Capt., H. Y D., good and cheap cement.
2003 Stevenson, A., model of Skerryvore lighthouse.
2351 Vignoles, C., model of Hilton railway
3502 Walker, J., rock lighthouses
— White, Brothers, Portland cement

In this Section there were also awarded the following number of medals to Exhibitors from the several places mentioned:—Canada, 2; New South Wales, 2; Victoria, 1; Austria, 8; Bavaria, 1; Belgium, 1; France, 32; Hanover, 1; Italy, 4; Mecklenburg-Schwerin, 1; Netherlands, 1; Norway, 4; Prussia, 7; Russia, 1; Sweden, 1; Switzerland, 1; Würtemberg, 1.

SECTION B. — SANITARY IMPROVEMENTS AND CON-
STRUCTIONS.

2239 Cliff, J., and Son, retorts for gas.
2331 Cookey, E. and Sons, valve for distributing gas.
2381 Finch, J., porcelain bath in one piece.
2291 Glover, G., and Co., apparatus for measuring gas.
2186 Jennings, Co., articles exhibited.
2330 Perkins, A. M., hot water apparatus for heating rooms, &c.
2390 Rosser, S. E., desiccating and warming.

2403 Spence, T., new material for filtering water.
2341 Stephenson, W., and Sons, earthenware gas retorts.
2411 Woolcock, W., stoves and warming apparatus.

In this Section there were also awarded the following number of medals to Exhibitors from the several places mentioned:—Austria, 3; Belgium, 4; France, 6; Hamburg, 1; Russia, 1; Sweden, 3; Switzerland, 1

SECTION C.—OBJECTS SHOWN FOR ARCHITECTURAL
BEAUTY.

2240 Architectural Pottery Co., mosaic, glazed tiles, bricks, &c.
2243 Dale, T. S., mosaic and ornamental floor, wall tiles, and glazed bricks.
2243 Bellman and Ivey, scagliola.
2121 Blanchard, M. H., terra cotta.
4831 Blashfield, J. M., terra cotta and pottery.
6831 Boote, Messrs., tiles and pottery.
2517 Burton, J. and E., Coalbrookdale Co., Davis and Co., Doughty, Evans, R., Exley, W., Jones, G. W., Maddy Wood Co., Maw and Co., Thorn, F. G., collective medal for encaustic tiles.
2425 Ecclesiological Society, wood carvings
2440 Forsyth, J., marble font and cover for Lord Dudley.

2431 Jackson, G., and Sons, carton pierre.
203 Lizard Serpentine Co., works made of serpentine.
204 Llangollen Slab and Slate Co., enamelled slate work and In ge slate slab.
214 Macdonald, A., granite used in building.
2137 McFarlan, W., and Co., iron ceilings.
2403 Magnus, G. E., enamelling slate.
6873 Minton and Co., earthenware, majolica, parian tiles, &c.
203 Pearce, W., jun., inlaid serpentine and steatite tables, columns, &c.
2440 Poole, H., and Son, mosaic and decorative works in stone and marble
2441 Serpentine Marble Co., marble font and pedestals.
2440 Slater (architect), design of exhibits by H. Poole and Son.
2446 Thomas, John, carved chimney piece.
2317 Wyatt, Digby, forms and colours in articles exhibited by G. Maw.

In this Section there were also awarded the following number of medals to Exhibitors from the several places mentioned:—Malta, 2; Austria, 2; Belgium, 4; Denmark, 1; France, 14; Greece, 2; Italy, 2; Netherlands, 2; Prussia, 6; Russia, 3.

CLASS XI.—MILITARY ENGINEERING, ARMOUR AND ACCOUTREMENTS, ORDNANCE AND SMALL ARMS.

JUROR WHO WAS AN EXHIBITOR.

Westley Richards, Rifle Maker, Birmingham.

SECTIONS A AND B.—CLOTHING AND ACCOUTREMENTS, TENTS, CAMP EQUIPAGE, AND MILITARY ENGINEERING.

2505 Adair, Col., model of London and adjacent country.
2325 Department of Inspection of Fortifications and the Royal Engineer Establishment at Chatham.
2571 models of fortifications, barracks, and hospitals.
2551 Ducane, Capt., E. F., R.E., application of iron to fortifications.
2336 Fawke, Capt., R.E., pontoons
2551 James, Col. Sir H., R.E., mode of reducing maps.
2551 Jones, Sergeant-Major, application of sheet iron to gabions &c.
2362 Lovell, Col. G. R., R.E., gun shield.
2390 Royal Medical Department of the War Office, ambulances and other appliances for medical service in the field.
2551 Topographical Department of the War Office, maps.

In these Sections there were also awarded the following number of medals to Exhibitors from the several places mentioned:—France, 4; Spain, 2; Switzerland, 1; Turkey, 1.

SECTION C.—ARMS AND ORDNANCE.

2506 Adams, R., breech-loading small arms.
2510 Blake, F. T., spring guns and rifles.
2519 Birmingham Military Arms Trade, commercial value of products
2511 Blakey, Capt., cast-iron ordnance.
2619 Bland, Capt., phantom target.
2515 Brazier, J., gun-locks and breech-loading actions.
2517 Chevalier, electric target.
2527 Daw, G. H., breech-loading guns and rifles.
2729 Deagull, E. D., breech-loading in guns.
2531 Ebrall, S., guns and rifles.
4109 Elswick Ordnance Co., articles exhibited.
2337 Fox, Lieut.-Col. A. Lane, parabolic theory for range of projectiles in vacuo.
2389 Gibbs, G., guns and rifles.
2541 Gisborne, F. N., electric target.
2540 Gladstone, H. and Co., novelty of invention in Captain Hayes' seamless skin cartridges.
2042 Greener, J., locks.
2551 Lancaster, C. W., rifles and cannons.
2558 Lang, J., fowling-pieces.

2561 London Armoury Co., rifles and revolver pistols.
2565 Manton, John, and Sons, guns and rifles.
2569 Mont-Storm, Wm., converting Enfield rifle into breech-loader.
2600 Royal Carriage Department, Woolwich, articles exhibited.
2601 Royal Gun Factories, Woolwich, articles exhibited.
2601 Royal Laboratory, Woolwich, articles exhibited.
2603 Royal Small Arms Factory, Enfield, articles exhibited.
2722 Sharpe, D., pendulum for obtaining correct inclination of ship's deck;
2612 Whitworth Rifle and Ordnance Co., guns and rifles.
2613 Wilkinson and Son, swords, rifles, and fowling-pieces.

In this Section there were also awarded the following number of medals to Exhibitors from the several places mentioned:—Austria, 1; Bavaria, 1; Belgium, 7; Brazil, 1; France, 11; Italy, 6; Prussia, 5; Russia, 8; Spain, 2; Sweden, 2; Switzerland, 3; Turkey, 2; United States, 1.

CLASS XII.—NAVAL ARCHITECTURE, INCLUDING SHIPS' TACKLE.

JURORS WHO WERE EXHIBITORS.

J. D'A. Samuda, Ship Builder, London.

H. D. Cunningham, F.R.G.S., Portsmouth.

SECTION A.—SHIPS FOR PURPOSES OF WAR OR COMMERCE.

2711 Coles, Captain C., R.N., revolving cupolas.
2529 Denny, Brothers, W., sectional model of screw steamer.
2051 Gray, J. W., and Son, ships' fittings.
2584 Griffiths, R., screw propellers.
2548 Hornsey, W., telegraphs and gongs for steam vessels.
2630 J. Jones, Jun., protection of ships of war.
3035 Elsakbir, drawing of the Persia.
2586 Laird, J., jun., and Co. of Iron Ship Building Co., models of the North-Eastern and Himalaya.
2537 Pierey, G., Admiralty Modeller, model of Victoria and Albert.
2710 Rennie, G., and Son, floating dock.

2719 Russell, J. S., naval architecture.
2725 Thames Iron Works and Ship Building Co., models of steam vessels.
2750 Thompson, D., machinery for building boats.

In this Section there were also awarded the following number of medals to Exhibitors from the several places mentioned:—Austria, 1; Denmark, 1; France, 1; Russia, 1; United States, 1.

SECTION B AND C.—LIFE BOATS, BARGES, AND VESSELS FOR AMUSEMENT, AND SHIPS' TACKLE AND RIGGING.

2779 Brown, Lennox, and Co., ships' cables and anchors.
2751 Davis and Co. fluid compass.
2757 Halkett, P. A., portable boat for exploring expeditions.
2783 Herbert, G., Leacon & co.
2817 Lords Commissioners of the Admiralty, compasses.

2815 Lords of the Admiralty, diffusion of their charts.
2793 Martin, C., a clear.
2755 Parkes, H. P., chain cables and chain work.
2756 Peace b. G., refuge buoy boat &c.
2756 Royal National Life Boat Institution, boat combining the qualities of a life boat, and good transport lug carriage.
2757 Searle, E., racing boats for lakes and rivers.
1710 Siebbald, Melame, chain cables.
2512 West, J. G., and Co., liquid compasses.
2514 Wood, Brothers, and Co., chain cables and chain work.

In this Section there were also awarded the following number of medals to Exhibitors from the several places mentioned:—New South Wales, 1; New Zealand, 1; Nova Scotia, 1; Tasmania, 1; Denmark, 1; France, 6; Norway, 3; Russia, 2; United States, 1.

CLASS XIII.—PHILOSOPHICAL INSTRUMENTS AND PROCESSES DEPENDING ON THEIR USE.

JUROR WHO WAS AN EXHIBITOR.

C. Wheatstone, F.R.S., Deputy Chairman, Professor of Experimental Philosophy, King's College, London.

2446 Adie, P., sextants, telemeter, &c.
2440 Alfred, T., apparatus relay and telegraphic apparatus.
— Babbage, c. calculating machine.
2836 Beale, Prof., animal tissues for microscopic observation.
— Beckly, registering anemometer.
2857 Bennison & Frond, chronometer apparatus in platinum.
2864 British and Irish Magnetic Telegraph Co., telegraphic apparatus.
2807 Buckingham, J., 6-inch object glass.
2871 Butters, T. E., parallel glass for optical instruments.
2874 Cowells, L. P., minimum thermometer.
2876 Chance, Bros., electric lights and optical glass.
2801 Commissioners of Northern Lights, reflectors for lighthouses.
2580 Cooke, T., and Sons, equatorial telescopes.

2859 Dallmeyer, J. H., equatorial telescopes.
2880 Darker, J. H., microscopes and microscopic photographs.
2899 Darker, W. H., crystals for investigations in physical optics.
2892 De Grave, Short, and Fanner, balances.
2895 De la Rue, W., astronomical photographs.
2897 Elliott, Brothers, philosophical instruments.
2899 Field, J. C., apparatus for electric telegraph cables.
2903 Griffin, J. J., apparatus for chemical research.
2903 Grubb, T., large equatorial telescope.
3001 Gutta Percha Co., application of material submarine telegraph cables.
2911 Hicks, J., minimum thermometer.
2912 Highley, S., microscopes.
2914 Holmes, F. H., electro-magnetic light.
2916 Horne and Thornthwaite, hexapteron.

2865 Kew Observatory, instruments for observing terrestrial magnetism.
2922 Kingsley and Son, balances for scientific purposes.
2929 Ladd and De Gong, balances for telescopic purposes.
2923 Ladd, W., stands for microscopes, induction coils.
2930 Negretti and Zambra, meteorological instruments.
2941 Norman, J., microscopic objects.
2944 Pastorelli, F., and Co., levels and surveying instruments.
— Peters, micrometer pantograph.
2743 Pillischer, M., students' microscopes.
2952 Powell and Lealand, object glass.
2953 Ross, T., microscopes and telescopes.
2954 Sax, J., balances for scientific purposes.
2959 Simms, W., and Co., telegraphic apparatus.
2961 Silver, S. W., and Co., conductors insulated with caoutchouc.

2964 Smith, Beck, and Beck, microscopes and optical instruments.
2965 Smyth, C. P., rotatory ship clinometer.
2962 Spencer, Browning, and Co., sextants, quadrants.
2968 Stanley, W. F., mathematical instruments.
2973 Sugg, W., photometric apparatus.

2076 Tree, J., and Co., mathematical scales.
2981 Varley, C. F., telegraphic apparatus.
2985 Woulnam, F. H. binocular microscope.
— White, James, marine galvanometer.
2990 Wilkins & Co., parabolic reflectors for lighthouses.
In this Class there were also awarded the following

number of medals to Exhibitors from the several places mentioned:—Austria, 4; Bavaria, 2; Belgium, 2; France, 25; Hanover, 1; Hesse Cassel, 1; Italy, 3; Netherlands, 1; Portugal, 1; Prussia, 8; Rome, 3; Saxe-Coburg, 1; Saxony, 1; Sweden, 2; Switzerland 3; United States, 1; Würtemberg, 1.

CLASS XIV.—PHOTOGRAPHY AND PHOTOGRAPHIC APPARATUS.

JURORS WHO WERE EXHIBITORS.

A. F. J. Claudet, F.R.S., Photographer, London.
C. T. Thompson, Official Photographer, Science and Art Depart., London.

3031 Amateur Photographic Assoc., photographic excellence.
3030 Bedford, F., photographs.
3019 Breese, C. S., views on glass of clouds, waves, &c.
3061 Caldesi, L., photographs of antiquities.
3349 Dallmeyer, J. H., lenses.
2893 De la Rue, W., photography for astronomical science.
3074 Fenton, R., fruit and flower pieces; photography.
— Frith, views in Egypt.
3091 Heath, Vernon, landscape photography.

— Beckley, photographs of spots on the sun.

3101 James, Col. Sir H., R.E., photography.
3117 London Stereoscopic Co., photographic views.
3123 Mayall, J. E., photographic productions.
3127 Mudd, J., landscapes.
3129 Negretti and Zambra, photographic transparencies.
3133 Piper, J. D., pictures in landscape photography.
3136 Ponting, T. C., iodised sensitive collod.on.
3140 Pretsch, P., photographic printing.
3147 Robinson, H. P., photographic manipulation.
3149 Ross, T., photographic lenses.
3150 Rouch, W. W., photographs.
3133 Sidebotham, J., landscape photography.

3167 Talbot, Fox W. H., photographic engravings on copper and steel.
3179 White, H., landscape photography.
3182 Williams, T. R., photography.
3187 Wilson, G. W., pictures of clouds and shipping.
In this Class there were also awarded the following number of medals to Exhibitors from the several places mentioned:—Canada, 1; India, 1; Jersey, 1; New South Wales, 2; Victoria, 4; Austria, 4; Baden, 1; Bavaria, 1; Belgium, 1; France, 37; Greece, 1; Hesse Cassel, 1; Italy, 2; Prussia, 6; Rome, 2; Russia, 1; Saxony, 1.

CLASS XV.—HOROLOGICAL INSTRUMENTS.

JURORS WHO WERE EXHIBITORS.

Charles Frodsham, Sec., Chronometer Maker, London.
E. D. Johnson, Chronometer Maker, London.
Sylvain Mairet, Watchmaker, Locle, Switzerland.

3814 Adams and Sons, productions.
3223 Barraud and Lund, productions.
3216 Bennett, J., watches and clocks.
3227 Blackie, G., chronometers.
3229 Brooks, S. A., watch jewelling.
3335 Cole, J. F., mechanical excellence.
3236 Cole, Ths., taste and design.
3238 Cooke, J., and Sons, turret clock.
3290 Crisp, W. B., marine chronometers.
3742 Delolme, H., clocks and chronometers.
3247 Dent and Co., chronometers and turret clocks.
3244 Dent, M. F., and Co., chronometers and watches.
3293 General and Callard, pendulum, with new balance springs.
3354 Guidbet and Rambal, excellence of work.
3355 Guillaume E. and C., ingenuity in repeaters.

3703 Hewett, S. and J., Prescott Committee, chronometers and watches.
3276 Hinton, J., excellence.
3271 Jackson, W. M. and S., excellence.
3275 Klaftenberger, C. J., excellence and variety.
3276 Kullberg, V., general excellence.
3279 Loseby, J. K., chronometers, astronomical and turret clocks.
3280 M'Lennan, pocket chronometers.
3284 Molyneux, W., Prescott Committee, chronometers.
3284 Moore, B. and J., three clocks.
3289 Moule and Capt, centre seconds and keyless watches.
3291 Parkinson and Frodsham, chronometers, watches.
3285 Pendleton, B., Prescott Committee, chronometers and watches.

3291 Poole, J., chronometers and watches.
3300 Rotherham and Sons, excellence and cheapness.
3293 Saggerson, E., repeating movements, chronometers.
3894 Sewill, J., excellence in watches.
3303 Smith and Sons, turret and house clocks.
3320 Walker, J., watches, railway watches and clocks.
3321 Walsh, A. P., chronometers and watches.
3324 Webster, R., watches.
3745 White, E., watches.
32-5 Wycherley, J., Prescott Committee, chronometers.
In this Class there were also awarded the following number of medals to Exhibitors from the several places mentioned:—Austria, 3; Baden, 3; Denmark, 1; France, 14; Hamburg, 1; Norway, 2; Portugal, 1; Prussia, 4; Saxony, 1; Sweden, 2; Switzerland, 21; Würtemberg, 1.

CLASS XVI.—MUSICAL INSTRUMENTS.

JUROR WHO WAS AN EXHIBITOR.

J. Schiedmayer, Musical Instrument Maker, Zoffingen.

3044 Besson, F., brass wind instruments.
3406 Bevington and Sons, organs.
3463 Boosey and Ching, harmoniums.
3306 Boosey and Sons, Praxten's flute.
3570 Brinsmead, J., piano.
3573 Broadwood and Sons, piano.
3575 Cadby, C., piano.
3577 Challen, C., and Son, tone in piano.
3379 Chappell and Co., harmoniums.
3381 Clinton and Co., flutes.
3258 Collard and Collard, piano.

3092 Distin, H., brass instruments.
3093 Dodd, J., bows and silvered strings.
3406 Gretner and Sandilands, piano.
3406 Boosey and Co., piano.
3647 Higham, J., cornets.
3696 Hill, W. E., tenor, and excellence of bows.
3112 Hopkinson, J. and J., piano.
3193 Kirkman and Sons, pianos.
3420 Köhler, J., brass instruments.
3425 Metzler, G., and Co., brass instruments.
3432 Pohlmann and Son, piano.

In this Class there were also awarded the following number of medals to Exhibitors from the several places mentioned:—Austria, 1; France, 11; Germany, 4; Italy, 2; Norway, 1; Prussia, 5; Saxony, 4; Switzerland, 2; United States, 2; Würtemberg, 6.

CLASS XVII.—SURGICAL INSTRUMENTS.

3483 Ash, C., and Sons, appliances in dental surgery.
3485 Daffey, W. H., crutches, abdominal belts, and spinal supports.
3486 Darling, J., sponge gold for stopping teeth.
3489 Gigg, H. H., orthopedic instruments.
3491 Brown, S. S., elastic supports for abdomen and leg.
3402 Coxeter, J., surgical instruments.
3503 Darrach, W. F., surgical, obstetric, and dental instruments.
3896 Ernst, F. G., orthopedic instruments.
3598 Evans and Stevens, surgical instruments.
3509 Evrard, J., tooth extraction instruments.
3512 Ferguson, J. and J., surgical and obstetric instruments.

3522 Gray, J. & Co., surgical and obstetric instruments.
3624 Grossmith, W. R., artificial legs and arms.
3540 Hilliard, W. B., surgical instruments.
3561 Hooper, W., water cushions and beds.
3583 Lawson, Buxton, and Co., surgical, dental, and obstetric instruments.
3640 Leonie, T., and Co., artificial teeth.
3542 Longdon, F., and Co., elastic supports for the abdomen and legs.
3547 Masters, M., artificial legs and arms.
3544 Matthews, W., surgical instruments.
3557 Norman, S. jun., artificial legs.
3559 O'Connell, J., feeding bottle for children.
3568 Penn, J. F., surgical instruments.

In this Class there were also awarded the following number of medals to Exhibitors from the several places mentioned:—Austria, 1; France, 9; Prussia, 6; Saxony, 1; Würtemberg, 1.

CLASS XVIII.—COTTON.

JUROR WHO WAS AN EXHIBITOR.

Dollfus, Deputy-Chairman, Manufacturer, France.

3640 Ashworth, E., and Sons, thread.
3641 Auld, Berrie, and Mattieson, Scotch muslins.
3644 Broom, J., and Brothers, sewing thread.
3646 Carlile, J., Sons, and Co., sewing threads.
3650 Christy, W. M., and Sons, towels and blankets.
3651 Clark and Co., sewing thread.
3650 Clark, J., jun., and Co., sewing thread.
3-51 Clarke, J. P., sewing cotton, &c.
3652 Clark, J. and P., sewing thread.
3653 Crewdson and Worthington, goods.
3660 Dickins and Co., cotton line yarns in threads.
3659 Evans, J., and Co., thread.

3659 Faulkner, H., cotton twine.
3664 Goodair, Slater, and Smith, long cloths.
3663 Greenwood and Whittaker, water twist shirtings.
3671 Hollingworth, J., and Co., yarn and thread.
3670 Horrockses, Miller, and Co., shirtings.
3672 Jack, J. H., jaquard muslin curtains.
3674 Johnson, J., and Fildes, quilts, cotton blankets.
3677 Kerr and Clark, sewing thread.
3678 Kesselmeyer and McIndoe, cotton velvet.
3683 Martin, Johnson, and Jouls, dimities and damasks.
3685 Morgan, J., candlewicks.
3687 Outram, H., and Co., cotton cloths, figured muslins.

3604 Phillips, J., fancy quilts.
3601 Smith, W. J., and Co., cross quiltings.
3691 Swann and Barker, muslins.
3699 Syminton, H., and Co., mulls, jaconets, &c.
3604 Williams, J., muslins, &c.
3695 Yates, Brothers, and Morewood, shawls.
In this Class there were also awarded the following number of medals to Exhibitors from the several places mentioned:—India, 1; New South Wales, 2; Queensland, 3; Austria, 8; Belgium, 4; France, 27; Hanover, 1; Italy, 3; Portugal, 1; Prussia, 5; Russia, 2; Saxony, 4; Switzerland, 11; Sweden 7; Würtemberg, 4.

CLASS XIX.—FLAX AND HEMP.

JURORS WHO WERE EXHIBITORS.

William Charley, Linen Merchant, Belfast.
Ch. de Browkere, Pres. of Cham. of Commerce, Roulers, Belgium.
G. Mevissen, Chairman, Privy Councillor of Commerce, Cologne, Zollverein.
J. Moir, Flax Manufacturer, Dundee.

3799 Austie, J., sash, blind, and picture line.
3730 Barbour, W., and Sons, sewing threads.

3732 Baxter, Brothers, and Co., coarse linen and sail cloths.

3734 Bell, R., and Co., damask goods.
3759 Brown and Liddell, diapers and linen.

2740 Browne, W., cordage, ropes, lines, and twines.
2741 Buckingham, J., rope web in ·tting, sacking, &c.
2745 Clibborn, Hill, and Co., bird's eye diapers.
2746 Connor, F., printed drills.
2747 Coverton and Nayler, English and flax tows.
2749 Dagnall and Tilbury, cocoa and mixed matt'ng.
2750 Dewar, D., Son, and Sons, common table linen.
2753 Dunbar, McMaster, and Co., linen sheetings.
2754 Dunbar, McMaster, and Co., linen yards, threads.
2784 Edward, A. and D., and Co., linen duck, &c.
2787 Fenton, Son, and Co., plain linen.
2761 Fraser, D., and Son, sail canvas, duck tarpauling.

5745 Grimond, J., and A. D., jute carpeting, Hessians.
3771 Hind, J., and Sons, brown and bleached linens.
3772 Holdsworth, W. B., and Co., hemp and flax yarns.
3774 Johnston and Carlisle, yarns and bleached linen.
3779 Marshall and Co., drills, threads, and plain linen.
3785 Masier, H., and Co., linen and handkerchiefs.
3782 Miller, O. G., dry spun linen and tow yarns.
3784 Moneur, A., and Son, sackings for grain, &c.
3790 Paterson, J., jute carpeting.
3792 Richardson, J. N., Sons, and Owden, linens.
3791 Sinleton, J., and Son, goods of flax and jute.
7399 Stuart, J. and W., fishing nets and twines.

3801 Thomson, D. J., and Co., jute carpeting.
3803 Walker, J. and Co., sail cloth, especially for yachts.
3804 Walker, J., and H., jute yarns, sacking, baggings.
3845 Wilford, J., and Sons, white and fancy drillings.
3860 Yeoman and Co., drills, ducks, huckabacks, yarns.

In this Class there were also awarded the following number of medals to Exhibitors from the several places mentioned:—Austria, 8; Baden, 2; Bavaria, 1; Belgium, 11; France, 14; Hanover, 1; Italy, 4; Netherlands, 3; Norway, 2; Portugal, 1; Prussia, 13; Russia, 3; Saxe Coburg, 1; Saxony, 2; Spain, 1; Sweden, 2; Switzerland, 1; Würtemberg, 8.

CLASS XX.—SILK AND VELVET.

Henry Brocklehurst, Reporter, Velvet Manufacturer, Macclesfield.

JURORS WHO WERE EXHIBITORS.

José Reig, Spain.

Baron von Diergardt, Privy Councellor of Commerce, Viersen, Zollverein.

3442 Alsop, Downes, Spilsbury, and Co., brald.
3443 Ballance, T., and Son, black silks.
3445 Beckham, Pownall, and Co., plain and fancy silks.
3446 Birchenough, J., fancy silk scarfs.
3451 Campbell, Harrison, and Lloyd, plain and fancy silks.
3452 Carr, T., and Co., sewing silks, and twists.
3453 Carter and Phillips, plain and fancy ribbons.
3454 Cash, J. and J., plain and fancy ribbons.
3455 Chadwick, J., silk fabrics.
3457 Christy and Co., hat plushes by machinery.
3504 Clabburn, Sons, and Crisp, silk shawls.
3459 Corns, W. W., and Co., fancy silk scarfs.
3460 Courtauld, S., and Co., black and coloured crapes.

3461 Cox, R. S., and Co., fancy and plain ribbons.
3462 Critchley, Brinsley, and Co., fancy silk scarfs.
3468 Franklin, W., and Son, plain and fancy ribbons.
3471 Grout and Co., black crapes.
3476 Keith and Co., furniture silk.
3477 Kenney, Moon, and Co., silks, plain and fancy.
3478 Le Mare, E. R., silk made by power.
        Owen, Brothers, designs.
3481 Peel, Greenhalgh, and Co., and G. Whyatt and Son, silk union velvets.
8492 Potts and Wright, serments.
3641 Ratliff, J., and Son, plain and fancy ribbons.
9586 Saikeld, J., and Co., spun and dyed sewing silk.
3587 Scanner, T., silks and moire anti que.

3854 Slater, Buckingham, and Slater, fancy scarfs.
3891 Smeale, W., serpents and scarfs.
3995 Thompson, W., and Co., yarns spun from silk waste.
3898 Walters, D., and Sons, furniture and silk fabrics.
3909 Wanklyn, W., silks, handkerchiefs, &c.
3909 Watson and Henley, velvet and plush.
3001 Winkworth and Procters, fancy silk.

In this Class there were also awarded the following number of medals to Exhibitors from the several places mentioned:—Austria, 2; Baden, 1; China, 2; France, 79; Algeria, 1; Italy, 20; Japan, 1; Prussia, 12; Russia, 3; Spain, 3; Sweden, 3; Switzerland, 8; Turkey, 8; Würtemberg, 1.

CLASS XXI.—WOOLLEN AND WORSTED, INCLUDING MIXED FABRICS GENERALLY.

JURORS WHO WERE EXHIBITORS.

Wm Clabburn, Joint Reporter on Mixed Fabrics, Shawl Manufacturer, Norwich.
H. Hudson, Woollen Merchant, London.
G. Larmour, Manufacturer, France.
G. Oldroson, Commission Merchant, Belgium.
G. Sella, Woollen Manufacturer, Italy.
H. S. Way, Deputy Chairman, Woollen Warehouseman, London.
M. Gaussen, Late Manufacturer, France.
Lacoreux, Member of the Senate, Belgium.
S. Pepper, Woollen Manufacturer, Austria.
T. Zehelle, Saxony.

3035 Akroyd, J., and Son, furniture, dress goods.
3047 Armitage, J. and R., waistcoatings.
3945 Birchall, J. D., wool and cotton warp.
3946 Bird, O., negretts.
3053 Bonus, G., and Son, cotton and wool coatings.
3054 Bliss, W., and Co., kerseys and serges.
3057 Bullinger &c, J. and F., and Jones, poplins.
3055 Bradford Chamber of Commerce for the Bradford Worsted District, yarns.
3054 Ditto, alpacas and mohair goods.
3057 Ditto, Orleans cloths, plain and figured.
3058 Ditto, Coburg, Paramatta, and other cloths.
3960 Ditto, Italian summer cloths.
3962 Ditto, mixed and moulted worsted goods.
3963 Ditto, fancy goods, alpaca, mohair, worsted, &c.
3964 Ditto, worsted goods, merinos, says, shalloons, &c.
3965 Ditto, moreens.
3967 Ditto, wool shawls, delaines, and shawl cloths.
3968 Brushwaise and Co., cloths for linings.
3974 Bull and Wilson, imeskins for hunting trousers.
3979 Carr, L., and Co., elysians, witneys, furlanwear, &c.
3980 Carter, W., and Geister, H., cloaking cloths.
3985 Cochrane, J. and W., Scotch tweeds, &c.
3992 Cook, Son, and Wormald, blankets.
3995 Cooper, D. and J., cloths and fancy coatings.
3994 Craven, J., plain worsted cloths.
4004 Crook, W., woollen tartans.
4007 Cubitt, Wilson, and Hemsall, Utrecht tapestry.
4011 Davies, R. S., and Sons, scarlet superfine cloths.
4017 Day and Watkinson, Bedford cords and doeskin
        bookbus.

4004 Day, Nephew, and Co., cotton warp.
4006 Dickson and Laings, shepherds' plaid tweeds.
40 23 Dixon, T. D., cotton warp cloths.
4031 Dobson and Riley, fancy trouserings.
4011 Early, L., and Son, Witney blankets.
4018 Eddowes and Co., blue, black, and coloured cloths.
4026 Firth and Sons, sealskin cloakings.
4977 Kenny, Moon, and Co., silks, plain and brocatelles.
4976 Gott, B., and Sons, light union tabbies, kraps, &c.
4043 Hargreave and Nusseys, cotton warp elysians.
4047 Hattersley, G., and Son, cotton warp, &c.
4051 Hemingway, J., woollen yarns for carpets.
4054 Hinde, F., and Son, Paramatta.
4057 Holdsworth, J., and Co., furnitures.
4061 Hooper, C., and Co., clastics, &c.
4065 Hunt and Co., military cloths.
4 66 Hunt, Whitetholham, and Co., livery cloths.
4370 Jay, G., and Son, mohair and alpaca yarns.
4673 Jowitt, J., and T., Bedford cords.
4079 Kerr, Scott, and Kilner, woven shawls.
4083 Leach, J., and Sons, flannels.
4084 Leach, J., and Sons, flannels.
4085 Lees, O., tartans and shawls.
4086 Marling, Strachan, and Co., black and blue cloths.
4191 Middleton and Answorth, crinolines.
4107 Morgan, J., and Co., woollen tartans.
4118 Paton, J. and D., and Co., wool on tartans
4127 Pease, H., and Co., mixed fabrics and yarns.

4121 Pim, Brothers, and Co., Irish poplins.
4148 Reid and Taylor, Scotch tweeds and maude.
4138 Ripley, R., woollen yarns.
4111 Roberts, Jowlings, and Co., cloths.
4133 Saker, S., and Co., plain and fancy doeskins.
4138 Scott, A., and Son, coleon warp cloths.
4144 Smith, H., and Son, witneys.
4147 Speirs, D., and Co., woven woollen shawls.
4151 Stanton and Son, billiard and hunters' cloths.
4162 Stead, J., and Sons, fancy waistcoatings.
4162 Thresher and Glenny, flannel for shirts.
4163 Tolson, Brothers, fancy waistcoatings.
4166 Turner and Nuter, fancy dress fabrics.
4160 Wade, John, and Son, cotton warp cloths.
4047 Walker, Birrell, and Co., fancy mohair cloakings.
4187 Walker, Joe, and Sons, printed sealskin rugs.
4173 Wandle Felt Company, felts.
4184 Wilks, Dick, and Seaton, flannels and dyed wools.
4188 Wilson, and A., worsted yarns.
4161 Wrigley, John, and Son, livery cloths.

In this Class there were also awarded the following number of medals to Exhibitors from the several places mentioned:—Canada, 1; New South Wales, 1; Prince Edward's Island, 1; Queensland, 1; Victoria, 1; Anhalt-Dessau, 1; Austria, 26; Belgium, 15; France, 74; Netherlands, 7; Prussia, 29; Russia, 6; Saxe-Altenburg, 1; Saxony, 16; Spain, 6; Sweden, 5; Turkey, 7; Würtemberg, 1.

CLASS XXII.—CARPETS.

J. Brinton, Secretary, Carpet Manufacturer, Kidderminster.
P. Graham, Deputy Chairman, Upholsterer, London.
H. L. Lapworth, Carpet Manufacturer, London.
W. Whitwell, Carpet Manufacturer, Kendal.

4131 Crossley, J., and Sons, carpets, rugs, &c.
4703 Downing, G. F., seamless floor-cloth, 10 yards wide.
4741 Hare and Co., floor-cloths, &c.
4763 Harrison, S., floor-cloth in panel, &c.
4764 Henderson and Son, samples of various carpeting.
4270 Humphries and Sons, carpets.

4947 Kirdon and Powell, floor-cloths, table covering, &c.
4956 Leather Cloth Co., leather-cloth, &c.
4102 M'Neill, E., and Co., kamptulicon floor-cloth.
4793 Morton and Son, velvet and Brussels carpets.
4796 Sons wald, H. M., bordered Wilton carpet.
4991 Templeton, J., and Co., carpets without se m.

1140 Treutrail, F. G., and Co., kamptulicon.
4973 Watson, Bortor, and Co., Axminster carpets.

In this Class there were also awarded the following number of medals to Exhibitors from the several places mentioned:—India, 8; Austria, 1; Belgium, 3; France, 6; Algeria, 1; Saxony, 1; Turkey, 4.

CLASS XXIII.—WOVEN, SPUN, FELTED, AND LAID FABRICS, WHEN SHOWN AS SPECIMENS OF PRINTING AND DYEING.

JURORS WHO WERE EXHIBITORS.

F. Leutenberger, Calico Printer, Austria
J. S. Stern, Merchant, Manchester.
A. Neild, Calico Printer, Manchester.

3860 Ashdwall, W., and Co., dyed smalls silk drains.
4307 Bradshaw, Hammond, and Co., madder and garancine work.
4308 Butterworth and Brooks, madder and garancine
4612 Dewhirst, S., and Co., morocco leather.
4593 Ewing, J. O., and Co., printed and dyed Turkey red cotton fabrics.
4316 Grafton, F. W., and Co., madder and bleck chintz
4317 Hands, Son, and Co., dyed shaded silk skeins.
4521 Litchwood, Wilson, and Co., madder styles.

4322 Lockett, J., Sons, and Leake, cylinder engraving for calico printing.
4574 Macnab, J., Jaconets, madder, or steam styles.
4853 M'Naughton and Thom, madder and garancine.
4378 Mandelly, B., and Co., printed and dyed Turkey red cotton fabrics.
4398 Newton Bank Printing Co., madder and garancine.
4458 Ormerod, R., and Co., fancy cotton ribbons.
4444 Richardson, B. S., silk skeins dyed
4458 Smith, S., and Co., dyed mixed fabrics

4359 Stead, M'Alpine, and Co., madder styles.
4540 Stirling, W., and Sons, printed and dyed Turkey red cotton fabrics.
4549 Thomson, J., and Co., printed woollen carpets.

In this Class there were also awarded the following number of medals to Exhibitors from the several places mentioned:—India, 2; Anhalt-Dessau, 1; Austria, 6; Belgium, 3; France, 37; Hesse Cassel, 1; Italy, 1; Netherlands, 1; Portugal, 1; Prussia, 7; Russia, 3; Saxony, 2; Spain, 2; Switzerland, 3; United States, 1.

CLASS XXIV.—TAPESTRY, LACE, AND EMBROIDERY.
JUROR WHO WAS AN EXHIBITOR.
Daniel Biddle, Lace Manufacturer, London.

4381 Abraham, R., and Sons, ornamental altar cloth.
4382 Adams, T., and Co., curtains and lace.
4387 Allen, C., Irish point lace.
4383 Bagley, J. W., Johnston Valenciennes, lace.
4386 Barnett, Maltby, and Co., silk laces, net, and
3815 Brown, Sharpe, and Tyars, embroidered muslin.
4390 Copestake, Moore, Crampton, and Co., machine and hand-made lace.
4397 Cowan and Co., Scotch embroidery.
4400 Dunnicliff and Smith, imitation Valenciennes lace.
4406 Evans, R., and Co., upholstery and dress trimmings.
4409 Forrest, J., and Sons, Irish point lace.
4411 Goblet, H. F., Irish crochet lace and needlework.
4412 Godfroy, G., point and other lace.

4417 Herbert, Thos., and Co., crochet and muslin lace.
4419 Heymann and Alexander, plain net lace.
4420 Higgins, Eagle, and Hutchinson, British lace.
4422 Howell, James, and Co., hand-made lace
4423 Hyde, Mrs., needlework, upholstery, and trimmings.
4424 Hyde, Archer, and Co., needlework, upholstery, and trimmings.
4426 Jacoby, R., and Co., imitation of Valenciennes lace.
4427 Jones, W., and Co., gold lace embroidery.
4431 Lester and Sons, Maltese pillow lace.
4433 Macarthur, D., and Co., muslin and lace.
4437 Mallet, H., imitation of Spanish lace.
4439 Manly, G. N., Irish lace.
4442 Norticote, S. H., and Co., real and imitation lace

4448 Radley, E., upholsterers' trimmings.
4449 Reckless and Hickling, lace shawls and flounces
4454 Riego de la Branchardiere, Melle. E., crochet lace
4456 Robinson, H., real and imitation lace.
4457 Stillwell, Son, and Ledger, gold lace embroidery.
4461 Vickers W., articles of black silk lace.
4462 Whittingham, T., and Wilkin, carriage lace.
In this Class there were also awarded the following number of medals to Exhibitions from the several places mentioned:—India, 3; Malta, 1; Austria, 9; Belgium, 26; Denmark, 1; France, 40; Greece, 1; Italian Islands, 3; Italy, 7; Portugal, 1; Prussia, 2; Rome, 1; Russia, 7; Saxony, 1; Spain, 2; Switzerland, 7; Turkey, 4; Würtemberg, 7.

CLASS XXV.—FURS, FEATHERS, AND HAIR.
JURORS WHO WERE EXHIBITORS.
J. A. Nicholay, Deputy Chairman, Furrier, London.
E. B. Roberts, Secretary, Furrier to the Hudson's Bay Company, London.
C. Nightingale, President of Section, Feather and Hair Merchant, London.

SECTION A.—SKINS AND FURS.
4199 Bevington and Morris, seal mantle and furs.
4627 Dodd, J. S., and Sons, sheep and fancy wool rugs.
4301 Drake, R., muffs.
4303 Ince, James, furs.
4304 Jeffs, H., furs.
— Kleitik, preparation of a Bengal tiger and boa constrictor.
4507 Poland and Son, furs.
4510 Smith, G., and Sons, furs and skins.
4511 Tussaud, Brothers, making artificial felt.

In this Section there were also awarded the following number of medals to Exhibitions from the several places mentioned:—India, 1; Natal, 1; Newfoundland, 1; Nova Scotia, 1; Tasmania, 1; Austria, 1; Belgium, 1; France, 2; Hesse-Cassel, 1; Netherlands, 1; Prussia, 1; Russia, 9; Sweden, 1; Turkey, 1.

SECTION B.—FEATHERS AND MANUFACTURES FROM HAIR.
4557 Booth and Fox, bed feathers and eider down quilts.
4559 Carter, H. H., wigs.

4572 De Costa Andrade and Co., ornamental feathers
4943 Douglas, R., excellence of work.
4573 Pemberton, A., elastic brushes.
4577 Truefitt, H. P., wigs
4578 Truefitt, Walter, wigs.
4582 Weekens, C. A., plaiting brushes.
4583 Webb, E., fancy coloured horse hair seating.
In this Section there were also awarded the following number of medals to Exhibitions from the several places mentioned:—Austria, 1; Bavaria, 1; Belgium, 1; France, 5; Prussia, 1.

CLASS XXVI.—LEATHER, INCLUDING SADDLERY AND HARNESS.
JURORS WHO WERE EXHIBITORS.
Piret Pauclet, Leather Manufacturer, Belgium.
Henry Brace, Wholesale Saddler, Walsall.
J. A. Owen, Saddler, London.

SECTION A.—LEATHER, AND MANUFACTURES MADE OF LEATHER.
4 19 Bevington and Morris, leather and wool rugs.
4620 Bevington and Sons, skins for several uses.
4621 Boak. A., leather for saddlers' purposes.
4500 Clark, C. and J., dyed wool, and sheep skin rugs.
4621 Clark and Sons, currying.
4768 Crouble, H., leather.
4632 Fitch, J. J., and Co., colours and finishing of morocco, calf, and sheep skins.
4683 Franklin, W. and J., work for saddlery purposes.
4768 George, J., furniture leather.
4626 Hepburn and Sons, millboards, buckets, and hose.
4649 Lamvert and Co., Cordovan leather.
4648 M'Rae, J. and J., buff hides.
4633 Norris and Co., pipe-hose, &c.
4654 Poole, J. and Co., currying of leather for boot and shoe purposes.
4835 Pullman, R. and J., chamois leather.
4637 Roberts and Co., dyeing of goat and sheep leather.
4649 Shaw and Morris, superior coach leather.
4661 Stockil, W., boot fronts curried.

4685 Sutton, W., Cordovan leather.
4687 Wilson, Walker, and Co., dyed skinners and other leathers.
4694 Winter and Son, dyed wool, sheep skin rugs.
In this Section there were also awarded the following number of medals to Exhibitions from the several places mentioned:—New South Wales, 1; Victoria, 1; Austria, 5; Baden, 1; Bavaria, 2; Belgium, 8; Denmark, 2; France, 23; Algeria, 1; Frankfort, 3; Hanover, 1; Hesse, Grand Duchy, 6; Italy, 1; Luxemburg, 1; Norway, 3; Portugal, 1; Prussia, 3; Russia, 5; Saxe-Altenberg, 1; Saxe-Coburg, 1; Saxony, 2; Switzerland, 3; Würtemberg, 4.

SECTION B.—SADDLERY AND HARNESS.
4682 Benton, E., saddlery and harness.
4684 Blackwell, S., dumb jockey.
4690 Callow, T., and Son, whips
4692 Cooper, M., saddles.
4695 Cowan, J., Scotch cart harness.
6047 Cox, S., bridle-bits.
4701 Dunley, J., cart harness.
4707 Garrett, J. and H., military officers' accoutrements

4702 Lilian, H., whips.
4704 Garnett, W., saddles.
4705 Gibson and Co., army and ordinary saddles.
4757 Gordon, A., carriage harness.
4712 Haynes and Son, saddle trees.
4717 Hinkson, J., sad lery and harness.
4726 Linnen, W., saddlery and harness.
4629 Marten, W. H., racing and walking saddles, whips
6151 Maxwell, H., and Co., military spurs.
4733 Merry, S., saddlery and harness.
4735 Middlemore, W., saddlery.
4754 Orrton, F. B., saddlery and harness.
4737 Oldfield and Son, harness.
4746 Sanders and Adeney, reins and whips.
4749 Weir, J., saddlery and harness.
4751 Whippy, Steggall, and Co., harness and saddlery.
In this Section there were also awarded the following number of medals to Exhibitions from the several places mentioned:—India, 1; New South Wales, 2; Victoria, 1; Austria, 1; Denmark, 1; France, 2; Hamburg, 1; Netherlands, 1; Prussia, 1; Spain, 1.

CLASS XXVII.—ARTICLES OF CLOTHING.
JURORS WHO WERE EXHIBITORS.
Geo. Christy, President of Section, Hat Manufacturer, London.
J. B. Allen, Hosier, Nottingham.
Henry Gregory, Secretary, Straw Bonnet Maker, London.
K. T. Bowley, Secretary, Bootmaker, London.
Aloys Isler, Straw Manufacturer, Wildegg, Switzerland.
Huber, Reporter, Director of the Chamber of Commerce of Stuttgart, Germany.
James Medwin, Bootmaker, London.

SECTION A.—HATS AND CAPS.
4804 Ashton, J. and Sons, silk hats.
4806 Carrington, S. and T., shell hats and soft felt.
4810 Douglas and Co., Scotch caps.
4811 Ellwood and Sons, ventilated helmets.
4820 Tress and Co., shaping of silk hats.
In this Section there were also awarded the following number of medals to Exhibitions from the several places mentioned:—Austria, 3; Belgium, 2; Brazil, 2; Bremen, 1; Denmark, 1; France, 5; Greece, 1; Hesse, Grand Duchy, 1; Italy, 2; Netherlands, 1; Norway, 1; Portugal, 1; Russia, 2; Saxony, 1; Spain, 2; Sweden, 1.

SECTION B.—BONNETS AND GENERAL MILLINERY.
4812 Ennor, Son, and Denrum, artificial flowers.
4848 Veill, D., artificial flowers.
4949 Welch and Sons, hats, Glengary caps.
In this Section there were also awarded the following number of medals to Exhibitions from the several places mentioned:—Victoria, 2; Austria, 1; France, 37; Greece, 2; Hanover, 1; Italy, 2; Portugal, 1; Prussia, 1; Spain, 1; Switzerland, 3; Würtemberg, 1.

SECTION C.—HOSIERY, GLOVES, AND CLOTHING IN GENERAL.
4867 Ashwell, T., and Co., hosiery.
4875 Car wright and Warners, merino hosiery.
4880 Dicksons and Laings, lambs' wool hosiery.
4883 Ennor, T., and Sons, gloves.

4889 Fownes, Brothers, and Co., gloves.
4893 Harris, R., and Sons, worsted and other hosiery.
4855 Hitchcock, G., and Co., trimmings and India's dresses.
4905 Linklater, R., Shetland knitted hosiery and shawls.
4906 Macintosh, C., and Co., waterproof garments.
4915 Morley, J. and H., silk hose.
4916 Mundella, Hine, and Co., hosiery by steam power.
4924 Salomons, A., stays, crinolines, and corsets.
4975 Sangster, W. and J., umbrellas and parasols.
4928 Silver, S. W., and Co., leather clothing.
4929 Sinclair, R., and Co., linen articles.
4932 Tillie and Henderson, linen articles.
4939 Smyth and Co., Balbriggan cotton hosiery.
4944 Thomson, W. T. and C. H. and Co., crinolines.
4937 Ward, Sturt, and Sharp, cotton hosiery.
4910 Wells, J. S., circular made hosiery.
In this Section there were also awarded the following number of medals to Exhibitions from the several places mentioned:—Austria, 17; Belgium, 4; Denmark, 2; France, 37; Greece, 2; Hanover, 1; Italy, 2; Portugal, 1; Prussia, 5; Russia, 1; Saxony, 4; Saxe-Weimar, 1; Spain, 2; Sweden, 1; Switzerland, 7; Turkey, 5; Würtemberg, 4.

SECTION D.—BOOTS AND SHOES.
4961 Allen, C. E., boots and shoes.
4962 Aldoff, J. G., good closing.
4983 Bastin, C., boots.
4968 Bird, W., ladies' boots and shoes.

4972 Brown, E., blacking and waterproof varnish.
4980 Erlam, J., India-rubber shoes.
4982 Gibson, J., boots.
4990 Hall, J., p—l boots.
4996 Ince, I., p—l boots.
4995 Hensley and —, leather boots.
4996 Heffron, J. and C., —.
5001 Hamilton, J., bootmaker.
5002 Love, W. and J., — and sole leather goods.
5031 Pratt, S., waterproof boots.
5040 North Irish leather rubber Co., rubber goods.
5044 Robert, A., les—s and shoes.
5030 Peal, S., waterproof boots.
5056 Walker and Co., waterproof work.
5070 Play, P. G., wholesale work.
5018 Walker and Kempson, wholesale work.
In this Section there were also awarded the following number of medals to Exhibitions from the several places mentioned:—India, 1; New South Wales, 1; Austria, 6; Belgium, 2; Brazil, 2; Denmark, 1; France, 10; Malta, 2; French Indies, 1; Hanover, 1; Hesse, Grand Duchy, 2; Portugal, 1; Prussia, 1; Russia, 1; Sweden, 2; Turkey, 4; Würtemberg, 1.

CLASS XXVIII.—PAPER, STATIONERY, PRINTING, AND BOOKBINDING.
JURORS WHO WERE EXHIBITORS.
Charles Cowan, President of Section, Paper Manufacturer, Edinburgh.
E. Hoesch, Zollverein.
Adam Black, M.P., President of Section, London.
Ch. Girardet, Manufacturer of Fancy Leather Works, Austria.
W. Spottiswoode, F.R.S., Her Majesty's Printer, London.
Ch. Saal, F.S.A., President of Section, Type Founder, London.

SECTION A.—PAPER, CARD, AND MILLBOARD.
5051 Barling, J., paper, millboards, &c.

5080 Hook, Townsend, C., and Co., writing papers
6093 Morley, J. W., millboards.

1057 Routledge, T., paper from half stuff.
5088 Saunders, T. H., writing papers.

[4091] Turnbull, J. A., and J., drawing and other boards.

SECTION B.—STATIONERY.

[5102] Arnold, P. and J., writing inks.
[5104] Banks and Co., black lead pencils.
[5105] Bartley, R., account books.
[5106] Bauerfeinder and Co., pasteboard boxes.
[5213] Branston, F. W., show tablets.
[5112] Brookman and Langdon, drawing pencils.
[5116] Brown, W. and Co., account books.
[5124] Cohen, H. S., pencils.
[5127] Dobbs, Kidd, and Co., stationery and lace papers.
[5127] Goodall, C. and Son, playing cards.
[5135] Goodall and Lauxdale, account books.
[5138] Hceginson, Mrs., paper flowers.
[5141] Hyde and Co., writing ink and sealing wax.
[5147] Johnson and Rowe, leather card cases.
[5219] Johnson, J. M., and Son, show tablets.
[5148] Jones and Causton, account books.
[5148] Jones, Owen, playing cards and illuminations.
[5150] Law and Son, bookbinders' cloth.
[5151] Lett- and Sons, diaries.
[5155] Marcus, Ward, and Co., account books.
[5116] Martin, T., seals.
[5161] Mordan, F., gold pens.
[5261] Newall, J., line ornaments and lace paper.
[5167] Reynolds, J. and Sons, playing cards.
[5174] Turner, Brothers, account books.
[5091] Turnbull, J. A. and J., drawing boards.
[5182] Warenson, H., sealing wax.
[5184] Wedgwood, H., and Sons, manifold writers.

[5187] Wilson, J. L., bookbinders' cloth.
— Woolf and Sons, black lead pencils.

SECTION C.—PLATE, LETTERPRESS, AND OTHER MODES OF PRINTING.

[5302] Austin, R., printing oriental books.
[5203] Bagster, S. and Sons, polyglot Bible.
[5206] Bell and Daldy, publications.
[5204] Bradbury and Evans, nature printing, ferns.
[5214] Bradbury, Wilkinson, & Co., photo printing.
[5216] Brooks, V., chromo-lithography.
[5217] Caston, H. W., and Co., type founding.
[5304] Clay, R., Son, and Taylor, printing woodcuts.
[5274] Day and Son, chromo-lithography.
[5726] Dickes, W., oil colour printing.
[5728] Electro Printing Block Co., electro blocks.
[5320] Faithfull, Miss, printing by female labour.
[5232] Figgins, V. and J., type cutting and casting.
[5243] Hanhart, M. and N., chromo-lithography.
[5247] Hughes and Kimber, plates for engraving.
[5304] Knight, C., English Cyclopædia.
[5754] Leighton Brothers, printing by machinery.
[5755] Leighton and Leighton, wood engraving, &c.
[5256] Linton, W. J., engraving for surface printing.
[5757] Longman, Green, Longman, Roberts, publications.
[5258] Low, F., Son, and Co., publications.
[5900] Maclure, Macdonald, and Macgregor, lithographic printing by machinery.
[5263] M'Queen, Brothers, plate printing.
[5263] Miller and Richard, type cutting and casting.
[5269] Murray, J., publications.

[5271] Parsons, Fletcher, and Co., printing ink.
[5273] Patent Type Founding Co., type cast and dressed by machinery.
[5281] Smith, H. and Son, printing ink.
[5283] Smith, Elder, and Co., publications.
[5706] Standidge and Co., lithography.
[5786] St-phenson, Blake, and Co., type casting.
[5291] Wallis, George, auto-typography.
[5/95] Watts, W. M., oriental types.

SECTION D.—BOOKBINDING.

[5300] Hayday, S., and Sons, Bible work.
[5310] Bedford, F., ornamental binding.
[5311] Hene, W., and Son, cloth work.
[5312] Chatelin, A., hand tooling.
[5315] Holloway, M. M., elegance of design.
[5872] Jenner and Knewstub, ornamental leather work.
[5317] Leighton, J., designs for binding.
[5654] Longhem, W., execution in leather work.
[5395] Riviere, R., taste in design.
[5326] Westleys and Co., solidity of work.
[5827] Wright, J., Trustees of late, blind tooling.

CLASS XXIX.—EDUCATIONAL WORKS AND APPLIANCES.

JURORS WHO WERE EXHIBITORS.

Dufau, late Director of the Institution of the Blind in Paris, France.
Bapst, Inspector-General of Elementary Education, France.

[4417] Abbott, R., maps and mathematical apparatus.
[4137] Arundel Society, printing in colour.
[4384] Ashmead, G. B., eyes and stuffed birds.
[5389] Bartlett, A. D., birds.
[5365] Bell and Daldy, educational works.
[5367] Betts, J., maps.
[5174] Black, A., and Co., educational works.
[5371] Blackwood, W. and Son, A. K. Johnston's Atlas.
[5434] Blind Asylum, Bristol, manufactures.
[5375] British and Foreign Bible Society, translations.
[5458] British and Foreign School Society, publications.
[5455] Brockedon, W., and Co., Cumberland lead.
— Bracciani, drawing models.
[4436] Caswell, Petter, and Galpin, educational works.
— Colenso, Bishop of Natal, mathematics.
[1422] Conwell, Dr. James, educational works.
[5326] Cranborne, Viscount, labours on behalf of blind.
[5513] Cremer, W. H., sen. toys.
[5515] Cremer, W. H. jun., toys.
[5461] Cromwell, J. M. and H., mathematical instruments.
— Currie, J., educational works.
[5392] Damon, R., fossils.
[5544] Dark, M., and Sons, collective medal for cricket.
[5543] Dark, R., tackle.
[5463] Darton and Hodge, educational works.
[5351] Day and Son, coloured diagrams.
[5555] Department of Science and Art, productions.
[5546] Duke and Sons, cricket balls.
[5361] Elliott, Brothers, section and models.
[5519] Gilbert, W., foot-balls and foot-ball shoes.

[5097] Chambers, J., educational works.
[5097] Chambers, J. R., minerals and fossils.
[5403] Dale, J. J., instruction in elementary science.
[10 Others, education of the blind.
[4574] Hall, A., Victor, and Co., Wenlo's works.
[4574] Hanmer, G. H., educational models.
[4400] Highley, S., educational collections.
[44-3] Home and Colonial Training Institution, works.
[5484] Hughes, O. A., typography for the blind.
[5443] Hullah, John, musical publications.
[4540] Jaques, J., and Son, toys and games.
[5487] Johnston, W. and A. K., physiology.
[4429] Joseph, Myer, and Co., objects designed for education and amusement of children.
[5435] Kaullck, stuffed animal.
[5430] Lloyd, W. A., for the benefit of life vivarium.
[5401] Longman, Green, Longman, and Roberts, educational works.
[5400] Macmillan and Co., educational works.
[5449] Montanari, A., wax dolls.
[5476] National Society for the Education of the Poor, works exhibited.
— Nelson and Sons, maps.
[5419] Oliver and Boyd, educational works.
[5502] Philip's Imperial Atlas, H. 1111, model of school-house.
[5546] Pierott, H., toys.
[5405] Potts, R., works on geometry.
[5505] Reeves and Sons, artists' materials.
[5501] Reformatory and Refuge Union, school furniture.
[5417] Religious Tract Society, publications.

[3118] Reynolds, J., diagrams employed in instruction of adults.
[5397] Staley, Rev. N. J., "book hawking."
[5508] Roberson and Co., drawing.
[5600] Robertson, C., elementary collection of zoology.
[5573] Roth, H., physical education.
[5503] Rowney, C. and Son, lead pencils.
[5513] School for the Indigent Blind, productions.
— Smith, William, Dr., works on history.
[5517] Society for promoting Christian Knowledge, education generally.
[4424] Sandford, E., geographical publications.
[5547] Statham, W. E., scientific collections.
[4578] Sunday School Union, books and apparatus.
[5131] Walton and Maberly, educational works.
[5453] Wolff, E., and Son, pencils and crayons.
[3618] Wright, B., elementary geology.
[5436] Wyld, J., geographical publications.

In this Class there were also awarded the following number of medals to Exhibitors from the several places mentioned:—Bahamas, 1; British Guiana, 5; Canada, 4; India, 9; Jamaica, 1; Natal, 4; New Brunswick, 1; Nova Scotia, 3; South Australia, 3; Tasmania, 3; Victoria, 3; Western Australia, 1; Austria, 23; Bavaria, 7; Denmark, 2; Belgium, 4; France, 70; Algeria, 3; Mauritius, 1; Hesse Cassel, 1; Hesse, Grand Duchy, 1; Italy, 19; Netherlands, 1; Norway, 1; Portugal, 1; Prussia, 3; Russia, 1; Saxe Coburg, 1; Sweden, 4; Switzerland, 1; Württemberg, 1.

CLASS XXX.—FURNITURE AND UPHOLSTERY, INCLUDING PAPER HANGINGS AND PAPIER MACHE.

JURORS WHO WERE EXHIBITORS.

Wm. Holland, Upholsterer, London.
John Jackson, Carton Pierre Manufacturer, London.
L. Tuglieu, Cabinet Maker, N. Germany.

J. G. Grace, Decorator, London.
Jos. Ferguson, Upholsterer, N. Germany.
Inem Jones, Vice-President Royal Institute of British Architects, London.

SECTIONS A. AND B.—FURNITURE AND UPHOLSTERY, PAPER HANGINGS, AND GENERAL DECORATION.

[5760] Ingledew, C., dining-room and library chairs.
[5390] Jeffery and Co., paper hangings.
[5761] Johnstone and Jeanes, fancy cabinet.
[5750] Jones and Willis, church furniture.
[5762] Kendall, T. H., articles for furniture.
[5463] Kershaw, T., decoration for walls.
[5762] Leach, J., sideboard in oak.
[5772] Litchfield and Radclyffe, marquetre furniture.
[5735] Magnus, G. E., enamelled slate bath, billiard table.
[5783] Morris, Marshall, Faulkner, and Co., furniture.
[5598] Poole & Maggillivray, jewel stand and two chairs.
[5767] Prentice, Cowian, and Co., imitations of woods.
[5958] Rodgers, J. and J., Sheffield, painted wall.
[5608] Rogers, W. G., wood carvings.
[5844] Seddon, T. L., canopies for carriages.
[5873] Taylor, J., imitations of woods and marbles.

[367] Tomlinson, inlaid tables of Derbyshire marbles.
[5859] Toms and Luscombe, bird tables, &c.
[5861] Trollope, J. and Son, carved chimney-piece.
[5843] Tudsbery, R. J., carvings from nature.
[5849] Wallis, T. W., carvings from nature.
[5862] Webb, W. F., carvings from nature.
[5855] Whytock, R. and Co., pollard oak sideboard.
[5662] Wright and Mansfield, decorative furniture.

In these Sections there were also awarded the following number of medals to Exhibitors from the several places mentioned:—Ceylon, 2; India, 5; New South Wales, 1; New Zealand, 1; Nova Scotia, 1; Austria, 6; Bavaria, 3; Belgium, 5; Brazil, 1; Denmark, 3; France, 37; Frankfort, 1; Greece, 1; Hamburg, 1; Hesse, Grand Duchy, 2; Ionian Islands, 1; Italy, 12; Mecklenburg-Schwerin, 1; Netherlands, 1; Norway, 1; Prussia, 1; Rome, 6; Russia, 3; Spain, 1; Sweden, 1; Switzerland, 1; Württemberg, 1.

CLASS XXXI.—HARDWARE.

JURORS WHO WERE EXHIBITORS.

H. E. Hoole, President of Section, Stove Grate Manufacturer, Sheffield.
V. Paillard, Bronze Manufacturer, France.
G. Stobwasser, President of Section, Manufacturer, Berlin, Zollverein.

A. Tyler, Deputy Chairman, Brass Founder, London.
Goldenberg, Manufacturer, France.

SECTION A.—MANUFACTURES IN IRON.

[5975] Avery, W. and T., scales and weighing machines.
[5971] Bally, W., and Son, iron work.
[59-6] Barnard, Bishop and Barnards, cast iron gates.
[59-3] Barton, J., stable fittings.
[59-6] Benham and Sons, cooking apparatus.
[19] Bennett, T., gold-leaf.
[5981] Bennett, W., smoke consuming grates.
[5900] Billinge, J., hinges.
[5901] Binks, Brothers, wire ropes.
[5990] Bolton, T. and sons, copper telegraph wire.
[1901] Bradford, F., washing machine.

[59-8] Branah and Co., locks.
[6002] Brown and Green, kitchen range.
[11sC] Brown, Lennox, and Co., construction of a vice.
[59] Buck, G., lightning conductors.
[1606] Bullock, T., and Son, buttons.
[6901] Butler, J., and Sons, wire.
[6011] Carron Company, range-stoves.
[6017] Chubb and Son, iron safes.
[6018] Clark, T. and C., and Co., hollow ware.
[6019] Coalbrookdale Co., articles exhibited.
[6021] Comfort, J., wire.
[6025] Cottam and Co., economic conservatories.

[6026] Cotterill, E., locks.
[6031] Day and Millward, scales and weighing machines.
[6032] Dawes, E., kitchen ranges.
[6033] Deller, T. A., horse-shoes.
[6043] Dudley and Sons, kitchen ranges.
[6045] Edelsten and Williams, wire and pins.
[6048] Edwards, F., and son, stove grates.
[6049] Evans, J., and Co., kitchen range.
[6058] Feetham, M., and Co., grates.
[6059] Field, W., and Son, horse-shoes.
[6007] Finley, J., dog-grates.
[6073] Firmin and Sons, military ornaments.

6065 Flavel, S., and Co., kitchen ranges.
6071 General Iron Foundry Co., cooking apparatus.
6077 Glass, Elliott and Co., wire ropes.
6091 Greening, N., and Sons, wire cloth.
6085 Griffiths and Browett, hollow ware.
6093 Hammond, Turner, and Sons, buttons.
6074 Handyside, A., and Co., fountains and vases.
1675 Hargreaves, W., washing machine.
1916 Harrison, W., machine for making ice.
6090 Hawkins, J., and Co., bits, spurs, and stirrups.
1099 Heaton, B., and Sons, coils.
1101 Hevens, E., kitchen ranges.
6102 Hiatt and Co., police handcuffs.
6103 Hobbs, Ashley, and Co., locks and safes.
6105 Hopkins, J. H., and Sons, tinned dish covers, &c.
6119 Iles, C., thimbles and pins.
6117 Janes and Sons, self-boring wood screws.
6119 Jeakes, C., and Co., kitchen ranges and stoves.
6122 Jenkins, Hill, and Jenkins, iron and steel wire.
6124 Jones and Rowe, kitchen ranges.
6126 Keith, G., ice safes.
6127 Kennard, R. W., and Co., iron castings.
6128 Kenrick, A., and Sons, enamelled hollow ware.
6129 Kenn, G., articles of domestic economy.
6131 Knight, Merry, and Co., railway lamps.
6132 Leoni, S., gas burners.
6138 Linley, T., and Sons, forges and bellows.
6140 Mander, Weaver, and Co., work in aluminium.
6149 Martineau, F. E., and Co., machine-made hinges.
6131 Maxwell, H., and Co., spurs.
6162 Nettlefold and Chamberlain, screws, &c.
6171 Onions, J. C., bellows.
6173 Patent Enamel Co., enamelled hollow ware.

6177 Peyton and Peyton, bedsteads.
6180 Pierce, W., cottage grates.
6183 Potter, T., "Una and the Lion."
6185 Price, C., and Co., locks.
6186 Prior, G., iron safes and locks.
6193 Radclyffe, T., kitchen ranges.
6192 Reynolds, J., wirework.
6205 Robinson, A., and Sons, steel wire.
6210 Scott, J. W., solid leather buttons.
212 Smith, E., and Co., iron wire.
6312 Stickley, J., gold-leaf.
9222 Stuart and Smith, bronze hall table.
6000 Summerscales, W., and Son, washing machine.
6226 Tann, J., iron safes and locks.
6230 Tisdard, Jr. V., and Co., scales.
622c Tucker and Reeves, articles exhibited.
6235 Tylor and Pace, pierced work for blinds.
6241 Warden, J., and Sons, bolts and nuts.
6245 Watkins and Keene, bolts and nuts.
6242 Watkin, W., and Co., spades.
6244 Webster and Horsfall, steel music wire.
6246 Wenham Lake Ice Co., refrigerator.
7251 Whitfield, T., and Co., frying-pans.
6055 Williamson, W., washing machine.
6254 Wilkins and Weatherly, wire ropes.
6257 Winfield, R. W., and Son, bedsteads.
6263 Wright, P., anvils and vices.
6265 Yates, Heywood, and Drabble, cast iron articles.
Section B.—Manufactures in Brass and Copper.
6280 Benhams and Froud, workmanship.
6283 Bischoff, Bross, and Co., water meter.
6289 Croll, Hall, and Co., gas meters.
6294 Duckham, H. A. F., gas water governors.

6300 Glover, G., and Co., gas meters.
6301 Glover, T., dry meters.
6301 Guest and Chrimes, brass articles.
6303 Hardman, J., and Co., perfection of workmanship.
6307 Hart and Son, perfection of workmanship.
6313 Hinks, J., and Son, lamps.
6320 Lambert, T., and Son, brass articles.
6321 Leslie, M., workmanship.
6327 Messenger and Sons, workmanship.
1044 Newton, Keates, and Co., workmanship.
6333 Philip, C. J., workmanship and design.
6336 Prosser, W., and H. J. Standly, flint light.
6343 Shakspeare Art Manufacturers Co., workmanship.
6349 Strode, W., sun burner.
6350 Sugg, W., gas burners.
6353 Thomason, J., and Co., workmanship.
6351 Tonks, W., and Sons, workmanship.
635x Warner and Sons, chinning bells by machinery.
Section C.—Manufacture in Tin, Lead, Zinc, &c.
6376 Chatterton, J., lead and black tin.
6379 Dixon, J., and Sons, Britannia metal wares.
6352 Gilbert, J. A., and Co., grocers' fittings.
6345 Loveridge, H., and Co., japanned wares.
6391 Wilson, R., and W., marks and plate warmer.

In these Sections there were also awarded the following number of medals to Exhibitors from the several places mentioned:—Victoria, 1; Austria, 10; Baden, 1; Bavaria, 12; Belgium, 18; Denmark, 3; France, 30; Hanover, 3; Hesse, Grand Duchy, 1; Hesse, Cassel, 1; Italy, 4; Netherlands, 1; Norway, 1; Prussia, 27; Russia, 3; Saxe-Meiningen, 1; Saxony, 2; Sweden, 6; Switzerland, 2; Würtemberg, 3.

CLASS XXXII.—STEEL.
JURORS WHO WERE EXHIBITORS.

J. Brown, President of Section, Mayor of Sheffield, Sheffield.
Thos. Jessop, steel Manufacturer, Sheffield.
Wm. Matthews, Past Master Cutler, Sheffield.
F. Werthdim, Vice-President of the Chamber of Commerce, Vienna, Austria.

Section A.—Steel Manufactures.
6427 Bessemer, H., converting crude iron into steel.
6428 Boulton and Son, needles and fish-hooks.
6430 Cammell and Co., steel railway springs.
6434 Gillott, J., metallic pens.
6435 Goodman, D., pins and needles.
6437 Hinks, Wells, and Co., metallic pens.
6440 Kirby, Beard, and Co., needles and pins.
6441 Knights and Co., needles and pins.
6448 Milward and Sons, needles and fish-hooks.
6446 Mitchell, W. (Birmingham), metallic pens.
6446 Mogg and Co., needlework fishing tackle.
6452 Myers and Sons, metallic pens.
6468 Naylor, Vickers, and Co., steel bells.
6.30 Page, W., and J., cork-screws and steel toys.
6462 Perry, J., and Co., metallic pens.
6466 Shortridge, Howell, and Co., steel in bar and sheet.
6486 Smith and Houghton, plano, pinion, and steel wires.
6481 Thomas and Sons, needles.

6462 Townsend and Co., machine needles.
6403 Turner, M., and Co., metallic pens.
6490 Turton, Brothers, files.
Section B.—Cutlery and Edge Tools.
6480 Addis, J. B., screw tools.
6483 Allarton and Powell, awls.
6484 Baker, W., and Sons.
6491 Brookes and Crookes, cutlery.
6499 Eadon and Sons, saws and machine knives.
6500 Eastwood, G., joiners' tools.
6503 Fuller, J. H., stocks and dies.
6305 Gibbins and Sons, scissors.
6310 Greaves, E. A. and W., planes.
6312 Hannah, A., tools for boring wood.
6315 Harrison, J., files.
6316 Hawcroft and Sons, razors.
6320 Howarth, J., tools.
6323 Jowitt and Son, files.
6327 Linneker, R. and J., scythes.

6320 Mappin and Co., cutlery.
6328 Mappin, Brothers, cutlery.
6350 Marsh, Brothers, and Co., brace bits.
6351 Mechi and Bazin, cutlery.
6341 Parkin, J., machine knives and pruning hooks.
6351 Peace, Ward, and Co., files.
6.45 Rodgers and Sons, cutlery.
6341 Raynor and Cooke, pruning knives.
6331 Steer and Webster, saws and edge tools.
6333 Taylor, H., engravers' tools.
6.36 Unwin and Rodgers, cutlery.
6367 Wade and Sons, scythes.
6361 Wilkinson, T., and Sons, saws and scissors.
6361 Wilkinson, Son, and Co., cutlery.
6363 Westenholm and Son, cutlery.
In these Sections there were also awarded the following number of medals to Exhibitors from the several places mentioned:—Canada, 2; Austria, 6; Belgium, 2; France, 17; Hanover, 1; Italy, 2; Prussia, 9; Russia, 1; Saxony, 1; Switzerland, 2; United States, 2; Würtemberg, 2.

CLASS XXXIII.—WORKS IN PRECIOUS METALS AND THEIR IMITATIONS, AND JEWELLERY.
JURORS WHO WERE EXHIBITORS.

Fred. Elkington, Silver Plater, Birmingham.
J. Hunt, Goldsmith, London.

6207 Angell, J., jewellery, gold and silver plate.
Armstead, H. H., Ourran Shield and Keats testimonial.
6603 Berry, W. E., gilt metal work.
6604 Bell, J., and Co., groups in aluminium.
6606 Benson, J. W., argentine and electro-plate.
6628 Bragg, T. and J., gold bracelets, brooches, &c.
6621 Collis, G. R., silver and electro-plated services.
6614 Dixon J., and Sons, Sheffield and electro-plate.
6633 Gerrard, R. and S., and 66, silver plate.
6629 Hancock, C. F., jewellery and precious metals.
6638 Keith, J., church plate.

6510 Lambert and Co., chased shield, cistern, beaker.
6516 London and Ryder, jewellery, diamond work, &c.
6652 Marshall, W., and Co., gold and silver jewellery.
6655 Martin, Hall, and Co., silver and electro-plate.
6663 Morel, Raphael, designing and modelling.
Morel, Leonard, repoussé work.
6656 Parker and Stone, gold chains and jewellery.
6668 Phillips, R., gold and silver, coral, &c.
6601 Priest, Co., silver, silver and electro-plate.
6601 Reid and Sons, silver and electro-plate.
6467 Smith and Nicholson, silver and electro-plate.
6668 Spencer, jewellery.

Vechte, Antoine, repoussé shield.
6576 Wilkinson and Veal's, silver plate and jewellery.
Wilson, W. Albert, dessert service.
In this Class there were also awarded the following number of medals to Exhibitor from the several places mentioned:—Ceylon, 1; India, 4; New South Wales, 7; South Australia, 8; Austria, 8; Baden, 2; Bavaria, 1; Belgium, 1; Brazil, 1; Bremen, 1; Denmark, 3; Egypt, 2; France, 34; Hesse, 1; Frankfort, 1; Hesse, Cassel, 1; Italy, 7; Japan, 1; Malta, 1; Netherlands, 1; Norway, 1; Prussia, 5; Rome, 1; Russia, 4; Spain, 1; Switzerland, 3; Würtemberg, 2.

CLASS XXXIV.—GLASS.
JURORS WHO WERE EXHIBITORS.

James Hartley, Glass Manufacturer, Sunderland.
D. Jones, Member of the Chamber of Commerce at Charleroi, Belgium.

6745 Lavers and Barraud, stained glass windows.
6737 Powell, J., and Sons, sinned glass windows.
In this Section there were also awarded the following number of medals to Exhibitors from the several places mentioned:—Belgium, 7; France, 11; Italy, 1; Prussia, 3; Section B.—Glass for Household Use and Fancy Purposes.
6742 Copeland, cut glass.
6764 Dobson and Pearce, table glass lustres and girandoles.
6767 Green, J., table glass chandeliers and lustres.

6771 Kilner, Brothers, bottles and glass.
6777 Lloyd and Summers, flint and enamelled glass.
6778 Naylor, F. J., stained glass.
6791 Pellatt and Co., table glass and chandeliers.
6792 Powell, J., and Sons, flint glass.
6751 Powell, J., and Sons, enamelled glass.
In this Section there were also awarded the following number of medals to Exhibitors from the several places mentioned:—Austria, 7; Bavaria, 2; France, 11; Portugal, 1; Prussia, 1; Russia, 1.

CLASS XXXV.—POTTERY.
JURORS WHO WERE EXHIBITORS.

6721 Field and Allen, stained glass windows.
6723 Hardman, J., stained glass windows.
6727 Heaton, Butler, and Co., stained glass windows.
6721 Holland and Co., stained glass windows.
6731 Morris, Marshall, Faulkner, and Co., stained glass windows.
6735 O'Connor, M. and A., and W. H., stained glass windows.

6839 Battam and Son, Greek reproductions.
6883 Blashfield, J. M., terra cotta works.
6883 Blanchfield, J. M., terra cotta works.
6834 Boote, Messrs., encaustic tiles.
6838 Bromwich, W., printed earthenware.
6-84 Brown, Westhead, Moore, and Co., productions.
6844 Copeland, W. T., porcelain enamels.
6815 Dimmock, J., and Co., printed earthenware.

6848 Doulton and Watts, stoneware.
6841 Dixon, Bird., and Nephews, china and earthenware.
6936 Grainger, G., and Co., semi-porcelain.
6396 Kerr, W. H., and Co., decorative porcelain.
6907 Kennedy, Powell, and Co., earthenware.
6930 Lockett, J., insured earthenware.
6971 Minton and Co., decorative porcelain, majolica.
7141 Pelham, J., terra cotta works.

6801 Rose and Co., decorative porcelain.
6 49 Teigne, F., decorative porcelain.
6 41 Wedgwood, J., and Sons, decorative earthenware.
In this Class there were also awarded the following number of medals to Exhibitors from the several places mentioned:—Australia, 3; Bavaria, 2; Belgium, 1; Denmark, 1; France, 14; Italy, 2; Prussia, 1; Saxony, 1; Spain, 1.

CLASS XXXVI.—DRESSING CASES AND DISPATCH BOXES, AND TRAVELLING CASES.
JURORS WHO WERE EXHIBITORS.

F. West, Cutler, London.

6931 Allen, J. W., Dressing Case Manufacturer, London.
6890 Asprey, C., general exhibition.
6855 Day and Son, workmanship.
6919 Gebhardt, Rottmann, and Co., utility and economy.

6942 Jenner and Knowsigh, general exhibition.
6991 Leuchars, W., dressing cases.
6941 Southgate, J., excellence in cheap cases.
6955 Toulmin and Gale, workmanship.

F. West, Cutler, London.
In this Class there were also awarded the following number of medals to Exhibitors from the several places mentioned:—Austria, 4; France, 7; Hesse, Grand Duchy, 1; Russia, 3.

CASSELL'S ILLUSTRATED EXHIBITOR.

1862.

Introductory.

May-day in the "good old times" was, we are told, a day of mirth and festival—gaiety under greenwood boughs and boisterous merriment in baronial halls. The times have changed indeed. For now, instead of Labour making merry under patronage, and consenting, at certain times and seasons, to put on holiday garb and be gay to order, it asserts itself boldly, and shows its power, and might, and irresistible greatness in Crystal Palaces and International Exhibitions.

Who is it that mourns for the days that are gone,
When a noble could do what he liked with his own;
When his serfs, with their burdens well filled on their backs,
Never dared to complain at the weight of a tax?

Not many, we fancy. In the "good old days," the idea of Labour being equal to anything but production, at the command of Wealth, would have been scouted. In the "good old times" there were, beside

EXTENSION OF THE INTERNATIONAL EXHIBITION BUILDING FROM THE EAST.—EXHIBITION ROAD.

1

May-day gaieties, horrors of frequent famine, relentless law, suppression of free speech, bigotry, persecution, the gallows, and the block! True, the ragged remnants of some of these still remain. But, year by year, they are fluttering in the wind of public opinion, and wasting, unregretted, away. The Chivalry that was once a light in the world, has paled before the sun of Education; and the learning that, in "the good old times," was confined to the few, now, day by day and hour by hour, widens its beneficent circle. It has reached the people; and will still widen and widen, till, at last, it will embrace within its all-encompassing arms the toilers and moilers of the earth, even to the least of their children.

The May-day of this year of grace eighteen hundred and sixty-two, unlike the May-days of the poets, may be said to be a real, substantial Festival of Labour. Look around. Every step we take in the International Exhibition reminds us that without labour this beautiful building and its costly multifarious contents could never have existed. Here, in friendly rivalry, all the nations of the earth are represented by the products of the soil; by aid of plough and spade, and axe and mattock; by aid of loom and shuttle, and needle; by aid of painter's brush and engraver's burin; by aid of workman's hammer, and chisel, and plane, and saw, and file, and lever, and rule; by aid of steam and electricity, and machinery in endless forms and bewildering variety; by aid of water, and fire, and hard-named chemicals; by marbles wrought into shapes of beauty, and metals dug from the bowels of the dark mine and fashioned into grace, and strength, and utility; by whirring wheel and wonder-compelling contrivances; by musical instruments and scientific appliances; by all the exquisite forms into which silk, and cotton, and hemp, and flax, and worsted have been woven, and spun, and felted, and drawn; by pictures painted by the sun itself; by innumerable delicate shapes of glass and pottery, and iron and steel, and copper and brass and zinc, and a hundred other metals; jewellery, gold and silver; myriads of beautiful and curious things, collected at vast expense of time and money, from all parts of the habitable globe — pictures, sculptures, books — all the gathered evidences of wealth, and refinement, and civilisation, go to make up a whole unequalled in the history of the nations from the beginning of the world. The student wishing to discover for himself the various processes of manufacture through which the crude metal passes ere it reaches us in its familiar marketable form, can note the rough ore through all forms of manufacture, to the finished article; the artist can trace the means by which greatness has been reached; the mechanic the steps whereby success has been accomplished; the merchant the gradual rise of wealth-winning products, from the dawn of an idea to its brilliant completion; the statesman the means by which peoples rise into power and consideration; the historian the social life of the world, as exhibited in its material success; the poet the up-springing and forward march of that intellectual progress which is destined eventually to break down the barriers of prejudice, and pride, and coldness, and exclusiveness among the nations, and to waken in the hearts of the people that love of the true, the honourable, the kind, and the beautiful, that must ennoble and sanctify, and that all will acknowledge as "a joy for ever!"

Eleven years since, May-day witnessed a scene as impressive as, and in many respects more imposing than, that enacted at the International Exhibition. The presence of our beloved Queen and her royal consort, Albert the Good, gave to the ceremonial of 1851 an impressiveness and meaning hardly realised by the inauguration of 1862. Both Exhibitions may be said to owe their peculiar grandeur and state to the late Prince Consort. To him is undoubtedly due the credit of having given a world-wide fame and reputation to an idea originally borrowed from the annual exhibitions of cattle and agricultural implements in large provincial towns. Something of gloom and regret could not but be present to the minds of all who took part in the brilliant ceremony of our May-day, when they reflected that the author of the Festival lay cold in his grave, and that the Queen, mourning in her widowhood, could not take part in the event of the day. But the influence of her Majesty, though without her actual presence, gave lustre to the imposing ceremony of the inauguration of

the International Exhibition of 1862. The following official programme of the ceremonial will give a correct idea of the state opening of the International Exhibition of 1862.

"The Queen, being anxious to mark her interest in the success of an undertaking, in promoting which the Prince Consort had taken a most active part, has notified her wish that the opening of the Exhibition should bear as much as possible the character of a national ceremony. Her Majesty has therefore been pleased, under the present impossibility of herself performing that ceremony, to appoint his Royal Highness the Duke of Cambridge, K.G., his Grace the Archbishop of Canterbury, the Lord High Chancellor, the Earl of Derby, K.G., the Lord Chamberlain, Viscount Palmerston, K.G., G.C.B., and the Speaker of the House of Commons, to be her representatives to conduct it in her name.

"Her Majesty's Ministers and the Royal Commissioners for the Exhibition of 1851 will attend in the procession, and her Majesty's Commissioners for the Exhibition will invite the Royal and distinguished persons at the head of the respective foreign commissions, and the foreign ambassadors and ministers accredited to this country, to take part in the ceremony.

"Her Majesty's Commissioners will seek the co-operation of the guarantors of the Exhibition, jurors, members of both Houses of Parliament, heads of the church, universities, law, army, navy, and volunteers, the municipalities, scientific and artistic institutions, the local and other committees aiding the Exhibition, &c., in giving to the state opening a national character. For such persons there will be a number of reserved seats, but the number is necessarily limited. Whilst desiring to meet the wishes of all, her Majesty's Commissioners must reserve to themselves full power of dealing with the arrangements according to their discretion. Her Majesty's Commissioners request that gentlemen occupying officially reserved seats will appear in uniform official, or court dress.

"The principal ceremonies will take place under the two domes and along the whole length of the nave. The official reception of her Majesty's representatives, and of distinguished visitors taking part in the ceremonial, will be held in the central south court. The procession will start from this point, and proceed to the west dome. Here will be a chair of state, and, after a verse of the National Anthem has been sung, an address will be delivered by the Earl Granville, K.G., Chairman of Her Majesty's Commissioners for the Exhibition of 1862. The procession will then move down the nave to the east dome, where the musical performances (a grand overture, by Meyerbeer; the inaugural ode, by Sterndale Bennett; and a grand march, by Auber) will take place; after which a prayer will be offered up by the Bishop of London, and the Hallelujah Chorus and the National Anthem will be sung. The opening of the Exhibition will be declared by his Royal Highness the Duke of Cambridge. The procession will then proceed to the picture galleries, and the barriers will be removed."

In conformity with the royal wish, the Inauguration Ceremonial on the 1st of May was conducted with all pomp and grandeur. The royalty, the nobility, the state, the church, the law, the science, art, literature, commerce, and industry of the nation were all represented; while as regards foreign countries, the Exhibition of 1862 was even better attended by European and other notabilities than its progenitor of 1851. The pageant was altogether a grand one, and worthy of the metropolis and the country. Flashing helmets and glittering jewels, sumptuous robes and unique costumes; feathers, stars, crosses, and all the bravery of fashion, intermingled with good effect: and when to these we add the charm of music and the inexplicable influence of youth, beauty, and refinement, it is easy to conceive that the opening of the Palace of Industry was an event that will long dwell in the minds of the glittering throng that on May-day graced by their presence the wonderful building at South Kensington.

As we have no space in this Number to describe in detail the grand Inauguration of the Industrial Palace for 1862, we must content ourselves with presenting to our readers the ode by Tennyson, the Poet Laureate, which was chanted right heartily, yet tenderly, by 5,000 voices.

THE FESTIVAL ODE.

Uplift a thousand voices full and sweet,
In this wide hall with earth's inventions stored,
And praise th' invisible universal Lord,
Who lets once more in peace the nations meet,
Where Science, Art, and Labour have outpour'd
Their myriad horns of plenty at our feet.

O silent father of our Kings to be,
Mourn'd in this golden hour of jubilee,
For this, for all, we weep our thanks to thee!

The world-compelling plan was thine,
And, lo! the long laborious miles
Of Palace; lo! the giant aisles,
Rich in model and design,
Harvest-tool and husbandry,
Loom and wheel and engin'ry,
Secrets of the sullen mine,
Steel and gold, and corn and wine,
Fabric rough or fairy fine,
Sunny tokens of the Line,
Polar marvels, and a feast
Of wonder out of West and East,
And shapes and hues of Art divine!
All of beauty, all of use,
That one fair planet can produce,
Brought from under every star,
Blown from over every main,
And mixt, as life is mixt with pain,
The works of peace with works of war.

And is the goal so far away?
Far, how far, no man can say;
Let us have our dream to-day.

O ye, the wise who think, the wise who reign,
From growing Commerce loose her latest chain,
And let the fair white-winged peacemaker fly
To happy havens under all the sky,
And mix the seasons and the golden hours,
Till each man find his own in all men's good,
And all men work in noble brotherhood,
Breaking their mailed fleets and armèd towers,
And ruling by obeying Nature's powers,
And gathering all the fruits of Peace and crowned with all her flowers.

So much for the general idea of the Great International Exhibition of 1862. In order that our readers may obtain a tolerably clear idea of the nature of the World's Fair, it will be necessary that we should say something of

THE BUILDING.

It will be remembered that the Exhibition of 1851 took place in a building every way unique and original. The structure was composed entirely of iron and glass, and presented an aspect which was well denominated "fairy-like." Re-erected, with many modifications, improvements, and additions at Sydenham, the Crystal Palace may be pronounced the most wonderful and attractive edifice in the world.

In few respects does the building itself now standing at South Kensington bear comparison with its predecessor of 1851. It can by no means be called a Crystal Palace; for though there is a vast quantity of iron and glass employed in its erection, its walls are of brick and its roof of wood. It was not probably thought necessary in 1862 to repeat Sir Joseph Paxton's idea of 1851, beautiful as it was; but in no essential respect does the International building fail in meeting all its requirements. Moreover, the necessity of retaining a large portion of the present building as a permanent structure for future exhibitions, rendered unadvisable its erection in glass.

THE SITE.—The International Exhibition building is erected at Kensington Gore, on a piece of ground belonging to the Commissioners for the Exhibition of 1851, by whom it was purchased with the surplus funds arising out of the Crystal Palace at Hyde Park. It lies between Prince Albert-road on the west, Exhibition-road on the east, and Cromwell-road on the south. It therefore presents three fronts; while adjoining it, and occupying the space between the Cromwell-road and Kensington Gore, are the gardens of the Horticultural Society. A glance at the ground plan (which we hope to be

able to insert in our next number) will render the situation of the building familiar to the visitor. The Exhibition may be reached from the City by several roads, and great facilities are offered by the railroad and omnibus proprietors for easy access. The tenure of the land is legally vested in the Royal Commissioners, who have leased the whole of that part of the building facing the Cromwell-road to the Society of Arts, by whom it will be kept as a permanent structure.

THE DESIGN.—The building for the Exhibition of 1862 is erected from the designs of Captain Fowke, Royal Engineers, to whom was intrusted the plans for the Kensington Museum, adjoining. The most remarkable difference between the Exhibition buildings of 1851 and 1862 lies, as we have already said, in the abandonment of glass as the staple of the building, this material being only resorted to for the purpose of lighting. It was a courageous and perhaps doubtful act on the part of the Commissioners to repudiate a novelty in structural arrangement which had received such éclat from the brilliant success which attended its experimental adoption in 1851; but it is said that the experience of that memorable year, and that since obtained at Sydenham, has proved that glass and iron are materials not to be depended upon for architectural purposes, as regards the permanent resistance of the weather; while as to the regulation of light in a building, glass is intractable, rendering the adoption of endless contrivances to obtain shade necessary for the most ordinary purposes. When the exhibition of pictures is desirable, no amount of contrivance can render glass walls effectual. At the Crystal Palace at Sydenham the picture gallery is inclosed and separated from the glass shell of the building. Captain Fowke reverts to the use of old-fashioned bricks and mortar for the main walls of the building. In external aspect it certainly has not the gossamer lightness of the Palace of 1851; but internally, whilst the provoking glare which habitually pervaded that fairy-like structure, and which called into requisition an endless amount of screening, is avoided, the body of light obtained is ample to give effect to the building and its varied contents.

GENERAL PLAN OF THE BUILDING.—The building for the Great International Exhibition of 1862 occupies a space of twenty-six acres, inclusive of the machinery and other annexes. The main building, as seen in the ground-plan, is in the general form of the letter I ; the upright limb, in which the machinery is placed, having a frontage towards Prince Albert's-road, and being backed by the gardens of the Royal Horticultural Society. Within the building proper the general idea of the nave of 1851 has been adopted; but, instead of the arched transept, which gave so much character to the Hyde Park Palace, two huge glass domes have been erected at either end. The nave is 85 feet wide, and 100 feet high—13 feet wider, and 40 feet higher than that of 1851—with side aisles, over which run the galleries. The main block is 1,152 feet in length, by 600 feet in width. The machinery annexe is 870 feet long, by 200 feet wide. Thus, while nearly 700 feet shorter than the Hyde Park Palace, it is much wider and higher.

The domes, or transepts, form the most novel features of the building. They form, at either end of the nave, great octagonal halls, 160 feet in diameter, surmounted by glass domes, 200 feet high from the floor. These domes are the largest ever built : St. Paul's being only 108 feet in diameter, and St. Peter's at Rome 139 feet ; while the diameter of the new dome over the reading-room at the British Museum—the largest hitherto constructed—is but 140 feet. The floors of these dome-covered halls are considerably raised above the floor of the nave, and therefore afford the best situations from which the visitor may obtain a good view of the interior. A small iron railing runs round each gallery, both inside and outside the dome. Upon the raised platform or dais in the centre of each hall are fountains, &c., surrounded by shrubs. These are the angles are staircases, communicating with the nave and side aisles. The building viewed from end to end, previous to its being filled with objects, presented an aspect something like a cathedral, to which a Manchester warehouse and a railway shed had somehow most unaccountably become connected. Now, however, that the

VIEW OF THE NAVE FROM THE EASTERN DOME, PREVIOUS TO THE INAUGURATION FESTIVAL IN 1851.

ALBERT THE GOOD

LONDON, 1851 · LONDON, 1862

ART SCIENCE MANUFACTURE TRADE

NEW YORK, 1853 · PARIS, 1855

THE EARTH IS THE LORDS AND THE FULNESS THEREOF

INTERNATIONAL EXHIBITIONS.
A MEMORIAL DESIGN BY H. ANELAY.

galleries are filled, and the straight lines of the pillars are broken here and there by the introduction of flags, and the floor is covered with various large objects, and the public crowd about in every direction, the effect, though infinitely inferior to that presented at the Crystal Palace, Hyde Park, is certainly very picturesque. Galleries run all round the nave, as in 1851. These, with the roof, are supported by iron columns, placed in pairs, at a distance of fifty feet apart, and banded midway in their height. The galleries occupy a length of upwards of a mile and a half; some of them are 50, and others 25 feet in width.

Besides the main building and galleries as seen from the domes, there are two glass courts (each 250 by 200 feet), two central courts, and other inclosed spaces. In these alone does the visitor recognise any likeness to the beautiful Crystal Palace.

The space occupied by foreign exhibitors in the galleries is as follows:—On the south side, France occupies 28,350; the Zollverein, 16,962; Spain, 1,875; Portugal, 1,250; and Italy, 6,875 square feet. On the north side, and in the galleries of the western transept, Austria has 9,796; Belgium, 10,787; Switzerland, 4,500; Denmark, 1,250; Norway and Sweden, 1,750; Russia, 3,250; Turkey, Egypt, and Tunis, 8,050; and Greece, 25 square feet. The gallery space is occupied by silks, printed woollen goods, muslins, and light articles.

The level of the ground being 5 feet below that of the surrounding roads, enabled Captain Fowkes to adopt an ingenious expedient. The visitor *descends* from the dais into the nave and transepts by flights of wide steps, and *ascends* into the picture galleries and the galleries of the Industrial Exhibition.

The Picture Galleries occupy three sides of a quadrangle. The largest gallery faces the Cromwell-road. This is 1,150 feet long, 50 feet wide, and 50 feet high above the ground-floor—being about as long as the gallery at the Louvre at Paris.

The passage from end to end of this great picture gallery is uninterrupted, although the entrance is in the centre of it. The construction is of substantial brick-work. The piers at the entrance are 14 feet wide, and 7 feet thick; and the foundations throughout are of concrete, 5 feet thick.

The walls are lined with wood, and the pictures hung to the height of not more than thirty feet. The lighting is on the principles so successfully demonstrated in the Sheepshanks Gallery, which was the first public gallery perfectly lighted by day and gas-light. These principles require that the quantity of light should be as great as possible, be subject to control, and obtained from above; and that the rays from the skylight incident on the pictures should in no case be reflected by their varnished surfaces, so as to strike the eye of a spectator while standing at a convenient distance for examining the pictures. The inflexibility of these principles, and the necessity for perfect ventilation, have regulated the architectural treatment of the present structure, at least as far as the picture galleries go. As the light *must* come from the top, and the pictures *must* hang on the walls, there could therefore be no window-spaces in the upper walls. The greatest damage has been done to pictures for want of proper ventilation; the miasma from crowds is most injurious, if not effectually removed. In this gallery ample provision is made for ventilation in the only right and effective places. Not to waste valuable space, a floor has been provided beneath the picture galleries, lighted from the sides. Given, therefore, these conditions of lighting, ventilation, and economy of space, as principles which must not be impaired by any considerations of architectural design, it would be interesting to see produced a better structural design for realising them than the present. Time will show how the exterior may be decorated. In the principal galleries are suspended the largest oil-paintings and cartoons; but auxiliary picture galleries for water-colour drawings and small pictures, architectural designs, engravings, &c., face the Exhibition and Cromwell Roads.

A careful study of the ground-plans will presently give to the reader a better idea of the distribution of space in the International Exhibition than can be conveyed by almost any amount of verbal description. In brief, then, the building at South Kensington provides,

on a scale hitherto unattempted, four main objects: 1. *Picture galleries*, which require to be solid structures, secure from all accidents of weather, extremely well ventilated, and lighted at the top. 2. Ample spaces, of different forms, and lighted in different ways, for the *exhibition of works of industry*, arranged in courts and galleries. 3. Platforms and wide passages for *ceremonials and processions*; and 4. Accommodation for *refreshments*.

The Roof of the entire building is of wood, coated on the outside with felt, and meeting in the centre at an angle, like Westminster Hall, and other ecclesiastical structures. It is supported by serviceable arches of timber, springing from the iron columns, at a height of sixty feet from the floor. The roofs of the picture galleries are covered with slate. With regard to

The Decorations of the building, much difference of opinion has been expressed; but this was during the progress of construction, and before a good idea could be formed of the general effect. The columns generally are painted a bronze green, with edgings of buff down their angles, and bands of bright red at their roots, their heads, and their junctions with the galleries. The ornamental iron work along the front of the galleries is also painted a bronze green, backed with red cloth. The roof of the nave is painted grey, with a pattern in light flowers and arabesques; the girders are painted alternately red and blue, relieved on the edges with a broad buff line. Each girder or spanner along the nave has the name of a country painted on it. The columns or shafts are painted the same bronze green, and their capitals are alternately painted blue and red, with gilded mouldings, which give them a very pretty appearance. The whole of the decorations have been confided to Mr. Crace, than whom no more able man could be found.

The large circular window in the tympan of the entrance under the east dome is filled in with stained glass, by Mr. Hartley, and has a very brilliant effect. This window is 30 feet in diameter, and forms the disc of the monster face for the clock exhibited by Messrs. Dent and Co. The face of the dial is 45 feet in diameter, and the figures of the hours are upwards of 6 feet in length. The wall in which this circular window is set is elegantly decorated, the western window is also filled in with coloured glass. Inscriptions run round the belt of the domes, and at the ends of the nave and transepts. In the English portion of the building the texts and quotations are in English; but to foreigners the poor compliment has been paid of supposing that they do not understand our language, and they have been treated to inscriptions in Latin. Whether foreigners have a more intimate acquaintance with Latin than English we cannot say; but, if a second language was considered necessary, we should have thought that the one which would have been more generally intelligible would have been the French. The inscription round the eastern dome is a portion of the prayer of David, when invoking a blessing upon the great palace which he had commenced, and which he left to his son Solomon to complete. The words are: "Both riches and honour come of Thee, and Thou reignest over all, and in Thine hand is power and might, and in Thine hand it is to make great." In the western dome the inscription, in Latin, is also taken from the words of David's prayer (1 Chron xxix. 11): "*Tua est Domine magnificentia, et potentia, et gloria, atque victoria; et tibi laus; cuncta enim quæ in cœlo sunt, et in terra tua sunt, tuum Domine regnum*" (Thine, O Lord, is the greatness, and the power, and the glory, and the victory, and the majesty: for all that is in the heaven and in the earth is thine; thine is the kingdom, O Lord, and thou art exalted as head above all)." At the end of the nave joining this dome are the words: "*Gloria in excelsis Deo, et in terra pax.*" At the south end of the western transept the inscription is: "*Deus in terram respexit, et implevit illam bonis suis*;" and at the north end: "*Domini est terra, et plenitudo ejus.*" At the east or English end of the nave are the words in English: "The earth is the Lord's and the fulness thereof." The east transept has at one end a line of Cowper's: "Alternately the nations learn and teach;" and at the other: "Each climate needs what other climes produce."

This expedient of giving the inscriptions in Latin is somewhat burlesqued by the placard liberally placed about the walls during the progress of the building—" No smoking allowed "—which appears in French, German, Italian, Dutch, Spanish, and Portuguese: " *Il est défendu de fumer;* " " *Das rauchen ist verboten;* " " *Non e permisso di fumare;* " " *Het is verboten te rooken;* " " *No es permitido fumare;* " " *Nao he permittido fumar.* "

It will bo seen by the ground-plan that the building is, as it were, divided into two halves, both on the basement and in the galleries; one half being devoted to Great Britain, and the other to foreign nations and the Colonies. In like manner, the Picture Galleries are divided into English and foreign.

The contractors for the building are Messrs. Kelk and Lucas, who for this structure have entered into a brief partnership. The price to be paid for the whole building is £300,000, though one-third of this amount is conditional on the gross profits exceeding half a million, as they did in 1851. The contractors, therefore, risk £100,000 on the success of the Exhibition, though in all human probability there is not the risk of a shilling. The Crystal Palace, in Hyde Park, cost only £80,000, and the materials at the close of the Exhibition were purchased by the Company formed for the purpose of erecting the Sydenham Palace at £75,000 more. Thus, in 1851, the building stands, in every respect, the test of comparison with its Kensington rival.

The laying out of the ground and the works commenced on March 1, 1861, and the whole was delivered over to the Royal Commissioners on the 12th of February in this year. On the whole, the new building, being of brick, iron, and wood, is perhaps the cheapest ever erected. The bricks were supplied by Messrs. Smeed, of Sittingbourne, in Kent, upwards of ten and a half millions having been used.

The iron castings were executed at the Stavely Iron Works, Derbyshire, under the direct superintendence of the proprietor, Mr. Barrow. The quantity of iron employed is something astonishing. There are 166 round columns for the nave and transepts, 12 inches in diameter, connected with an equal number of square pilasters; 312 eight-inch round columns, and 140 twelve-inch square columns for the galleries; 138 eight-inch square columns for the clerestory windows, and 160 ten-inch square columns supporting the floors of the picture galleries; 62 round columns supporting the roofs of the glass courts, and various smaller columns. If all the iron columns in the building were placed end to end, they would reach a distance of upwards of five miles; or say, from the Kensington Museum to Whitechapel Church. Besides these there are 1,165 girders, 11,600 feet of pipes, 15,000 feet of gutters, 14,000 feet of railing, 1,000 brackets, 750 trusses and girders, 1,400 shoes, and other iron castings, the weight of the whole of which is estimated at about 5,000 tons. The castings were all delivered on the ground by the 1st of last October, about the period of the year, indeed, at which the Hyde Park Palace was begun.

The wrought iron was supplied by the Thames Iron Company, and is estimated to weigh about 1,250 tons. It was principally used in the construction of the domes; the duty of fixing the bolts, bracings, trusses, and railings for which, was intrusted to Mr. Ashton, gentleman, who superintended the like operations for the Crystal Palace at Hyde Park and Sydenham. The bracings, trusses, &c., were wrought by the contractors.

The woodwork was executed, in nearly similar quantities, at the works of Mr. Kelk, at Grosvenor Canal, and at the yard belonging to Mr. Lucas, at Lowestoft, Essex. About 26,500 loads were consumed in the building and scaffolding. Much of the framing, &c., was prepared on the ground.

For the clerestory lights of the nave and transepts, about 30 miles of sash-bar and glass have been expended; for the top lighting of the galleries, about 50,000 feet superficial of glass and framing; and for the lighting of courts, &c., a quantity almost as large.

The centre area of the picture gallery is to be the property of the Society of Arts, as a permanent structure for future exhibitions. Should a surplus arise from the Exhibition, as there doubtless will, the disposition of it will be left to the decision of the guarantors. The Exhibition building, so quickly and so substantially erected, so capable of almost any amount of after decoration—for which, indeed, provision is

made in the charter of incorporation—will be evidence of the skill, if not the taste, of its designers and contractors, and prove a monument of disinterested public spirit on the part of the guarantors, and of the success of voluntary unassisted effort.

During the progress of the building upwards of two thousand workmen were constantly employed, of course, to those employed by the exhibitors towards the completion of the structure. Besides these, there were armies of labourers to do the rougher work—the carrying, lifting, and removing of bricks and mortar, timber, iron, &c.; for your regular skilled mechanic always has his attendant workman. Every girder, pillar, and truss was tested previous to being set permanently in its place, and not a foot of flooring but was treated as though on its stable and durable qualities depended the whole success of the enterprise. Indeed, every precaution has been taken to render the building fully capable of meeting all demands that can by any possibility be made upon it.

As to the exhibitors in this great World's Fair of 1862, hardly a name of any eminence in art, science, commerce, literature, trade, or manufacture is absent; while, in the foreign half of the building, every European country, and most of the centres of civilisation in every quarter of the globe, are represented.

The fine art portion of pictures, drawings, statues, models, and engravings is a welcome and appropriate addition to the industrial display. Both portions of the Exhibition are large, comprehensive, and highly interesting. Nothing, indeed, so fine and so complete has hitherto been seen.

The picture galleries are certainly the most spacious and noble in existence, not even excepting the long gallery of the Louvre. The lighting is also as successful as could be hoped; and the collection of British art now brought together is finer than has ever been known: in every department we are above competition, except in the representation of battles and military spectacles, in which the French surpass us.

The arrangement and design of the building is such that the exhibited articles have been generally arranged in three great divisions.—

1. Fine arts, in the galleries especially provided for that department.
2. Raw materials, manufactures, and agricultural machinery, in the main building and the eastern annexe.
3. Machinery requiring steam or water power for its effectual display, in the western annexe.

The exhibiting space in the building has been divided equally between British and foreign exhibitors—our Colonies occupying a portion of the space on the British side. The industrial portion of the display has, throughout the whole building, been divided into thirty-six classes, under the general heads of raw materials, machinery, and manufactures. These classes are filled by about 23,500 exhibitors; 16,000 coming from the leading Foreign States, 2,000 from the Colonies, and 6,000 from the United Kingdom. The number of British exhibitors in 1851 was certainly much more numerous—a fact that may possibly be attributable to certain want of arrangement among the exhibitors themselves—while the foreigners have increased threefold. Nearly 10,000 applicants claimed space, of whom all but about 2,000 were in the industrial department. Had the claims of all the would-be exhibitors been complied with, a building seven times the size of the South Kensington Palace would have been requisite. A judicious system of cutting down was therefore necessary, and even the most sensitive exhibitor will acknowledge that the Commissioners and their Secretary have exercised great skill and admirable judgment in their selection. The greatest number of applicants, and consequent rejections, was in the iron, metal, and general hardware department; the smallest number was in mining and metallurgy. As was said by the Prince Consort of the Great Exhibition of 1851, " there is beauty in utility;" and even the most severe of critics will scarcely deny that, in that regard, there is beauty in Captain Fowke's design. At any rate, if it fall short of the airy lightness of the Crystal Palace of Hyde Park, it is at least solid and substantial, as becomes the English character. Moreover, that substantiality has been obtained at the smallest possible cost—another really English recommendation.

An able writer graphically describes the scene at the building previous to the opening. "The most energetic exertions," he says, "were bent upon its completion by the 1st of May; a man is killed on one day, a boy is crippled for life on another; a great contractor looks on complacently at the chaos of work, or touts, through his servants, in several languages, for orders for fittings; clerks of works hurry about with papers, dogged by foremen and labourers; groups of workmen stand in convivial groups, and take hourly refreshment from overflowing beer cans; a dozen men congregate round a hole, or a piece of timber, or balance themselves upon swinging scaffold poles, and act as if six hundred years were allowed them in which to complete the building; hangers of pictures shut themselves up in the galleries (by strict official orders), and do their work in solitude and silence, as if it were a mystery of Isis; sappers and miners seem to spend half their lives in taking instructions from clerks about canister stoves; exhibitors look in to learn something from observation about their space, and shake their heads when they see the rain dripping through the glass from a thousand crevices; authorities, who have more respect for stone statues than for the well-advertised reputation of Messrs. Kelk and Lucas, decline to send in heavy works in this order of art until the flooring of the picture galleries is largely strengthened; clumsy carts come rumbling slowly into the centre of the building with overhanging loads, and the horses shake their harness as they hear the thunder of the falling timber under the eastern dome. All this may be active work, and there may be 1,000, or there may be 2,000 working men in the building; but every plank that is laid down or raised, every nail that is driven in, certainly puts the structure in a worse position." One half of the southern courts — once pleasingly called the "open or glass courts" — is now boarded off for the great French arena, and much of the space that looked so charming during the progress of the building is now shut off from the nave and transepts. But perhaps this closing up of open spaces in both ends of the Exhibition was necessary in order to obtain room for the sort of hangings of carpets, tapestry &c. Of course in these expressed during the progress of a design must be subject to modification. As a whole, now that the Exhibition is complete, there seems little reason to complain of the appropriateness of the spaces placed at the disposal of each exhibitor.

So much for the building. In future numbers we shall endeavour to present our readers with illustrations of all the principal and notable objects in the World's Fair of 1862. As an instalment of our design, we have pleasure in giving a picture of Mr. Foley's portrait statue of Oliver Goldsmith. This statue is in bronze, and will be found in the principal picture gallery facing the Cromwell-road. It is afterwards to be erected in front of Trinity College, Dublin, and is now exhibited by the subscribers, of whom there were more than 2,000.

BRONZE STATUE OF OLIVER GOLDSMITH. BY J. H. FOLEY, R.A.

THE ROYAL TROPHY. BY MR. J. DURHAM, AND MR. AND MRS. THORNYCROFT.

The Royal Trophy.

JUST within the main entrance from the Cromwell Road, and forming the principal object in the noble hall, the visitor will notice the famous sculptural group we have selected for illustration. It consists of a colossal portrait statue on a pedestal, within the sub-base of which are portrait busts, and at the advanced corners emblematical figures of Commerce; Peace, with the olive branch; Plenty, with the well-filled horn; a hunter, and a fisherman. The principal figure is an emblematical treatment of her Majesty's statue (the Queen, with the attributes of Peace), by Mr. J. Durham. It was intended as the crowning object in the group commemorative of the Great Exhibition of 1851; but, in accordance with the royal wish, it will—in the complete work, to be erected in the Horticultural Gardens—be superseded by a statue of the Prince Consort, in his robes as Grand Master of the Bath; from the design of the same artist, who is now engaged upon the work. Under these circumstances, and as a fitting memorial of the originator of the Exhibition, it was determined to place this statue of the Queen near the main entrance of the building. As will be seen, an attempt has been made to embody in one group portraits of the royal family. In the centre face of the base, which is an irregular octagon, the royal arms are displayed, immediately above which is the bust of Prince Albert, which has been recently executed by Mr. Thornycroft. The other faces of the base contain, in their several niches, busts of the Princesses Frederick William (the Princess Royal), Alice, and Beatrice; while the features of the emblematical figures at the advanced corners are those of the Princess Helena, as Peace; the Princess Louise, as Plenty; Prince Leopold, as the Fisher-boy; and Prince Arthur, as the Huntsman. The treatment of the whole subject is noble and graceful.

In the International Exhibition sculpture does not—at least, in the British half of the building—take quite so prominent a part in the general display as it did in 1851, there being shown comparatively few original designs. Nevertheless, our most famous sculptors, both deceased and contemporary — Nollekens, Flaxman, Westmacott, Chantrey, Wyatt, Bailey, Behnes, Bell, Foley, Gibson, Lough, Macdowell, Marshall, Noble, Theed, Thomas, the Westmacotts, and the Wyons—are all well represented. To the joint work of Mr. Durham, Mr. Thornycroft, and Mrs. Thornycroft—the last of whom is responsible for the statuettes in the lower pedestal of the royal group—too much praise cannot be accorded. It should be stated that the statue of the Queen will finally be cast in bronze.

Eleven Years of Progress.

THE glory of 1851 was revived in all its pomp and magnificence on May-day, 1862. The Great Exhibition of 1851 was the first experiment of the kind; and now that its value and significance have been fully comprehended, the public mind is prepared to relearn the lesson to be learned, and to profit by the teaching. In the convocation of the nations at South Kensington we but perceive the realisation of an idea that twelve years ago was hardly understood, and certainly not fully appreciated, by the great bulk of the world's thinkers and actors. But if the majority were slow to recognise the true significance of the World's Fair in 1851, it is satisfactory to believe that the seed then sown has fructified and borne good fruit. In a thousand ways our national taste has been improved by the experience gained then and since. In a thousand ways our ideas have been enlarged and liberalised. In a thousand ways the people are better prepared to accept the teachings of science, and the results of experimental philosophy. The Exhibition of 1851 did for the nation what foreign travel does for the individual

PLAN OF GALLERIES.

A Picture Gallery, British School.
B, C Picture Gallery, British School.
D Paper, Stationery, &c., Class 28.
E Horology, Class 15.
F Surgical Instruments, Class 17.
G Philosophical Instruments, Class 13.
H Dressing Cases, Class 36.
J Lace, Class 24.
K Woollens, Class 21.
L Flax and Hemp, Class 19.
M Silk and Velvet, Class 20.
N Mixed Fabrics, Class 21.
O Dining Room.
P Cotton, Class 18.
Q Printed and Dyed Goods, Class 23.
1 France.
2, 3 Zollverein.
4 Egypt.
5 Austria.
6 Belgium.
7 Russia.
8 Switzerland.
9 Holland.
10 Sweden.
11 Norway.
12 India.
20 Spain.
21 Portugal.
22 Italy.
The Central Tower is occupied by Photography, &c.
Sculptures, Bronzes, &c., are distributed throughout the Picture Galleries and various parts of the Nave and Courts.

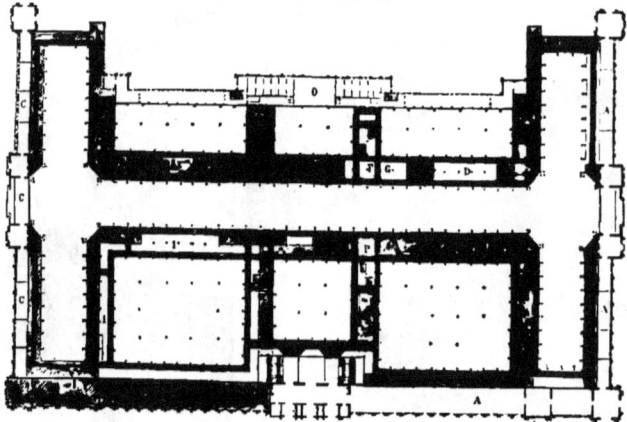

Briton. It taught it to be less insular in its notions, and more generous in its estimation of others. If this assemblage of all the countries of the world to the display of their industrial and artistic achievements was intended—as in the mind of its august originator it surely was—to illustrate the progress of each, and to show the backward how to mend their pace, and the foremost the open road to a yet nearer approach to perfection, it follows that periodical stock-takings and comparisons with our neighbours cannot but be highly advantageous both to us and to them. The only question is, what interval of time should elapse between each exhibition. Ten years appears a reasonable period, and the Society of Arts—whose share in the carrying out of Prince Albert's idea has been as considerable as it has been honourable—did well to propose the International Exhibition of 1862. Two years since it began to collect facts of every description illustrative of the progress of the world during the last decade. Most striking have been the results communicated through the industry and keen perception of the gentlemen to whom it entrusted the collation of the necessary intelligence. From the reports of Mr. William Hawes, the Registrar-General, Mr. C. M. Willich, Colonel Owen, and Sir Cusack P. Roney, we learn that the population of Great Britain since 1851 has increased by four millions, and that London itself contains an extra half million, for its share of the increase. Half of this population, it was further explained, were persons from fifteen to fifty, and one-fourth were too young to derive any benefit from the Exhibition of 1851. With the population had grown also the means of transporting them from place to place. England in 1862 possesses 4,045 miles of railway added on to the 6,055 it had in 1851. Moreover, many new lines have been opened since, all more or less calculated to bring foreigners in larger numbers and with greater facility to our shores; while the managers of foreign railways have been at length converted by our example, and have learned to create additional traffic by return tickets, excursion trains, and reduced rates. The Atlantic Ocean, too, is now bridged over by four times the number of regular lines of steamers, and the cost of the passage is diminished 30 per cent. New York, Boston, Portland, and Quebec are linked by a chain of railways of threefold intricacy to that which connected them in 1851. India is nearer to us by several days, and the voyage to Australia is shortened by half. The West Indian colonies have also participated in the general approximation; and South America and Africa are now permanently and regularly communicated with, which they were not before.

So much for the improved means of responding to the idea of an International Exhibition now possessed by the world, and the increased numbers to whom its practical lessons will extend. To still further illustrate this part of the subject, we take from the "Official History of the Exhibition," compiled by Mr. Hollingshead, the following concise summary of our industrial, social, and scientific progress since 1851:—

"Most important discoveries have been made in the preparation of colours for painting and dyeing, producing what are called the 'Aniline' series. Great economy has been effected in the manufacture of glass, and a process has just been made perfect for transferring photographs to that material. The manufacture of agricultural implements, and especially the application of steam power to them, has been so improved and extended, that it is now a highly important branch of trade.

"Photography, hardly known in 1851, has become an important branch of art and industry, used alike by the artist, the engineer, the architect, and the manufacturer.

"Marine telegraphy, only just accomplished in 1851—the public communication with Dublin having been opened in June, and that with Paris in November, 1852—has now become almost universal, linking together distant countries.

"The electric telegraph has become universal, and in every direction facilities for communication have been increased.

"We have repealed the duties on soap and paper, the only manufactures the prosperity of which was then thwarted by excise restrictions.

"We have abolished all taxes on the dissemination of knowledge, and have given increased facilities for the circulation of knowledge by post.

"We have repealed the import duties, or very nearly so, on raw materials, the produce of foreign countries, to compete with our own.

"Old industries have been stimulated and improved. New industries have arisen.

"In fine art, painting, and sculpture, it is hardly possible, except in very extraordinary periods, that a marked change can be observed in a single ten years, but this country certainly holds its own as compared with the productions of other countries.

"In the manufacture of iron, improvements have also been made; new bands of ore have been discovered, and day by day we are economising its production; and a metal between iron and steel is now produced at one process, which heretofore required two or more processes, alike expensive and difficult.

"In steam power, especially that applied to railroads and to ocean steam navigation, economical appliances have advanced rapidly.

"The use of coal for locomotives, in place of coke, and superheating steam and surface condensing in ocean steamers, tend to increase the power and economise the cost of those powerful engines of civilisation.

"In ship-building the past ten years have produced great changes.

"Our navy and mercantile marine have alike advanced in scientific construction and in mechanical arrangements. The ocean steamers which were then employed in the postal service included but one of two thousand tons; now there are many of nearly double that tonnage, with corresponding power and speed, increasing the facility and decreasing the risk of communication with our colonies and foreign countries.

"In printing, great advances have been made. By the perfection of chromatic printing, views of distant countries have been brought within reach of almost every class, displacing works which neither improved the taste nor gave useful information; and by the application of most expensive and most beautiful machinery to the printing of our daily journals, we have been enabled profitably to meet the increased demand caused by the cheapness of our newspapers. Invention and mechanical contrivance have thus kept pace with the requirements of intellect and the daily increasing love of knowledge."

To the effect of reasoning cogent and earnest as this, energetically impressed on the public mind, and more especially addressed to the commercial and manufacturing interests—already half converted by their own practical good sense—is due the International Exhibition of 1862. This second of a series of periodical displays of the industry, art, and taste of the world's workers will render manifest and stimulate our progress in all that tends to enlighten, purify, and exalt. In the important achievement of an International Exhibition—an exhibition for practical use, and not for mere empty and vain-glorious display—the memory of the Prince Consort will be preserved imperishably, perhaps more lastingly than by any monument, however solid and enduring; for in the pages of history his noble and philosophical mind, his quiet, unobtrusive greatness, will preside, like a protecting genius, at the portal of a new era in civilisation.

Turning now from mere generalities to hard facts, let us endeavour to show the reader

HOW TO SEE THE EXHIBITION

to the best advantage.

And first, in order to place the visitor in a fair position properly to estimate the value of the Great Industrial Show, we must make him acquainted with the

CLASSIFICATION OF OBJECTS

determined on by the Commissioners, and issued in February last.

The amount of space, covered and uncovered, which the designs of Captain Fowke placed at the disposal of the Commissioners for the three industrial sections, is 1,231,000 square feet, of which one-half had to be reserved for passages. The claims for a share of this space amounted to nearly 9,562—of which all but 2,000 referred to the industrial department. But as may be imagined, a large proportion of them were destined to be rejected, not a few of the proposals sent in being so wild as to appear the emanations of lunatics. The winnowing process being applied to these, the result has been that nearly 5,500 British exhibitors remained the chosen representatives of excellence

(Continued on page 14.)

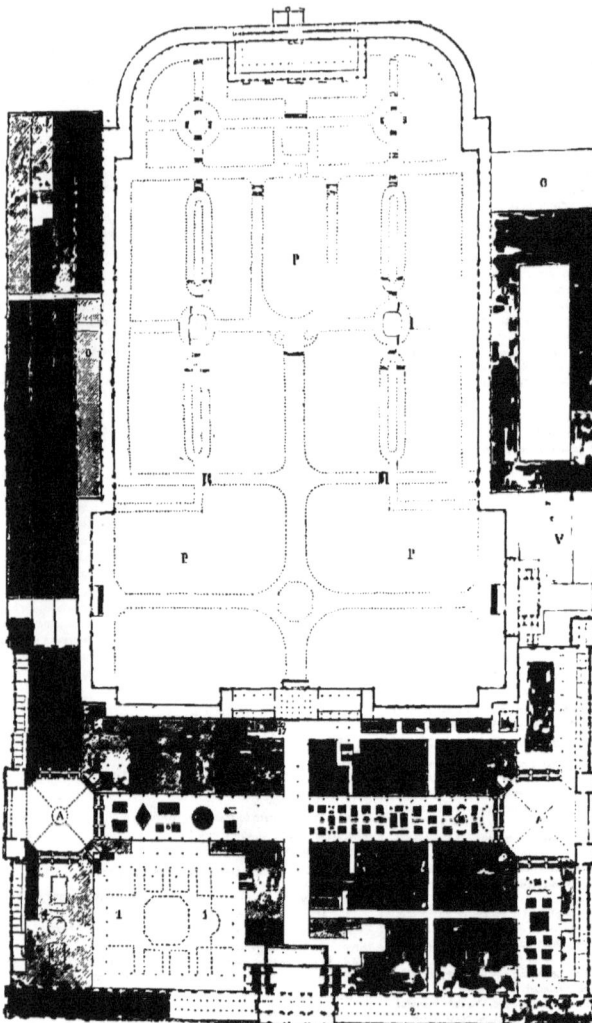

GROUND PLAN.

EXPLANATION OF
REFERENCES
ON
GROUND PLAN.

British Side and Annexes.

AA Eastern and Western Dome.
B Furniture, Class 30.
C Civil Engineering, Class 10
D Military Engineering, Class 11.
E Naval Architecture, Class 12.
F Glass, Class 34.
G Pottery, Class 35.
H Precious Metals and Jewellery, Class 33.
J Iron and Steel Works, Classes 31 and 32.
K Sheffield Court, Class 32.
L Leather, Saddlery, &c., Class 26
M Skins, Furs, and Feathers, Class 35.
N British Machinery, Classes 7 and 8; 1, 4, 5, 6, Foreign Machinery.
O Refreshment Rooms.
PP Royal Horticultural Gardens
Q Agricultural Implements, Class 9.
R Machinery, Class 7.
S Animal and Vegetable Substances, Class 4.
T Food, Class 3.
U Chemicals, Class 2.
V Mining Products, Class 1.
X Music.

Foreign Side.

1 France.
2 Hanse Towns.
2 Carriages—United States, North Side.
3 Zollverein.
4 South West Transept—Zollverein.
5 North-West Transept—Austria.
6 Belgium.
7 Holland.
8 Switzerland.
9 Denmark.
10 Sweden.
11 Russia.
12 Turkey.
13 Greece.
14 Brazil.
15 Costa Rica
16 Gusta Mala.
17 Peru.
18 Ionian Islands, China, and Japan.
19 British Colonies
20 Spain.
21 Portugal.
22 Italy
23 Rome.

In the Plan the main passages are left white; the main entrances lead to the east and west domes, to the picture galleries, and from the Horticultural Gardens, with the central transept between. The staircases to the galleries lead up from the domes and the central transept. The Inquiry Offices, Post-office, and Retiring Rooms will be found under the four corner towers. The annexes are reached through the transepts from either dome.

French Bronzes.

For ornamental works in metals the French have long been celebrated; nor will the present Exhibition by any means tend to lessen the pre-eminence they possess. In bronzes—which, by the way, are more often coloured zinc—they are confessedly very great. Nearly sixty exhibitors show bronzes, of various kinds and degrees of beauty and excellence, in the shape of tazzas, statues, candelabras, lamps, &c. The group here engraved is selected from the fine show made by Messrs. Barbezat, of Paris, whose display will be found just within the French Court from the nave. Nothing can be finer than some of the castings shown by this firm, to say nothing of the exquisite taste with which they are arranged. Among the most prominent of the exhibitors of bronzes, we may mention the names of Delafontaine, Galopin, Rollin, Cleaumont, Popon, Daubree, Hadrot (the inventor of the well-known table lamp), Deniere, Bayer, Lionett, Vitoz, and Malifat. The latter firm have, if possible, a finer show of the smaller description of table bronzes than they had in 1851. These Paris firms make their several displays so picturesque, that there is always about them a crowd of admirers, especially now that the French Courts are completed.

The art of bronze-founding attained its greatest height of excellence towards the middle of the last century, when it gradually declined, and towards the termination of our last war with France had almost died out of public estimation. But the necessity for other works than cannon revived the manufacture; and from 1817, when Lemot cast his statue of Henry IV., which stands on the Pont Neuf at Paris, it has as gradually grown in popularity, till in our day it is employed in the production of numerous articles of beauty and utility.

The ordinary proportion in which the various metals are mixed to form bronze for statuary are, for every 100 parts—copper 91 10 parts; zinc, 5 53; lead, 1 67; and tin, 1 70. Many of the French table bronzes are coloured, after casting, by a preparation of metals in nearly similar proportions. Works to be exposed to the atmosphere are generally allowed to retain the colour of the metal as it leaves the furnace.

GROUP OF FRENCH BRONZES. MM. BARBEZAT, PARIS.

(Continued from page 11.)

and progress, and the total horizontal space allotted to them, viz., 386,700 square feet, was decided in the following proportions among the different classes :—

SECTION I.—RAW MATERIALS.

Class 1.—Mining, quarrying, metallurgy, and mineral products.
This class is exhibited in the south court of the eastern annex: 433 British exhibitors occupy 8,400 square feet of floor space. R. Hunt is the superintendent.

Class 2.—Chemical substances and products, and pharmaceutical processes.
South-eastern passage: 205 exhibitors, with 3,100 square feet of floor space. Classes 2, 3, and 4 are under the superintendence of C. W. Quin, F.C.S.

Class 3.—Substances used for food, including wines.
Eastern side of eastern annex: 163 exhibitors, occupying 4,500 square feet of space.

Class 4.—Animal and vegetable substances used in manufactures.
Eastern side of eastern annex: 247 exhibitors, occupying 7,500 square feet.

SECTION II.—MACHINERY.

Class 5.—Railway plant, including locomotive engines and carriages.
The various objects in this class are exhibited in the eastern and western annexes. The machinery in motion, both British and foreign, will be found in the western annex. Classes 5, 6, 7, and 8 occupy 113,532 square feet of floor space. In Class 5 are 83 British exhibitors. Mr. D. K. Clark is the superintendent of Classes 5, 7, 8, and 10.

Class 6.—Carriages not connected with rail or tram-roads.
South-eastern court: 116 exhibitors.

Class 7.—Manufacturing machines and tools.
Western annex: Principally machines in motion. Two general divisions are observed in this class—machinery employed in weaving and spinning, and machines and tools employed in various manufacturing operations: 241 exhibitors in the British end.

Class 8.—Machinery in general.
Western annex: 252 exhibitors. The machinery in this class comprises a great variety of ingenious contrivances for all kinds of labour-saving appliances.

Class 9.—Agricultural and horticultural machines and implements.
West side of eastern annex: 150 exhibitors, occupying 38,800 square feet.

Class 10.—Civil engineering, architectural, and building contrivances.
This class is exhibited in the south court. It is divided into three sub-classes:—1. Civil engineering and building contrivances; 2. Sanitary improvements and constructions, such as ventilators, &c.; and, 3. Objects shown for architectural beauty, such as vases, fonts, &c. 164 exhibitors occupy 13,962 square feet of space.

Class 11.—Military engineering, armour and accoutrements, ordnance, and small arms.

Class 12.—Naval architecture, ships' tackle.
Both these classes are exhibited in the south court, and occupy together 12,610 square feet of space. The first is in three divisions: —1. Clothing and accoutrements ; 2. Tents and camp equipages; and, 3. Arms, ordnance, models of fortifications, barracks, &c. Class 12 is also divided thus:—1. Ship-building for purposes of war and commerce ; 2. Boat and barge building, and vessels for pleasure; and, 3. Ships' tackle and rigging. Class 11 has 195 exhibitors ; class 12, 150. Major Moffat, Superintendent.

Class 13.—Philosophical instruments, and processes depending upon their use.
This class is exhibited in the north court of the gallery, and in it are shown optical, magnetic, surveying, and other like instruments. In it are 149 exhibitors, with 7,625 square feet. C. R. Weld, Superintendent.

Class 14.—Photographic apparatus and photography.
This class will be found exhibited in the central tower and gallery, on the north side of the building: 165 exhibitors ; 2,966 square feet. P. Le Neve Foster, M.A., Superintendent.

Class 15.—Horological Instruments.
The clocks and watches, chronometers, mercurial and other timepieces, exhibited in this class, will be found in the gallery of the north court. About 170 exhibitors occupy 2,700 square feet of floor space. The superintendent of classes of 15, 28, and 38a (art designs for manufactures), is Mr. J. Leighton, F.S.A.

Class 16.—Musical instruments.
The musical instruments will be found in the north court, under the superintendence of Mr. C. Hoosé. All kinds of contrivances for producing harmony from metal, wood, and animal substances, are shown by 91 exhibitors, who occupy 5,890 square feet of floor space.

Class 17.—Surgical instruments and appliances.
The objects in this class are also exhibited in the gallery of the north court, under the superintendence of Mr. J. R. Tracr, F.R.C.S. ; 134 exhibitors occupy 2,475 feet.

SECTION III.—MANUFACTURES.

Class 18.—Cotton.
Cotton goods of various kinds are shown in the south gallery by 63 exhibitors, with 4,654 square feet of floor space, independent of upright hangings.
Classes 18, 19, 20, 21, 22, 23, 24, and 27, are under the superintendence of Mr. G. Wallis, with his assistants.

Class 19.—Flax and hemp.
Manufactures in this class are shown in the gallery of the southeast transept, by 81 exhibitors, in 6,483 square feet, besides hanging space.

Class 20.—Silk and velvet.
The manufactures in this class are to be found in the south-east gallery ; 64 exhibitors occupy 4,722 square feet.

Class 21.—Woollen and worsted, including mixed fabrics generally.
The objects in this class will also be found in the south-east gallery : 235 exhibitors, occupying 21,093 square feet.

Class 22.—Carpets.
Various specimens of carpets, shown by 44 exhibitors, will be found under the north-east gallery, and on the gallery walls.

Class 23.—Woven, spun, felted, and laid fabrics, when shown as specimens of printing or dyeing.
All the articles exhibited by 51 British manufacturers in this class will be found in the south-east gallery, and occupy about 3,500 square feet of the floor, besides much vertical space.

Class 24.—Tapestry, lace, and embroidery.
The objects in this class also occupy part of the south-east gallery ; 86 exhibitors have 5,087 square feet.

Class 25.—Skins, fur, feathers, and hair.
This class is divided into three sub-classes : A, skins and feathers ; B, feathers ; and C, manufactures from hair : 68 exhibitors occupy 1,316 square feet in the south transept court.

Class 26.—Leather, including saddlery and harness.
This class also occupies a part of the south transept court ; 196 exhibitors have 4,563 feet of floor space.

Class 27.—Articles of clothing.
In this class are shown, not clothes, in the widest sense of the word, but caps and bonnets, hosiery, gloves, boots, shoes, and gaiters. In the south-east angle of the building, 201 exhibitors occupy 7,500 square feet.

Class 28.—Paper, stationery, printing, and bookbinding.
The articles exhibited in this class are paper, card, and millboard, general stationery, plate, letter-press, and other modes of printing : with bookbinding " in all its branches." 225 exhibitors occupy 6,250 square feet of space in the gallery of the north court.

Class 29.—Educational works and appliances.
The objects in this class will be found in the central tower, where 234 exhibitors occupy 4,344 square feet, in showing books, maps, diagrams, and globes ; school fittings and furniture ; toys, and games of an instructive character; and illustrations of elementary science. J. G. Fitch, M.A., is the superintendent.

Class 30.—Furniture and upholstery, including paper-hangings and papier-maché.

This is a large class, occupying the north court, and consisting of furniture and upholstery, carvings, paper-hangings, and general household decoration, besides numerous articles for ecclesiastical purposes, in carved wood, papier-maché, &c.: 258 exhibitors occupy 25,272 square feet. Classes 30, 33, 34, 35, and 37 are under the care of Mr. J. B. Waring, F.R.I.B.A.

Class 31.—Iron and general hardware.

This class occupies the south court, under the superintendence of Mr. T. A. Wright, who also has the care of Classes 6, 32, and 36. The space occupied by 409 exhibitors is 25,522 square feet.

Class 32.—Steel, cutlery, and edge tools.

This class occupies the transept, south court: 127 exhibitors have 13,316 square feet.

Class 33.—Works in precious metals, and their imitations, and jewellery.

This class is located in the central division of the south court: 84 exhibitors have 7,968 square feet of space.

Class 34.—Glass, for decorative and household purposes.

The objects in this class are also shown in the south court, by 81 exhibitors, with 15,680 square feet of space; besides much stained glass being erected vertically, in order to obtain the necessary light.

Class 35.—Pottery.

Various articles, illustrative of the ceramic art, are shown in the central division of the north court, by 62 exhibitors, with 5,475 square feet of space.

Class 36.—Manufactures not included in previous classes.

In the gallery of the north court, 31 exhibitors show dressing-cases, writing-desks, portmanteaus, &c., in 2,800 square feet.

It will thus be seen that Section I. occupies 26,500 feet; Section II., 195,540 feet; and Section III., 165,663 feet; making a total of 380,708 square feet for 5,500 exhibitors.

SECTION IV.—MODERN FINE ARTS.

Class 37.—Architecture.

North-east gallery, facing Exhibition-road.

Class 38.—Paintings in oil and water colours, and drawings.

Principal picture gallery, facing Cromwell-road.

Class 39.—Sculpture, models, die-sinking, and intaglios.

Shown in the principal picture gallery.

Class 40.—Etchings and engravings.

North-east gallery, Exhibition-road.

The object of the Exhibition being to illustrate the progress and present condition of Modern Art, each country will decide the period of Art which in its own case will best attain that end.

LETTERPRESS PLAN OF THE EXHIBITION.

By means of the following simple arrangement of type the reader will at once understand the position of the several trophies, &c.

The Exhibition of British Art in this section includes the works of artists alive on, or subsequent to, the 1st of May, 1762.

It is not proposed to award prizes in this section.

Prices will not be allowed to be affixed to any work of art exhibited in this section.

One-half of the space allotted to Section IV. is given to foreign countries, and one-half reserved for the works of British and colonial artists.

The arrangement of the works of art within the space allotted to each foreign country is entirely under the control of the accredited representatives of that country, subject only to the necessary general regulations.

The British Colonies, whose claims were more easy to deal with, obtained 12,822 feet, which were detached from the British side. In 1851 the Colonies, as a whole, had scarcely been represented. They now stand out in the following proportions :—

	Square feet.
East Indian Colonies, exclusive of India	300
Australian Colonies	1,650
South African	640
West African ...	200
Mediterranean	400
North American	5,895
West Indies ...	837
	12,522

Of the allotment of space in the foreign half of the Exhibition, we need only state that the largest amount has been granted to the French exhibitors, who number nearly 4,000.

Prizes, or rewards for merit, in the form of medals, will be given in Sections I., II., III.

These medals will be of one class, for merit, without any distinction of degree.

No exhibitor will receive more than one medal in any class or sub-class.

An international jury will be formed for each class and sub-class of the Exhibition, by whom the medals will be adjudged, subject to general rules, which will regulate the action of the juries.

Each foreign commission will be at liberty to nominate one member of the jury for each class and sub-class, in which staple industries of their country and its dependencies are represented.

Her Majesty's Commissioners have resolved that an industry shall be ranked as a staple one which has twenty exhibitors in a class, or fifteen exhibitors in a sub-class. But Her Majesty's Commissioners give to each foreign commission the alternative of sending a specified number of jurors, determined by the experience of past exhibitions, and by the relative spaces allotted to the several countries.

Life-size Statuary in Porcelain.

MANUFACTURERS have long been familiar with the production of statuettes in Parian and other descriptions of ceramic ware; but nothing on so extensive a scale as this statue has hitherto been attempted. To the eminent firm of Daniel and Co., of New Bond Street, is due the credit of producing this famous figure of a famous man. But not upon English workmen were the English manufacturers enabled to rely for the production. The potteries of Worcestershire and Staffordshire shrank from the responsibility of undertaking so large a statue in porcelain. The risk of breakage and unequal shrinking in the process was too great- the idea of life-size statuary was too novel, and altogether the experiment was too bold for even Wedgwood or Kerr. Having conceived the idea, Messrs. Daniel were not, however, to be baulked in the execution of a statue in pottery. They applied to a clever Frenchman, and he, with characteristic national intrepidity, designed, modelled, and executed the work; and that he succeeded, the proof lies before us, and may be made evident to any visitor to the International Exhibition. The statue is upwards of six feet in height. Great artistic taste is displayed in the treatment and pose of the figure; and so ably have the difficulties in its production been met and combated, that we doubt not statuary porcelain will soon become very popular. The cost of a life-size figure in unglazed pottery is about a fourth of that of marble; and it seems, therefore, not unlikely that the example of the bold Frenchman will be speedily followed.

The story of Palissy the Potter is too well known to need repetition. Every schoolboy is acquainted with the enthusiastic struggles of the self-taught potter of the sixteenth century with his deferred hopes, his sickening trials, and his first triumph. The experiments in which he spent so much time and money- half a century of perseverance and poverty- the beautiful art he studied, the exquisite works he produced, and which even now reach a high price in the market—the intimate connection which all his life existed between his religious opinions, staunch Huguenot as he was, and his labours as an artist-workman—his years of biting poverty, and his brief period of Court favour under Catherine de Medicis—all the history of "poor Master Bernard of the Tuileries" is replete with interest and instruction; for, strong in faith and persevering in effort, he triumphed in his laboratory — but was, alas! doomed to suffer imprisonment for his opinions, and, at last, died in the Bastile.

PALISSY THE POTTER.

Fine Arts in the Exhibition. 1.

THE great and distinguishing characteristic of the present Exhibition is, undoubtedly, its Fine Art department. The visitor will wander through the nave and courts of the wonderful building, and admire the immense variety of unique, curious, strange, and common-place

The main gallery, as already explained, is equally divided between the works of British and foreign artists. Among the former will be found the masterpieces of our principal artists, ranged in somewhat the following order : —On the south wall, the works of Hogarth, Gains-

MARBLE BUST OF THE PRINCESS ALICE. BY MRS. THORNYCROFT.

objects there on display; but he will return to the picture galleries and sculpture court again and again, to be again and again delighted. The pictures provide a never-ending source of gratification to all : for in the famous galleries, to which the visitor at once enters from the main entrance in the Cromwell Road, there are to be found all the chefs-d'œuvres of modern art. The main British gallery runs to the east of the entrance ; the smaller galleries, to the north, being devoted to water-colour drawings, engravings, architectural designs, &c.

borough, Wright, Wilson, West, Northcote, Opie, Singleton, Lawrence, Fuseli, Callcott, Danby, and Poole. Many other works of artists not quite so well known to fame are also to be found on the south side of the gallery.

Returning by the north wall, we have the best works of Martin, Collins, Constable, Mulready, Etty, Eastlake, Stanfield, Pickersgill, Frith, Meadows, and others.

The foreign galleries are devoted to works of art illustrative of

3.

the French, German, and Italian schools, with specimens from Austria, Norway, Sweden, Russia, Belgium, Rome, Switzerland, Spain, and the United States.

It was originally intended to confine the sculpture to the picture galleries and a special sculpture court. But since the opening of the Exhibition, various important alterations have been made in the arrangement of the objects in the domes, naves, and transepts. In the place of some of the trophies which then encumbered the nave, we have now, at both ends of the building, many exquisite specimens of the plastic art. The purely industrial part of the Exhibition—the ground floor—is now graced by the presence of noble pieces of sculpture by all the best artists of England, France, Italy, and other countries. In a previous page we gave an illustration of the royal group in the entrance hall from the Cromwell Road. We have now pleasure in presenting to our readers a beautiful engraving of one of the busts in the base of the trophy. It is that of the Princess Alice, sculptured in marble by Mrs. Thornycroft, an artist whose works have obtained an European fame. The likeness to the royal lady is said to be excellent, and the artistic treatment of the bust is everything that could be

desired. The work is the more interesting from the fact that the Prince Consort himself superintended and "touched" upon the clay model.

All doubt as to the excellence of the sculptural and pictorial display made in the Exhibition is now at an end. As we walk through the British Nave and Foreign courts, the eye is everywhere arrested by forms of beauty and grace. Marbles and bronzes claim our admiration, and the picturesque makes bold head against the utilitarian. This is especially the case on the foreign side of the palace, where, as in 1851, the tastefulness of the display often compensates for the unsubstantial prettiness of the material out of which it is evolved. Thus we have in the French courts zinc castings painted to imitate bronze; plaster figures treated with some chemical, in order to assimilate them to marble; deal wood painted to look like ebony; and engraved pewter putting on the dignity of silver, while even silver itself wears a masque of the more precious metal.

We content ourselves with a passing glance at these objects, reserving for future pages a fuller and more complete account of the Fine Arts.

The Exhibition Open.

By this time all the world knows that the State Opening of the International Exhibition took place on Thursday, the first of May, Eighteen Hundred and Sixty-two. A description of the imposing ceremony is necessary in these columns, though it appears somewhat after date, because the "Exhibitor" is intended to form a permanent record of this year's great industrial jubilee.

The morning of May-day broke gloriously over the metropolis, and before the hour at which business is usually commenced, the streets leading westward were full of company. Carriages of all descriptions brought visitors from all quarters, and a vast throng of sight-seers assembled at every point whence a good view of the out-door procession could be obtained. All along the line of route, the windows were filled with well-dressed spectators, and about the building itself thousands upon thousands assembled.

The first of May will henceforth be marked in the annals of England as an important epoch, for on that day, eleven years apart, the nations met in friendly rivalry, and the dawning of a brighter era for the human race began to be perceived and understood. Surely sang the poet Cowper—

"There is need of social intercourse,
Benevolence and peace, and mutual aid
Between the nations."

The "need" of which the poet—ever the true politician—had eloquent prevision nearly a century ago, is now freely acknowledged. The "social intercourse" he advocated, and which was so dimly understood in his day, is now growing, rapidly and healthily, by means of International Exhibitions, and all the real blessings that follow in their train. The barrier that of old interposed between the free interchange of ideas among the peoples of the world are, year by year, breaking down; and trade, commerce, and civilisation begin to assume their position as civilisers.

All who look with a philosophical eye upon the International Exhibition cannot but regard it as one of the most effective agents of social and scientific progress. The invitations that were sent forth far and wide for the transmission of products with which to fill the building, were indeed so many missives of peace and good-will; and the results have so far justified the anticipations of the promoters of the scheme as to warrant the prophecy of a success, both morally and commercially, beyond all precedent.

But to return to the May-day ceremony. It was in all respects worthy of the occasion. In a previous page we referred in general

terms to the programme observed. We have now, therefore, only to fill up the hiatus by placing on record in our columns the order in which the State Opening was performed.

At half-past twelve the doors of the building were closed, and no more season ticket holders were admitted. At one o'clock the Queen's Commissioners, together with his Royal Highness the Duke of Cambridge, K.G., his Grace the Archbishop of Canterbury, the Lord High Chancellor, the Earl of Derby, K.G., the Lord Chamberlain, Viscount Palmerston, K.G., G.C.B., and the Speaker of the House of Commons, entered the principal gateway in the Cromwell Road, their arrival being made known by a flourish of trumpets. Her Majesty's Ministers, the Foreign Commissioners, and other persons distinguished by title, nobility, office, learning, or position, who had waited their arrival, now joined the Royal Commissioners, and formed in procession in the following order:—

Trumpeters of the Life Guards in State Uniforms.
Contractors' Superintendents.
Decorator, Draughtsman, Surveyor.
Superintendents of Exhibition Arrangements.
Her Majesty's Commissioners' Superintendents of Building Works.
Contractors and Architect.
Council of Horticultural Society and Secretary.
Council of the Society of Arts, and Secretary.
Deputation of Ten Guarantors of the Exhibition.
Assistant Secretary to Her Majesty's Commissioners.
Secretary of Finance Committee.
Financial Officer.
Members of the Building Committee, and Secretary.
Special Commissioners for Juries, and Secretary.
Chairman of Juries.
The Right Hon. Lord Taunton, President of the Council of Chairmen of Juries.
Acting Commissioners for Colonies, Dependencies, &c.
Foreign Acting Commissioners.
The Lord Provost of Glasgow. The Lord Mayor of York.
The Lord Mayor of Dublin. The Lord Provost of Edinburgh.
Macebearer and Swordbearer of the City of London, preceding
The Right Hon. William Cubitt, the Lord Mayor of London.
G. J. Cockerell, Esq., W. H. Twentyman, Esq., Sheriffs of London and Middlesex.
Presidents of Foreign Commissions.
Her Majesty's Commissioners for 1851, and Secretary.
Her Majesty's Commissioners for the Exhibition of 1862, and Secretary.—

The Right Hon. the Earl Granville, K.G.,
His Grace the Duke of Buckingham and Chandos,
Sir C. Wentworth Dilke, Bart.,
Thomas Baring, Esq., M.P.,
Thomas Fairbairn, Esq.,
F. R. Sandford, Esq., Secretary.
The Right Rev. the Lord Bishop of London, accompanied by the Rev.
John Sinclair, M.A., the Archdeacon of Middlesex, and the
Rev. W. J. Irons, D.D., the Incumbent of the Parish.
Her Majesty's Ministers,
(Not being either Commissioners for the Exhibition of 1862, or Special
Commissioners for the opening.)
Her Majesty's Special Commissioners for the opening:—
His Royal Highness the Duke of Cambridge.
His Grace the Archbishop of Canterbury.
The Right Hon. Lord Westbury, Lord High Chancellor.
The Right Hon. the Earl of Derby.
The Right Hon. the Viscount Sydney, Lord Chamberlain.
The Right Hon. Viscount Palmerston.
The Right Hon. the Speaker of the House of Commons.
Royal Personages attending the opening:—
His Royal Highness the Prince Oscar of Sweden.
His Royal Highness the Crown Prince of Prussia.
Gentlemen in attendance on Royal Personages.
Pipers of the Scots Fusilier Guards.

The grand procession, starting from the south centre of the nave, proceeded through the lines of spectators to the western dome.

On the dais was a richly gilded throne, on a splendid rich Turkey carpet, and under a canopy of velvet and cloth of gold, from which was suspended the royal banner, and the banner of the Prince Consort. Nine red and gold chairs formed a semicircle about the throne; the steps, the dais, and the greater portion of the space in front being railed off from the general body of spectators, and covered with crimson cloth. Here was stationed a band composed of musicians from the several regiments of the Guards, the whole forming an *ensemble* grand and imposing in the extreme.

At the moment of his Royal Highness the Duke of Cambridge reaching the throne, at the right hand of which he stood, the National Anthem was sung by the choristers, two thousand strong, in the great orchestra under the eastern dome, with an instrumental accompaniment such as has seldom before been heard.

At the conclusion of the National Anthem, the Earl Granville, K.G., Chairman of her Majesty's Commissioners, read the following address:—

"May it please your Royal Highness and my Lords Commissioners:— We, the Commissioners for the Exhibition of 1862, humbly beg leave to approach her Majesty through you, her illustrious representatives on this occasion, with the assurance of our devotion to her Majesty's throne and Royal person.

"And first of all it is our melancholy duty to convey to her Majesty the expression of our deep sympathy with her in the grievous affliction with which it has pleased the Almighty to visit her Majesty and the whole people of this realm, in the death of her Royal Consort. We cannot forget that this is the anniversary of the opening of the first great International Exhibition eleven years ago by her Majesty, when his Royal Highness, as president of the commissioners of that Exhibition, addressed her Majesty in words that will not be forgotten. After stating the proceedings of the commission in the discharge of their duties, he concluded with a prayer, that an undertaking 'which had for its end the promotion of all branches of human industry, and the strengthening of the bonds of peace and friendship among all nations of the earth, might, by the blessing of Divine Providence, conduce to the welfare of her Majesty's people, and be long remembered among the brightest circumstances of her Majesty's peaceful and happy reign.'

"When we commenced our duties, and until a recent period, we ventured to look forward to the time when it might be our great privilege to address her Majesty in person this day, and to show to her Majesty within these walls the evidence which this Exhibition affords of the soundness of the opinion originally entertained by his Royal Highness — evidence furnished alike by the increased extent of the Exhibition, by the

earnestness with which all classes of the community have sought to take part in it, and by the large expenditure incurred by individual exhibitors for the better display of their produce and machinery. We can now only repeat the assurance of our sympathy with her Majesty in that bereavement which deprives this inaugural ceremony of her Royal presence; and whilst bearing mournful testimony to the loss of that invaluable assistance which his Royal Highness was so ready at all times to extend to us, we have to offer the Queen our dutiful thanks for the interest evinced by her Majesty in this undertaking, by commanding your Royal Highness and your Lordships to represent her Majesty on this occasion.

"Our respectful thanks are also due to their Royal Highnesses the Crown Prince of Prussia and Prince Oscar of Sweden, the presidents of commissions for those countries, for the honour which their Royal Highnesses have done us in coming to England for the purpose of attending this ceremony. In the attendance of his Royal Highness the Crown Prince of Prussia, we recognise a cordial deference to the wishes of our Sovereign, and a tribute of affection to the memory of his illustrious and beloved father-in-law.

"It now becomes our duty to submit to her Majesty a short statement of the circumstances connected with the realisation of the scheme for holding a second great International Exhibition in this country, the necessary powers for conducting which were conferred upon us by the charter of incorporation graciously granted to us by her Majesty in the month of February, 1861.

"In the years 1858 and 1859 the Society of Arts, a body through whose exertions the Exhibition of 1851 in a great measure originated, had taken preliminary measures for the purpose of ascertaining whether a sufficiently strong feeling existed in favour of a decennial repetition of that great experiment to justify an active prosecution of the scheme. Although the result was stated by the Society of Arts to be satisfactory, the outbreak of hostilities at that moment on the Continent necessarily put a stop to further proceedings.

"The restoration of peace in the summer of 1859, however, enabled the consideration of the question to be resumed, although at a period so late as to render it necessary that the Exhibition should be deferred till the present year; and the Society of Arts obtained a decisive proof of the existence of a general desire for a second great exhibition in the most satisfactory form, namely, the signatures of upwards of 1,100 individuals for various sums of from £100 to £10,000, and amounting in the whole to no less than £450,000, to a guarantee deed for raising the funds needed for the conduct of the Exhibition.

"The commissioners for the Exhibition of 1851, mindful of the source from which their property and their continued existence as a corporate body arose, and of one of their earliest decisions, that any profits that might be derived from that exhibition should be applied 'to purposes strictly in connection with the ends of the exhibition, or for the establishment of similar exhibitions for the future,' without hesitation placed at our disposal, free of all charge, a space of nearly seventeen acres on their Kensington Gore estate, which was at first considered sufficient for the purpose of the Exhibition, but to which at a subsequent period a further area of upwards of eight acres (being all the land which could be made available for those purposes) was added to our application, when the original space proved to be insufficient. For this grant of a site we have to express our thanks.

"To the Governments of foreign states and of her Majesty's colonies our acknowledgments are justly due, for the manner in which, with even greater unanimity than in 1851, they have responded to the appeal made to them to assist in this undertaking. In this cordial co-operation we find another proof that the time had arrived when a repetition of the Exhibition of 1851 had become desirable in the common interests of all nations.

"A similar tribute is due from us to those of her Majesty's subjects who appear as exhibitors, or who have placed at our disposal many valuable works to illustrate the branches of British art, and in this respect our grateful thanks are especially due to her Majesty.

"The arrangement and design of the building are such that the exhibited articles have been generally arranged in three great divisions:—

"1. Fine arts, in the galleries especially provided for that department.

"2. Raw materials, manufactures, and agricultural machinery, in the main building and the eastern annexe.

"3. Machinery requiring steam or water power for its effectual display, in the western annexe.

"Within these divisions the classification adopted is in most respects

THE INAUGURAL CEREMONY ON MAY DAY—THE PROCESSION DOWN THE NAVE TO THE READING OF THE ADDRESS.

the nations of the world may be drawn together in the noblest rivalry, and from which they may mutually derive the greatest advantages."

Immediately afterwards, the Earl of Granville went through the formal ceremony of presenting to the Duke of Cambridge the "Key of the Exhibition," which is, in fact, a master key of all the locks throughout the building, and which has been wrought entirely by hand out of a solid piece of steel, by Messrs. Chubb. It was on this occasion enclosed in a crimson velvet bag.

The procession was then re-formed, and proceeded along the north aisle of the nave to the eastern dome, the various bands playing, and the pipers of the Scots Fusilier Guards bringing up the rear.

On the platform, seats under the eastern dome were reserved for the principal personages, among whom were the Duchess of Cambridge, and her daughters, the Princess Mary and the Grand Duchess of Mecklenburg-Strelitz. The diplomatic corps, the ex-ministers, ex-chancellors, the Japanese Ambassadors, with a large number of noblemen and gentlemen who did not join in the procession, were also assembled on this spot.

Then was performed the special music, at which a full chorus, collected for the occasion from all parts of the country, and more than four hundred instrumentalists assisted. The first piece was Meyerbeer's grand overture, followed by the admirable ode by the Poet Laureate, magnificently composed as a chorale by Sterndale Bennett. The words we have already given; but we cannot express the wonderful simplicity and harmony of this exquisite chorale—poetry and music blending in a way that will long linger in the hearts of the vast multitude that day present. It was, indeed, a grand work, and produced a most profound sensation. The deep silence that prevailed enabled every syllable to be heard, and at its close, long and prolonged applause resounded through the palace.

The last of the special performances was a grand march by Auber, full of melody and great masses of sound.

At the conclusion of the orchestral performances, the Bishop of London offered an impressive prayer, and Handel's sublime Hallelujah Chorus followed. Scarcely had the musical thanksgiving ceased to vibrate through the dome, than his Royal Highness the Duke of Cambridge rose and proclaimed "the Exhibition open." The procession once more formed in order, and proceeded to the picture gallery; the trumpets took up the notes sounded by the orchestra, the barriers were removed, and the visitors at last roamed at will through every part of the building.

Thus, then, was the Great International Exhibition of 1862 thrown open to the public. All that was great and grand, all that England—nay, Europe—could produce, gave *éclat* to the ceremonial. All that is beautiful and useful is assembled at the world's great show-room at South Kensington, and well may we believe that there were but few present on that memorable May-day whose hearts did not bent responsive to the sentiment conveyed in the opening lines of Tennyson's noble ode:—

"Uplift a thousand voices, full and sweet,
In this wide hall, with earth's inventions stored.
And praise th' invisible, universal Lord,
Who lets once more in peace the nations meet,
Where Science, Art, and Labour have outpoured
Their myriad horns of plenty at our feet."

THE EASTERN DOME AND TRANSEPTS.

We will now suppose the visitor to enter the building by one of the doors at the eastern end from the Exhibition Road. He will presently find himself under the Great Eastern Dome. Before him is the Nave; to his right hand is the north-east transept, and to his left the south-east transept; while farther on, and adjoining the nave on either side, are the north and south courts. The situation and aspect of the nave and courts will be best seen by reference to the plans given.

First and foremost among the beautiful we notice MINTON'S

MAJOLICA FOUNTAIN, in the centre of the eastern dome. This fine work of art was not completed on the day of opening, and, indeed, at the moment at which we write can hardly be said to be entirely finished. It is composed of the kind of earthenware called majolica ware, and was designed by the late John Thomas, a sculptor of great talent and exquisite taste. This novel application of manufacture, probably the largest work of this kind ever undertaken, forms, like Osler's glass fountain in the Hyde Park Palace in 1851, a very attractive point in the present Exhibition. This magnificent work is no less than 36 feet high by 39 feet in diameter, and may be thus briefly described:—At the summit is a group, larger than life size, of St. George and the Dragon; four winged figures of Victory, holding crowns of laurel, encircle a central pavilion, on the top of which the group rests; underneath is a series of smaller fountains of varied shapes and sizes, which receive the water, and spread it as required. One of these is after the model of a fountain designed for the Queen's dairy at Windsor, by the late John Thomas, the sculptor, a man of rare genius. The fountain for Windsor was modelled under the personal superintendence of the late Prince Consort. The outer basin of the St. George's fountain is ornamented with an oak-leaf, alternating with the rose of England, and is divided by eight flower vases. The whole arrangement of the heraldic colouring is considered very perfect, and the imitation of the steel armour on the arms and legs of the colossal figure is especially deserving of notice.

Looking south, we have a large gas custom of wrought iron for the tower of Hereford Cathedral, and immediately beyond is the elegant WROUGHT IRON SCREEN for the same cathedral. Both this and the corona have been produced by Messrs. Skidmore and Co., of Coventry, from the designs of Mr. G. C. Scott. The screen is 36 feet long and 35 feet high. It consists of hammered iron and copper, with figures of angels, &c., in bronze, and a central figure representing our Lord rising from the tomb. The panels are filled in with mosaics of various coloured stones, &c. It is altogether a splendid specimen of art manufacture.

Beyond the screen there is a lofty GOTHIC BELL-TOWER, with a peal of nine cast steel bells, manufactured by Messrs. Naylor and Vickers, of Sheffield. Around are grouped various specimens of steel, in order to show the application of that metal to the manufacture of ordnance and every kind of arms, railway metals, &c.

Opposed to them we have a trophy of LONDON HARDWARE—a collection of modern metal-work, from original designs, in four compartments.

Then comes DENT'S TURRET CLOCK, which strikes the hours on a bell weighing about four tons, and the quarters on four smaller bells. The wheels of the clock are of gun-metal, and each of the dials are seven feet in diameter.

Specimens of steel by Bessemer's process are followed by Messrs. WARNER'S EIGHT BELLS, which are fitted with chiming apparatus, so as to be rung by one man. The largest bell weighs about a ton. Towards the south-east entrance are the COALBROOK DALE GATES, and other works in cast iron. These beautiful gates are 54 feet wide, and 25 feet high. Adjoining is a fountain in iron work, 25 feet high, with a statue of Oliver Cromwell, and figures of Peace and War.

The space on the east side of the transept abutting on the office, and underneath the gallery is cut up by the columns into a series of bays. These have been made into separate enclosed courts, which have been mostly assigned to individual contributors. Here Messrs. Hardman, of Birmingham, and Messrs. Hart, of London, have fitted up one of those bays as a mediæval court, with fine ecclesiastical furniture, statuary, and decorations. Close behind them is a bay appropriated to the exhibition of chandeliers and lamps. Between them and the dome, also underneath the gallery, is the space occupied by objects shown for architectural beauty—a series of works in stone and plaster, of a higher decorative character than those falling under the more generic term of building materials.

Passing again across the dome, we come to the Colonial trophies in the north-east transept. The Eastern, Australasian, African, Mediterranean, North American, and West Indian possessions are all well represented. The trophies include a gilded pyramid from Victoria, 40 feet high, representing in bulk all the gold sent from that colony ; a timber column from Tasmania, 90 feet high ; a section of coal from Nova Scotia ; a timber structure formed of native woods from New Brunswick, and a trophy of Canadian timber.

An ORGAN, by Foster and Andrews, of Hull. This fine instrument has 46 registers, 2,475 pipes, six composition pedals, two sforzando pedals, and one pneumatic combination pedal ; it is 30 feet high, 22 feet wide, and 14 feet deep. Previous to the opening, this organ stood in the centre of the nave, as shown in our engraving ; but it has since been removed to the side of the north-east transept. The organ of Messrs. Wills, which stood immediately behind it, has also been removed to the end of the British half of the nave.

We will now walk down

THE NAVE.

The trophies in the British half of the nave are not arranged in quite so much order as we could have wished. Of some of these we may speak hereafter at greater length. They meet the eye somewhat in the following order :—

Decorative furniture in the mediæval style.

Decorative furniture in the modern style, by Crace, Jackson and Graham, and others.

Drinking fountains, by Earp, of Lambeth ; sculptured stone, enriched with Swiss, Devonshire, and other coloured marbles.

A mounted statue of Lady Godiva, by Fuller, in plaster, coloured to imitate bronze, on a Norman pedestal.

An assortment of the various kinds of leather and skins, with a machine for testing the strength of leather, paper, &c., exhibited by Bevington and Sons.

Woollen goods, from Bradford, exhibited by Titus Salt.

A 160-pound rifled cannon, by Whitworth.

A collection of Birmingham small arms, consisting of rifles, pistols, swords, and bayonets, &c. ; exhibited by Bentley and Playfair, Joseph Bourne, Cook and Son, Cooper and Goodman, Hollis and Sheath, King and Phillips, Pryse and Redman, W. L. Sargant, W. Scott and Son, Joseph Smith, Swinburn and Son, Tipping and Lawden, William Tranter, Thomas Turner, James Webley, Joseph Wilson, and B. Woodward and Sons.

A rifled cannon, by Sir W. Armstrong.

On the side opposite the food trophy are the wrought iron gates of Messrs. Barnard, of Norwich. This beautiful specimen of work consists of a pair of centre and two side gates, supported on four substantial iron piers. They have been designed with a view to combine cast and wrought iron in such a way, that the more massive parts, having weight to carry, should be of cast metal, and the lighter framing, with all the ornamental work, forged. In accordance with this idea, the piers and the girders 'over the gateways are of cast iron; the gates themselves, the scroll-work over them, and the panels and mouldings of the piers and girders are of wrought iron. The only enrichments attempted in the castings are slightly raised patterns in places, and the solid heraldic animals on the piers. The gates are framed of square bars, and filled with devices, copied from Nature, composed of the vine, hawthorn, ivy, and wild rose. The principal piers are about 18 feet high, the pedestals of these are 3 feet square, the shafts in proportion, above which are capitals enriched with foliage in wrought iron, the whole being surmounted by griffins supporting shields. These shields bear the monogram of the firm, to be replaced by the arms of those by whom the gates may be purchased. In the shafts are introduced panels of wrought iron, in which the stem and foliage of the oak form a groundwork, which is interlaced by convolvulus, bryony, smilax, periwinkle, ivy, &c. The external piers are of a similar character, but reduced in height. The scrollwork over the central gates is a combination of oak and holly branches, with the old double rose. These surround a shield bearing the Arms of Norwich, over which is a knight's helmet. The scrolls over the side gates are composed of branches and flowers of the hawthorn. The whole has been designed and superintended by Mr.

Thomas Jeckyll, of Norwich, and manufactured under the direct superintendence of Messrs. Barnard. They have been placed in their present position and fitted by Mr. Ames, to whose care is owing much of the success attending this exquisite specimen of hammered iron work.

Next we come to the trophy of animal and vegetable substances, placed in the compartments of an hexagonal pile, standing upon steps and surmounted by a dome, designed by Mr. Leighton.

The lighthouse of Messrs. Chance, of Birmingham, here arrests attention. This useful object is fitted with dioptric apparatus of the latest invention and most approved style.

At the sides we see large equatorial telescopes, respectively by Cooke and Sons, York ; J. Buckingham, Walworth Common ; Dallmeyer, Bloomsbury-street ; and Grubb, Dublin.

Philosophical instruments from the Kew Observatory, Richmond, consisting of self-registering magnetometers and meteorological apparatus, exhibited by the British Association for the Advancement of Science.

Lighthouse apparatus, consisting of lanterns for light-ship, lenses, &c., exhibited by Messrs. Wilkins, of Long Acre.

A collection of dressing-cases, travelling-bags, writing-cases, caskets, and other articles, designed by Mr. Waring.

The FOOD TROPHY, a really tasteful arrangement of various articles used for food. Of this we shall have more to say in another page.

China, consisting of her Majesty's dessert service, made at the Worcester Porcelain Works, and exhibited by Messrs. Kerr and Binns.

Cases containing elaborate works in gold, silver, and jewels, by Hunt and Roskell, and Harry Emanuel.

An exquisite arrangement of pottery, by Messrs. Copeland, of which we shall also have more to say.

We now reach

THE FOREIGN NAVE.

Here the centre is kept tolerably clear, but on either side are trophies and groups of statuary, bronzes, furniture carvings, jewellery, bijouterie, &c.

On the south side is the entrance to the French court, which occupies a large space ; and next to this is the Spanish trophy, and some furniture from Italy. On the north side are arms from Turkey ; a jasper column, candelabra, vase, and Siberian trophy, from Russia; some large anchors, granite pillars, and a sledge, a block of silica, and a model of a ship, from Norway; arms, and an anchor, a statue of zinc, some guns, and marble and granite columns, from Sweden ; china and sculptures from Denmark ; pianos and carved wood work from Switzerland ; diamonds and silver from Holland; and statues from Belgium; with a great show of stearine and other candles.

MIDDLE AVENUE.

The north and south British open courts are closed in on their west side by the Middle Avenue, which runs across the building from the central entrance in the Cromwell Road to the central entrance of the refreshment arcades leading into the Horticultural Gardens. This avenue is filled with trophies placed at intervals down its centre, the first of which, near the Cromwell Road entrance, is a large group of statuary, followed by a mezzo-relievo, by Alfred Gatley, representing the "Passage of the Red Sea," and intended for the Miller Mausoleum, near Edinburgh ; a temple, in coloured statuary marble, by Gibson and others; and a clock, by Benson, striking the hours and quarters on five bells, the largest weighing 22 cwt. The works are 300 feet from the dial, which is situated in the great central tower, the connections being carried underground. The weights exceed a ton, and are 200 feet from the works. Next to this comes an architectural model of Strasburg Cathedral ; and, after crossing the nave, a trophy of linen from Belfast, a trophy of imports from Liverpool, and a fountain, designed by the late Mr. Thomas, the sculptor.

VASE IN PARIAN. BY MESSRS. MINTON AND CO.

found the wonderful displays of Mr. Minton, and Messrs. Copeland, Messrs. Rose and Daniel, Sir J. Duke, and Messrs. Kerr and Binns; the latter firm show, in the nave, a portion of the service they lately manufactured for her Majesty the Queen. This service is executed in enamel, in the style of the enamels of Limoges, but on a turquoise ground. We have engraved one of the most charming objects in the Continental rivals. The works of Minton, Copeland, Daniel and Rose, and others, will be examined with intense interest, not only on account of the inherent beauty of the objects themselves, but for the fact that a great improvement has taken place in the manufacture since the Exhibition of 1851, when the Sèvres porcelain ranked as the first of its kind.

Pottery in the Exhibition.

WE resume our remarks on the Pottery in the International Palace of Industry and Art.

The potter's art is one with which mankind became very early acquainted. Frequent allusions to the "potter's wheel" in the Old Testament, and in the historical accounts of Oriental nations, make us familiar with this fact. And if any further evidence were required,

the cleaner and more shapely drinking vessels supplied from Staffordshire, Worcestershire, and Lambeth.

Not to speak at length, however, of its history, we may state that all pottery is composed of earth, or plastic clay, moulded into shape, hardened by baking or exposure, and rendered impervious to water by means of a sort of glass coating, known as a glaze. Under the name

ENGLISH PORCELAIN BY MESSRS. ROSE AND DANIEL.

we find it in abundant instances all over the world. Vessels of baked clay and moulded earth are discovered among the ruins of the most ancient cities—in Egyptian tombs and Persian mausoleums—among the rubbish of once famous palaces and the *débris* of extinct American cities. In all places and at all times, where men have gathered into families, and risen above the condition of mere savages, there the potter's art has, in some way or other, found a home. Even the South Sea Islanders are gradually putting away their gourds, in favour of

of pottery we may include all kinds of ceramic ware—for whether we call it earthenware, porcelain, flintware, delf, china, terra-cotta, ironstone, or what not, it is still produced in very much the same way, from very much the same sort of material. The rough, yellow, glazed basin out of which the beggar takes his broth, and the common cup whence poverty drinks its tea, is of the same identical family as the delicate vases in Sèvres, Dresden, or Worcester, though perhaps rather distantly related.

4.

In the Palace of Industry pottery is well represented in all its departments. The arrangement of Class 25 reflects the highest credit on the taste of Mr. Waring, the superintendent; and perhaps no part of the admirable display at South Kensington will attract more attention than the courts under his control. We have adverted briefly to the fountains and vases of Messrs. Minton; and we have now pleasure in placing before our readers a picture illustrative of the charming objects shown by Messrs. Daniel, of New Bond Street, in conjunction with Mr. Rose, of the Coalport China Manufactory. In this case manufacturer and seller have combined in producing a most exquisite and tasteful display in porcelain, of rare excellence and beauty. Messrs. Rose and Daniel have some delightful specimens of porcelain, of the kind known as Rose du Barri. It is impossible, in a wood engraving, to do more than indicate *form*. The visitor must examine for himself the gold and gilding on the vases—the exquisite colours, turquoise blue and blush-rose, on the cups and saucers—the delightful paintings, executed by a pupil of Etty's—the entrancing landscapes and figures on plates and dishes. Notice the varied and beautiful forms in which the tried skill and educated fancy of the artist-workman now appear. How cunningly shaped the clay—how carefully selected the pigments, and how wonderfully well laid on—how cautiously glazed and baked, in order to produce an array of such entrancing loveliness! Who will be surprised to find that this unique dessert service of turquoise and gold has already been secured? People of all tastes will pause before the stall of Messrs. Rose and Daniel; and when they come to consider that the objects they see before them are the results, not of art, in the usual signification of the term, but of a most widely-spread and useful manufacture, they will doubtless be glad to know that all that gallant show is produced by English workmen.

The ceramic ware, known as the Rose du Barri, is a manufacture quite distinct in form of decoration from that of any other kind of pottery. It is essentially painted porcelain—the very finest of earthenware, on which is pictured, in exquisite style, and in their natural colours, landscapes, fruit, flowers, &c. If we were allowed to take one of these pretty plates or vases, and hold it up to the light, we should find it to be semi-transparent, with the figures finished with the care, minuteness, and brilliancy of an enamel. Indeed, to such perfection has painting on porcelain been brought of late years, that the employment of artists of considerable eminence has been found necessary, and hence various branches of the manufacture have risen into the rank of absolute art. To the establishment of schools of design and art-manufacture we may naturally look for still further advances in this direction.

We are able to show but few examples of the great variety of styles and designs in vases, plateaux, flagons, &c., exhibited by Messrs. Rose and Daniel. We wish we could by engraving convey a perfectly correct notion of the gems in painting and enamel in their stall; but to perfectly appreciate their display, one must go and examine the Paul Potter landscapes, and other paintings, on a vast variety of porcelain, in diverse form and degrees of beauty.

People of cultivated taste, equally with those of simple likings, are always attracted strongly by pottery and porcelain. See in the Exhibition how bright-hued flocks of fair ladies, both married and single, hover lovingly over "sweet" tea services, and "sweetly pretty" vases, and evince as unmistakable a desire to finger each and every object of their passionate regard, as the ladies in Sterne's tale did to touch the wonderful nose of Slawkenbergius. There also are to be seen shoals of gentlemen porcelain fanciers, who are quite as anxious as the ladies to feel and handle, and twist and turn the dainty little things which are spread about so lavishly for inspection. Noting all this excitement, it is not difficult to realise one of those great china crazes of the past, when some high and mighty personages became porcelain mad, and crowds of little people went porcelain mad also; that time, for instance, when Augustus of Saxony exchanged a regiment of dragoons for some old china vases; or the period when Charles, King of Naples, worked as a potter in his own palace, and had before the gates of that palace

a shop, in which the productions of the Royal manufactory were sold.

Among the visitors to this magnificent collection of pottery and porcelain, there are, of course, numbers who appreciate fully the immense value to historians of the pottery work. It has been truly remarked that articles of fictile ware are at once the most fragile and the most enduring of human monuments. Stone crumbles away, ink fades, and paper decays, but the earthen vase, in some quiet but forgotten receptacle, survives the chances and changes of time. In their power of traversing accumulated ages, and affording glimpses of ancient times and peoples, fictile articles have been compared to the fossils of animals and plants, which reveal to the educated eye the former conditions of the globe.

After a rapid survey of what has been as yet unveiled by exhibitors of pottery and porcelain, both British and foreign, we confess to feeling a justifiable pride in the productions of our pottery towns. Just step into the well-arranged china establishment in the Exhibition belonging to Messrs. Minton and Co., of Stoke-upon-Trent. Glance at those divine little vases of Celadon china, with their delicate white cords and lovely fern leaves. There is one of those vases which is not quite so charming as the others. Its beauty has been marred by a quantity of tasteless gilding. In the manufacture of majolica vases this firm is clearly unapproached and unapproachable. Many of their articles are magnificent triumphs of the potter's art, but some few of the designs are singularly repulsive. There is a huge vase adorned with villanous-looking satyrs' heads. The spectator turns with disgust from those vicious, pallid faces, those horrid pale pink lips, and ugly protruded pale pink tongues. There is a grand pair of porcelain vases with large, boldly painted wreaths of roses and handsome snake handles, to which the hue of dead gold has been imparted. That large and beautiful article with those lordly rams' heads looking forth from its sides, is poised upon the shoulders of some three or four pretty little children, whose faces cannot be seen, for they are bent earth-wards, in a manner rather suggestive of pain than pleasure. When you see Atlas carrying the world on his shoulders, you glance at the lusty fellow's splendid muscular development, and have no fears that the huge ball will break his spine and crush every square inch of his body. But here the idea is very different. The little vase-bearers are mere babies, and should be flying about in a carriage drawn by doves, instead of groaning under a huge burden of marble. We have an illustration of this fine vase on page 24.

Etruria is well represented in the Exhibition by the grandson of the celebrated Wedgwood. The manufacture of these beautiful vases of light-blue jasper has only recently been revived. They were out of fashion, it seems, for some twenty years or so. There is a huge specimen, with lovely white bas-reliefs, representing a sacrifice, and some fine heads of goats and wild boars, with magnificent borders of oak and laurel leaves. It is the largest thing of the kind ever made, being three feet high and two feet across at the top.

Alderman Copeland's collection of parian figures is surpassed by that of no other exhibitor. We particularly direct attention to the statuette of Beatrice.

     "With regal step, and look wherein disdain
         Was pictured, still proceeding, thus she said
     (Like one who does her bitterest taunt retain):
         'Yes, I am Beatrice—regard me well.'"

In the glass cases of Alderman Copeland are to be seen some exquisite specimens of landscape painting in porcelain, as well as other noteworthy objects. But as we shall return to the ceramic display in the Exhibition, we shall have an opportunity of speaking further on the Copeland stalls, as well as the Sèvres and Dresden porcelain displayed in the Foreign half of the building.

OBJECTS IN THE EXHIBITION BELONGING TO THE QUEEN.

The articles belonging to her Majesty, exhibited by her permission in the case of Messrs. R. and S. Garrard and Co., are the Koh-i-Noor diamond, shown as a specimen of diamond-cutting; three large and fine rubies from the treasury at Lahore, mounted as a necklace in gold and enamel in the Indian style, with large diamond pendant; and an ornament for the centre of the table, representing the Palace of the Alhambra, executed in silver, silver-gilt, and enamel. Round the base of this is a group of horses, portraits of favourite animals, the property of her Majesty; on the lower portion of the base, which is designed to represent a ruin, are introduced the flamingo and vulture, and also various plants, natives of Arabia.

The other articles exhibited are a jewelled and enamelled cup, in silver-gilt, the gift of her Majesty and the Prince Consort to their grand-child and god-son, the Prince Frederick of Prussia, on the occasion of his christening. The cup is designed with emblems and figures typical of baptism; on the stem are the arms of England and Prussia, and on the base a group of St. George and the Dragon. There is also a tazza-form cup, presented by her Majesty the Queen to the Hereditary Duke of Baden, on the occasion of his christening.

The cup is treated in the Renaissance style, with emblematical wreaths of wheat and vine, symbolical of the sacrament, surmounted with a group typical of baptism; on the body are introduced the arms of England and Baden.

A richly-chased christening bowl, in Renaissance style, with winged figures supporting coronet and wreaths of flowers, is added to this. On the edge of the bowl is an emblematic figure pouring water. This cup was presented by her Majesty the Queen to the daughter of his Excellency Count Bernstorff, on the occasion of her christening.

Other articles exhibited by her Majesty, in the case of Messrs. Hunt and Roskell, are—

A vase, by Antoine Vechte, in oxidised silver, damascened—subject, "The Centaurs and Lapithæ;" on the pedestal are groups and entablatures illustrative of the same subjects; and

A vase and pedestal, by Antoine Vechte, in oxidised silver, marine composition. The bassi relievi represent Venus and Adonis, and Thetis presenting to her son Achilles the armour forged by Vulcan.

The Foreign Half of the Building.

WE resume our walk through that wonderful avenue between the two domes.

At the moment at which we write, hour by hour, day by day, week by week since the opening, it has been assuming something more of order; and with order comes grace, and beauty, and enchanting interest. It is impossible that in a visit or two the stranger can calmly make up his mind to the careful examination of a single section of the building. Is it not much more likely that he will walk wonderingly and admiringly through the nave, and make flying visits now and again into the courts on either side, and linger a moment at this tasteful stall, and before that beautiful object, and then back again to gaze through the now exquisite vista, studded with evidences of the commerce, the wealth, and the refinements of the world? Centuries of civilisation have been needed to achieve the results now laid before the eyes of the multitude who throng the world's fair at Kensington. Improvement upon improvement, invention upon invention, hard thinking, and active, unremitting working—each and all has been necessary to the accomplishment of the great whole here laid before our astonished eyes. Just stand for an instant in the gallery of one of the domes, and look before you. The roof with its delicate, pearly-grey decorations, and the columns of pale bronze and gold, cover and inclose a space in many respects unique and unequalled. It is not fair to compare Captain Fowke's building, even as decorated by Mr. Crace, with the Crystal Palace; but, taken by itself, we are bold to affirm that the structure of the International Exhibition is infinitely more worthy of commendation than many critics would have us believe. But then glance at the contents. See from our vantage-ground the well-dressed throng winding in and out among the trophies, here an obelisk, there a statue; in one place a case of jewels glittering in the sunlight, in another the flashing of a thousand rays of varied hues through shapes of fairy-like crystal or the pendants of graceful chandeliers. Surely, few sights can be more gratifying to the eyes. And then, from divers parts of the building, come sounds of music, mingling—who shall say how harmoniously?—with the indescribable hum of the multitude, and blending the whole—palace, people, and treasures—into one bewildering scene of delight!

Descend we again into the nave, now bright with orange trees and statuary, and cleared in the central space of all large objects likely to intercept the view from end to end. The new arrangement of the nave has vastly improved the aspect of the interior, which now assumes more than ever the completeness and symmetry that so charmed us all in the Crystal Palace of Hyde Park.

Starting from the central avenue, let us walk westward into the domains of the foreigner. Here Italy first claims our regard: and if we only once venture into her courts, we shall soon be lost in admiration of the noble groups of statuary and mosaics exhibited by Rome and Tuscany. We glance a moment—though an hour's examination would scarce suffice—at the Sybil and the Cleopatra of Mr. Storey, the American sculptor; we gaze in speechless admiration at the tinted statuary of our own Gibson—that lovely Venus, and that exquisite Cupid; we pause for a little before the swords of Victor Emmanuel and Cialdini—the former inscribed with the magic words, "The Independence of Italy;" and then wander back into the nave.

Here is the Spanish trophy, consisting of models of gun-carriages, and various curious mechanical contrivances in regard to arms. A rifled brass cannon, with six deep grooves, and the shells with corresponding projections standing beside it, is perhaps the most noteworthy object in this trophy. The grooves are so arranged that in loading, the shells screw in and out of the weapon. The workmanship of this gun, not of the highest description, was performed at Barcelona.

Every person will see and admire the fine cast-iron gates of MM. Barbezat and Co., of Val d'Ozne, facing the nave, and hung with exquisite tapestry, from the looms of MM. Braquemi, of Aubusson. The design in the largest piece is illustrative of the story of "La Belle au Bois Dormant," and is copied from a drawing by M. Mazerole. See the attitude of the awakening princess in the central group, and notice the whole execution of the beautiful design, the harmony of the delicate colours, the soft fall of the exquisite drapery, and the wreaths of flowers forming the border, wrought in a pattern studded with gems. Very marvellous and brilliant is the execution of the whole work.

Just below this are a pair of beautifully-carved cabinets, by M. Fourdinois, to which we shall have occasion again to refer. They present great masses of such delicate carvings as have scarcely ever been exceeded.

Gold and silver work, imitative bronzes, diamonds, and other jewellery, succeed. See the silver work of M. Rudolphi, and the silver and other works of MM. Christofle, executed for the Mayor of Paris, and destined to glitter and grace the tables in the Hôtel de Ville de Paris. This exquisite service is thus described:—The candelabra and surrounding objects are composed of a composite metal alloy, such as is often used for electro deposits. The surface of this is afterwards covered with silver. This peculiarity of appearance consists, in this instance, in the blending of colours, which range from deep gold to a pure silvery white, the intermediary tints being various pale shades of green. A spacious plateau of silvered glass, the frame of which is relieved by various depths of gold, supports a large frame, the heraldic symbol of the Corporation of Paris. The vessel is shaped like an ancient galley. On the deck is a raised *parois*, sustained by caryatides, and bearing the emblematical statue of the town. The four caryatides personify Art, Science, Industry, and Commerce. At the prow is an eagle, drawing the ship towards its future destiny, the Genius of Progress lighting its path. On the poop of the vessel stands the figure of Prudence, her hand on the helm. Groups of tritons, sea-nymphs, and dolphins surround the golden hull. The two extremities of the glass plateau are occupied by groups of sea-horses.

The lofty clusters of candelabra already mentioned are connected at their base with the frame of the plateau. Some particulars in the history of this work are worth recording. Messrs. Christofle and Co. received the commission last November, and it was not until the beginning of the present year that they were in possession of the models from which the casts were to be made. It may, therefore, be considered a wonderful example of dispatch; and, indeed, there is no doubt as to its being the largest galvano - plastic work ever produced within the time. The general plan of the service was given by Baron Haussman, Senator-Prefect of the Seine. The sculpture was executed under the superintendence of M. Baltard, Director of the Architectural Works of Paris, and Inspector of Fine Arts; by MM. Diebolt, Maillet, Thomas, Gumery, and Mathurin Moreau, artists, who have each gained in turn the grand prize of Rome; and by MM. Rouillard, Capy, and Auguste Madroux.

We pass on. Beyond the gates of MM. Barbezat, we find, still facing the nave, various specimens of beautiful satin damask, exhibited by MM. Carthiau and Corbière, resplendent in colour and chaste in design. Further on we notice a fine black marble mantelpiece, decorated with bronze; and still farther westward, we come to the splendid bronze works of M. Marchand. Many of these are from the designs of M. Piat, the draughtsman of the mantelpiece. This work

SIR CHARLES WENTWORTH DILKE, BART., ONE OF THE ROYAL COMMISSIONERS.

is Grecian in style. The dominant idea of the artist has evidently been to construct a sort of altar to Minerva. In the lower portion of the work the body is of black marble, in which slightly incised lines and patterns, produced by the action of acids, have been introduced and brought out with colour and gilding. The piers are massive and elegant in design, and in the panel of each is a bronze figure of a Grecian sage. A bronze egg and tongue moulding runs below the bold and chaste pediment, in the centre of which is a grotesque head, while on the apex is a fine gilt figure of Minerva, with server helmet and shield, and holding a spear reversed. We walk through a vast vista of beautiful shapes in bronze, silver, marble and iron, with here and there a cascabinet, a group of Sèvres porcelain, or a carpet from the Gobelins, till we reach the western dome. Here, indeed, we come upon a perfect marvel of each and various trophies — the King of Prussia's triumphs in Berlin pottery in the centre. Bronzes again, with the magnificent cataof candelabra and polished columns in jasper and porphyry, from Russia. Berlin, Dresden Vienna, Sèvres, Paris all combine to make up a fine mixture. Nevertheless, they are said to be outshone by Rose and Daniell's England. Mintons and the other exhibitors of English porcelain. In fact, we overlook the Continental manufacturers in 1851 and since then we have passed them. Who does not remember our triumph in glass and porcelain at the Paris Exposition in 1855?

Russia, Germany, Austria, Prussia, and other countries crop out into the nave, each exhibiting some specialty. All are worthy the most minute examination, and all will be pronounced fine; but in many respects good workmanship, especially in cabinet work, has been sacrificed to show. In this respect the visitor will do well to notice the cabinet chairs and tables shown on the side of the nave opposite France.

In the Zollverein, however, there are some good specimens of real, genuine work, nobly executed. Austria also has, as in 1851, some massively grand specimens of decorative furniture, some few pieces of which intermingle picturesquely with the sculpture and silver work in the nave. Especially worthy of notice are the wax and stearine candles exhibited in the nave by the Belgian manufacturers, and the group of Swedish bronzes in the centre.

We may not pass unheeded the curious, though rather meagre collection of objects shown by the Turkish Government, consisting for the most part of articles of clothing, silver, food, fruits, and cereals. They are arranged with taste, and what few objects are seen in the nave are seen to great advantage.

The countries bordering on the nave are—on the south, Italy, Spain, Portugal, and France; and on the north side, Belgium, Holland, Switzerland, Denmark, Sweden, Norway, Russia, and Turkey. All these have objects placed conspicuously in the wide avenue through which the great public must certainly take its first walk. In their courts behind, they have, to some extent, disposed of their productions according to the Commissioners' classification—the heavier goods on the ground floor, and the lighter ones in the galleries. The several countries occupy about the same position above and below stairs. Thus, France holds the greater part of the south-west court, and the galleries above; the Zollverein—the German free-trade union—has the south-west transept, with its galleries, with the Hanse Towns located near; while Austria has the north-west transept and its galleries. The western dome is a sort of common ground, in which each and all are represented.

The western annexe is a sort of long continuation of the north-west transept. As we shall have, by-and-by, to speak at length of the machinery in motion, we need not linger among the whirring wheels just now.

Let us take a peep into Austria. The objects she shows in the nave can be taken to include a fair specimen of the whole display, only as a break may be said to be a sample of a house. In the Austrian court will be found various kinds of vegetable products, besides silk, flax, wool, woods, and all kinds of raw materials. Thirty-

six industrial classes are furnished by about fifteen hundred exhibitors.

As the foreign half of the building further develops itself, we are surprised and gratified at the improvement made since 1851, in the more useful and less showy objects exhibited; and we have no doubt but that all visitors will share in our delight. To be sure, Russia sends us no great malachite doors, but then how rich and valuable are her furs, and how complete her show of cereals! Switzerland, too, is prominent in carvings, watches, printed muslins, embroideries, straw plait statuettes, and jewellery.

Belgium, again, is rich in minerals, and cotton and linen manufactures—to say nothing of her various food products. She also sends us some fine statuary in bronze and marble.

See that admirable and spirited group in the nave, "The Combatants." It is a representation of the old Runic fashion of duelling—two men strapped together, and fighting with knives to the death. The story of the fatal encounter, from its first outbreak to the widow weeping before the uncouth Runic stone which marks the grave of husband and lover, is simply but forcibly told in bas relief beneath the group, some of which are literally copied from the old Runic originals. These fine statues are cast in zinc, bronzed over. The whole group is, beyond a doubt, the most spirited and life-like in the building. The practice of thus coupling antagonists has long been known to the northern races,

THOMAS FAIRBAIRN, ESQ., ONE OF THE ROYAL COMMISSIONERS.

and the tradition of this particular duel is almost equally familiar to Swedes, Norwegians, and Danes. The youths engaged in this mortal strife are first seen, in the sculptured narrative encircling the base, sitting together drinking. The next stage is a quarrel, caused by some familiarity on the part of one of them with the betrothed wife of his companion. She is then seen endeavouring to prevent their encounter; and lastly, we find her plunged in grief, and prostrate before a Runic stone, on which is sculptured a rude representation of the youths struggling together.

Then, again, we may linger awhile in Egypt, with its interesting and valuable collection of raw produce, arms, and carvings; and pass into Greece, which has no frontage in the nave. Here we shall be charmed with Byzantine paintings, curious pipes, and curious gold and silver embroidery. A small case is fitted up like a modern drawing-room, filled with groups of models, clothed in the picturesque national costume, in which crinoline for the ladies and pegtop trousers for the gentlemen strangely mingle with gold embroidery, lace, and jewels.

Costa Rica, with its roots, seeds, ores, oils, woods, cottons, shells, bird-skins, india-rubber, sugar, tobacco, gold, silver, and copper, comes next. Then Brazil, with a fine show of native oils and minerals, silver filagree, and even photographs. Next Peru, properly represented by silver, gold, and precious stones—corn, wine, wool, cotton, and many antiquities. Next Uruguay, with skins, marbles in the rough, and ores as they are dug from the mine. Afterwards China

and Japan, with the multitude of curiosities, and we are once more on the British side of the Exhibition.

In this rapid survey we have followed the course most probably adopted by the visitor. No one who is not a scientific observer, or a writer for the press, goes to the Exhibition with a plan in his head, or if he does he is soon obliged to abandon it, as the jurors did when they began their examination a week or so after the opening. Nevertheless we shall return, from time to time, to the foreign countries, and endeavour to point out to our readers some of the more prominent objects, amid the multitude of useful and beautiful things exhibited by each.

The Royal Commissioners.

THE classification adopted by the Commissioners is not certainly that which will be followed by the visitors in their wanderings through the building. Instead of taking Class 1 as the first to be examined, they will probably walk into the furniture court, or the hardware court, on either side of the nave, and therefore begin with Classes 30 and 31. But it must, of course, be understood that this system of classification is merely adopted for the purpose of properly arranging the objects exhibited, and by no means as a guide to visitors. Previously to describing the several courts, we think it right to introduce the portraits of two gentlemen, to whose untiring exertions and indomitable perseverance very much of the success of the Exhibition is owing.

Her Majesty's Commissioners are five, but the real work of the Exhibition is practically left in the hands of his Grace the Duke of Buckingham, Mr. T. Fairbairn, and Sir C. Wentworth Dilke. Mr. Baring, as might be expected, is too fully engaged in commerce to give much time to the Exhibition, and the Earl Granville has too many demands upon his attention to be able to put aside matters of state for matters of taste. From the known antecedents of the two gentlemen we have chosen as the representatives of the Royal Commissioners, it is certain that in whatever respect business habits and enlarged views are likely to benefit the Exhibition, such habits and such views will be adopted. As Secretary to the Commissioners of the Exhibition of 1851, Mr. Dilke contributed, with Mr. Cole and Mr. Digby Wyatt, very largely to the triumphant success of that brilliant undertaking. He is also well known, not only from his long and honourable connection with literature, but also from the fact, that as Chairman of the Council of the Society of Arts, he worked manfully in keeping that valuable institution always before the public; and there is little doubt that his connection with the International Exhibition will redound not only to his own honour, but also to the immense benefit of the great undertaking.

The name of Mr. Thomas Fairbairn is one intimately connected with industrial progress and social improvement. All who know the name of Fairbairn—and who does not?—know it for one intimately connected with vast enterprises, in which wonderful machinery and fertile invention go hand in hand. William Fairbairn, the father of the Royal Commissioner, is himself a representative man; for he is not only a practical engineer, but he is also a Fellow of the Royal Society, a Corresponding Member of the National Institute of France, and President of the British Association for the Advancement of Science. In all that the father has proved himself great, the son is also excellent. And more; for Mr. Thomas Fairbairn has identified himself intimately with the progress and encouragement of education, and the study of the Arts. As Chairman of the Art Treasures' Exhibition in Manchester, in 1857, he greatly distinguished himself. At her Majesty's visit to the cotton metropolis in that year, the honour of knighthood was offered him; but holding a position as head of one of the largest engineering establishments in the world, he respectfully declined the tempting distinction. Mr. Fairbairn is a magistrate and a deputy-lieutenant for the county of Lancaster; but as one of her Majesty's Commissioners for the Exhibitions of 1851 and 1862, he stands before the world, not alone as a great manufacturer and a wealthy gentleman, but also as a man of taste, judgment, and great executive powers. In the Fine Arts department of the International Exhibition will be found many examples of Mr. Fairbairn's knowledge and taste in the arts, in the shape of pictures and sculptures—in most instances either the result of direct commissions to the artists, or of judicious purchases at the Royal Academy, and other exhibitions.

With these two gentlemen as active managers, there seems little doubt—if any ever existed—of the final and complete success of our World's Fair of 1862. It is but fair to say that their efforts are well seconded by Mr. Sandford, the Secretary.

Stained and Painted Glass.

THE display of stained and painted glass in the Exhibition is varied, interesting, and attractive. Both sides of the building show capital specimens of good genuine work, artistically designed. Thirty-five British manufacturers are represented in Class 34; and though in 1851 there was a larger number of exhibitors, the quantity of stained and painted glass shown was less than now. France is represented by the national manufactory of St. Gobain, and fourteen private firms; Austria, by three exhibitors; Prussia, by four manufacturers; Russia by the Imperial Glass Works of St. Petersburg; Sweden, by the Bromo Glass Works, Westgothland; and even Mecklenburg-Schwerin, by M. E. Gillmeister.

Among the British exhibitors whose works will attract special attention in this Exhibition, few will deserve it better than the Messrs.

Cox, the church decorators, of Southampton Street, Strand. As an instance of the proper application of colours and the subordination of forms to the purpose of stained glass windows, the specimen we have chosen for illustration is very successful. The window itself will be found in the gallery of the south court, about the centre. Its effect would have been much better had the light been more concentrated; for it will be recollected that the best position for a stained glass window is one in which the sun's rays pour directly through and upon it, and the side from which it is viewed is comparatively dark, as, in fact, in a church.

The stained glass in the Exhibition is shown in several places. In the east and west transepts, on the British side, will be found some very fine examples, as well as in the windows under the east and west entrances. A window in the west transept, by Messrs. Heaton, Butler. and Bayne, of Carrington Street, Euston Road, will be much admired, particularly one executed for the Harpenden Church, with the Acts of Mercy for its subject. For an illustration of this beautiful window, see page 33.

Messrs. Baillie, of Wardour Street, Oxford Street; Messrs. Hardman and Co., of Birmingham; Messrs. Lavers and Barraud, of Endell Street; and Messrs. Hetley, of Soho Square, also have some really fine specimens of stained glass. Attention will also be drawn to the painted window exhibited in the south gallery, by Messrs. J. Ballantine and Son, of Edinburgh, in which are shown portraits of the principal Church reformers from Calvin to Chalmers. A fifteenth century hall window, representing the patron saints of Great Britain—St. George, St. Andrew, and St. Patrick—surmounted by the royal arms, will be much admired. Of course the well-known names of Chance, Claudet, Holland, O'Connor, and Warrington will be found attached to numerous excellent examples of stained glass, both for ecclesiastical and domestic purposes. The visitor should especially notice the examples of the progress in the art from the twelfth century to the present time, as shown by Mr. Warrington, Sen., of Connaught Terrace; and the painted glass window executed for St. Anne's Church, Westminster, exhibited by Messrs. Ward and Hughes, of Frith Street, Soho.

Great improvement has been made since 1851 in the manufacture of stained glass. The colours being all transparent, and to be viewed by means of light transmitted through the windows, great care is necessary in their selection; for, like the pigment used in fresco work, the original tints change most remarkably during the process of drying. Numerous colours, especially those with a metallic base, which have

STAINED GLASS SIDE WINDOWS,

a beautiful effect when applied cold, on paper or canvas, are quite incapable of being used in glass painting, from the changes consequent on vitreous fusion. The means whereby the wonderful results before us are achieved are comparatively simple; but, like all simple things in art or manufacture, a certain indefinable tact, habit, or method is necessary for their proper and successful application. To state the mode of manufacture in a sentence, it is easy to say, "When

certain metallic oxides or chlorides, ground up with proper fluxes, are painted upon glass, the colours fuse at a moderate heat," and so produce the design. But something more, very much more, is necessary. Besides the artist to make the original design upon paper, there must be the artist-workman to transfer it to glass, the chemist to nicely calculate the various proportions of the several colours, the careful workman to "fire" or fix the colours on the glass, and the artistic plumber to place the several pieces together, so as to form, when completed, one harmonious whole. The beautiful art of glass staining has, during the last few years, been restored to its true position among the Christian arts. Its ancient splendours have been revived, and that which is justly regarded as one of the most interesting accessories of ancient architecture has, by the labours of earnest men, been reproduced for the enrichment of our churches, public buildings, and private dwellings.

The revival of the decorative arts generally (among which glass staining holds no mean place) is owing to several causes, among which may be mentioned the restoration of numerous old buildings, the rapid increase of churches, the general spread of artistic knowledge, and the increasing apprehension of the fact that objects of utility may also be rendered objects of beauty and attraction, without detracting from their fitness for their original purposes. These causes combined have directed an amount of attention to stained windows especially, which a few years ago would have been deemed chimerical.

But this decorative art has not, even yet, attained to that general appreciation which it enjoyed in olden times, though the appliances for its manipulation were then far more limited than at present. Its magnificent effect, however, in both sacred and secular edifices; its recognised appropriateness for monumental purposes, owing to its imperishability, attractiveness, and scope for sacred illustration; combined with the extraordinary reduction in the cost of its production—are, however, rapidly bringing it into the general favour which it merits.

It will facilitate the comprehension of the principles and resources of glass staining, if we briefly sketch the rise and progress of the art till it reached its climax in the fourteenth century, and its subsequent decline until it became all but extinct in the eighteenth century,

BY MESSRS. COX AND SON.

towards the end of which it was again cultivated to a limited extent, and gradually assumed a higher character, until, in recent years, it has received an impetus which has again raised it to its true place as one of the noblest, most beautiful, most fascinating arts of the age.

Glass, as a substance, was discovered and used at a very remote period; the Egyptians, 3,000 years ago, as well as the Greeks and Romans, being evidently acquainted with its use; but its application as a transparent protection for the interior of buildings against the weather, was unknown until about the eighth century, when glass was first adopted in the construction of churches, though its introduction into dwellings was not general until several centuries later.

Immediately glass was used for windows, the opportunity it afforded for decoration suggested itself, and was freely taken advantage of. Specimens of work as far back as the twelfth century are still preserved, and though they are frequently classed with early English, yet, when discriminating the various styles, we find they possess peculiarities of their own, and are interesting as being early efforts in an art which in course of time attained such distinguished eminence, and was at length so completely identified with Christian architecture that no ecclesiastical structure was considered complete without having its transparent walls variously and richly decorated. The abbey church of St. Denys,

STAINED GLASS WINDOW, BY MESSRS. COX AND SON.

in France, exhibits the most perfect examples of this period, being supposed to date about the beginning of the twelfth century.

Succeeding to the rude Norman efforts, we have the early English style, corresponding with the first pointed period of gothic architecture, extending from about the year 1150 to 1280.

The stained glass of this period, until near its close, resembles in most characteristics that of the previous century. The design of the window was composed of simple but beautiful geometric forms, and

the colouring was intense and gem-like, red and blue generally predominating. The foliage was an adaptation of Grecian and Roman ornament, always conventionally treated, but becoming more natural towards the close of the period. The figures, though often rude and treated in the most abstract manner, were forcible and effective. Some of the windows were composed almost entirely of coloured glass; these are perfect mosaics of the most vivid, intense, and gem-like tints, excluding more light than others, but imparting an extremely solemn and impressive effect.

The decorated style, corresponding with the secondary period of pointed architecture, prevailed from 1280 to about 1380.

The artists had now attained the mastery over the principles of design and colour, had acquired confidence in their own powers, and boldly exhibited the originality of their genius in works of surpassing beauty and grandeur.

The leading characteristic of this style is the natural forms of its ornament. The attempt to imitate classical models was abandoned, and to the woods and fields the painter went to learn the varied forms of beauty Nature draws. The leaves of the ivy, oak, maple, and most other well-known trees, may be recognised in the productions of this period. The simple geometric forms of the preceding centuries now gave place to more elaborate combinations. The use of a canopy over figures and subjects became general; and running patterns, in imitation of weeds, flowers, and plants, filled up the details of the windows, according to the untrammelled fancy of the artist.

The figures are more refined than the early English, and the drapery more flowing and ample. They are severe in drawing, and closely resemble in character those in the illuminations and sculptures of the time.

It was during this period that glass painting attained its purest

STAINED GLASS. 14TH CENTURY WINDOW—THE ACTS OF MERCY.   MESSRS. HEATON, BUTLER, AND BAYNE.

5.

and most perfect development; and when we consider the exactness and excellence of the designs, the beauty of the ornaments, the rich harmonious contrast of the colours, and the expressiveness of the human figures introduced, it is impossible to withhold our admiration, even when regarding the windows simply as decorations. But, in addition to these merits, the deep religious feeling exhibited in the sacred illustrations, and the perfect adaptation of the whole to the architecture, deserve our highest commendation.

The art of glass staining, as now generally practised, must not be confounded with glass painting. The latter is a method of painting with semi-transparent enamels on white glass, which are afterwards fused, so as to incorporate the colour with the surface of the glass. This method was practised a few years ago, to the exclusion of the former. It is well calculated to produce a pictorial effect, but is costly, and, as we now think, unsatisfactory. It may be considered a sister art to enamel painting on copper, differing only in the pigments being semi-transparent instead of opaque, the system of using them being similar. Reynold's window in New College Chapel, Oxford, and the east window of St. George's, Windsor, are favourable examples of the style. There are also many fine Swiss paintings of this kind, in which the colours are remarkably brilliant. The colours, however, as used in England are indifferent, and liable to peel off when exposed to the atmosphere.

Glass staining, on the other hand, though requiring specialities of manipulation, is similar in principle to mosaic painting, which consists in imbedding small pieces of homogeneous coloured glass in cement, by which means the most beautiful and imperishable works are produced.

A stained window consists of multitudes of small pieces of translucent glass, united together with bands of lead. The colour is generally produced by mixing oxides of metals with the liquid glass before it is blown into sheets or circles, thus rendering it homogeneous. In other cases, as in ruby glass,[*] the colouring matter is on one side only of the glass, extending from about one-eighth to one-sixteenth of the entire thickness, the remainder being white. In this case it is called "flashed," or "veneered" glass. Fluoric acid removes this veneer, leaving a white figure on a red ground. There are many instances of this process in fifteenth and sixteenth century windows, especially where the pieces of glass were too small to be worked with lead, as in minute charges in heraldry; but at that time, fluoric acid being unknown, the colour was ground away with fine sand. There is much of this work in the fine east window of Beauchamp Chapel, Warwick.

Previously to the middle of the fourteenth century, each colour was leaded up separately; but afterwards we occasionally find the white glass partially stained with various tints of yellow, and in course of time the practice became general. Silver is the basis of this stain, and is the only true stain used to this day. The tint varies with the chemical mixture of the glass, and the quantity of stain applied; old glass taking a much richer colour than what is now commonly used. This is probably owing to the small proportion of iodine in the kelp which is used as an alkali in the manufacture, for we find that a glass made purposely with kelp will take a stain equal to the old material.

It is a remarkable fact that silver will act as a stain, either used in a metallic state, or in combination with any other substance. The iodide of silver acts the most readily; but the most convenient form is the sulphuret of silver and antimony. We are not aware that its true chemical action has been ascertained, but are of opinion that, at the high temperatures to which all the glass is submitted, the silver will leave its combinations to form silicate of silver.

* We suppose the old masters made their ruby glass according to the receipt in the Bolognese Manuscript, "Segreti per Colori." Take 1 lb. of copper, and melt it, and when it is melted, add 4 ozs. of lead, and incorporate them well with each other, and throw the mass into cold water, and it will be broken small like grains of corn; then grind it as fine as you can, and stir it into the glass, and it will become red glass for making paternosters and other articles.—Mrs. Merrifield's "Practice of Ancient Painting."

A stained window, however, somewhat differs from a mosaic painting, in respect that the outlines and shadows are painted with an opaque enamel, afterwards fused into the glass at a full red heat.

In producing a stained window, the coloured design is first prepared on a small scale, and afterwards the figures and other parts are drawn to the exact size they are to appear in the window. In these working drawings or cartoons it is customary to mark the division of each piece of glass, and the exact place of the leaden bands with double lines, the width between them showing the width of lead to be used. These bands, instead of being unsightly in the completed window, are turned into a means of rendering the design more effective and definite; and few persons unacquainted with the structure of a stained window would conceive it to be composed of thousands of small pieces of glass, held together with strips of lead. The cartoon being coloured and approved of, a piece of tracing muslin of the same size is placed over it, on which is marked out with a fine black line the sizes and colours of the pieces of glass which will hereafter compose the window. This is called the cutting-drawing. On this drawing the glass-cutter places the white and coloured sheets of glass, cutting with a diamond the various shapes. The outlines, and such shading as is absolutely necessary (and no more), are now painted on with the opaque enamel. In the case of a "subject" or figure, the various small pieces are fastened on to a large sheet of glass, with a mixture of bees' wax and rosin, which enables the painter to judge what the effect of the completed work will be. During this process, the glass has to be once or twice submitted to a full red heat, in order to "burn in" portions of the painting, which cannot very well be executed all at once. Most of the glass in stained windows is fired twice, and sometimes thrice.

The kiln in which the glass is fired is composed of an iron box, on an average about two feet long by fourteen inches wide, and twelve high, with grooves on each side to sustain iron plates, on which the glass is placed, in a bed of very dry powdered whiting, which prevents the glass, when fired to a state of semi-fusion, from adhering to the iron. This iron kiln is set above an ordinary fire box, with a fire slab between, and imbedded in carefully constructed brickwork—the flues being so constructed that the flames may play completely round the iron box, which is never allowed to come in contact with the body of the fire. This arrangement allows for a gradual heating of the whole mass, and prevents the glass from breaking through the too sudden increase of temperature. There are sight-holes in front of the kiln, through which the interior may be examined at any time. These are left open during the earlier part of the process, that the fumes of the oils used in painting the outlines may escape, before they are converted into carburetted hydrogen. When the interior of the kiln is seen to be of the required temperature—which, although called a full red heat, can only be judged of by much experience—the fire is withdrawn, and the kiln and its contents are allowed to cool slowly.

The annealing of the glass is a point that should have more attention paid to it than it generally receives. If the kiln is opened too quickly, the contents will of course fly to pieces, so that a certain amount of annealing is compulsory. But it frequently happens that glass which has remained intact during the construction of a window, or even for months afterwards, will, on a sudden change of the temperature, show its want of sufficient annealing by falling to pieces. As a rule, the glass in stained windows cannot be annealed too much, for, although so fragile, no material is more exposed to changes of temperature.

The kiln is opened about twelve or fourteen hours after the fire is withdrawn, and the glass is carefully examined, to see that it is properly fired, which is known by a slightly glossy appearance. The glazier then begins his work. After placing each piece of glass in its right place on the cutting drawing, he selects the proper leaden bands with which to unite the parts together. These leaden bands have a groove on each side to admit the glass, and are made of various sizes, to suit particular classes of work, the best and strongest having the flanges in the form of segments of circles, instead of flat leaves. The ancient glass stainers coat their metal into the required form at once; but the plan now adopted is first to cast a bar of lead, and then pass it through grooved rollers of the pattern desired.

A common lattice, or diamond-shaped window, exhibits glazing in its simplest form, and in a similar, though more complicated manner, the lead in a stained glass window surrounds each separate piece of glass. The joints are then well soldered together, and additional strength is imparted by cementing the whole with red lead and oil, carefully worked into the hollows of the leaden bands. Thus, each completed section of a window forms one strong sheet of stained glass, which it would require wilful violence to injure.

The window is now fixed in a suitable position, and carefully examined; alterations are made, if required, and at last, carefully packed, it is sent to its destination.

Having erected our window, let us now see if it agrees with the true principles of decorative art, and if it fulfils the requirements of a stained window. As a decoration, then, does it harmonise with the architecture it is designed to enrich ? Is it suitable for its position in the building ? and does it form an appropriate part of the building itself?. Although a stained window may present evidences of originality, care, and skill, both in drawing and colouring (without which no good work has ever been produced), yet, if its purposes are overlooked, it cannot be regarded as a successful production. It was in the strict fulfilment of the above requirements that the perfection of old windows mainly consisted, for none can enter an ancient sacred building without being struck with the harmonious, satisfying completeness which the noble stained windows impart to the edifice; and this, we contend, not produced solely by the use of an excellent material, but by careful attention to the many details and trifles which are necessary to the attainment of a perfect work.

Messrs. Heaton, Butler, and Bayne, of Cardington Street, Hampstead Road, exhibit several very beautiful stained glass windows, both in the north window of the west transept and in the gallery of the south aisle, Class 34.

In the west transept they have a thirteenth century window, executed for the south aisle of St. Alban's Abbey; subjects, the Baptism of Christ and the Passage of the Red Sea. A fourteenth century window, executed for the transept of Harpenden Church; subject, Acts of Mercy. This window is shown by a very fine engraving on page 33. A fourteenth century window, illustrative of the Burial of Our Lord. In the gallery of the south aisle they exhibit a sixteenth century window; subject, the Adoration of the Wise Men. A transept window, executed for Skulthorpe Church, the subject of which is the History of Ruth. East window for Langton Church, illustrating the Life of Our Saviour. A fifteenth century hall window, representing the Patron Saints of Great Britain and Ireland—St. George, St. Andrew, and St. Patrick, with the Royal Arms.

It would have been much more satisfactory to the exhibitors of stained glass, if a place with a better light had been provided. As now placed in a diffused light, it is impossible to see any of them to the advantage they deserve. Their inherent beauty is such, however, that in any position they will be admired.

Arms in the Exhibition.

ONE remarkable phase in the International Exhibition did not escape the attention of the Poet Laureate. He noticed—as no intelligent visitor can fail to notice — that side by side with the evidences of wealth, luxury, and peace, were exhibited the deadly implements of war—

> "Brought from under every star,
> Blown from over every main,
> And mixt, as life is mixt with pain,
> The works of peace with works of war."

Classes XI. and XII. are devoted to Military and Naval appliances; armour, accoutrements, ordnance, and small arms; models of ships, lighthouses, lifeboats, gunboats, batteries, and other means of offence and defence.

These classes are severally represented by trophies in the nave. In each trophy an endeavour has been made to embody the main idea of military and naval warfare. Thus, groups of Armstrong guns and other great pieces of canonry stand as the representatives of ordnance; models of the different classes of ships in the Royal navy, from the "Great Harry" to the "Warrior"—from our first armed vessel to our last impregnable—with various other "strange sea-things," represent naval architecture; while the manufacture of the more portable weapons of warfare is fully and satisfactorily characterised in the Birmingham Small Arms Trophy shown in our engraving.

This is one of the most successful of the so-called trophies. In fact, it is really a very beautiful object, considering that it is composed entirely of muskets, rifles, bayonets, swords, pistols, revolvers, and other deadly weapons. The form of the structure is that of a four-sided pyramid, with projecting angles. On each side are shown weapons of various kinds arranged in symmetrical order, while locks, trigger-guards, and other portions of the Enfield and other rifles are made to do duty as a sort of decorative fringe about the principal figures. The summit of the trophy is formed of a bristling fringe of bayonets and ramrods, so arranged as to reflect the light which falls upon their polished surfaces, in a most successful manner. Nor is this mere glitter and show the main end of the Birmingham Small Arms

Trophy. The curious visitor will admire the armes de luxe — pistols and sword-hilts decorated in the most wonderful manner with gilding and carvings in ivory and ebony; damascened blades and barrels, with all the elegance and beauty that can be given to metal. But he will also learn something of the mode of constructing the barrels of these powerful playthings of fight. At the base of the trophy are cases in which are shown the several stages of manufacture, from the half-fused lump of horse-shoe nails to the finished weapons. We can trace the volunteer's rifle through all its forms: first, the rusty-looking nails; then the semi-melted mass; then the whole rolled out into a flat bar, which, we see, has been presently twisted into a spiral, and last of all welded into the form of the perfect barrel, of one single piece of homogeneous metal. Beside the barrels are the nipples, the triggers, cocks, and other parts of the weapon, also shown in their several parts and stages; a most instructive and suggestive picture. The principal Birmingham manufacturers have contributed to this trophy. Among the well-known names of the armourers and sword cutlers of our great workshop are those of Messrs. Bentley and Playfair, Cook and Son, Goodman, Hollis, W. L. Largant, W. Scott and Son, Joseph Smith, Swinburn and Son, Tipping and Lawden, W. Tranter, Thomas Turner, James Webley, Joseph Wilson, and B. Woodward and Sons. Altogether, the Small Arms Trophy may be considered, in a pictorial point of view, as one of the successes of the nave. It is designed with taste, constructed with skill, and presents a very attractive contrast to the various surrounding objects.

Not less interesting is the Armstrong Trophy, from the Royal Arsenal at Woolwich. Whatever be the merits or defects in the Armstrong gun—and these we cannot enter into—there can be no dispute as to the ingenuity and skill with which the collection of this unique and tastefully arranged display has been carried out.

This trophy has been said to resemble a Christmas tree—certainly rather a formidable-looking one—around the base of which, and clustering upon its branches, are seen the various parts of this scientific and complicated weapon—from the rough bar to the highly-finished metal—together with the various tools and instruments used

EAST WINDOW OF ST. PHILIP'S CHURCH, EARL'S COURT, KENSINGTON. MESSRS. HEATON, BUTLER, AND BAYNE.

CONTRACTORS TO HER MAJESTY'S WAR DEPARTMENT

THE SMALL ARMS TROPHY IN THE BRITISH NAVE.

in its construction. Especially interesting is a glass bottle, containing spirals of steel, just as they have been cut and curled cold from the chisel of the workman, and bearing the inscription—"Good workmen are known by their chips." Mr. Anderson, the superintendent of this trophy, under Major Moffat, furnishes the following very satisfactory account of it:—A broken bar of the rough iron lying at the base shows that the raw material out of which the gun is made is of the very best quality. The next piece in order shows the bar twisted into a spiral form; this has been done upon a mandril, suitable in size to the bore required, and the iron now has the shape of a twisted hollow tube, such as the threads of a corkscrew would resemble if pressed close together. The next form shows that this twisted hollow tube has been welded together; then specimens are shown bored, rifled, and turned. Towards this this tube is strengthened by others similarly manufactured, shrunk on, and welded over it again and again, until the required thickness and strength are obtained. Up to this point the gun differs but little from any wrought-iron cannon; and to form a tolerably correct idea of a breech-loading Armstrong gun, let us take, for example, an ordinary cannon, and continue the bore clean through the breech till we have a hollow tube open at both ends. The shot and charge may now be passed into the barrel at the breech; but as it must be prevented from expending the force of the charge in a wrong direction, a stopper is required to close up this opening in the breech, and this is the weak point in the Armstrong gun; for to admit this stopper, plug, or ventpiece, an opening has to be made clean through the section of the gun, greatly in excess of the size of the barrel or the chamber. The breech of the gun, against which this plug is to bear, is formed like the seat of an ordinary conic valve, and to keep the plug up against this seat, that portion of the gun behind the plug is bored out to an increased size, in order to receive a nut, which keeps the plug in its place. This nut is also bored out the same size of the chamber of the gun, so that the shot and charge passes through it when the plug is removed. With one exception, all the Armstrong breech-loading guns in the collection are of this description. That exception is a .70-pounder wedge gun, to which is attached a very ingenious piece of mechanism, which keeps the touch-hole closed until the wedge is properly adjusted; so that, even in the hands of inexperienced gunners, there is little danger of accident in working the gun.

Among the items that adorn the trophy are models of the solid shot used for testing the gun. That for 110-pounders is about eight feet in length, and weighs about 1,000lb.; and the shot for testing 12-pounders weighs 120lb. One of the guns shown has been subjected to eighty-seven of these proof shots, and another to 391, and both guns are stated to be uninjured. As an evidence of the excellence of the material employed, and the perfection with which it is put together, a shaving is shown, cut from one of the welded coiled cylinders, and measuring 430 feet in the curl, the probable total length of which is 1,462 feet.

The heaviest piece of ordnance in the Exhibition is the Prince Alfred Gun, a muzzle-loading rifled cannon, manufactured by the Mersey Shot and Iron Company. This powerful weapon is thus described:—"This gun is 12 feet long, 3 feet in diameter at breech, and weighs 10 tons 15 cwt. Before rifling, it carried a spherical shot of 136lb. weight, and will now carry an elongated shot of from 500lb. to 600lb." Alongside this gun is shown a plate of wrought-iron, 4½ inches thick, which was placed as a target, and backed with 18 inches of solid teak, and broken by a shot weighing 136lb., impelled by charges of from 20lb. to 30lb. of powder. The shattered and ruined plates speak volumes in favour of the destructive power of the gun. The same firm produced the ordnance which first broke the heavy iron plates of the Government target. In May, 1856, they broke a wrought-iron plate of 4½ inches thick (the first ever broken) by a spherical shot of 282lb., with a charge of 25lb. of powder from the 13-inch "Horsfall Monster Gun." There is also shown a diagram of the comparative ranges of the 68-pounder smooth bore, the Armstrong 110-pounder, and the Monster Gun, from which we extract the follow-

ing:—"Point-blank range of the 68-pounder, 310 yards; the Armstrong, 340 yards; the Monster, 600 yards. At 3 degrees' elevation: The 68-pounder, 1,470 yards; the Armstrong, 3,325 yards; the Monster, 1,800 yards. At 7½ degrees: The 68-pounder, 2,430 yards; the Armstrong, 2,570 yards; the Monster, 2,980 yards"—the initial velocity being uniformly in favour of the Monster Gun. The same firm exhibit a breech-loading rifled gun nine feet long, mounted on a field-carriage.

The visitor may now examine the Blakeley 200-pounder Pivot Gun, manufactured by Messrs. Fawcett, Preston, and Co., of Liverpool. Mr. Lancaster exhibits a 100-pounder oval-bore cannon, which has fired 604 rounds at angles over twelve degrees of elevation. Mr. Parsons of London also shows a very ingenious breech-loading cannon of small calibre. The Whitworth Ordnance Company exhibit six pieces, thus described:—A 1-pounder muzzle-loading rifled cannon, mounted; a 6-pounder muzzle-loading, and a 6-pounder breech-loading gun, a 12-pounder brass rifled field-piece, a 32-pounder rifled ship's cannon, and a 70-pounder; with an assortment of projectiles of various weights, solid shot and shell, from 1-pounder to 70-pounder. They also exhibit one of the flat-fronted projectiles which were fired through the armour-plates and side of the Trusty during the official trials at the Nore. This projectile, though slightly shattered at the point of contact with the plate, and shortened or stove up by the blow, is still whole. The bore of the Whitworth cannon is hexagonal in the cross section, and the rifle pitch is equal to twenty times the diameter of the bore. The solid projectiles are usually cast and then planed. One man, it is said, will mould 200 of the 1lb. shot per day, or plane the same number in the same time. We understand that the average ranges obtained from a 12-pounder Whitworth rifled gun, with a 12lb. shot and 1½lb. of powder, are at point blank 380 yards; at 1 degree elevation, 900 yards; at 10 degrees, 4,500 yards; and at 35 degrees, 10,000 yards, or nearly six English miles. The charge of powder usually employed is equal to one-sixth of the weight of the shot. The proprietors of this gun claim for it great penetrating power, and for their flat-fronted projectiles the capability of retaining this power only slightly impaired after passing a considerable distance through water. The drill of the gunners with the rifled muzzle-loading Whitworth is similar to that practised for the ordinary smooth-bore cannon.

Messrs. Moore and Harris, of Birmingham, show a large number of beautiful sporting guns, breech-loaders, rifles, &c. Messrs. Mortimer and Son, of Edinburgh, exhibit an improved rifling and sight for volunteer's rifles. Mr. Newton, of Chancery Lane, has an ingenious portable camp fire-place. Mr. Parsons, of London Bridge, has some valuable specimens of breech-loading fire-arms. Single and double rifles, both military and sporting, with locks on various patent principles, are shown by the Breech-loading Gun Company, of Great Portland Street; and repeating pistols and rifles are exhibited by many eminent manufacturers.

These, and a number of other kinds of weapons, will attract considerable attention. A variety of shot, shell, gun-carriages, &c., are shown in the British half of the building; but it must not be supposed that similar objects are absent from the foreign departments. In the French, Austrian, Russian, and Spanish courts will be found many fine specimens of ordnance and small arms, some of the latter ornamented with great taste and skill. A gun trophy, consisting of models of gun-carriages and other appliances of war, is shown by Spain—once the foremost of European nations; and now, after long decay, exhibiting signs of renewed vitality. In the Indian and Chinese courts will also be found many curious and ingenious specimens of arms. Of course, it is no part of our design to question the policy of nations in continually manufacturing great iron ships, monster guns, powerful batteries, shot-proof forts, and other deadly appliances for securing what is called the "balance of power." We merely notice these various and complicated objects in the "EXHIBITOR," as evidences of manufacturing science and skill. Whether England and France, and the other great powers, would not better expend their resources in cultivating the arts of peace than the arts of war, is a question that must be discussed elsewhere.

Civil and Naval Engineering.

In the south-west and south courts will be found a large number of highly-interesting models, illustrative of civil engineering, architectural, naval, and building contrivances. Among these will be found, either as models or as the actual objects, various kinds of furnaces, armour for ships, gas apparatus, hoists for machinery, bridges, docks, window-shutters, iron castings for railways, gates, &c.; chimney-pots; domestic articles in terra-cotta, marble, alabaster, stone, and wood; models of ships, boats, marine steam-engines, screw-propellers, tents, rudders, light-houses, ferry steamers, &c. We select a few of these.

Messrs. J. Tylor and Sons, of Warwick Lane, exhibit a model of their improved diving apparatus, as used in laying the foundation of piers, bridges, breakwaters, docks, &c.

Messrs. Heinke Brothers, of Great Portland Street, show some very excellent helmets and diving dresses. They have effected several improvements in this apparatus, by which the diver is enabled to remain under water for any length of time. The diving dress is an invaluable aid in the recovery of property from wrecks, in subaqueous engineering, and in pearl and sponge diving. The diving dress is used in conjunction with the Diving Bell. Messrs. Heinke are submarine engineers to the English, French, Russian, Spanish, Portuguese, Sardinian, Canadian, Peruvian, Brazilian, and Indian Governments.

MODEL OF DIVER IN WATERPROOF DRESS AND HELMET.
MESSRS. HEINKE BROTHERS.

A FLOAT FOR DISCHARGING SCREW COLLIERS.

This patented invention is illustrated by a complete model in the International Exhibition, Class 10, No. 2,262. The owners of the vessel are Messrs. William Cory and Son, of Commercial Road, Lambeth; and the engineer is Mr. J. H. Adams, of Grove Hall Terrace, Bow.

The float is to be used in the stream; and vessels intended to be unloaded will be brought alongside immediately they arrive, and will leave the river as soon as they are discharged. Thus the delay of locking vessels in and out of a dock is avoided, and great despatch obtained. The float has a level flush deck and flat bottom, draws only a few feet of water, and is of considerable breadth in proportion to its length. It is 90 feet beam, and is therefore very stable, so that the weighing operations can be performed with accuracy. The ends are angular, to enable two barges to be fastened at each end for the reception of coals. The sides are of sufficient length for two of the largest steam colliers to be moored alongside and discharged at once. Three of Sir William Armstrong's hydraulic weighing-cranes are provided, to work out the cargo from each collier. There are shoots, to convey the coals without breakage into the barges; and the surface of the shoots is formed with screen-bars, for separating the small coals. The four end cranes deliver the coals directly into the shoots. There are two elevated platforms upon the deck, which run from end to end of the float. The two centre cranes deliver the coals into trucks, which run on a tramway upon this platform, and the coals from these two cranes are in this manner conveyed to the shoots. The hold of the float will be occupied by the engines, boilers, and machinery of the cranes; and also by a complete gas-works, which have been constructed for lighting the float throughout, to enable the workmen to perform their operations at night. Each crane will lift 60 tons of coals per hour, and a steamer of 1,200 tons cargo may be discharged, either by night or day, in ten hours.

MODEL OF DIVING APPARATUS. J. TYLOR AND SONS.

VIEW OF THE STAGING FOR DISCHARGING SCREW COLLIERS AND OTHER VESSELS   W. CORY AND SON.

Messrs. Cory have similar machinery on an extensive scale in operation at the Victoria Docks, on fixed buildings of a novel construction, which, with other peculiar contrivances and arrangements for storing and shipping coals, were designed by Mr. Adams. Screw colliers of the largest class are constantly under discharge, night and day, in these docks.

The Fruit and Food Trophy.

MUCH has been written and said about the trophies in the nave of the Exhibition. Some have regretted their erection, but the larger number of visitors have certainly admired their symmetry, and learned something from their teachings. The trophy illustrative of Class III. — substances used for food —is particularly suggestive in the latter respect. It is an hexagonal pile, containing specimens of all kinds of edibles, from wheat to wedding cakes, pickles to potatoes, chocolate to confectionery, biscuits to beans, cattle food to concentrated cocoa, tea to tobacco —which is certainly not an edible—sweetmeats to seeds, and cakes to curry. In fact, this elegant group consists of samples from a very large number of articles of agricultural produce, dry-saltery, grocery, and confectionery, besides wines, spirits, and liqueurs.

The trophy was designed by Mr. Alfred Gilbert, the architect. As will be seen by our illustration, it is a really attractive and pleasing object. In the centre rises a column, on which is inscribed the names of the several exhibitors, surmounted by a globe, with a figure of Ceres with her horn of plenty. From the top of the column depend garlands of foliage and flowers, with fruit intermixed. Its base is surrounded by baskets of fruit, modelled in wax by Mr. K. Sandell, of Chiswell Street, Finsbury. From cornucopias on either side issue a profusion of fruits in sugar, furnished by

Messrs. Schooling and Co., of Whitechapel, the space between being filled with specimens of the various articles mentioned above—jars of jellies and sauces, vases of tea in the leaf and coffee in the berry, packets of various cereals, bottles of pickles, &c. Heads of goats, rams, and stags are at the several angles, while round the fascia Mr. Hallet, of Brighton, shows his "Pedigree Wheat," the immense ears being arranged on a black velvet ground, so as to form the words "pedigree wheat" in English, French, and German. The wheat has been produced on the same principle as that adopted in the breeding of animals. The largest ears were selected, and from them the finest grains; and so on each year from 1857 to 1860, till this result is gained ; the two original ears together contained 87 grains, — after four years' repeated selection, a single ear contained 123 grains, and is nearly twice the size of an ordinary ear of wheat.

Below the main body of the trophy is an elegant arrangement of rockwork, filled with plants and flowers, supplied by Messrs. Carter and Co., the eminent seed merchants and florists of High Holborn. They also supply fresh flowers daily to such portions of the trophy as require them.

A most admirable feature of this trophy, and one that appears to be highly approved by visitors, is that of the series of drinking fountains. These fountains are supplied with pure, crystal-like

THE FRUIT AND FOOD TROPHY.

water, filtered during its transit from the main, by a patent process invented and manufactured by Mr. Dahlke, of Bolingbroke Gardens, Battersea. The mode of filtering adopted by this gentleman is found so simple in its operation, and so perfect in its results, that it will probably supersede the cumbrous mode at present in use. The general arrangement of the trophy has been carried out by Mr. Ainsworth (Chairman of the Trophy Committee, and senior partner of the firm of Carter and Co.), Mr. Dahlke, and Mr. Gilbert, the architect.

On the day of the grand opening, many of the flowers and other objects in the Food Trophy were ruthlessly destroyed by the well-dressed throng, who, in their anxiety to gaze on the Duke of Cambridge, the Prince Oscar, and other notabilities, crowded over the rockwork, swarmed up the great lighthouse, and occupied every spot from which

a sight could be obtained. But the damage was repaired next day; and, ever since, the public have refreshed themselves at the fountains, and examined the curious things in the trophy with untiring interest; and, as a whole, this trophy will well repay examination. It has been erected, at the express request of the Royal Commissioners, by a number of gentlemen, to whom great credit is due; and at a cost of several hundreds of pounds. It should be mentioned that large quantities of the several articles of food here represented will be found on the eastern side of the eastern annexe, where also are many curious and interesting objects in chemistry, &c. The eastern annexe is a long continuation of the north-east transept, through which it is reached. Entrance may also be had from the Exhibition Road to this most important section of the Exhibition.

Curiosities in the Great Exhibition.

VISITORS will naturally look out for the curious, after having feasted their eyes on the great, the wonderful, and the valuable. We propose, therefore, to devote a few pages occasionally to the description of some of the smaller objects exhibited. These, though scarcely appropriate for illustration by means of engravings, will be found highly interesting.

CAFFRE LUXURIES.—A very interesting portion of the Exhibition is the collection (in the North-east Transept) illustrating the habits and modes of life of the Caffre. His great luxury seems to be snuff, and here are every variety of snuff-boxes and snuff-spoons, generally carried in his back hair, along with his nose scraper and other useful articles; and some of them show considerable skill in carving. A few of the Caffres smoke, and by sticking a reed with a bowl made of soap-stone at the end of it into a cowhorn, which they fill with water, they manage to extemporise a very rude kind of hookah. Their greatest ingenuity, however, is shown in their musical instruments. The Caffre lyre is a bent bow strung with twisted hair, which, beaten with a stick, will give out some four or five distinct tones; while the Maca-bere piano, which is a series of strips of wood, each backed by a sounding chamber, formed of the rind of some dried and hardened fruit, has one or two notes very nearly approaching to the music of a cracked bell. The extraordinary top-knots which are the most dis-tinguishing feature of their simple costume, are well illustrated by a specimen which was torn off the head of a native in a scuffle at D'Urban some little time ago. Two or three articles of red pottery ware, which belonged to the famous Moshes, are surprisingly excellent in quality. There is a smoothness and finish about them which proves considerable proficiency in the art. In timbers the colony appears to be rich, for there is an immense variety shown, some of them possess-ing great durability, while others are useful only for ornamental purposes. Two of them rejoice in very singular names: the "sneeze-wood," which is of extraordinarily tenacious fibre, and stands exposure to the weather admirably, is so called from the pungent qualities of its saw-wood; and the "stinkwood," which is a furniture wood some-what resembling dark walnut, while green, gives out a most dis-agreeable odour.

GLUE.—The manufacturers of glue and gelatine exhibit in great numbers, and show glues of very superior quality, both in strength and transparency. An idea of the tenacity of good glue may be gained from the fact that one of the makers shows two pieces of wood having a square inch of surface that were united by glue, and required a force of more than five hundred pounds weight to effect their separation.

ARTICLES IN CORAL.—The coral show, in the Precious Metals Court, is a perfect mermaid's cave. Of this beautiful material, Mr. Phillips, of Cockspur Street, justly claims the distinction of exhibiting the choicest and most varied collection ever seen together. It consists of every description of ornament in fashionable use, and of cabinet specimens of rare and matchless beauty; most of them having been carefully collected during several years for the present Exhibition.

The inherent beauty of the material, showing every gradation of colour—from pure white to pale pink, from deepest red to jet black—and its consequent fitness for personal decoration, originally induced Mr. Phillips to select it as a medium to supply the place of the costlier gems of the toilette. During the last fifteen years, the demand for the finer qualities of coral has extended all over Europe.

INDIAN PAINTING.—People who pay a series of visits to the Exhibition would do well to begin one day by ascending the staircase that commences just inside the turn-tables, and, turning to the right, to make a regular round of the galleries. First, they will find some splendid engravings, principally Hogarth's, and a set of very curious Indian pictures, the production of native artists. Nobody will refuse to linger a moment before the quaint but accurate representation of the Kaiserbagh, or the painting—which defies all rules of perspective—of the coronation procession of the late King of Oude. Two or three of the "common people" are very properly being trampled in the fore-ground by the elephants, because they have neglected to get out of the way, and the artist has taken special care to make them of such hideous countenances as entirely to satisfy the spectator that they richly deserve their fate.

GERMAN CLOTHING.—Some very valuable facts may be obtained by an inspection of the case of an Austrian tailor, in the South-west Gallery. He displays what it is to be supposed he conceives to be real bargains in wearing apparel. There is a hunting-coat, which a label informs us was made for "The Right Hon. Count Westphalen," and which would astonish Melton Mowbray; and a "summer paletot" of very ordinary materials, marked at the uncommonly low price of twelve pounds sterling. Now, there is not the slightest doubt but that any London tailor would supply the article for three pounds; and, as there are forty millions of people in Austria, of which five must certainly wear paletots, that great empire might save forty-five millions sterling annually by relaxing her tariff, and allowing her subjects to wear summer paletots of British manufacture. Dress-coats and great-coats are marked at similar extravagant prices; so that it would be well worth while for the Austrian visitors to make a few inquiries as to the prices of wearing apparel with us, before they return to their own country.

AMERICAN NOTIONS.—In the court devoted to the United States, just within side the south-east entrance, are several admirable "notions" and productions. There are patent rope walks not three yards long, and yet capable of making rope of any required longitude; wonderful washing machines, that dispense with all human labour, and fire engines calculated to throw, with the aid of steam, any quantity of water to any required height or distance. There are beautiful paintings by Cropsey and Kellog; pianos, which are pro-nounced to be of superb tone by first-rate London judges; and last, though not least, the new cereal preparation, "Maizena," (the rather mysterious name of which may be read without any further word of explanation on every wall in London upon which a bill could be possibly posted. This "real blessing" to housewives and cooks is a sort of flour carefully prepared from the finest portion of the maize or Indian corn, and is so rich in mucilage as entirely to supersede the use of eggs in the preparation of custards or puddings. It has been used for both purposes, and in the preparation of blanc-manges in the refreshment rooms since the opening of the Exhibition, and is pronounced by every one who has tasted it to be a valuable as well as economical addition to our culinary resources. One of its most valuable properties is, we understand, its adaptability to the weak stomachs of invalids—a circumstance which alone would justify us in directing attention to the case of the Maizena exhibitors.

A NEW MATCH.—Among the most extraordinary substances shown is a new material called "Parksine," from the name of its discoverer, the product of a mixture of chloroform and castor oil, which produces a substance as hard as horn but as flexible as leather, capable of being cast or stamped, painted, dyed, or carved, and which, above all, can be produced, in any quantity, at a lower price than gutta percha. Another most valuable invention is also shown here in some improved safety matches by Bryant and Mays. These curious matches, which in outward appearance are like other lucifers, cannot be ignited either by friction, fire, or percussion, or in any way except by being rubbed on the side of the box in which they are contained. This most important improvement is effected by separating the chemical substances which produce fire by friction, and placing one-half on the head of the match, the other on the side of the box.

AUTOMATON ANIMALS.—Near to the western boundary of the French Court are certain automatic birds and animals, the former of which flutter about and sing most naturally, and the latter of which play, much to the amusement of the juveniles, on guitars, violins, drums, &c. The hare, which performs on the guitar, is a wonderful creature. He not only thrums the strings, but he winks, moves his nostrils after the manner of hares, opens and closes his eyelids, as if in sleepy enjoyment of the music, which is not particularly good; but, as Dr. Johnson said of the novel which a lady wrote, "The wonder is not that it is done badly, but that it is done at all."

WONDERFUL CALCULATING MACHINE.—Visitors should notice, in the North Court Gallery, Class 13, Mr. Babbage's extraordinary calculating machine, which will work quadrations and logarithms up to seven places of figures. It was the account of this invention, written by the late Lady Lovelace—Lord Byron's daughter—that led the Messrs. Scheutz, of Stockholm, to improve upon it to such an extent as not only enabled the machine to calculate its tables, but to print its results. This improvement was at once bought up by the English Government; but it is not now shown at the Exhibition, as it is very busy at Somerset House, night and day, working out annuity and other tables for the Registrar-General.

MICROSCOPIC WONDERS.—The collection of microscopes is unequalled, and with them Mr. Norman shows (in the North Court Gallery, Class 13) a wonderful series of microscopic slides, containing minute sections and preparations of almost every conceivable object, animal or vegetable, from sections of the tooth of a lion to the liver or skin of a man—from the lungs of a boa constrictor to the palate of a toad or the tongue of an alligator. One of the most curious instruments in this extraordinary collection is a machine exhibited by Mr. Peters, for microscopic writing, which is infinitely more wonderful than Mr. Whitworth's machine for measuring the millionth of an inch, which excited such astonishment in 1851. With this machine of Mr. Peters it is stated that the words "Matthew Marshall, Bank of England," can be written in the two-and-a-half millionth of an inch in length, and it is actually said that calculations made on this data show that the whole Bible can be written twenty-two times in the space of a square inch. We must leave a detailed description of this most extraordinary instrument to another occasion, and content ourselves now with simply saying that the words to be written microscopically are written in pencil, in ordinary characters, on a sheet of paper at the bottom of the instrument. But the pencil with which this is done

communicates by a series of levers and gimbals with another minute pencil and tablet at the top, by means of which the ordinary writing of the pencil and the pencil for the microscopic writing both move in unison, though the motion of the latter is so graduated that a stroke of a quarter of an inch at the bottom is only a stroke of a quarter of a millionth of an inch at the top, the shape and character of both marks being, nevertheless, precisely alike in outline. As a matter of course, the microscopic writing at the top is only visible under powerful magnifiers, and the object of the machine is chiefly to mark banknotes with certain minute signatures, for the prevention of forgery. Such a precaution, no doubt, would prove an effectual stopper on counterfeit notes, if only all tradesmen supplied themselves with microscopes to examine them, just as a little ordinary care would now detect any forgery.

THE "PROCESSES COURT."—This court, which is close to the Pottery, is a never-failing source of attraction. Here there is, besides the exceedingly interesting pipe manufactory of Mr. Reynolds, a number of processes well worth seeing. Mrs. Lavinia Jones, of Bradford-on-Avon, Wilts, shows her miniature Albion printing press, which she hopes to introduce, not merely as a source of amusement in parlours or libraries, but as a means of inducing ladies to learn typography, so that they may, if cast upon the world, have a resource against starvation in their own exertions. Some of Mrs. Jones's specimens in various languages, and produced from the miniature press, are exceedingly elegant. Opposite this little stand Messrs. Day, of Queen Street, Lincoln's Inn Fields, exhibit the processes of chromolithography as applied to the production of some views of the Exhibition. Messrs. J. and H. Robinson and Co., of Milk Street, Cheapside, have at work a silk velvet loom capable of producing but half a yard per day of fine velvet. It seems strange that with all the advance in mechanical science there has never yet been produced a silk velvet loom capable of throwing its own shuttle, and cutting the pile of the web. Messrs. Pinches make and roll medals by a powerful press, and Messrs. H. Milward and Sons, of Redditch, show by models and samples the process of needlemaking. Messrs. Kennan and Sons, of Dublin, have, among other machines, a sculpturing machine at work, and right well it seems to serve its purpose; and all over the court there are sewing machines, the mere enumeration of the proprietors or inventors of which would occupy more space than we can spare. To the uninitiated each sewing machine seems twin brother to its neighbour.

LARGEST BLOCK OF COPPER ORE IN EUROPE.—The fame of the Burra-Burra copper mines of South Australia is well supported. There is a block of ore, which stands on the visitor's right hand as he enters the Australian Court, and which we believe to be by far the largest and richest mass of its kind ever sent to Europe. Its weight, which is nearly seven tons, has been a cause of some delay in its appearance at the Exhibition, as for a time great difficulty was found in unshipping it from the hold of the Murray. There it is now, however, a marble-looking mass, flaked with vivid green and intersections of granite. Its yield of metal is estimated at more than 30 per cent. The malachite, also, is fine, especially the large table of that singular carbonate, the mineral character of which is belied by its stone-like appearance. But there are here some curious nuggets of the veined green substance which in 1851 was first familiarised to the English public by a grand display in the Russian Court of the Hyde Park Exhibition. We do not remember to have seen anything so strange, so beautiful in its way as the large lump of malachite, thickly encrusted over nearly the whole of its surface by blue crystals.

GRAPHITE.—Near the Russian specimens of pietra dura, &c., there has just sprung up a new trophy, containing specimens of graphite from the recently-discovered mines of the substance in Siberia. The exhibitor, Mr. Alibert, deserves great praise for the pains he has been at to give an ornamental appearance to a substance otherwise not very attractive. Statuettes, busts, hands, &c., are carved out of it with considerable artistic skill, and though this is quite beside the usual purposes to which plumbago is applied, it could hardly present itself in such fine company without this homage to the beautiful.

Furniture and Decoration.

IN the centre of the North Courts, on the right hand side from the Eastern Dome, will be found most of the furniture and household decorations belonging to the British exhibitors. Part of the space thus filled is inclosed, and devoted to what is called the Mediæval Court. Here will be found a number of very fine pieces of furniture suitable for ecclesiastical decoration — a reredos executed by Mr. Earp, from a design by Mr. Street; a couple of swell organs, in the Gothic style; some fine Gothic church furniture; and a Gothic casket, by Messrs. Fisher, of Southampton Street; and various carvings by Messrs. Cox and others.

The Mediæval Court has been arranged by Mr. Burges, the eminent Gothic architect, who, assisted by Messrs. Slater and Morton, has ably carried out the views of Mr. Beresford Hope, whose speciality appears to be a revival of ancient forms in modern times. Great skill has been displayed in the arrangement of the various beautiful objects exhibited in this court, to which the leading manufacturers have liberally contributed. The visitor will examine with pleasure a portion of the reredos for Waltham Abbey, and the cartoon of the finished work, as well as the various specimens of Glastonbury chairs; and the 13th century bookcase, exhibited by Mr. James Forsyth, of Edward Street, Hampstead Road. This quaint but beautiful piece of furniture is a reproduction in all respects —shape, carving, colouring, and general tone—of the sort of receptacles in which the monks kept their manuscripts, and before which they performed those wonders of illumination and minute caligraphy, it has lately become a fashion to imitate, if not to rival. We are enabled to give an illustration (on page 46) of this excellent work.

The same exhibitor has also some very beautiful specimens of carvings in wood and stone in the Mediæval Court and other parts of the building. In this page we have an engraving of the font executed by him for the Earl of Dudley, and now fixed in Witley Church. In the Mediæval Court an exact model of the font appears, as designed by Mr. S. W. Daukes, the well-known architect. The lower part of the work consists of a richly-carved basin in Caen stone, supported by four winged angels, sculptured in the same material, and surmounted by a carved oak cover, the upper figure on which is intended to represent John the Baptist. The style of the work is true Renaissance, and the motive of the whole is well sustained. An appropriate inscription—"Suffer little children to

MODEL OF FONT IN WITLEY CHURCH, MR. JAMES FORSYTH.

come unto me, and forbid them not, for of such is the kingdom of heaven"—runs round the base of the cover.

Here also—the work of the same exhibitor—are some fine carvings in oak, intended for the bench-ends of the choir in Chichester Cathedral; the high tomb erected to the memory of the late Lord Cawdor; one of the circular panels, with an open cut subject, for Chichester Cathedral; and some other beautiful specimens of genuine carving. Many of the latter are from the designs of Mr. William Slater. In the Mediæval Court will also be found a carved font of Ancaster stone, exhibited by Messrs. Kirk and Parry, of Stanford, Lincolnshire. This font has a beautifully carved cover, executed by Mr. David Sharp, a young and rising artist, who shows a bracket in the classical style against the walls of the adjoining court.

The very remarkable works exhibited in the Mediæval Court will attract considerable attention. The visitor should especially notice Mr. Redfern's casts of sculptures of the Ascension, for the Digby Mortuary Chapel, at Sherborne; as well as some specimens of mediæval carvings; the cast of Dr. Mills' monument at Ely Cathedral, from the design of Mr. Scott, the Gothic architect; the metal-work and furniture shown by the Ecclesiological Society; and the new frontal executed for Peterborough Cathedral by various young ladies, and exhibited by the Dean of that ancient city.

But as we shall possibly return to the Mediæval Court, we proceed to notice some other pieces of furniture shown in Classes X. and XXX.

The sideboard in *carton pierre*, executed by Messrs. George Jackson and Sons, of Rathbone Place, Oxford Street, is certainly a most successful application of this style of decorative art. One of the advantages of work in this material is that it does not warp or shrink through heat. The caryatides supporting the entablatures of this sideboard are models of grace and good taste. They are from the same mould as those which support Mr. Harry Emanuel's unrivalled jewel case.

Messrs. Jackson also exhibit a Greek candelabrum, executed under the direction of C. R. Cockerell, Esq., the eminent artist; a pair of griffins and candelabrum between; a Louis XVI. door, admirably designed; various mouldings, ovals, centre flowers for ceilings, cornices for libraries and drawing-rooms, and a compartment for a decorated ceiling, intended to show the advantages of *carton pierre* in respect of lightness, sharpness of detail, and completeness of relief. But the triumph of the Furniture Court will be found in the sideboard and various objects contributed by Messrs. Jackson and Graham, of Oxford Street. Of these we shall have something to say by-and-by. For the present we content ourselves by calling the visitor's attention to their surpassing excellence of workmanship and beauty of design.

A gilt cabinet and looking-glass by Mr. C. Nosotti, of Oxford Street, may be considered an excellent specimen of modern house decoration. This elaborate piece of furniture is executed entirely from designs furnished by Mr. Nosotti's own English workmen; and all the moulding, carving, gilding, &c., is done on his premises. In drawing-room decoration and gilt work generally—especially in frames for looking-glasses, pictures, and prints.—Mr. Nosotti bears the palm among the English exhibitors; nor have we seen anything in the foreign half of the building to exceed them for beauty of composition and excellence of execution.

Messrs. Wright and Mansfield, of Great Portland Street, also exhibit some finely-carved and gilt cabinets, book-cases, girandoles, &c., with *plaques* of Wedgwood ware tastefully introduced here and there.

Notice also the old-fashioned furniture of Messrs. Toms and Luscombe, the decorative furniture of Messrs. Morris and Co., of Red Lion Square; the artistic decorations for dining and drawing-rooms, by Messrs. McLachlan, of St. James's Street; the cabinets shown by various firms; the Taunton sideboard; and, generally, the furniture shown by Messrs. Gillow,

Grace, Fisher, Jenner and Knewstub, Lawford, Seldon, and Jones and Willis. But as it is impossible to do more than glance at these on the present occasion, we shall endeavour, in another page, to give the reader some illustrative specimens of the most important and noteworthy among them.

The paper hangings, carvings, and other wall decorations, will also claim a more extended notice. Meanwhile, we may mention that since 1851 a great advance has been made in domestic furniture. We are no longer shocked by inconsistencies or repelled by anachronisms. Our Jacksons and Gillows, our Fishers and Trollopes have no need to fear competition with their Continental rivals. If none of them show in their furniture the massiveness of Austria, or the flimsiness of France, they, at least, avoid the homeliness of America, or the tawdriness of Russia. Grace in design and thorough integrity in workmanship are the chief characteristics of British furniture and household decoration; and while these are earnestly sought and unhesitatingly adopted, our manufacturers need have no fear of commanding the markets of the world—to say nothing of the constantly increasing demands for home consumption.

The collection of British furniture—rich and noble as it is—has two great defects: it is badly placed in the building, and is without attendants to explain its merits. Fragments of rich mantel-shelves, hall-fittings, and massive dining-tables that would not disgrace a Venetian palace, stand in solemn silence before admiring crowds, without even a descriptive ticket attached to

CHIMNEY-PIECE IN CARTON PIERRE.   MESSRS. GEORGE JACKSON AND SONS.

them. The open, cheerful southern courts would have given more space in which to display their delicate beauty, and would have attracted more visitors than the cramped northern courts.

Pianos, as articles of furniture merely, are entitled to especial notice: their claims to attention as musical instruments are tested daily, and with great satisfaction, by thousands of visitors. Approaching the Furniture Courts from the foreign nave, we come first to musical instruments. Notice the handsome instrument in a walnut case, inlaid, by Hopkinson; and, at the back, the oak piano with carving, in the style of decoration of the time of Charles I. The next court is occupied jointly by Collard and Broadwood; both of these firms show instruments worthy of their great fame. In Broadwood's compartment are some interesting models, and parts illustrating the construction. We notice, at the back of this court, Challen's double-action piano, in case of walnut and marqueterie. Messrs. Kirkman and Son show several fine pianofortes. The case of the Grand nearest the nave should be carefully examined; it is a magnificent specimen of parquetry.

The visitor should "make a note of" the suite of bedroom furniture in sycamore and alnus woods, shown by Bird and Hull, of Manchester. The designs are peculiarly elegant. Purdie, Cowtan, and Co., of Oxford Street, exhibit a dining-room fireplace, with wall-decoration in imitation marbles, ebony, walnut, and purple wood. The pictures occupying the panels of the two side compartments are specimens of water-glass, or stereo-chromic method of fresco. The works of Trapnell, a beautiful walnut bedroom furniture, and the carpets of Filmer, from designs by the students of South Kensington, occupy a portion of this court. In the next two courts a handsome book-case in oak, with cast-iron mountings; a sideboard by Caldecott, of carved English oak; Topling's carpets; Ogden's sideboard of carved oak, beautifully relieved with slabs of walnut; and Thurston's billiard-table, attract deserved attention. The latter is made of oak, from drawings by Mr. J. M. Allen, in the style of the fifteenth century. The panels of the sides and ends are carved in low relief, illustrating the history of the

THIRTEENTH CENTURY BOOKCASE.   MR. JAMES FORSYTH.

Wars of the Roses, supported by eight legs, each composed of four clustered columns, with richly foliated cups. It has a central crocketed shaft, with carved spurs on a square moulded base. The various panels represent the "Departure of the Duke of York from Ludlow Castle, 1455;" "Battle of St. Albans;" "Death of the Duke of Somerset, and Reconciliation of the Duke of York and the Queen;" "Battle of Blore Heath;" "The Earl of Shaftesbury leaving Middleham Castle"—from necessity, these two subjects are chronologically reversed; "The Desertion of Sir Andrew Trollope and Veterans from the Fortified Camp of Ludlow, 1459;" "Somerset released at Colchester;" "Warwick's Triumphant Entry into London;" "Battle of Northampton;" "Desertion of Lord Grey de Ruthyn;" "Battle of Wakefield Green, and Death of the Duke of York;" "Death of the Duke's Son on Wakefield Bridge;" "Great Battle at Towton, 1461, in the midst of a Terrible Snowstorm" (the Lancastrians being nearly all), "Battle of Mortimer Cross," "Battle of Barnet, and Death of the Earl of Warwick," "Battle of Tewkesbury, Defeat of Margaret, and Death of Edward Prince of Wales." Messrs. Thurston also exhibit a model of a patent combination billiard-table, easily convertible into a dining or supper table, the cushions being large and easy to turn down.

Messrs. ———, Son, of Berners Street, exhibit a superior extended ———— dining-room table, of the finest English make, in ———— oak; the framework of Italian design, with scroll supports, ornamented with festoons of

fruit, &c., manufactured on a novel plan to open to an increased diameter by an extension of the framework, the top being preserved entire, and quarter-circle leaves being introduced in several series round the circumference, thus preserving at all sizes the perfect circle.

In comfortable and useful furniture, Mr. Brown, of Piccadilly, celebrated all over the world for his easy chairs, stands prominent. He has sent a "perfect folding couch" in brass, and also "marvellous chairs" in iron and brass. These chairs and couches are novel and peculiar from their extreme comfort and ease, as also their portability and simplicity, rendering them highly desirable for the army and navy, and peculiarly so for invalids, as any desired elevation may be obtained without removing the person reclining. They are also graceful and light in appearance, and when made in brass for drawing-rooms very elegant. A very useful garden or verandah chair is also shown, and a novelty in a revolving stool for cricketing or yachting. The army and navy have long made use of these very portable and elegant pieces of furniture.

Mr. A. Sedley, of Regent Street, exhibits a fine silver equilibrium chair, which, in addition to an extremely elegant appearance, possesses every requisite that the most fastidious lounger can desire. It is almost **self-acting, and requires no exertion** to adjust it perfectly to the sitter's fancy. A side-board, also by the same firm, is worthy of notice. It is made of dark brown and light oak, with a large plate-glass back, and is more remarkable for elegance of form and good outline than for exuberance in ornamental detail. The style is Italo-Elizabethan, and there is a clock case, a novelty which harmonises nicely with it; also, a brass bedstead, or rather the foot end is a novel, ingenious, and elegant application of metal to such an article of furniture.

GILT CABINET AND LOOKING GLASS. MR. C. NOSOTTI.

Turkey carpet, they are very graceful. **They are largely used for halls, corridors, churches, and picture galleries.** Wright's pearl table, Egan's cabinet-table, the decorations of Hayward, are all of them works which we can heartily urge our readers to examine, if their time will allow of their so doing. The next court is one of the most attractive of this group; it contains examples of the works of Skidmore's Art Manufactures Company. The most prominent object here is the tomb of Bishop Pearson, to be placed in Chester Cathedral. The tomb itself is a beautiful work in stone and marble; over the recumbent figure of the bishop is a magnificent canopy of metal-work, similar in character to the Hereford screen. In the glass-case containing examples of the smaller works of the Company is an exquisite cover of the book of the Gospels. It is of chased silver, with *champ-levé* enamelled border, and corner-pieces and centre in niello-work. A silver flagon, enriched with enamels and crystal globes on the handle, is very pleasing.

There are some very excellent specimens of decorative furniture in the foreign half of the building; but, in their desire to shine in colour and curious form, many exhibitors

Mr. Arrowsmith's solid parquet floors (a mosaic of woods), as aids to decoration, attract much and deserved attention in this court. Being manufactured by machinery, they are produced very cheaply, and they are extremely durable. As a border to a room, round the fringe of a | have neglected the solid qualities of good workmanship, which we in this country consider necessary to beauty and indispensable to utility. In carved cabinets the foreign show at the Exhibition is fine, but in household furniture it is somewhat weak.

48

CASSELL'S ILLUSTRATED EXHIBITOR, 1862.

IRON HOUSES, &c.

Messrs. Samuel Hemming and Co., of Moorgate Street, have, in Class X., several samples of iron buildings, and iron roofing for portable houses, adapted for all climates We here show the interior of a church recently erected by them for the Colonies. Their portable iron houses are simple in construction, perfect in arrangement, efficient in character, and easy and inexpensive of carriage. They are also exceedingly neat and comfortable in all their arrangements. The chief advantages are durability, economy of space, and aptitude of erection. To describe one iron house is to describe the main points of all. They consist of a timber framing, 4½ by 3 inches; but in some instances the framework is made of iron. The walls and roofs are corrugated iron; the ridge capping of the same material. The walls are lined on the inside with half-inch boarding, covered with canvas ready for papering, leaving a space of 4½ inches through-out the entire building between the iron and the woodwork, by which means complete ventilation is effected, and the temperature in summer much lessened, and increased in winter. Each house is adapted for 4½ inch brick-work, or any non-conductor, which may be applied at any time, if considered necessary, after the completion of the building. The

ceilings are lined with half-inch boarding on the under side of the ceiling joist; then to be covered with canvas, papered, and distempered. The flooring and joists are the same as an ordinary building. The doors are four panels, with good locks and hinges. The sashes are glazed with crown glass to the foot, and all the fittings are complete. All necessary skirtings, beads, architraves, and other mouldings, are provided. The erections are either put together with iron screws and bolts, and may be re-erected by inexperienced persons in a very few days, every part being numbered to correspond and lettered as directed ... by the builder. The roof girders, pillars, girders and other ... portions of the church shown in the engraving are of iron, while the pews, screens, &c., pit, and well, are of course of ... the usual materials. It may not be thought that iron for houses is incapable of decoration. A glance at the picture will show that, on the contrary, it is admirably adapted for giving lightness, grace, and durability to an edifice. But its especial advantage is that it may be forced in England, taken to pieces, packed, and re-fitted in any part of the world with the utmost ease and facility. Such portions as are necessary are cast, but all the ornamental parts can be constructed of hammered iron, and coloured to any design, or otherwise decorated.

MODEL OF IRON CHURCH. MESSRS. HEMMING AND CO.

The British Colonies.

A MOST interesting and important section of the International Exhibition is that devoted to the British Colonies. They occupy the whole of the north-eastern transept, and a portion of the north courts next those devoted to furniture, altogether about 15,000 square feet, of which India has nearly a fifth.

The Colonies, which were almost unrepresented in 1851, appear now in their true proportions. Canada, New South Wales, Nova Scotia, Prince Edward's Island, and the other North American Colonies, are placed in a group; while the Australian and Eastern dependencies, in like manner, stand side by side.

In the centre of the transept there are ranged, by way of trophies, various prominent productions of the Colonies. Thus, we have agricultural implements, hardware, and homespun. The visitor will also observe some highly interesting drawings in crayon, the colour and artistic finish of which reflect great credit on their exhibitor, Mr. F. Locke; one, a picture of Niagara, is wonderfully truthful.

The iron ores of Canada are very important. That chiefly worked is the bog iron ore, which is spread out in patches over the surface of the country. It is largely melted at the Radnor furnaces, Three Rivers, and is chiefly used for cast-iron railway wheels, a pair of which are exhibited that have traversed a distance of 150,000 miles, and show but slight signs of wear.

The specimens of the Bignor ore beds of Marmora are exceedingly interesting. The lead of Canada is not at present of great practical

CANADIAN COURT.—NORTH-EAST TRANSEPT.

the timbers of Canada shown in a tall mass of pine slabs, and oak beams, birch poles, and other woods, that grow and thrive beneath the snow. Victoria is represented by the great gilt obelisk, meant to represent to the eye the actual bulk of all the gold found in the colony since 1851. Tasmania shows whale boats and timbers; while the East and West Indies, our Mediterranean possessions, Queensland, and our African settlements, each appear by some characteristic sign.

Were it not for the fact that many eminent scientific men had willingly assisted Dr. Lindley in the arrangement of the multitudinous objects contributed by our Colonies, the visitor would experience great difficulty in comprehending their value and importance. We propose to notice briefly the principal articles exhibited by each colony.

UPPER AND LOWER CANADA show various specimens of timber, ores, and minerals, together with many of the products of their fisheries,

importance, but the copper ores are particularly good and abundant. A large mass of native metallic copper, 450 lbs. weight, is very striking. The amount of Canadian gold exhibited is not more than about £500 in value.

The Canadian building stones are admirably shown; blocks of a cubic foot, with the different faces, showing the appearance of the stones in the rough, when dressed, and also polished, are exhibited. Among the samples are numerous limestones, dolomites, sandstones, granites, syenites, marbles, &c. What would not English architects give for a bed from which dolomite or magnesian limestone could be obtained in unlimited quantities? the formation being 150 feet in thickness; the stone free from any substance producing stains, its colour improving with the weather, and not marred by the growth of lichens. Gypsum, or plaster stone, also used as manure, is shown

7

in fine specimens, and is especially abundant, selling in the unground state as low as two dollars per ton. Lithographic stone, of very good quality, has been recently discovered, which is well worthy the careful observation of our lithographers.

Among the less valuable, but by no means unimportant, minerals are mica, in sheets twenty inches square; thunbago, of excellent quality; buhrstones nearly equal to the best French varieties; phosphate of lime, or apatite, so valuable as a substitute for bones or coprolites in the manufacture of artificial manures; and many others, all of them indicating a bright fortune for the manufacturing prosperity of the Canadian people.

Although concerning the scientific geologist to a greater degree than the general public, we should commit an act of injustice if we passed over unnoticed the admirable illustrative mineral collection arranged and described by Mr. Henry Hunt.

The collection of forest woods and timber from the Canadas has been most carefully and scientifically made and arranged. The mere catalogue of the various kinds would occupy several columns of our space; but, as each specimen is fully labelled and described, the visitor to the Exhibition may examine for himself the interesting gathering.

From the excellent Catalogue issued by the Canadian Commissioners, we learn that "Canada exports annually about 30,000,000 cubic feet of timber in the rough state, and about 400,000,000 feet, board measure, of sawn timber. The revenue derived by the province, during 1860, for timber out in the forests, amounted to about 500,000 dollars. Of the sixty or seventy varieties of woods in our forests, there are usually only five or six kinds which go to make up these exports so vast in quantity ; the remaining fifty or sixty timber trees are left to perish, or are burned as a nuisance, to get them out of the way. By showing in the markets of the world that we have these valuable woods, and can furnish them at such unprecedentedly low prices, we shall secure additional purchasers. The collections here named were made chiefly in reference to this point, and are, in their nature and in their intrinsic value, it is believed, well adapted for that purpose.

"In extent, in the variety and value of its woods, the great forests of deciduous trees of North America surpass all others ; and the most remarkable of this great mixed forest is that growing in the valley of the St. Lawrence. The western coasts of both continents, in high latitudes, furnish only or chiefly the coniferæ. The high summer temperatures and abundant summer rains are, unquestionably, those conditions of climate necessary to produce these peculiar forest trees. The western coasts of both continents, in high latitudes, have the necessary moisture, but not the high summer temperature ; the western prairies east of the Mississippi, and the vast deserts west of it, have the summer heat, but not the moisture ; hence the absence of all trees in the one region, and of the deciduous trees in the other. If the people of this country had a more correct appreciation of the riches which they possess in these mighty forests, they would not, surely, so unnecessarily destroy them."

NOVA SCOTIA sends various kinds of minerals and timbers, besides several specimens of birds, fishes, and quadrupeds, excellently preserved in a manner that closely imitates life. A group of furniture in the centre of the court, and some beautiful carving, will also attract attention. In both Nova Scotia and Canada are exhibited sleighs, and various sorts of carriages.

The minerals in the Nova Scotian Court are remarkably characteristic. Coal is particularly well represented. A column thirty-four feet in height, showing the thickness of the seam, is a prominent object in the north-east transept. The Albion mines, from which this specimen was obtained, yield 70,000 tons annually, of which a large portion is exported to the United States, and another part to Canada, to reduce the iron ore to the metallic state. There are also specimens of interest from the ten-foot seam at Cow Bay, Cape Breton, nearly the whole of which is used by a gas company at New York. In addition to these there are three samples of a nine-foot seam from Lingan; and a six-foot seam from Sydney, in Cape Breton—all these

belonging to an extensive coal field, the thinnest seam of which is about five feet.

The Provincial Government of Nova Scotia exhibit about £4,000 worth of gold in quartz, and specimens of the valuable iron ore of the province ; this is chiefly hematite, which occurs in veins ten feet thick, and specular iron ore. Much of this iron is reduced by charcoal, and is almost all purchased by the Sheffield cutlers, being ranked by them very near the best Swedish in quality. Among the other economic minerals may be noticed samples of their gypsum, which occurs in a deposit fifteen miles in extent, and of which large quantities are exported to the United States. A good cabinet of the minerals characteristic of the country is shown by Professor Howe.

NEW BRUNSWICK shows specimens of iron ore, hydraulic limestones, and coal ; but the most interesting mineral exhibited is a new substance, termed Albertine, or Albertite coal. This is a peculiar mineral, burning with a flame, leaving little ash, and yet differing from bitumen, which it much resembles in its bright, lustrous appearance and great lightness, and by its not melting readily. It has been most profitably employed in the distillation of hydro-carbon, or burning oils, and has been the subject of a law-suit, as contradictory in its scientific evidence as that given in the very celebrated but by no means creditable case of the Boghead coal, or Torbane Hill mineral.

In the centre of the transept will be seen a trophy formed of Indian dresses and moccassins. They are profusely decorated with beads of different colours, arranged with some taste. There are also furs of the beaver, fox, lynx, bear, and other animals, peculiar to the province ; together with some interesting specimens of native woods. Against the wall will be seen a large number of domestic articles, such as pails, hoops, brooms, the work of the inmates of the Penitentiary of St. John's.

NEW SOUTH WALES, in the International Exhibition, abounds with evidences of the material wealth and comfort of its inhabitants. Gold, iron, copper, cotton, silk, flax, oil, and wine appear in profusion, in many shapes of beauty and utility. More than three hundred specimens of native woods are shown, both in a manufactured and unmanufactured state.

In gold, New South Wales is especially strong. The small case that faces the nave contains some splendid nuggets, and samples of gold in quartz and in a manufactured state. The new Australian sovereign, which it is proposed to make a legal tender in this country, is shown alongside of its English namesake.

Immediately above this case are two samples of native gold, modelled by Mr. Julius Hogarth, and representing two of the most characteristic of the Australian animals, the emeu and the kangaroo. The skill shown in these works is very great ; a more truthful resemblance of an emeu was never executed. In addition to the nuggets and samples of gold and auriferous quartz which are shown by the Royal Mint at Sydney, there are two most instructive cases, exhibiting the various deposits encountered in sinking for gold, the character of the gold obtained, and specimens of the bed-rock on which it rests.

The iron ores of the colony are chiefly brown hematite, and magnetic iron ore ; they are very widely distributed. These ores differ very much from the ordinary ironstone, as they can be reduced by fuel alone, without the addition of any flux: the earthy matters of the ore form a fusible slag without admixture.

The coal-fields of New South Wales have attracted the attention of the Home Government, and samples of two tons or more have been sent from each colliery for trial by the Lords of the Admiralty. The experiments are now in progress.

VICTORIA exhibits some most interesting specimens of the various products of her soil, and the industry of her inhabitants. Gold obtained by quartz crushing and washing, as well as tin ore and antimony, are also shown. Antimony is now being worked at M'Ivor, and arrangements are making for the working of the thick veins of iron ore that exist in many parts. A singular mass of meteoric iron is exhibited, weighing several hundredweights, and containing the usual additions of nickel, &c.

QUEENSLAND, the latest of our colonies, which has only separated from New South Wales some two years since, exhibits some fine specimens of copper ore.

TASMANIA is a rising colony, and exhibits coal, iron, lead, gold, and precious stones, as well as several articles of jewellery. Samples of very good sandstones are shown, both in the rough and converted; and a cube of close-grained red granite, of very fine colour, and capable of receiving a good polish; nor must the serpentines and black marbles be overlooked, some of the latter being quaintly curious for their singular markings. Among the more singular minerals is one known as "dysodile," a soft, brown, inflammable mineral, which burns with much flame and smoke, however, to a very disagreeable odour; it appears to consist of a foliated schist, studded with minute points of mineral resin. Though scarce in Europe—being found only at Mellili, near Syracuse, in Sicily, and in Hessia—it occurs in seams seven feet in thickness in Tasmania. On an emergency, it can be used for fuel, to which application its fœtid odour when burning is, however, a serious drawback; it is, however, obviously capable of being utilitised as a material for the distillation of the hydro-carbon oils, paraffin, and similar products.

The court which contains the articles sent from BRITISH GUIANA is full of interest. In all our English literature, one of the most charming and one of the least known works is Sir Walter Raleigh's "Discovery of the Large, Rich, and Beautiful Empire of Guiana." Written with the glowing eloquence, the curiosa felicitas of style and diction that characterised the prose of the Elizabethan era, it has all the charm of a novel, all the accuracy of a chart. The vivid descriptions of natural scenery and objects which mark its pages will no longer seem exaggerated to those who, at South Kensington, cast a glance at the collection furnished by British Guiana. Were Sir William Holmes, the chief commissioner from that colony, to re-edit the work of his illustrious precursor, he would find no reason to alter or abate its glowing terms. Nothing in the whole Exhibition is more charming than the collection of stuffed birds exhibited in this court. It is not an aviary; it is a kaleidoscope! From the purest white to the most intense scarlet—from glowing and burnished orange to clear and vivid green—there is not a colour which cannot be found represented in this collection. Close by we have a large assortment of stuffed monkeys, interesting to the naturalist, amusing to the children, but rather sad, perhaps, to the quiet observer. They are so like! The serpents of the colony are also represented; and there is a certain wild and terrible beauty in their coiling, curling, crouching forms. One is perpetually reminded in this court, alike of the wild fertility of tropical life and the myriad dangers to which it is exposed. The very woods have a sombre beauty about them. Even in their names there are poetical suggestions. There are cabinets of "tiger-wood;" there are walking sticks of "purple-heart." Interesting, not less from its own merits than from other associations, is the model, executed in pith, of an Indian hut, containing all necessary Indian furniture, including war clubs, idols, hammocks, sieves, and spears. The modeller is himself an Indian, and dwells upon the shores of the Upper Berbice river. He bears a name which must needs be disappointing to the lovers of romance—to the admirers of Fenimore Cooper, Mayne Reid, Louis de

Bellemare, or Gustave Aimard; he calls himself simply "Robert Saunders." However, his work is good; and there are few exhibitors of whom one would think with a kindlier interest than of this poor fellow, carving a rude reproduction of his hut when his day's toil is done, and then sending it over the sea. Another model of an Indian hut, or "buck-house," is exhibited by Mr. Curtis. A large collection of the insects of the colony includes a "thorough-bred" tarantula; and nearly forty varieties of a certain animal, the members of whose family are so numerous in Russia that an imaginative English traveller in that country asseverates that he could hear them bark.

The contents of this court include a jewel-case, constructed of forty-five different woods; a necklace, formed of the teeth of the huge cayman; some specimens of the red paint with which Indian warriors or Indian squaws "enamel" their faces, in a manner not entirely unknown to more civilised nations; models of fruit, which—being executed not in wax, but in papier-maché—will bid defiance to the fiercest rays of heat that dart down through the eastern dome; a large selection of farinaceous articles, such as cassava bread; an assortment of green ginger, pepper-pods, and castor-oil plants; a quiver containing the blow-pipes through which darts, impregnated with the mysterious South American poison, are projected at a foe; the skin of a jaguar, adapted for domestic use as a common rug; and a wonderful variety of walking-sticks, with noble and sonorous names, such as "Gasparillo Colorado."

TRINIDAD, which occupies a part of the same court, has also a rich and varied show. Of cocoa, the finest specimen is that grown on the Soconusco estate, and exhibited by Messrs. Burnley, Hume, and Co.; one of the partners in which firm, by the bye, is a son of the renowned representative of Montrose. An article even more interesting is a certain sample of cotton, which has been recently valued by Messrs. Littledale and Co., of Liverpool, at no less a price than 2s. 6d. a pound. Beautiful in colour, and apparently of a fine, long staple, it seems to be well worthy the attention of those manufacturers who do not wish to see Lancashire starve whenever America quarrels. The collection of woods sent from Trinidad is almost incredible, in the number of its varieties; and the mineral productions of the island are also fully represented. There are large specimens of crude asphalte, taken from the "Pitch Lake," which is situated in the south-western division of the island—a pitch lake of a dreary and Stygian aspect, on the shores of which Raleigh stood, nearly two centuries and a half ago, and of which notices occur in the journal of his final expedition. It was in the neighbourhood of this lake that he waited to hear what success had attended the attempt of his son and of Captain Keymis upon the Spanish settlements. Rumours of disaster and defeat came to him day by day, until at last the old hero, worn and wasted by so many years of imprisonment and sorrow, closed his journal with the solemn and pathetic words, "Waiting until I hear the truth." He heard it soon enough; and it meant the ruin of his enterprise, and the death of his darling son.

JAMAICA, BARBADOES, ST. VINCENT, and other West Indian Islands, are well-represented. The fibres of these colonies are both too numerous and too important to be dismissed with a cursory mention.

Furniture and Decoration.—II.

Now that the shilling visitors are swarming into the building, and the monetary success of the International Exhibition of 1862 is secured, writers and visitors will have an opportunity of calmly considering the value and quietly examining the quality of the vast and multitudinous display within its walls. Leaving the teachings of the Exhibition to themselves on the minds of the multitude as best they may, and as they cannot fail to do, we pursue our remarks on the domestic and decorative furniture with which the Palace of Industry abounds. Having already briefly noticed some of the more

prominent objects in Class 30, we may be excused if we offer a few remarks on the general principles which seem to influence the manufacturers and exhibitors in this section of the World's Bazaar.

It would lead us too far from our purpose to inquire into the causes of the popularity of Gothic forms: suffice it that the Gothic is popular, and that in church building it is now recognised as the most acceptable style of architecture. Such being the case, it follows as a matter of course that the furniture and decorations of Gothic buildings should also be uniformly Gothic. Hence, during the last few years—

especially since 1851—there has sprung up a trade which, under the name of "ecclesiastical decoration," bids fair to greatly influence the domestic furniture of our own times. Much of the mediæval style of architecture is undoubtedly poor and bad, but then we must recollect of these forms be desirable or otherwise, we do not undertake to say, but that the phenomena of revival in this direction is characteristic of the age can scarcely be denied. Even in the International building itself we see a tendency towards Gothic teachings through

CHURCH FURNITURE.—MESSRS. COX AND SON.

that our architects, decorators, and manufacturers are but pupils in a new school. To the late Mr. Pugin, and to the learned enthusiasm of Messrs. Burges, Slater, Norton, and others, we owe the revival of those forms in furniture and house decoration which were once universal in England. Whether the development and popularisation the mechanism of such ordinary materials as brick, iron, and glass. We have had enough of the mill and factory principle of building, and more than enough of the cold and heavy style of eighteenth-century furniture. The imaginative mind of to-day wants something warmer and more suggestive—something, in both houses and their decorative fitting, which will appeal directly to the sense of the beautiful, and the love of the picturesque. Hence, in our churches, halls, and dwellings, we have lately cultivated a preference for a higher art than satisfied our forefathers. Form and colour, artistic carvings and curious mouldings, tessellated pavements and painted ceilings, graceful wall-paper in flat designs, and appropriate furniture in carved woods and colours—all show the influence of what, for want of a more appropriate word, is known as eclecticism in the national taste. We see it in our streets daily. The use of red brick, relieved in colours by horizontal black bands; the forms of window-openings and doorways, roofs and chimney stacks, and other peculiarities of the pointed style of architecture, clearly show the growing taste of the people for the principles of an essentially Gothic style.

This growth of popular taste has been responded to by a proportionately improved standard of general artistic attainment. In our dwellings engravings are no longer the usual adornments, and square tables, heavy chairs, cumbrous bookcases, awkward cabinets, and shapeless pianos our usual furniture. Pictures and furniture of graceful form have taken, or are taking, their place. The double chest of drawers and the square looking-glass have given way to the architectural wardrobe and the mirror, in a finely-carved and appropriate frame. Finish of execution and truthfulness in manufacture have superseded the dull and heavy styles in domestic appliances which distinguished

the eras of Anne and the four Georges. With the monstrous curled wig, and the abominable flapped coat of our forefathers, have departed dining-tables difficult to move, and uneasy chairs too heavy to lift. Pre-Raffaelitism has descended from art to manufacture; and the improvement in detail which was made first manifest in Royal Academy pictures, has advanced to illustrated books and household decoration.

The application of the art of design to the furniture and implements of ordinary life is by no means to be overlooked in our examination of the contents of the International Bazaar at South Kensington. In 1851 we were in many respects behind our Continental rivals as regards these necessary adjuncts to comfort and convenience in our homes. The very superiority of our mechanical appliances had conduced to the undue depression of the art element of manufactures. It followed upon the extreme subdivision of labour, and the combined rapidity and economy of production, that the less obviously useful qualities of good taste, elegance, and fitness had come to be comparatively disregarded. The divorce of beauty from utility was one of the great facts substantiated by the Exhibition of 1851; and from that discovery we may date a real desire and energetic endeavour to remedy the evil. Our schools of design, initiated as far back as 1837, received a new impulse, and the elementary education of our workmen proceeded upon a far more satisfactory basis than hitherto. It is true that the public scarcely demanded a more tasteful

CARVED CABINET.—MESSRS. FARLEY AND CO.

CARVED OVAL MIRROR FRAME.—MESSRS. JENKINS AND CO.

condition of the public mind on this question. The *Illustrated Exhibitor*, and various other periodicals of that date, pointed out the direction which art manufacture was desired to take in all coming time; and now we have the satisfaction of knowing that our workmen are no longer behind, but are in the van of the foreigner in all matters of taste as regards furniture and house decoration. Our Jackson and Grahams, our Gillows, our Fishers, our Cox and Sons, our Mintons, our Oslers, and our White and Parlbys have fully demonstrated our superiority over the manufacturers of France, Russia, and Austria. The triumph of Paris and Berlin lasted only four years; for in the Exposition Universelle of 1855 our manufacturers competed successfully for the chief prizes in the most important branches of French manufacture, and upon which France

holstery. No visitor to the Exhibition will, we think, deny that real advance has been made in these respects.

It is scarcely necessary to insist on the ways in which the growing taste for the beautiful may be further fostered and advanced. Practically, patronage may be bestowed on art-manufacture by the selection of the best designs at the upholsterers, the mercers, the carpet warehouse, the china-shop, and the print-sellers; but a more complete encouragement of art in this direction may be given by the steady perseverance of teachers in advocating elementary drawing as a regular branch of youthful education. The importance of a more general cultivation of art in England is a text that hardly needs a commentary. It is not merely in a moral point of view that whatever refines and elevates life is desirable for the comfort and well-being of the people, but, in the present state of commerce, the development of the art-element of our manufactures has a positive material value. Time was when this country, through the aid of its coal, iron, and machinery, feared no rivals in its great task of supplying the markets of the world. This condition of things is rapidly changing; other nations tread on our heels in the quality of the products of their manufacture, and almost undersell us, through the advantages they possess of cheaper labour and lower rates of profit. But if, in addition, we allow foreign manufactures to be manifestly superior to our own in general taste, form, colour, or harmony, or in their adaptation to the purposes for which they are intended, the balance of trade will soon turn against us. But, happily, our manufacturers, our merchants, and our trades-men are now fully alive to the necessity of active exertion. The step we have gained since 1851 must not be lost. Education and manu-facture must proceed hand-in-hand. No element of success can be safely disregarded by those who enter the world-wide competition of modern commerce.

oak reredos consists of five compartments, with coved ogee canopies overhanging, with crockets, spandrils, finials, and pinnacles richly carved with the leaves and fruit of British plants and trees. The middle rail contains an enriched moulding of the foliage of the maple tree. The lower panels are filled with tracery, having the leaves of the passion flower in the spandrils; on the cusps are the flowers them-selves, supporting a crown of thorns, in the centre of which is the sacred monogram. The upper panels are filled with the Command-ments, the Lord's Prayer, and Creed, written on slate; the centre compartment has a cross and scroll, with inscription richly illuminated in colour, on a gold ground. It is 11 feet 6 inches long, and nearly 10 feet high. The altar table in front is carved in oak; tracery of elaborate character is interspersed with spandrils of natural foliage, and sur-mounted by palm wreaths, springing out of the vases which form the buttresses; there are also twenty small carved cups, and a richly carved moulding running round the edge. On page 52 we have shown various of the objects exhibited by Messrs. Cox, collected into

REREDOS CARVED BY MACHINERY.

So much for the general idea of improvement in art-manufactures. We now proceed to lay before our readers some evidence—necessarily weak and insufficient, from the very nature of the medium through which they are shown—of the advance we advocate.

Messrs. Cox and Son, of Southampton Street, Strand, have cha-racteristically shown how machinery may be applied to the manu-facture of such articles of furniture and church decoration as need the aid of carving. At their works in Lambeth they produce various articles by means of machinery. But it must be understood that the machine merely produces the rough work, which has afterwards to be finished by hand. The reredos and altar table, pictured in this page, is shown in the Mediæval Court as a specimen of what can be effected by the carving machine; but beside it is a piece of finished work, by which we perceive how much the mind and skill of the workman may improve the merely mechanical roughing of the pantagraph. This carved

a group. Attention will also be called to the carved oak eagle lectern and pulpit. This latter is of Corsham Down stone, and dis-plays considerable novelty in design and vigour of treatment. It is profusely carved with imitations of foliage, small animals, birds, &c. At the base of the oak tree, represented by the pulpit, are clinging wild plants and ivy. It is exhibited as a proof of what may be ac-complished by the carving machine, some of the under-cuttings being twelve inches deep. In Class 7 may be seen in operation the machine by which these carvings have been produced.

Messrs. White and Parlby, of Great Marylebone Street, exhibit a ceiling in their new cement, a cabinet and frame, console table and frame, toilet glasses, girandoles, candelabrum, &c.; also, Louis the Sixteenth's drawing-room door and architrave; all in excellent taste. Messrs. Jenkins and Co., of Fleet Street, show some glass frames, carved and gilt, in good style.

Fine Arts in the Exhibition — II.

SINCE the opening of the Exhibition many fine works in sculpture have found their way into the naves and domes, interspersed pleasantly with orange trees, and other tropical plants and flowering shrubs. This is a great improvement upon the original design, which was to confine the sculpture to the Picture Galleries and to a court of its own.

We shall have occasion to speak of the sculpture groups as we proceed in our examination of the works of Foley, Bell, Gibson, Munro, Marshall, Watson, and other English artists; and also to notice the foreign exhibitors in this department. Sculpture holds a very high and deservedly important place in the International Exhibition. The collection of busts alone is remarkable; and as for life-size statuary, there are in the building upwards of two hundred groups—in marble, plaster, and bronze.

Of the works of living sculptors the tinted "Venus" of Gibson and the "Brother and Sister" of Woolner are acknowledged masterpieces. Without undertaking to pronounce on the disputed point as to whether colour is an enhancement of the beauty of statuary, we think we may say that Gibson's "Venus" is really a fine work. It is tinted in the slightest possible manner, so as merely to soften the general effect of the marble, and to give a faint appearance of life to the figure. Mr. Gibson has not adopted the conventional idea of Venus, but has represented her as the goddess of marriage — a beautiful and dignified matron, with a tortoise at her feet. The

statue was executed at Rome, in 1852, and has been ... by ... of the owner, after remaining in the sculptor's ... several years, the admiration of all connoisseurs.

Much has been written ...
alleged deterioration in those ...
and the greater advances in ...
last ten years in the sister arts of p...
and increasing. Mr. Palgrave, the C...
ment Inspector of Schools, has under...
to speak in terms of condemnation at th...
works of living sculptors ...
without knowledge and t...
leaning towards one particular s...
and indeed, towards one particular ...

his criticisms are deservedly ...
as worthless, at least by all who h...
form opinions of their own. He ...
condemnation of the works of Baron M...
cotte, Mr. and Mrs. Thornycroft...
Mr. Marshall and his workshop coat...

TRIAD ...

MUSIC

STATUETTES IN PARIAN—MESSRS. COPELAND.

lodge among those who are rich enough to become patrons of sculptors. That the public themselves are partial to the art, the growing taste for Statuettes in Parian and biscuit ware seems evidence enough. But the perfection of modelling can only be obtained through life-size sculpture. When—as in the Manchester Art 'Treasures' Exhibition—we see chiselled marbles of half or quarter life-size, we fear for the future of sculpture. What, then, should sculptors themselves do to revive the taste among the wealthy? It is not every day that a Thomas Hope can afford to give to the world a Thorwaldsen, or that a corporation like that of the City of London can be induced to offer commissions to half-a-dozen educated artists. Why do not our sculptors try their chisels on some material less costly than the

alabaster, both for its warmth of colour and adaptability for working. That colour, applied with moderation and refined taste, is not alien to severely pure sculpture, we know from the examples of Phidias and Gibson. Monumental effigies would be more common if patrons were not deterred by the vast costliness of blocks of foreign marble; and we are glad to see that, in this respect, sculptors are beginning to use their chisels more freely upon the products of our own quarries.

Modern millionaires have shown less discrimination than Mr. Hope and the late Earl of Ellesmere in the use of their abundant means for the encouragement of sculpture; but might not communities of less wealthy men join together to produce beautiful works in this art?

PAUL AND VIRGINIA—GROUP IN PARIAN.   MESSRS. COPELAND.

marbles of Paros or Carrara? Surely there is warrant enough in our old churches for the employment of a cheaper material; and stone, of fair quality and sufficient endurance, is by no means scarce in the quarries of Caen, Devonshire, Portland, and Yorkshire. If cheap sculpture were desired, why could not our Gibsons and Marshalls try the beautiful alabaster of Derbyshire, or the delicate serpentine of Cornwall, which may be obtained in blocks of any size, and in all gradations of colour? In Hardman's Mediæval Court, in the south-east Transept, there is a "Virgin and Child," in variegated marble, with only the face and hands white. We presume the heads of the figures have been joined to the main block. No material is better suited for sculpture, in connection with Gothic architecture, than English

There is excellent precedent for such combined action. It was from the guilds of craftsmen and shopkeepers that Donatelli, Ghiberti, and their fellows received commissions for their immortal works in Florence.

The sculpture in the International Exhibition is much of it very fine, much of it only mediocre, and some of it poor in design and faulty in execution. In the foreign courts—especially those of Rome and Italy—many good works are displayed; and here and there in the Nave and Picture Galleries we come upon a beautiful figure or a spirited group by an English artist. Of these we shall have to speak in another page; but we cannot refrain from calling attention to the "Shakespeare Group," by the late John Thomas, the "California," by Hiram Powers, whose "Greek Slave" was one of the gems of the Hyde Park Palace of 1851, and the "Cleopatra," by Story.

In Portrait sculpture the present Exhibition is particularly rich. The sculptors who for the last hundred years have given us resemblances in marble of the great men of the world, are all here—Nollekens, Banks, Chantrey, Flaxman, Watson, Foley, and others of our own countrymen; while Canova, Dannettée, and two or three other names, represent the art of France, Italy, and Germany. There is considerable interest in portrait marbles, and we regret that their costliness acts as a bar to their greater popularity among the wealthy classes; but, as regards the general public, there is certainly no lack of appreciation for works of real merit. It is to be lamented that so few opportunities are afforded for the display of good sculpture. It is true that in the Crystal Palace and in the South Kensington Museum there are a large number of valuable casts from English and foreign works of repute; but they lose half their utility from their unfortunate juxtaposition with other works of art and industry with which they have no kind of relation.

In the Exhibition there is indeed a hall devoted to the display of modern sculpture; but in order to familiarise the mind of the public with the chefs-d'œuvre of the art, they should not be placed in lines, as in the Italian and Roman courts; but each particular statue should have, as it were, a shrine of its own—an architectural frame, as in the Vatican and the Louvre—in which the Apollo and the Laocoön might be studied to advantage. How much architectural accessories lend to a statue may be seen in Gibson's majestic sitting figure of our beloved Queen, in the throne room at Westminster; though, unfortunately, the scale of the marble is too great for the apartment, and the attendant allegories strike one as rather obtrusive. But enough for the day. We are not desirous of lecturing on art, though we wish to convey to our readers some correct ideas of its influence and value as an educational medium. Having touched upon sculpture, we shall by and by have something to say about painting. The pictures and engravings in the International Exhibition demand separate and distinct notice. They cannot be dismissed in a column.

The works we have engraved to illustrate our remarks are to be found in Messrs. Copeland's stall in the British nave. They consist of statuettes in Parian, and are remarkable as showing how successfully this kind of art manufacture can be produced. The group of "Paul and Virginia" is very gracefully modelled, especially the heads. A large number of other subjects in Parian will be found attractive; notably those reduced from well-known groups. The only fear is that in their reproduction, mere prettiness may be esteemed above power, and that the public taste for sculpture may thus be debased instead of improved. These statuettes must, and undoubtedly do, diffuse a knowledge of fine works, and improve the general taste of the people by familiarising their eyes with beautiful forms; but it is, nevertheless, true that noble sculpture can only be fully appreciated in life size or even heroic groups. Though our St. Paul's and Westminster do not contain many excellent works, the sculpture in them has certainly the effect we refer to on the minds of all visitors.

Curiosities in the Exhibition.

ALUMINIUM.—The display of works in aluminium, and its alloy with copper—which the manufacturers, with a slight laxity of technology, denominate bronze—is highly attractive, from its novelty, as well as from its intrinsic merit and beauty. Here is an example of one of the great strides which industrial art has made since the Exhibition of 1851. It is true that the existence of the metal had then been known for some twenty-four years, but the want of a process by which it could be produced in quantity, and in a workable shape, kept it in the rank of a scientific curiosity. The discoveries of M. Deville attained this desideratum, and here we have an example of the extent to which the taste and skill of the manufacturers have profited by this new resource. The metal is shown in many varieties of form—cast into ingots, drawn out into fine wire, wrought into reflectors, spun into lace, and fashioned into many ordinary and scientific implements. Its lightness may be judged of by the fact that an aluminium sextant of the ordinary size weighs only 1lb. 9oz., whereas a brass one of the same dimensions would weigh 3lb. Its superior inaccessibility to corrosion is shown by the juxtaposition of a fragment of it with a piece of silver, in a sulphureous solution, which has blackened the latter, but left the former intact.

OLD DRESDEN CHINA.—Near the Turkish Court, but farther west, and shown in the Nave, is some fine Danish porcelain, from the Imperial factory at Copenhagen. The only real re-production of old Dresden china is exhibited here, in the form of a dinner-service, manufactured for Prince Louis of Hesse, and which, as a sample of high-class manufacture, and as a really good copy of the old Dresden type, is one of the best specimens of foreign porcelain in the building. The shapes of these pieces are, perhaps, not what modern manufacturers would call shapes at all, though all porcelain amateurs will at once understand what we mean, when we say that in this set the quaint, old, serviceable forms, the delicate painting, bright glaze, and perfect figure-moulding of old Dresden have really been perfected at Copenhagen. Compared with this excellent work, the Dresden Court itself shows only modernised conventionalities, in which more of the faults than the beauties of the old ware are reproduced,

FIRE-ENGINE ARRANGEMENTS.—Captain Bent is the officer who has the superintendence-in-chief of the fire arrangements, and under him are one engineer, four sub-engineers, and nine firemen, of which number at least eight are always on duty in different parts of the building, while close at hand a company of Sappers is stationed, from whom considerable assistance and support would, of course, be received. There are six engines, ten stand-pipes, twenty-four dozen of fire-buckets, twenty-four hand-pumps with pails, 120 lengths of hose, and three hose-reels, with an adequate proportion of tools. The water supply consists of a 9-inch main, which runs east and west throughout the entire length of the building, and which is again intersected at right angles with 4-inch service pipes. The eastern and western annexes are similarly supplied, and the galleries and roof with smaller service pipes. There are a large number of stopcocks, and no less than 107 hydrants, or fire-cocks.

FOREIGN ENGLISH.—The following choice specimen of English composition is daily distributed in the Western Annexe:—"Balthasar Danzer, manufacturer of Bellows a Munic, recommends his theny-producing apparatus made for the irrigation of tender plants and calculated dr destroying plant lice. Price Lt. s. 15. His second apparatus intended for domestic use serves for the pur pore of destroying bugs batles cock rachos and all other noisome chafers in house a Kitchens. Pr: 6s. 0d."

A SINGING BIRD IN METAL.—Another little "lion" is the watch-maker's case in the Swiss Court, where the exhibitor is pestered with the applications of fair petitioners for a song from the wonderful little bird, which, jumping up out of a splendid gold box, sings and hops about as if it were alive.

THE TALKING INSTRUMENT.—The display of the famous talking instrument is viewed with much curiosity. Only one other instrument of the same kind exists in the world, though in this the difficulty of clearly pronouncing the "th" has been altogether overcome. It is said, however, that in the machine about to be exhibited in a few days not only is the pronunciation perfect, but even in several languages,

COAL-TAR PRODUCTS.—The new aniline colours from the benzole of coal-tar are well represented. Perkin's case (south-east passage of Eastern Annexe), showing the manufacture and application of aniline purple or mauve, is well worthy a long inspection, as it shows the entire series of changes from the crude and fœtid coal-tar, and naphtha obtained from it, through the series of benzole, nitro-benzole, aniline, sulphate of aniline, to the precipitation of the splendid mauve by bichromate of potash. It also shows all the re-agents employed in the process, and the waste materials, including the refuse black pigment employed in the manufacture of the printing-ink used by some of our cheap contemporaries. The auxiliary substances used in the dyeing processes are also shown, and the mauve in a crystalline state, when it resembles the gorgeous lustre on the wings of some green tropical beetles; and also in bulk a small pillar, about the diameter and twice the height of a man's hat, being worth £1,000, the quantity of colouring matter it contains being enough to dye the heavens with purple. Nor is the case of coal-tar products exhibited by Simpson and Co. less attractive. Here the magenta, or rose aniline, is shown, and our readers will perhaps be surprised to hear that this splendid red colour forms brilliant metallic green crystals, and that the huge crown formed of this substance contains nearly £200 worth of material, and was crystallised in a vat containing solution to the value of many thousand pounds.

AUTOMATON MUSIC.—The finely enamelled mechanical casket of M. Golay Leresche, of Geneva, attracts crowds of admiring listeners, as well as spectators, for this casket is not only a sight to see, but a sound to hear. A shepherd boy, answering the notes of a bird on the bough of a tree, fingers his pipe, and bids it discourse most eloquent music. The song of the bird is deliciously natural, and the motion of the boy's fingers in controlling the stops of his instrument is perfect.

A JEWELLED HOUSE-SHOE.—Among the jeweller's work behind the Prussian case under the Dome is a collection from Herr Joseph Friedman, of Frankfort, which includes, among other "elegant" trifles, a tiny clock set in a horse-shoe with turquoise nails. In what school of jeweller's art did the designer learn to shoe a clock?

KING JOHN'S BARONS AT THE EXHIBITION.—A great ornament has been added, since the Opening Day, to the eastern daïs, by placing under the arcades of the stairways Elkington's series of the Magna Charta Barons, executed for the House of Peers. Of course, the originals are now in the Peers' Chamber; but these are the models from which they were executed, which have been themselves bronzed and relieved with gilt, and are in no way to be distinguished from these which nightly loom down from their niches over Government and Opposition.

THE USEFUL AND ORNAMENTAL COMBINED.—The works from the Berlin Royal Prussian Iron Foundry, exhibited in the centre of the Zollverein Transept, at the bottom of the stairs descending from the platform under the dome, are worth especial attention. Near the group of works from the Berlin Iron Foundry is another of the odd notions in which these German courts are somewhat rich. It is a suit of armour treated as a stove. The gentleman who likes old armour in his hall, and also wishes his hall to be warmed, may here see how the legs of a man-at-arms may serve for stove pipes, and his whole substance may be so dealt with that potatoes can be baked behind his breastplate, and a pot of coffee be kept warm under his helm.

THE SAVAGES' PAINT.—In the colonial department—the South-east Transept—there are exhibited many varieties of clays and pigments. Among others there is the wilgi, with the qualities of which the natives are well acquainted, and which would, no doubt, prove of service in the arts and manufactures of this country. The natives adorn themselves with this earth, just as our ancestors decorated themselves with the blue dye of the saffron. In order to appear in full costume, the Western Australians—we do not, of course, mean the settlers, but the aborigines—saturate themselves thoroughly with grease, and having formed this adhesive surface, they rub their bodies over with this light red ochre!

A MILKING MACHINE.—The latest Yankee invention is exhibited in the shape of a mechanical "cow-milker," which does the work more effectually than the neatest-handed Phyllis, and doubles the ordinary process in results. Spectators are amused, and ask "What next?" but a great many think that the old machine has solid recommendations to the bucolic mind.

WEST AUSTRALIAN TIMBER.—The Jarah tree of this colony grows to enormous proportions, and is a most durable and serviceable wood. Six planks, cut out of one tree, have been sent to London; they are 120 feet long, five feet wide, and seven inches thick. As they cannot be conveniently shown in the building, they have been placed in the horticultural gardens.

THE OLD TIMES AND THE NEW.—From the Duchy of Saxe-Altenburg are seven exhibitors; one Herr August Hou of Altenburg being the only exhibitor of cross-bows (not toys) within the building. So times change. The cross-bows are gone, and the suit of mail is an "ornament for your fire stove!"

The Netherlands Contributions.

HOLLAND—a country connected politically, commercially, and socially with Great Britain—is exceedingly well represented in the Great Exhibition of All Nations. The Netherlands—for under this name is comprised the principality popularly known as Holland—shows well in thirty-three classes; and her court, on the north side of the nave, between Belgium and Switzerland, is really one of the most attractive in the palace.

In animal and vegetable substances used in various manufactures, in cereals and timber, paper and printing, furniture, iron, and hard-ware, pipes, snuff, tobacco, and saddlery, woollens and blankets, silks, damasks, and mixed fabrics—good and substantial, though not very tasteful in design—Holland and her colonies merit considerable attention from the visitor.

In the centre of the court will be seen and admired various groupings of woollen goods, handsomely encased in a sort of cabinet, surmounted by flags artistically arranged.

Near at hand are several musical instruments, of fine tone and good workmanship; as well as some really excellent specimens of cabinet ware, in curious and expensive woods. The cabinet in Amboyna wood, with pilasters in palisander, in colour somewhat darker than rosewood, is much admired. Considerable ingenuity is displayed in some of the furniture—secret springs, concealed drawers, and other mysterious arrangements rewarding the patience of the searcher. A tall bureau, with a pair of steps, which fly out of its side to enable one to reach its upper shelves, is certainly a novelty; and a console table, which may be converted at pleasure into a sideboard, may have much merit; but neither of the objects recommend themselves greatly to English tastes.

Considerable skill is shown in some of the Dutch carvings—especially the Brabant Pulpit—finely executed in oak, and boldly designed.

Several curious machines, in brass and iron wire, used by the Dutch women in dressing and adorning their hair, will excite attention; as we presume would also a full-sized crinoline, of, say, twenty steel hoops, if shown in China or Japan. Silver manufactures, with filigree, from Java and the Dutch colonies; stones for building pur-poses, ores, gold lace, and military uniforms, well-designed silver plate, together with a miscellaneous collection of objects, comprising Dutch cheeses, and strong liquors in squat bottles, oils of rape and other seeds, biscuits, glue, sugar-glue, and sweetmeats, will be found under the galleries.

Glass, pottery, and manufactures in leather are also abundant; but the most prominent, and certainly the most valuable, of the Dutch contributions is the famous diamond, the "Star of the South," which is shown in the nave, facing the principal entrance to the court.

The diamond merchants of Amsterdam have long been famous for the brilliancy of their gems, and the exquisite taste with which they are cut. The "Star of the South" was discovered in Brazil, some five years since. It is of an oval shape, very pure in colour, which is what connoisseurs call "pink-white," in contradistinction of the tint assumed

Steam-power is brought by Messrs. Coster into extensive operation in the process of diamond-cutting. The first step is to rub two sur-faces together, on the proverbial principle of "diamond cut diamond." By this process they receive their first rough general shape. The numerous small facets are then cut at the mill, by means of swiftly-revolving plates of metal, on which is placed a mixture of diamond-dust and olive oil. The extraordinary rapidity with which the wheels revolve may be seen by any visitor who goes into the machinery annexe, where Messrs. Garrard are actually cutting and polishing diamonds before the very eyes of a curious and inquiring public. Nothing more interesting can be seen than the way in which a gem

THE NETHERLANDS COURT.

by the Koh-i-noor, which is "white-white." The art of diamond-cutting is carried on almost exclusively at Amsterdam, where several large mills have been established. This peculiar trade is, strange to say, almost entirely in the hands of persons of the Jewish persuasion. It is said that of the 28,000 Jews residing in Amsterdam, nearly half of them are employed in the various industries connected with the cutting and polishing of diamonds. The "Star of the South" belongs to a company of shareholders in England, France, Holland, and Brazil. It was cut and polished at the establishment of Messrs. Coster, one of the largest in the Dutch metropolis. They hold one share in the gem, and have displayed great care and taste in bringing it into its present condition of almost unapproachable beauty.

of purest ray serene," like the "Star of the South," is brought to the perfection and beauty necessary for the tiara of an empress or the coronet of a countess. The diamond which flashes and sparkles, and reflects every ray of light which falls across it, is, after all, but a bit of carbon!—an idea rather consolatory to those who possess no diamonds, but are perfectly acquainted with the valuable properties of charcoal.

In the Netherlands Court there is seldom so great a crowd as to prevent the visitor making a careful examination of its various objects of attraction; but for the studious inquirer after knowledge we advise a tolerably long stay. He will not waste his time; for, next to foreign travel, an inspection of the products of other countries is the most profitable.

Naval Architecture, &c.

CLASS XII. consists of ships' boats, rigging, nautical instruments, life-boats; models of vessels, docks, and lighthouses; anchors, cables, compasses, life-belts, and various life-saving apparatus. These useful objects will all be found in the south court, under the superintendence of Major Moffatt. The Lords of the Admiralty are themselves exhibitors of an interesting series of models, representing the old and new styles of vessels for the Royal navy; and a very instructive lesson may be learned by a comparison between a full-rigged frigate of the time of the last Exhibition, and the redoubtable Warrior of the present day.

The Commissioners of the Trinity House, of the Northern Light, Edinburgh, and of the Ballast Board, Dublin, have some exceedingly valuable models of the beacons round our dangerous coast. A model of the American system of boat-building by machinery is also shown. By this system a boat may be constructed in a few hours, complete, from the logs of squared timber. Models of submarine vessels, gun-boats, floating batteries, steering apparatus; in fact, naval appliances generally, may in this class be studied. And whether the visitor be learned or unlearned, scientific or simple, he cannot fail to profit by his examination.

We propose to select a few of the more important objects in this interesting class for illustration by pen and pencil.

Messrs. Pile, Spence, and Co., of West Hartlepool, have a model of a Graving Dock, of new invention; the object of which is to facilitate the raising and lowering of ships or vessels out of the water, for the purposes of repair or inspection. The modes hitherto adopted to effect these ends have been rather rude and cumbrous.

Fig. 1, a longitudinal elevation; Fig. 2 is a front elevation of the dock entrance; Fig. 3 is a plan corresponding to Fig. 1; and Fig. 4 is an end view of a floating pontoon, having a vessel supported thereon. The improved floating dock consists of a series of columns, A, arranged at equal distances asunder in two parallel lines. The columns, A, are pillars of wrought-iron, the lower extremities of which are firmly fixed to the bottom pontoon or lift, and act as air-tubes to admit the air into the pontoon or lift as the water is pumped out. On the upper extremities of the columns, A, is built a platform, B, which is carried completely round the dock, as shown in the plan, Fig. 3, of the engraving. The columns, A, serve also as guides for the floating pontoon, F, which extends from end to end, and from side to side of the dock.

A series of tubular apertures, corresponding to the number of the columns, A, are made in a vertical direction through the pontoon, F. These openings encircle the columns, A, and are sufficiently large to admit of the pontoon rising and falling easily. The outer end, H, of the

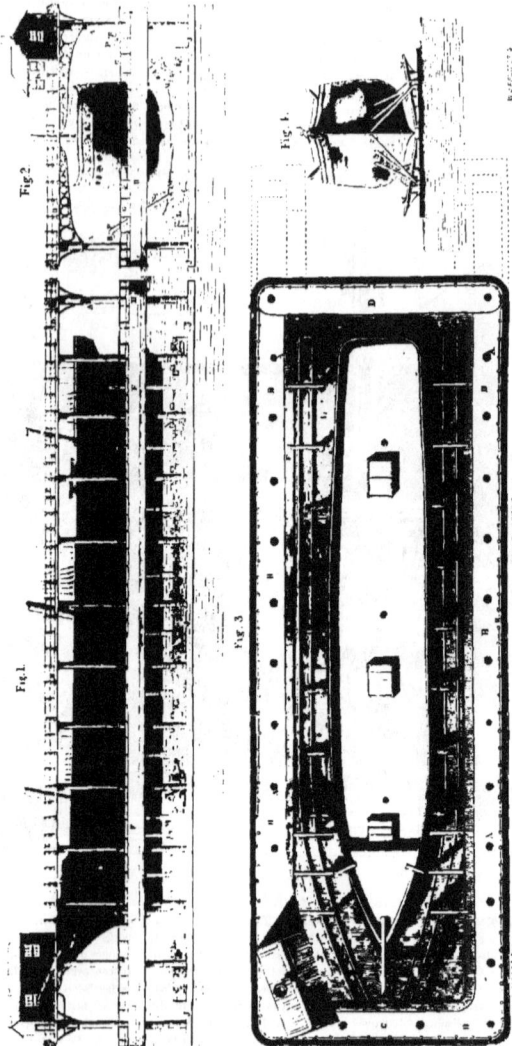

PATENT GRAVING DOCK. MESSRS. PILE, SPENCE, AND CO.

pontoon, is formed in two parts, and these are made to swing back, when required, by means of a rack and pinion, or other mechanical contrivance. The floating pontoon, F, has pendent from its lower side a series of chains, I, the lower ends of which are secured to the submerged pontoon, J, by means of which chains the submersion of the pontoon or lift is regulated to any depth. This elevating pontoon, J, is constructed of iron, thoroughly water-tight; it carries the columns, A, which are securely fixed thereon. It is so arranged that it may be partially filled with water, so as to give it a greater specific gravity than the surrounding fluid, in order that it may be submerged with facility; upon discharging this water from the pontoon, sufficient buoyant power is imparted to it to lift a vessel out of the water.

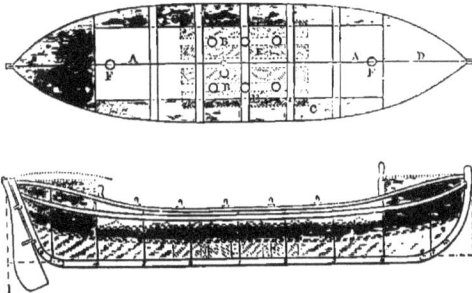

MODELS OF LIFEBOATS EXHIBITED BY THE ROYAL LIFEBOAT INSTITUTION.

In addition to the pontoon, J, there is a secondary pontoon, L, which is constructed so as to be easily attached to it; this pontoon is made to any required size, according to the weight of the vessel to be lifted, and is attached to the pontoon, J. Upon this secondary pontoon, L, the cradle, M, and chock-blocks, N, for preventing the ship from heeling over, are arranged. Prior to the vessel being docked for examination or repair, the pontoon, L, is secured to the lower pontoon, J, as shown in the end view, Fig. 2, of the accompanying plate. The vessel is then floated into the dock, and the pontoon, J, is raised by pumping air into, or water out of, the interior thereof, the vessel being kept meanwhile equidistant from the columns, A. When the pontoon, L, touches the keel of the vessel, the blocks, N, are brought be-

When it is desired to remove the ship from the dock, the pontoon, L, is cast off from the pontoon, J, and she is floated out thereon. To float the ship from off the pontoon, L, after repairs, the pontoon and ship are again brought into the dock and placed over the elevating pontoon, J; water is then let into both pontoons, J and L, and they sink accordingly, leaving the ship floating on the surface. The elevation, Fig. 4, shows the ship floating upon the pontoon, L, and free from the dock.

Messrs. G. Rennie and Sons, of Holland Street, Blackfriars, also exhibit a model of their patent Floating Graving Dock, lately constructed. The engraving on page 64 shows the general appearance of the apparatus, which was constructed for the Spanish Government, and is capable of lifting vessels of 5,000 or 6,000 tons dead weight.

Floating docks of similar construction are suitable for localities where masonry graving docks are difficult and expensive to execute, or where there is but little rise and fall of tide; and will be found to be of service now that vessels of iron are so much in use both in the royal and mercantile navies.

The model exhibited is almost identical with the large floating dock constructed for the Spanish Government for the arsenal of Ferrol. The ends are both open, so that no gates are required, and merely the sides are closed in, against which the shores of the ships rest when docked.

The vessel and dock are lifted by the buoyancy of the lower compartment till the vessel is out of the water. The engine and pumps are placed on the upper part of the side walls, for pumping the water out of the several chambers of the base or lower compartment. The tops of the sides are used as buoyant chambers, to prevent the possibility of the dock sinking altogether through carelessness in handling.

The arrangement exhibited shows three shallow flat horizontal slipways, radiating from a common centre. This system is intended for places where there is but little rise and fall of tide, as in the Mediterranean; and is now being carried out at the Spanish Royal Arsenal at Carthagena, in conjunction with the floating dock.

In order to dock a vessel by this means, it is first raised out of the water by the floating dock; the latter, with the vessel on it, drawing about ten to eleven feet of water, is then to be hauled into a shallow basin, which is so arranged that the way on the base of the floating dock is level with the ways of the slips in it. The floating

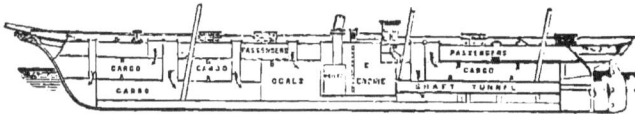

MODEL OF MR. C. LANGLEY'S UNSINKABLE SHIP.

neath the hull, in order to keep the ship in an upright position. The blocks, N, are drawn down the inclined surface of the cradle by means of the chains, O, which are carried away below the cradle, and on to windlasses fitted for the purpose on the platform of the pontoon, F. The bow and stern of the ship is further steadied and supported by means of the shores, P, which are jointed to the pontoon, L, so that they may be readily thrown back out of the way when it is desired to release the vessel. When the ship is floated over the cradle, M, and rests upon the blocks, N, the shores, P, are brought up against the bow and stern of the vessel by the chains, Q, which may be actuated in manner similar to the chains, O. Or the chains may be made fast to eyes screwed into the cradle, M, the slack of the several chains being taken up on spindles actuated by means of the winch handles, R.

dock is then lowered by admission of water into the base or floating chamber till it rests on the bottom of the basin. The vessel is then hauled off, and can be repaired at leisure. This operation can be repeated as often as desired with the same floating dock, until the slipways are occupied with the number of vessels they are capable of containing.

To place the vessels in the water again, the operation is simply reversed. The model shows only three slipways; but this number may be increased, so as to obtain the required accommodation. In case of repairs of a simple description, or such as will take a short time, or when merely an examination of the bottom of a vessel is required, the operation of hauling-off is not necessary, the vessel being merely lifted out of the water by the floating dock, examined, and afterwards allowed to float again by submerging the dock.

The Royal Lifeboat Institution exhibit models of their excellent boats; and it is greatly to be regretted that they were not permitted by the Commissioners to show a lifeboat as used on their various stations round the coast. The principle of the lifeboat is much the same, whoever be the maker,—namely, the construction of a vessel incapable of being turned over in the water. Air-tight cylinders, cork-fitted chambers, &c., are necessary to attain this end. The boats and their transporting carriages are well worthy examination. The lifeboat of the National Lifeboat Institution possesses the following qualities:—1. Great lateral stability. 2. Speed against a heavy sea. 3. Facility for launching and taking the shore. 4. Immediate self-discharge of any water breaking into her. 5. The important advantage of self-righting if upset. 6. Strength. 7. Stowage room for a number of passengers. By an ingenious contrivance, the boat, with her crew on board, is launched off the carriage. With their oars in their hands, they are thus enabled to obtain headway before the breakers have time to beat the boat broadside on the beach. The hauling up of the lifeboat on her carriage is accomplished with equal facility. Plans of lifeboat houses, designed by Mr. C. H. Cooke, the hon. architect of the Society, are also exhibited. Specimens of the gold and silver medals of the Institution presented to persons who save life from shipwreck at the risk of their own, also of the life-belt and life-buoy used by the crew of the lifeboats of the Society, and of the lifeboat telescope, by Dollond, as well as a lifeboat liquid compass by Dent, are shown; and specimens of the barometers supplied to the Institution's lifeboat stations, and of barometer model indicators. Many lives have already been saved through the indications of the barometer. By means of the barometer indicators seamen in an offing can distinctly see at a distance of two or three miles the state of the barometer. A large wreck chart of the British Isles for the past year is also shown by the Institution. During that period the number of casualties on our coasts was 1,494, from which 884 lives were lost, but happily 4,024 persons were rescued during the same period from these disasters, of which 734 owe their lives immediately to the services of lifeboats.

Mr. James Basire, of King Street, Westminster, exhibits a model of the unsinkable ship invented and patented by Mr. C. Langley, of Deptford-green Dockyard. This model represents the unsinkable and fire-proof ship Briton. The longitudinal section now engraved represents the disposition of the cargo, shaft-tunnels, boiler space, cabins for passengers, &c. The lower deck, marked A, is made of iron, water-tight, and fitted with water-tight trunks, to communicate with the upper deck, so that access can be had at all times distinct from the other decks. By this plan, if the vessel's bottom is torn out, the water can only get into the space under the lower deck, the trunks preventing it going into the other holds. The deck, marked B, is also made of iron, as well as the trunks. These decks give the means of fitting iron storerooms and divisions for other purposes; and the more

fittings put in, the more secure is the ship against fire or combustion, which is localised. E is engine and boiler space, which is inclosed by iron walls, so that if water gains access it is confined, and can be pumped out by separate pumps. The model is made to show the principle of the invention, which can be adapted to every kind of merchant, transport, or war ship.

Of the various forms of fatal accidents to which mankind is liable, drowning in sea voyages is in by far the largest proportion. The majority of instances of sailors and others falling overboard, and lost before help can reach them, either never come to our knowledge, or pass unheeded in the crowd of events that daily press upon our notice.

It requires a catastrophe like the loss of the Amazon, or the Birkenhead, the Queen Victoria, the Austria, the Pomona, or the Royal Charter, with all its attendant horrors, to bring us to think of and appreciate the perils incident to navigation.

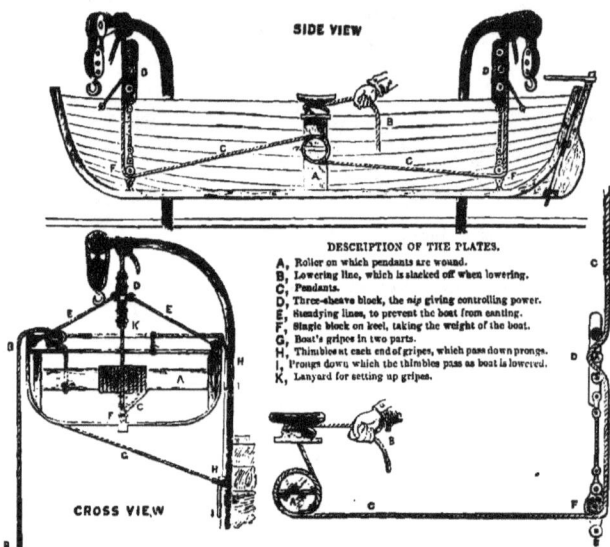

SIDE VIEW

CROSS VIEW

DESCRIPTION OF THE PLATES.

A, Roller on which pendants are wound.
B, Lowering line, which is slacked off when lowering.
C, Pendants.
D, Three-sheave block, the nip giving controlling power.
E, Steadying lines, to prevent the boat from canting.
F, Single block on keel, taking the weight of the boat.
G, Boat's gripes in two parts.
H, Thimble at each end of gripes, which pass down prongs.
I, Prongs down which the thimbles pass as boat is lowered.
K, Lanyard for setting up gripes.

MR. CLIFFORD'S METHOD OF LOWERING SHIPS' BOATS.

During the space of only a few months of 1859-60, not less than 1,184 persons lost their lives at sea from the destruction of six ships; and it was officially stated that upwards of 1,000 men are annually lost from American ships alone, by falling or being washed overboard, while the numbers lost from British ships are probably equally large.

One of the chief causes of this lamentable loss of life is the want of any means for lowering the boats speedily and safely in case of accident to the ship. On the occasion of the loss of the Amazon, the Parliamentary report stated that the supply of boats was ample, but "that the means of lowering boats evenly, and readily disengaging the tackles, &c., are desiderata wanting throughout the naval service;" and that "it may be expected some useful means for supplying these defects may be devised." This expectation has been realised. Mr. Charles Clifford, of Fenchurch Street, shows a model of his invaluable method of unhishing, lowering, and releasing ships' boats from vessels, either sailing or at rest, without the possibility of overturning, by one of the crew sitting in the boat. The importance of this invention cannot be too highly estimated. The nature of the invention will be seen by reference to the engraving in p. 63. Clifford's system has been approved and adopted by the Admiralty and every naval department of the Government, by the surveyors at Lloyd's Register of British and Foreign Shipping, by the Institution of Civil Engineers, and most of the leading Steam Companies. After repeated competitive trials, it is the only plan made compulsory in all ships chartered by H.M. Emigration Commissioners, the Council of India, and the Marine Board of Melbourne. The Committee of the Royal National Life Boat Institution, consisting of some of the first naval men of the country, passed a vote of thanks to its inventor on account of the number of lives it has saved, a list of which the Journal of the Institution, Jan. 1862, gives in the following words:—

"We think we shall be rendering a service to the great cause of humanity, by giving every possible publicity to this invention, as in most of the instances we record the men have fallen overboard in heavy gales, and when the ship was moving rapidly

the want of such means of instantly lowering a boat, it is hoped some one will be found with sufficient spirit and humanity practically to test this challenge.

On slacking off the lowering-line, B, the roller, A, revolves, and the pendants, c c, are unwound evenly as the boat descends into the water, when the pendants being tapered at the ends, overhaul themselves, and the boat is perfectly free. The controlling power is obtained by the blocks, D D, which act like a sailor's "turn and a half" on the boat on each pendant; the nip of the blocks exist only when they sustain the weight of the boat, and cease when it reaches the water. This power in the block to decrease the weight of the boat, and thus enabling the man attending the lowering-line to control the descent whatever the weight may be, but yet allowing it to run free the moment the lowering-line is let go, is its chief feature, and that which fits it for the purpose to which it is here applied, and for which it was specially designed.

Instructions for Lowering. One of the boat's crew takes charge of the lowering-line, B, and with one round turn on the cleat, slackens off

MODEL OF RENNIE'S FLOATING GRAVING DOCK.

through the water; the officers in command stating their firm belief that but for it they would have been lost; and also that the lowering and disengaging the boat being the result of the single act of one man only, is the chief cause of its great success. In some cases the entire crews of ships when foundering or wrecked, in collision, and suddenly sunk, or on fire, owe their preservation to it."

The committee appointed by Admiralty order to report upon this apparatus, expressed its unanimous conviction "that no captain, whether in the Queen's or mercantile navy, should be permitted to put to sea without it."

In the House of Commons, Admiral Berkeley said "that in every trial which had been made of it, its use had been attended with complete success, and he hoped to see it universally adopted."

Mr. C. Clifford states that he is prepared to unlash, lower, and entirely disengage from any ship, either stationary, under weigh, or going at any speed, in a gale, or in smooth water, a boat laden with a full crew, against any other invention or crew in the world, for any sum of £100, to be given for placing a lifeboat on an exposed part of our coast. As hundreds of our best seamen are annually lost through

off slowly. The pendants let themselves by the thin... down the proper... When the boat reaches the water, the line is let go, the pendants overhaul themselves, and the boat perfectly free. Thus by this one simple act of the one man the boat is unlashed, lowered, and released from the ship.

Mr. Henry Cunningham, R.N., of Bury House, near Gosport, Hants, exhibits a model of a self-reefing topsail, &c.

By this invention topsails can be reefed and unreefed from the deck, without sending any one aloft. It is also applicable to topgallant-sails and other sails. This invention is now in use on board several thousand ships belonging to the mercantile marine, and also on board many of H.M.'s ships, and the old, defective, and dangerous method of reefing by the men going aloft and out on the yards, is rapidly giving place to the new method. It is computed that many hundreds of lives have been already saved by it. It has been found that sails wear at least one-third longer than on the old plan; ships, too, can be navigated with fewer regular seamen, and, from the ability to make and shorten sail so easily, sail can be carried on longer, thus considerably abridging the duration of the voyage.

An Hour in the Horticultural Gardens.

ONE of the great attractions of the Crystal Palace at Sydenham—in fact, the charm of the place—is its delightful sweep of garden, lawn, and pleasure-ground. To some extent the International Exhibition enjoys a similar advantage, in its contiguity to the beautiful Gardens of the Royal Horticultural Society. It is not, we think, generally known that admission to these Gardens may be easily obtained by the general

Bazaar." Thus it will be seen that visitors may either go from the Palace to the Gardens, or from the Gardens to the Palace, at a very cheap rate. On Fridays the charge for visitors to the Gardens is half-a-crown ; and on Saturdays five shillings. A good view of the Horticultural Gardens, with all their wealth of greenery and flowers, and architectural adornment, and statuary, and music, on such terms for

GREAT FRENCH FOUNTAIN IN THE HORTICULTURAL GARDENS.

public. On Mondays, Tuesdays, Wednesdays, and Thursdays, during the remainder of the Exhibition season, the price of entrance to the general public is sixpence, if from the building ; a shilling, if to the Gardens alone ; and eighteen pence, including admission to Gardens and Palace. The principal entrance is in the Kensington Road ; but the one most convenient to visitors will be found in the Exhibition Road, nearly opposite the temporary erection known as the "International

the privilege, is not very costly, but the pleasure is certainly very great.

Nothing is more pleasant than to walk out from the building—spacious, well-ventilated, and admirably filled as it is with evidences of the world's treasures in manufactures and objects of art—and to enjoy for an hour or so a stroll among the arcades, or on the green sward, or into the well-stocked and exquisite conservatory. The rippling of running water, and the plash of cascades and fountains—what so deliciously cool and refreshing, after an instructive examination of machinery, raw materials, and pictures?

Day by day the growing beauties of the Horticultural Gardens unveil themselves; day by day they make a more and more charming addition to the main display within the building. Cascades murmur musically on the ear, and refresh the eye, dazzled with multifarious forms and colours. Military bands entertain the company several times during the day with their enlivening strains. Statuary, in bronze and marble, is placed here and there about the Gardens, and becomes a marked feature in the noble walks and terraces; and only from this place can a thoroughly good view of the International Exhibition Building be obtained. Its aspect from the Gardens is Captain Fowkes's strong point. Here we are enabled to take in the whole architectural design, and actually see both domes at one time. The narrowness of the Cromwell Road is a most unfortunate circumstance, with respect to the view of the Palace from that position. In truth, a building of its peculiar character, on so extensive a scale, should have been placed in the centre of a great park. The view as given on page 63 cannot really be had; for, in order to enable the eye to include the entire façade from east to west, greater distance is necessary than that which is allowed by the houses in Cromwell Road. As in history, so in architecture and scenery: in order to comprehend the whole plan of a great design, or a complicated series of events, it is premiss absolute that the spectator should view either the one or the other from a sufficiently distant point of observation.

Several objects in the Horticultural Gardens will well repay examination. ' Here, at the junction of four main walks, is the fine equestrian statue of Charles Albert, the last King of Sardinia, by Baron Marochetti. This work, though much abused by a gentleman who sets himself up as a critical judge of all fine art productions, is really fine. Beyond are two French fountains, of exquisite design and perfect finish. One, by Durenne, is a good specimen of casting; and the other, shown in our engraving, is a fine monumental work produced at the foundry of M. Barbezat and Co., the successors of André, at the furnaces of the Val d'Osne, in Paris. M. Barbezat had decreed to him the Cross of the Legion of Honour in 1844, and a Medal of Honour in 1849; the Council Medal at the Great Exhibition of 1851,

and the Medal of Distinction at the Exposition Universelle at Paris in 1855. His works are no less artistic than beautiful; and among the bronzes and iron works in the Exhibition, we find objects designed by artists of high class—Liénard, Mathurin, Moreau, Alfred Jacquemard, and Charousse. On page 13 will be found an engraving representing a group of bronzes from the display of Messrs. Barbezat. Animals in bronze, with vases and statues in like material, will also be found scattered about the Horticultural Gardens, by Barbezat and Durenne. The fine cast-iron gates near the Refreshment room will also repay examination. That essentially garden statue, in colossal proportions, of Milo of Crete, from the foundry of the Brothers Miroy, Paris, likewise claims the tribute of such high praise that we cannot regret its banishment from the French Court, and its presence in the Gardens. But the work which will attract all visitors is the Memorial of the Exhibition of 1851, by Durham, at the head of the cascade just in front of the great conservatory. All who remember—and what man of twenty does not?—the grand industrial jubilee of that year, will look with interest on this reminiscence of its royal founder.

At various periods during the summer, flower shows, and special meetings of the fellows and their friends, are held in the Horticultural Gardens; and we know of no sight in London so eminently characteristic. All the wealth, the nobility, the talent, and the beauty of the land are represented on these occasions. Not alone are the flowers and shrubs the points of attraction; the crowds of fashionable and aristocratic company certainly present a picture unequalled and unique—not to be witnessed in any other country in the world.

To wander, then, among these beautiful parterres; to mingle, even for an hour, with the elite of the world's favourites; to forget, amid the profusion of bright objects everywhere surrounding us, the wear and tear of life, the worry of business, and the anxiety of professional toil; to revel in enjoyment; to escape from the dull round of every-day existence; to feel that other things than buying and selling, and producing and competing, are really worth living for in this beautiful world of ours; to gain a healthful glow of pleased excitement, and to indulge in a little profitable idleness—surely these experiences are cheaply bought by a visit to the Gardens of the Royal Horticultural Society.

The British Colonies.

WESTERN AUSTRALIA IN THE EXHIBITION.—This colony stands alone in being the only one which continues a penal settlement. Here the Robsons and the Redpaths of society at home are provided for; and it is a somewhat interesting fact that in the exhibition now made by the colony the handiwork of one at least of these famous criminals is represented. A cabinet has been sent to the Exhibition, to the construction of which Robson, it is said, devoted some portion of his time and talents. That which, however, is of the most importance is, that the cabinet illustrates the many excellent varieties of wood, suited to cabinet purposes, which the colony possesses. Western Australia is particularly rich in timber. There is a famous tree, called the tooart, which has been used to a small extent in the construction of one of our crack line-of-battle ships—the Hannibal—and which is said to be as durable as the British oak. The sandal wood of the colony has long been highly prized in Singapore and China; the eucalyptus grows to a height of two or three hundred feet—it has a fine grain and a beautiful colour; and from the Shea oak excellent spokes and felloes for wheels are made. To show the durability of the timber, there are exhibited some posts and piles of the jarrah, which have lain for many years in land and water, and neither the white ants nor the all-consuming toredos have made any impression upon them, and the surfaces which have been planed still take a high polish. Minerals abound in this favoured colony, and there are specimens of lead and ores shown of

unusual richness, and some copper ores, which are said to contain seventy per cent. of metal. There is a lump of lead from the Geraldine mine, which forms part of a mass weighing upwards of one ton; and a bar of iron sent from the Royal Engineer department, formed from native iron, which was tested against a Swedish bar, and gave a result of from five to eight in favour of the Western Australian specimen. There are useful clays and pigments, too, in great number.

The gums and resins of this colony are very valuable, and there are specimens of tanning barks, which deserve the special notice of persons engaged in the leather trade in this country.

The leathers exhibited speak highly for the value of these substances for tanning purposes. Some black harness leather is equal to some of the best specimens shown on the English side. The kangaroo skin makes very good leather; it is soft, pliant, and tough, and is said to wear well for boots and shoes. A small parcel only of wool is shown, but, judging from this, it would appear that the colony is well suited for producing large quantities of this material. Some fibrous materials are shown, which seem to be well adapted for paper-making, or even for the manufacture of ropes and cordage; among others, some specimens of string, made from the fibrous rush, which grows plentifully on the banks of the Swan river. The silver wattle bark is also of a very fibrous character; while some bark from the paper bark tree, which is said to be very easily reducible to pulp, is well worthy the notice of those who are now casting about for new and fresh materials to aid in the manufacture of paper. Furs, feathers, and lace are represented by a rug of the opossum skin, a mat of pelican down, a victorine of parrots' feathers, the skin of the emu, a lady's muff made of the feathers of the parrot, a collection of very pretty feather-flowers, and feathers of the white, black, and tipped cockatoo, emu, and night-owl. Wheat, and various descriptions of grain, preserved and potted meats, including the dainty kangaroo's tail, mullet, whiting, and salmon, are shown; olive-oil and eggs of the emu—a very good article of food—and many varieties of vine grown in the colony. The great value of these colonial displays is, that they familiarise the British public with the productions of our varied colonies, and convey a much more accurate notion of their resources, and of their value as places for settlement, than can be obtained by any other means. The specimens exhibited in this court confirm in a striking manner the accuracy of the description of the Colonial Secretary, viz.:—

"That the country is subject to no extremes of heat or cold. Cattle have never been known to die from lack of water, and in the very driest weather there is a sufficient supply of food for them. Exposure to weather by night or day appears to produce no ill effects on the constitution of the colonists, many of whom, for months together, rarely sleep under any beyond the most temporary dwellings. Snow is never seen, ice only in the depth of winter, and then but in the very early morning. As in New Zealand, both maize and potatoes ripen in this country, and the latter crop is grown to a considerable extent. The apple and the pear, the orange, banana, fig, peach, and apricot, with the melon and the vine, grow luxuriantly, and may be seen ripening at the same time. The colony is peculiarly adapted to the growth of the vine, on the cultivation of which much attention is bestowed, and which is likely to prove very remunerating. English tropical vegetables are largely cultivated, and yield profusely. Attention is also being directed to dried fruits, and specimens of figs and raisins that have been sent to the periodical horticultural exhibition for competition are little inferior to those imported from Europe."

The following is a copy of a letter written by the Duke of New-castle, the Secretary for the Colonies, to Dr. Lindley, the Superintendent of the Colonial Department at the Exhibition:—

"My DEAR DR. LINDLEY,—Now that the Colonial Department of the International Exhibition is very nearly complete, I must express to you first, my thanks for the trouble you took in showing me all the various productions, and next, my extreme admiration of the spirited and successful manner in which the colonies, with scarcely an exception, have responded to the invitation of the Commissioners to send specimens of their natural products and their industry, for the information, and, I may well add, the instruction of the nations of Europe. It is impossible that such a display of what the colonial portions of the British Empire can produce should be without a very material influence upon the future prospects and prosperity of each of them. In gold and other metals, in cereal produce, in timber, in wool, above all, in cotton, the visitors to the Exhibition will find the English colonies eclipsing all competitors; and I am much mistaken if foreigners will not find in the department allotted to them more to excite their admiration and wonder than in the more showy and artistic displays, which do so much credit to the taste, energy, and manufacturing power of the mother country. I assure you that not only officially, but individually, I am delighted at the position before the world which the colonies have assumed in the Exhibition."

After so flattering a testimony to the value and interest of the show made by Western Australia, we fancy our readers will not fail at their next visit to the Palace to wander into the north-east transept, and gather for themselves some further illustrative facts concerning the great variety of useful and ornamental objects exhibited.

MACHINES FOR WORKING IN WOOD.

SINCE 1857, no branch of mechanical invention has been more prolific than that which is devoted to the working in wood by machinery. A quarter of a century ago, crude planing machines were only beginning to struggle into notice, while the mortising, tenoning, moulding,

and chamfering machines, now so common, were unknown, at least in this country. In America, machinery of this kind has always received great attention, and the display which her citizens made in this branch of industry in 1851 has doubtless tended to stimulate the invention and enterprise which have produced the interesting collections now to be seen in the western annexe. Nor do these collections, ample and interesting as they are, exhaust the subject; indeed, they must only be regarded as samples of this class of machinery. One firm that exhibits only six machines have over two score in their catalogue. This firm, Messrs. Samuel Worssam and Co., of Chelsea, exhibit a fine large circular saw, and a wonderful planing machine. It can plane, groove, and tongue boards or planks thirteen inches wide and six inches thick at the rate of fifty feet per minute, and reduce their thickness at the same time. A fine tool also is their portable deal frame; it is capable of sawing two deals of fourteen inches by four inches at one time. It is fitted with an air cylinder, which balances the frame. As the saws descend, a partial vacuum is created in the cylinder, which acts as a buffer at the time of the stroke, thus giving the frame so easy and steady a motion that it can be driven at the rate of 250 strokes per minute. This frame is also fitted with a silent feed, which not only works without noise, but acts with the greatest nicety. The other machines exhibited by this firm are the general joiner; a mortising machine, with square hollow chisel and an auger working inside—an ingenious and valuable machine for mortising hard wood; a moulding machine; and a tenoning machine. The collection of Messrs. Powis, James, and Co., adjoining that of Worssam's, is not less interesting, though none of the machines are seen in motion. These wood-working machines are situated just beyond the engineers' tools in the centre of the western annexe. Messrs. Powis and Co. exhibit a combined timber and deal frame, which will take in 24 saws, and work with an 18-inch stroke at from 150 to 200 strokes per minute. They also exhibit a band-sawing machine—a tool which they have done much to improve by their patent adjustment for regulating the tension of the saw. They also exhibit a planing machine, a double tenoning machine, a moulding machine, and a small hand mortising machine, the value of which may be judged of by the fact that upwards of 3,000 have been sold within the past ten years. Near these exhibitors, and fronting on the eastern passage, Messrs. Greenwood and Batley, of Leeds, exhibit, with other machinery, a variety of wood-working machines. The most prominent of this class is a lock-bedding machine, of exquisite workmanship. It is one of a series of nineteen machines for making the stocks of Enfield rifles, and is similar to those used in the Small Arms Factory, Enfield-lock. The object of this machine is to cut out the recess for receiving the gun-lock. An iron fac-simile of the recess is fixed in the machine alongside the stock, and a dummy tool follows all the intricacies of the recess, while a cutter performs a similar movement in the gun-stock, assimilating the recess in the stock to the one in the iron gauge. This machine is capable of cutting out 60,000 stocks per annum. A Blanchard lathe, for turning irregular figures, prepares the stock for the lock-bedding machine, and also turns shoe-lasts, spokes for wheels, &c. The other wood-working machines exhibited by this firm are a curvilinear ribbon saw, a Kinder's patent shaping machine, a mortising machine, and a machine to joint the staves of casks, samples of the work of which are also shown. Among their machines for working in iron is a self-acting rifling machine, and a machine to make percussion caps for the army, capable of producing 30,000 caps per hour. They also exhibit a patent machine for making boots and shoes, which will rivet a shoe together in fifty seconds; a machine to make the rivets from a coil of wire deposits them in helic boxes to supply the riveting machine. In the passage which crosses the annexe at this point, Messrs. Cox and Son, church-furniture manufacturers, of Southampton Street, Strand, have a wood-carving machine, which, when in motion, attracts great attention. Its method of operation is somewhat similar to the lock-bedding machine of Greenwood and Batley; but it is capable of producing several fac-similes at one operation.

THE INTERNATIONAL EXHIBITION BUILDING, FROM THE SOUTH.

Designs for Wall and Floor Coverings.

It is not many years since—quite within the memory of young men and women—when our carpets, wall papers, hearth-rugs, and painted panels were detestable in design and bad in colour. Even now we have hardly got rid of our national partiality for ugliness. Manufacturers still turn out thousands of carpets and tens of thousands of hearth-rugs in colours and patterns that are offensive to the eye, and unfitted to their special purpose by reason of their designs being in relief and sham picturesqueness, instead of flat and geometrical. What can be more false or in worse taste than a carpet covered with flowers, or a hearth-rug representing a lion or a dog? They are bad, because they are untrue to Nature. We do not tread upon flowers, or wipe our feet upon the backs of lions or dogs.

So also with the papers with which we cover our walls. In colour and plan, the old-fashioned patterns are worse than ugly; they are false. Wall-papers, like carpets, should not form the most conspicuous furniture of a room. They should be bright, but not too bright; picturesque, but not grotesque. We have seen parlour walls in respectable houses representations of castles and lakes, boats and birds, and balloons, and other monstrosities repeated in every strip of the pattern, till the eye grew tired and the head ached with gazing on their frightful fascinations. Again, who has not seen patterns, in other respects unobjectionable in colour, so badly designed in point of balance, that the walls appeared to be tumbling forward, or sinking slantingly to the earth?

But all these objectionable phases of decoration are rapidly disappearing. Artistic taste is taking its right place in the workshop, and the uneducated mind is in course of getting some degree of refinement even through such simple mediums as carpets and wall papers. In the International Exhibition, both in

ANMINSTER PILE CARPET.   MESSRS. SEWELL AND CO.

the British and foreign halves of the building, we are glad to observe numerous evidences of improvement in these respects.

We have selected a few good objects in illustration of our position that floor and wall coverings should not only be bright and pretty, but that they should be appropriate to their purpose—conventional in

a single piece, and the pattern consists of a fine geometrical arrangement of flat ornaments, richly arabesque, with scrolls, trellis-work, shields for crests or monograms; but, withal, consistent in design and simple in treatment. Indeed, this is a carpet which in all respects vies with the productions of Aubusson and Tournay.

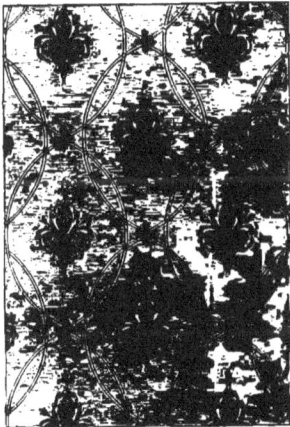

DESIGNS IN LEATHER CLOTH.   THE LEATHER CLOTH COMPANY.

their treatment rather than naturalistic—suggestive of the things represented in their designs rather than directly imitative.

In the preceding page we have the design for the fine Axminster carpet exhibited by Messrs. Sewell, Hubbard, and Bacon, of Soho. Now, here we have a capital pattern in brilliant colours; but both pattern and colours are entirely subservient to their proper purpose. The carpet is a carpet, and not a picture on the ground. It is woven in

The designs in this page, intended for wall hangings, are in every way good, because, again, they are simple and appropriate. They are copied from the articles contributed by the Leather Cloth Company, Cannon Street. Leather cloth of this kind is extensively used, both at home and abroad, for wall hangings, table-covers, seats of chairs and couches, linings of carriages, fancy bags, hassocks, &c. Many of the patterns—which, it will be observed, are all flat and conventional—are printed in gold, and in some cases the pattern is embossed. Of the material itself, we are informed that it combines durability with elegance, at a cost of about one-tenth that of leather. As wall covering, it has the advantage of being printed in oil, and is therefore

The designs from the papers shown by Messrs. Filmer were obtained by competition from the pupils of the Government School of Art at South Kensington. They consist of six conventional treatments of flowers in their natural colours. The two we show represent the

DESIGNS FOR PAPER HANGINGS.　MESSRS. SCOTT, CUTHBERTSON, AND CO.

capable of being easily cleansed; in its design, however, we recognise the possession of educated taste in its producers.

Four designs for wall papers appear in this page: two by Messrs.

blackberry and the passion-flower. Each pattern, by both firms, is printed in various colours from several blocks in the ordinary way, and each is fitted alike for either wall papers or furniture hangings.

DESIGNS FOR PAPER HANGINGS.　MESSRS. FILMER AND SON.

Scott, Cuthbertson, and Co., of Whitelands, Chelsea; and two by Messrs. Filmer and Son, of Berners Street, Oxford Street. Those of the first firm are in the Gothic, or ecclesiastical style, and are commendable for finish, colour, and fitness for their special purpose.

Especially soft, rich, and appropriate is a Persian pattern, shown by the latter firm. The passion-flower pattern obtained the second prize in competition, the designer being Mr. J. Randall; the blackberry pattern was designed by Miss Mary Julyan. The first prizes were severally obtained by Mr. H. H. Lock and Miss Charlotte James. All may be taken as evidence of advance in the right direction. The carpets will be found in Class 22, North-East Gallery; the wall papers in Class 30, North Court.

Messrs. F. G. Trestrail and Co. exhibit (in Class 4, Eastern Annexe) various designs in kamptulicon floor cloth, one of the patterns of which we show in the engraving.

The border surrounding the centre pattern is printed on ordinary kamptulicon, manufactured from india-rubber, gutta-percha, and cork. This material is fast superseding the old oil-cloth, being noiseless, warm, elastic to the tread, impervious to wet, indestructible by

printing in oil colours, which retain their brilliancy for a length of time. Colours may be worked into it, too, in the process of manufacture, so as to produce imitations of marble, which wear out only with the material itself. Lastly, it will stand any climate in the world.

The pattern is in imitation of the ancient Carthaginian mosaics, and is quite fitted for its purpose, being in keeping at once with the character of the material to which it is adapted and the end to which it is applied.

The designs we have here given are only samples of a vast number that might be selected from those stored in the International Exhibition, as specimens of suitable and tasteful decoration for materials for

PATTERN OF KAMPTULICON.—MESSRS. TRESTRAIL AND CO.

damp, and, from its extreme durability, much more economical. It is in use at Windsor Castle, Buckingham Palace, the British Museum, and all the Government offices. In the Houses of Parliament it has been down nearly twelve years.

It is, however, the kamptulicon on which the centre pattern is printed that Messrs. F. G. Trestrail and Co. specially claim as a novelty and improvement. It is a patent article, manufactured from oxydised oil, with or without a fibre, and, at considerably less cost, has the advantage of ordinary kamptulicon, with others in a greater degree. Being coloured through and through, it will always preserve the same appearance, whatever the amount of wear to which it may be subjected; and it may be scrubbed and even pumice-stoned with advantage. From the nature of its composition, it is better adapted for

covering the walls and floors of our homes. They show that our manufacturers are devoting themselves to the study of the means of rendering the most ordinary objects of utility at once pleasing to the eye and in accordance with the true principles of taste. Formerly it was considered enough if materials of this kind possessed qualities sufficient to answer the actual purposes for which they were intended. Paper, to cover walls, and cloth, to cover floors, were certainly produced; but that was all. Manufacturers now have become alive to the fact, that, in addition to this, their materials must possess design, or they will speedily be beaten out of the field by foreign competitors. These instances show that, having turned their attention to the subject, they can meet any rivals in the field on equal terms, and are surpassed by none in the excellence and beauty of their work.

Furniture and Decoration.

From the Furniture Courts we might fill our pages with pictures, so rich is Class 30 in carvings and works of real beauty. Since 1851 art-manufacture has taken a most decided stride; and that, too, in the right direction—the direction of good taste combined with good workmanship.

In this page we engrave a carved ebony cabinet, from the collection of M. Gros, of Paris. This gentleman shows several fine pieces of furniture in carved wood, ornamented with bronzes; besides marquetrie and mosaic work in rich variety. In decorative furniture, the French

friezes of them ornamented with the hop plant, springing from shields. The frieze of the centre division has a richly carved shield, with barley springing from each side, the shield itself being enriched with fruit. The angles of the pedestals are canted to form a background for richly-carved chimeras with leopard's heads, which appear to support the slab. Above the slab, and over the pedestals, are plinths, enriched with carved panels, the one representing a wine cup entwined by the vine, and the other a tankard surrounded by the hop plant. Upon these plinths are placed two female caryatides, the one

CARVED CABINET. M. GROS, PARIS.

are in no respect behind their Continental neighbours. If they lack the solidity we so much admire, they have at least abundant taste and constructive skill.

Among the most prominent of the exhibitors in the Furniture Court are Messrs. Jackson and Graham. This eminent firm show various exquisite specimens of cabinet work. Facing the nave the visitor will notice their fine buffet or sideboard. This work is a work of rare beauty, in pollard oak, enriched with carvings in brown English oak. It is 10 feet long by 12 feet 6 inches high. The doors of the pedestals are niched, with figures of boys gathering grapes, and reaping, and the

10.

with attributes of the field and forest, the other of the ocean and river. These figures support the cornice and pediment, which has a boldly-carved shield in the centre, with festoons of fruit hanging gracefully from it, and partly resting upon the cornice. The caryatides are flanked by richly-carved pilasters, the one representing game, surmounted by the head of a retriever watching the spoils of the day, and the various other denizens of sea and stream surmounted by the head of an otter. The centre and side panels of the upper part are filled with silvered glass.

They have also a fine walnut-wood wardrobe, nine feet long, in three

MESSRS. THURSTON AND CO. CARVED BILLIARD TABLE.

inlaid with various woods, the caps and bases finely carved, which support the cornice and pediment; the latter has a shield in the centre from which spring rich festoons of flowers, in marqueterie work. The corners of the plinth and cornice are rounded, and a hollow worked upon the angles of the wardrobe to receive columns inlaid and carved *en suite* with the pilasters, to complete the support of the cornice. The doors on each side of the centre have small oval mirrors, surrounded by rich floral marqueterie work.

Notice their decoration for the side or end of a drawing-room, in the style of Louis XVI., panelled and enriched with mouldings, and relief ornament, gilt. The centre panel fitted with silvered plate glass, and the side panels with rich crimson silk, of thrice the ordinary width, designed and manufactured expressly for exhibition. A chimney piece of Algerian onyx, the pilasters and frieze enriched with bas-reliefs of bronze, chased and richly gilt, will well repay examination. The object selected for engraving is a cabinet of ebony, inlaid with ivory, the centre inclosed by doors, with oval medallions of hymeneal subjects, in bronze, highly chased and gilt, the ends open and rounded, the plinth, columns, and frieze all enriched with mouldings and ornaments of bronze, finely chased and gilt, and surmounted by a slab of the finest Algerian onyx.

Messrs. Jackson and Graham also exhibit a piano—the interior by Messrs. Erard, the case of fine Amboyna wood, richly inlaid in various ornamental devices, musical trophies, and flowers of fine marqueterie work; the front, above the fall, of very finely perforated purple wood, in which are framed three finely-executed paintings, on porcelain, that in the centre representing a group of children playing upon musical instruments, upon the left of which is a medallion, with a boy playing the Pandean pipes, and on the right another medallion, with a boy playing cymbals—a small drawing-room chair, very finely carved, and richly gilt, in the style of Louis XVI. and an *etagère*, of ebony, inlaid with ivory. Altogether, their show is quite equal to their well-sustained reputation.

In Class 22, they also show a very beautiful patent Axminster carpet, 25 feet by 18 feet, the ground of rich Marone colour, with crimson rosettes, the centre with group of flowers, on white ground, surrounded by rich brown and gold ornamental framing, intersecting with the border, which consists of arabesque scroll-work, on white ground, with shields and festoons of flowers at each corner. Upon the margin, outside the border, a light arabesque ornament has been introduced. They have also various samples of different designs, some with borders of velvet pile carpet, woven by steam-power, in Jacquard loom; and a sample of patent tapestry velvet carpet. These may be taken as good examples of design, in the direction advocated in our columns.

Messrs. Thurston and Co. show a carved oak billiard-table, of good

divisions. The plinth, cornice, and end panels inlaid with lines, and ornamental corners of Amboyna, purple-wood, and holly. The centre door has a panel of silvered glass, and on each side are pilasters richly design and admirable workmanship; as well as their Patent Combination Billiard-table, which may be converted at pleasure into a dining-table, the cushions being hinged, and made to turn down.

The carved oak table, shown in our engraving, has been executed by Mr. J. O'Shea, from designs by J. M. Allen, Esq. It is carved in the style of the fifteenth century; the panels at the sides and ends are in low relief; and the story told is illustrative of the Wars of the Roses. The table is supported on eight legs, each consisting of four clustered columns, with richly-foliated caps, having a central crocketed shaft, with carved spurs, on square, moulded base.

The history carved in oak begins with the Departure of the Duke of York from Ludlow Castle, in 1455; then follows the Battle of St. Albans, with the Death of the Duke of Somerset, and the Reconciliation of the Duke of York and the Queen; next we have the Battle of Blore Heath, followed by the Earl of Salisbury leaving Middleham Castle. These two subjects are, from necessity, chronologically reversed. Then comes the Desertion of Sir Andrew Trollope and his Veterans from the Fortified Camp at Ludlow, in 1459. Next we have Somerset Repulsed at Calais; Warwick's Triumphant Entry into London; and the Battle of Northampton. In regular sequence then follows the Desertion of Lord Grey de Ruthyn, the Battle of Wakeford Green, and the Death of the Duke of York. Afterwards we see the Death of the Duke's Son on Wakefield Bridge; the next, the Battle at Towton, in 1461, in the midst of a terrible snow-storm, when the Lancastrians lost more than 28,000 men; the Battle of Mortimer Cross; the Battle of Barnet, and the Death of the Earl of Warwick. Lastly, we have the Battle of Tewkesbury, the Defeat of Margaret, and the Death of Edward Prince of Wales. This work, as a whole, is one of the most important in its class, and is therefore deservedly admired.

MINTON'S MAJOLICA FOUNTAIN.

IN the next page we have an engraving of the famous Majolica fountain under the east dome. We have already referred to this beautiful work in porcelain, which, like Osler's crystal fountain in 1851, is unique and beautiful. It was designed by the late John Thomas, the eminent sculptor, from whose plans the minutest details have been fully carried out. It stands 36 feet high. Four winged figures of Victory, holding crowns of laurel, encircle the central pavilion, on the top of which rests the group of St. George and the Dragon. Beneath we have a series of smaller *jets d'eaux*, one of which, the stork, was originally modelled for the Queen's dairy at Windsor, under the personal superintendence of his late Royal Highness the Prince Consort.

The water of the fountain has several times been perfumed by M. Rimmel, with considerable success. The eastern dome is, in consequence, the most popular part of the building. Here every afternoon may be heard the strains of beautiful music from the Grand Pianofortes of Messrs. Kirkman and others, and here beauty and fashion meet and mingle with the representatives of labour—the working men and working women of our world. On crowded days—and almost every day is crowded—the eastern dome is a sight to behold!

MINTON'S MAJOLICA FOUNTAIN

The Processes Court.

YOUNG'S TYPE COMPOSING AND DISTRIBUTING MACHINES.

ONE of the most interesting courts in the building is that devoted to certain manufacturing processes. On page 43, we referred briefly to the principal objects of attraction in this court; we now lay before our readers a pictorial and verbal description of one of the most curious of the many ingenious processes, namely, Mr. Young's method of composing and distributing printing-types by machinery.

THE TYPE-COMPOSING MACHINE, WITH ATTENDANT.

THE DISTRIBUTING MACHINE.   THE JUSTIFIER.

We offer no opinion as to the ultimate effect this machine may have on the printing trade, but simply publish the inventor's own account of its uses:—"For some time past," says the patentee, "the necessity for discovering a means for increasing the speed of setting up types, and superseding the present slow hand method, has been strongly felt. Whilst printing from the composed types has, by the improvements in the steam press, been carried to a most advanced stage, setting up by hand is not now done more quickly than it was four hundred years ago, by the earliest printers. In order to save a few minutes time in printing, large sums are paid for improved steam presses, when the use of a well-devised composing machine would save a much greater portion of time, by preparing the types expeditiously for the press. With the present slow method of composition, it is only by the exercise of the most wonderful degree of method, surprising skill, and most untiring energy on the part of every one concerned, that the daily newspaper is so unfailingly supplied to its readers. To show how much of this laborious effort would be saved by the use of the composing machine, a single example will suffice. Let it be supposed that, half an hour before the usual time of putting to press, important news arrives, enough to extend over three columns of the paper—or say 45,000 types have to be set up in thirty minutes by hand ; this would require the assistance of ninety compositors, each having a scrap of paper put into his hand to set up, in such a manner that it may tally with his neighbour's piece, technically called 'making even.' With the machines, only six players, and, therefore, only six pieces of copy, instead of ninety, would suffice to set the quantity up, while twenty-two justifiers would justify the same ; and, besides that, the system would afford immense facilities for correction. It must be remembered, too, that for this very work steam presses are waiting to throw off copies at the rate of 20,000 per hour, so that the saving of the few minutes would be a gain of 1,500 copies. The late Mr. James M. Young, fully convinced of the importance of such a labour-saving machine to the printing trade, applied himself during many years with great skill and unwearied energy to its perfection, and finally succeeded, within a few months of his death, in completing a most efficient type-composing machine, and also that most desirable adjunct, a good type-distributing machine."

These are the machines shown in the Processes Court, and, by means of engravings, in the preceding page.

The Type Composing Machine is provided with separate compartments, called "reservoirs," for all the letters of a fount, and each reservoir is provided with a small lever, which, by means of a rod, is connected to a key, like those used in a piano-forte. When a key is struck by the player, it pushes a type out of the reservoir, by means of the lever mentioned above, and the type is thus caused to slide down an inclined plane, and thence into a receiver, where it is set up side by side with other types, by means of a beater. Thus each type or letter can be set up by a player in the order required by a compositor's copy. This is now done with a speed of from 12,000 to 15,000 types set up in an hour's time.

· The Justifying Apparatus is intended to replace the compositor's stick. The compositor places the galley, filled with the long lines of type set up by the composing machine, slides one of them into the apparatus, divides it into the proper width of the page, and having justified it, moves a handle, which depresses the completed line, and thus makes room for a succeeding one. It is found that a compositor can, by this means, justify at the rate of 4,000 to 6,000 types per hour.

The Distributing Machine separates all the different letters of a fount, that may have been used for printing, into different channels, ready for use in the composing machine. This is effected by one or more pairs of nippers, which take every type singly from the reservoir in which all the types have been placed, and allow it to slide down an inclined plane, the upper part of which moves on a hinge. The thin or lower-case types slide down to the bottom of the fixed inclined plane, but the thicker or upper-case letters are retained on the movable incline which, on being raised, drops them into an appropriate recep-

tacle, whence they are then taken and re-distributed, by passing down a separate channel of the inclined plane. The thin or lower-case letters that have arrived at the bottom of the inclined plane, are pushed into the grooves of a revolving chain. This chain, in moving, passes underneath plates, which are made of different widths, in order to cover only certain nicks cut cr cast on the edge of the types, and situated in different parts of their length, from 1-16th to 12-16th of an inch from the tail of each type. When, therefore, a type passes underneath a plate which allows its nick to be exposed, it is pushed from off the chain by means of a scraper, which passes over the plate on to a tilting inclined plane. This plane, in its descent, allows the type to slide down, by means of an inclined channel, into a receiver, where it is set up by means of a beater, as in the composing machine. The distinguishing nicks are somewhat like those used by type-founders; 71 per cent. of the types require only one nick, 20 per cent. only two nicks, and the remainder have three nicks. One distributing machine, attended by two boys, will distribute and prepare for the composing machine from 14,000 to 18,000 types per hour. A saving of 50 per cent. in the cost of composition is effected by the use of these machines.

In connection with printing apparatus and machinery, there are in the Exhibition many curious and remarkable objects. A writer in the Daily Telegraph thus refers to an interesting group :—"To those who find their way into the machinery annexe, a group upon its western side seems very attractive, and certainly it is worthy inspection. The group consists of two printing presses, a type foundry, and a type-composing and a type-distributing machine; while not far off is a paper-making machine. One of the printing presses is Pettor and Galpin's 'Belle Sauvage' Machine, the great feature of which is its compactness, cheapness, and noiseless working. The other is a perfecting machine by Mr. John Ross, of Leith, which, when we examined it, was turning off rapidly Cassell's large Illustrated Bible. But it is on the type foundry and the machines for composing and distributing type that the chief interest of the group is centred. The foundry machine casts, cuts, polishes, and squares the type, so that when the type is thrown out it may at once, without any hand process, be transferred to the cases of the composing machine. The foundry is the invention of Mr. Johnstone, of Red Lion Square. The type-composing machine, which we have seen 'set up' the equivalent of two and a-half of these lines in small pica in fifty-six seconds, is the invention of Mr. Mitchel, of New York, and is now extensively used in several printing establishments in America, while there are, we are told, nine of these machines in use in England and Scotland, two of them being in the printing-office of Messrs. Spottiswoode and Co. The distributing machine, also the invention of Mr. Mitchel, is very complex, but perfectly automatic, and must be seen to be understood."

A SULTAN'S PRESENTS.

AMONG the curious or valuable objects recently added to the contents of the building, Mr. Emanuel exhibits two of the most singular. These are a mirror and a stereoscope, made by order of the late Abdul Medjid for one of the ladies of his harem. We have all heard a good deal about Oriental extravagance, and these two articles are in themselves almost as strong proofs of the fact as any to be found in this country. The mirror is a small oval toilet mirror, for a lady, about a foot wide, but its pillars and draw-stand beneath are of pure gold, exquisitely chased, and the frame of the mirror itself is a curved gold scrollwork of flowers, which are heavy with gems. This, however, is really a very beautifully designed and executed work of art, and so far, notwithstanding its immense cost, the Sultan might be justified in wishing one of his ladies to possess it. But the stereoscope stand has nothing to recommend it but its value. It is an ordinary-shaped box stereoscope of ivory, on a pillar and stand of the same material, set all over, as thickly as plums in a pudding, with diamonds, emeralds, and rubies. The value of these two little presents for one of the ladies of the harem is about £15,000.

SAFETY APPARATUS ON RAILWAYS, &c.

INVENTIONS for the preservation of life under any circumstances should always claim public attention. The universal adoption of machinery in manufactories renders the use of "the lift" so essential in most large houses of business, that any modification of the present mode of construction, tending to decrease the risk of accident, must be viewed with satisfaction by a very large class who need the assistance of such contrivances. In Class 10 (South-West Court), among other inventions of a similar character, we notice a couple of working models of an ingeniously contrived piece of mechanism, patented by Mr. Marcus Brown Westhead, of Manchester.

the box or cage within a few inches, and that instantaneously. This is a double security in the event of the rope breaking, as the machine, in that case, does not depend upon the action of the governor alone. It has been proved that the greater the weight of the cage or box and its contents, the more safely it is secured; for the heavier the load the greater will be the resistance of the cams, as they will take a much firmer hold of the guides or uprights. Some alteration of the plan, as shown in fig. 1, makes this invention equally applicable to the cages used in coal and other mines, where it is essential that the momentum of the cage should be gradually reduced in the event of over-speed. This inven-

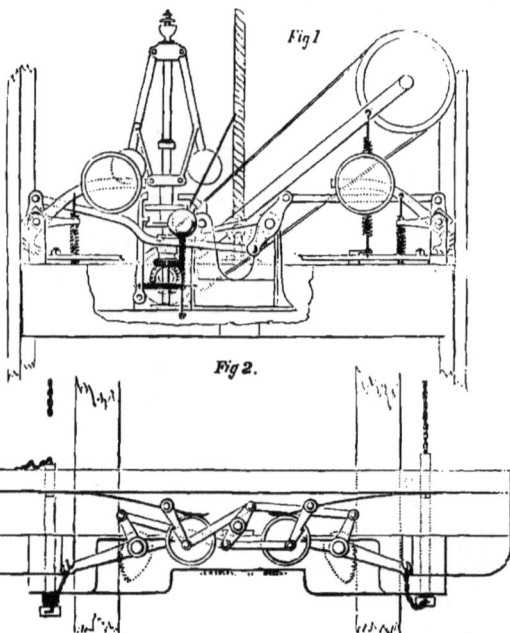

Fig 1.

Fig 2.

PATENT HOIST GOVERNOR, AND PATENT SAFETY RAILWAY PLATFORM LIFT.

Fig 1 represents a patented apparatus, used in the northern districts of England, for preventing accidents to life and injury to property, in hoisting and lifting machinery. The machine is attached to the upper side of the ascending and descending chamber, or cage. It is simple in construction, and easily kept in order, and has already proved itself, in many instances, to be a secure and efficient apparatus for the purpose intended. It is evident that, no matter what the cause of the cage or box travelling at too great a speed, the expansion of the governor, from an excessive rate of motion, must, per force, operate upon the other portions of the machine, and thus permit the cams or wedges to be instantly projected against the uprights or guides of the shaft or well-hole, and so arrest the box. A small-weighted lever falls, if the rope of suspension is severed, and thereby catches

tion combines the peculiar and important advantage, viz., the springs to insert the cams are not brought into action except at the required time, thereby preserving their elasticity unimpaired.

Fig. 2 is a plan for preventing accidents to railway platform lifts. These hoists are extremely dangerous, in consequence of the liability of one or more of the suspending chains breaking. By this invention the platform is evenly and simultaneously arrested at its four corners, in the event of one or all of the suspension chains being fractured by too great a load, or from the alternations of temperature affecting unequally the nature of the metal employed in the manufacture of the chains. It is, moreover, advantageous in its application, as the platform can be readily adjusted or repaired, whenever requisite, without having to stay the platform.

SODA-WATER MACHINES.

Few things are more simple in appearance, or less suggestive of the application of powerful machinery, than a bottle of soda or seltzer-water. The young gentleman who indulges in a "cool draught" in the morning little imagines the trouble taken to procure it; and perhaps it may be information to him, and to many, when we state that the bottling of all kinds of aërated waters is at once a dangerous and complicated business: dangerous, from the fact that the glass frequently breaks in the process of bottling—the workmen being

and pressed firmly against a suitable packing-ring, on the under side of the filling-piece, the air is excluded, and the otherwise dangerous operation entirely prevented. A further improvement is the application of a small steam cylinder, combining in one machine the apparatus for making the soda-water and a steam-engine for driving the same, which, being connected to the same shaft, the fly-wheels answer the purpose of both.

The machine produces 2,500 bottles per day (or over 200 doz.), and the principal features of the invention are the mechanical contrivances

PATENT STEAM SODA-WATER MACHINE AND BOTTLING APPARATUS.　MR. D. FLEET, WALWORTH.

obliged to wear masks and thick leather gauntlets; complicated, from the nature of the operation of forcing a certain determinate quantity of gas into a given quantity of water.

One of these machines—exhibited by Mr. Fleet, of Walworth—we have chosen as illustrative of the system of making and bottling aërated and mineral waters.

The steam soda-water machine exhibited by Mr. Fleet is an improved method of manufacturing and bottling soda-water, lemonade, ginger-beer, and all kinds of mineral waters and aërated drinks, by means of a patent screw bottling apparatus, which forces the cork into the bottle without the aid of a mallet; and being elevated by a treadle

for the entire exclusion of all atmospheric air and the ease with which it can be worked by non-professional men.

The great success which has attended its working by the exhibitor proves that from its solidity of construction, power, and completeness, it is a great acquisition to this increasing branch of trade.

Mr. Fleet's steam soda-water machine and bottling apparatus is worth the attention of chemists and others interested in the manufacture of mineral waters. It is economical in cost, at the same time improving the quality of the article produced; and, from its compact and portable nature, is inexpensive in freight, and well adapted for exportation.

The Prizes and the Medal.

THE jurors have issued their report, and the list of the prize-holders is now published. In the original plan laid down by the Royal Commissioners, it was indicated that " Prizes, or rewards for merit, in the form of medals," should be given to the most prominent exhibitors of " raw material, machinery, and manufactures," the three sections of the classification observed in the industrial portion of the Exhibition. It was further announced that

" these medals will be of one class, for merit, without any distinction of degree. No exhibitor will receive more than one medal in any class or sub-class. An international jury is formed for each class and sub-class of the Exhibition, by whom the medals will be adjudged, subject to general rules, which will regulate the action of the juries. Each foreign commission will be at liberty to nominate one member of the jury for each class and sub-class in which staple industries of their country and its dependencies are represented.

" The juries are required to submit their awards, with a statement of the grounds of each, to her Majesty's Commissioners, before the 15th day of June. The awards will be published in the Exhibition Building, at a public ceremony. They will immediately afterwards be conspicuously attached to the counters of the successful exhibitors, and the grounds of each award will be very briefly stated. If an exhibitor accepts the office of juror, no medal can be awarded in the class or sub-class to which he is appointed, either to himself individually, or to the firm in which he may be a partner. The medals will be delivered to the exhibitors on the last day of the Exhibition."

These several conditions have been complied with. On the 15th of June the jurors submitted their awards, and on the 11th of July the state ceremony took place, at which these awards were made public. The official circular relative to the declaration of the jurors' awards, was to the following effect:—

1. The declaration of the awards of the juries at a State ceremony on Friday, 11th July, 1862, at one o'clock, will be made by an International representative body of royal and distinguished personages, especially named by the various nations which have taken part in the Exhibition.

2. The Queen has named his Royal Highness the Duke of Cambridge, K.G., as her Majesty's representative to receive and distribute the awards to the exhibitors of the United Kingdom and its colonies and dependencies. The special representatives of foreign countries will receive and distribute the awards to foreign exhibitors.

3. The various ceremonies will take place in the Exhibition Buildings and in the Horticultural Gardens, which will be treated as part of the Exhibition for that day.

4. The special representatives will be received by her Majesty's Commissioners on the upper terrace of the Horticultural Gardens, if the weather be favourable; if unfavourable, in the conservatory; and the International juries will then deliver their awards to the special representatives.

5. The special representatives, after receiving the awards, will pass in procession along the arcades to the Exhibition Buildings, and at various stations will deliver the awards to the chairman of the British Class Committees, to the Colonial Commissioners, and to the Foreign Commissioners in or near those parts of the buildings where the principal objects of each class or country are placed.

6. Upon the arrival of the special representatives at the different stations for distributing the awards, the national airs of the respective nations will be played by military bands, British and foreign. After the distribution, &c., the procession will assemble again on the upper terrace, when " God save the Queen " will be performed by all the military bands.

7. The public will be admitted between the hours of 10 and 12.30 by season tickets, or by special tickets, to be purchased before the 8th July, at 5s. each. On and after that day the price will be 7s. 6d. each. Tickets will be ready for issue on the 30th June.

8. Exhibitors who may not have season tickets may obtain a free ticket of admission upon personal application at the offices in the Exhibition Road, on or before the 8th July.

All the ceremonial observances passed off successfully ; though the large number of prize medals awarded, and the fact that all the medals were of one class, caused surprise in the minds of many. But when we come to consider the high degree of merit evinced in the works exhibited in nearly all the classes, our wonder is rather that the prizes were not greater in number. It may happen that the jurors have overlooked some who really deserved distinction ; but, on the other hand, it must be remembered that they have had a very difficult task to decide amid so many contending claims.

The ceremony was very grand, and altogether English in character ; impressive, yet free from ostentation ; gay and lively, without being boisterous.

The list of prize-holders will be given in another number. For the present we content ourselves with producing fac-simile representations of the Prize Medal—the same size as the original.

PRIZE MEDAL—OBVERSE.

PRIZE MEDAL—REVERSE.

11.

The design of this beautiful work of art was produced by Mr. Daniel Maclise, R.A., and the execution of the medal in bronze was entrusted to the experienced hands of Mr. Wyon, of the Royal Mint. Britannia is seen seated, armed; yet bearing the emblems of peace—the olive branch and the laurel wreath. Behind her are three female figures, representing the fine arts; while Science, Manufactures, and Agriculture kneel in front to receive their several wreaths of distinction. Various implements, suggestive of commerce and industry, are introduced. On the other side of the medal is a wreath, bearing in its centre an inscription appropriate to the occasion—"*honoris causa,*" for the sake of honour. It is intended, we believe, to have the name of the holder of each medal engraven round the rim. Altogether, the medal of the International Exhibition of 1862 is a work entirely worthy the great occasion for which it was designed.

Curiosities in the Exhibition.

WOOD-WORKING MACHINES.—We recently referred to some of the curious and valuable machines for working in wood, exhibited in the Western Annexe. Our attention has since been drawn to other contrivances of similar character. The visitor will notice with admiration some pieces of machinery exhibited by Mr. R. H. Thompson, of her Majesty's dockyard, Woolwich. There is a universal joiner, a horizontal sawing and tree-felling machine. Messrs. Forrest and Barr, of Glasgow, exhibit a planing and moulding machine, adapted for ship-yard work, and a finely-finished machine, arranged for working mouldings only, with some samples of its work. Close by is a neat horizontal saw frame, exhibited by Mr. William Geeves, of Islington. Messrs. Thomas Robinson and Son, of Rochdale, are also exhibitors of some first-class wood-working machines, several of which are to be seen at work at certain times each day, and when in motion they are generally surrounded with an eager group of spectators. At the extreme north end of the Western Annexe the visitor will find the French collection of wood-working machinery. The samples are not numerous, and the principal exhibitor is M. J. L. Perin, of Paris. There are few machines in the Exhibition that merit and receive as much attention as M. Perin's band-saw and its productions. A large share of the credit, however, is due to the skilful manipulation of the attendant workman. The unique samples of workmanship exhibited along with the machine, especially the artistic device commemorative of the Exhibition, are excellent of their kind. But, apart from these considerations, a peculiar interest attaches to M. Perin's machine, for he was the first to bring the band-saw into successful operation. It is said that M. Perin has made a fortune by his invention. His saws are in operation in all the dockyards and arsenals of France, as well as very generally throughout the Continent; and one, we believe, is in Woolwich Arsenal. Adjoining M. Perin, Messrs. Frey and Son, of Belleville (Seine), exhibit a substantial portable saw-frame for cutting heavy timber; and Messrs. Longard and Son, of Cautelcu (Seine Inf.), a planing machine. There are also in this section last-machines, machines for shaping wheel-spokes, and a variety of others for wood-working purposes, all more or less different from those in general use in our own country. The largest collection of this class of machinery exhibited by any foreigner is shown by Mr. J. Zimmerman, of Chemnitz, in Saxony. It comprises upwards of two dozen machines for wood and iron work, and their finish and general getting-up will compare well with any in the class to which they belong. These machines comprise several features peculiar to themselves. They are situated in the north-east corner of the Annexe, out of the way of the great stream of visitors.

CURIOUS WATCHES.—Among the recent additions to the World's Show, Mr. Benson exhibits round the base of his Great Clock a curious collection of antique watches, with a view of illustrating the gradual rise and progress of watch-making to the present time. These curious old relics vary from 100 to 250 years old. Nearly all are of the ordinary vertical construction, but have a piece of catgut, instead of a winding chain, and are, of course, without pendulum springs. Some of the oldest of these are the smallest, and many of them are finished with the utmost nicety, and even now remain in working order. The largest watch in this collection is one which belonged to that redoubted Parliamentarian, Pym; though there is another, almost equally huge and massive, which has no fewer than six hands, and which shows the month, day of the month, day of the week, hour, minute, and second, with the daily age and quarters of the moon. Another antique specimen from Nuremberg—the birthplace, so to speak, of pocket watches—is almost equally curious. A very handsome and large one is shown, with an enamelled case, enriched with pearls, the works in which are so arranged as to play a variety of tunes, like a musical snuff-box. This, however, is a comparatively modern English specimen, taken at the general "loot" of the Chinese Emperor's Summer Palace, at Yuen Min Yuen. The progress made since those days is exemplified by a series of chronometers and chronograph watches, the latter of which mark time to tenths of seconds. All these are shown in cases ornamented with designs, for which prizes were offered at the various Government Schools. Some of them are of great beauty.

PRAYER CYLINDERS. — In the Indian collection (North-east Gallery) there are many curious and remarkable objects. Among others are the Prayer Cylinders—a common brass cylinder, filled with printed prayers, which the natives spin and turn round, and every revolution counts as so many prayers said. In some parts near Thibet, where the strictest Buddhism prevails, these prayer cylinders are made of great size, and turned by water power, so as to do the praying of the whole village in which it works, without a moment's cessation. This easy method of invocation is so extensively practised by all the natives, that printing in Thibet is confined almost exclusively to the production of the innumerable prayers required by the people. The printing blocks used for this purpose, in Thibet and Darjeeling, are shown in one of these cases. They are cut in coarse wooden blocks, and in workmanship are apparently on a par with what Caxton's first failures must have been.

THE MUSICAL BOXES from Geneva attract great attention. Messrs. Auber and Linton show a beautiful piece of mechanism, which, though no novelty, has a crowd of admirers. It is in the shape of a small musical box, just large enough for the waistcoat pocket, out of which, when the lid is opened, pops up a pretty little bullfinch, who pipes a song, fluttering his wings in the most natural manner possible. The plumage, the action, and the peculiar note of the bird are imitated with wonderful exactness.

THE TERROR.—One of the most interesting models in the Naval Court is that of the Terror, which accompanied the Erebus in Sir John Franklin's last voyage. With her broad bluff bow, with her strengthened sides, and with her plates of iron for cutting through the ice, she gives one the due impression of immense power and stability.

MODEL MUMMY CASE.—In the Egyptian Court is a most curious object—a sort of model mummy case. By the side of the body sits the soul, and on the side of the coffin are inscribed prayers, supposed to be addressed to the body by the soul, beseeching it to remain undisturbed until the day of resurrection, when the two will be found together again.

WEST AUSTRALIAN DELICACIES.—Among other substances used for food are cases of preserved meat, including kangaroo tail—said to be of delicious flavour—and 50 ounces of jelly-seaweed, prepared from 63 lbs. of the living weed, and capable of producing 100 quarts of jelly, or blanc mange.

The Zollverein Contributions.

UNDER the title of Zollverein—literally "toll union"—the following German States exhibit in the South-west Transept and the galleries above :—the Duchy of Anhalt-Bernburg, the Duchy of Anhalt-Dessau-Cothen, Grossherzogthum Baden, Bavaria, Brunswick, Frankfort-on-the-Maine, Hanover, Hesse-Cassel, the Grand Duchy of Hesse (Hesse Darmstadt), the Principality of Lippe, Nassau, the Grand Duchy of Oldenburg, the Kingdom of Prussia, the Kingdom of Saxony and Principality of Reuss, the Grand Duchy of Saxony, the Duchy of Saxe-Altenburg, the Duchy of Saxe-Coburg Gotha, the Principality of Schwarzburg-Sondershausen, Würtemberg, and Mecklenburg-Schwerin. The German towns of Bremen, Hamburg, and Lubeck, under the designation of the "Hanse Towns," also exhibit in the South-west Transept. This free-trade union for the adoption of a uniform system of import duties is of comparatively modern formation. In 1841 it was renewed for twelve years, and in 1858 the German Diet again renewed it for a further period, which subsists till 1865.

Prussia makes the largest show, her contribution appearing in each of the classes, from raw materials to fine arts. In "Raw Material" section, the Zollverein is especially well represented. The mineral products of the entire Zollverein department have been collected together, and are advantageously displayed in one large room near the south-west angle of the building. This arrangement gives a facility for examination and study that contrasts remarkably with the difficulty felt in going through the other Zollverein classes, each of which is split up into as many divisions as there are exhibiting States.

The mining products are arranged very systematically. First come the products of the coal measures, then brown coal and peat. The different metallic ores follow next in order ; these are naturally succeeded by the metals and metallic products ; the rocks and earths used in building and manufactures succeed, and the collection concludes with the rock salt and products of the salt springs.

The distribution of the different minerals in the Zollverein is rendered more evident by the suspension on the walls of the court of a series of valuable geological maps, which are placed in the closest possible proximity with the objects whose distribution they are intended to illustrate.

In chemicals, too, the German States show well ; but our space will not allow us to do more than mention one or two of the main objects of attraction in this department. Aniline colours, from coaltar, are shown, as are also some curious products from cinchona bark, and a variety of cheap candles and soap, produced from what we in this country consider waste materials.

The display of pottery and porcelain is superb. There is some little specimen of almost every kind that can be named, but the strength of the exhibition is given to the two valuable kinds of earthenware—the pottery of Henri Deux, and the porcelain of Dresden. There is a goodly collection of majolicas, and some admirable bits of Palissy ware. From the royal manufactories of Berlin and Meissen, in Saxony, the ceramic show is very fine. Conspicuous among the trophies under the western dome, is the display of porcelain made by the King of Prussia. Especially noticeable are two fine busts, in parian, of the Crown Prince and Princess of Prussia, which are actual portraits in their minute resemblance to the originals. In this class, also, Dresden has entered the field in great force. Some of the Dresden chandeliers, mirror frames, and groups of figures are real marvels of ceramic excellence, both as to colouring and form of figures and outline.

The large iron foundries of Berlin and Hanover send several large ornamental works in bronze ; and two colossal couching lions come from the latter town, to add to the effect of the German Courts.

Among the industrial branches connected with science and art, specimens are exhibited from the printing-offices of Berlin, Brunswick, Gotha, with globes and maps from the different States of the Zollverein. A good collection of photographs is exhibited, chiefly from Munich ; and the portrait, life-size, is shown of his Royal Highness the Prince of

Wales, taken on his journey to the Holy Land. Bavaria also sends a collection of very excellent drawing-pencils.

Colours for printing and lithography are sent from Frankfort-on-the-Maine and Hanover ; toys principally from the Duchies of Saxony and the city of Nürnberg ; clocks from the Grand Duchy of Baden ; and straw-plaiting from the Black Forest. The models of the new Exchange building at Berlin, the Dorschauer railway bridge, and the sloping plain of the Oberlaendische Canal, in East Prussia, are peculiarly interesting to architects.

Professor Hyrtl has supplied anatomical preparations, illustrative of the construction of the inner organs of the ear in nearly two hundred different animals. Beginning from the diminutive mouse of the Italian hills, he proceeds, through many intermediate stages, as far as the auditory organs of the immense whale ; and, to explain the phenomena of the present world by those of a past creation, even takes into his very interesting collection the antediluvian bear, the primeval ichthyosaurus, and some other monsters of a period now belonging exclusively to palæontological researches.

Under the western dome are shown the splendid silver plate presented by the burgesses of Berlin to our Princess Royal, on her marriage with Prince Frederick William, now the Crown Prince of Prussia ; and an exquisite silver shield, the offering of the Rhenish nobility to the youthful bride and bridegroom. With the historical and mythical suggestions are represented the good wishes of the donors to the newly-wedded couple, whose betrothal is represented in the centre. Round the rim are little scutcheons of enamel, bearing the names of the subscribers. The work is a fine one, though perhaps inferior to the Dreamer's Shield, shown by Messrs. Elkington.

In the Russian Court will be found many of the toys with which English children are familiar—some of them, indeed, identical with those shown by Messrs. Cremer, in their toy trophy in the British nave. Bronze ornaments, cork models, lamps, photographs, swords, guns, and pistols, with some really good statuary, will be discovered in the crowded courts of Germany. Furniture of all kinds, and a considerable quantity of gold and silver ware, with clocks from the Black Forest, and philosophical instruments, looking glasses, and many products of the loom, as well as various agricultural implements, will be found in the Baden courts. At the end of the court, within the transept, is the Grand Duke of Baden's popular Orchestrion, exhibited by M. Welte, of the Black Forest, the largest and most wonderful piece of musical clock-work in the Exhibition. On each side of the Orchestrion there are the rival Farinas, with their eau-de-Cologne, patronised by visitors apparently without much care as to which is the "real, genuine, neat as imported" article.

The Rhenish provinces send specimens of arms and cutlery, pianofortes from Leipzic and Berlin, and harmoniums from Stuttgardt ; also silk goods from Crefeld and Bielefield ; woollen and worsted, linen and cotton fabrics from Prussia, Saxony, and Würtemberg. The display of varnished leather from Mayence, Worms, and Rhenish Prussia, and of fancy leather goods from Offenbach, Frankfort-on-the-Maine, and Berlin, will also attract attention. Examples of jewellery and ornaments in gold are sent from Hannau, Pforzheim, and Frankfort-on-the-Maine ; and of works in amber from the Prussian shores of the Baltic.

In the machinery department will be found many remarkably fine specimens of manufacture. The iron and steel work includes an immense cast-steel steam-hammer from the foundry of Krupp, in Westphalia, and several fine locomotives and steam-engines.

In the fine arts, the German States show conspicuously ; what is called the German school of painting being in no way behind the schools of Great Britain and France. Altogether, the Zollverein collection will well repay careful examination. Our engraving is taken from the centre of the transept, and shows the circular heading of the wall at that end of the building, with the inscription, *Deus in terram respexit et implevit illam bonis suis.*

NORTH-WEST TRANSEPT ZOLLVERLIN.

Substances used for Food

On the eastern side of the Eastern Annexe will be found many specimens of things familiar in most households — specimens of teas, coffees, sugars, cocoas; preserved meats, fruits, and vegetables; dried and preserved meats, compressed hops, with various kinds of beverages. Dr. Hassall shows a case of bottles, illustrative of the adulteration in sweetmeats, confectionery of all kinds, grocery, pickles, &c.; and perhaps no illustration of the kind was ever so complete and so instructive. But with adulterations are also shown some really beautiful preparations of sugar, isinglass, &c. Messrs. Schooling, Vickers, Phillips and Co., and Martineau and Sons are large exhibitors of "pan sweets," confectionery, Everton toffee, sugar, tea, &c.; while Messrs. Fortnum and Mason have a case of most beautifully preserved fruits, dried nuts, and other adjuncts of the dessert, including some rarities, such as cassava bread, coquilla, ivory nuts, &c.

We have shown for illustration two of the most remarkable objects in this class, namely the wedding cakes exhibited by Mr. Richard Holland, of Chester, and Mrs. Maria and Mr. Richard W. Shackle.

This magnificent specimen of bridal cake was manufac-

WEDDING CAKE. MR. DOLLAND.

tured by Mr. Bolland, of Chester. It was designed and ornamented by Mr. W. Dolland, and is a highly successful production of their united talent and enterprise. The cake, which has been greatly admired for the beauty of its adornments and for its elegance and artistic skill, stands upon a circular pedestal of eight inches, the height of the cake itself being four feet. The base is surrounded by an elaborate gold ornament; at each corner are the royal arms, beautifully moulded in gold relief; the other parts being filled by figures, representing cupids with quiver, bow and arrow, holding birds' nests, surrounded by garlands of roses. The design for the cake is shown in three compartments; in the first are panels, representing Providence, Wisdom, Innocence, and Happiness, in bold relief, on a blue ground, from designs by the late Alderman Boydell, formerly Lord Mayor of London. At the four corners are Gothic niches, emblematical of Marriage. The niches are supported by pillars of Gothic architecture, with appropriate columns. At the summit of each arch is a female bust, with reclining figures on either side. Around the second compartment are festoons of flowers, interspersed with the national emblems, the rose, thistle, shamrock, and leek; and the other parts filled with armorial bearings of the various kingdoms of Europe. The crown of the cake is ornamented with cornucopias, medallions, banners, and rich foliage, the turtle dove, and clusters of orange blossoms; the whole surmounted with a beautiful kneeling figure of Flora, bearing a vase filled with every description of the choicest flowers. The weight of the cake is about 2 cwt., and the whole of the ornaments are moulded, cast, or otherwise worked out in sugar.

Mr. and Mrs. Shackle, of Jeffery's Terrace, Kentish Town, exhibit the bride cake shown in our engraving, as well as two vases of flowers in colours, the whole manufactured in pure sugar, without any kind of metallic colouring, the flowers not being of cambric, as is usual.

The whole design is five feet in height and three in diameter. Commencing at the base, the cake is decorated with three ribbons, with the mottoes, "Liberty and Justice," "Rule Britannia," "Peace and Plenty," alternating with a festoon of rose, thistle, and shamrock. Round the sides are nine coats of arms, with nine large scollop-shells, each supported with scrolls, filled with honeysuckles, forget-me-nots, emblems of the bond of love, taste, &c. On the top of the shells, three Cupids, with a ribbon inscribed "Love." Six scrolls alternate with shells and arms, supporting a vase, containing myrtle and jessamine, emblems of friendship and love. Round the edge is a row of shells, filled with roses and lilies. Then above is another cake, adorned round the sides with

BRIDE CAKE. MARIA AND RICHARD W. SHACKLE.

cluster-leaves and rose-leaves projecting from the edge of the top cake, and doves flying out between the cluster-leaves. On the top are three scrolls, with initials, and three friendship bows, with six light pillars. Inside the temple is an altar, with the flame of Love in the centre, and six small doves flying from the six corners of the altar, with each a scroll, containing a motto—Peace, Love, Hope,

Unity, Faith, Truth; and six large doves, with olive branches, between the pillars. Round the entablature are six ribbons, with mottoes of Humility, Wisdom, Charity, Patience, Perseverance, and "Never Despair." The dome supports three large silk flags, with the mottoes, "Health and Happiness to the Bride and Bridegroom," "The earth is the Lord's, and the fulness thereof," "God save our gracious Queen." Then three Cupids, with doves resting on them; and three small pillars, supporting a canopy over two doves in a rose. Then three cornucopias, with the Union Jack, Royal standard, and Prussian standard; orange - blossom and myrtle, emblems of bridal festivity. Above the whole is a vase, filled with honeysuckle, orange-blossom, lily of the valley, jessamine, and forget-me-nots.

We regret to say that this magnificent specimen of the confectioners' art has been destroyed since it was delivered in the building, the exhibitors sustaining a loss of £100. The fragments have been put together as well as possible, and even in its present state it forms a highly attractive object.

In this department of the Exhibition will be found many highly curious and interesting objects. Here, for instance, are to be seen a large number of flavouring substances, a few drops of which convert a mere syrup into a delightful confection of raspberry, strawberry, pine-apple, currant, peach, pear, or nectarine. Most of these flavourings are prepared from substances that have no affinity with the fruits whose names they bear; and all are perfectly harmless. Here, also, are various kinds of albumen, jellies, isinglass, and other preparations of animal and vegetable tissue; preserved fish and vegetables, with concentrated essences of meats. Examples of all the beverages in use among civilised nations find a place in Class 3 in the British Annexe.

Furniture and Decoration.—IV.

THE Furniture Courts, both on the British and Foreign sides of the building, are especially attractive; much more so, indeed than they were in 1851, in consequence of the better taste displayed in the manufacture of the several articles exhibited.

In the objects we have chosen for illustration there will be observed not only considerable grace and harmony of design, but also what we have always believed to be inseparable from good taste, namely, good workmanship. In the glasses, &c., shown by Mr. Page, of Coventry Street, these qualities are especially observable; no less, however, are they to be commended in the contributions of Mr. Wilkinson, of Old Bond Street.

tive furniture; that is to say, the tastes which may belong to well-to-do people. For the mansion, the hall, the lodge, and the villa there is abundance of choice; but for the six or eight-roomed house in the suburbs, for the cottage of genteel poverty, and the house of enforced economy, there is actually nothing whatever shown. Hardly a chair for a sovereign, or a table for less than five. We should have been pleased to have seen some effort made to produce good, cheap furniture, in pretty shapes; but the exhibitors generally do not appear to have thought it necessary to bring such articles to South Kensington, even if they

GILT CONSOLE TABLE AND GLASS, GIRANDOLE AND CHEVAL SCREENS.   MR. H. M. PAGE.

Among the ornamental furniture in the British Court, that of Messrs. Wright and Mansfield will also be noticed. Observe a book-case of wild cherry-wood, with medallion in the centre of the back in Wedgwood-ware—the design, and the medallions of the frieze and door-panels, after Flaxman. A pair of girandoles, carved and gilded; a handsome Erard's oblique pianoforte; a boudoir book-case of sycamore, with panels of Wedgwood; and a candelabra, carved and gilt, are also very good.

Some very excellent decorative furniture is shown by Messrs. Morris and Co., of Red Lion Square; Messrs. Trollope and Son, and indeed, by several of the well-known London and provincial firms. All sorts of tastes are consulted by the exhibitors of carved and decora-

possessed them. An exception in this respect may be made in favour of Messrs. Heal, of Tottenham Court Road, whose show seems intended to attract the eyes of middle-class, rather than rich and noble purchasers. But, perhaps, with the example of Austria in 1851 before them, exhibitors are anxious to show, not what they could produce of the cheapest and, at the same time, most tasteful character, but that which was best calculated to impress foreigners with an idea of the great wealth and careless ostentation of their principal customers. Be this as it may, the furniture exhibited in the South Courts is sufficiently massive, decorative, and graceful to command universal admiration. The majority of sight-seers may possibly take pleasure in looking at drawing-room suites they cannot afford to purchase, and examining chairs and tables on which and at which they would be afraid to sit or to dine; but some would certainly have welcomed examples of plainer and more useful objects. Nor is this fault—if fault it be—confined to the British side of the building. With the exception of some cottage furniture in the American department, all is intended for purchasers with incomes of from one to ten thousand a-year. It is certainly very delightful to witness such triumphs of mechanical and artistic skill, and to know that there are really people in the world rich enough to buy them.

Of course it will be understood that in the above remarks we by no means deprecate the use of expensive and elegant furniture. On the contrary, the efforts made by the manufacturers of our country, equally with those of foreign lands, to produce excellence in every department, should be warmly encouraged. And this encouragement can only come fairly and legitimately from the possession of great wealth and good taste. In furniture, no less than in pictures, engravings, sculptures, and bronzes, purchasers have the future of art-manufacture entirely in their own hands. Nor can there be any manner of doubt that periodical exhibitions must tend to improve the taste of both workmen

and the general public. As an instance of good taste in respect to furniture of a decorative character, we notice the carved gilt frame and sideboard exhibited by Messrs. McLauchlan and Son, of Printing House Square. The design is both graceful and original.

In this page we introduce a fine specimen of cabinet work, exhibited by Messrs. C. Wilkinson and Son, of 8, Old Bond Street. This drawing-room cabinet consists of a bookcase with large glass and frame above, in fine walnut-wood. All the ornaments are either in relief or inlaid, of white holly. The top of the bookcase, which is glazed with plate glass, is of jaune Fleuri marble. The carvings are emblematical of the Four Seasons. The same firm also show a wash-stand, on pedestals of Savannah pitch pine, with mouldings and ornaments in relief of purple wood, with porcelain tile top, made in one piece, and decorated border en suite, with the chamber ware; a lady's toilet table, and glass en suite with the above; a walnut drawing-room chair; a gilt occasional table, Louis XVI.; a library chair, stuffed back and seat, in morocco; an oak sideboard, with enrichments of Potts's patent electro bronzes. The whole of the furniture displayed by Messrs. Wilkinson and Son is of a superior description.

DRAWING-ROOM CABINET. MESSRS. WILKINSON AND SON.

Carvings in the Exhibition.

WOOD CARVING IN CLASS XXX.

RECOLLECTING the emulation aroused in the minds of British wood carvers by the display of foreign workmanship in the Exhibition of 1851, we cannot wonder that our countrymen have this year made efforts to take a foremost place in the great competition for excellence in design and handicraft. It is too much the fashion (a pernicious one, we think) for the patrons of art to extol the foreign workmen, forgetting there may be an equal amount of latent genius at home for producing works of an ornamental or decorative character. The consequence is that our own workmen are discouraged; they have not only to rival the foreigner, but to contend against this prejudice. Another

now and then obtained considerable commissions for church work—received laudatory comments for having equalled Michael Angelo or Grinling Gibbons—but generally submitted to execute any kind of ornamentation, whether creditable to Art or not. In fact, the name of Grinling Gibbons has been used to the detriment of the workman, for, as a rule, if the latter did anything in imitation of the great master, English patrons begrudged the payment. We speak of what may be called ordinary ornament of the class which it is now well understood Gibbons simply supervised.

To have accomplished all attributed to him, he must have lived three hundred years, instead of the space allotted to man. His excel-

CARVED JEWEL CASE. MR. W. H. BAYLIS.

great obstacle to the advancement of the wood carver at home has been the want of a proper school either for acquiring the rudiments of his art, or where, when his work was accomplished, it could be shown for his advantage. Of course the Trade Society has worked as effectually as it possibly could in providing the means of communication between its members, and an excellent class library for their study and improvement; but, in truth, until the Council of the Architectural Museum offered prizes to all workmen, the best effort of any one of them was at once deposited in a mansion or palace of the commoner or noble, without the chance of exciting any ambition amongst the younger members of the profession, or enabling those of maturer years to mark the progress of the art. Occasionally, public attention was aroused by something startling accomplished by a new aspirant for honours, who soon subsided into the position of assistant to some one else, and was as soon forgotten, save in a small circle; whilst the leaders in trade

lent works may well be praised for their truthfulness and finish, but the modern workman considers very confidently that they are not unapproachable; all that is wanted is proper remuneration for the work bestowed.

The results achieved by the Architectural Museum competition are highly gratifying to the Council, and have been, and will be, of essential service to the Art workman. If we needed an instance in point, we could not do better than refer to the production of one of the exhibitors of 1862, Mr. W. H. Baylis, of 69, Judd Street, whose Jewel case, one of the best pieces of carving in the Exhibition, we have selected for illustration. A glance at the exquisite work, even through the medium of wood-engraving, will be sufficient to warrant our choice.

Mr. Baylis's contributions are four in number; the first being a specimen of rich and elaborate moulding, size 2 feet by 8 inches.

This gained a first prize at the distribution in 1860, at the South Kensington Museum, and was much praised by Mr. A. J. Beresford Hope, the President of the Architectural Museum. The second is a frame (in chestnut wood), in a conventional style of ornament, suitable for a miniature or other purpose, size 18 inches by 12. Next in order is another frame, carved in lime-tree, displaying various flowers, wild and cultivated, with remarkable delicacy and finish; its size is 20 inches by 15.

The remaining production is a Jewel Casket carved in boxwood. At first sight it arrests attention by the beauty of its general outline. Each corner shows the head of a puma, grotesquely treated, and conventionally winged; from the mouth of each bunches of flowers depend, falling gracefully over the sides. The lid is surrounded by a well-executed group—a bird expiring in the coils of a serpent. The rest of the ornamentation is elegant and tasteful, though what may be termed conventional. It is said that the price of this casket is 200 guineas. In size it is about 20 inches by 8, and about 10 inches deep. Mr. Baylis is a young man of the self-taught class, the class from which success in art naturally springs. It is evident he has not servilely followed any master, but, striking out a path of his own, has produced most pleasing combinations, and furnished worthy examples of modern English art. They are not only to be admired

surmounted by an oak cover, carved in English oak, by Mr. David Sharp. The work is well designed and admirably executed. In the centre of the cross-like cover, there is a carved figure of our Saviour, a very marvel of skill and good taste. Mr. Sharp also shows a carved bracket on his own account, which will be found above the doorway leading from the outer Furniture Court to the Colonial Department.

Mr. Bryer, of Southampton, exhibits his admirable little work, the "Moment of Victory," which attracted so much attention when shown in Colnaghi's, in 1858. It is a reproduction in boxwood of Fraser's picture of a game-cock exulting over a fallen foe, while peasants and others are looking on admiringly. His chief work in the Exhibition is an altar-piece, from Rubens' "Crucifixion," carved in English oak. It is about five feet in height by three feet in width. This fine work will be found at the south-east corner of the central Furniture Court, where it attracts considerable attention. It is in very bold relief, the front figures being very nearly detached, the whole carving being nine inches in depth. Mr. Bryer has been eminently successful in giving a good expression to all the many figures in the striking group. There is throughout a very graceful treatment of drapery, which has that peculiar flow and elegance which distinguish the best ages of sculpture, and mark the intense love of the artist for his work; finish without toilsomeness, conventionality without stiffness, combined with natural

SIDEBOARD IN CARTON PIERRE. MESSRS. GEORGE JACKSON AND SONS.

for strikingly natural feeling, but for their very bold, off-hand execution. There is no appearance of laborious effort, or unnecessary anxiety, but rather a repose and vigorous touch which are not often united in so young an artist. These works will be found standing by themselves in the passage leading from the Nave to the centre of the Furniture Court.

Many other fine specimens of carving grace the present Exhibition. Notice those exhibited by Mr. Perry; Mr. Forsyth, of the Hampstead Road; Mr. Walker, of Notting Hill; Mr. Kendall, of Warwick; and Mr. Stevens, of Taunton, whose mahogany sideboard, a work of considerable merit, is crowded with representations of game, fish, fruit, &c.

The veteran Rogers, whose carvings have been so long and so deservedly admired, has a stand of most exquisite works in the Furniture Court. But, as we shall probably illustrate some of these, we refrain from further detail. Mr. Rogers will be remembered as having produced the "Prince of Wales's Cradle," by command of the Queen, and other fine carved works, which were shown in the Hyde Park Exhibition in 1851. Taste and skill in this direction appear to belong of right to the family; for Mr. Rogers's son also shows some very excellent carvings in wood.

In the Mediæval Court there is a font of Ancaster stone, exhibited by Messrs. Kirk and Parry, of Sleaford, Lincolnshire. This font is

case and mastery of beautiful form. This work cannot fail to add to the artist's reputation. Mr. Bryer also exhibits, in the same court, a carved canary, in full song; a spaniel, in alabaster, from the life; a lectern eagle, in oak, the property of the Rev. James Lyon; and an altar, the property of Mrs. W. Iremonger, of Wherwell Priory—all of them noticeable for their varied excellences.

In this page we also introduce a good specimen of imitative carving by Messrs. George Jackson and Sons, of Rathbone Place. The work is executed in carton pierre, a cheap and excellent substitute for wood, especially when the design is large. On page 46 we have another specimen from the contributions of Messrs. Jackson. It was wrongly called a sideboard, when it, in fact, is a design for a chimney-piece.

On the foreign side of the building there are some very fine specimens of carving, especially in the French and Swiss Courts. Nothing can exceed the delicate beauty of some of the smaller specimens of Swiss carvings in soft white wood; but it is to be regretted that these works, generally the production of uneducated peasants, do not improve in a ratio consistent with their popularity. What cheap Swiss carvings were in 1830 they were in 1851; and just what they were in the latter year they are now—very pretty, very delicate, and very deficient in the nobler qualities of art.

Brass Instruments in the Exhibition.

MR. DISTIN'S SAX HORNS.

EVER and anon, amid the sounds of music from the crowd of pianos in the Exhibition, will be heard the long, clear, piercing, beautiful note of a single instrument, which is heard from end to end of the building. It is the call of one of the Sappers and Miners, and is produced from one of Distin's famous brass horns.

Without entering minutely into the theory or science of acoustics, it is well known that the manufacture of wind instruments has really become a "fine art," based upon essentially scientific acoustic principles. Men very early discovered a mode whereby they could produce sounds in imitation of and differing from their own voices by means of artificial appliances. The feathered songster created the idea of music, and then the instrumentalist began his work. To quote a writer of the early part of the present century: "As the materials of music had birth with Nature herself, so their employment in the production of melody was divided by the earliest race of man."

One of the largest and perhaps best show-cases in the Exhibition of Art and Industry is that of Messrs. H. Distin and Co., of Great Newport Street, Leicester Square. In it may be seen some of the finest specimens of brass and silver instruments exhibited by the British manufacturer.

Some very highly-finished specimens of the Kœnig horn, the saxophone, the cornet, and the ventil horn are placed in this case; which instruments we are induced to illustrate, and to state that their prices are more moderate than any instruments of the kind we have yet seen.

It is an interesting fact to notice the steady increase of talent in this branch of trade, while it will be well remembered that but few years have elapsed since all our brass musical instruments were made on the Continent: we may say every improvement that was introduced into them came from abroad. The wonderful appliances of mechanical power are in this branch of manufacture very great. They enable the instrument-maker to supply the public at a very much lower rate than he could do some few years since. Indeed, the advances in them are so great, that we are induced to give our readers an outline of their mode of manufacture.

The manufacturer commences with a mere sheet of brass, which, passing under the machine, is cut into the requisite size to make the tubing. The strip of metal is then turned in the shape of a pipe, until the edges meet closely. In this form it is submitted to the action of the brazing-forge, and the edges become literally welded together. The next operation is "pickling," in a chemical bath, in order to clean the metal from the effects of the brazing. The crude instrument now passes on to an upright "draw-bench," worked by a chain, strap, and fly-wheel; this is to make it perfectly cylindrical inside and out. The mandril is passed through a thick steel plate, closely fitting it; the wheel is set in motion by the tremendous power of the "draw;" the mandril, with the tube on it, is pulled through perfectly straight in its length, and completely round in its form. The next thing is to bend the tube into the various curves required, either in a ventil horn or cornot, at the same time that the cylindrical form is maintained. The bending and twisting of those tubes, without flattening or breaking them, has always puzzled the uninitiated. We will explain why. If a

tube has only to receive a gentle curve, it is filled with melted pitch. When the pitch hardens it gives "body" to the tube, prevents indentations in the bending, and is easily taken out by re-melting. When, however, the bend is very sharp, like the "crank" or "crooks" resembling the letter U, pitch will not answer. In such cases molten lead is poured into the straight tube, and allowed to cool; by its affinity for brass it is capable of being turned to any form.

When the desired shape has been arrived at, as lead melts at a much lower temperature than brass, the tube is placed under the influence of an adjusted flame, and the lead very readily pours out of the tube, leaving its brass skin in all its purity and beauty of form. In the end or "bell" of the instrument, some of which are twelve inches in diameter at the mouth, the edges of the pattern from the sheet brass are first brought together in the way described for the straight tubes, but the "bells" are not placed in the draw-bench. They are placed upon mandrils of their own particular shape, and carefully hammered until the gauge pronounces them of "perfect fit." The common blow-pipe is now a valuable agent. A small jet of gas, the mouth of the blow-pipe behind it, the foot on the treadle of the bellows, and a white heat may be obtained in a very few seconds.

With respect to the very small shanks, they are fitted into a die and stamped up at once. The straight and curved pieces are next given out to the various workmen to fit up for their respective uses. When each has done that which is required of him, he passes the work on to the next man, whose duty it is to continue it; and thus it proceeds until the instrument is so far advanced as to require the mouthpiece. This important part, as well in the manufacture as its use, is at first a piece of rough, unshapen brass or silver; but with the aid of the lathe, it soon assumes its required form. The construction of this portion of the instrument is comparatively simple. Crooks, shanks, pistons, slides, springs, bells, mouth-pieces, and all are now placed in the hands of the fitter, who soon converts that which but a few hours before was a piece of flattened metal into a cornet, or other instrument of elegant form, ready to discourse sweet music for many a day to come. After the instrument has passed the hands of the fitter, it is

"put to the test," and soon receives the stamp, and other marks, to notify its capability of action or use, though not, of course, finished sufficiently for the educated eye of a musician. It now, therefore, undergoes the process of polishing, which is too simple to require any description. Now it is again sent for examination, and is tried most carefully, in competition of tone, with an old instrument. The highly practised ear of a musician soon pronounces it perfect or defective, as the case may be, in tone and register. This ordeal is the last; and the instrument is now placed in the show-case, to await its future master —the whole process having been performed in as little time as, a few years back, was required by an English firm to manufacture one bend of an instrument.

The French Court in the Exhibition.

and its flowered seats are triumphs of skill. Again we invite the attention of the visitor to the exhibition of articles from the Imperial Manufactory of Porcelain at Sèvres. Exquisite in form, though perhaps hardly so successful in colour as of old, are these charming vases, jugs, plates, cups, &c. Look at that beautiful kind of pottery called celadon, on account of the brittleness of its nature. It is only made at Sèvres, and is exceedingly difficult to produce. Several fine vases in this nave have attracted almost universal attention. Perhaps it may be interesting to our readers if we describe the mode of manufacture. First, the vase is modelled, and the figures painted on with a brush; then the vase is put into a glaze, after which it is gradually and tenderly introduced into an oven. Just look at those raised white figures on that fine stone-coloured ground. Place a light within the vase when the shades of evening have fallen, and vase and figures suddenly assume the loveliest of rose-coloured tints. In M. Hadret's fine collection of porcelain, all visitors are struck with the beautiful articles in celadon, made for the Emperor and Empress of the French. These consist of an oval vase and two lamps. On one of the latter is finely painted the head of Napoleon III.; on the other is an exquisite

ENGRAVED SILVER JUG.

likeness of the Empress Eugénie. Then, again, there is the famous Rose du Barri pottery, with its lovely landscapes, painted up to a finish equal to enamel; and the biscuit paste, so light and delicate; and the pure white china of Limoges, in which most of the tea and coffee services of Parisian cafés are produced, and the strange but remarkable Palissy ware. Most persons know how fond that enthusiastic designer, Bernard Palissy, was of constructing plates and dishes representing the bottom of the sea, covered with shells, pebbles, and seaweeds, fishes and snakes, and how he gave to those plates and dishes, with their contents, the names of rustic places, and also how speedily this strange species of ware became the fashion in France and England. Perhaps the strangest article of Palissy ware in the French court is a large oval looking glass, with a frame which would have delighted the great Bernard himself, covered as it is with lizards, fishes, tortoises, marine plants, frogs, beetles, seashells, and surmounted by a naked little urchin who lustily blows a conch. Underneath the fish and reptile mirror are a great number of plates and dishes, which swarm with strange creatures, and jugs in the shape of sea-monsters, with mouths horribly agape. In one of the dishes the principal figure is a pike, the skin of which is excellently rep-

SILVER CANDELABRA.

SILVER CENTRE-PIECE.

dered. Grouped round this ravenous creature are lizards, shell-fish, leaves, &c. In another dish, a handsome snake seems engaged in mesmerising an unhappy frog. In the third, a well-developed perch wonderfully natural in form and colour, is the piscatory centre of attraction.

People of the most contrary tastes are fond of pottery and plate. In the French court both tastes may be gratified. Gold and silversmiths' work is exhibited by most of the best makers in France, besides a vast quantity of *bijouterie*, and what is called Palais Royale jewellery. In the latter M. Villemont is paramount; while in silver work Christofle, Debain, Odiot, and Rudolphi bear the palm.

We have already mentioned (page 13) the bronzes in the French court; but of the furniture, the carvings in ivory and wood, the

the printer, Spain by Murillo the painter, and America by Franklin —all representative and historical men. The outer portion of the work consists of the arms of the various nations, encircled with wreaths, foliage, and emblems. In shape the whole is a fine oval; but in order to enable us to print the design on one page, we have been obliged to remove the extreme border, portions of which are seen at the corners of the engraving.

This beautiful composition has been produced in enamel on gold. The enamelling a plate of these dimensions—17 inches by 10—offers incalculable difficulties. The enamelling of gold is seldom employed in goldsmiths' work, though in small objects of jewellery it is very usual. The process is as follows:—The plate of metal, after having been beaten out, in order to obtain the necessary convexity, is

ARTICLES IN SILVER PLATE. M. CHRISTOFLE, PARIS.

national produce and the manufactures of France, we must reserve remark for another occasion. Suffice it that the courts over which are placed the bust and arms of Charles Louis Napoleon, by the grace of God and the will of the people Emperor of the French, are among the most attractive in the whole Exhibition.

In the next page we have engraved a representation of a fine enamelled shield by M. Payen. The design is intended to symbolise the nations exhibiting at the Great Industrial Palace of 1862. In the centre is an oval, at the lower part of which are figures representing Justice and Concord. At the right and left are seen the nations, represented by female figures, coming to receive the laurel crowns distributed by the genius of Progress, assisted by Humanity. The figures each carry a scroll, inscribed with a name celebrated in their several nations. England and France are in the foreground, and below them, at the foot, is a medallion with the legend, "Science, Art, and Industry," supported by appropriate winged figures. At the right hand of England stands Watt with the steam-engine; while France is attended by Palissy the potter, Germany by Gutenburgh

engraved in bas-relief, after which it is thoroughly cleansed, sulphuric acid being a principal agent employed. It is then enamelled; after which it is placed in the midst of a clear fire, and in a short time the union of the metals is completed, and nothing remains but to polish and fit it for exhibition. The designer of this fine work has overcome all the difficulties of the jeweller, the enameller, and the goldsmith. M. Payen is a true artist, because he was originally a perfect workman. He is associated in this beautiful work with the well-known Paris goldsmiths, Gobert, Dierterle, and Chabot.

M. Payen was nine years in completing this surprising work; and if its merits depended merely on the difficulties he has surmounted, it would be entitled to great consideration. We are too often apt to estimate the worth of a thing by the cost and labour of its production; but in this case the object is worthy of high praise for its intrinsic merit.

Various noble groups in silver and bronze will be seen in the French Courts. Artists—not merely artisans working to pattern—are employed by the producers of the various *articles de Paris* shown in the International Exhibition.

Fine Arts in the Exhibition.—III.

FOLEY'S STATUE OF LORD HARDINGE.

THE sculpture in the International Exhibition may, as a whole, be considered very fine. All the modern artists, and most of the great sculptors of the last hundred years, are represented in various parts of the building, both on the British and Foreign sides. In one room

have been found for the works of Bailey, Munro, Macdowell, Hancock, Davis, Woolner, Mr. and Mrs. Thornycroft, and others. The works of Raphael Monti, Story the American, Benzoni, Baron Marochetti, and other foreign sculptors, also attract great attention and deserved admiration. "Sculpture," says the writer of the Historical Intro-

EQUESTRIAN STATUE OF THE LATE VISCOUNT HARDINGE.   BY J. H. FOLEY, R.A.
Drawn for "CASSELL'S EXHIBITOR" by Melville, and Engraved by Best.

in the Picture Gallery, are shown fine examples of the works of deceased British artists. Here are to be seen the *chefs d'œuvres* of Banks, Flaxman, Chantrey, Westmacott, Wyatt, and others. In the Roman Court will be found Gibson's "Tinted Venus," of which we shall have something to say in a subsequent page; and places of honour

ductions to the several sections of the "Fine Arts Catalogue," "has never been so conspicuously represented as in the present Exhibition. In Assyria, Egypt, Greece, and Rome this art stood first in popular estimate, roused the deepest interest, and was practised by the ablest men. During the middle ages, Sculpture, though less decidedly an element

13.

in religion, held her own still, in union with architecture, in England, France, Germany, and Italy, filling the churches with bas-reliefs and monuments, and preceding everywhere the sister art of painting in her renewal and development. Even the sixteenth century—that time of crisis between triumph and degradation—by reproductions of ancient work, or by its employment for decoration and display, gave a kind of third life to sculpture. But by 1750 the art had fallen to the lowest point, at once in technical skill, vitality of meaning, and general estimation; nor can it be said that the efforts of later years have as yet, in any real sense, restored it to its former glories. Sculpture awakens but a cold, feeble, artificial interest, the brief enthusiasm of personal patronage or pedantry. If it appeals at all to popular sympathies, they are the sympathies of ignorance for mechanical trick or mechanical grandeur, for more mass or for mere minuteness: not for deep or tender feeling, truth to nature, freshness of invention, refinement in handling, loftiness in aim,—for those qualities, in a word, without which the block in the mountain side is far more living than the statue.

"Whence this deathly decline in an art second to poetry alone in antiquity and nobleness? It cannot be that modern life has no place or desire for sculpture. * * * Sculpture, of all arts the most arduous in execution, is at the same time the most delicate of nature: like some tender and sympathetic living creature, if not understood, she fades and perishes. If few modern sculptors of merit for all time in imaginative work can be named—if the prevailing schools of the last hundred years must be divided mainly between the ornamental, the pedantic, and the common-place—not without certain groups only characterised by extravagance or emptiness—these judgments should not be given without great reserve as regards the individuals who have suffered from the long train of external depressing influences. That such classes should comprise so many minor sculptors is not wonderful, when men by nature so highly gifted as Canova and Flaxman have been able to carry the art so little onward, and have left no permanent effect except from the defective side—Canova turning his followers to operatic sentimentalism, Flaxman to antiquarian revival. Yet the Italian, by the grace and finish of his early works, appeared to his contemporaries the restorer of a lost art; whilst the neglected Englishman, whom Canova praised with the liberality of genius, possessed a loveliness of invention, a sense of simplicity, an instinctive poetry and grace, which, in a more appreciative age, would have placed the name of Flaxman with the best of his contemporaries in national estimation. If, however, the favourite subjects of these men, of Thorwaldsen, Gibson, and other distinguished artists are remembered, it is intelligible why imaginative sculpture should be the fallen art she has long been, praised by patrons, meaningless to the world at large. Will it not at some time appear one of the strangest of delusions, that a mythology, dead for two thousand years, should have been fancied a living interest to the nineteenth century?

"One branch of sculpture, however, remains, which has always maintained more or less of life; and to this, with the recovery of a more vital manner in architecture, and the re-union of the arts so long divorced, we may fairly look with hope for the future. For Portraiture, since mastery in it was first reached (hardly before the age of Alexander), has remained, and must always remain, the foundation of excellence in sculpture, as it will finally be recognised in regard to painting. Men are a little less unwilling to compare the semblance with the reality; and wanderings from nature are more easily traced, or censured with greater freedom. It is true that here also the general false position of the art appears. How few public or monumental statues can be named which do not fail, often utterly, from the conventional classical style, bringing with it feebleness in modelling and tameness in outline—from meretricious trick, or shallow artifice —from vacuousness and slovenly execution! Conspicuously placed as they are, how few have any interest or influence over the thousands who would be 'moved as by a trumpet' by the real effigy of a Richard, a Wellington, a Newton, a Napier, a Peel—even of the Sovereigns in their succession, or men of local mark and position!

To foreigners who visit Trafalgar Square or St. Paul's—to Englishmen who know Berlin and Paris, the Louvre and the Santa Croce—it will be needless to add more, or give the list of recognised too-familiar failures. But Foley, Rauch, and Rietschel may be properly named amongst the few honourable exceptions."

The truth of these trenchant remarks will be admitted by all who examine the sculpture in the International Exhibition. Some bright exceptions to the general rule of mediocrity will, however, be noticed and prized; and among them, few so conspicuous as the noble works of Gibson, Woolner, and Foley.

In the *Central Avenue*, which divides the British from the foreign half of the building, stands the splendid colossal *Equestrian Statue of the late Lord Hardinge*, by Mr. Foley. The work in the Exhibition is of plaster, coloured to imitate bronze. The original statue stands in a conspicuous situation in Calcutta, where it has been erected as a memorial of the intrepid soldier who won his spurs in many a fierce encounter, beneath the burning sun of India.

This well-known group was executed in 1857. It is admitted to be the finest work of the kind ever seen in this country; and it is to be hoped that the wish expressed by so many artists and persons of taste will be eventually fulfilled—namely, that another cast in bronze may be made for the ornamentation of the metropolis. We entirely echo the sentiment expressed at a meeting of artists, that the work is highly honourable to British art, and that a subscription ought to be raised for its reproduction and exhibition at home.

For some time previous to its transport to India, the "Hardinge" was publicly exhibited at Burlington House, Piccadilly; and the general opinion of the critics was that nothing so complete and so entirely original had hitherto proceeded from the *atelier* of an English sculptor. The highest authorities in art concurred in this conclusion; and now all the world has an opportunity of estimating its truth.

The likeness of Lord Hardinge is preserved with remarkable fidelity, and the contour of the head is grand and vigorous. The horse is modelled from Lord Hardinge's favourite charger, "Meanee," which bore him through the whole of the Sutlej campaign. The ease and grace of the lines are remarkable; the pawing foot, the tail lashed inward against the hind leg, the arched neck, the well-formed mouth, and the open, fiery eye, express impatience for the charge, and contrast finely with the calm earnestness and dignity of the rider. Who would suppose that the sculptor who produced the "Ino," and drew tears from all eyes by a marble representation of maternal woe, could have so well succeeded in characterising the heroic in bronze, instinct with life and natural grandeur? "Mr. Foley," says one of the critics, "has placed Lord Hardinge, as the Greeks would have done one of their 'horse-taming' heroes, on horseback. He bestrides, and rules the coquettish and feigned passion of his favourite Arab; his head is bare; a simple military cloak, classic in its few strong folds, falls over his shoulders, and leaves the arms reasonably free; by his side is the straight, heavy, business-like sword of Napoleon, given to the old Peninsular chief by Wellington, to whom, we suppose, it fell with other *spolia opima*. The plain, military surcoat, and the long boots and spurs were all the elements of a soldier's dress given to Mr. Foley to shape and arrange, and he has used them with skill, and rendered them subservient and not antagonistic to form."

The proportions of this fine group are, as we have said, colossal; and the whole conception bears the impress of genius—the work being treated in so masterly a manner as to call forth enthusiastic admiration from all beholders. Nothing finer in its own class is to be seen in the Exhibition, or, indeed, in Europe. Amid all the sculpture in the International Exhibition it is unsurpassed in masterly execution and nobility of idea. A few such statues as these distributed throughout the metropolis would relieve us from the odium, so liberally thrown upon us by foreigners, of being fond of public monuments, and yet possessing few worth looking at.

We shall have again to refer to the sculpture in the World's Fair at Brompton.

Silber Plate in the Exhibition.

Works in the precious metals are abundant and valuable in the International Exhibition. Excluding jewellery—of which there is a finer and richer show than was ever before witnessed under one roof—the Silver Plate, in its various forms, is an exhibition of itself. Both British and Foreign manufacturers seem to vie with each other in the exquisite taste and immense value of the several objects exhibited. Who can walk down the nave, and fail to admire the beautiful specimens of silversmiths' and goldsmiths' work — fit reminders of the triumphs of the great Italian, Benvenuto Cellini?

In the cases, on the English side, of Messrs. Hunt and Roskell, Garrard, Hancock, London and Rider, Harry Emanuel, Widdowson and Veale, Attenborough, Benson, of Ludgate Hill; Dodd and Son, Shaw and Son, of Birmingham, Wilkinson and Co., of Sheffield; and Derry and Jones, of Birmingham, will be found some of the most tasteful and exquisite articles in silver, whether shown as *articles de luxe*, or simple domestic appliances. So also on the foreign side. We have in the French department beautiful specimens of *repoussé* work and enamelling ; and in the Zollverein, Austrian, Italian, and Spanish Courts are seen magnificent objects in oxydised silver, and other forms in which the precious metals are made to subserve our wants and luxuries.

A few of these we have engraved ; not so much as specimens of the whole group, as selected articles exhibiting good taste in design, and integrity in manufacture. On page 96 we gave a representation of the wonderful enamelled shield of M. Payen, of Paris; we now show the famous table service of Messrs. Christofle and Co., and some objects from the cases of Mr. Benson and Messrs. Derry and Jones.

As works of art, some of the objects in silver plate are highly creditable. The visitor cannot fail to notice the vase by Antoine Vechte, in oxydised silver, damaskeened,

ENGRAVED SALVER.

shown among the Queen's plate, by Messrs. Hunt and Roskell ; and the basso-relievo, representing Venus and Adonis, and Thetis presenting to her son Achilles the armour forged by Vulcan. But, perhaps, the most ambitious and the most successful work in silver is the Table exhibited by Messrs. Elkington. It is called the "Dreamer," and is the work of M. Morel Laduil, a pupil of Vechte. The work is engraved in silver, in what is called the *repoussé* style — that is, the raised figures are beaten up from the back, and then sculptured. This style was successfully practised by Cellini and others. The design is worked out in the most poetical manner imaginable, and is, emblematic of 'sleep and dreams.' The table rests on a substantial tripartite foot, at which recline the labourer, the warrior, and the minstrel. They are seated amid the poppy and other narcotic herbs, which twine round and upwards, and so form the stem to support the top of the table. The table top is formed of three divisions, but each blends so harmoniously with the other that the whole forms one complete illustration of the dreams of the figures at the base. The labourer dreams of peace and plenty, fruit and flowers, wine and corn, and other produce of the earth. The troubadour is dreaming of love (represented by a beautiful female figure, surrounded by Cupids), of folly, of fortune, and of poetry, each being represented by artistically formed figures; while the soldier dreams of victory, a figure bearing the laurel branch, followed by Honour. Fame with a trumpet, and the Muses, who write his name in the page of history. The engraving of each figure is as fine as though it were intended for a separate work, though the whole design is in the strictest harmony. The border of the table is formed of a fantastic combination of figures, representing the horrors of the nightmare. From the centre rises the

FLOWER STAND.

FLOWER STAND.

SILVER PLATE, SHOWN BY MR. BENSON.   PRIZE MEDAL.

their base with the frame of the plateau. Some particulars in the history of this work are worth recording. Messrs. Christofle and Co. received the commission last November, and it was not until the beginning of the present year that they were in possession of the models from which the casts were to be made. It may, therefore, be considered a wonderful example of dispatch; and, indeed, there is no doubt as to its being the largest galvano-plastic work ever produced within the time. The general plan of the service was given by Baron Haussmann, Senator-Prefect of the Seine. The sculpture was executed under the superintendence of M. Baltard, Director of the Architectural Works of Paris, and Inspector of Fine Arts; by MM. Diebolt, Maillet, Thomas, Gumery, and Mathurin Moreau, artists who have each gained in turn the grand prize of Rome; and by MM. Rouillard, Capy, and Auguste

easily gratify their love of the beautiful by possessing articles of graceful pattern, and classic design, in a material less intrinsically valuable.

There is in this section of the Exhibition a great deal of fine work, known generally by the French term, *repoussé*. Plate for presentation, and race-cups, are the best known specimens of this class of work, and foreigners are largely employed in this country in its production. The hammer and wooden mallet play important parts in getting up *repoussé* articles. If the design for a race-cup, for instance, is to be got up in silver, a sheet of that material is first cut into the form of the object, when developed on a plain surface. It is then beaten into a hollow dish by means of a mallet. When a proper degree of concavity has thus been given, the bases for the ornamental projections are formed

SILVER SALVER, CENTRE PIECE, TEA SERVICE, GOBLETS, ETC. MESSRS. DERRY AND JONES, BIRMINGHAM.

Madroux. It is needless to say that Messrs. Christofle have obtained the Prize Medal in the Exhibition of 1862. M. Rudolphi, also a principal exhibitor of silver work, has likewise obtained a Prize Medal for his grand show in the French Courts. Prize Medals have likewise been awarded to exhibitors of works in precious metals from Italy, Austria, Germany, Spain, and many other countries.

In the various objects exhibited by Messrs. Derry and Jones' firm, equally with those of Messrs. Benson and others, considerable taste and skill are displayed, not only in giving elegance of form and classic beauty of outline to the objects themselves, but also in adapting them to their several uses. The candelabra, tea services, salvers, goblets, &c., are produced both in silver and electro-plate; purchasers, therefore, who may not care to go to the expense of the silver, may

by the hammer, the silver plate being moved as required over bars of iron, or more properly speaking, small anvils. Skilful manipulation is here required. In order to produce more exactly these projections, or, if need be, to form indentations, the silver vessel is filled now with a composition of pitch and other ingredients. This allows of the administration of blows with punches on the exterior at particular points, without destroying other parts of the work. When the relief is fully modelled up, the finishing touches are given by the use of the graver. The pitch is next melted out and the inside is cleaned, and it may be gilt and burnished. This is a general way is the mode of producing *repoussé* work; but, of course, there are intricacies and niceties about the art which require skill, practice, and taste for their development.

Musical Instruments in the Exhibition.

PIANOS.

MANY and handsome—beautiful in appearance, and exquisite in tone—are the Pianos shown in the Musical Court of the Exhibition, close to the Central Avenue. The British exhibitors, as might be expected, show to great advantage, though there are many fine instruments in the foreign half of the building. Messrs. Broadwood, Collard, Kirkman, Brinsmead, Allison, and other of our first-class makers, have spared no pains to let all the world see how the pianoforte has improved from its old model, the virginal of the time of good Queen Bess.

Every day may be heard the tones of some of the best pianos in the Exhibition, as touched by the educated fingers of some among the best native and foreign performers. Of the many fine instruments, we have selected two for illustration: one for its fine tone as a box of music, the other principally for its admirably - designed case. Too much carelessness has been exhibited by makers in the form and ornamentation of the piano, which may now be really considered a peculiarly English musical instrument. In our first illustration we have the pianoforte exhibited by John Brinsmead, of 15, Charlotte Street, Fitzroy Square; with model of the action, and

PICOLO PIANO IN CARVED CASE. MR. JOHN BRINSMEAD. PRIZE MEDAL.

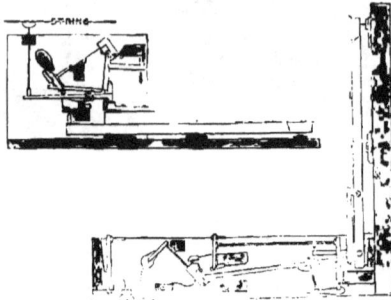

DIAGRAMS SHOWING THE ACTION OF MR. BRINSMEAD'S PIANO.

also a model of grand action on same principle—those patented by him in February last, with compensating tubulated backs.

Of the great improvements attained since 1851, this action stands pre-eminent. Its great advantages are—the most perfect check repeat hitherto discovered—the check acting with the slightest movement of the keys, which have attained that sensibility of touch

so much needed by the profession, and conveying from the performer to the hammer acting on the string all the delicacy of action of the finger expressing the feeling of the player, from the most powerful to the softest quality of tone.

In the escapement of this action, the hammer relieves itself from a block on the end of the key; the set-off and repeat being attained by one movement. Thus, the touch of the most rapid performer never fails to elicit a distinct note. Again, the lever and hopper being superseded in the mechanism of this action, the full force of the blow is transmitted direct from the string to the hammer; while, in the ordinary action, the sticker is hinged from the butt with leather, and connected with levers by leather clothing, the underside of the lever having a piece of box cloth, which forms an elastic cushion for the hopper to strike against. From the consequent and necessary interposition of these clothings, a portion of the power of the blow is absorbed; while, in this action, the sticker is connected with the butt by a bushed centre, resting on the adjusting block and the end of the key, and is the only medium from the hammer, thus gaining its superiority of power. In the construction of the case, iron supports are scientifically introduced in front of bracings, forming square abutments against metal plates from the bottom block, and bent side to the wrest or tuning-pins' plank, thereby rendering it impossible for the case to yield to the great pull of the string; carrying out a perfect compensating principle, and ensuring the instrument standing to one pitch, however variable the temperature of climate; as the iron supports in the front of the wood bracings and the strings contract or expand in the same proportion. Thus, we have in this instrument all the modern improvements combined with the principle patented by Mr. Brinsmead.

Our next illustration shows the beautiful carved oak piano exhibited by Messrs. Allison and Sons, of Wardour Street. This elegant and finely-toned instrument is designed in the prevailing style of Charles I., when the stiff and formal ornament of Elizabeth had given place to a more graceful and flowing outline.

The entire design is made in accordance with the purpose of the instrument—namely, the production of musical sounds. Kneeling angels, playing upon harps, form the brackets for the support of the keyboard. Busts of Jubal, Miriam, and David, with carved portraits of Handel, Haydn, and Mozart, on enriched panels, form the ends; the cheeks having busts of singing angels, surrounded with richly-carved foliage. The lower portion of the front has three perforated panels, enriched with armorial bearings, and the monogram of the owner, and is divided by two caryatide figures. The upper part is supported on each side by angels, cut in full relief, playing upon harps. Above are female figures, holding scrolls of music, which show the commencement of

"Gloria in Excelsis." The centre is divided into three panels by richly-carved semi-detached pillars beneath circular arches, the centre key of which is a bust of Her Majesty. The panels themselves are all richly carved, and in the centre is St. Cecilia playing upon a hand organ. In the side panels are angels holding scrolls in their hands, with the legend, "Glory to God in the highest, and on earth peace." In the spandrils of these two side compartments are portraits, carved in full relief, of eight of the various British warblers, the nightingale, skylark, treelark, robin, linnet, blackcap, bullfinch, and goldfinch. The spandrils of the arches contain cherubim. The cornice is also elaborately pierced, so that every means has been taken to insure the full emission of sound. The lower frieze is of foliage, with small birds, and monogram intertwined. The large upper one is a choir of twenty-seven angels, each playing upon a different musical instrument, from the earliest known example down to the most modern. The name-board is richly chased with ornamental devices, and the monogram of the owner is again introduced in relief. Wherever mouldings are required, they have been elaborately ornamented. The interior of the instrument has by no means been neglected, for three strings have been placed to each note, and the blow given by a new patent check escapement action. We understand that the value of this instrument is three hundred and fifty guineas.

Messrs. Allison also exhibit a fine pianoforte, in walnut-tree and gilt mouldings, with carved pillar truss, and the new patent check action. They likewise show their "Improved London Model" pianoforte in rosewood. This is one of their ordinary instruments, suitable for the school-room and boudoir. In the fret-front there are no fewer than 575 holes, and it has the patented back and wrest plank, with registered key board. The price of such a piece of music is, we believe, £30; and for general practice no better piano is needed.

A very curious and complicated affair is a piano. Its interior, to an uneducated eye, is a world of strings, and pedals, and strange-looking mechanism. The strings, stretched to the full amount of tension, give, we are told, a "pressure of several tons;" yet such is the ingenious arrangement of the machine, that the whole is brought into instant action by the slightest touch of a lady's finger.

Of the relative merits of the various beautiful instruments shown on the British side, it is quite impossible to pronounce any opinion; but if their interior arrangements are as good as their exterior embellishments—and the power of musical sound constantly heard in the Exhibition warrants this belief—why, then, we may well conclude that there is assembled at South Kensington a collection of the finest instruments in the world.

The strange names by which some of the pianos are known will surely puzzle a non-professional visitor. For instance, we find one cottage-piano described as a "tubulated," another as "equipollent," and a third as fitted with an anti-blocking hopper; while a "grand" is called a microchordon, and a "square" an "iron clipper plated," with propeller action. But all these have doubtless their peculiar excellences.

In the foreign half of the building there are some very fine specimens of pianos. Visitors who linger late in the evening are frequently attracted to the Austrian Court, by the sound of music, vocal and instrumental, which, by its soft and pleasant character, contrasts very favourably with the harmonic strife of the morning. The vocal portion of this entertainment is executed by Mr. Franz Holzhuber, an assistant to one of the Austrian exhibitors of iron work, and who, in the evening, when his work is done, sits down to one of the fine pianos from Vienna, and very soon collects an audience by his masterly way of singing those fine German songs, so little known in this country. This prevalence of musical accomplishment is, we find, a peculiarity of the Austrian department, as even the workmen have made the extramural refreshment houses they frequent quite popular, by their fine glee and chorus singing.

Another instrumental performer is Mr. Pohl, from a village in Bohemia, who has revived the public interest in the almost forgotten glass harmonica. This interesting instrument, which has all the dreamy sweetness of the Æolian harp, with the advantage of being under the control of a player, has a remarkable history attached to it. It was at first simply an arrangement of drinking-glasses, the credit of the invention being given, not inappropriately, by Dr. Franklin, to a Mr. Puckeridge, a gentleman from Ireland. This gentleman and his instrument were, unfortunately, burnt together, and the invention passed through many vicissitudes, until the time when we find two fashionable ladies astonishing the Vicar of Wakefield's family with their brilliant talk about "Shakespeare and the musical glasses," the latter being the Harmonica, alluded to by Dr. Franklin. It was subsequently condemned by the mad doctors of the period, on the ground that railway travelling is condemned by the mad doctors of our period, namely, that its music was dangerous to the mental health; and so it slumbered until now, when it turns up in a very complete form in the International Exhibition of 1862. Its wild, exceedingly sweet, and almost unearthly tones can be heard with great distinctness in the Austrian Court, of an evening, where Mr. C. F. Pohl, the exhibitor, may be found occasionally bringing out hymns and chorales, literally with "a wet finger," and with a most charming effect. The instrument consists of an axle, upon which are arranged in chromatic succession glasses of different sizes and colours, the successors of the primitive "tumblers" of the Irish inventor.

CARVED OAK PIANO. MESSRS. ALLISON AND SON.

Fine Arts in the Exhibition.—IV. Sculpture.

Having already expressed an opinion generally on the sculpture in the International Exhibition, we may now notice one or two of the more prominent groups exhibited by our own and foreign artists. In this page we introduce an engraving of a new work, which has on all hands been admitted a *chef-d'œuvre* of modern art. It is by Mr.

stood that "The Brother and Sister" are portraits. The design and general finish cannot fail to delight, not only artists and connoisseurs, but all who gaze upon the group. The form of the nude child and the texture of its flesh are almost perfect—if perfection be an admissible term in art—and contrast admirably with the breadth and

BROTHER AND SISTER—A GROUP IN MARBLE.   BY J. P. WOOLNER.

Woolner, a young sculptor, whose works would have made a much more decided impression on the public mind had he not been so injudiciously praised by his friends. This fine group in marble represents two young children, seated in a position at once tender, natural, and graceful. The work has been executed for Mr. T. Fairbairn, one of the Royal Commissioners, and it is generally under-

graceful flow of the drapery in the other figure. As a model of style, "The Brother and Sister" is certainly worthy of all praise, so perfect are the lines, and so pure the whole composition.".

Several works by the same artist are also exhibited. In portraiture he appears to particular advantage, as is evidenced by the busts of William Fairbairn, the father of the Royal Commissioner; Professor

Sedgwick, Rajah Brooke, Professor Maurice, and the Poet Laureate. In the model for the statue of Lord Bacon, erected in the new Museum at Oxford, we see Mr. Woolner to better advantage than in the busts. The only fear seems to be that the very excellence for which he is now praised may cause him so to repeat himself as to fall into the fatal gulf of mannerism, where so many young and promising artists have found a grave for their reputations.

Foley, Watson, and Woolner have been selected by a critic, who claims to understand and appreciate sculpture, as artists who have boldly renewed and consistently followed the severe style of the sculptors of classic times. Their works are truthful, dignified, and conscientious; earnest in expression, inventive in arrangement, and, withal, exhibiting that simple tenderness and finish in execution, without which marble hardly approaches the semblance of reality, be it elaborated never so carefully. Much of what we admire in sculpture we admire because we have been taught to reverence the antique. A figure which, therefore, is built up from recollections of the master-pieces of Greece and Rome—a posé borrowed from this great work, and a thought from that, an expression from some famous group in the Vatican or the Louvre, and a method of imitating, rather than initiating, natural style and original manner—such a figure passes muster, and is at once taken to be a great work. Such was the judgment passed on Powers' "Greek Slave;" and such is the tone of approval with which the "Cleopatra" of another American artist, Mr. Storey, is everywhere greeted. Not, however, that this work is destitute of merit; on the contrary, it is very fine. But it is not original. It, with many other statues shown in the Roman Court, is but a reflection of the antique. The genius that wakes up an answering fire in the breast of the gazer is not apparent in the sculptured marble. In order to attract attention, some sculptors, again, have recourse to means hardly admissible within the region of high art. But for the exquisite method of manipulation—the real, indisputable genius in the works of Gibson—it is at least doubtful whether his tinted statues would have been so warmly appreciated. But when a sculptor descends to certain tricks of art—such, for instance, as covering the face of a statue with a thin marble veil, through which all the features are distinctly visible; or throwing an artificial light upon it: both of which artifices have been resorted to by Mr. Raphael Monti—then, we think, we may fairly regret the necessity for such modes of appealing to public sympathy.

Nevertheless, thousands will admire the "Veiled Nun," and the "Lady in the Turkish Harem." But that proves only that thousands are not educated up to the mark when appreciation of the beautiful and the true in art calls for no such adventitious aids to popularity.

Of an altogether different style of art—truer and more natural, and appealing more directly to every man's and every woman's nature—is "The Grapplers," exhibited in the Foreign Nave, just opposite the Swedish Court, and represented on page 108. This spirited group is a representation of two men strapped together after the old Runic fashion of duelling, and fighting to the death with knives. The story of the fatal encounter, from its first outbreak to the widow weeping before the uncouth Runic stone, that marks the grave of husband and lover, is simply but forcibly told in bas-relief, beneath the groups, some of which are literally copied from the old Runic originals. These fine statues are cast in zinc, bronzed over, and, even allowing for some slight faults, which are probably due to the metal itself, the whole group is beyond a doubt the most spirited and life-like in the building. The practice of thus coupling antagonists has long been known to the modern nations; and the tradition of the muscular duel, here pictured in bronze, is almost as familiar to the Danes, Swedes, and Norwegians as our story of "St. George and the Dragon" is to our own British youth. The men engaged in this mortal struggle are first seen, in the sculptured narrative around the base, drinking together. The next stage is a quarrel, caused by some familiarity on the part of one of them with the betrothed wife of his companion. She is then seen endeavouring to prevent their encounter; and lastly, we find her plunged in grief, and prostrate before a Runic stone, on

which is sculptured a rude representation of the youths struggling together. This is, indeed, a fine group, natural, vivid, and life-like.

We may just glance at a few of the works which visitors cannot fail to notice with approbation. The "Giotto as seen by Cimabue" is a good and conscientious work, by Mr. Ambuchi. Every one recollects the "Eagle Slayer" of John Bell, which in 1851 stood in bronze, under the Coalbrook Dale dome, in the middle of the wonderful glass nave. Well, there is the original statue in marble; together with the "Dorothea heads," so familiar to the public by means of Copeland's statuette. Then we have the "Sabrina " of Cardwell, in marble, pure and lovely; the "Cupid caught Flying," of Davis; the "Titania Asleep," watched by a Fairy," by Earle; the "Lions and Lionesses" of Gatley, whose fine bas-relief of "Pharaoh and his Army in the Red Sea " will be found in the Central Avenue; the "Venus," "Pandora," and "Cupid," of Gibson, in the new style of tinted statuary. The busts of Brougham, Palmerston, Clarendon, and Carlisle, by Jones; the "Clie " of Lawler; the "Comus" of Lough; the "Day Dream," exquisite in thought and amazing in execution, of Macdowell; the "Paolo and Francesca," from the entrancing "Story of Rimini," by Munro; the "Purity" of Noble; the "Young Emigrant " of Papworth; the "First Mirror" of Sharp; the "Bard " and the " Prodigal's Return " of Theed; the "Skipping Girl " of Mrs. Thornycroft; the "Boys struggling for Grapes," by Tarupp; the "Peri" of Westmacott, and the "Britomart," from Spenser's "Faerie Queene " of Wyon—all works that will carry the fame of our British sculptors farther and farther, and sustain their reputation for originality of design and integrity of treatment, even when compared with the best works of foreign artists. France may well be proud of her sculptors: for who can gaze on her "Napoleon" of Louis Rochet, the "Cornelia" of Cavelier, the "Theseus" of Barye, or the "Meditation" of Bonnassieux, without acknowledging the great merit of these designers?

The Italian and Roman Courts are places of delight for all who take interest in works of sculpture. But for these, and the German and other foreign schools, we must delay our examination. The beautiful groups, busts, single figures, and bas-so-relieves, shown in the foreign courts, cannot be dismissed in a paragraph. We would, however, just draw attention to a pair of bronzes, by Hebert, one representing "Faust and Margaret," and the other "Romeo and Juliet." The figures are well treated, especially those of Margaret and Romeo, and the costume is managed without stiffness. A pair of figures, representing "Paul and Virginia," are also very gracefully modelled, especially the heads, which, by the way, are repeated in a pair of busts, and show thus the grace and purity of their design, to much better advantage. A figure of "Columbus," seated and surrounded with nautical accessories, is remarkable for its vigour and simplicity, the attitude and the expression of the countenance both admirably expressive of calm and dignified confidence. A companion figure of "Galileo" poring over a globe is nearly as good. A very fine group, life-size, of "Boys with a Swan," in the French Court, is scarcely to be distinguished from bronze. Two figures of the same metal, silvered, with gilt ornaments, and representing two "Varlets" in the costume of the pages in the Maximilian procession, are remarkable for the swaggering boldness of their attitudes, and the care and finish of every detail in the costume. They are designed by Salmson, who has a special celebrity for these moyen âge varlets. By far the finest, as it is the most expensive, display of cast bronzes in the French Court is that of Barbédienne, who stands pre-eminent in his profession. His platform is laden with copies of all sizes of many of the finest works of sculpture, ancient and modern, remarkable equally for their fidelity to the originals in form and proportion, and in every minute detail of expression. The small copies are produced by a mechanical process of reduction. Of a very high quality in art, though different in treatment from any we have already noticed, are the animal designs of Julius Hachnel, of Schmiedeng, in Prussia. Distinct, says a critic, as are these works in subject, there is a greatness and a grace about them, which raises his work to an excellence, within its sphere, not inferior to that of the 'Arthur and Constance.' The Giraffe in her stateliness, the Lion in his strength and his repose, have been rendered in no extant sculpture with a truth and insight like Haelmel's. The works of such men, whenever we meet them, supply more or less a measure of what serious sculpture can reach. Let us hope that spectators, comparing excellence in modern art with real life, and then again with what has been done by master-artists of old, will gradually learn to praise and encourage such work alone as agrees with the one and only standard – Nature. Give us but this, and sculpture will soon follow the brighter fortunes of painting.

Furniture and Decoration.—V.

WE again recur to a class of subjects that cannot but possess considerable interest for all home-loving people—namely, domestic furniture and decoration. We have already referred to the mediæval and Gothic forms of furniture, now so popular; and in another page expressed regret that so few articles capable, from their high price, of oak, walnut, ebony, and gold. In the upper part are two life-size figures of Vintage and Harvest; between them an oval frame, containing a mirror, but designed to receive a painting (if required), trophies of fruit, corn, &c., are introduced. The lower part is supported by figures of boys on pedestals; the central panels are

LIBRARY TABLE IN OAK. MR. THOMAS KNIGHT.

being admitted within the doors of ordinary people, are exhibited. But there are a few shown in the British side of the building, which are at once excellent and economical in cost, and of first-rate description—admirable in design, perfect in workmanship, and entirely adapted to their several uses.

Our first illustration shows us a LIBRARY TABLE, exhibited by Mr. Thomas Knight, of George Street, Bath. This table is of oak and ebony, surmounted by a cabinet occupying its whole length, containing drawers on either side, and a desk in the centre, which, when shut, forms an ornamental panel, with malachite, lapis lazuli, cornelian, and serpentine; and when open, discloses an arrangement of the materials necessary for correspondence; just such a table, in fact, as a diplomatist might sit in front of, and take a pride in, but for the possession of which an ordinary author might sigh in vain. The same gentleman has also a chair, in ebony, covered with silk, in the style of Louis XV., a most desirable and elegant piece of furniture.

Mr. James Lamb, of Manchester, shows a fine sideboard, in pollard arranged to form one connected relievo of game, fish, &c. Groups of fruit and vegetables fill the carved end panels. Designed by W. J. Estall; modelled by Hugues Protat.

Mr. Lamb also exhibits dining-room chairs, in embossed and gilt morocco leather; and a marqueterie cabinet, of Thurgau and other woods, in the style of Louis XVI.

We have incidentally alluded to the show of excellent furniture from the well-known establishment of Messrs. Heal and Son, of Tottenham Court Road. We have now an opportunity of presenting to our readers pictures of the objects themselves. They consist of a BEDSTEAD, WARDROBE, and TOILET TABLE, with GLASS, designed especially for the firm by an eminent draughtsman, in the style of the period of Louis XVI. The whole of the articles are made of mahogany, enamelled in pure pearl white; the ornaments are principally foliage and tracery, in carved wood, and gilded. The furniture for the bedstead, and the eider down quilt that covers it, are made of rich silk damask, of cerise colour, lined with white silk; and

THE GRAPPLERS—A GROUP IN BRONZED ZINC. BY JEAN PETER MOLIN, SWEDEN.

the decorations are also of white pearl-work, with the exception of the head-cloth, which is of rich white silk, embroidered in colour to correspond with the curtains.

has been engaged in the decorative part of the work, the object of the exhibitors being to produce articles of domestic furniture which should combine elegance of design and the highest class of art manu-

MAHOGANY BEDSTEAD.   MESSRS. HEAL AND SON.

The TOILET TABLE is quite unique in design, with a looking-glass in the centre, and cases on either side for the brushes, jewellery, &c., necessary to the proper adornment of a modern English lady. The WARDROBE is in like style, carved and gilt. The best available talent

facture with a simplicity of style and effect, which should render them suitable for a nobleman's or a gentleman's mansion. It may also be mentioned that these goods were designed and manufactured entirely by Englishmen. Messrs. Heal and Son would, we think, have done well to have shown some of the cheaper descriptions of furniture, for which their house is so justly celebrated. We understand that it was their original intention to have done so, but that they found the space awarded them quite insufficient for their purpose. It is not, therefore, surprising that they exhibit the more expensive, if not the more useful and available, of the articles they manufacture.

The specimens of ORMOLU, shown on page 112, are from the case of Mr. S. Wertheimer, of New Bond Street. This gentleman makes a fine show; the cabinet, *étagères*, and council table being really handsome evidences of what is daily accomplished by our great manu-

In all parts of the Exhibition is seen this desire to be first in each particular branch of trade or manufacture; and it speaks well for Great Britain, that the jurors, though composed partly of foreigners, have awarded so many prizes among her exhibitors. In the furniture and decorative classes, this is especially observable.

The last engraving we have in this section of the EXHIBITOR represents a library table, in the Pompeian style, by Messrs. Howard and Co., of Berners Street, who also show a book-case, and various other articles similarly decorated. The ornamental work introduced into the decoration of these pieces of furniture is all carved below the

TOILET TABLE. MESSRS. HEAL AND SON.

facturers. The articles in ormolu, grouped together in the engraving —candlesticks, inkstands, and work-box—are elaborately decorated with figures in parian, coloured and otherwise ornamented. The amount of ingenuity, contrivance, and arrangement expended upon furniture is scarcely conceivable. The most common objects of domestic utility have, of late years, been made ornamental. Tables, couches, chairs, &c., have received a degree of attention hitherto unthought of. Mechanical difficulties in the production of elegance have been successfully overcome, as we see in the instance of Mr. Wertheimer's ormolu articles; and the introduction of woods, marbles, metals, &c., of various colours into domestic appliances, is evidence sufficient of the determination of our manufacturers not to be outrun in the race of excellence.

general surface of the object, so as to preserve the delicate work from the effect of friction. The more prominent ornaments are gilt bronzes, of English manufacture. The workmanship is of the highest class. This fact may be tested "by the drawers within the pedestals of the table being turned in any way, when they will be found to fit with the nicest accuracy." We quote the latter sentence from the exhibitors' own description; and we understand that the jurors did actually so test the assertion. But it would, perhaps, be dangerous for ordinary visitors to accept the invitation. Drawers *might* fall and be broken, and then a conscientious public would doubtless blame itself.

A suit of bedroom furniture, in polished deal, with imitation marqueterie and inlaid work, by Messrs. Dyer and Walls, of Islington, will well bear examination. They are among the very few articles of furniture intended for middle-class purchasers.

Messrs. Filmer and Son, of Berners Street, have some excellent furniture in Class XXX. Among other articles is a circular extending dining-table, of fine English pollard oak, the framework of Italian design, with scroll supports, ornamented with festoons of fruit, &c. It is manufactured on a novel plan, to open to an increased diameter by an extension of the framework, the top being preserved entire, and quarter-circle leaves introduced in several series round the circumference, thus preserving at all sizes the perfect circle. The movement of this table combines extreme simplicity with the utmost certainty of action; it is fitted with a screw and cog mechanism (by Hawkins), by the operation of which the whole framework is expanded simul-

forming two easy chairs and two settees, which are constructed to fit together, and can be formed into a complete and elegant centre seat.

We have already referred to the fine buffet shown by Messrs. Jackson and Graham, and the furniture shown by Messrs. Jallow and Messrs. Holland. We have only, therefore, to draw attention to the furniture of a few other exhibitors. Messrs. Litchfield and Radclyffe, of Hanway Street, Oxford Street, show, among many other noticeable objects, a carved ebony and ivory upright cabinet on stand, inclosed by doors, inlaid with cornelians, marble in columns, plinths, &c., the inside lined with silvered glass, and decorated with groups, and fine specimens of Sèvres, Dresden, Berlin, Vienna, &c., from their large collections of most of the European porcelains.

Mr. Walter McFarlane, of Glasgow, shows a fine OAK BOOK-CASE

WARDROBE. MESSRS. HEAL AND SON.

taneously; the leaves being placed, are all fastened by the same means at once, thus enabling one person, without assistance, and in a few minutes, to arrange a table sufficiently large to dine thirty or forty people.

Two pollard oak dining-room chairs, of Italian design, with stuffed panelled backs, covered with morocco leather to accord with the table, and an easy chair to match, are also shown by this firm.

An easy chair, the frame carved in walnut wood; the back arranged with an oscillating spring, combining the comfort of an ordinary lounge with the pleasant motion of a rocking-chair, will attract attention. Notice also the movable convertible ottoman for the centre of rooms, richly carved in the style of Louis XVI., the ground-work finished in white enamel, with mat and burnished gold relief; covered with rich figured silk. This ottoman is made in four separate parts,

with brass mountings. This piece of furniture is designed with a boldly projecting base, above which it is divided into five compartments, enriched with moulded baffets, enriched with a band of holly berries. Over each division shields of varied designs support semi-circular panelled tablets in line with and breaking upon the cornice. These are to be surmounted with bronze busts of celebrated men; the tablets contain the name, whilst the date of birth and death are inscribed on the shields below; the two centre shields bear family monograms. All the letters are of bronze, and in design characteristic of the different periods in which they lived. A curved pediment crowns the centre compartment, the tympanum of which is occupied by the exhibitor's crest in bronze. A bust of the Queen is to be placed on the pediment; and above the cornice is a light bronze cresting. The doors are fitted in with glass, and have crank handles of an elaborate

spiral form, with serpents outward. The hinges have projecting barrels of similar design, all in bronze. The details
have been studied with due regard to the nature of the
materials, the object aimed at being to combine truth, fit-

for drawings and prints, and the case is so arranged as
to serve also as a portfolio rest. . . . .
woods; the panels painted by Messrs. M . . . . Marsh . .
and Co., illustrating the . . . .

SPECIMENS OF ORMOLU. MR. S. WERTHEIMER. PRIZE MEDAL.

ness, and beauty with a certain degree of expressiveness and individuality. The wood work is by Robert White and Son, Glasgow; the
bronze crest and letters by Messrs. Elkington, of Birmingham, the

letters by King R . . . .
house Sculptor by th . . . .
. . by th . . . . the same . . . .

LIBRARY TABLE IN THE POMPEIAN STYLE. MESSRS. HOWARD AND SON. PRIZE MEDAL.

other bronze work is of Glasgow manufacture. Mr. Thomas Seddon
shows various articles of furniture, executed from designs by Messrs.
Pritchard and Seddon, architects. Among these is a case of shelves

celebrate its completion; and in the upper panels are represented in
of ornamental carving, metal work, embroidery, weaving, stained glass,
and mosaic work."

The Contributions of Rome to the International Exhibition.

ROME, in the Exhibition, occupies a position similar to that which she has politically—behind Italy, and under the wing of France. In the World's Show, however, her place is prominent, by reason not only of the productions of her own subjects, but of those who range artistically under her banner. The entrance to the Roman Court, from the nave, is through the passage between Italy and Spain; but from the south door in the Cromwell Road the visitor passes at once into the middle avenue, and hardly pausing to admire the Royal group, by Durham,

Indian corn and other cereals from the Pontine marshes; an oil mill, and various tools for gardeners; a few guns and other weapons; some exquisite photographs; various articles in silk fabrics, embroidered stuffs suitable for priestly robes, &c.; lace made by prisoners, and tapestry worked in the hospital of St. Michael; two or three beautiful specimens of bookbinding; a large number of articles in imitation of lapis lazuli, malachite, porphyry, alabaster, &c., such as tables, pavements, and inlaid work; a few scissor- and razors; some Roman pearls

STATUARY IN THE ROMAN COURT.

finds himself amid the exquisite sculpture shown by the exhibitors who date their letters from the Eternal City.

In what is called the "Industrial" part of her display, Rome appears by about fifty exhibitors, in eighteen classes. The Pope himself is an exhibitor, with Cardinal Wiseman, the Minister of Commerce, the Società Romana, and others. Calcareous stones and argillaceous earths for the construction of artificial marbles; lava, bricks, cement, and other building materials; potash, salt, and alum;

and ornaments made from them; bronzed lamps, reliquaries, breviaries, tazze, and a model or two of parts of St. Peter's—these are objects by which Rome holds her own in the commercial and industrial display. But in sculpture she is pre-eminent.

The Roman Court possesses great interest for all who can appreciate the wonderful charm and power exercised upon the mind by sculptured forms. The tinted statuary of our English sculptor, Gibson, provokes endless discussion among spectators. The "Cupid" is a very

15.

spiral form, with serpents entwined. The images have projecting bezels of similar design, all in bronze. The details
have been studied with due regard to the nature of the
materials, the object aimed at being to combine truth, lit-

for drawings and prints, suitable for a library, workdesks
to serve also as a portfolio rest, . . inlaid with various
woods; the panels painted by Messrs. Morris, Marshall,
and Co., illustrating the fine arts as follows:—"*Archi-*

SPECIMENS OF ORMOLU. MR. S. WERTHEIMER. PRIZE MEDAL.

ness, and beauty with a certain degree of expressiveness and individuality. The wood work is by Robert White and Son, Glasgow: the
bronze crest and letters by Messrs. Elkington, of Birmingham; the

tecture, by King René and his Queen, considering the de-
house : *Sculpture,* by the same, ... *Pse-
ing,* by the same, decorating its walls. M . . . by the same, . . .

LIBRARY TABLE IN THE POMPEIAN STYLE. MESSRS. HOWARD AND SON. PRIZE MEDAL.

other bronze work is of Glasgow manufacture. Mr. Thomas Seddon
shows various articles of furniture, executed from designs by Messrs.
Pritchard and Seddon, architects. Among these is a case of shelves

celebrate its completion; and in the upper panels are representations
of ornamental carving, metal work, embroidery, weaving, stained glass,
and mosaic work."

The Contributions of Rome to the International Exhibition.

ROME, in the Exhibition, occupies a position similar to that which she has politically—behind Italy, and under the wing of France. In the World's Show, however, her place is prominent, by reason not only of the productions of her own subjects, but of those who range artistically under her banner. The entrance to the Roman Court, from the nave, is through the passage between Italy and Spain; but from the south door in the Cromwell Road the visitor passes at once into the middle avenue, and hardly pausing to admire the Royal group, by Durham,

Indian corn and other cereals from the Pontine marshes; an oil mill, and various tools for gardeners; a few guns and other weapons; some exquisite photographs; various articles in silk fabrics, embroidered stuffs suitable for priestly robes, &c.; lace made by prisoners, and tapestry worked in the hospital of St. Michael; two or three beautiful specimens of bookbinding; a large number of articles in imitation of lapis lazuli, malachite, porphyry, alabaster, &c., such as tables, pavements, and inlaid work; a few scissors and razors; some Roman pearls

STATUARY IN THE ROMAN COURT.

finds himself amid the exquisite sculpture shown by the exhibitors who date their letters from the Eternal City.

In what is called the "Industrial" part of her display, Rome appears by about fifty exhibitors, in eighteen classes. The Pope himself is an exhibitor, with Cardinal Wiseman, the Minister of Commerce, the Società Romano, and others. Calcareous stones and argillaceous earths for the construction of artificial marbles; lava, bricks, cement, and other building materials; potash, salt, and alum;

and ornaments made from them; bronzed lamps, reliquaries, breviaries, tazze, and a model or two of parts of St. Peter's—these are objects by which Rome holds her own in the commercial and industrial display. But in sculpture she is pre-eminent.

The Roman Court possesses great interest for all who can appreciate the wonderful charm and power exercised upon the mind by sculptured forms. The tinted statuary of our English sculptor, Gibson, provokes endless discussion among spectators. The "Cupid" is a very

15.

pretty child, and the "Venus" a very lovely woman. Much has been heard of the statue which Mr. Gibson has coloured very, very slightly, and has gifted with a pair of gold ear-rings. It is a sweet figure, and (says a public writer) we are not so bold as to express timidity on the delicate point which must be raised as soon as absolute and pure form is invaded by painting. Submit Mr. Gibson's Venus to the crucial test of comparison with the untinted marble statues in the same court, and it is hard to say that his is the least pure. The attitude is exquisitely graceful, and the significance of the Venus de Medici is carried out by the position in which this modern goddess gathers up the folds of her white drapery with one hand, while with the other she holds the golden apple. A peculiarity is noticeable about her throat, which is crossed by slight wrinkles, or, as one might say, ripples, by way of rendering the uglier word in a very subdued sense. This is considered by Italian judges to be a beauty; and perhaps when Mr. Gibson is at Rome, he not only does as they do there, but thinks as they think.

The position of the various noticeable pieces of statuary and other works of art in the Roman Court, will be best shown by a diagram.

she grew up, their feelings of enmity against the white man, and conducted herself in all respects as became an Indian maiden. With bow and arrow, and scalping-knife, she was a terror wherever she went. At last she was taken and brought a captive in the very house of her parents, of whom she knew nothing but as enemies. But her mother happening to sing a song that had hushed her babe to sleep, the old air came like a revelation upon the startled ear of the maiden, and woke up the slumbering memories of forgotten childhood. In the sculpture she is represented listening to the song of her mother—memory and old affection struggling in her countenance.

"Love Captive," by Engell; "Zephyr and Flora," by Ives; and the "Fortune Teller," by Guglielmo, are all fine examples of modern sculpture. Near the entrance of the Court from the Central Avenue is a bust of Cardinal Wiseman; and towards the centre a mosaic gothic table, carved out of a single block of Carrara white marble, and inlaid with mosaics. The top is inlaid with rose antique, malachite, and lapis lazuli, and upon it, in small medallions, are represented objects of the chase, the centre being left for the arms of the purchaser.

ITALY.

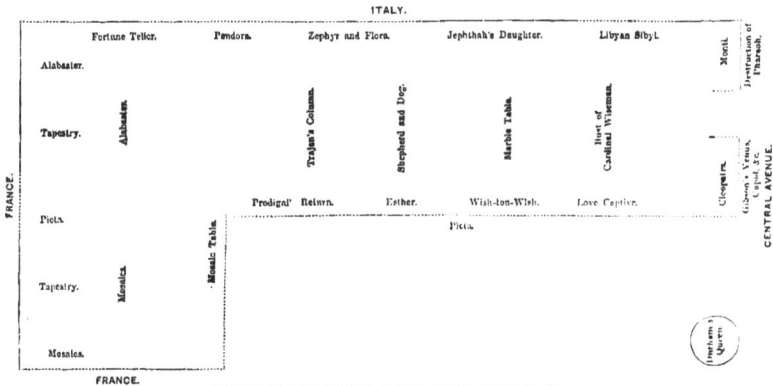

POSITION OF THE PRINCIPAL OBJECTS IN THE ROMAN COURT.

Next in attractive interest amongst sculptures, are the "Cleopatra" and "Sibyl" of Mr. Storey, an American artist. There is none of the conventional and voluptuous beauty about the "Cleopatra." The form and features, though handsome, are of purely Egyptian type, and the expression of the face is one of thought and intellectual power. Both the face and figure of the "Sibyl" are grandly suggestive of the moody abstraction of one really possessed of the powers of divination, looking gloomily forward in the long chapter of human woes.

As, in the Hyde Park Exhibition of 1851, the "Broken Drum" became one's favourite, so the "Shepherd and his Dog" achieves great popularity. A boy offers a piece of bread to his dog, and suddenly draws his hand away; the dog bounds and barks, and it is this moment which the sculptor has fixed. The group tells its own tale—the laughing boy, the eager dog, and the accessories. Every one will understand it, and so marvellous and expressive is the execution that every one will admire. It is the work of a young sculptor, Mulpieri, but he will not be for long an unknown one.

Four statues by Mozier, another American artist studying at Rome, attract great attention—"Esther," the "Wept of Wish-ton-Wish," "Jephthah's Daughter," and "Ruth"—all works of great merit. The Wish-ton-Wish is the name of a valley in which the Puritan Fathers settled; and the "Wept One" was a child stolen from her parents by the Indians. Dwelling among the savages, she shared, as

The foot, also of Carrara marble, has groups of soldiers, in the costume of the Middle Ages, clustered about it. Signor Monachesi is said to have been eleven years engaged in producing this magnificent specimen of modern mosaic. Other tables, of like character, will also be looked upon with interest, especially one intended as a present to her Majesty the Queen, from his Holiness the Pope. The pietà by Giacometti, —the Madonna, Magdalen, and St. John, bending over the body of the Saviour—holds the place of honour in this Court; while at the front and at the side are other pietas—that in the front by Schubert, and that on the other side by Achtermann, an artist so famous for this class of work, that he is known in Rome as the Christaro (the "Christ Maker"). Galley's wonderful bas-relief of the "Destruction of Pharaoh and his Host" is one of those works on which a volume might be written, and still something may be left unsaid; it is so full of suggestion, so admirable in conception, and so perfect in execution.

In the Picture Gallery Rome shows well, and the artists cannot but gain largely in the world's estimation from the works there exhibited. In the paintings of the foreign schools we notice the absence of the very qualities which we in England consider indispensable to success, namely, lightness of treatment and purity of atmospheric effect; but in subjects of genre character—interiors with figures, &c.—many of the Italian pictures will bear comparison with the best of those by our own artists.

Machinery in Motion.—I.

THE WESTERN ANNEXE is a place of great attraction for all those visitors to the Exhibition who go to learn rather than to lounge—for the Shillings, in fact, rather than the Season Tickets.

Of the immense variety of objects of interest in this department it is, however, almost impossible to present anything like a general idea; for what information beyond that contained in the catalogue should we convey, if we were to say that in the Western Annexe there were locomotive and marine engines; machine tools; woodworking tools; papermaking machines; cotton-spinning machinery; silk-throwing and spinning machinery; vacuum pans and sugar-mills; steam-engines, looms, corn mills; steam cranes, hydraulic machinery, centrifugal pumps, ice-making machines, printing machines, paper-cutters, and steam-hammers? We fancy that a rather hazy and confused notion is conveyed by a paragraph informing the reader that in the Western Annexe will be found engine and boiler fittings, including tubes and trap-work of all kinds; furnaces and furnace-bars; smoke-consumers; traction-engines; steam-engines; washing, wringing, and mangling machines; railway carriages and wagons, railway wheels and axles, railway gates, turn-tables, and traverses; fire-engines; flour and other mills; driving bands; bread-making machinery, pressure gauges; brewers' and confectioners' machines; beer-engines and fountains; double-action refrigerators, for brewing and distilling; boilers and cowl; copper and brass work; quartz-crushing machines; silk and flour-dressing machines; steam and vacuum gauges and salometers; telegraphs; indicators; brick-making machines; rotary engines; needle-making apparatus; Jacquard looms; fire-engines, and steam-engines for making iced waters.

Nor do we get a much clearer idea of the vastness, the importance, the value, and the interest of the Western Annexe and its varied contents, when we say that the inquiring visitor may examine for himself the curious processes in manufactures belonging to many interesting trades—steel-pen makers, pin and needle-makers, button-makers, medal-strikers, gold chain manufacturers, engine-turners for watches, type-casters, type-printers, lithographic and copper-plate printers, earthenware and porcelain-printers, potters, brick and drain-tile makers, glass-blowers, turners in metal, ivory, and wood; glove-makers, pillow-lace makers, and wood-carvers. We have said but so many words, conveying so many separate ideas, it is true, but not distinctly or vividly. The writer can but assist the mind of the reader to realise a word-picture; and, in respect of description, is much less favoured than the draughtsman, whose art allows him to present the picture itself. When, however, picture and written description are combined, there is less difficulty in producing a satisfactory train of thought. This great advantage belongs especially to illustrated literature. However

1.—PLATE LATHE, SELF-ACTING.

2.—MUIR'S EIGHT-INCH FOOT LATHE.

vivid the "word-picture" may be, it is infinitely inferior to the poorest wood-engraving in conveying a clear notion of a strange or unfamiliar object. To say of a watch, for instance, that it is a combination of wheels moved by a concealed spring, producing motion in the hands on the dial, is but to present a jargon of words, to him who never saw a watch; while but to show to the eye of a savage or a child the picture of a watch-face, with its hands pointing to the hours and minutes, is to produce on the mind of that savage or that child a distinct and ineffaceable impression. What ordinary objects in domestic use are to savages and children, machinery and machine processes are to the general public - the mass, the million, the people!

This brings us at once to our subject. Instead of attempting a "word-picture" of the Western Annexe as a whole, we prefer to present representations of some of its more important contents. But it will be necessary, in order to assist the reader's comprehension of this most interesting portion of the International Building, that we should preface our remarks by a short account of the Annexe itself.

Briefly, then, the Machinery Department is substantially fitted up to provide steam-power and the means of transport for heavy materials. A single line of railway runs from end to end on each side; six double-flue boilers, 30 feet by 6½ feet in diameter, are built in at the north end, communicating with a chimney 75 feet high, which has a diameter of 10 feet at the base. Two hundred elegant iron columns, of the Doric order, have been raised at intervals 10

3.—SELF-ACTING RADIAL DRILLING MACHINE.

feet apart, and 10 feet high above the floor, supporting 2,000 feet of shafting, 2½ inches in diameter. Two thousand feet of steam-pipe, having a graduated diameter from fifteen to eight inches, are laid down in a bricked subway, or pipe culvert, side by side with 2,000 feet of exhaust-pipe, 18 inches in diameter.

In this department many of the very heavy goods were delivered, and were unloaded by two travelling steam cranes, capable of lifting five tons each. The steam-power supplied here is from 400 to 500 horses; and two pumps are placed in this Annexe to work the two great French fountains exhibited in the Horticultural Gardens. There is also a travelling crane, capable of lifting 2½ tons, in two twelves. The largest steam cranes are in the French section, where

two are exhibited, of 60-horse power each. With this preface, we may at once proceed to examine the

MANUFACTURING TOOLS

EXHIBITED BY MESSRS. WILLIAM MUIR AND CO., BRITANNIA WORKS, MANCHESTER.

These consist of Lathes, Drilling Machines, Shaping Machines, Slotting and Planing Grindstone Apparatus, and Screw Stock and Screw Tackle; together with a couple of patent improved Copying Presses. It is almost needless to say that Messrs. Muir have been awarded a "Prize Medal."

Fig. 1 shows Muir's Self-acting twelve-inch centre Duplex Lathe for sliding and screw-cutting—headless geared head-stock, with wrought-iron steel mandril, running in hardened cast steel conical bearings, guide at the screw the foot of the foot and the patent self-acting screw bearers, held 25 feet long, with slide bars, clamp now and now tree, rack and pinion for quick return by hand, the slide rest having two bottom motions for driving back to fast slides. The machine also possesses a facility versing motion for changing right to left hand, and also cutting work and changing the side of which there twenty-two feet. This lathe is especially adapted for cutting screws expeditiously and for other turning-work in general, especially for preparing the parts of these machines—headstocks, &c.

Fig. 2 is a representation of a foot-lathe with two treadles, and useful for screw-cutting, &c. This lathe is designed particularly for use on board steam-ships, where the want of a screw at the right moment might endanger the safety of the vessel. For the colonies and India, where wages are low and steam-power is not always readily obtainable, this lathe is found especially adapted. A workman and an assistant are able to produce with a lathe of this description as much work as will ordinary steam-power lathes of like capacity.

Fig. 3 is a Powerful Self-Acting Radial Drilling Machine, with vertical elevating slide, radial arm, movable throughout an arc of 180 degrees, to drill holes up to 10 inches diameter. This machine is particularly adapted for drilling ends of boiler plates, large cylinders, and all work of a massive character, as it can take in an object 9 feet high,

All holes within range of the machine can be drilled without removing the object.

Fig. 4 is a Central Duplex Lathe, of similar capacity to that shown in the first figure.

Fig. 5 is a Self-Acting Slotting and Shaping Machine, with a variable stroke up to 6 inches. It will take a wheel 3 feet in diameter, and has self-acting transverse and circular motions.

Fig. 6 is a Self-acting Vertical Double-geared Drilling Machine, with circular revolving table, on a radial bracket, which can be raised or lowered on a vertical slide, by means of a worm-wheel, so that when the work is once fixed, a hole can be drilled on any part of it without moving it. This drill is provided with a hardened steel back-nut, which entirely prevents any back-lash in the spindle.

Fig. 7 is Muir's Universal Shaping Machine, with a variable stroke from half an inch up to six inches. This machine will plane an object two feet long, or circular work of twelve inches in diameter; and can be changed to plane round, hollow, or flat surfaces, without re-fixing the article operated upon.

Full justice cannot be done to these and other machines of like character without minute examination. To see how shavings of cold iron are curled away under the plane like ribbon, how slices of iron are cut like cheese, and how particles of steel fall like so much sawdust from the tireless drills; to see with what ease and strict regularity every portion of the machine does its work, and to know that without such appliances as these we could have no railways, no iron bridges, no Crystal Palaces—in fact, none of those large engineering works in which iron is largely employed; to witness the means and to think of the ends to which such means are indispensable, we must go to the Exhibition, the greatest school in the world. In throwing a glance over the magnificent display of machinery to be found in the Western Annexe, it is impossible to avoid being struck with the progress made, even in the short period which has elapsed since 1851. This is evinced by the number of contributors and the excellence of the specimens exhibited, both by Englishmen and foreigners. And though the arrangement of this department was attended with great labour and difficulty, on account of the ponderous nature of the articles, and other circumstances, it is worthy of remark that it was the most complete of any on the opening day, so earnest were the contributors in their endeavours to have everything in as perfect order as possible, that the noble specimens of their ingenuity and skill might be seen in the most favourable circumstances. The last International Exhibition was well calculated to astonish the reflecting observer; but engineering science has since then hurried onward with giant steps. If, however, we look on this occasion for absolutely new inventions, we shall scarcely succeed in finding them. New inventions are but rarely made in machinery; and, though it would not be reasonable to suppose that nothing is left to be invented by future research, we are to look for the results of successful ingenuity rather in the improvement or the perfection of what has been already devised, or in giving to it a greater power or a wider range of usefulness, than in the suggestion of any combinations which have never been thought of before. In this sense we shall find abundant matter for the gratification of our curiosity or the increase of our knowledge; immense marine engines and locomotives, most complete in every detail; powerful lathes, drilling and shaping machines, steam-hammers, and steam-cranes; castings and forgings of unprecedented magnitude—numberless ingenious and powerful mechanisms, meet us at every turn, and almost overwhelm ordinary minds with their vastness, their seeming complication, and their wonderful capabilities. The eye unaccustomed to examine the productions of skill and science is, on such an occasion, rather dazzled than instructed; and however the uninitiated may admire what he sees, he can derive but little improvement from it, unless accompanied in his rambles through this maze of wonders by some friendly guide, who may select for him what is most worthy of his notice, and explain the most remarkable properties and details. Such a guide the ILLUSTRATED EXHIBITOR seeks to become. We shall, therefore, return, from time to time, to the Western Annexe, and explain, by pen and pencil, some of the numerous wonders and mechanical novelties it contains.

Messrs. Muir also show a Patent Apparatus for Grinding Edge Tools. The stones are regulated by means of a right and left-hand screw, and a lateral motion is given to one of them by means of a cam, thus enabling the workmen to grind their tools with a degree of accuracy hitherto unattainable, and also doing away with the dust arising from the use of the "turning down" stones, so injurious to the bearings of all machinery.

A complete set of Screwing Tackle will also be found with Messrs. Muir's machines. In these the dies are so made that one will serve as a guide and the other as a cutter, which can be sharpened on a grindstone. The taps are fluted in a superior form for cutting. The cutting edge is a radial line through the section of the tap, which is found by experience to take about one-third less power than taps that

1.—CENTRAL DUPLEX LATHE.

have been hitherto used. The angle of the thread is 55 degrees for all diameters, rounded top and bottom. The same firm also exhibit a couple of Improved Copying Presses.

STEAM-HAMMERS.

AMONG the many objects of interest in the Western Annexe, connected with iron manufactures, is a machine-hammer, shown by Mr.

5.—SLOTTING AND SHAPING MACHINE.

T. W. Cowan, of Greenwich, which is deserving of special attention. It is driven by a strap, and upon the hammer being raised, the air in the chamber above being compressed by the upward stroke of the hammer, it immediately expands upon the down stroke, and causes the hammer to fall with any force required, up to 48 cwt. For a light blow the air is compressed under the piston, and by the simple turning of a handle the blow can be regulated to the fractional part of an ounce. The number of strokes can also be regulated by an apparatus for throwing the machine out of gear, and allowing the strap to run on a loose wheel. Another good feature in this machine is the fact

of its requiring no foundation, and the whole arrangement is so simple that a boy would be capable of working it.

Messrs. Robert Morrison and Co., of the Ouse Burn Engine Works, Newcastle-upon-Tyne, also show a fine steam hammer, with hammer bar and piston forged solid together. It is to be seen in full operation daily.

It possesses a power of 20 cwt., and, like that above-mentioned, can be regulated to a blow of any force, from the forging of a railway sleeper to the cracking of a hazel nut. The hammer-bar is forged in one solid piece, with the piston and claw for holding the different faces required for various kinds of work. Two small steel rings are inserted in grooves turned in the piston, and render it effectually steam-tight, without the introduction of bolts, junk-rings, or any additional part calculated to destroy its solidity and simplicity.

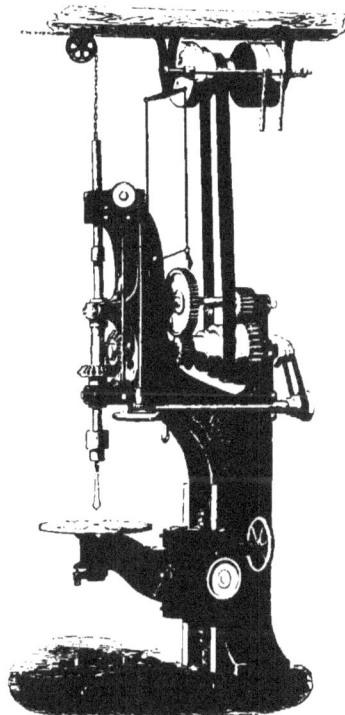

6.—SELF-ACTING VERTICAL DOUBLE-GEARED DRILLING MACHINE.

The momentum of the bar in rising, and its impact with the forging in its descent, regulate the action of the valve to the greatest nicety. After the delivery of the blow no more steam is admitted; and, as it requires scarcely an eighth of an inch opening of slide to raise the bar while working with heavy blows on red-hot iron, the full force of the bar, without any check from the steam below, is obtained at the commencement, the reduction in thickness of the forging, consequent on the blow, being sufficient to open the slide, to admit the requisite amount of steam to lift the bar, the momentum of which being unchecked in its upward course, opens the slide considerably more in that position, and admits the steam more freely at the top of the piston, so that in all cases a very firm and powerful blow is obtained.

Naylor's "Patent Single or Double Action Steam-Hammers" are exhibited by the Kirkstall Forge Company, Leeds. These hammers possess many admirable qualities, being completely under the control of the workman in charge, and capable of repeating the stroke with great rapidity.

With these steam - hammers must be mentioned the instrument exhibited by Krupp, of Westphalia, who has some excellent machinery and castings. All the steam-hammers are variations upon Nasmyth's original plan—a steam-hammer, of great size and power, being shown by the celebrated Patricroft firm, with punching, dividing, and other machines.

Why the claims of these exhibitors in Class 7 have been overlooked, it seems difficult to understand; but then, perhaps, the jurors better understood and appreciated sewing - machines than steam-hammers.

A Toy and a Necklace.—A pretty toy is shown in the Canadian department. It consists of thin slabs of plaster, in which pieces of agate are inserted in the shape of butterflies. They look like so many sheets of paper covered with the treasures of a collection of these beautiful insects, and would make a tasteful ornament for a boudoir or drawing-room table.— Another novelty is a genuine Chinese necklace, of the finest Orient pearl, part of the loot of the Summer Palace, and which has found its way to the case of Mr. Emanuel. It is very beautifully strung, and ornamented with green jade, a very precious article in China. It might be worn at a London ball without any alteration. The value of this costly spoil of some princess of the Flowery Land is set down at £1,000.

The Work of a Needle.—Those who take an interest in the results of that great domestic institute, the needle, will do well to look at a raised crochet counterpane, which is exhibited in Class 24, South-east Gallery. It is, both in design and workmanship, the unassisted production of a London sempstress, and is certainly a monument of patient and well-directed industry. The detail of its stitches would delight the Statistical Society. There are roses embroidered on it containing 2,696,370 stitches; leaves, 191,880; grapes, 58,851;

stars, 50,100; flowers, 14,620—grand total, 2,921,821 stitches; and all done in three months, by Jane Berwick, whose name must not be left out of the chronicle of the Exhibition. Since the days of the royal lady who wrought the Bayeux tapestry, there has never been such an amount of stitching done in so short a period. We must not omit to state that there were used in the making of this wonderful counterpane 62,000 yards of crochet cotton, and that the sempstress worked twelve hours each day.

In the Architectural Gallery there is a model at which few who have heard of the Indian mutiny will look with unmoistened eye. It is the monument which has been erected by the Indian Government over the well at Cawnpore, with an inscription :—"Sacred to the perpetual memory of a great company of Christian people, chiefly women and children, who, near this spot, were cruelly massacred by the followers of the rebel Nana Dhoondopunt, of Bithoor, and cast, the dying with the dead, into the well below, on the 15th day of July, 1857." The original is built of Chunar sandstone, with a gate of gun-metal, and will ultimately be ornamented with a piece of sculpture, the gift of the late Earl Canning, and which is now in the hands of Baron Marochetti. The model, which is in Agra soapstone, was made by native artists, and is on a scale of half an inch to the foot. It is simple and unornamented, and but for the associations connected with it, would probably not attract much notice.

Terra - cotta Vases and Figures.—The terra-cotta works of Mr. Blashfield have excited as much interest as admiration among our foreign visitors. These beautiful figures and vases are made entirely from the clay of oölitic beds in Northampton and Lincoln, mixed with flint-glass, sand, and in some cases with fossil bones, ground together, and after being moulded and fired, the objects come out as sharp as if they were carved with a chisel. Here are shown some wonderful imitations of Portland stone in terra-cotta—literally, baked earth. These imitations were undertaken, at the request of the late Prince Consort, for the material for the urns placed round the mausoleum of the Duchess of Kent at Frogmore. There were many failures in this attempt, but at last the imitation was perfected, so that, while the material is really as durable as flint-glass, there is to the eye no difference between these urns and those carved in Portland stone. There are terra-cottas of every kind shown here—pure white, stone colour, red and gray, all of equal hardness, and equal finish in their modelling. Some of the tazzas have basins from seven to eight feet in diameter—almost large enough for swimming-baths.

7.—UNIVERSAL SHAPING MACHINE.

Stained and Painted Glass.—II.

HAVING already spoken at considerable length (*ante* page 30) on the general subject of Stained Glass windows, we have only now to introduce engravings of the very excellent examples exhibited by Messrs. Lavers and Barraud, of Endell Street, Long Acre. These two lights are executed in the first style of the art, while as regards their design, we think little exception can be taken to the breadth and grace of the outlines or the integrity of the details.

Of course it will be understood that, from the very nature of stained glass, no adequate notion of the fitness of a design can be seen in an engraving. The picture, to be seen properly, must be viewed by means of transmitted light, as in a church. There the proper degrees of brilliancy and shade blend together, and form one harmonious whole. In the Exhibition the stained glass is generally so placed that the light shines *upon* instead of *through* the painting: the consequence is, that the lead-work used in joining the several pieces of stained glass together to form the design, is far too prominent, and the lustre of the colours is not sufficiently demonstrated. This is a great misfortune; but, like other shortcomings in the International Exhibition of 1862, it is nobody's fault. To be sure, we might have expected of Mr. J. B. Waring, the superintendent of Class 34, a little more judgment and taste; but then, when we recollect that this gentleman had also under his care the objects shown in the Furniture Courts (Class 30), the Precious Metals Courts (Class 33), the Pottery Courts (Class 35), and some pictures (Class 37), we can easily understand that he would have been rather over-worked previous to the Opening Day, especially as he had allotted to him only two assistants. We might have expected of Mr. Crace, the superintendent of decoration, some little care in the proper placing of the stained glass, did we not remember that this gentleman had the painting of the roof and the colouring of the columns to occupy all his attention; or we might have hoped from Mr. R. A. Thompson, the general superintendent of arrangements within the building, some more careful oversight, did we not know that this gentleman had far too much already on his hands, in spite of his six assistants, to look after everything. Thus it has happened that stained glass has come very badly off in the general placing of the exhibited objects in the industrial portion of the World's Show. Nevertheless, Messrs. Lavers and Barraud have been deservedly rewarded with a Prize Medal. Among the producers of stained glass, they stand in the first rank, as will be evident to all who examine the engravings we here introduce. These examples of a very valuable and interesting branch of art-manufacture are every way commendable—drawing, glass, and colouring being all that could be desired. They have attracted considerable attention from all classes of visitors.

STAINED GLASS. LAVERS AND BARRAUD, ENDELL STREET, LONG ACRE. PRIZE MEDAL.

DECORATIONS FOR A DRAWING ROOM OR BOUDOIR. MESSRS. TURNER, LONSDALE, AND CO. PRICE £1,054.

Curiosities in the Exhibition.

AMERICAN BREECH-LOADING RIFLE.—The American Breech-loading Rifle has, since it gained the Prize Medal, been left out in the Military Court for public examination. The interest which this weapon excites among military visitors, foreigners as well as English, is very great. In the Military Court the breech apparatus is shown fitted to the Enfield, Whitworth, cavalry, and other rifles, and its incontestable superiority over the European inventions of the same kind can be seen in an instant. Since its appearance in the Exhibition the attention of foreign officers has been more particularly drawn to it, and the result is that one great continental Power is in treaty for the supply of 50,000, as soon as they can be made.

NEW OBJECTS IN THE EXHIBITION.—The little singing bullfinch is now realising as much as £10 and £12 per day for the Lancashire operatives, though he has now a formidable rival in another warbling automaton at Mr. Emanuel's case. This latter is scarcely larger than a common bee, yet it skips out of its little box, and trills and flutters about with the vehemence and fulness of note of a grown skylark. A good many beautiful and interesting objects have recently been added to the various courts and classes; in fact, to those devoted to art-manufactures, such as jewellery, porcelain, glass, &c., almost daily additions are made. In glass, Messrs. Dobson and Pearce have just brought in a very small engraved cup, much larger than an ordinary tumbler, but so exquisitely engraved that it found a purchaser at the enormous price of fifty guineas the first hour it was seen. No piece of Venetian glass of the same size ever fetched such a sum. Messrs. Pellatt's engraved glass has also attracted such admiration that the firm has received orders to make large dessert services of the same kind for the Prince of Wales and the Viceroy of Egypt, each of which is to be so elaborate in design that many months will be required to complete them. Mr. Naylor has also been equally fortunate in the additions to his beautiful collection, some of the best of the pieces in which have been purchased by the Princesses Alice and Helena. In porcelain, also, some beautiful objects have been added to the collections shown by the Royal Worcester Works, Minton, Rose and Daniell, and Copeland.

THE EXHIBITORS AND THE JURORS.—Holders of Prize Medals are not altogether content; while those who have obtained none, express themselves sometimes very strongly indeed. Some evidence of an overt act of rebellion against the decision of the jurors is to be seen just at the entrance of the precious metals department, where it attracts considerable public attention and curiosity. It is the case of Mr. Forrer, "artist in hair," and who has the honour of exhibiting the royal arms over his goods. Mr. Forrer, it appears, got only "honourable mention," at which he was so indignant as to put a placard in front of his case, denying the justice of the award, and appealing to the general public; whilst at the same time he challenged all artists in hair to produce anything like his work, either in design or execution. Upon this the Commissioners took summary action. They sewed up Mr. Forrer's case in a canvas bag, and placed a sapper on guard to see that the arrangement was not disturbed. Mr. Forrer threatens legal proceedings, but, in the meantime, the case remains shrouded in sackcloth and mystery. The jury of Class 7a have entirely overlooked the machinery employed in the great staple of the country —plain cotton weaving? In no single award, whether it be "medallic," or the lofty distinction of "honourable mention," have this jury even noticed this class of machinery. There is no kind of machinery so extensively used, and there can be none more important. It has now been decided that the delivery of the Medals and of the Certificates of Honourable Mention to the exhibitors cannot take place till after the close of the Exhibition, when it will be made at a public ceremony in the building, to which will be admitted all the exhibitors, the holders of all classes of season tickets, except those for one shilling days, and the public on payment of £1.

COVENTRY RIBBONS.—The visitor to the south-east gallery will view with admiration many specimens of exquisite ribbon and silk goods from Coventry. An altogether new and interesting product of the loom is a well-manufactured kind of ribbon containing pictures, poems, verses, mottoes, flowers, and other designs, intended to be used as book-markers, neck-ties, scarves, &c. One specimen has Tennyson's poem of "Lady Godiva," every letter and word complete, and perfectly readable. Another series of ribbons of this kind is exhibited by Mr. Slingsby, of Park Street, Coventry. Here we have scarves, badges, and collars for Freemasons, Odd Fellows, Foresters, and other of the friendly societies; neck ribbons for the several Temperance Societies and llands of Hope; and various distinctive emblematic "regalia" used by the various "orders," all correctly designed, and exquisitely beautiful in colour and manufacture. Some of the book-markers, with the Lord's Prayer, the Creed, selected texts, &c., will certainly become popular. Any plan whereby the peculiar industry of Coventry can be encouraged, deserves recognition and patronage; and we have therefore pleasure in directing the attention of visitors to the show of ribbons in Class XX.

THE LETTER LOCK.—In the Hardware Court there is shown more than one of those fallacious letter locks. Many visitors will read with amazement the thousands of millions of permutations necessary before the lock can be opened. One exhibitor states that a reward of £200 "will shortly be offered" to any one who can perform this marvellous feat. A burglar would not set himself down for a thirty years' siege of a "letter lock," and wait until he had exhausted all the changes. He would know a much simpler mode of opening it without force, or failing that, he would give the "letter lock" a tap with the hammer, and the sesame would open at once! This would not, of course, entitle him to the promised reward; but if the lock were on a banker's safe, it would enable the thief very readily to get at the contents!

THE TARTAN TROPHY.—In the south-east gallery is the Tartan Trophy, consisting of specimens of tartan plaid, by several exhibitors. In an industrial point of view, it deserves special notice; for in the straths and glens of the far north there is many a home made cheerful, and many a hearth brighter, for the employment afforded to the poor cotter's family in spinning and weaving the native wools, and forming them into those socks, and tweeds, and plaids, of the value of which there are but few sportsmen or anglers who will not bear a ready witness. Some of the tartans are of great beauty. An idea may be formed of the variety of lands into which these famous Scotch dresses are being introduced when we state that the identical class of Highland dress which was worn at Culloden in the days of "Prince Charlie," the use of which was prohibited for a time after the rebellion of '45, was actually worn but recently by the Prime Minister (himself a Scotchman) of the King of the Sandwich Islands, on a great state occasion!

THE GREAT ORGAN.—Just at the entrance to the north-western transept is placed the great organ, exhibited by Messrs. Forster and Andrews, of Hull. We have before referred to this fine instrument, and now give a few of the particulars furnished to the jurors. The whole of accessory movements (as composition pedals, &c.) are labelled similar to the registers. Sforzando pedal No. 1 couples the great to the swell; sforzando pedal No. 2 couples the pedal organ to the great. When this pedal is down and the various couplets drawn, the full power of the instrument is concentrated on the great organ and pedals, and although 46 pipes will speak for each key pressed down, and 51 for each pedal, the touch remains the same as for a single pipe. The patent combination pedal acts simultaneously on the stops in the various organs, producing eight different combinations from one pedal. The movements in the interior are principally direct action. Improved pneumatic movements are applied to the great and pedal organs, which also act on the whole of the couplets. The bellows are blown by Joy's Patent Hydraulic Engine, supplying wind to the respective portions of the organ at four different pressures, the heaviest of which is nine inches. The scales of the flue pipes are by Professor Toepfer, of Weimar, on the proportion of 1 : $\sqrt{8}$. This arrangement obviates a weakness which is sometimes noticed in the treble part of the instrument. The wood pipes, from the 4 feet pipe upwards, are made of Swiss pine. The large pedal open diapason and 16 feet metal diapason have conical valves under the feet. This form of valve was introduced by Foster and Andrews in 1850, and used since then with perfect success. The pipes on the soundboards stand directly over their wind. The organ is tuned in equal temperament. The pitch is that lately sanctioned by the Royal Society of Arts; C giving 520 vibrations in a second. The registers are arranged at an angle of 45°. The pedal keys are a combination of the concave and radiating principle. The total number of pipes is 2,475, with registers, 46. It will be remembered that this organ stood in the British nave on the opening day, as shown in our page 4. As it was found to somewhat obstruct the view of the nave and impede the free passage of the visitor, it was removed by the Commissioners to its present position. During each week visitors have an opportunity of judging of its merits as a musical instrument, a fine performer occasionally playing overtures, &c.

India at Brompton.

IN the Exhibition of 1851 India was very gorgeously represented to the eye of the multitude, but very inadequately to those who looked beyond "barbaric gold and gems," and who strove to find something which would better exemplify the resources of this quarter of the world, than was shown in the conventional magnificence of howdahs, or gaudy horse trappings. Magnificence, and Oriental richness, however, are not wanting to some portions of the present collection, but it is the richness of shawls, embroideries, and textile fabrics as articles of trade—the India here is not the mere surface splendour of Rajahs and Nabobs, but the India of productiveness and resources, as it is now fast becoming under its new form of Government. The whole of this collection has been brought together and arranged under the care of Dr. Forbes Watson, with the assistance of Mr. Aston, Deputy-Keeper of the India Museum at Fyfe House. Under such administrators the visitor naturally expects a good collection, and his highest expectations will not be disappointed. The most suggestive, but the least generally attractive portion of the display, is at its entrance, where one of the great tests of a country's value is shown by a collection of its raw materials and natural products. Beyond these come its manufactures—native locks that would puzzle Hobbs to pick; cutlery from Salem that should astonish Sheffield. Beyond these are weapons, damascened in gold, and then some few specimens of gold and silver work, and enamelled jewellery, of such workmanship, and offered at such prices, as have amazed and almost alarmed the goldsmiths of other nations. Beyond the jewellery are cases of ivory carvings and inlaid goods, then specimens of carved furniture, the like of which, we believe, has not been seen before in England; and beyond these again are the textiles, the wonderfully-woven carpets of cotton, wool, and silk, the Dacca muslins, the gorgeous tissues of Kincob, the gold-worked shawls of Delhi, the embroidery of Scinde, the imitative cashmere of Umritzir, and the thick, costly, sad-coloured fabrics of

"Kashmir," the shawls of which every one has heard of, but few have seen—the real shawls of Cashmere. An Indian shawl is popularly supposed to be a mixture of gold and brilliant colours, while on to almost any and every scarf or shawl coming from the East, has been tacked the name of "Cashmere." Those who wish to be learned in the matter of these exquisite fabrics, the manufacture of which, it is to be feared, is dying out, ought now to visit the India Court, where they can trace every step of the process, from the first rough groups of dirty hair and wool that are sheared from the shawl goat, down to the cleaned wool and hair, the wool twisted, dyed, and woven at last into those wonderful patterns of sad colours which make the thick Cashmere shawl. Near these wonderful cases of textiles are shown a few specimens of a work which, in its best examples, is almost peculiar to the natives of Goojerat. These are the steel objects, inlaid with the arabesques in gold. Formerly it was almost entirely used for decorating armour, shields, and blades of weapons. Now none of these are made, and the natives confine the manufacture entirely to such things as paper-knives, caskets, jewel-boxes, &c. Some exquisite specimens of these are shown; and as only moderate prices were asked, they were all bought up before the Exhibition was open a week.

Perhaps the most important fact we have had to record since the Opening Day, is the arrival of eleven bales of Indian cotton, of superior quality, and beautiful in colour, grown from American seed in the district of Dharwar (North Canara), Bombay Presidency. It was gathered at the end of February, left Dharwar by a new route, for the new harbour of Sedashegar, on the 16th of May, and is now at the Exhibition, having been only two months in transit.

The Fine Arts are represented by a good collection of engravings, photographs, and drawings. Among the varieties may be mentioned the pottery from the School of Industrial Arts in Madras, as well as from Bangalore and North Arcot.

Household Decoration.

HOW to build, fit, furnish, and decorate a house has long been a difficult problem. To build your house, when the design has been determined on, and the money is ready at your banker's, seems easy enough; but then there is the decision about the style of house to be made—the claims of Italian to be balanced against Gothic, and Elizabethan against Composite—which may mean anything, from a decorated palace to a gabled cottage. But presuming the architecture of the house to be finally settled, then comes the question of its furniture and decoration. These must, of course, depend greatly on taste and the fitness of the various articles of furniture for the apartments they are to adorn. But notwithstanding "all appliances and means to boot," with no lack of wealth, and no disinclination to spend it, the furnishing of a house is really a very delicate affair. It is not, perhaps, a very troublesome matter to place appropriate chairs, tables, wall-papers, and window-curtains about a cottage or eight-roomed villa: but enlarge the villa into a mansion; fill it with its morning-rooms, drawing-rooms, reception-rooms, library, billiard-room, and study; make up your mind to furnish and decorate all your apartments with good taste, and spare no expense in so doing; then, when you have undertaken all this, request the advice and opinion of your friends, and you will discover that you have incurred a wonderful amount of very serious responsibility.

Manufacturers have of late exhibited great anxiety to make the fittings and decorations of all classes of houses accord with the architectural pretensions of the houses themselves. More especially has this been the case in the dwellings of the wealthy. In the application of the arts of design to articles of utility, great progress has been made during the eleven years which have elapsed since the Great Exhibition

Machinery in the Exhibition.—II.

PRINTING·MACHINES.

WE take the following very excellent account of the Printing Machines

of type by casting was invented by Schœffer, and, although the invention of the lever or American mould, about the beginning of the present century, rendered the work of the type-founder somewhat more easy, the 'Jury Reports' of 1851 say that 'since the invention of casting types by Peter Schœffer, a process which goes back to the origin of printing itself, this art has made but little progress.' But, notwithstanding this report, it is believed that the casting machine, invented in Germany, and improved in America, was in the possession of at least one British firm in 1851. Messrs. Johnson and Atkinson, of Red Lion Square, along with Messrs. W. H. Mitchell and Co., and Messrs. Potter and Galpin, occupy a court in the Annexe, between the wood-working and the paper machinery, where the process of manufacturing is, without the aid of manual labour, may every day be seen in operation. The type leaves the machine finished, requiring no subsequent cutting or trimming. The mould exhibited by Messrs. Besley and Co. (the successors of Messrs. R. Besley and Co.) on the contrary, leaves the 'gate,' or metallic excrescence formed at the opening through which the melted metal flows into the mould, to be removed by hand. But, even with this drawback, the attendant of this machine states that it can turn out 2,000 types an hour. Messrs. Potter and Galpin's 'Belle Sauvage' Printing Machine is exhibited under the number 1,685, and stands in a prominent position, near the south end of the western passage of the Annexe. This is a finely-finished machine, and occupies but little space. Though strong and well-built, it is sufficiently light to admit of its being erected in a press-room. The working parts are very simple; it runs easy, and with very little noise. The one on exhibition is a double-crown machine; and, though occupying less working space

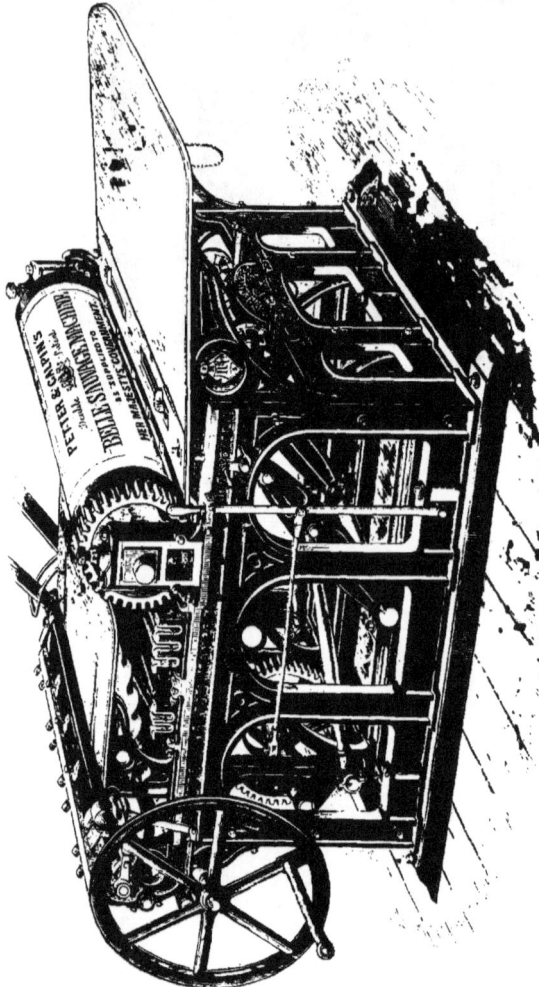

exhibited in the World's Fair at South. Kensington from the *Morning Star*:—"About the middle of the fifteenth century, the manufacture

than a double-crown press, it can be driven, either by hand or steam power, at the rate of from 1,000 to 2,000 impressions per hour, according to the capacity of the layer-on and class of work on hand. The cylinder being made to rest while the white sheet is taken and the printed one delivered, ample time is afforded to lay the sheet correctly up to the register gauge. When if by accident the sheet has not been laid up in time, the layer-on has it in his power to stop the cylinder without stopping the machine, and so prevent the blanket from being inked. By this means he is also enabled, before printing the sheet, to ink the forme two or more times at pleasure, as in the case of posters, or other heavy, solid formes, where more than an ordinary charge of colour is required. We believe that there are over two hundred of the 'Belle Sauvage' machines now in use.

"Mr. William Conisbee, Waterloo Road, exhibits a Main's Patent Printing Machine for bookwork and job printing. This machine is employed on regular job work in the Exhibition, which is turned

power, and at the same time to carry the expansion of the steam to a great extent for the purpose of insuring the utmost amount of economy in fuel.

The cylinders are respectively ten and twenty-one inches in diameter, and the length of stroke is two feet in each case; one external steam jacket, fed direct from the boiler, embraces both cylinders. The steam enters the small cylinder at the full pressure of the boiler, and when the piston has travelled half its stroke, is cut off, and expanded through the remainder of the stroke; it is then exhausted into the wrought-iron reservoir, shown by dotted lines under the bedplate (this reservoir being jacketed with high-pressure steam from the boiler). Here the steam is stored up until the crank of the larger cylinder, which is at right angles to that of the smaller one, has brought its piston to the end of the stroke, when the slide valve of the

MESSRS. MAY'S DOUBLE CYLINDER HORIZONTAL ENGINE.

out in a very creditable manner. A working model of Hoe's printing machine is to be seen on the west side of the western passage; and close by, Messrs. D. and J. Greig, of Edinburgh, exhibit a paper-cutting machine, lithographic, copper-plate, and photographic presses, &c., which for finish and workmanship will compare favourably with any in the same class. E. and W. Ullmer show a single-cylinder gripper machine of their own manufacture, which seems a compact, serviceable machine.

"Near the north end of the Annexe a couple of French machines are exhibited, one by M. C. Alanget, of Paris, and the other by M. A. B. Dutartre, also of Paris. These have both horizontal cylinders, and are larger than any of the British machines exhibited, except that of Mr. Ross. A few presses, manufactured by Messrs. Dingler and Wolff, at Zweibrucken, in Bavaria, and a printing machine, by Dr. C. F. Heintz, of Munich, about completes the list of foreign machines of this class in the Western Annexe."

MESSRS. MAY'S DOUBLE CYLINDER HORIZONTAL ENGINE.

This "Uniform Power, Expansive, Double Cylinder Horizontal Steam Engine" is designed especially with a view to obtain uniform rotative

large cylinder opens, and admits the steam from the above-mentioned reservoir, and, as in the smaller cylinder, it is again cut off at half stroke, expanded through the remainder of the stroke, is cut off, and exhausted into the condenser, which may either be a surface-condenser, as in the case of the engine exhibited, or an ordinary one, according to the circumstances of each particular case. The air-pump, which is placed vertically, as being preferable to horizontally, is worked by a connecting rod from the end of the crosshead of the large cylinder.

The nearest approach that it is possible to obtain to perfectly uniform rotative power, is arrived at in this steam engine.

In connection with the above-described engine, is exhibited "Perkins' Patent Surface Evaporator Condenser," the advantages of which may be summed up as follows, viz.:—the supply of perfectly pure water to the boiler, which infallibly prevents all incrustation and priming; the more regular supply of water to the boiler; the condensers are cheap and very portable; dirty or salt water is capable of being used for condensation, and existing high-pressure engines may, by its use, be converted, at a moderate cost, into condensing engines, and a very considerable increase of power obtained, without any additional consumption of fuel.

TROTMAN'S ANCHOR.

IN Class XII., South Court, is exhibited a model and a drawing of the famous Anchor invented by Mr. J. Trotman, of Cornhill. Messrs. Hawks, Crawshay, and Sons, of Newcastle-on-Tyne, also exhibit a model of this valuable instrument. In the first case it is the model of the anchor belonging to H.M.'s yacht Victoria and Albert which is shown, and in the latter it is the model of the anchor to the famous frigate Warrior.

The distinguishing feature peculiar to Trotman's anchor is the palm being set at an acute angle to the line of strain, and differing from that of the arm: in action, it is found to bite the ground instanta-

palm and arms of Porter's, and other anchors, being identical, the ordinary anchor, likewise, in action, is a mere scraper, accumulating, as it were, the loose surface, instead of biting and retaining its fulcrum of resistance in unbroken ground; its form rigid and inflexible, a mass of iron, one third of which is never available, and really mischievous—as the upper arm is ever liable to be fouled, or hooked, by the cable of other ships in crowded anchorages—presenting always a dangerous projection to ships' bottoms, in shoal water, tidal harbours, and rivers. The principle of Trotman's anchor obviates these objections. It is flexible in its parts, each contributing its portion of duty to the whole, and adapting itself to every emergency.

TROTMAN'S ANCHOR. PRIZE MEDAL.

neously as a ploughshare, and by reason of the vibratory motion of the arms, the pressure of the upper arm on the shank imparts increased penetration to the lower arm in the ground; or, in other words, the heavier the strain, the more tenacious the holding properties. It possesses other advantages besides strength, and holding-power more than doubled; viz., freedom from fouling the cable—increased efficiency with reduced weight, affording very material relief to ships' bows in a head sea—facility of transport to or from ships by means of boats—convenience of stowage—elasticity of form, which enables it to sustain sudden strains or jerks at short stay-peak, and concussion, when let go on hard or rocky bottoms.

Comparison suggests the following conclusions:—the angle of the

THE BLAKELY CANNON.

HAVING already noticed this fine specimen of ordnance in a previous page of the EXHIBITOR, we have only now to present our readers with an engraving of the noted 500-pounder itself. It will be found, together with other pieces of ordnance, in the South Court, at the eastern end of the Nave. In our illustration, the figure of a man

BLAKELY'S ORDNANCE. PRIZE MEDAL.

introduced, in order that the reader may estimate the size of the cannon by comparison. The exhibition of arms and ordnance in the South Kensington Palace throws an altogether new light upon the dreams of "universal brotherhood," "peace," and the "good time coming," about which so many amiable enthusiasts indulged in writing and talking during the year 1851.

Tapestry in the French Court.

FRANCE has long been celebrated for the production of a very beautiful kind of carpet, and also for that sort of embroidery upon canvas known as tapestry. The Imperial manufactories of Gobelin, the Savonnerie, and Beauvais are famous all over the world; and in the International Exhibition the magnificent results of the labours of their artist-workmen are deservedly admired. We have already expressed our opinion upon the subject of designs for carpets and tapestry; there is, therefore, no necessity to renew our protest against rocky landscapes, country scenes, horses, dogs, hawks, eagles, tiger-hunts, fortune-tellers, minstrels, cava-liers and beautiful dam-sels—much less against the telling of a story, or the illustrating of a fable, in the produce of the loom. Suffice it, that there is no lack of this kind of picture-manufac-ture in the show of French tapestry. The design shown in our en-graving is executed in beautiful colours, partly in silk and partly in worsted; and but that we told the reader it actu-ally represents a carpet, he might take it for an oil picture, a mosaic, a piece of wood - carving, the painting upon a dessert dish, or a work in silver *repoussé*. In the old times, when tapestry hung in natural folds over the bare walls of châteaux and mansions, there was good excuse for the representation of figures of men and ani-mals; but now that such productions are framed, and hung flat against the sides of rooms, or placed upon floors as co-verings, it appears to us that they should not be made to represent pic-tures with designs in re-lief.

The collection of woven and embroidered carpets and tapestry in the Exhibition is very rich and interesting. The tapestry carpets of the Gobelins and the Savonnerie are seldom valued at less than from two to three hundred pounds each, some of them ranging as high as five thousand pounds; one, for instance, in the Exhibition is valued at that amount, which necessarily con-fines the use of such articles to a very limited circle. This class of goods may be termed the hot-bed produce of the State, being forced at an enormous cost of labour and capital, but assuredly not for the improvement and extension of the general carpet trade of France; the style, the character of the designs, and the *tout ensemble* of the work, placing them far beyond the reach of imitation by the humbler

17.

and more useful branches of the manufacture. The next in richness to the Gobelins are the productions of Sallandrouze and Rogier, called the Aubusson and Felletin carpets. They are manufactured in the department of La Creuse, and are both long and short nap. The Messrs. Gravier also produce velvet-nap carpets, which present an exceedingly rich appearance, though their ordinary price is about one-fifth of those manufactured by the State.

"Unfortunately," says M. Flachat, writing of the French manu-facture, "the general arrangement of our habitations has precluded us from the use of carpets. In this respect we are much behind the Eng-lish, and even the Dutch. A progress of this kind is necessarily dependent upon that of other con-veniences, and our first step to ensure it must be the suppression of the duty upon foreign wools, in order that our manu-facturers may produce cheaply, as well as su-perbly, this useful arti-cle." A step in this di-rection has been made by France in the treaty of commerce concluded lately by Mr. Cobden.

The Western Division of the French Court facing the nave is hung with some excellent spe-cimens of *tapisserie de Reps*, from the looms of M. Morceau, who was the inventor of this fabric, and is still the most eminent of its manufacturers. The co-lours are bright, and the patterns generally cha-racterised by good taste; and one specimen, with medallions of flowers and gold scrolling, on a blue ground, is especially charming. The same exhibitor shows a new species of tapestry, which he calls *tapisserie St. Maur*, a triumph of in-dustrial progress and ar-tistic beauty. It is made with the Jacquard loom, and although previous attempts have been made to produce similar results by the same process, none have been crowned with such complete suc-cess. It is hard to say which is the loveliest among the specimens shown, the principal being two table-covers, two curtains, and a covering for a sofa. In the latter, one of the most exquisite designs in flowers that could be conceived is charmingly thrown up by a silver-grey ground; the design is good, and the colours are equally remark-able for delicacy of tint and richness of tone. But the reflection which must strike every one is, that such a work of art is much too lovely to sit upon. In all that is shown by M. Morceau of this new material, the

FRENCH TAPESTRY—THE WOLF, THE FOX, AND THE APE.

same commendable characteristics are apparent—chaste elegance of pattern, and a combination of softness of shading with brilliance of hue. The texture is finer than that of the Aubusson tapestry, so that it is better fitted for use in furniture which is necessarily open to close inspection, and we are informed that it can be produced at about one-half the cost.

We have but few specimens of carpets or tapestry in the British half of the Exhibition to vie in magnificence with the productions of the Gobelins or Aubusson; but we manufacture a humbler kind of carpet, which comes within the means of less wealthy purchasers, and is often distinguished by good taste in design, as we have already shown. In quality and price the Brussels, velvet, and tapestry carpets of England are unequalled by any productions of a similar kind on the Continent. But though we have little to fear from the competition of

our neighbours, we have a great deal to learn—namely, the fine and practical taste which they pre-eminently possess. Examine their carpets, wherever there is no limit to taste and fancy, and you will find such a charming combination of colours, and so subdued a tone, that it is scarcely possible for the eye to be disconcerted, however grotesque and bizarre may be the furniture of which they form the natural background. It is comparatively easy to blend the bright and prominent shades of wool, as colour is so largely absorbed by the latter; but to harmonise the pale and subdued tints, so as to form a pleasing contrast to almost any conceivable combination of furniture, is the result of a long-studied attention to the laws which regulate and influence taste. In this particular the French have long been thought to be far a-head of us; but recent specimens render the assertion doubtful.

Curiosities in the Exhibition.

How Distance and Depth at Sea are Measured.—Mr. Walker, of Birmingham, shows a new patent Ship-log. In this ingenious device the register and rotator are combined, and the principle by which the speed of the vessel is recorded is identical with that of the "tell-tales" at the Exhibition. As there are 6,120 feet in a nautical mile, the sixtieth part of this number will be 102; and *this* is called a minute-knot. Of the four dials which compose the registering part of the log, the finger of the first will have made one revolution when the machine has passed through six minute-knots, or the tenth part of a mile. At the end of a mile the finger of the second dial will have revolved—the fingers of the third and fourth requiring, respectively, ten and a hundred miles for a complete revolution.—The same exhibitor's sounding-machine is ingenious. Here, again, we have two registering wheels, the smaller of which makes one revolution in ten fathoms, the larger going round in 150 fathoms.

A Portable Life-boat.—In the South Court is "a new Life-boat," which attracted the attention of the late lamented Sir John Franklin. It is the invention of Mr. Halkett, and consists of a curved cylinder of India-rubber cloth for the sides and ends of the boat, which become distended when inflated with air. This life-boat can be rolled up and stowed away, so as to take up no more room than a spare sail. It seems well adapted for explorers, and parties having difficult postages to make between navigable lakes and streams.

The Smallest Locomotive in the World.—This pretty little toy, really a working steam-engine, is two and a quarter inches—or less than one's little finger—in length, and it weighs scarcely an ounce. Its cylinders are of one-eighth of an inch in diameter; the stroke of each piston is one-fifth of an inch; the driving-wheels are five-eighths of an inch across, and the wheels are six in number. With its silver boiler, gold dome, chimney, and its 296 parts, it is the greatest, while the smallest, wonder of the annexe. The maker is a Mr. Myers, an amateur mechanician, living at Birkenhead, who has arranged for the application of heat to get up the steam by the tiniest of all little spirit lamps, and who puts upon the "Little Wonder" the price of £100. This elegant piece of workmanship will be found in the Western Annexe.

Toledo Blades.—Among the newest of Spanish manufactures are placed some specimens of one of the oldest. Here is a splendid assortment of the famous "old Toledos," one of which is shown bent into a circle. So strong and stout—so supple and pliable—enriched with glittering hilts, and bearing ornamental tracery upon their bright blue blades—these swords are really very beautiful objects.

Jewels.—The finest in the Exhibition is the Koh-i-noor; the next in beauty is the Star of the South; and the third in size is the property of Mr. Dresden. Its weight is 76½ carats, and it is a conspicuous

object in the case of Messrs. Garrard, who display, besides this and the larger diamond belonging to her Majesty, a notable collection of jewels, including the large engraved ruby in the necklace taken from the treasury of Lahore, now also the property of the Queen. The characters inscribed on this Indian jewel are Persian, and the dates refer to the Mohammedan era. Then there are the Nassock diamonds, which were purchased of Messrs. Rundell and Bridge for the Marquis of Westminster, and are exhibited by his lordship in the case of Messrs. Hunt and Roskell. Though these jewels have been re-cut less judiciously than the Koh-i-noor, it is said that they would readily sell for double the price at which they were obtained by the marquis, and which was £13,000.

Models of a Spanish Bull Fight.—A collection of the elegant Malagan figures is to be seen in the Spanish portion of the nave. They represent the various stages of the bull fight, from the first attack of the picador, with the tantalising diversions of the chulillos and bandilleros, the *coup de grace* of the matador, and the final exit of the victim at the heels of the mules who drag him ignominiously from the arena. Some of the exciting incidents of this barbarous national amusement are represented with great spirit. Groups in the same material, and with the same artistic finish, are exhibited by Cubero, of Seville.

The Champion Emeralds of the World.—The largest cut emerald in the world is a prominent feature of the very rich and tasteful collection of Messrs. London and Ryder; and the largest emerald, being uncut, is in the sumptuous show of Mr. Hancock, where it looks, to an untaught eye, like a square mass of rough rock-crystal that has been stained green. Messrs. London and Ryder's emerald boasts a very romantic history. It was once in the possession of Runjeet Singh, "the Lion of the Punjaub," and for many years it graced the state-saddle of that prince. The stone weighs 377 carats; it is cut octagonally, and is 2½ inches long, and 2½ inches wide. Inasmuch as an emerald is a six-sided crystal, some idea may be formed of the size of that particular stone from which the jewel in question was cut. The colour is remarkably pure throughout, and in the centre a space is clear and perfect to about the size of a two-franc piece. The gem has been lent for exhibition by the Maharajah Duleep Singh, whose diamond belt, manufactured for him by the same firm, also appears in their case.

The Largest Ruby in the World.—In the case with the emeralds is seen an extraordinary ruby; but what with bad cutting, and what with having been drilled, this Oriental jewel is in a sad state of deterioration. It was originally the property of Tippoo Sahib, and once formed the eye of a Hindu deity. Its value is £4,000. By its side is shown a very beautiful opal, of large size, the prismatic tints of which are perfectly dazzling.

Japan at the Exhibition.

THE small but highly-interesting collection shown under the name of Japan should not be overlooked by visitors. All who do examine it leave it with regret that the collection is not larger, for there is scarcely an object shown which does not give some new and special insight into the habits of this extraordinary people. It is unnecessary to say that this collection is not forwarded by the Japanese themselves. It is not, therefore, a representative exhibition, either of their arts or industry, such as they possibly might wish to show. It is simply a series of cabinets, containing specimens of the industrial and art manufactures of the country, collected by the very few individuals who have seen it, the chief exhibitor being Mr. Rutherford Alcock, her Majesty's Envoy to the Tycoon. As we have said, therefore, only enough is shown to excite our admiration, and stimulate our wish to see more. But, small as is the collection, it is large enough to prove the skill of the people in their own manufactures, and in ours, too; and, above all, to show that the general disposition of the people leans to broad, comic fun. There is only one Leech in England, but in Japan there must be hundreds, if not thousands. To be satisfied of this, one has only to examine the wonderful collection of little metal buckles for fastening the dress, shown by Mr. Alcock. The designs in some of these are irresistibly grotesque, and at once recall to mind the little black wood-cuts with which Mr. Leech began his connection with *Punch*. Probably every object in this collection is by a different artist; yet, though in some the designs are so minute as to require a magnifying-glass to see them well, all are treated with the same broad humour, so that it is impossible to avoid downright laughter as you examine them. There is one figure of a man timidly venturing to coax a snarling dog, which is inimitable in its funny expression, and so also is the expression on another's face, who is frightened by a ghost. All these works, the reader must remember, are not mere sketches, but are solid little pieces of metal work, the background being of bronze and the raised figures in relief being either gold, silver, steel, or platinum, or, as in most cases, of all four metals intermixed. It is evident from the platinum being so freely used here, that the metal must be much more common with the Japanese than with us, and that the secret of melting it, to which our chemical knowledge has only just attained, has long been known to them. In the adaptation of bronze to ordinary domestic purposes, such as ink-stands, tobacco jars, candlesticks, and the like, there is wonderful ingenuity shown. There is a bronze tripod candlestick so ingeniously hinged that it folds up into the size of a small envelope, and not much thicker. By the side of this case is shown an object which is one of the most curious of all in the whole building. It is a small window-blind, made apparently of rods of twisted glass strung together. The rods are as hard, as clear, and as sharp as glass. Let the visitor examine it attentively, and then believe, if he can, that it is made of *rice*. Of all who have seen or who are yet to see this wonderful little screen of rods, we venture to say not a hundred will believe them other than what they seem to be—pure glass. Yet Mr. Alcock asserts that they are made from a gelatine of rice, and his statement is borne out by the fact that, hard and sharp as they are, they sound, when knocked together, like sticks of soft wood. In the side of the case where the metal buckles are shown we find in a collection of ivory carvings fresh proofs of the art, skill, and comic genius of the people. Let any one examine the litter of puppies sprawling over each other; the grotesque look of pain on the face of the woman who has been started by a fox, and tumbled forward with her fingers under the edge of a basin; the triumphant aspect of the companion figure, who has succeeded in clapping his basin down on the fox. Yet, notwithstanding their wonderful finish, all these figures are so small that they might be worn as brooches. Opposite this case is one of porcelain, in which is a large plate that represents two Japanese ladies wearing French bonnets and shawls, with deeply-flounced silk dresses, spread out by such an amplitude of crinoline as even our belles

seldom venture on. One has a telescope, with which she is pointing to the sea with an air of fashionable nonchalance, while the other figure, to still further exemplify European habits, has her gloved hand filled with green apples. In the background are two other Japanese ladies, dressed in the costume of the country, and who are shrinking with horror and astonishment from their strangely-attired sisters. This ceramic caricature tells its own tale. The attitude of the European Japanese lady pointing to the sea, whence the barbarians are to come, the fidelity with which our dress and very walk is copied, all show it to be meant as a warning satire of what will result to Japanese costumes and customs if once the Europeans are admitted within the pale of their strange community. It is a curious illustration of their manu-facturing skill, that a passing joke like this should be represented in such a costly medium as this beautifully-finished porcelain. The specimens of egg-shell porcelain shown in this case are, if anything, almost thinner than egg-shell. Even the renowned specimens of this china made at Worcester are more earthenware compared to them.

The show of arms and armour is not great, though the Japanese, as might be expected from a people among whom the sword is an insignia of rank—the first three lay classes having the right to wear two—manufacture blades of the most exquisite temper. A good weapon is handed down as a heirloom from generation to generation, and so sharp and well-balanced are the blades, and so dexterous are the people in the use of their favourite weapon, that their best swords-men can, it is said, cut a man in two at a single blow. Among the weapons here is a formidable, short, double-edged sword, taken from one of the party of assassins who attacked the house of the English Embassy at Jeddo by night, last year. The best Japanese sword-makers, it is said, get as much as £100 for a single blade. This sum, however, is, perhaps, not very great among a people who possess gold in such profusion that its value appears to be estimated at little more than twice or three times that of silver. The coinage is shown in the collection. The silver coins are thick and square; those of gold are large, but thin, and have the corners rounded off. The largest coin of the latter kind is about three inches long by two inches broad, yet its value is only equal to thirty shillings of our currency. It is certainly thin, but there must, nevertheless, be at least £3 worth of gold in it. Yet, amply as they seem to be supplied with gold and silver, the Japanese have found their way to a paper currency; and their notes for various amounts, all of which are oblong, like the coins, are shown near the money. In paper, the manufacturers of Japan have un-doubtedly attained an excellence and skill of which we in Europe know nothing. Here are paper waterproof coats, paper leathers, paper parasols, and paper pocket-handkerchiefs. Some of the paper leathers are as strong, apparently, as any hides that ever left a tan-yard. There is a large collection of the different kinds of paper used for paper-hangings, for writing, printing, and for wrapping up parcels, and, in fact, the different qualities and kinds of paper seem infinitely more numerous than our own, and in their combinations are efficiently applied to such purposes as are not thought of here. The different specimens of printing are also shown. There is a Japanese Court Guide—a Directory which gives the names, ranks, and abodes of all the notabilities of the empire; there are a set of Japanese playbills—for the theatre is even a more fashionable place of resort in Jeddo than in London—a Japanese encyclopædia, and some children's story books, which the comic genius of the people enables them to illustrate with the most racy humour. At the eastern end of the court is a most valuable collection of Japanese drugs and surgical instruments. Of the value of this pharmacopœia we can, of course, give no opinion, beyond saying that all their medicines seem derived from herbs. Their surgical instruments, however, are as numerous and as formid-able as if the Japanese were accustomed to have railway accidents on a colossal scale every day in the week. One thing is evident of their

The Exhibition Carpet.

THIS carpet is a *spécialité* in the manufacture of "Axminsters," and was meant to show what machinery is really capable of producing in this particular branch of the manufactures of Great Britain._ It is intended as a screen or panel for wall-decoration, after the manner of the Gobelin tapestries; and was specially designed, under the direction

with branches of palm, depending from which are large swags of fruit, symbolical of Peace and Plenty. At the base are the English and French flags, supporting the Rose, Thistle, and Shamrock, with a blue ribbon, bearing the motto, "*La reciprocité est la base vraie et durable de la paix*"—"Reciprocity is the true and lasting basis of peace."

"A FURTHER PROOF OF FRIENDSHIP."—AXMINSTER CARPET. MESSRS. TAPLING AND CO.

of Mr. Thomas Tapling, by Mr. William A. Parris, of London, for the International Exhibition. The design is meant to commemorate the recent Treaty of Commerce between France and England, and contains figures, considerably larger than life, of the Emperor presenting the Treaty to the Queen, as "a further proof of the friendship of the French nation." The principal subject is surrounded with an elaborate frame-work of laurel and oak-leaves, in gold colour; the panels, of a rich marone, having an interlaced ornament, running alternately, of the rose and bee, emblematical of the two countries. The French emblem is again introduced on a shield at the top of the design, surmounted

Such a work in this manufacture has never before been attempted in this country; and it is scarcely necessary to add that, dealing with so novel a design, there were many difficulties to contend with.

The carpet measures 22 feet by 18 feet, is woven in one piece, and occupied in its manufacture only three months from the date on which the artist's original design was completed.

Unfortunately, in common with other carpets in the Exhibition, it is hung in a cross light, which greatly mars the effect, both of drawing and colouring.

Agricultural Implements.—Eastern Annexe.

THE Eastern An-
nexe is one of the
most important por-
tions of the Exhibi-
tion, for here will be
found, not only va-
rious mining, quar-
rying, metallurgical,
and mineral products;
the several chemical
substances, and phar-
maceutical processes;
substances used for
food, and chemical
and vegetable sub-
stances used in manu-
factures, but a show
of Agricultural Im-
plements such as was
never before gathered
together.

When, says a re-
cent critic, we con-
sider that about two-
thirds of the popula-
tion of this country
derive their income
from the produce of
the land, by being
either engaged in ag-
riculture, or depen-
dent on it, and that
there are three and
a half million persons
directly employed in
it throughout the
United Kingdom, this
great basis of industry
assumes an import-
ance not quite con-
sistent with its being
thrust into a wretched
leaky lean-to, which
presents all the ap-
pearance of an after-
thought. It looks as
though, in the origi-
nal design, no thought
was entertained of the
beautiful machinery
which now adorns the
Eastern Annexe; but
that, being impor-
tuned for space, the
Commissioners, at the
last hour, threw up a
shed, and gave it a
French term to hide
its ugliness. Upon
entering the building,
the difficulty is to
find this shed; and when the certainty of its position gradually dawns
upon the mind, the painful necessity one is under of leaving all
that is beautiful, in making a timorous dive through the unknown
terrors of a dark tunnel to reach it, imparts to the mind a feeling of
revulsion, and a disinclination to pass to what looks like a chamber of
horrors beyond. The sense of duty, however, being too strong for

VIEW IN THE EASTERN ANNEXE.

these sensations, we press on through a portion of the Colonial department, on the right of the Eastern entrance, leave the Post-office and the trophy of Tasmanian woods behind, together with Cowper's free-trade motto, "Each climate needs what other climes produce;" traverse a court just described, hung with geological maps, and filled with mineral and rock products; navigate the dark passage, catch a glimpse of an open court, where old boilers, packing cases, and wind and rain have it all their own way, and gain assurance as we land amid Burgess and Key's familiar reaping machines, and the eye strikes along the gilded structures ranged against the main wall on the left, and catches such names as Barrett, Ransome, Hornsby, Robey, Garrett, and others.

The ground space allotted to the Implement Manufacturers, one of whom does a business with Russia alone, in engines, of £10,000 annually, is about 16,900 square feet. Three-fourths of the exhibitors cannot show a sample of each implement they make; and yet the room is well occupied, and the machines sufficiently huddled together to make the work of observation in some instances difficult, in others impossible. On the left side of the open court, which runs parallel with the Exhibition Road, will be found the shed in question, 51 feet broad, and a little more than 300 feet long, with an angle at either end of 30 square feet. This length is divided into four lines of stands, one on each side, and two up the middle. Up the main aisle are thirteen stands, sixteen feet broad, with full space in front for the public. The two rows of stands up the middle are each six feet wide, and a path of six feet intervenes between these last and the twenty stands on the other side, which have only a width of seven feet accorded to them. This is all. If the ground space was not sufficient, exhibitors were at liberty to erect galleries at their own expense, which they have done in numerous instances, at an outlay of several hundreds of pounds; in all cases with great taste, and in some cases with an architectural enrichment excelled in none of the courts in the building. Richard Garrett and Son's design (as shown in our engraving), perhaps the most perfect of its kind, catches the eye from every point. The harmony of colour and unity of parts produce an exceedingly pleasing effect. Buff, white, and gold are the colours employed below; the gallery balustrade is of pale violet, and bears the gilded name of the firm. Along it, at intervals, are placed the royal arms, gilded; and in the centre a cumulative group of emblematical female figures in white.

Hornsby and Sons, of Grantham, must have also incurred considerable expense, and have given to their designer a perfect carte blanche for the exercise of his taste. The effect of an exceedingly pretty plan, painted in white, and pink, and gold, and gallery with green and gold balustrade, adorned with enrichments, and crowned with a bust of the late Prince Consort, could not be otherwise than pleasing. Ransome and Sims, of Ipswich, have erected a pretty structure; and Barrett, Exall, and Andrewes, of Reading, Bentall, of Maldon, Clayton and Shuttleworth, of Lincoln, Samuelson, and Priest and Woolrough, "on

the line," have done the best in various fashions to beautify the bare walls of this place. When we visit the building we notice that the fairy wand of industry is extended over the edifice in course of erection by the Howards, of Bedford; but beside it, at the northern end, stands out, complete and triumphal, the arch-like structure of our steam ploughman, John Fowler, with emblematical figures, a surmounting three-furrow plough, and niches for resultant sheaves of golden-headed wheat.

But to descend from generalities to particulars, we notice first the

IMPLEMENTS OF MESSRS. GARRETT AND SON.

This firm, whose works are at Leiston, Suffolk, exhibit, among many other machines, a combined Threshing and Dressing Machine, which embraces many good points. The whole blast necessary for dressing the grain is produced by one fan, and can be regulated by means of valves to suit any description of grain. This machine is also fitted with an improved revolving screen, by which four perfect separations are made, and the grain delivered into four sacks, viz., best corn, seconds ditto, tail corn, and seeds, the chaff (a very great improvement) being delivered quite free from the seeds. For extent, variety, and workmanship, the collections of Messrs. Garrett and Son will compare favourably with any in the building.

IMPLEMENTS OF MESSRS. RANSOME & SIMS.

This eminent firm exhibit a fine collection of Portable Steam-engines, Thrashing-machines, Steam-reapers, Mills, Chaff-cutters, Ploughs, and Harrows.

Among the most important of these is a "Patent

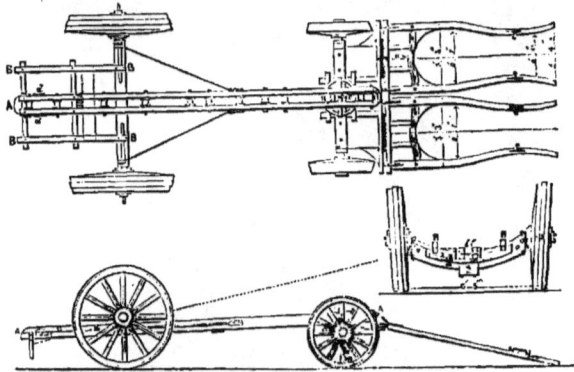

SECTION OF AGRICULTURAL WAGON. MESSRS. RANSOME AND SIMS.

Double Blast and Finishing Steam-thrashing Machine." The drum has patent wrought-iron reversible beaters, which wear four times as long as the common beaters, and are not liable to breakage; they do not injure barley in thrashing. The shaker has a rotary movement, and not only performs all the operations which the crank or reciprocating shakers perform, but also returns the short straw and grain to the riddles, thus dispensing with the cumbrous reciprocating machinery required for this purpose with other non-rotary shakers.

The screen is self-cleaning, without the aid of brushes, pickers, or blasts of air, and is also adjustable to suit any quality of grain. The frame-work is all prepared and shaped by machinery. The mortices and tenons are thus better fitted than is possible by hand-labour, and the utmost durability is secured. If a frame-work is not solidly made, the various bearings are apt to get out of line, more power is required, and greater wear and tear ensues. The spherical locking-gear removes all twist from the frame when on uneven ground, and thus prevents heating and cutting in the bearings.

Every part of the machine is under the eye of the attendant, and all necessary adjustments can be made with great facility, many of them while the machine is at work. These machines are extensively used in England, Russia, Australia, and other corn countries.

Among the machines shown in the gallery erected by this firm are a "Model of a Patent Victoria Self-Raking Reaper." The grain is delivered at one side in sheaves, by a continuous rotary motion. Sheaf-delivery reapers have previously had an intermittent reciprocating movement to drive the delivery rakes. The platform turns up,

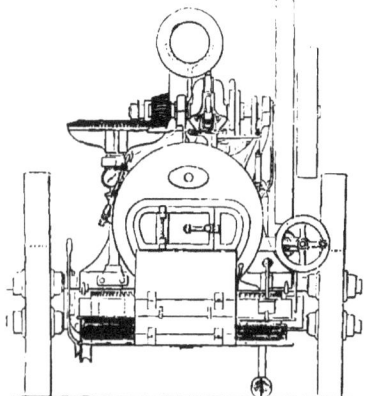

SECTION OF STEAM THRASHING MACHINE. MESSRS. RANSOME AND SIMS.

and thus the machine will pass through a narrow gateway. The platform and cam which guide the rakes are connected by levers, which cause the cam to follow the undulations of the ground exactly in accordance with the platform, and thus keep the rakes always at the same distance from the platform. These are entirely new features in reapers.—"A Patent Balance Horse Rake." The driver rides, and his weight is used to balance the teeth, so that the rake, although so large, is more easily cleared of its load than the ordinary hand-rakes. — "Biddell's Patent Oat Mill." The columnar stand with tripod foot. The roller with hardened steel cutting edges, supported by cast iron, is cheaper and more durable than case-hardened wrought or cast rollers.

Messrs. Ransome and Sims have, of course, obtained the Prize Medal. They also show various medals obtained at previous exhibitions—in all, sixty-six. These medals have been awarded for excellence in all kinds of machinery

and implements, from steam-engines to ploughs—a position of greater merit than if they had all been awarded for the same article.

The machinery shown by this firm generally is notable for adaptation to the purposes for which it is intended, good proportion in strength of the various parts, excellent workmanship combined with suitable materials, and facility of repair when working parts are worn out or broken. From the

IMPLEMENTS OF MESSRS. ROBEY & CO., OF LINCOLN,

we select a "Traction Engine and Thrashing Machine." The engine is a ten-horse power double cylinder, and attached is an endless chain traction engine, mounted, improved, and manufactured by the exhibitors. The diameter of each cylinder is 7¼ inches. It has link motion reversing gear, governors, strong tender to carry engine driver and fuel, water tank, and very efficient hand-steering apparatus, or shafts for horse steerage. It also possesses Robey and Co.'s patent fire-box, the advantages of which are to economise the consumption of fuel, to prevent the escape of fire from the fire-box, dispensing with the loose ash-pan, and as a substitute introducing a three-inch water space beneath the fire-bars, which gives a large amount of heating surface, and forms a space for the sediment, which can be blown out of the boiler by a blow-off cock underneath the fire-box. The ash-pit door forms a damper, by which the draught may be regulated with the greatest nicety.

This engine is simple in construction, easy of management, has great power with a small consumption of fuel, and is readily turned in a very small space—suitable for ploughing, thrashing, corn-grinding, saw-mills, and wherever machinery is used. It draws a load of from fifteen to twenty tons on an ordinary road with ease, and with little noise, at a speed of five or six miles an hour. It is extensively patronised both in this country and abroad.

Robey and Co.'s Portable Combined Thrashing, Shaking, and Dressing Machine, for finishing the corn for market, is constructed to thrash all kinds of grain without injury to either straw or kernel. The drum and breasting are made exclusively of wrought iron and wood. It has a very simple and efficient straw shaker, which delivers the straw perfectly straight and clear of corn; the cavings and chaff are separated and kept distinct. The corn, when dressed once over, is passed through an improved barley horner, which is fitted with a self-acting delivery valve, whereby choking is prevented, and regular chopping insured. It has also a very effective finishing apparatus, containing Patent Corn Screen, which removes all capes or whites from wheat, and purifies the grain from all filth, dust, fur,

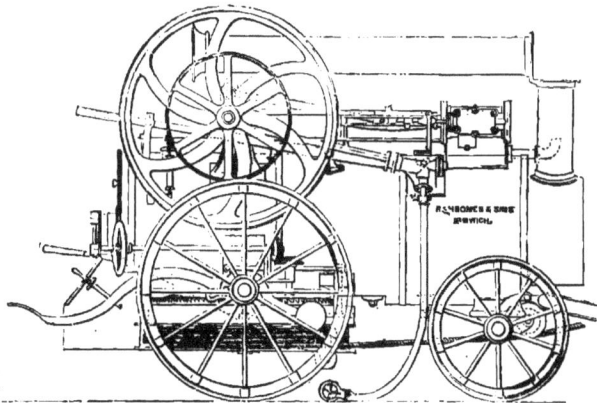

SECTION OF STEAM THRASHING MACHINE. MESSRS. RANSOME AND SIMS.

smuts, small seeds, &c. Also a double blasted blower, which takes out all extraneous matter liberated from the corn while passing through the chopper and screen, and separates the light tail corn from the best, delivering both best corn and tailings into their proper sacks. The above machine is peculiarly adapted for grain in very bad condition, or when very full of crow needles and rubbish. It can be worked either as a single or double dresser, and delivers the corn on either side.

The arrangements are very simple, all working parts being on the outside and easy of access. The machine stands remarkably steady when at work. It is mounted on wood wheels and patent axles, the drum fitted with Goucher's patent beaters. Our illustration represents the engine as it appears when conveying its machine or apparatus from one place to another. From the

EXHIBITS OF MR. EDWARD HAYES,

of Stoney Stratford, Bucks, we select the Self-acting Windlass for Steam Ploughing. Our illustration is a sketch taken on the estate of his Grace the Duke of Grafton, at Wakefield Lawn, Northamptonshire, a beautiful and picturesque part of the county, bounded by the ancient Forest of Whittlebury, and abounding in historic interest. Near the spot still stands the Queen's Oak, under which King Edward IV., in 1464, met, for the first time, the lovely widow, Elizabeth Woodville, the ancestress of the present royal lady. Here some interesting trials in steam cultivation have recently taken place, through the invitation of his Grace the Duke of Grafton, who kindly placed a piece of land at the disposal of Mr. Hayes, to test the merits of his patent self-acting windlass, previously to its being placed in the International Exhibition. A silver medal was awarded to this windlass at the Royal Agricultural Show at Leeds, 1861. Among the company present on the occasion were his Grace the Duke of Grafton, the Duchess of Grafton, Lord Euston, the Hon. Colonel Douglas Pennant, Lady Pennant, the Hon. George Fitzroy, Captain J. C. Mansel, with a number of the leading agriculturists of the neighbourhood, who took great interest in the working of the machinery. The results of the trial were considered

very good; the piece of ground allotted being completed during the daytime, and a portion cross cultivated after the moon had risen. More than usual interest was taken in these trials, in consequence of the novel application of steam power, through a very ingenious windlass, to the tillage of the land. The chief anxiety of the Royal Agricultural Society, and those most interested in the application of that wondrous agent, steam, to till the land, has been to find the best means to yoke the ordinary portable steam-engine, now numbering their hundreds in almost every county in England. This has been done by the self-acting windlass of Mr. Hayes. The windlass is detached from the engine, and driven by a strap, as the thrashing machine has been; the engine and windlass being drawn by horses, to and from the work to be done, as the engine and thrashing machine have been. In thrashing corn by steam, the engine is not stopped; neither is it in cultivating the land. When the cultivator reaches the headland, the plough or cultivator is instantly stopped by the anchorman waiting to receive the same. The engine has not even any portion of its steam shut off; nor is it really necessary that the engine-driver should be in sight of the work being done. The stopping and starting is much more quickly done than in the ordinary method of stopping and starting, the engine requiring only one man to superintend engine and windlass. As signals are not a necessity, it will be perceived that work can be done in fogs and by moonlight. This adaptation is considered of great value. The steam horse never tires. By a double set of hands, the ploughing need not cease night or day. The main distinguishing features of the windlass are:—It is so constructed as to use with advantage the simple and ordinary portable engine with one cylinder, and so employ much of the capital already expended in the steam-engine for agricultural purposes. One man superintends both engine and windlass. The anchor-man at each headland stops the implement without stopping the engine.

TRACTION ENGINE AND THRASHING MACHINE. MESSRS. RODEY AND CO.

SELF-ACTING WINDLASS FOR STEAM-PLOUGHING. MR. EDWARD HAYES.

Wood-cutting and Carbing Machinery.

MESSRS. POWIS, JAMES, AND CO.

HAVING already referred (p. 67) to the machines for working in wood, we have now pleasure in directing the attention of the reader to illustrations of the machines themselves, as exhibited by Messrs. Powis, James, and Co., of Watling Street. These gentlemen have produced a

when changes are required to suit the various classes of work. The same attention is also apparent in the arrangement of the working parts, which are all easily accessible, the cutter-heads being forged solid on the spindle, a great improvement over older inventions.

The second figure shows the Improved Moulding Machine.

1. COMBINED MACHINE FOR PLANING, EDGING, TONGUING, GROOVING, AND MOULDING.

number of most admirable contrivances for the saving of labour and the cheapening of productions in building and other appliances.

Our first illustration shows the Patent Combined Machine for planing, edging, tonguing, grooving, thicknessing, and moulding, and which operates on all four sides of the timber at one time. This

This is a very useful machine to joiners, for mouldings, skirtings, &c. The machine will cut top and bottom mouldings, up to nine inches in

2.—IMPROVED MOULDING MACHINE.

is a very ingenious apparatus, and must be seen in operation before a correct estimate of its working accuracy is likely to be made. It has a variable feed, and is well adapted for every class of moulding, as well as floor boards. As in the endless band-saw machine, the patentees have here also consulted the principle of uniform pressure; the manner in which the pressure is applied to the feed-rollers giving great facility

3. - MACHINE FOR MORTISING, TENON-CUTTING, AND BORING.

width, at one operation. It has a movable table, and can be fed with great rapidity. In squaring up door stiles it is found of considerable service, as a number of them may be passed through together edge-

18.

ways, so as to attain a uniform width. Its workmanship is clean and accurate.

The third figure shows the Patent Combined Machine, for mortising, tenon-cutting hard and soft wood, and boring wood or iron. This is perhaps one of the most interesting of Messrs. Powis, James, and Co.'s production. It is a beautiful little apparatus, simple, powerful, and expeditious, and is, we believe, the only one patented in the United Kingdom for doing three kinds of work by one machine. It is self-feeding, and requires only unskilled labour for its attendant, or is not likely to break or get out of order, and will do as much work (even with unskilled aid) as eight good workmen with the chisel and mallet.

The Improved Patent Combined Timber and Deal Frame is so contrived as to answer a double purpose. It is very efficient, yet simple, the effect of the invention being to render it of easy adaptation and working. The bulk of timber to be operated on it is supported by the saw frame by means of a "roller feed," the timber being carried forward on two iron carriages, running on rails, and provided with wrought-iron screw clips, for holding the timber in position. One great advantage of this frame over the old kind is that the pressure and binding rollers, when not required for cutting deal, may be wound up and put out of the way, instead of needing complete removal. When required as a deal frame very little preparation is necessary, the fence being made in one piece, ready to drop in its place. Here may be cut round or square logs, up to twenty-four inches diameter, or two twenty-four by seven inch deals, or any size under, the timber carriages being arranged so as to allow the curve to be followed in crooked logs. The frame can be driven from above or below, and can be used on a tidal river, as no excavations are required underneath,

4.—COMBINED TIMBER AND DEAL FRAME.

except a pit for the sawdust, a matter of great moment where promises are subject to flooding. The workmanship throughout is excellent, and the material of first-class quality.

The Endless Band Saw Machine is provided with a compound spring adjustment (never before adopted), to prevent the fracture of saws from the sudden expansion, contraction, &c., to which they are unavoidably liable in the course of daily use. In the ordinary machines, the bearing which carries the saw wheel is a fixture, and therefore no allowance can at any time be made for sudden strains. In Messrs. Powis's improvement the top spindle or bracket, or bearing, carrying

the saw wheel is allowed to move freely up and down a dovetail slide, which is connected with a compound adjusting lever. Two adjusting rods pass through the end of this lever, in communication with boxes containing springs, on which the saw-wheel rides, and thus, when sawing sharp curves, an expansion of the saw takes place, and in all those other cases where the saw is required to be eased on the wheels carrying it, this combined mechanical adjustment comes into immediate operation. The action of the springs is compensatory for any sudden demands—the saw is allowed to ride easy and soft on the wheels, and the slack caused by expansion is immediately taken up without the tightening of the wheel a second time, as in the old inventions. Considering that the evils of carelessness on the part of attendants, and the misfortunes unavoidable, are thus prevented, this improvement may be certainly called a success, in its most important feature of economy. This machine cuts twenty-two inches deep, and the table is made to shift on the angle to, suit any class of work. It is of finished order, perfect in adaptation and design, and already in extensive and successful use in the mining, ship-building and manufacturing districts of this and other countries.

Next we have a Six-horse Horizontal High-pressure Engine, exceedingly simple, inexpensive, and compact, constructed with great accuracy, lightness, and strength, and of the most approved design. Those connected with machinery know the value of smoothness and ease in the working parts, and the engine under consideration is perfect in these respects. It is supplied with pump, governor, throttle and stop valves, blow-through cocks, and grease-urn to cylinder. Each motion-block is cased with brass, so as to hold oil to lubricate the bottom bars; indeed, Messrs. Powis have been particularly careful that all the working parts of the engine should be well lubricated—a very important point. These engines are constructed of the best material, and are admirably adapted for the driving of the various wood-cutting machines we are now noticing. Throughout the Western Annexe—so richly stored with machines for working in iron and wood—none contribute a more interesting display of wood-cutting machines than the above-mentioned firm. Many of them are masterpieces of automatic skill, and all are evidently the results of deep thought, consummate professional skill, and thorough knowledge.

5.—ENDLESS BAND SAW MACHINE.

Bookbinding.

WE have selected our illustration from the extensive show of Messrs. Leighton, of Brewer Street, Golden Square, which contains an extremely good collection in this important branch of art manufacture. Their contribution to the Great International Exhibition consists of volumes of every variety of size and style, from the most elaborate specimens in morocco to simple calf-bindings. The book from which our engraving is taken is a copy of "Shakspere," in morocco, in the Elizabethan style. It is richly illuminated with the arms and autograph of the poet. On the edges is a painting of "Shakspeare reading his plays to Queen Elizabeth," which does not show when the volume is shut, the design having been drawn before the edges were gilt, so that the picture is only seen upon opening the book. Among the curiosities of Art-manufactures exhibited, these specimens are to be commended for originality, ingenuity, and taste.

These exhibitors do not show so much for minute "finishing," as for substantial work, in combination with good design. We would direct attention particularly to a folio volume, "L'Inferno di Dante," bound in black morocco, inlaid in coloured leathers, and richly gilt, with design of the serpent and apple enveloped in a shower of golden flames, which is very Venetian in character.

In addition to Messrs. J. and J. Leighton's show of extra leather bindings, they display processes connected with the restoration of missing portions of imperfect books, as copper and woodcut illustrations; also letterpress, which are produced by them in MS fac-simile; plates reduced from folios to 8vo size, by the photo-zincographic process; likewise samples of paper-splitting (which is often very useful in bookbinding). There are also shown a choice assemblage of book-plates—produced by them for various literary collectors.

Most of the patterns in "extra" or library bindings are produced by impressing on the covers a number of separate tools, arranged by the "finisher" himself into forms according to his taste, and in many cases without artistic help.

One of the greatest faults of the book-binder, foreign as well as British, consists in the over elaboration of designs, without due regard to leading features. This, however, is a fault that does not apply to the works under notice, which are highly meritorious.

In the same case are several specimens of the richly-variegated Spanish leather (now so scarce), which affords a pleasing variety to the ordinary calf-bindings, which, with a copy of "Burnet on Painting," in red morocco, with a chaste pattern in gilt lines, and a "Tennyson's Poems," in green morocco, richly gilt; also "Lyra Germanica," in purple morocco, are works of which a bookbinder may justly be proud, as they display the skilful hand of an artistic workman.

THE EXHIBITION SHAKSPERE: MESSRS. J. AND J. LEIGHTON. THE DESIGN BY LUKE LIMNER.

Mediæval Furniture.

We have now to present our readers with a couple of illustrations from the group of furniture by Messrs. Hindley and Son, of Oxford show the adaptation of that style to modern requirements, when carefully managed. Too often it is rendered ungraceful and clumsy by

MEDIÆVAL BOOKCASE. MESSRS. HINDLEY AND SONS.

Street. We select these in order to show how good taste and ability may be worthily combined.

The bookcase is in mediæval style, and has been designed to the affectation of extraordinary proportions and shapes, scarcely possible to be useful. In this piece of furniture it has been the study of the manufacturer to preserve and to exhibit the solid construction of

CARVED SIDEBOARD. MESSRS. HINDLEY AND SONS.

minent throughout, having a plinth on which rise the perpendicular supports, formed into plain, strong brackets below, terminated with Gothic foliage, beautifully varied, and surmounted by pillars above, elaborately carved, with traceried ornament, and finished with handsome capitals and entablature, highly enriched with tracery and foliage. The panels of the doors are a specimen of what may be executed in wood by first-rate designers and carvers, being exceedingly light and elegant ; the upper ones being open to show the books, the supported on two antique lions. The upper part has a silvan plate-glass centre—available for a piece of fine art carving, or a picture instead—set in a frame, between pillars and panels of carved work. There are many carved mouldings of great richness; and the scrolls, panels, capitals of the pillars, and the entablature, cornices, and vases, are also most elaborate in design and execution. The chief ornamental parts exhibit the bay-leaf, the ivy, and the acanthus ; and, though executed with extreme delicacy and lightness, are yet strong and genuine in construction, carved in solid wood, and their lightness is the effect of the expression produced by workmanship of the highest class.

A noble piece of work, exhibited by Messrs. White and Parlby, of

tions of which plan have been adopted in various important public buildings. The right-hand illustration is of a fine old engraved Venetian looking-glass, adapted as a choval glass, by a stand of richly-carved ebony, inlaid with ivory. This piece of work was manufactured for

ARCHITECTURAL DOME   MESSRS. WHITE AND PARLBY.

Great Marylebone Street, and a couple of examples by Messrs. Litchfield and Radelyffe, completes our review of the furniture in the

and is the property of the Right Honourable the Earl of Craven, whose crest and cipher are introduced into the ornamentation of the frame. The left-hand illustration is of a carved upright cabinet on stand, inlaid with cornelians, marble, in columns, plinths, &c.; the inside lined with silvered glass, and decorated with groups and fine specimens of Sèvres, Dresden, Berlin, and Viennese porcelain, selected from the

CARVED CABINET   MESSRS. LITCHFIELD AND RADCLYFFE.

VENETIAN CHEVAL GLASS.   PRIZE MEDAL.

British Courts in the International Exhibition. One illustration shows the application of Messrs. White and Parlby's new cement to the formation of curved and ornamental surfaces, successful applica-

stock of Messrs. Litchfield and Radelyffe, at their warehouse, Hanway Street, Oxford Street. Marqueterie, ebony, and inlaid furniture, of a very superior description, is shown by this firm at the Great Exhibition.

Mats and Matting.

THE specimens of Cocoa-nut Fibre, and the manufactures therefrom, exhibited in Class 1, Eastern Annexe, are numerous and excellent. The fibre is obtained from the husks of the cocoa-nut (*cocos nucifera*), and has been long made use of by the natives of Ceylon and India for the manufacture of ropes and coarse fabrics. Since its introduction into this country, some twenty years ago, its use has increased daily, the best proof that it has been rightly bestowed is found in the fact that all his competitors freely acknowledge the justice of the Jurors' award. There are so few instances of this kind that it is pleasant to record such when they occur. Our illustrations are the Pompeian door-mats "Salve" (*Welcome*), and "Cave Canem" (*Beware of the Dog*), and are taken from the specimens exhibited by Mr. Treloar.

DESIGNS IN COCOA-NUT FIBRE.   MR. TRELOAR.   PRIZE MEDAL.

until it has become an important article of industry, giving employment to thousands of hands. The annual importation of *coir* (the commercial name by which the fibre of the cocoa-nut is designated) is said to amount at the present time to upwards of 8,000 tons, in value somewhere about a quarter of a million sterling. Besides the

The introduction of colour into the mats and matting has been attended with great success, and many of the patterns exhibited are most artistic in their design and treatment. Much might be written in commendation of cocoa-nut matting did our space admit; but visitors to the Picture Galleries cannot fail to have noticed the

POMPEIAN DOOR-MAT IN COCOA-NUT FIBRE.   MR. TRELOAR.   PRIZE MEDAL.

fibre imported, a considerable quantity is broken up from the husk in this country, and used chiefly for making brushes and brooms for household and stable purposes, the imported fibre being almost entirely used for cordage, floor-matting, mats, and sheepfold nets.

Although there are many exhibitors of cocoa-nut fibre manufactures in Class 4 whose works are very good, the single distinction of a medal has been given to Mr. T. Treloar, of Ludgate Hill; and perhaps

excellent specimen which covers that vast area, and which has added so much to their comfort.

For an illustration of the manifold uses of the cocoa-nut tree in its native latitudes, we refer our readers to the Ceylon Court, in the North-east Transept, where they will find a stand covered with articles, "the produce of a cocoa-nut," associating itself with nearly every want and convenience of life.

The Leather Court

MESSRS. SWAINE AND ADENEY'S WHIPS.

THE Leather Court will be found on the south side of the building, just behind the Civil Engineering Department. About one hundred and thirty-five exhibitors have 4,583 feet of floor space. Sheep, hog, and seal-skins; goat, calf, horse, deer, and other hides; enamelled, curried, patent, and coloured leathers; saddlery, bridles, and other harness, will here be admired. One of the most striking objects in this Court is the case of whips and canes shown by Messrs. Swaine and Adeney, of Piccadilly, who have obtained the Prize Medal. The members of this firm call the attention of equestrians and equestriennes to their whips, which they confidently, and with justice, proclaim to be the guineas. In order, however, to show the elaborate manner in which the handles of the whips are carved in silver and gold, we subjoin views of the two sides of the new Exhibition Whip, especially prepared for the World's Show of 1862.

It may perhaps be considered by many that the ornamentation of the handle of a whip is a simple matter; but if they will examine some of the whip-handles in Messrs. Swaine and Adeney's case, they will speedily change their opinions. Elaborate chasing and carving in silver and other metals affords ample scope for both designer and workman. In the design for the Exhibition whip, for instance, it will be seen that allegory has been well employed to good purpose.

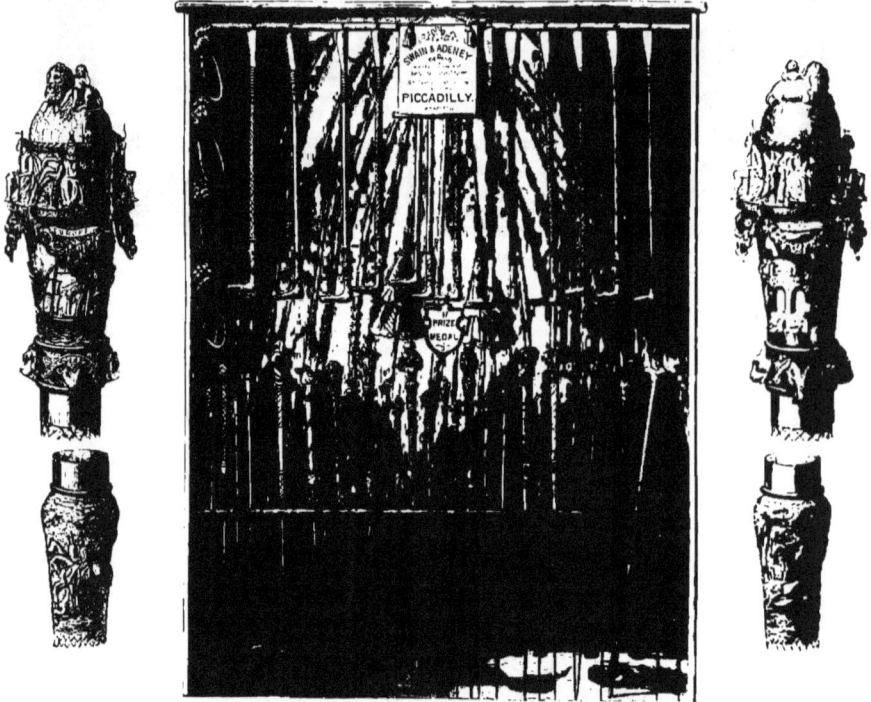

CASE OF WHIPS AND CANES. PRIZE MEDAL, MESSRS. SWAINE AND ADENEY.

"one thing needful" for all who mean to "witch the world" with noble horsemanship. Here are whips wherewith to win the Derby; whips for the state-coachmen and postillions on drawing-room days; ladies' phaeton whips, contrived "a double debt to pay," and be at once both whip and parasol; in fact, every variety of the flexible *Fouet*, except that particular one which is intended to "whip creation," and which, of course, can only be found in the American department. This case of whips—inadequately shown in our engraving, from the very nature of the articles themselves—is worth upwards of a thousand

Figures typical of Europe, Asia, Africa, and America are seated round a globe surmounted by the British lion, while below we have Peace and Commerce represented by ships, railroads, bales of merchandise, &c., the whole united by wreaths of flowers and conventional ornaments. The ring-classes are illustrations of hunting and racing; and both them and the mounts are finished in the most chaste and elaborate manner.

In the Leather Court will be found gigantic butt hides of tanned leather, some of which are actually ten feet square.

VIEW OF THE FOREIGN NAVE FROM THE WESTERN DOME.

19.

Silver Plate in the Exhibition.—II.

WORKS IN THE PRECIOUS METALS EXHIBITED BY MESSRS. ELKINGTON AND CO.

THE Precious Metals and Jewellery (Class 33) shown by British exhibitors occupy a large court on the south side of the Nave, next the Central Avenue. This position is one of the most prominent in the building; and the beautiful objects shown provide a never-ending source of attraction for visitors of all countries and conditions. Here

1.—ENAMELLED CANDLESTICK—GREEK STYLE.

the Koh-i-noor flashes and sparkles beside the jewellery shown by Messrs. Hancock, Lambert, Phillips Emanuel, London and Ryder, Garrard, Hunt and Roskell, and the other exhibitors of gems and trinkets. Eighty-four exhibitors in the Precious Metals Court have nearly eight thousand square feet of space, inclusive of passages. Here will be found rare jewels, exquisitely set; gold and silver filagree,

3.—ENAMELLED SILVER TAZZA—POMPEIAN STYLE.

bijouterie, and all the witcheries of female ornamentation, in the way of tiaras, brooches, ear-rings, finger-rings, bracelets, sleeve-links, chains, pins, studs, &c.

But these form only part of the gallant show; for in the same cases in which shine diamonds, rubies, sapphires, pearls, opals, and emeralds, there are various fine works in gold and silver, such as centre-

pieces, shields, race-cups, presentation vases, dinner and tea-services, &c., most of which may be considered rather as coming within the realm of fine art than as mere manufacture.

2.—ENAMELLED CANDLESTICK—"THE BUTTERFLY."

This is especially the case with the objects exhibited by Messrs. Elkington and Co., from whose cases we have selected various fine works for illustration. In the manufacture of artistic works in silver, bronze, and other metals, the Messrs. Elkington stand in the

4.—ENAMELLED SILVER TAZZA—POMPEIAN STYLE.

very first rank. They have an especial appointment by her Majesty the Queen, and their works are known all over the world as possessing the highest degree of finish combined with educated taste and rare manipulative skill. In their works at Birmingham are produced a vast variety of useful and ornamental articles in the precious metals, and also in less costly materials coated with silver by means of the electro-galvanic process. This process of gilding and plating was patented by the Messrs. Elkington in 1840, and has since become a very important branch of industry. Various other manufacturers and foreigners have since adopted and practised it extensively. The advantages of plating by this process are the application of a white metal, approximating to silver in hardness and colour (as a base instead of copper, as in the old system of plating), upon which suspended in the trough. The metallic base of electro-plated articles of the finer kind is generally formed of German silver, or a hard, white metal composed of nickel, zinc, and copper, the several parts being held together by hard solder, which fuses only at a very high temperature. Under the old method of producing designs in plated silver, the figures and ornaments were cast in silver; but electro-plated goods are cast in white metal, and, after being rifled or cleared, are introduced into the galvanic bath, and receive a deposit of silver equally on all their parts. The electro process is now largely used in the production of duplicate engravings, such as those from which our illustrations are printed, copper being deposited instead of silver on the surface of the mould. In the old system of silver-plating, heat and pressure were employed, and the superficial covering of the article effected previous to the manufacture or shaping of the article itself. A piece of silver or gold is placed upon an ingot of the metal to be plated. They are then introduced into a furnace, with a flux between the two surfaces. At a given point of heat fusion of the two surfaces takes place, and complete adhesion is effected. The ingot is then rolled out into sheets between steel rollers, by the ordinary process, and the object manufactured of the combined metal. The objection to this plan is, that when the superior metal wears off, the inferior base is exposed, and the article rendered comparatively valueless. When the voltaic action is carefully conducted—as in the examples shown by Messrs. Elkington—very beautiful surfaces are produced. In electro-gilding, solutions of the oxide of gold in the cyanide, or the ferrocyanide of potassium, are usually employed. Many specimens of this kind of gilding may be seen in the English and Foreign Courts.

With this explanation—which, we believe, will not be unwelcome

6.—SILVER TANKARD.

the real silver is deposited by electricity; secondly, the removal of all restraint as to the form of the object to be plated—the most elaborate ornaments and the most complicated designs producible in silver being equally obtainable by the electro process; thirdly, permanency of plating, the coating of silver becoming, by the agency of electricity, one body with the metal on which it is deposited, rather than a mere covering; lastly, economy in cost and durability. By this process, works of art of the highest character may be cheaply multiplied; and copies of the smallest trinkets or the largest statues, possessing all the accuracy and beauty of the original designs, are produced with exact precision and perfection.

The discovery, or rather application, of the principle of the electrotype process is due in this country to Thomas Spencer, of Liverpool. He is said to have made the discovery by observing the exact copy in metal of some imperfections at the bottom of a cell in one of his scientific experiments which he had been using for scientific experiments. The electrotype differs from the magneto process only in so far as the exciting agent is produced by the immersion of zinc, platinised silver, &c., in a solution of sulphuric acid, which is connected by wires or rods with the deposit trough. In this solution is suspended the article to be gilt or silvered; the strength of the solution is maintained by plates of the metal, of the same kind as that which is to be deposited, being

G.—SILVER-GILT CLARET JUG.

to our readers—we may proceed to notice some of the exquisite articles shown in our engravings.

Figures 1 and 2 are of enamelled candlesticks—the first in the Greek, and the second in the modern style of ornamentation. We lately explained the principle upon which enamelling on gold and silver is produced. Though large objects in enamel are now seldom made, the manufacture is by no means new. Trinkets, and other small objects in enamel, have been found in various excavations, proving that the art was practised by the ancient inhabitants of this island. At Oxford there is preserved the enamelled jewel made by command of King Alfred; and about the tomb of Edward the Confessor, in Westminster Abbey, there are various specimens of the art. The gold enamelled cup given by King John to the burgesses of Lynn, in Norfolk, and many other specimens, prove that the art was commonly practised in the Middle Ages.

The Tazzas, in the Pompeian style, belong to an enamelled silver dessert service of forty pieces, and are deservedly admired. For graceful design and excellent workmanship, they are perhaps unequalled by any similar work in the Exhibition.

Next we have a pair of silver tankards, exquisitely engraved; near them, in the case, are the Queen's Prize Cup, presented by Her Majesty to the Royal Mersey Yacht Club Regatta, last year, and won by the exhibitor, C. T. Couper, Jun.; a pair of candelabra, modelled from a design of his late Royal Highness the Prince Consort; a silver equestrian statue of "Godiva," the property of the Queen, by whose permission it is exhibited selections from various portions of a service of plate for a hundred persons, manufactured for H.R.H. the Duke of Brabant, by whose permission they are shown; a silver-gilt and oxidised "Challenge Shield," presented by Lord Ashburton, and won by Rugby scholars at the Wimbledon Rifle Contest last year; the silver-gilt prize claret jug, offered by the National Rifle Association, won by Captain Horatio Ross, the champion shot, last year, at the Wimbledon meeting; a silver equestrian statuette of Her Majesty the Queen, modelled by J. H. Foley, and adorned with bas-reliefs, commemorative of the Queen's visit to Warwickshire (in the panels of the pedestals), by A. Williams, the well-known artist in silver. This

7.—"THE DREAMERS"—SILVER REPOUSSÉ TABLE.

statuette is the copyright of Messrs. Elkington, who can, therefore, make reproductions of it in silver or bronze. Then there is a fine

silver and bronze group of "Guy, Earl of Warwick, and the Dun Cow." This formed the Race Cup at Warwick in 1854, and is exhibited by the winner, H. Padwick, Esq. Near it is a group in silver, designed and modelled by the late E. Jeannest, the subject being "Charles the First discovering the Body of his Standard-bearer, De Verney, after the Battle of Edge-hill." Another fine group is the "Flight of Amy Robsart, conducted by Wayland"—from Sir Walter Scott's "Kenilworth," and which formed the Race Cup at Warwick in 1860. It is exhibited by permission of the winner, the Right Hon. the Earl of Strathmore. Forming part of the same trophy is the silver inkstand presented to Costa by the Sacred Harmonic Society and the Crystal Palace Company, in commemoration of the oratorio of the Handel Festival of 1859; and a silver group presented by the Birmingham Choral Society to the same composer — the subject being taken from the oratorio of "Eli." Various centre-pieces and plateaus, vases, rifle cups, trays, tazzas, and statuettes occupy places of distinction in the Elkington trophy; but, perhaps, the most famous piece of work is "The Dreamers" —a repoussé table by Morel Ladeuil, an artist scarcely second to Vechte, his preceptor, in this description of work. We have already (page 99) mentioned this fine work; but now that we are enabled to present an engraving of it to our readers, we may give the artist's own explanation of his beautiful design.

This work, says M. Ladeuil, is intended to portray the poetic influences of Sleep, by the picturing in dreams of the ideal pursuit after Happiness in our waking existence.

To carry out the idea with simplicity, the artist has limited himself to three principal figures, symbolising Agriculture, Music, and War, who, in the persons of a husbandman, minstrel, and soldier, are sleeping on the tripod base, surrounded with the instruments of their various callings, habited in the picturesque costumes of the Middle Ages, and grouped about the stem; round which is intertwined

robed with Music; Folly, with her cap and bells; and Fortune, who, kneeling on her emblematical wheel, scatters gold, unmindful of where it falls.

The third dream is that of the Agriculturist, and is one of Peace and Plenty. The figures here bear offerings of the fruits of the earth, intertwined with flowers; a Bacchante also holds the wine-cup to receive the juice of the grape; following in the train is a Cupid, bearing the no less important wheat sheaf. This group is completed by a figure bearing a cornucopia, emblematic of abundance.

The border is a fantastic creation, in the German manner, of monsters and reptiles, being intended to represent how hideous fancies will sometimes mingle with the fairer visions of the night.

"Galatea" is a reproduction of a jug, by Briot; and, as well as the "Indian Combat," is considered a very fine specimen of silver work.

In page 151 we have a silver dish, with medallions emblematical of the "Elements"—Earth, with the cornucopia, reclining on a bank of flowers; Air, represented by a flying figure, followed by birds of passage, and attended by the winds; Water, by a river goddess, sitting on a throne of aquatic plants, and bearing the emblems of command, in the midst of the sea, in which are seen dolphins, &c.; and Fire, by winged demons carrying the bolts of Jupiter through clouds of flame and smoke: the whole surrounded by an appropriate border of conventional ornaments.

In page 152 are shown a pair of *repoussé* tazzas, representing Night

9.—SILVER TANKARD WITH IVORY MEDALLIONS, ILLUSTRATIVE OF THEATRICAL ART.

11.—ENAMELLED VASE.—POMPEIAN STYLE.

10.—SILVER TANKARD.—INDIAN COMBAT.

12.—SILVER JUG.—CHALIA.

and Morning—the one scattering flowers on the earth, and the other throwing a veil of darkness over all the landscape, while the stars peep out, to add their glory to the scene. Both figures, "Aurora" and "Night," are attended by their appropriate emblems—the one, by Love with a torch, and a child distributing dew from a vase; and the other, by a bat flying fearfully, fitfully by. Nor should these perfume-burners in enamelled copper be passed over. The silver enamelled dessert-service, in the Pompeian style, is a splendid specimen of art-workmanship; and so are the great Indian vase, the mauresque epergne, the centre-piece discovering "Æsop's Fables," and an inkstand in the style of Louis XIV. The Indian and Renaissance tea-sets are also in the highest style of art-workmanship, and will challenge comparison with anything of the kind in the Exhibition.

The wonders of Messrs. Elkington's vast establishment are most striking in the shops, where, in vast baths, great statues lie gathering strength hourly, that they may presently bear the brunt of the elements upon lofty pedestals. The head of Mr. Durham's "Europe" (part of his memorial of the Great Exhibition of 1851) is being emancipated from its copper mould by the help of heavy pincers. Foley's "Caractacus" still lies in his copper bath; but the figures and statues for Wellington College; Hancock's "Beatrice;" figures of her Majesty the Queen, and of her late lamented Consort; great pieces, also by Durham; and for Balmoral "The Malcolm Canmore"—these are among the great works which have issued of late from Messrs. Elkington's magic baths.

13.—SILVER DISH, ILLUSTRATIVE OF THE ELEMENTS.

But to see the works of Messrs. Elkington to advantage, a visit should be paid to their manufactory at Birmingham.

Thousands of people remember the delight with which, when metal was first deposited upon a metallic surface by the agency of electricity, they made copper impressions of little plaster medallions. They wondered to see the warm film of copper come upon the leaded surface. That which was the toy of their youth has become a great and magnificent industry. Since the time when the electro process was a plaything, noble works have been set in enduring metal by it. It has deposited statues and bas-reliefs for the House of Lords; it has produced the statues that are to decorate Wellington College. On the other hand, it has elaborated for the households of the middle, ay, and of the humbler classes, articles for use and ornament which, forty years ago, were the exclusive enjoyment of the rich.

The visitor who mounts the stairs to the splendid show-rooms passes two rows of statues executed for the House of Lords, which have all grown under the electric fingers of this renowned firm. One of these is shown in an illustration on page 153. The show-rooms exhibit the gorgeous results of the industry that is going on round about them. The costly, and the elegant and cheap, are side by side. The factory can send forth an Alhambra table, or it can—as at the other works a mile distant—turn out one thousand dozen of spoons, that shall be within reach of all purses, in a week. In this spoon and fork department, five tons of "german" is used every six days. Each mill, or machine, in a room we visited, could cut 140 dozen small forks, and 80 dozen large, per diem. Spoons are counted by the 300 dozen. They lie about in vast discoloured heaps. The annealing in rotary ovens, the pickling in aquafortis between each process; the soldering, hammering, &c.; the smoothing and filing; the silver-pointing, where the solid silver tips are fastened upon the forks; the finishing, where the girls, by dozens, are using, first, the rottenstone and oil, then the "red" from the potteries, and, lastly, the rubbing of the hand, which gives the "bloom"—these are processes which must be seen to be properly understood.

The art department of Messrs. Elkington's establishment is one that cannot but present attractions for all classes of visitors. The fret and toil that are going on to produce splendours for Elkington's part in the Exhibition are wonderful. Here is the most wonderful of all spirit-rapping; for, by the help of magic taps given by little hammers, behold the magic dream which M. Morel Ladeuil reveals upon this silver table, "The Three Dreamers."

The skilful artist of this magnificent work has also executed a raised silver vase, still the effect of his magic rapping. The subject of this work was evidently inspired by the Exhibition. Steam and the electric telegraph are here represented by two female figures, with outstretched wings, supported by fantastic monsters. At the base four children, perfectly modelled, hold emblems of the voltaic battery, photography, the screw-propeller, and the Jacquard loom. The bas-reliefs suggest the sciences which marshal discoveries, and industry and skill which apply them. One child, in meditative attitude, leans upon a pneumatic machine, in company with Astronomy and Chemistry, who are surrounded with books and philosophical

14.—"MORNING"—A TAZZA IN SILVER.

15.—"NIGHT"—A TAZZA IN SILVER.

instruments. Industry—also a child—has various manufactures in his vicinity; and here is Mercury, representing Commerce. Upon the books and tablets the names of great and greatly useful men are engraved. This Exhibition vase is capped with a bold Genius of Industry; but the piece cannot be completed in time for the Exhibition, a fact greatly to be regretted.

Leaving the noisy workers, we pass to the vast store-rooms. To judge by the thousands of packed tea-pots, one would think that the Maine Liquor Law had become universal law.

But to fairly appreciate all the useful and ornamental development of which the electro process has proved itself capable, it is necessary to spend days in an establishment like that of Messrs. Elkington and Co. Here may be seen in perfection every variety of the electro process; in one part are the mighty figures modelled by Durham for his Great Exhibition Memorial, lying in their copper baths; in another are the frailest branches receiving their thin coat of gold. Wandering from room to room, from shed to shed, from courtyard to courtyard, the visitor is bewildered with the constant variety of skill and ingenuity brought to bear upon common objects of daily life; and specimens of all these are to be seen in the Elkington Trophy, before which—in the British Nave of the Exhibition—we invite the reader to pause and study; certain that his time will be well employed—for while he admires, he cannot but learn.

Bronzes in the Exhibition.

THE bold barons who wrung Magna Charta—the "great charter of English liberty"—from King John, seem as fitly to occupy their places in the Great Exhibition of all Nations as they do in the House of Lords. Every visitor will remember the figures of these grim warriors, standing at the angles made by the junction of the Nave with the Eastern Dome. They are the original plaster casts—bronzed, and made to look like the real metal—of the statues now placed in niches in the Peers' Chamber of the Palace of Westminster.

The fine statues of the eighteen barons who signed the important document called "Magna Charta" were cast in bronze by Messrs. Elkington, from designs by Westmacott, Thornycroft, the late John Thomas, and other eminent sculptors. In the Exhibition there are nine of these—six on the steps of the Eastern Dome, three on each side, and three in the Elkington Trophy, in the Nave. These are Langton, Archbishop of Canterbury, by John Thomas; Almeric, Master of the Knights Templars, by P. Macdowell, R.A.; and Norfolk, Earl of Arundel, by T. Thornycroft. The six other knights in the People's Palace at Brompton are Saher, Earl of Winchester, by Westmacott (the noble figure shown in our engraving); Robert Fitzwalter; Eustace de Vesci; the Earl of Hereford; and Robert, Earl of Clare. Of course it will not be expected that we should criticise these fine statues. Having been admitted into the Parliament House of the nation, we must needs accept them as true representations of the veritable warriors who, sword in hand, forced the timid and cruel John into a grand submission; but as to their reproduction in bronze, from the clay models of the sculptors, we may speak in terms of high praise. The sharp, clear outlines, and the crisp edges of the metal, show that in the founding the Messrs. Elkington exercised their usual care and educated taste.

While on this subject, we may mention the statue of "Goldsmith," by Foley, a representation of which we gave on page 8 of the EXHIBITOR, and the bronze copy of Mr. Henry Weigall's bust of his Grace the "Duke of Wellington," both produced by Messrs. Elkington, and both shown in the International Exhibition. Of the latter work a competent writer observes:—

"This bust, which was modelled in the autumn of 1851, from sittings given to the artist expressly for the purpose, is distinguished from all others we have seen by its remarkable fidelity—fidelity both of form and of expression. It is evident that the artist has not allowed himself to be biassed by any pre-conceived notion of what a hero ought to be. He has studied the venerable English nobleman who was then and there sitting before him—the veteran soldier who had been long enjoying that peace he had so mainly assisted in procuring for his country—the practised statesman who had retired from the arena of political conflict; he reverently studied and followed Nature, and he who does this will never

SAHER, EARL OF WINCHESTER. DESIGNED BY J. S. WESTMACOTT, AND CAST BY MESSRS. ELKINGTON.

lose his reward. There is more of the real man here than we have found elsewhere. The signs of age have not been fastidiously avoided. We have that breadth of the lower part of the face which is occasioned by the falling cheek and the compressed lip; but, nevertheless, in no representation of the Duke that we can call to mind is the mouth so full of expression. It is firm and resolved, and the brow, too, is still the seat of power, though an air of benignity is diffused over the whole countenance. The light from many a domestic hearth has been playing over the stern features of command—playing over them very gracefully, but not obliterating them. The attitude or position of the head is also admirably selected. The artist has faithfully rendered that slight stoop, or forward inclination, which of late was visible in the Duke, without impairing in the least the dignity of his subject, for more of the expression of a bust depends upon the manner in which the head is placed upon the shoulders than is generally understood. Neither can we leave unnoticed the judicious adoption, in this instance, of the modern costume in preference to the classic toga, or that ideal drapery which, as a general rule, we should still wish to see retained in sculpture. It is altogether such a work of art as would have done no discredit to the studio of Chantrey, and we are very much mistaken if Mr. Weigall has not manifested in this, and in other efforts of his art, a kindred genius to that of our great bust-sculptor."

Having drawn the attention of our readers to the most prominent of the bronzes in the English half of the building, we may briefly notice other good specimens of casting. In the French Gallery are a pair of groups worthy examination—one representing "Faust and Marguret," and the other "Romeo and Juliet." In another part of the French Court there is a very remarkable display of zinc castings, coated with bronze, and approaching, in appearance as well as in execution, with wonderful closeness to the beautiful metal for which they are so economical a substitute. These are briefly noticed, with an illustration, on page 13. A very fine group, life-size, of boys with a swan, is scarcely to be distinguished from bronze. Two figures, of the same metal, silvered, with gilt ornaments, and representing two "varlets," in the costume of the pages in the Maximilian procession, are remarkable for the swaggering boldness of their attitudes, and the care and finish of every detail in the costume. They are designed by Salmson, who has a special celebrity for these *moyen age* varlets. By far the finest, as it is the most extensive, display of cast bronzes in the French Court, is that of Barbédienne. His platform is laden with copies of all sizes of many of the finest works of sculpture, ancient and modern, remarkable equally for their fidelity to the originals in form and proportion, and in every minute detail of expression. The small copies are produced by a mechanical process of reduction. The Russian bronzes are also very fine. One large group is an allegory of the introduction of Christianity in an idolatrous land. An armed figure, bearing the sign of man's redemption, places his foot on a hideous log, carved into a roughly grotesque and diabolical semblance of the human form. Another figure, that of an old man, with the attributes of a river deity, and perhaps intended to typify some Russian province, crouches at the knee of the Christian knight, and strives to grasp the senseless idol which the nobler intelligence spurns under foot. Next to this composition, the design of Professor Pimenof, is a model by the same artist, for a monument to a Russian admiral. The smaller and more novel bronzes are chiefly representations of animal life, full of vigour, naturalness, and individuality. There are hunting groups, which give one a vivid picturesque idea of sport in Russia.

One little work shows a Muscovite huntsman in at the death. There are two hounds only in the group; from one of them the man drags the fox, and the other slinks away as if from a cut of the lash. In a similar design a second huntsman has cut off the fore-feet of a hare, and has flung them to his dogs, one of which mumbles and tosses the dainty morsel in true houndish manner. The horses are the most admirable parts of these bronze pictures, for such they may aptly be termed. Every hair is marked; every vein stands forth; and so wonderfully is the texture of the coat imitated, as it would appear after a trying run, that it positively looks wet. The horses stand with their necks stretched out, their knees seeming to tremble, their chests sunk, their tails drooping, their nostrils distended. Three single figures, equally forcible and highly finished, though not so striking as subjects, are the property of the Emperor.

The Swiss Court.

Six centuries ago the name of Switzerland had never been heard of. Three hundred years ago there was only one Switzerland; we have at the present day three nations, or fractions of nations, making up one community under that name. The French Swiss, Calvinistic, dogmatic, philosophical, take to watchmaking as their calling, a calling combining ornamental art with mathematical precision. The German Swiss spin and weave, a steady, regular, positive pursuit, befitting a people with an eye to the useful. The Italian Swiss, comparatively a small flock, and lately admitted into the Confederacy, continue true to their Southern lazy propensities; they contribute hardly any one article to the world's show; they sit in the shade of their own fig-trees, till their corn-fields, dress their vineyards; and, where their mountain districts are barren, they migrate in masses, and offer the services of their strong arms, or carry their minor industries into the cities of the plain.

The French cantons—Geneva, Lausanne, and Neufchâtel—attempt to monopolise the watch trade of the world. It is a branch of business that suits them admirably. The French Swiss are called French because French is their polished language; not, indeed, that they have much in common with their Gallic neighbours either in race or character, or in the popular idioms fast dying away amongst the lowest classes. The French Swiss are Burgundians; like the Belgians, a cross between the German and the Celtic tribes, with some of the best, and some, perhaps, of the worst qualities of either stock. They pride themselves not a little on the purity of their French, which they set high above the Parisian, but they speak it slowly, emphatically, deliberately, somewhat pedantically, perhaps, precisely as a travelled, reclaimed, and very nice Yankee might be made to pronounce the Queen's English. The Genevese and Vaudois are schoolmasters par excellence. The great doctrinaire school which reigned in France under Guizot sprung up at Geneva. That queen of blue-stockings, Madame de Staël, could flourish nowhere so well as on the shores of Lake Leman, and Rousseau could nowhere have written his "Emile"—that system of education aiming to reduce the human mind to a philosophical piece of clockwork—so well as in that community destined to fill the world with its wheels within wheels.

A Great International Exhibition was hardly required to make us acquainted with Geneva watches, seeing that it is hardly possible to go down any main street without seeing a shop window with a display of Geneva watches. The Swiss watchmakers have achieved a success.

In England, perhaps, where more solid brains prevail, it would seem as if more substantial ware ought to find favour; but it is a fact, notwithstanding, that, even in England, out of ten watches sold by the day, nine are of foreign workmanship, and the Swiss supply by far the largest share.

Well, of these pretty Swiss baubles, intended for use no less than ornament, we have a most charming display. There are ten or twelve houses from Geneva—Lang and Padoux, Baume and Lerard, Moulinié et Lagrandroy, &c.,—not only claiming the merit of timepieces of the greatest precision, but also rivalling each other in the production of those trinket watches, watches to be inclosed in a bracelet, in a brooch, in a crown-piece, in a ring almost, which seem the ne plus ultra of minute workmanship. Masterpieces in the same style, of equal merit, are sent by Audemars, Aubert, and others, in Canton Vaud; and by Courvoisier, Grosclaude, &c., from Chaux-de-Fonds, and other localities in Neufchâtel. Some of these master workmen exhibit the whole of their workshops, with the various pieces—wheels, hands, cases, and other parts that go to the composition of a watch. It is, of course, impossible for a mere looker-on to test the real qualities of these complicated machines; but the whole of the apparatus seems, in most instances, to be got up with great neatness and accuracy, and the result ought to be nicety and precision. Of the mere external attractiveness of these machines, he who runs may speak with confidence. Taste is consulted in all its peculiarities, even in its mere whims. Artists of very high pretensions give the design for the endless variety of cases and faces: there are gold engravings by Alphonse Dubois, and by Fritz Kundert, both of Chaux-de-Fonds, some of whose specimens have been made for this Exhibition, which may challenge competition with anything that may be achieved in the same style by the artists of any other country. All this concentrated talent is called into activity by the watch and jewellery trade of French Switzerland; all is subservient to its interests. It would be important to inquire how large a population of those cantons is supported in great ease and comfort by that single, almost exclusive, line of profitable business.

In most of the eastern German cantons, especially Zurich, St. Gall, Appenzell, Glarus, &c., industries of a very different kind are at work—woollen and cotton factories, which do not seem to be here largely represented; and machine embroidery, tambour work, and other frame and hand embroidery, of which we have capital specimens, especially by Rudolph Ranch, and Stäheli, both of St. Gall; Steiger-Schoch and Eberhard, and Tanner and Koller, both houses of Herisau, in Appenzell.

There is a great variety of silk, riband, and other manufactures, chiefly from the cantons of Zurich and Basle, which, however, do not seem likely to excel those of Lyons and Spitalfields, though Switzerland carries on a very brisk trade in such articles, probably by offering her wares at low prices. There is one pleasant feature in Swiss manufactories in general, and it is that much of the work connected with them is carried on by the workman in his own home. As you cross some of the happiest, though naturally poorest, districts of Appenzell,

Glarus, &c., you are agreeably struck with the multitude of women and children busy at their looms, at their frame, or with their spindle, at the door of the cottage, whence the goodman issues forth with his team and plough on his way to the field, where more solid work demands stronger exertion.

Berne, Geneva, Vaud, and other cantons send specimens of their *stutzen*, or rifles, plain and solid, somewhat ponderous weapons, claiming but little attention for external workmanship, but to which any one will feel disposed to take off his hat who knows how much of the pride and happiness of Swiss independence rests on the general proficiency of the whole population in the use of those apparently uncouth and common-place tools—any one who witnessed the stern resolution with which such weapons were everywhere brandished when the Con-

federacy was threatened with the attack of a Power of vastly superior forces at the opening of the year 1857.

The Swiss have shown excellent good sense this time in sparing us all that farrago of carved beech-wood, all those chamois, chalets, and other knick-knacks without number of which every hotel, every cabin, by lake, glacier, or waterfall, is a shop in the Bernese Oberland, as well as every nook and corner of the forest cantons. Travellers, especially English travellers, have been sufficiently bored and pestered with such toys in their progress through that Alpine region, and, we repeat, we ought to be thankful to the Swiss for not filling their galleries with these too famous wares, and might well wish that their brethren of the Austrian and Zollverein departments had been equally considerate. The Swiss exhibit in the Nave some good wood and ivory carvings

Terra-Cotta.

TERRA-COTTA—literally, "baked earth"—is largely employed in the production of various kinds of garden ornaments and economic statuary. Of this material Messrs. F. Hahn Danchell and Co., of

water, to be placed in cisterns; and constructed for softening from 100 to 100,000 gallons of water per day. Water-testing Apparatus, requiring no knowledge of chemistry, to ascertain the presence in water

OBJECTS IN TERRA-COTTA. MESSRS. DANCHELL AND CO.

Red Lion Square, produce a variety of filtering, water-softening, and water-testing apparatus, in elegant forms, as may be seen by reference to our engraving. These may be thus briefly described:—Cistern Filters, to be placed direct into house cisterns, and capable of yielding from two quarts to two gallons of water in a minute, according to size. Fountain Filters, to be connected either with the service-pipes direct from the main, or with the supply-pipe from the cistern; and capable of yielding from two quarts to two gallons per minute, according to size. Portable Household Filter, of stoneware, from one to ten gallons size. Portable Table Filters of porcelain, earthenware, terra-cotta, &c., from one to four gallons size. Self-regulating Apparatus for softening

of any deleterious substance in solutions. Arranged for domestic use, hydraulic engineers, sanitary officers, and others.

Having the contract for supplying the Exhibition with filtered water, numerous very novel designs in vase and fountain filters will be found in use in various parts of the building. Mr. Danchell has published a treatise on "Water and its Impurities," which will be read with interest by all who care to drink the "pure element."

CARVED STONE PULPIT.

This Pulpit is exhibited by Mr. Jones, of Bradford-on-Avon. It is a specimen of the White Bed Farleigh Down stone, and is intended to

CARVED STONE PULPIT.   MR. DANIEL JONES.

material than the Bath stone for building purposes, when the cost of material and labour are considered. The different quarries produce shades of difference in the colour and quality of the stone; and from all the quarries the Farleigh Down may be selected as the most agreeable in colour, in soundness, and in adaptability to mouldings and Gothic tracery.

At Mr. Daniel Jones's place of business there are interesting varieties of beautifully executed columns in this stone, as well as substantial and elegantly designed chimney-pieces, &c., all offered at moderate prices.

This firm has been established for nearly a century, and has erected hill, overlooking the ancient town of Bradford, so many genuine works of great interest have been produced.

We leave our readers to the pleasure of examining these curious fossil districts, and the "torrc" of Bradford; meanwhile, an examination of the pulpit executed by Mr. Jones cannot but command considerable attention. It will be found near the Canadian Court, among various objects of interest in the building trade, exhibited for their architectural beauty. Here will be found stones and earths of various kinds, both in their natural and manufactured states. The capability of terra-cotta and the softer kinds of stones for various useful and ornamental works has never before been so completely demonstrated.

Benson's Great Clock.

ONE of the most admired pieces of workmanship in the Exhibition is certainly Benson's Trophy Clock—the largest which has yet been manufactured in this country, excepting the great Westminster clock. It will strike with sufficient force to obtain a tone from a bell of equal weight to the Westminster bell.

This fine piece of mechanism has already been noticed in our columns; but as we now present

our readers with a picture of the clock and its case, we may be excused if we offer them a more detailed description.

The frame of the movement is nearly 10 feet long, made of strong iron planed to a fine surface, and firmly bolted together, having three great wheels measuring over two feet in diameter each; they are made

MR. J. W. BENSON'S GREAT CLOCK.

of the finest gun metal, as are all the other wheels, cut and finished by the engine. All the pivots work in gun metal bosses fitted in plummer blocks; these plummer blocks have never been applied to clockwork before, and the a.vantage gained is that they allow of any portion of the clockwork being removed without disturbing the remainder when it requires cleaning, &c. The clock chimes the quarters on four bells; the chimes are the same as those of St. Mary's, at Cambridge, but so arranged that by their intonation they denote 2nd, 3rd, and 4th quarters, as the case may be, and it strikes the hour on a fifth bell. These five bells weigh 50 hundredweight, and are from the foundry of Messrs. Mears, having a compensating pendulum measuring over all 15 feet, which vibrates once in two seconds. The motive power is obtained by iron weights of nearly a ton, which are placed in one corner of the south front of the Exhibition building, some 200 feet from the clock itself; being connected with the clock by means of pulleys and lines carried under the floor of the Exhibition. The dial of the clock is placed in front of the building over the grand entrance in Cromwell Road, at a distance of nearly 300 feet. It is 9 feet in diameter, was designed at the South Kensington Museum under the superintendence of Mr. Cole and Captain Fowke, and manufactured by Mr. Magnus, in his enamelled slate.

The special peculiarity in the clock, however, is a new double lever remontoir, the application of which diminishes the friction or retarding force, and will allow of great motive power—even to the extent of several tons—being used, without disturbing the time-keeping qualities of the clock. It is always necessary when there are great disturbing or impeding forces to overcome—such, for instance, as the wind blowing against the hands of the clock, or the dial being at a great distance from the movement, as is the case with this clock—that a great motive power should be employed, and the advantage, therefore, of this new invention is palpable, by preventing irregularity in time-keeping occasioned by the necessity of employing such great motive power hence the superiority of this arrangement in clocks where great motive power is indispensable.

The entire finish is of the highest class. The foundations on which rest the clock and its case were erected by Messrs. Kelk and Lucas, in solid brickwork, and sunk some

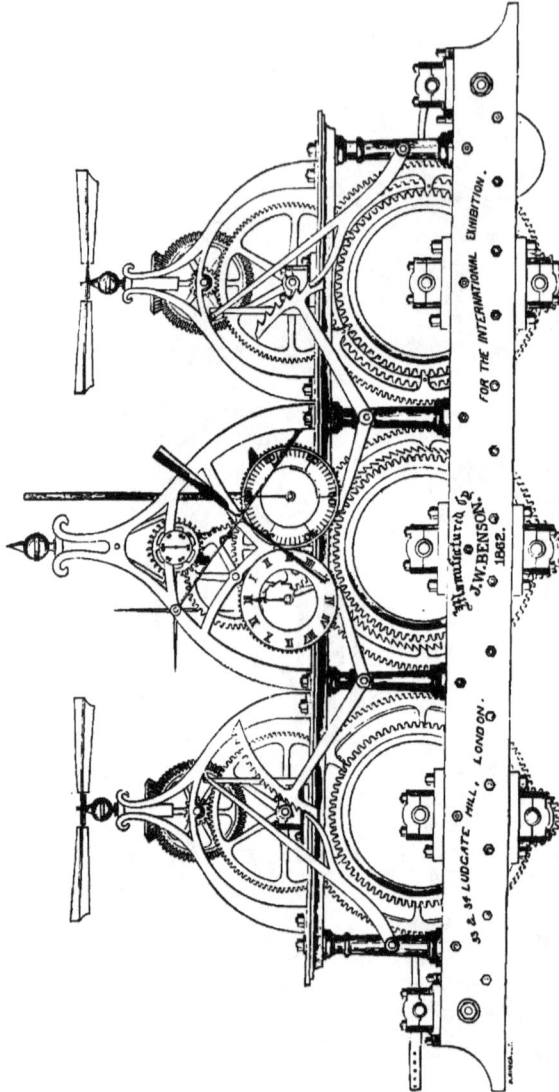

Manufactured by J. W. BENSON. 1862.

"MOVEMENT" OF THE GREAT CLOCK.

FOR THE INTERNATIONAL EXHIBITION.

33 & 34 LUDGATE HILL, LONDON.

fifteen feet below the floor of the Exhibition. The ironwork is by Potter of South Molton Street, who also cast the four dials to be placed at the cardinal points. Messrs. Jackson, of Rathbone Place, have fitted with their beautiful composition the exterior of the clock-case, which is decorated by Mr. Crace. Messrs. Minton have laid their encaustic tiles round the base. The entire structure of the clock-case is from designs by Mr. Leblle, of the South Kensington Museum.

If Mr. Benson's reputation as a clockmaker rested upon this one instrument alone, it would be perfectly safe. Without referring to other turret and large clocks he has produced, there is in the Exhibition clock ample evidence of originality and integrity of workmanship to mark him as a highly scientific and accomplished horologist. This is the most important piece of clockwork produced in England since the last Exhibition.

The measurement of time by public clocks has always been considered of great importance. It was so thought some six hundred years ago, when a public clock was first erected, the expense of which was paid by a fine which was levied upon the then Chief Justice of the Queen's Bench. We might mention many other instances for a more modern date. Public or church clocks are important objects of utility

The reason of this is, that persons are often employed to make and fix the clock who have not sufficient practical and scientific knowledge for the purpose. To obviate this, great care should be taken in selecting

THE "RAPHAEL" DRAWING-ROOM CLOCK.

THE "MICHAEL ANGELLO" LIBRARY CLOCK.

—of great convenience in the mutual intercourse of life, for public meetings, the services of the Church, and all commercial transactions; and it is often to be regretted that public clocks are so constructed, and so little attention is paid to them, that they sometimes become a public nuisance instead of a boon.

a good manufacturer, and one who, for his reputation's sake, will pay the greatest attention to the mathematical construction of the machine; sparing no pains or labour in the finish of all its acting parts, and, at the same time, employing the best materials that it is possible to obtain. Two great objects should be kept constantly in mind: firstly, the accuracy of the clock's performance — secondly, its durability; and these objects can only be obtained by employing proper materials, by constructing the machine on correct mathematical principles, and by executing the work with great accuracy. With this view the clock should be so made, that in case of necessity any one part can be removed without interfering with the remainder. The escapement should be Graham's dead-beat, which is considered the best practical escapement known, and specially adapted for this particular sort of clock. The pendulum ought (where it is possible) to be what is technically called a "two seconds," with a heavy bob and wooden rod, unless extreme accuracy is required, when a compensated pendulum is used; this, however, on account of the great attendant expense, is rarely done. The frame of the clock ought to be made of iron of a sufficient thickness and strength. The wheels should be made, where it is possible, of gun-metal or hard brass. It should have hardened steel pinions; expansion fly, to regulate the time in striking; repeating work, to prevent it striking the wrong number of strokes;

maintaining power, so that the clock will continue going while being wound; dial and hand on the movement to show the time inside the clock-tower, and by which to set the exterior hands; the whole of the wheels to run in gun-metal or hard brass bosses, answering to the jewel-holes in a watch; and various other improvements which are necessary for its correct performance.

As a church or public clock is intended for the convenience of the general public, the greater the distance at which it can be heard to strike, and to which the time shown on the face is made visible, the more it tends to fulfil that intention; and it would be well if architects and builders, when erecting churches and other large buildings in which it is proposed to place public clocks, would bear in mind this fact, and in designing the building make the dial or dials of a sufficient

excellent turret clock for the sum of forty guineas, at the same time that he makes others varying from that price to 3,000 guineas, as, for instance, the Great Clock for the International Exhibition.

The clock should be as near as may be to the dials, in order that the great friction of additional rod-work may be avoided. The pendulum should be well fixed, detached from the clock if possible, and as long as convenient, for the longer the pendulum the less will be its error. In ordinary church clocks a pendulum made of straight grained deal will answer every purpose; for if the clock be made well, the difference between a deal pendulum rod and a compensation one is almost inappreciable.

In all these particulars the Exhibition Clock of Mr. Benson is fully up to the mark. But it must not be thought that this exhibitor is prominent alone for the production of large turret clocks; on the

THE "GARLAND WEAVERS."

size to be of use to the public. This would also enable the clockmaker to furnish the dials with figures sufficiently bold to make the clock of general service in the neighbourhood in which it is placed. Another fact, to which great attention should be paid, is the situation and mode of hanging the bell or bells, so that when the clock strikes the hour or quarter, it may be distinctly and extensively heard.

Clockmakers in this country have made considerable progress in this branch of horological science. The French were formerly considered to have been far in advance of us in this respect; but the attention of practical and scientific men having been directed to the subject, numerous inventions and improvements have been introduced, by which church and turret clocks are rendered much less expensive than they were some years ago. Thus Mr. Benson, with the aid of steam-power, can produce at his manufactory a very durable and

contrary, he shows, both in the Exhibition and in his shop on Ludgate Hill, a variety of charming drawing-room and other ornamental table clocks. A few of those we have chosen for illustration.

The GARLAND WEAVERS is a handsome drawing-room clock, under a glass shade. The case is beautifully modelled, and gilt in the best style, with inlays of porcelain. The movement is of the most modern description, keeping time for fifteen days, and striking the hours and half-hours.

The RAPHAEL is a clock of similar value in respect to its works, in a tasteful case.

The instrument known as the MICHAEL ANGELO CLOCK is in bronze and marble; the figure of the great sculptor being modelled with true artistic feeling. Other clocks of a like character will attract attention, equally from their tasteful execution, and from their accuracy as timekeepers.

VIEW IN THE PICTURE GALLERIES.

Fine Arts.—The Picture Galleries.

Two departments of the International Exhibition offer special and peculiar attractions to visitors of all tastes—the Machinery Annexes and the Picture Galleries. We have already referred to the machinery; let us now say a few words about the pictures. Of course, it will be understood that in our columns only a very cursory view can be taken of the splendid and unrivalled collection of oil paintings, water colour and architectural drawings, etchings, designs, and engravings, which grace the walls of the beautiful saloons fronting the Cromwell Road. The severest of critics will find it hard to deny the merits of ample space and excellent proportions to the Picture Galleries. They are certainly the most spacious and noble in existence, not even excepting the Pitti and Uffizi, the galleries of Munich, Dresden, and other continental cities, most of which are divided into small compartments, or even the long gallery of the Louvre itself. For lighting they are perfect; and by the judicious breaks in their length, keeping one vast saloon as an effective and simple hall, the designer has relieved the tedium of pacing in front of walls hung with pictures for many hundred feet. On entering, the airy beauty of the great saloons containing the pictures will strike every beholder with delight. Nor are our foreign guests less nobly lodged. France has the larger half of a magnificent saloon, in which our allies have arranged some of those stupendous works in which they delight. The Russians are also well represented, and thousands of persons will now for the first time set eyes on a real Muscovite work. The character of each country will be found visibly written on the surface of these walls. When the eye takes in so many masterpieces of British Art, it will not fail to recognise the peculiarly domestic character of the nation and the school. It is only on such occasions as this that the real characteristics of our art become strongly perceptible. In the choice of subject—a very important indication—it is astonishing to see how homely we are compared with our classical and military neighbours—how very few big, heroic pictures of the grand style are found among us. We shine at home; our heroisms and our beauty seem kept for home use; and our artists labour in the feeling that makes the most pathetic of our songs home-songs, as our sea-songs—although sung under all skies—have ever been. There seems to be no place like home with an English artist, an English boy, or an English sailor.

The great Picture Gallery, running along the whole length of the Cromwell Road frontage, is divided into equal parts—the south-western angle being appropriated to foreign artists, and the south-eastern to the exhibition of works by the painters of the British school. The period of art represented is that between 1762 and 1862—a century of artistic progress. As far as Great Britain is concerned, full advantage has been taken of this hundred years; the contributions in the English department commencing with the works of Hogarth, who died in 1764, and extending, by regular gradation, through all the links of our best art, down to the works of the most celebrated painters of our own day. This is not so much the case with foreign countries, whose contributions are chiefly confined to the works of living artists.

The foreign division is distributed into eighteen sections, respectively representing France, Germany, Austria, Holland, Sweden, Norway, Denmark, Russia, Belgium, Spain, Switzerland, Italy, Rome, Greece, Brazil, United States of America, Portugal, and Turkey. In our hurried and necessarily brief notice, we commence naturally with the

BRITISH SCHOOL OF PAINTERS.—The collection of paintings by British artists is the finest and most complete ever brought together—more comprehensive, full, and truly representative than was the noble gathering at Manchester in 1857. At South Kensington we have good specimens of every known English painter within the last century; but when, as in the instances of Turner, Wilkie, Mulready, Poole, Hook, Maclise, Dyce, Philip, and others, the painters have different manners, there are generally examples of each. For

this result we have to thank Messrs. Creswick and Redgrave and the other managers of the Exhibition.

On entering the British Gallery, and turning to the right, the eye is immediately arrested, and filled with a magnificent display of the works of Sir Thomas Lawrence, Sir Joshua Reynolds, and Gainsborough; and under, and by the side of these, are the infinitely humorous pictures of Hogarth, whose "Harlot's Progress," and "Rake's Progress," the Election pictures, the "March to Finchley," and the "Marriage à la Mode," establish his claim to be esteemed one of the greatest satirists that ever lived, and a painter of most varied powers and the highest technical skill.

Among the many pictures by Sir Joshua Reynolds, we have here the portrait, from the Dulwich collection, of Mrs. Siddons, as the Tragic Muse, a good repetition of the Grosvenor picture—his greatest masterpiece, and one of the loftiest conceptions of semi-historical and allegorical portraiture that ever flashed into life, Minerva-like, from the brain of genius—beside a long range of portraits, a large proportion of which are the more valuable for being unfamiliar to the general public, and which have made a reputation here as the Nelly O'Brien did at Manchester. Next in public estimation among the painters of the Reynolds period is Gainsborough. He is represented by his glorious "Blue Boy," which will match with any portrait of the time for all the qualities of high art, and numerous female portraits of indescribable beauty and attraction. The landscapes by Gainsborough also show him to have been a painter of great taste and feeling.

After Gainsborough comes Romney, who has left an almost equally great name in art, and who in his day "divided the town" with Reynolds and other painters of portraits. The declining reputation of Sir Thomas Lawrence, another painter of portraits once immensely popular, will hardly be revived by the works from his pencil here shown.

Wilson, the contemporary of the then great masters of the British School, is represented by several of his well-known classical landscapes. Barry, whose fine paintings in the rooms of the Society of Arts are deservedly considered as among the most precious of the Society's possessions, is also to be seen in company with his brother artists.

Benjamin West is also welcome in the goodly company, if only for the good service he rendered to art by his boldness in representing contemporary subjects in a natural style; as in the "Death of General Wolfe," where modern costume takes the place of the absurd classical togas in which it had before his time been thought necessary to clothe great men in historical pictures. Opie, the "Cornish prodigy," is well represented in the Great Picture Gallery, as also are Harlowe, Northcote, Sir H. Raeburn, Crome, Stothard, Callcott, Hilton, Haydon, Fuseli, Shee, and other painters, who in those days took the town by storm. Their works will not now attract so much attention as the pictures by Briggs, Bonnington, Copley, Chalon, Newton, and our English Holbein—Nasmyth.

Stothard's "Canterbury Pilgrimage," so well known by the engraving, for its pure early Italian-like spirit, will be seen here as an old friend by all lovers of beautiful designs. Its graceful spirit shows better here than in the print, good as that is. "Diana Reposing," by the same, is a specimen of unusually strong colour; she lies nude under a canopy, around which flit little infant spirits, charmingly designed, and giving, through its opening, a vista of blue waters falling murmurously, and a star-lighted valley of bold character. There is strong Hellenic feeling in the famous "Greek Vintage,"—youth and flower-laden maidens dancing with joined hands over infants that trip lightly. Dashing and effective is the little composition, by Bonnington, of "Francis the First and his Sister;" he seated; she behind his chair, by an open window. "A Turk" has strong colour, indicating a system of art which has had immense influence on recent practice: for this the works of this painter deserve especial attention, more indeed than is generally given to them in England, where he is esteemed less than on the Continent; an odd thing enough. What a contrast we find between the last and Fuseli's preposterous "Satan Expelled from Paradise," a huge work, ridiculous in drawing and really almost childish in design! The "Nightmare" is hung too high to let its true character, as one of Fuseli's most meritorious works, be seen. It is notable for ghastly power.

We are fortunate in finding Hilton's magnificent altar-piece "The Crucifixion" here, it being a very noble composition. The figures of the weeping women at the foot of the Cross are admirable, as are those in the wings of the triptych, that on the right of the crowd before the gate especially. "The Angel delivering St. Peter" is somewhat conventional; the angel rather too tame. The sleeping guards are even commonplace. Hilton had a happier vein than either of these works shows, of which his "Ganymede," seen at Manchester, was a fine example. To compare him with that extraordinary genius Haydon, whose very best work, "The Judgment of Solomon," hangs on the opposite wall, is worth while. Hilton was never vulgar, but he was often weak; Haydon never weak, but often coarse: both drew finely in diverse fashions, both had valuable feeling, and, occasionally, happy colour. In the "Solomon" the two women contending for the child, as a group, express at once the power and the folly of Haydon. The woman in red is as fine a figure as any painter ever produced; she in yellow, to the front, about as vulgar a mistake as can be conceived. This artist's "Lazarus," at the Pantheon, Oxford Street, shows precisely the same contradictory character in the female figures. The figure of Solomon is truly grand in art; and in looking at this picture, one can well understand how it was that its painter contemned with such rashness the incapables of his time. It is a fervent, solid, noble picture, exceeding Hilton's by ages of intellectual power. How sad the temper that could mar so much!

Wilkie, as ever, shines among the painters of homely incidents —the genre school, as it is called, of which he was the principal revivalist. Who can look upon his "Village Fair," his "Cut Finger," his "Distraining for Rent," and other well known efforts of his pencil, and not acknowledge him a master of his art? Here is "Blindman's Buff," containing admirable composition in those figures of the two girls and the young man cluster about. The first is almost Hogarthian in character, while the second shows us Wilkie for himself in spirit, with unusual grace of design, as we may see again in the girl adjusting her shoe in "The Penny Wedding," truly a notable work. He seems to have felt his shortcomings in colour in "The Parish Beadle," but overcharged it with blackness. The Spanish pictures—of which there are more here than do credit to his fame—are naturalist of his decline.

Turner, another great painter of landscapes and sea-views, is not so fully represented as could be wished among the painters in oil. His later imaginative subject-landscapes have here no place; but his earlier, and, perhaps, finest style has a worthy example in the inimitable "Schaffhausen," with its rush of mighty waters, given with such force that the steadfast rock standing in the cataract seems moving in the current, and with all its mass slowly sliding past. Nothing can be grander than this, that when dealing with mere naturalism, the artist terrifies us so that the earth vibrates in fancy beneath our feet. Turner could hardly leave England when executing "The Seventh Plague of Egypt," which looks homely with all its grandeur of the vengeful cloud, and anything but Egyptian, notwithstanding the ghastly whiteness of that pyramid in the centre, grand as it is. This is naturalistic to its core—see the treatment of the road, encumbered with dead bodies, and compare the whole with that epic by F. Danby, "The Passage of the Red Sea," where the painter has gone on another principle. For mere life and simple beauty, suggestively given, no better picture is here than "The Guard-ship at the Nore," with the rain-cloud hovering over the line-of-battle ship, her signals telling with a glimmer as of light against it, and that pallid line of distant shore shining in the sun's latest gleam; the up-heave of the boat is a perfect study as the bold black wave tosses it. There is artful skill in "The Beach, Hastings," a warm, sunny picture, where the flat shore tells so perfectly with the bright waves and that cunningly-placed blue bundle

in the centre, which concentrates the cool tints, and has an echo in the fishing-boat's blue vane. Much faded is "The Mill and Lock," but it remains a miracle of tone, as the quaint mill stands with its delicious greys in shadow against the blazing sun and sky full of blood-red cirrus. Nor are the cool tones in the cavern of the opened lookchamber less admirable than the masterly truth and infinitely varied mass of shade projected to the front. This is perfect morning. Magnificent is "Dunstanborough Castle," in its sombre, greenish grey, and the mighty heave of the wave that wells against the rock in sullen oneness, as if some far-off storm had hunted it to the shore at last, but still unbroken.

Müller had more merely Oriental spirit than Turner; see his pearly-tinted "Rhodes," with its sweep of the armed bay and lovely sea. Mr. Stanfield is both landscape and marine painter, but in neither does he give us the full intense key of natural colour; his feeling for precise form expresses, within certain limits, what that of Turner for colour and tone achieved without restriction, except, in the example before us, that of intensity of key. One sees, on looking at Mr. Stanfield's "French Troops crossing the Tyrol," how little atmosphere it has, after Turner and Müller have filled the eye. There is more mist than atmosphere in that painted monody "The Abandoned;" in feeling, however, this comes near to Turner, with its heavenly rain of mild light falling upon the troubled sea. In it is little colour; there is less in "The Mass," which is only bright, but has been as seldom surpassed for still-water painting as "The Abandoned" has for water in violent motion.

Etty in two or three pictures supports his claims to be considered one of the greatest modern colourists. All the principal of the more modern artists, with scarcely a single exception, may be studied in some of the best examples; as, for instance, Constable, Müller, Danby, Stanfield, Collins, J. Ward, F. R. Pickersgill, Mulready in his earlier manner, as in the "Firing the Cannon," and his later, as in "The Bathers," and "Choosing the Wedding Gown," shown in our engraving; Leslie, two or three well-known pictures from Don Quixote, the "Merry Wives of Windsor scene," &c.; Frank Stone; the three principal portrait painters, Sir Watson Gordon, Knight, and Grant; Maclise, "Caxton Exhibiting a Proof Sheet to Edward IV.," and perhaps his finest oil picture, "The Banquet Scene, Macbeth;" Roberts, Sir Charles Eastlake, Hurlstone at his prime, J. and W. Linnel; Paton, the admirable Scotch painter of "Home—the Return from the Crimea;" Sir Edwin Landseer in several of his largest and most impressive Highland pictures; Leighton, the great picture of "The Procession of Cimabue;" Hook; O'Neil, the "Eastward Ho!" Solomon, Lance, John Faed, J. Clark, Horsley, Frost, Cope, Egg, T. S. Cooper, F. Goodall, Dobson, Phillip, Poole, E. M. Ward, "Charlotte Corday going to Execution," "The Fall of Clarendon," "The Antechamber at Whitehall," and "The Last Sleep of Argyll," a noble picture, as will be seen by our engraving; J. F. Lewis, "Scenes in the East;" Cook, Dyce, "Titian's First Essay in Colouring" and "Pegwell Bay;" Creswick, Webster, Poole, "Solomon Eagle Preaching during the Plague;" a fine sea-piece by the elder Meadows, an artist of taste and feeling; Ansdell, Lee, Herbert, "Two Magdalens;" Elmore, "The Tuileries, 1792," and many other painters. The pre-Raphaelites are well represented by Messrs. Millais, Holman Hunt, "The Light of the World," Brett, and Hughes. There is Mr. Martineau of whom the public know scarcely anything, who will take one of the foremost places among the pre-Raphaelites, with a remarkably elaborated picture, entitled, "The Last Day in the Old House." By Watts there is an excellent portrait of the Poet Laureate.

To Mr. Mulready the modern school of painting owes much brilliant colour. We may see, in pictures wrought by him nearly half a century ago, indications of the lustrous quality which is now the prerogative of every good painter. These walls display him fairly, not too well. If we take "The Bathers" as a fair sample of his flesh-painting we should do him injustice, seeing it is cold, thin, bloodless, and, with all the delicate drawing of the figures, shows disproportion. In the "Whistonian Controversy" the error is in fervid heat of colour,

CHOOSING THE WEDDING-GOWN. BY W. MULREADY, R.A.

THE LAST SLEEP OF ARGYLL. BY E. M. WARD, R.A.

but it is perfect in composition, expression, and design. There is a want of solidity about this artist's handling perceptible in nearly every picture here, mostly in the otherwise admirable "Burchell and Sophia," the best illustration of an English classic we know, which is saying a great deal. How manly is the grace of Burchell as he helps his mistress! how pretty her womanly pretence of ignorance! With "Train up a Child" artists would wish to rest the fame of this distinguished painter. The subject is two girls who have brought a little, daring, bold-eyed English urchin to give alms to three Lascars, that crouch by a park-wall, one of whom gratefully salutes him with Oriental gesture. The composition of this group is admirable, the colour of their dusky faces almost Titianesque in harmony with the garments they wear. No two art contemporaries were ever more contrasted than are Messrs. Mulready and Maclise. The last is best represented by "The Banquet Scene in Macbeth," for the "Mokanna Unveiling" seems only an illustration for an "Annual." The "Caxton," though a fine and expressive picture, is far below the first-named, with its effective tumult, varied expression, and the noble figure of Lady Macbeth. The painter, in managing the idea of the spectre, has been less fortunate than with the like matter in the Play-scene in Hamlet, now in the National Gallery. In both, the difficulty is to produce by natural means a shadow that is but a shadow to others, but to the guilty, miserable murderer an accusing spirit. The shadow of a substantial arm pours poison into the King's ear in the Play-scene, but in "Macbeth" nothing but a meaningless gloom sits in the chair of sovereignty, and might be as palpable to the torchbearers as to Macbeth. Thus far the picture falls short—that we are not let into the chamber of his brain, and feel not with the guilty conscience of the usurper, but simply wonder at the unaccountable substance, for such it is, that blanks his countenance so terribly.

Mr. Hook's salted sunny air has such blessed life in it as might do a sick man good even to think of. Who is not grateful to him for "Luff, Boy!" and does not enjoy the delicious balance of that boat upon the green-crystal wave as she yaws off a little from the wind, whence the command to keep her to it, vented so surlily to the rosy, ringletted urchin, who, heedless of his cap, puts the helm over with a will? Who that knows the sea does not recognise that chaplet of pearly bubbles that rises from beneath the net? The colour of those fish in the boat here is as fine a thing as can be produced in such art: perfect is the touch which gave it so freely. As a work of art, probably, "Whose Bread is on the Waters" is better than the last—a Cornish pilchard-fisherman and his boy in a boat, just at evening, when the sky gives an olive-green to the sea—and there is greater promise of change in tho air than we find in the above; a less obviously beautiful and, may be, more difficult theme. The action of the pair, as they stand up in the heeling boat, pulling in the net, the colour of the sea, and the bright sparkle of the fish that leap in the net, are inimitable. "Stand Clear!" a boat coming to the beach, with a bright, clear curve of hollow water springing under its keel obliquely, and drawing up the seaweed as it comes forward, tells well, as do the expression and action of the boys sitting on her gunwale, and that of the sailor furling the canvas. Bright and true as these are, they look rather flat, and in need of solid modelling. "The Brook" is a charming illustration of Tennyson's lyric:

> "And out again I curve and flow,
> To join the brimming river;
> For men may come and men may go,
> But I go on for ever."

A moral of the progress of life—a young man and an old one are in a cart, entering the shaded channel of a rivulet to a dark vista, while a baby, borne in a woman's arms, is carried across a rustic bridge into the sunlight of existence. In execution this is delightfully fresh and faithful. "The Marriage Feast," a Venetian costume-subject, shows beautiful colour and admirable composition, in the artist's early manner.

It matters not with what a man deals in art, so that 'he gets dramatic feeling out of it. Therefore popular justice has long ago

placed Sir E. Landseer amongst our greatest artists, and feels over sure to find interest and passion in his works. The Hogarth of Dogs fears comparison with none. Here, indeed, he compares least advantageously with himself, "The Portraits of Her Majesty and Prince Albert, 1842," being hardly worthy of him; nor is the much-praised "Bolton Abbey" more than a flimsy sketch, compared with "The Combat," "Night and Morning," and "The Drive" of deer in Glenorchy, with its fine tone and perfection of hide texture. At Manchester Sir Edwin was more worthily represented than here. Neither "The Combat" nor "The Sanctuary" fairly honours his dramatic powers as does the listening blood-hound, in the room through which his master has been borne to the deathbed. Of the Sheepshanks Gift, none of his best works, the humorous subjects, are here. We have but a few words for portraits per se, and those must be given to Mr. J. P. Knight's "R. J. Lane, Esq., A.R.A.," in admiration of its earnest expression and sound execution.

We should wrong our readers to avoid dwelling upon Mr. Poole's "Song of Philomena on the Shore of the Beautiful Lake," from Boccaccio—a pictorial dream, that seems filled with the pulsing throbs of the lute the singer holds, while her charmed companions listen, as we might, languidly resting, some reclining, some seated, some at length—all in graceful case, and all in pairs, the lover and the lady; while golden twilight melts into night upon the shores of that Elysian lake, whose form already recedes and faints before the eye. This is music in colour.—Mr. F. M. Brown's "Last of England" may be contrasted for colour with Poole's picture: an emigrant and his wife gazing upon the lost English shores; the ship at sea, and a keen wind blowing the foam from the crests of the angry waves as they rise in sunlight clear and cold—the whole healthy, bracing to the strong, if sharp and poignant and terrible to the weak. They sit on the poop: he mournful and bitter; she happy and confident in him, clasping his hand with a grasp that whitens his cold, purpled flesh, and showing from under her shawl a baby's tiny fist. Her world is limited; so she will take her life as it comes with him, and "suffer sorrow by reflection." He seems to buffet the world in angry fancy, and sits here brooding, brooding over all—his eyes enlarged to a fixed stare, angry gloom upon his face, his lips bitterly set, his face huddled within the coat's collar, and shaded by his broad hat. Behind, a set of sottish, coarse companions wrangle and smoke out their lives. The sharp, strenuous, frosty wind blows out the wife's ribbon in a gay streamer, dashes spray upon their covering, but does not bring a tear into her confident eyes. A noble picture, as finely wrought as it is finely thought. Turn now to Mr. Clark's "Draught-players"—an old man beaten by a boy, who, in cosy joy, nurses his knee, while the defeated, half-ashamed to be so, pretends not to discern his own error. He has been fairly beaten, after a long fight, too; for the dog, bored to death by its duration, has lain himself down with resignation, and sleeps; while a younger child has dived into his grandfather's pocket, and, unreproved, fished out the sacred silver watch for a leisurely examination.

We must be on our guard, says a recent writer, against attributing too much influence to what is called "Pre-Raphaelitism," if it be understood as the style of a school which grew up some sixteen years ago, among a knot of energetic and clever students of the Royal Academy; the merits and demerits of which have been the subject of fierce controversy, now nearly silent; and the good of which is bearing fruits with other kindred wholesome influences, while its extravagances are being gradually moulted and modified among the strong, or developing into palpably vicious consequences in the weaker members of the school.

Nothing is more apparent, on examination of the contemporary pictures in the English gallery, than the marked tendency to "realism and naturalism," i.e., the directest study of nature compatible with purposes of imitation on canvas. There is no general distinction between the earlier and later half of our international collection so characteristic as this; but it would be slanting our eyes to facts to attribute it to Pre-Raphaelitism. It had been in progress for thirty years before Pre-Raphaelitism was heard of; it had, indeed, won popular favour for Hogarth a century before the P.R.B. asserted their title. In the hands of Wilkie, Leslie, Newton, Mulready, Webster, and W. Hunt, for domestic incident; in those of Ward, Frith, Egg, Elmore, and others, for historic, or semi-historic subjects; in those of Turner, Constable, Collins, D. Cox, Calcott, Cooke, Stanfield, Roberts, Linnell, J. Lewis, Chambers, and Muller, for landscape, or landscape with life, realism had gradually been ousting Academicism or conventionalism from public favour. Its growth had, indeed, kept pace with the widening circle of picture-buyers. As our manufacturing wealth increased, our great manufacturers became picture-buyers, and their taste was all for the natural, as opposed to the conventional, in art.

Mr. Egg's picture "The Scene from 'Henry Esmond,'" is here,

them will bear a longer inspection. With us colour and effect is too often the sole end sought, with them they are too often despised as the means. The French pictures show the result of more thorough and complete artistic education, an education based upon a long and arduous study of the human figure—the great test of all noble design. French art has another characteristic almost entirely different from our own. It is essentially national, and far more frequently monumental. The French painter devotes himself not to the gratification of a half-educated class, to mean, trivial, childish, or commonplace subjects, but to the celebration of the great deeds of his country, and themes of sacred, poetical, or historical interest.

We must content ourselves with a mere enumeration of some of

LE QUART D'HEURE DE RABELAIS.—M. VETTER.

with its apt personation of Beatrice, its reverent expression of the enraptured Esmond, kneeling to receive the accolade.

Mr. Leighton's "Cimabue's Madonna carried through Florence" startled the world with a broad and bold revival in the true spirit of good Italian art. There is hardly a picture on the walls that is so full of light, so gracious, and yet so soft. The beauty of Florentine customs, and often seen processions in that city, has given Mr. Leighton full means and materials for his art, of which he has made such good use to produce this noble and graceful picture. The composition is admirable and effective, both in spirit and form. And so we might go on, but our space forbids. We therefore proceed to a very brief examination of the works in the Foreign Galleries.

THE FRENCH SCHOOL.—The contributions of our French friends are well deserving careful study. The pictures shown may not make so immediate an appeal to the eye as our own, but many of

the pictures which will be most interesting to the English visitor. The "Portrait of Mdlle. Rosa Bonheur," by Dubufe fils; "The Banks of the Nile," by Belly; "The Dying S. Francesco d'Assisi," a most impressive picture by Benouville; "St. Augustine and St. Monica," his mother, the only work, we regret to say, by Ary Scheffer; "The Spring," a female figure perfectly nude, and as perfectly pure, and the only example of the great master Ingres; "The Landing of the French Army in the Crimea," and "An Incident at the Battle of the Alma," two colossal pictures by the young painter, Pils, who, as the French say, is already plus fort que Horace Vernet (there is not one work by the latter). By Yvon there are small copies of the great pictures at Versailles, painted for the Emperor—"The Battle of Solferino," "Curtain of the Malakoff," "Gorge of the Malakoff," and "The Attack on the Malakoff"—all well known by engravings. "The Landing of the French Army in the Crimea," by Barrias—another colossal picture from Versailles), "The Two Friends," by Bellangé, a touching picture of two comrades lying dead on the battle-field in each other's arms; Gleyre's "Illusions perdu," badly translated "Illusions destroyed" (from the Luxembourg), "Lady Jane Grey," and "Henri III and the Duc de Guise," by Comte; Flandrin's over-finished portrait of the "Prince Napoleon;" "The Triumph of Martyrdom," by Bougereau; "Sisters of Charity," by Madame Henriette Brown exhibited at the French Gallery, Pall Mall, as "The Sick Child;" a noble "Study" of a nude figure seated on the edge of a precipice, with the face buried between the knees; and a portrait of "The Emperor," by the eminent painter Flandrin; "The Environs of Damascus," by M. Danzats, the French International Commissioner; Gérome's well-

but exquisite technically "Ploughing at Nevers," by Rosa Bonheur, the famous lady painter of cattle, whose "Horse Fair" created such a sensation among the art-critics a few years since. There are two portraits by Horace Vernet, of Marshals Bosquet and MacMahon, Duc de Magenta, but "The Battle of the Alma," in the catalogue has, we believe, not yet arrived; there are three of the minute and marvellously perfect pictures of Meissonier and charming examples of Troyon, Lambinet, Ziem, Marilhat, Edouard Frère. When we say that it is a collection by Delaroche, it need scarcely be added that there is not anything more worthy in the whole French collection. The collection of M. Pereire, wonderfully individual and distinct, with ... A.M ...

THE DYING CUIRASSIER IN THE HOSPITAL. M. CHARLET.

known picture of "Roman Gladiators saluting Tiberius in the Roman Amphitheatre," and "Rembrandt engraving a Plate in Aqua Fortis," "Embarkation of Ruyter and De Wytt," by Isabey; "The Arrival of Queen Victoria at Cherbourg," by Guidin; two Roman subjects by Hébert; Troyon's fine picture of "Oxen going to the Plough," from the Luxembourg; "Fortune and the Little Child," a picture painted in emulation and almost in imitation of Titian's "Sacred and Profane Love;" and a very interesting picture of "St. John;" "Charles V. and Louis XIV.," by Robert Fleury; "Good News—Magenta," by Laugée; "Arab Scouts," a good example of the distinguished painter Boulanger; the monkey "Alchymist," by Rousseau; a "Nymph carried away by a Satyr," by Cabanel, broad in subject and treatment,

in the reign of Diocletian, is founded on an ancient Christian that a nimbus floated over the head of ... ... is just now popular in the form of engraving. The "M ... Antom..." is not one of the painter's best work, for it was so ... work picture under the others, which might easily be overlooked. It is one of the most extraordinary productions of human genius, the other inspired ideal, on the same diminutive scale, for the intensity of the spiritual expression and marvellous subtlety of tone. These are "The Virgin in Contemplation before the Crown of Thorns;" "Good Friday;" celebrated in the midst of persecution by early Christians; and the "Return from Calvary."

The pictures we have selected for engraving are in their manner

peculiarly French—that is to say, poetic and yet homely. The
"Dying Cuirassier" represents one of those old soldiers, with whose
features we are so familiar in the pictures of Horace Vernet,
attended in his last moments by a devoted comrade. A somewhat
similar treatment prevails in the other picture, entitled "The
Invalid and his Children."

A capital bit of humour is M. Vetter's "Quart d'Heure de
Rabelais," showing how, when he could not pay his tavern bill, and

Roman washerwomen, "Lessive à la Cervara;" M. Cabanel's "Nymph
carried off by a Faun;" Hébert's "Les Cervaralles," with copper jars,
in the cavern well; the late Simon St. Jean's "Orange" peeled and
divided by its septa; also passing from the orange peeled by the
painter to the round world that a great king would have taken for an
orange, but did *not* contrive to peel and divide at discretion—there is
the late Adrien Guignet's "Xerxes," enthroned on a mountain by the
Hellespont, with a suggestive foreground of ruins, and his army, seen

THE INVALID AND HIS CHILDREN.

still less his journey on to Paris, he procured arrest, with its free
board and lodging to his destination, by labelling two packets of wood-
ash "Poison for the King," and "Poison for the Queen." There is
—to speak of mechanical effects—in the Rabelais picture some clever
painting of the innkeeper's glass screen, beyond which is the bar; and
from M. Vetter, in another picture, entitled "Le Départ pour la
Promenade," we have a capital figure in purple satin, conscious of the
looking-glass by which he passes. We should name also M. Curzon's

from the heights as a pigmy multitude spread in the wide plains below.
It is Xerxes seeing his host, suddenly weeping, because in a century
all these men will be dead. "Since life is so short, then," said Arta-
banus, "why should kings vex and shorten it by unjust wars?"

"At the head of the living painters of France," says Mr. Tom
Taylor, "stand by general consent Ingres and Delacroix. Each has
here only a single picture. That of Ingres is simply a nude figure
the size of life, entitled 'The Source' (in the English catalogue inac-

curately rendered 'The Spring'). A well-known French critic, speaking of English paintings in which young ladies are represented in scant drapery, says that he is always shocked when he looks at such pictures, because, although there is never anything shown that even a Puritan would care to conceal, the fair ones look so conscious, so much as though they were going to cry out 'for shame,' that out of very modesty he is compelled to turn aside his face. Certainly, neither in M. Ingres's picture, nor in any other of the many similar ones here, is there any reason for a like delicacy. They conceal nothing, but, like our first parents, are naked and not ashamed—though it may be not exactly from the same cause. M. Ingres's 'Source' we must suppose to be an illustration of a Greek idea. But the lady is certainly not a divinity, and certainly not a Greek—simply a disrobed Parisienne. The figure is admirably drawn—observe especially the skilful expression of hands and feet—cleverly though coldly painted, and—utterly uninteresting, except as the work of a man of eighty, in which respect it is almost a marvel.

"Delcroix's picture, the 'Murder of the Bishop of Liége,' is full of vigour and spirit, but exaggerated, murky, confused, and conventional, and, if one may say so of a favourite work of one who is regarded by Frenchmen as the prince of colourists, ill-coloured. As a principal work of one of the most popular of the rising artists of France, Gérome's 'Ave, Cæsar Imperator, morituri te salutant,' must not pass unheeded, and is a production of unquestionable power, careful study, and, despite some peculiarities of drawing and colour, of great technical skill; it will repay close examination. As examples of a class of pictures essentially French, may be noticed the tremendous 'Vision of Zachariah,' by M. Laemlein; Flandrin's magnificent study of a young man, though why he should have chosen such a spot to rest upon it is hard to imagine; the 'Pillory' of M. Glaize; and 'Illusions Perdu' of M. Gleyre. M. Gleyre's picture is the best of the favourite Parisian semi-poetical, semi-classical pictures in the room. It is the old allegory of man reviewing the departed joys of life; a commentary on the text 'Vanity of vanities,' not very hard to read, but sufficiently obscure."

M. Alexandre Cabanel's large "Glorification of St. Louis" is a grand and effective academical exercise. M. Glaize goes to Béranger's "Chanson des Fous" for the motto of his picture, showing how great and earnest men of this world have been pilloried in all ages:—

On les persécute, on les tue
Sauf, après un lent examen,
A leur dresser une statue
Pour la gloire du genre humain.

Upon a broad canvas he paints in the centre of his pillory, our Lord himself, over whom an angel holds the sentence, "They know not what they do." On either side are pilloried portrait-figures of Socrates, Æsop, Kepler, Galileo, Correggio, Palissy, Lavoisier; of Dante, Cervantes, Joan of Arc, Columbus, Denis Papin, Solomon Caus, and Stephen Dolet, whom even Calvin and Beza were content to think righteously burnt for an atheist, as he was not. In front sit the mockers—Misery and Ignorance on one hand, Violence and Hypocrisy upon the other. Of one of these men, Bernard Palissy, M. Louis Roux represents rather the power than the suffering, by showing him in a finely-painted picture as a teacher of the foremost scholars of Paris who came to his museum, the first public cabinet of Natural History, forming what he called "my little Academy," in 1575, to hear from him his discoveries of the first principles of more than one great science, to which he had penetrated as a close and reverent student of the works of God. This picture also may include portraits, for among Palissy's pupils then were Ambrose Paré, the king's surgeon, one of the great founders of the modern art of surgery, Richard Hubert his colleague; Lobel, who became physician to William of Orange and King James I.; with others of like stamp, philosophers, churchmen, nobles, foremost thinkers in their day.

In the late M. Benouville's picture of "St. Francis of Assisi," as he is carried dying to Sainte Marie des Anges, blessing the town of Assisi, nailmarks in his white, uplifted hands, there is some good

treatment of the figures of surrounding friars of his order. M. Charles Louis Muller paints "Madame Letitia, the mother of Napoleon," mourning the death of her son in her chamber at Rome. Dressed in black, she sits by the full-length portrait of the Emperor, the two old Corsican women, who were her household companions, at work near her; and she also with her distaff close at hand. "Celebration of Mass in the Reign of Terror," in a poor hut, for the Royal family during the flight to Varennes; broken power kneeling beside poverty, a peasant's son watching meanwhile at the door, is M. Muller's other picture. We miss in them both—good, as undoubtedly they are—the highest power of expression. This is the case also in M. Comte's two pictures, "Jane Grey" arguing with Bonner, Gardiner, and Feckenham, until her husband has thrown himself at her feet and asks pardon for having intended to forsake his faith; and the meeting at the Château of Blois, on the way to the communion-table, but also on the eve of the duke's assassination, of "Henry III. and the Duke of Guise."

Two boat-loads of victims of tyranny, "The Exiles of Tiberius," on their way to the barren island, where they will be left deprived of fire and water, are effectively represented by M. Barrias. But a finer work is M. Gérome's picture of the doomed gladiators in the amphitheatre before Vitellius, "Ave, Cæsar Imperator, morituri te salutant," which has already been exhibited in London. From M. Gérome, we have also a group of Italian pipers under a shrine; and a room interior, a piece of remarkably skilful painting. M. Caraud's "Madame de la Vallière taking the Veil in 1674;" M. Robert Fleury's "Charles V. at the Monastery of St. Just," urged by an ambassador from Philip I. to return to cares of state, and give his counsel in the critical affairs of Spain; the artist's picture of "Boileau and Racine reading their MSS. as historiographers to Louis XIV.;" and "The Soldier's Return," are all excellent specimens of the painters' peculiar style.

The German School.—The great German school of painting is well represented by the Zollverein and other German States. Prussia has sent nearly two hundred works of art in architectural designs, oil paintings, sculpture, and engravings, the productions of about a hundred and twenty artists. Berlin and Dusseldorf have each sent a fine collection of paintings, and the engravings from the former place are choice and numerous. Among the sculpture from Berlin is a case of medals by Carl Fischer. Only one specimen has been sent of Peter von Cornelius, and two of Oswald Achenbach. The oil paintings from Dusseldorf include a series of eleven pictures by H. Mucke, representing the life of St. Meinrad.

Bavaria has sent about forty works of art, chiefly oil paintings, by about twenty-seven artists, amongst which are seven pictures by Carl Wilhelm Müller. Saxony is represented by about twenty artists, in thirty paintings, drawings, and groups of sculpture; the Grand Duchy of Baden has sent a small Fine-art collection; and the Duchy of Brunswick, Frankfort-on-the-Maine, the Electorate of Hesse, the Duchy of Saxe-Coburg and Gotha and Wurtemberg are represented by about forty works of art, the productions of about thirty artists. North Germany and the Hanse Towns have also sent a small collection, Hamburg having contributed about twenty works, by about twelve artists. Among these are three pictures by F. Heunendinger, one being a picture of fairy life from a tale by L. Tieck, and three pictures by B. Mohrhagen. A cartoon, by Peter von Cornelius, of "The Four Horsemen of the Apocalypse," is the only work in the Exhibition that represents by its chief master one of the highest forms of modern German art. There is a cartoon of "Charlemagne meeting Duke Thessilio at the Monastery," by C. Adamo, and one of "The Deluge," by Herr August Hovemayer; and there are seventeen "Cartoons from the Odyssey," by Friedrich Preller. In cartoon also there is a very German and conventional study of "King Lear with his Fool," by Hermann Wislicenus. Somewhat allied to the cartoon painting are the illustrations, in long perpendicular strips, to Goethe's "Faust," "Prometheus," &c., by Herr B. von Neher; and the spirit of the cartoon-drawer and fresco-painter is expressed in miniature by the three frames of small sketches, painted in oil, by the Baron Hugo von Blomberg, twenty-seven in number, to illustrate Dante's "Divina Commedia."

THE AUSTRIAN SCHOOL, as it is called, is represented by about eighty oil paintings, sixteen water-colour pictures, nineteen pieces of sculpture, five engravings, and about ten architectural sketches. These are the works of about ninety-seven artists.

Austrian art, as may be easily conceived, is essentially imitative; though even in imitation there is a certain amount of tact in adaptation that almost amounts occasionally to originality. At one time her artists have gone to Rome, and looked at ancient art through the spectacles of Mengs and Winckelmann; at another, they tell us the painters of England have been their model; but we fancy it is as they were seen in English engravings; of late years Munich and Dusseldorf have plainly given the law, and now it is evident that the conqueror at whose proud foot Austria sits is France. In the Austrian pictures there is a good deal of honest, careful painting, and some character. "But," says one acute critic, "don't let your official catalogue lead you to suppose that Austrian painters form such conceptions of the 'Virgin and Child' as that assigned to Friedrich Ameling (No. 1,073). Ameling only intended to represent an ordinary, every-day Austrian mother, pleasant, plump, and homely, nursing a chubby boy, and entitled it, reasonably enough, 'A Mother with her Child;' it is the officious catalogue that has re-christened it the Madonna."

THE DUTCH SCHOOL.—Holland exhibits about one hundred and twenty oil paintings, by fifty-nine artists, and two engravings. Of the pictures, seven are by Dr. Bles and eight by P. Van Schendel. Belgium contributes about one hundred and thirteen oil paintings, by fifty-three artists, about twenty-six groups of sculpture, by sixteen artists, and two engravings. It has sent nine pictures by L. Gallait and eight by Madou. Switzerland sends more than one hundred pictures, by about fifty artists, amongst which are fifteen specimens of Jules Hébert, with a few sculptures and engravings.

The Dutch pictures hang next the French in the Foreign Gallery, and show admirably. Especially does Holland come well through the ordeal of criticism. Her painters exhibit no large pictures; but, true to the old style made famous by Teniers and the other grand old masters of the Low Countries, the paintings here shown are of the cabinet size, and are all worthy examination. For example, there are six or more Dutch drawing-room views by David Bles, that are nearly perfect in their own way; one (No. 1,228) almost a Meissonnier in size and finish, but with a tender homely feeling, such as Meissonnier never expressed. Nothing can be more simple than the theme or more refined than the treatment; it is merely a young mother rocking the cradle of her young first-born, over which the father leans and plays to it on his violin; but the unconscious, happy expression of the whole makes it quite a household idyll. Then there are other genre painters, Martens, Jamin, and the Ten-Kates, worthy associates of Bles; Bosboom, who paints quaint national interiors; Verveer, with his equally national and still quainter out-door scenes; Koekkoek's neat green-bordered canals; Van Schendels' never-ending candle-light subjects, affording constant wonder to the majority of visitors, to us infinite weariness; Springer, who paints architectural exterior on a small scale better than any other man in Europe; Israëls, who, having been studying Troyon and the French paysagists, works on a large canvas, yet paints national scenery with true Dutch gusto, and, as in "The Shipwreck" (1,253), native incidents with genuine pathos; and delicious fruit and flower pieces, by Uppink and Van Os. Among the younger landscape painters there is a growing effort after French style; and in some with enlarged space, there seems to have arisen a larger manner; with all its faults, Kugtenbronmer's "Forest Scene" is a good example of this order, and so are some of the pictures by De Haas, Mollinger, and others. Dutch art is always welcome to the lovers of domestic scenes; but then Dutch art is not high art, in the opinion, at least, of those who claim to speak and write with authority on these matters.

THE SPANISH SCHOOL.—The (so denominated) Spanish school is represented by about twenty-three artists, and thirty works of art in

oil painting, sculpture, and engraving. Valasquez and Murillo are only represented by the engravers. The Spanish school is altogether weak, both in numbers and quality.

They are, moreover, sometimes unpleasant in subject, and poor in treatment; though, in one or two, we fancy we can trace a memory—only a memory—of the style which once achieved a world-wide fame, and which has, even now, a host of imitators.

THE ITALIAN SCHOOL.—Italy, as might naturally be expected, is well represented in the Fine-art classes. About forty architectural designs, of various degrees of merit, by about thirty artists, and eighty oil paintings and drawings, by about sixty artists, form the display of pictures. About seventy groups of statuary and busts, some of them by English artists, have been sent in the sculpture class; and the engravings reach at least fifty, by about twenty-two engravers. C. G. Battista and Luigi Marchesi are represented by the most numerous specimens amongst the paintings; and the engravings include twelve plates by Luigi Calamatta, of Rome, and some works by Giuseppe Longhi, Raffaelle Morghen, and Leonardo da Vinci. Rome has sent about fifty-seven pieces of sculpture, by about thirty-six artists, including eight specimens of G. M. Benzoni; a great number of valuable cameos; a few fine drawings; a good many engravings; a small collection of medals; and a large group of mosaics, by seventeen artists, including a contribution from the Vatican. Its oil paintings number about forty-five, by about twenty-four artists, chiefly modern painters. Italy sends many works, of all methods of execution. Rome, as elsewhere, is distinct in the exhibiting space.

Italy has too long been content to dwell on her ancient glory. She has now thrown off the yoke of a foreign master; let us hope that in the lesser matters of art and literature she will soon become equally self-reliant. But let us not be supposed to imply that there are no good Italian paintings in the Exhibition. On the contrary, many are exceedingly clever, and most show considerable artistic dexterity. But there are certainly no works of power. We have heard, indeed, once and again, of men of more than promise—self-reliant, original, imaginative—emerging from the mass of public imitators, especially in Florence; but they are not among the exhibitors here.

THE RUSSIAN SCHOOL.—Russia sends more than a hundred works of art, by about sixty artists. Eight of them are oil paintings, three are architectural sketches, and seventeen are engravings. Amongst them is a collection of forty-seven medals exhibited by the Academy of Fine Arts of St. Petersburg, and a monument representing the Empress Catherine II., by Felix Chopin. The earliest picture exhibited is one by Anthony Lodsuiko, who died in 1773; and there are seven specimens of Axenfeldt, and five portraits by Levitsky Demetrius.

Among the Russian pictures many will be found that commend themselves to the visitor's earnest regard—striking subjects well handled. Russia spends freely, liberally, that her young painters may have good training at Rome, Munich, or Paris; they, in return, work doggedly, and return home excellent imitators. But some of them, or others who have not been so favoured, take to painting the men and scenes they see around them; and may thus, in good time, establish for Russia a vernacular art. Such are the storm scenes of Aïvazofsky; Popof's "Fair at Nijni Novogorod;" Scherwood's peasant groups; Fedotof's bourgeoisie; Jacoby's "Lemon-seller," with a phiz redolent of fun; and Eugène Duker's well-painted Livonian views.

THE SCHOOLS OF NORWAY, SWEDEN, AND DENMARK.—Norway is represented by about sixty works of art, by about twenty-one artists. Among some fifty oil paintings are nine specimens of Boe—pictures of flowers, fruit, birds, and scenery; six landscapes by Dahl, and eleven specimens of Tidemand, one of which we have engraved—figure pictures, in two of which the landscapes are painted by the former artist. Several portraits in ivory are in the small collection of sculpture.

SWEDEN is represented by about forty works of art in oil painting and sculpture, by about twenty-four artists. The rustic scenes of J. F. Hackert and Miss A. Lindegrin are the most numerous amongst the pictures.

THE ARTIST IN HIS STUDIO.   M. CHARLET.

We introduce in this page a very characteristic sketch of the "Artist in his Studio." Charlet is a painter belonging to the new school; imaginative, poetic, domestic, and yet, in a large degree, practical. The picturesque room in which he is seated, thoughtfully thinking out, perhaps, the design of his next picture, is very well executed; while the accessories—models, busts, books, painting implements, and flowers—all go to make up a subject replete with interest, and not without a certain amount of dry humour.

CATECHISING IN NORWAY. ADOLPHE TIDEMAND.

DENMARK has sent about one hundred and ten works of art, by about sixty-four artists, including six groups of sculpture by Thorwaldsen, and five by J. A. Jerichau. Among the oil paintings, E. Jerichau is the artist most largely represented.

The collection is such as cannot fail to enhance the estimation of Danish art in England. The same may be said of the contributions from other nations, whence, although, there may be less to miss in such a collection as this, there is much that is beautiful, and more that is original and strictly national—in art the healthiest sign we know. This is markedly true of the three Scandinavian nations—Sweden, Denmark, and Norway.

In the Norwegian and Danish collection there are many highly characteristic scenes and incidents, honestly painted, which go home to the hearts of all visitors. Such, for instance, is Exner's "Sunday Visit to Grandpapa." See how thoroughly natural is the best room of the comfortable cottage, in which, though made neat and smart for Sunday company, the chickens move about with an air of the most innocent security. Notice the curious furniture; the elaborate ornaments on the children's heads; the peculiar costumes; and withal the delighted look of the mother and grandfather, and the reverential air of the child, as it addresses its little, carefully-conned Sunday speech to the old man. In this and pictures of a similar character, the actual painting is, perhaps, just a little too feeble; but then it is very true in conception, and honest in treatment—as witness the design by Tidemand we have chosen for illustration. Here, as in other pictures of the same school, the purpose of the artist is thoroughly and conscientiously worked out. Schiött's "Offer of Marriage," and Madame Jerichau's nearly similar scene, show us, as in a photograph, how seriously and decorously such affairs are managed in Northern Europe—the father of the bridegroom, in each case, making the proposition to the parents of the bride, with all due formality. In the Norwegian department of the Picture Galleries there are several paintings which, in like manner, illustrate various national peculiarities.

. Swedish and Lap life and manners may be almost as well studied at South Kensington as in the actual countries themselves. Here are various landscapes, not always commendable, by the way, as works of art, possessing a strong feeling of locality; and Northern scenery is thus brought directly to our view. Some of the views —those of Gude, of Norway, for example—are, however, excellent as works of art; and there is a large sea-piece (1,573), "Early Morning off the Skaw," by Sörensen, of Copenhagen, in which the waves are as well drawn as though Stanfield were the limner, the water real sea water, and unmistakably wet, and the effect of dawn over a stormy sea admirably given.

THE BELGIAN SCHOOL.—Next comes the Belgian room, a room to linger long in, and return to again and again. Here the master-minds are the chiefs of the rival schools of Antwerp and Brussels, both men of genius, and painters of extraordinary skill. Gallait, of Brussels, has the popular suffrage ; but Leys, of Antwerp, is the object of even more intense, though more limited, admiration. Each has a European reputation; each may be regarded as the representative of the two great classes of historical artists of our time—the dramatic and the minute. Gallait has here nine pictures, all of large size. The largest, but least interesting, is his "Abdication of Charles V.," belonging to the Brussels Museum. His master-works are "The Last Honours paid to Counts Egmont and Horn," and "The Last Moments of Count Egmont;" both well known by Martinet's admirable engravings. The former, a commission from the town of Tournai, is one of the noblest gallery pictures in the building; large in style, forcible in expression, and deeply impressive. "The Last Moments of Count Egmont," belonging to the Berlin Museum, is no less grand in effect; and the head of Egmont has even a profounder sentiment. His more recent picture, "The Remorse of Delilah," is a fine conception, but feebler in treatment, and somewhat French in style. Slingeneyer, of Brussels, follows in the wake of Gallait; indeed, his "Christian Martyr under Diocletian " — every Continental painter of history has his "Christian Martyr" — divides the popular favour with Gallait's "Egmont and Horn." Pannels, of Antwerp, steers between the two, and has a couple of pictures, "The Widow of Artevelde," and "The Proscribed," which only want the vivifying touch of genius to be masterpieces.

In the other leading branches of art, Belgium is likewise great. Madou's quiet humorous subjects—"A Hat Hunt," "Trouble-fête," and the like, are universal favourites. By Dillens there are lively and

admirably painted scenes from the familiar life of Zeeland. Bossuet has some clever street scenes. By the veteran Lies there is a picture worthy of his fame, "Rapine, Pillage, and Conflagration." The satin dresses of Willems are worthy of Terburg, whatever the rest of the picture may be ; but he is an immense favourite with the admirers of painted satin, and those who care for this kind of dexterity will do well to look at his pictures. Then there are the conversation pieces of Alfred Stevens; the cattle pieces of Verboekoven, from whom our Cooper learnt to paint cows ; and many others of various orders, all excellent in their way, and altogether making up a collection that does no little honour to Leopold's tiny kingdom, and that would in itself form a very creditable and suggestive exhibition.

THE GREEK SCHOOL.—Greece has sent two oil paintings, five groups of sculpture, and eight engravings—the works of about fifteen artists; and the Ionian Islands are represented by about twelve pictures—the productions of seven artists. The sculpture from Greece consists chiefly of statues by L. and G. Phytalæ.

TURKEY, for the first time in the history of exhibitions, fills a place as an exhibitor of pictures. Five paintings have been sent by M. Paul Musurus Bey, and they comprise portraits and sketches of still life. The artist, who is the son of the Turkish Commissioner, is only twenty years of age, and therefore these works must be judged leniently.

AMERICAN ART.—The American Fine-art display is small, numbering about a dozen pictures and engravings, the chief of which is Mr. Cropsey's "Autumn on the Hudson ;" but several Transatlantic sculptors find places and an honourable welcome with England.

The great Continental schools of painting have not responded to our invitation to the great Art Festival at South Kensington with such frankness and alacrity as could be wished. The works of art sent from several countries convey but a very inadequate idea of the real position of those countries in the republic of genius ; many of the pictures and statues were only sent at the last moment. This has arisen partly, no doubt, from apprehensions respecting the difficulty and danger of transmitting works of art, and possibly from under-estimating the achievements of our own school. In the nature of things, the most eminent artists of Germany, the great mural painters in fresco and stereochrome—Overbeck, Cornelius, Kaulbach, Schnorr, and Hess —could not be fairly represented ; but even the painters of the well-known Dusseldorf school, for instance, many of whom could have contributed works in oil, are almost entirely absent.

Speaking of the combined industrial and artistic show at South Kensington, an eminent critic says :—"There is a peculiar propriety and usefulness in thus wedding the fine and useful arts. It is hardly possible to find now any branch of industry not susceptible of ornament and decorative treatment. And fine art is the fountain-head of all decoration. One of the great lessons of the Manchester Exhibition was this—that if fine art be fostered, ornamental art will take care of itself. We there saw that whatever was characteristic of painting and sculpture at any particular period was reproduced in what are now called art-manufactures. The artist was, indeed, in the old time, often the artificer also. There is nothing so well calculated to carry out the purposes of improvement and progress of international exhibitions and the wishes of their great founder in England as the placing the works of human genius and industry in juxtaposition. Nothing, moreover, will tend so much to lessen the utilitarianism and materialism with which, as a people, we are chargeable. We need not claim for art a moral, a chastening, and ennobling influence. This is conceded by all but the thoughtless. The old Greeks, we know, had but one word for the good and the fair."

WATER COLOURS.

Branching off right and left from each extremity of the main gallery, smaller galleries, on the same level, run at right angles along the Exhibition Road and Prince Albert's Road ; and, as far as the domes, the walls are entirely covered by paintings in oil and water colours, and drawings—an important addition to the attraction on this occasion, paintings not being included in the International Exhibition of 1851. These have been grouped together in Class XXXVIII.

In the catalogue of a collection gathered from public and private galleries, and liberally lent by many hundreds of art patrons, it is almost unnecessary to say that there will be found the names of all our principal painters in water colours—that truly national school of painting, founded by Cozens, Girtin, and above all by Turner, whose works illustrate both the commencement and the full perfection of the art. Those who laboured with them to extend its scope have not been overlooked, and Eldridge, Robson, Dewint, Fielding, Prout, and Varley, are well represented; while the works of Stothard, Barrett, and Cox lead up to the living representatives of this beautiful art. These specimens have been selected by Mr. Redgrave, R.A., inspector-general for art at the South Kensington Museum.

Many other known names might be added: Müller, by whose early death we lost an artist of brilliant promise; Cattermole and Haag, distinguished for figure-painting; Nash, Roberts, and Haghe, in architecture; Cooke and Duncan, for sea-pieces; Harding, G. Fripp, Gastineau, Boyce, Davidson, and many more, for different aspects of the landscape. These names bring us to our own days, and to the later developments of the art. Whilst recognising the merits of much that now fills our exhibitions with skilful and pleasant work, it cannot fail to be observed that water-colours appear to be passing beyond the earlier—may it not be added, the natural?—limits of the material, and engaging more and more in a rivalry with the effects and the methods of oil painting. The issues of this tendency are uncertain: it may hold sway for a time as a fashion, or lead to the establishment of another school of art, like that which of old was practised under the name of *Tempera*, and applied with eminent success in England to miniatures, in the seventeenth century. But, meanwhile, the peculiar facilities of water-colour painting expose it to danger from an opposite source.

ENGRAVINGS AND ETCHINGS.

The fine collection of British etchings and engravings—Class XL.—is divided, at South Kensington, into two sections; the first containing the works of deceased, and the second those of living, engravers. The former is divided into etchings, line engravings, mezzotints, stipple, and wood. The arrangement of each subdivision is a chronological one, not calculated according to the dates of the births or deaths of the artists, but as nearly as possible on the times when their principal works were published. The number of these represented is eighty-four; their engravings are about four hundred and fifty, and they occupy three hundred and twenty-seven frames. They are, with few exceptions, early proof impressions of the very highest quality.

The etchings do not call for special remark; but among the line engravings will be found the most celebrated works of Hogarth (those engraved entirely by himself), Browne, Woollett, Sir R. Strange, W. Sharp, the Heaths, Raimbach, the Cookes, and others of nearly equal importance.

The mezzotints are peculiarly interesting, and the wonderful productions of MacArdell, Pether, Dixon, Earlom, J. R. Smith, V. Green, and others, are sufficient to prove the unrivalled excellence of the British school in this branch of art.

The sections of stipple and wood engravings include many of the best specimens of Bartolozzi, Haward, Collyer, Striven, Bewick, Clennell, Williams, &c.

PLOUGHING. ROSA BONHEUR.

The department of living engravers is similarly subdivided, with an additional section of lithographs, but the arrangement of each subdivision is an alphabetical one. It contains about 300 works, by 68 engravers, which fill nearly 180 frames. With very few exceptions, the proofs are contributed by the artists themselves. The whole arrangement of this class has been undertaken by Mr. William Smith, assisted in the hanging by Mr. Colnaghi.

Of the many forms of what, from the stone employed at first as the plate, has been called Lithography, detailed notice will not be appropriate, as the processes belong more to mechanical agency than to pure art.

In wood-engraving the lines are in relief, the contrary to those in engravings on metal plates, and which therefore fit them for surface printing in conjunction with type. The first great English wood-

largeness in style, exactly analogous to the proof . . . . . . So little are perfection and greatness in art dependent . . . . . material.

If Bewick's peculiar excellence has not . . . . . . engraving has been both in France and England . . . . . wonderful height in finish and brilliancy. The art, however, lain too decidedly in this direction, as if in competition with . . . a vain struggle, which risks loss in the natural treatment and natural effects of the wood-cut. By a return within the strict limits fixed by the material, by moderation and study from nature, the admirable skill which a multitude of artists have attained will, no doubt, tend to bring wood-engraving before long to further . . . . . . excellent series of "Parables" which . . . . .

THE FUNERAL IN THE FROST. CHALDEE.

engraver—and, in fact, the father of the modern practice of the art —was Bewick. He "added an effectiveness in light and shade, a delicacy and variety to his work," which gave woodcuts henceforth an independent existence in pictorial expression. This great change—one of the most decided in the history of art—he effected by his unusual good sense truth to nature, and tenderness in feeling. His mode of engraving was to bring out the design, where possible, by white lines laid on black; to build, as it were, from darkness upwards to light. He thus followed the natural treatment or law of his material; for the lines cut into the wood-cut form the whites, as those cut by the line-engraver form the darks, of the impression; and the proper direction of each art is indicated by this difference. Bewick's other gifts are shown in the exquisite simplicity, truth, and invention of his well-known wood-cuts. These cannot be too carefully studied: they have a directness in reaching their point, a breadth and

It is . . . . perhaps, necessary to remind at once . . . . . . to the pictures and engravings, via the International Exhibition . . . . . . amongst industrial portion of the Great Show; yet a careful perusal of the picture-galleries. To understand and appreciate art requires a peculiar education; but to fully estimate a steam-engine at work, a model in action, or a piece of work in silver or bronze, a very slight acquaintance with history, or manufactures is only necessary. It has been our aim in this work to aid in disseminating a love for both, useful and the beautiful.

On reviewing the contents of the Picture Galleries, the intelligent visitor cannot but be much impressed with the works of our foreign friends. The beauty, attractiveness, and vivacity of the works that everywhere meet the eye, lead to a careful examination of the pictures themselves, and such an examination cannot but add to the visitor's delight and instruction.

THE GRECIAN COURT.

23.

Grecian Contributions to the International Exhibition.

THE sunny land of Greece is represented at the World's Show by about 280 exhibitors, principally in the classes belonging to raw materials and food products. In manufactures she is by no means prominent; but in the fine arts, as might be anticipated, something of the spirit which once actuated the world's conquerors is still discernible. Her position at South Kensington is peculiar, for she stands in the midst of Turkey, Brazil, Russia, and Peru. Thus:—

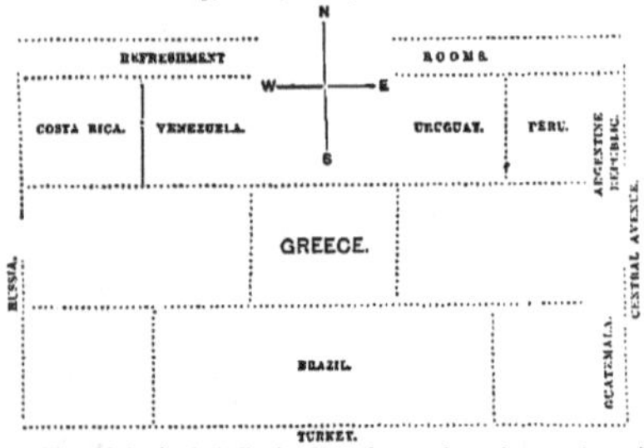
N
W
E
S
REFRESHMENT
ROOMS.
COSTA RICA.
VENEZUELA.
URUGUAY.
PERU.
ARGENTINE REPUBLIC.
GREECE.
RUSSIA.
CENTRAL AVENUE.
BRAZIL.
GUATEMALA.
TURKEY.

The old land of civilisation—the home of warriors, poets, and patriots—even now, in the degradation arising from a succession of foreign rulers, shows something of the grand old temper which shone so conspicuously in the struggle for independence years ago. At the entrance of the Grecian Court are numerous busts and statues of the famous chieftains and soldiers who assisted in the good work. Here will be seen a figure of Kodios, of whom the oracle had declared that the war would not succeed while he remained alive. The story goes that, resolved to sacrifice himself for the good of his country, he rushed into the thickest of the fight, and fell, pierced with a score of wounds; but, ere his life-blood ebbed quite away, he drew aside his cloak, and showed his face to the enemy—the chief whose loss had been declared necessary for the success of the cause for which he fought. In this statue he is seen unveiling his noble features. The statue of another great captain is here, who, after having slain a crowd of Turks, had his sword broken, when he was surrounded and killed by the enemy. This, and similar pieces of sculpture by young Athenian artists, will be viewed with pleasure, standing as they do in the centre of the court.

But, as regards modern Greek sculpture, there is little to be said that may not be said in a few sentences. While, as we have seen, a few good figures appear here and there, and a few fine groups are to be seen in the Grecian Court, it must be admitted that the modern artists have sadly degenerated from the grand models of Phidias and the followers of the classic school. Strange, that while the moderns go to the old Greek style for sculpture and architecture, the living artists of the Archipelago should be so far behind even the sculptors of less favoured lands! The antique is servilely copied by the moderns, but the spirit that actuated the production of the antique is lost. As in sculpture, so in painting. The Picture Galleries contain but five Greek pictures, the work of two Greek artists. Indeed, the show made by Greece in the fine art department is, on the whole, disappointing; though, as we have already observed, the few artistic works shown bear promise at least of future excellence, and a return to something approaching that exquisite taste in design and that delicacy in execution which once belonged to a great historical country.

Various specimens of *verde antique* marbles of Tinos appear in the familiar shape of Corinthian and Ionic columns; magnesite, or whitestone, and soft-soap clay, with green and white marble, and various specimens of minerals and marbles are interspersed with exquisite wood-carvings, minute in detail; ceramic clays, yet innocent of the potter's art; tea, tobacco, pulse, almonds, barley, figs, wheat, maize, walnuts, honey, linseed, raisins, currants, wine, spirits, wood, oil, tallow, timber, cocoons, naphtha, cotton, wax, boxwood, military and naval accoutrements, table-cloths, sheets, silk and woollen fabrics, lace, carpets, embroideries, goat-skin garments, hides, caps, furs, sandals, boots, account-books, electro casts, printed books, manuscripts, vases, pipes, cutlery, jewellery, and bones. So do the most familiar objects of every-day life intermingle with the memories of classic times, and the reminiscences of departed glories, in a collection at once rich, complete, and interesting; representing, as it does, the produce of modern Greece, beside the arts which made ancient Greece famous in the world's history. "In the sunny region of the Archipelago," writes an intelligent observer, "a bright young Greek, and a sententious old one, combine to give you, in excellent English, full information about the gold embroidery with which their case is filled, from neat tobacco pouches, up to the really gorgeous mitre of the septinsular archimandrite. Here are also Byzantine paintings, executed last year, but exactly in the same style as those of the times of the Comneni; pipes of ineffable suggestiveness, and all sorts of modern Attic *bric-à-brac*. Here will be found a case, the size of a small drawing-room, containing a brilliant group, ladies and cavaliers, in the picturesque national costume. You see the whole thing at a glance, and conclude that human vanity is the same everywhere, and that crinoline is universal." How strangely this reads in connection with our associations of the famous land which produced Herodotus, the father of history; Demosthenes, the prince of orators; Lycurgus, the model of lawgivers; and Alexander, the conqueror of the then civilised world!

Silver Work in the Exhibition.

HAVING already referred at some length to the works in silver exhibited by our French neighbours, and also to those shown by Messrs. Elkington and others, we may now proceed to introduce a few specimens from the cases of Messrs. Emanuel, of Portsmouth, whose case is always an object of great attraction, and Messrs. Primo and Son, of Birmingham; leaving the objects shown by Messrs. Hunt and Roskell, Messrs. Phillips, Garrard, and Hancock, for more particular examination to a future occasion.

Messrs. Emanuel have the honour to be jewellers and silversmiths to her Majesty the Queen and the Prince of Wales, and they have also supplied numerous works of art in the precious metals, as well as jewellery, to the principal courts of Europe. In the Exhibition they show a vast variety of those objects, exquisitely wrought, as well as some machinery of good workmanship, used in the production of the several wheels, pinions, &c., belonging to clocks and watches.

Our second illustration is a silver candelabrum belonging to a dessert service, allegorical of the International Exhibition, for which it was expressly designed and manufactured. The candelabrum has a beautifully cut glass basket on the top, for fruit or flowers. As portions of the branches can be removed, it is made applicable as an epergne. On the base is a large group, representing Britannia seated on a lion, and attended by an allegorical figure of Industry, distributing rewards to the representatives of the various nations of the world, who are represented laying the products of their several countries at her feet. The decorations of the whole of this service, which are of a floral character, are of an entirely novel design. The allegory is carried out in two epergnes, with figures of the Arts and Sciences. The centre pieces on page 184 belong to this service, which was designed and modelled by Mr. E. W. Clarke, and produced at the manufactory of the exhibitors. The centre pieces contains figures severally representing Europe, Asia, Africa, and America, with appropriate allusions in silver to the productions of the four quarters of the globe.

The Race Cup on page 184 belongs to a style of work much patronised, being both figurative, allegorical, and historical. The treatment of this particular specimen is very good, while the workmanship is equally worthy of commendation.

To notice all the objects in Messrs. Emanuel's case would occupy too much space. We may, however, briefly notice a silver tazza, designed and modelled by Mr. W. Clarke, representing scenes in the Holy Wars. The basi-relievi round the body of the work represents the battle between Richard Cœur de Lion and the Saracens; while the group at the summit is descriptive of the friendly meeting after the battle between Richard and Saladin. Another fine work is a silver candelabrum and epergne, with allegorical figures of Comedy, Dancing, and Music, designed by Mr. Emanuel, jun., for Edward Weston, Esq., by whom it has been lent for exhibition. The visitor will also notice a silver vase in the Louis Quartorze style, representing Perseus slaying the Dragon, and rescuing Andromeda. The bowl is richly embossed, while at each corner of the vase are figures of rampant horses. This work was designed and modelled by Mr. H. Morell. Another noticeable work is a silver "vase irregulier," with groups of wild horses, in various positions, executed in basrelief.

A silver jug, in alto-relievo, by Mr. Clark, is very characteristic. It is called an "Episode in a Steeple Chase," and shows how one of the sportsmen, in attempting to jump a stone wall, has come to grief, while others are gallantly charging the obstruction. The Homer tazza, designed and modelled by Mr. Morell, consists of a group in alto-relievo of Achilles in his chariot, the stem and base composed of armour shields, weapons, &c., copied from the antique. The body of the tazza surrounded with illustrations of the following subjects, from the "Iliad:"—"Diomed casting his Spear at Mars," "The Hours taking the Horses from the Car of Juno," "The Gods descending to Battle," "Hector's Body dragged at the Car of Achilles." This is really a very fine work, thoughtfully designed, and admirably executed.

Somewhat similar in treatment is a classic group in silver, representing "Thetis bringing her son Achilles the Armour forged by Vulcan," also designed by Mr. Morell. The following is the passage

POMPEIAN CANDELABRA. MESSRS. ELKINGTON.

from the "Iliad," book xix., which the artist has sought, and sought successfully, to reproduce in silver:—

"Tu vero a Vulcano allata inclyta arma accipe,
Pulchra admodum, qualia nondum quisquam vir humeris gestavit.
Sic sane locuta Dea armo deposuit
Ante Achillem ; illa vera sonitum-edidere facta-artificiose omnia."

The Tasso Vase is also from the design of Mr. Morell, whose classic taste is well shown in this elegant object, which is parcel gilt, the outline in the Italian style, and the ornaments in the cinque-cento period. The large group in alto-relievo illustrates "The Combat of Clorinda and Prince Tancred," portrayed in Tasso's "Jerusalem Delivered," canto iii. stanza 21 :—

"Meanwhile, Clorinda rushes to assail
The prince, and level lays her spear renowne 1 ;
Both lances strike, and on the barrel rontayle
In shivers fly, and she remains discrowned ;
For, burst its silver rivets, to the ground
Her helmet leaped — incomparable blow !—
And, by the rudeness of the shock unbound,
Her sex to all the world emblazoning so,
Loose to the charmed winds her golden tresses flow."
* * * * * *

One bas-relief represents "The First Interview of Prince Tancred and Clorinda at a Fountain" (canto i. stanza 47) :—

"To the same warbling of fresh waters drew,
Armed, but unhelmed and unforeseen, a maid :
She was a Pagan, and came thither, too,
To quench her thirst beneath the pleasant shade :
Her beautiful fair aspect, thus displayed,
He sees, admires, and, touched to transport, glows
With passion—'tis strange how quick the feeling grows :
Scarce born, its power in him no cool, calm medium knows."

The second bas-relief is descriptive of the scene in which the Prince rescues Clorinda from an attack of one of his followers (canto iii. stanza 20) :—

"One base pursuer saw Clorinda stand,
Her rich locks spread like sunbeams on the wind,
And raised his arm, in passing, from behind,
To stab secure the undefended maid ;
But Tancred, conscious of the blow designed,
Shrieked out 'Beware !' to warn the unconscious maid,
And, with his own good sword, bore off the hostile blade."

This beautiful work is the property of Captain Alexander, of Belgrave Square, by whose permission the manufacturers are enabled to exhibit it. Another noble work is a silver vase in the Grecian style, the bow, enriched with festoons of vine-leaves and grapes, in alto-relievo; with handles formed of winged horses, and the base ornamented with abundant foliage and bacchanalian heads. The first group in alto-relievo, on the base, represents the attack of the Trojans, Æneas and Pandarus, on Diomedes, resulting in the death of Pandarus, the rescue of Æneas by Venus, and the capture of Æneas's celebrated horses ("Iliad," Book V.) :—

"Thus, while they spoke, the foe came furious on, And stern Lycaon's war-like race began: Prince, thou art met. Though late in vain assailed, The spear may enter where the arrow fail'd."

The second alto-relievo represents the horses being unloosed from Juno's car by the attendant Hours ("Iliad," Book VIII.) :—

"She spoke, and backward turned her steeds of light, Adorned with manes of gold, and heavenly bright. The Hours unloosed them, panting as they stood, And heaped their mangers with ambrosial food."

This work is the property of the American millionaire, R. Ten Broeck, Esq., by whose permission it is allowed to be shown at the International Exhibition by the manufacturers:—

There is also a suite of articles in silver for the writing-table, of entirely novel design, consisting of inkstand, blotting-book, envelope-case, match-box, date-indicator, pair of candlesticks, penholder, seal, &c. The bodies of the articles are of engraved silver, and the wire mounts are in silver-gilt. Perhaps the most noticeable object in the case of Messrs. Emanuel is a silver shield, the outer circle of which is surrounded, in relief, with a frieze of horses and warriors,

taken from the celebrated Elgin Marbles in the British Museum. The centre of this shield is in alto-relievo, and is a copy of the classic cameo by Athenion, in the Royal Museum at Naples, illustrating "the Conquest of the Titans by Jupiter," described by Horace (Ode iii. 4—42:—

" . . . Scimus ut impios
Titanas, immanemque turmam
Fulmine sustulerit caduco,
Qui terram inertem, qui mare temperat
Ventosum, et urbes, regnaque tristia,
Divosque, mortalesque turmas."

Jupiter is represented in his car, drawn by four horses, and preparing to hurl his thunderbolts at the giants, who, in accordance with Ovid, are depicted by the artist as men of great stature, having serpents in the place of legs:—

"Sphingasque et Harpyias serpentipedesque Gigantas."
Ovid, Trist. iv. 7, 17.

This fine shield was designed by Mr. Morell, and manufactured by the exhibitors for the Right Hon. the Earl of Lonsdale, by whose permission it is now exhibited.

We have now mentioned the principal objects in the case of Messrs. Emanuel; and the conclusion to which we and all intelligent visitors come is, that their entire display is altogether worthy the reputation they have made for themselves as art-manufacturers of the highest class. Other exhibitors show a large variety of objects in silver and electro silver, some of which are worthy the attention and careful consideration of the visitor. They consist of presentation plate, prizes for rifle and archery meetings, candelabra, epergues, fruit-stands, flower-stands, plateaux, and artistic plate of every description;

SILVER CANDELABRUM.   MESSRS. E. AND E. EMANUEL.

dinner, tea, and coffee-services, wine-coolers, salvers, tea-trays, cruet-frames, liqueur-stands, candlesticks, toast-racks, soy and pickle-stands and frames, side-dishes, &c.; all of which may be characterised as possessing considerable merit in design, with undoubted excellence in workmanship.

The show made by Messrs. Thomas Prime and Son, of the Magneto Plate Works, Birmingham, consist of dinner, tea, and dessert services, &c., in silver and electro-plate, of exquisite design and good manufacture. The general aspect of their case will be seen in the beautiful engraving we introduce on page 185. The various objects shown may be thus briefly enumerated — an Italian epergne or centre-piece, and plateau, with figures of Tragedy, Comedy, and Music; a coffee and tea service, kettle and tray, designed after Greek models; a coffee and tea service, kettle and tray, richly engraved, wrought by hand, without the use of dies; enriched gothic communion service; a silver cruet frame with engraved bottles — the design and ornamentation in the Moresque style; engraved glass claret jugs, with plated mounts and handles; a silver claret jug, richly engraved; an inkstand of Moresque design; group in centre, "The Pet Lamb;" presentation trowel, part oxydised, and

gilt, the handle enriched with enamels; an engraved glass butter-dish and cover, with plated stand—Greek; pair of fish carvers, beaded handles; spoons and forks, Princess and other patterns, dessert, butter, and fish table knives; engraved waiters, various designs, &c. All these articles are grouped together with considerable taste, and, in the comparatively small space allotted them, the Messrs. Prime make a most rich and varied display.

Mr. Thomas, of New Bond Street, exhibits many beautiful and highly-finished specimens of the silversmith's art. His attention has evidently been directed to the production of such articles as would be required in daily use. There are also several specimens of *repoussé* work, which deserve notice on account of the general boldness of style and vigour of execution. The Bradgate Park Testimonial, a large rosewater dish or sideboard shield, the result of a penny subscription, subscribed for by the poorer inhabitants of Leicester, and presented to the Earl of Stamford and Warrington, is of a most elaborate character, and is a fine example of chasing. The small, but prettily arranged, case of this exhibitor contains numerous pieces of plate, ably modelled, and of a very high order of merit, many admirably adapted for racing,

SILVER RACE CUP.   MESSRS. H. AND E. EMANUEL.

yachting, volunteer, and other presentation prizes. Mr. J. A. Wheatley, of Carlisle, shows specimens of Cumberland lead, lead ore, Cumberland silver, jewellery, and a pretty design, known as the Cambrian cup. The body of the cup is composed of white glass of the form of a Roman urn, with Cumberland silver mounts, standing on an ebony plateau, designed to symbolise the peculiar features of Cumberland scenery. The same exhibitor also shows a paper-cutter, designed in the form of a Roman sword, ornamented with scroll work, and bearing on one side the words "Murus Sereri," and on the other "Luguvallium," the name borne by the city of Carlisle when a Roman station; a vinaigrette, the lid bearing a crown in frosted silver, surrounded by a wreath of thistles and roses entwined; a miniature portrait of Napoleon I. in water colours, by Colanton, representing the emperor in his coronation robes, and mounted in a splendid wreath of diamonds (the portrait is original, and was painted for the mother of Napoleon, and by her bequeathed to one of the old nobility of France); together with a few fine specimens of goldsmiths' work in gold; gem and enamelled brooches, bracelets, and gem and sig-net rings of new designs, manufactured by eminent London firms; and scarf pins, with a new safety guard, the invention of the exhibitor, suitable to sporting or valuable gem pins, being a security against loss, and very simple in operation.

Mr. B. Lee, of Rathbone Place, shows several suits of ladies' jewels, of new and elegant designs; ladies' brooches, bracelets, eardrops, rings, necklaces, chatelaines, necklets, crosses, lockets, pencil-cases, book-markers, charms, and riding-whips; gentlemen's Albert guards and keys, guard chains, pins, rings and studs. Miniature and device brooches. A choice collection of designs and specimens of hair devices for brooches and bracelets. A large bouquet of 80 flowers, formed of delicate shades of hair, and other novelties in the art of hair-working.

Messrs. Attenborough, of Piccadilly; Barker, of Birmingham; Jamieson, of Aberdeen, Lambert, of Coventry; Johnson, of Dublin; Payne, of Bath; and Wilkinson, of Sheffield, also show various capitally-designed objects, in silver and electro-plate, besides many British and foreign jewels. In fact, the workers in the precious metals all display, variety, richness, and taste, far in advance of the show made at any previous exhibition.

THE CAIRO JEWELLERY.

THE portion of the Egyptian Court which will excite most interest is the contributions from the Cairo Museum. The Viceroy, among his other titles to distinction, has the credit of being the first Mussulman sovereign who has formed a museum. Instead of destroying the monuments of antiquity, he has done all in his power to preserve them; and, under the care of the accomplished director, M. Auguste Mariette, who acts as his chief commissioner here, a collection is rapidly being formed at Cairo, which, though now only two or three years old, is, in some respects, already superior to any of the European museums. In one of the cases in this Court is exhibited a collection of ancient Egyptian jewellery, of extraordinary rarity, all the results of researches carried on by M. Mariette, at Thebes, and, with one or two exceptions, all forming part of the funeral ornaments of Queen Aah-Hotch, the mother of Amosis, the first king of the eighteenth dynasty. Without going deeper into the mysteries of Egyptian chronology, we may say that her Majesty lived about 1900 B.C., or five hundred years before the time of Moses, which will bring her somewhere about the time of Joseph. Visitors should bear this in mind, when they remark the beautiful finish of the workmanship, and the still brilliant colours of the stones with which they are ornamented. The savans are sure to cluster round this case, and to examine every ornament minutely; but, for the general public, it is sufficient to specify some of the principal objects. In the front of the case is a poniard, the blade of which is elaborately chased with figures representing the fight of a lion and a bull, and close by the hilt is the cartouche, or private seal of King Amosis. Behind is a diadem, of massive gold, in the front of which is a box, with the cartouche graven on it, supported by two exquisitely carved sphyuxes. The posterior portion is set with

coloured stones, lapis lazuli, cornelian, and turquoise, and it has a peculiar tongue rising above the head, which served to divide the hair of the wearer. A hatchet—the symbol of divinity—has on the blade a curious representation of Amosis sacrificing a barbarian captive, and on the handle a complete genealogy of his Majesty. A massive gold chain, pretty nearly a yard long, is suspended to a scarabaeus of marvellous workmanship, and near it is a collar of equal beauty, with three large golden bees suspended from it. The most curious article is a golden boat mounted on four wheels, with twelve oarsmen in silver, and a figure in gold seated in the midst, probably an effigy of the dead queen. This is supposed to symbolise the voyage of the soul after death, and may be regarded as another proof of the belief of the Egyptians in the immortality of the soul. The most elaborate of all the ornaments is a pectoral, or brooch, which represents King Amosis between two divinities, who are pouring over him the water of purification. Both sides of this ornament are beautifully finished—one side in gold, the other in coloured stones. There are a profusion of other ornaments—bracelets, rings, necklaces—in gold of excellent quality, all of which were found on her Majesty's person, and all of them, it is conjectured, made specially for her adornment in the coffin. The two great earrings are of a later date, and bear the cartouche of Rameses, of the twentieth dynasty. On the other side of the court is a case which contains a complete pantheon of the Egyptian deities, among which a beautiful figure of Isis is, perhaps, the rarest and most beautiful. In a small figure of an Egyptian demon, about the size of one's little finger, in blue enamel, is unique, and a great price has already been offered for it by the director of the Museum of the Louvre. The figures of the hippopotamus and the little hand below are remarkable for the beautiful shade of blue—the real bleu d'Égypte, which modern manufacturers have in vain attempted to reproduce. It has generally been believed that the Egyptians had no knowledge of the art of enamelling; but this theory is destroyed by these specimens, as well as by a votive vase found in the tomb of Amenophis (the Greek Memnon), which is ornamented with small plaques of various coloured enamels. The most curious object in the case is a sort of model mummy case. By the side of the body sits the soul, and on the side of the coffin are inscribed prayers supposed to be addressed to the body by the soul, beseeching it to remain undisturbed until the day of resurrection, when the two will be found together again. We have mentioned these articles because, though they are perhaps not altogether within the scope of the Exhibition, they are unique of their kind, and are certain to excite great admiration among all persons who take an interest in these subjects. Over this very complete illustration of ancient and modern Egypt is fitly placed a fine portrait of Mehemet Ali, the energetic founder of the modern prosperity of the country.

THE MANUFACTURE OF THE ARMSTRONG GUN.

THOSE who visited the Exhibition of 1851 will probably remember a few military rifles exhibited by the skilful gunmakers of France. There arms bore names then new and strange to English ears, such as "Carabine à tige," "Carabine Militaire Système Minié," and attracted very little attention except from those who were aware that they were precursors of a revolution in the science of projectiles, which must of necessity soon extend from small arms to artillery. From the moment that it became evident that the Minié and the Enfield in skilful hands could silence field guns, efforts were made by mechanics and artillerists both in this and other countries to introduce such improvements in the construction of ordnance as should restore to this arm its superiority of range. The accomplishment of this object was only to be effected by pursuing the same course in regard to artillery which had been so successful with the infantry. The introduction of the principle of rifling in ordnance, to throw a much heavier shot from the same calibre of gun, at once solved the problem; but the extra strain of the elongated projectile, over and above that of the round shot, involved the necessity of immensely increased strength, greater than could be obtained in cast-iron guns, however well fabricated. This led to the employment of wrought-iron and steel, and to vastly improved modes of manufacture, all of which are fully represented. The most prominent object, and at the same time one of the most interesting, is the War Department trophy, erected in the centre of the court, illustrating the manufacture of the famous Armstrong gun. In this fine series of specimens from the royal gun factories at Woolwich is shown the embryo Armstrong gun, first in the shape of a bar of exceeding tough compound iron, coiled round a mandril, and forming an open tube, some foot or foot and a half in length. It is then heated, and by repeated blows of a heavy steam hammer, welded into a perfectly homogeneous mass. The next process is that of boring it out to the required calibre of the gun intended to be made. A number of these cylindrical sections are then joined lengthwise to get the required length for the gun, by cutting a right angle groove on the outer edge of one section, and on the inner edge of another, fitting these two grooves to each other, and welding them into one length. When completed, this tube forms the inner core of the gun, being of the same thickness from end to end.

To give the additional strength at the breech, larger sections, of similar construction, are shrunk on, at a low red heat, to this inner core, until the required thickness is attained. The visitor will see that, by turning the screw-handle at the breech, and removing the vent piece, which slips into a slot cut to receive it, in rear of the trunnions, the gun is an open tube from end to end. The cartridge is inserted into the rear aperture, pushed forward by a rammer clear of the spot occupied by the vent piece, the vent piece is dropped into its place, the handle turned to secure it, and the gun is ready to be discharged. All the guns are rifled with a number of fine rectangular grooves. A number of beautifully-finished 9-pounder and 12-pounder Armstrongs, with several of larger calibre, are exhibited as forming part of the trophy. Forming part of the War Office exhibition, the visitor will find Armstrong guns of various calibre, from the 100-pounder naval or siege gun, down to the delicate looking little weapons which a strong man would find no difficulty in putting on his shoulder and carrying off, intended for mountain warfare, and to be transported on pack-saddles.

Miscellaneous.

NEW OBJECTS IN THE EXHIBITION.—There has been lately added to the Minton collection a fine memorial vase, presented by Her Majesty to the Princess Alice on her marriage with Prince Louis of Hesse. This work of art, which is of the most delicate material and workmanship, bears portraits of the Queen and the late Prince Consort on either side. Its prevailing colour is the famous gros bleu; and the medallions are in the style of the Limoges enamels. Several productions have been added to the collection within the past few days. Among these were a pair of exquisite vases, which exhibit the most finished skill on the part of the painter. They are of lilac tint, and the encircling groups of figures are of the same hue, painted so as to resemble the Antwerp bas-reliefs. Another object is a majolica plateau, of antique design, the subject of which is "Cupid stealing the thunders of Jove." Blended with the vigour and breadth of this peculiar kind of fictile art, the painting of the plateau possesses the quality of high finish and a remarkable brilliancy of colour.

WHILE speaking of additions to the Exhibition, we should not omit to mention a specimen of Zostera Marina, the substitute for cotton discovered by Mr. Harben, and exhibited by Messrs. Harben and Mountcastle. This interesting object will be found near the spinning machinery in the Western Annexe. In the same locality, but more removed towards the far end of the building, are placed the American flax and fibre machines of Messrs. Sanford and Mallory. The invention thus exemplified is noticeable for simplicity, cheapness, economy of labour, portability, and excellence of production. The weight is scarcely above five hundred weight, and with the aid of one machine about 130 lbs. of perfectly clean fibre may be produced by two persons in a day. A serious want is supplied by Messrs. Sanford and Mallory's machine, and its value will be especially recognised in India, and all climates yielding plants of the agave, aloe, plantain, yucca, and pineapple families.

MACHINERY AND HAND-LABOUR.—The Saturday Review says: "All that is to be seen at Brompton is a vast and ingenious system of joinery. Scarcely anything is made on the spot. There is absolutely not one solitary fragment of work—wood, iron, or glass, which is not executed by machinery. It would be perhaps difficult to point out one single square-inch of work which is due to skilled manual labour. The iron is all cast, the bricks are all machine-made, the wood is all machine-planed; the very capitals of the vast columns, the one and only feature in which ornament has been attempted, are all run in plaster moulds. The glass is all cast. All that man has to do is to screw and nail, and tie and mortice and cement ready-made materials together. It is the tendency of modern work to destroy skilled labour

which requires anything more than mechanical precision. It absorbs the man in the machine. The more the workman is brought down to the level of a piece of unerring and irresponsible machinery, incapable of praise or blame, the better he is fitted for our present great building works. No doubt this is the cause why this vast structure is probably the least satisfactory which has emanated from human skill."

THE AMERICAN REAPING MACHINE.—We have already alluded to the contents of the American court, which, although not very numerous, include several of those novel and ingenious inventions for which Brother Jonathan is remarkable. The court is, in fact, in a very similar situation to the American Court in 1851, being very sparingly but very curiously furnished. The great American "lion" of that exhibition year was M'Cormick's reaping machine, then as great a novelty as the cow-milker is now, but which since then has established itself completely as a most valuable agricultural invention. The inventor now comes to us again with an improved reaper, which he claims to be as great an improvement on his first invention as the first was on the methods of harvesting known to preceding generations. Former reaping machines had either required the labour of extra men to deliver the corn in sheaves, or had laid it in a continuous swathe. Mr. M'Cormick's invention in his present machine consists of a light revolving fan of four arms, one of which, by means of a wheel revolving in a "cam," picks up the corn with a delicacy and ease bordering on human intelligence, and deposits it in sheaves by the side of the machine, and outside of the track to be traversed by the horses in the next round. Nothing is left to be done but for the binders to follow and bind up the corn, without the aid of a rake. At the trial of reaping machines at the late meeting of the North Lancashire Agricultural Society, there were nineteen entries of reapers, and of these eight or nine entered the field. After a very few rounds the opinions of the judges were unanimously expressed that Mr. M'Cormick's machine was superior to all others on the ground; and to it was awarded the first prize of £15 and the society's medal.

MODEL OF THE EXCHANGE.—In the Eastern Annexe will be found a remarkable contribution by Messrs. Fauntleroy and Co., of Bunhill Row. It is a model of the west front of the Royal Exchange, composed of various specimens of hard and other woods to the number of 434, together with the cowge nut, or vegetable ivory, and the coquilla, colocan, and betel nuts. The model is designed and arranged by Mr. T. D. Roch, and the execution is due to Josiah Bennett, cabinet maker. A classified list of the various woods employed in the production of this model, together with a map or plan, is appended, in which each piece is numbered for reference. A very compotent acquaintance with the fancy wood trade may be acquired by an examination of this curious and valuable model, in which each piece is numbered for reference.

NEW PENTOGRAPH.—In the Berlin Court of the Zollverein M.

CENTRE PIXES FOR EPERGNE. MESSRS. L. AND E. EMANUEL.

Wagner exhibits an engraving pentograph applied to the production of those curious bas-relief engravings with which the public have lately become familiar. M. Perreaux exhibits his straight line dividing instruments, such as are used at Kew and by all the leading philosophical instrument makers. He also shows a novelty since 1851—a spherometer, for measuring the curves of object glasses. This instrument is of such extreme delicacy that, when adjusted to zero, even placing the hand on the ground glass plane beneath, from which the slender index works, is sufficient to deflect it instantly.

ODD CONTRIBUTIONS TO THE EXHIBITION.—Julia Pastrana's embalmed body having been declined by the Commissioners, they have not excluded a pig "preserved whole." A gentleman who proposed to display his feats with a flying machine, under the hollows of the domes, has been warned off; but if he imitates other persistent enthusiasts, the ladies may be astounded some fine morning, by his appearance in mid-air. Among other odd things that were offered, was a patent moustache guard, to enable soup-eaters to dine. A poetical catalogue of the whole Exhibition was proposed by a French gentleman, who intended to work up the reports, decisions, and minutes of the Commissioners into an epic poem!

FRENCH CALCULATING MACHINE.—In the gallery of the French department, on the left, as the visitor goes towards the west dome, he will find the calculating machine of M. Thomas—the Babbage of France. Unlike the elaborate instrument we have produced, it is so small as to fit in a compass not greater than that of a good musical snuff-box. Yet, by simply winding a handle, 18 seconds suffice to multiply 8 figures by 8. To divide 16 figures by 8 figures, only 24 seconds are required, and a square root of 16 figures is obtained within a minute. And all this is done by machinery!

GLASS PHOTOGRAPHS.—F. Joubert exhibits, in the French Court, a series of very beautiful pictures burnt in on glass, a marvellous adaptation of the photographic art in an absolutely new direction; and here perfect permanency is obtained, at least so long as the glass will last. By a pure photographic process he produces on the glass, in ceramic colours, a picture, which by exposure to heat in the furnace becomes burnt in like any other picture on glass or china. By an artistic manipulation he has produced effects in several colours, and a cheap and artistic ornamentation of our windows is brought within the means of the many.

Curiosities in the Exhibition.

EATING, DRINKING, AND SMOKING.

THERE are several exhibitors of preserved and cured provisions and potatoes, and one shows "azotised raw meat," &c.; others dry milk in powder, and concentrated milk in combination with cocoa. It has a singular effect to see the narrow, crowded eastern annexe turned into wine and beer vaults, with casks and bottles of beer with well known labels staring us in the face—certainly not very attractive to the eye, however pleasant to some palates, and necessary as they may be to "thirsty souls." Mr. A. Sharman treats the public to a new beverage from the fruit of the carob-tree, the same locust beans of which the cattle condiments are mainly compounded. Ciders and perries and British champagne are shown to the public, with artificial mineral waters, aërated quinine water, and filtered liquors by the Silicated Carbon Filter Company. There are nine exhibitors of manufactured tobaccos and cigars, snuffs, &c. The dietetic articles of teas, and sugars, and spices are scarcely represented at all; and the exhibits will convey but a poor representation of the extent and importance of the trade. Why are all our merchants, importers, and dealers, shut out? Were they excluded, or were they too apathetic to trouble themselves with the matter? But there are representations enough of many of those important products from India and the colonies, and on the foreign side. However, we should have liked to have seen some such collection of the general imports of London made, as that which the merchants and brokers of Liverpool have sent up. The trade and commerce of this port and metropolis entitle it to some collective and marked display.

GROUP OF OBJECTS IN SILVER. MESSRS. THOMAS PRIME AND CO., BIRMINGHAM.

24.

FOUNTAIN OF PERFUMED WATER.

VARIOUS FORMS OF RIMMEL'S PERFUME VAPORISER.

occasions it is that the water of Minton's Great Fountain under the Eastern Dome is perfumed with a subtil essence, popularly believed to be the secret alone of M. Eugene Rimmel, of the Strand, perfumer to their Majesties the Queen of Spain and the King of Portugal. But not alone in the Grand Nave and Transepts are these delightful perfumes to be found; in the Eastern Annexe M. Rimmel has a stand, which is always surrounded by curious and gratified crowds. Here is the celebrated Perfumed Fountain, into which ladies—and gentlemen, too — sometimes dip their handkerchiefs as they pass; with magic vines, bouquets, flowers, and rings for the holding of delicious scents, with perfume sachets, almanacks, &c., standing beside rows and piles of soaps, pomades, creams, pastes, elixirs, dentifrices, washes, powders, cosmetiques, and other essentials of the fashionable toilet. But, besides these, there is the Perfume Vaporiser, a newly-invented apparatus for diffusing the fragrance of flowers, and effectually purifying the atmosphere of apartments, ball-rooms, theatres, &c. The Vaporiser has been used on board Her Majesty's yacht, and at various public banquets and entertainments, with the greatest possible success. It is equally valuable in a sick chamber and in a close cabin at sea. The various forms of the caskets containing the aromatic fumigating material are shown in our engraving.

PENCIL-MAKING.

THE improved methods of making artists' pencils is illustrated in the Process Court, where the original of our portrait is seen daily

PENCIL-MAKING BY MR. S. D. COHEN'S IMPROVED METHOD.

fill the centre cavity of the cedar with one unbroken length of lead, thus rendering each pencil unvarying in its degree throughout, and obviating the inconvenience arising from the ordinary method of laying in several small pieces in succession, which snap at each joint, and incur the further inability of having different qualities of lead in one and the same pencil.

The fact that [...] cannot be easily [...] [...] Obtainable, is felt by [...] Why this difficulty has [...] explained. For many years the best pencils were manufactured from the Borrowdale lead, taken from the mine situate in Cumberland, the only one in the world yielding this valuable mineral.

The supply of plumbago in quantity sufficiently large for the manufacture of pencils has long ceased [...] quently forcing [...] quality have [...] After careful study Mr. C [...] succeeded in perfecting a process by which the powder and fragments of the Borrowdale lead (hitherto considered almost useless, can be consolidated and made of a consistency which will allow of its being formed into slips of the exact size, and the degree required for each pencil.

A CURIOSITY INDEED! On the principle of "better late than never," asked a deaf and dumb man, who calls himself the "White Knight," writes to the Commissioners from Scotland, offering for exhibition a pair of shoes in which he has walked 12,000 miles, and which are, nevertheless, still in excellent repair. He claims great originality in their construction, but will not undertake to send them unless the Commissioners guarantee all expenses by steam and rail.

This improved process obviates the necessity for any joint, and precludes the possibility of any variety of degree; while it imparts to the lead great tenacity, richness of colour, and the invaluable quality found in no other pencil, viz., *that of being easily rubbed out*. Mr. Cohen has the honour of supplying the Royal Family, Her Majesty's Government offices, and has received testimonials from the most eminent

SHERRATT'S ASTRONOMICAL CLOCK.

AMONG the "Educational Works and Appliances," in the Central Tower, will be found the ingenious instrument shown in our engraving. It is called a Time Globe, or Keeper, for showing the corresponding time at any place in the world. A terrestrial globe revolves on its axis, simultaneously with the pointer, or hand, together making one

THE "HYTHE BOOT." INVENTED AND EXHIBITED BY LIEUTENANT-COLONEL CARTER.

artists of this country, affirming the great improvement of his pencils on all others. These pencils supply the want so universally felt of a really good pencil at a moderate cost.

THE HYTHE BOOT.

COLONEL CARTER, of Monmouth, has discovered the secret of making a good, comfortable, easy boot for the use of soldiers, volunteers, sportsmen, policemen, fishermen, and indeed all persons used to much walking; and the secret, like all really useful inventions and discoveries, is so simple, and so natural, that we only wonder it has not been thought of before. It consists simply and really of putting a joint or hinge in the sole of the boot, in order that the natural action of the foot may not be impeded. Other advantages belong to the Hythe boot, which will be more readily understood by referring to the engraving. First we have a figure showing the natural bend of the foot when walking; next we see the sole of the boot, and the dividing line or hinge for facilitating the natural bend of the foot; the next figure shows the large opening of the Hythe boot, which renders it easy to put on and off; then follow two others, the one showing that, by two straps buckled, the large opening can be effectually, neatly, and quickly closed; and the other, how the trousers can be worn with this boot, on muddy roads, or in the fields or moors. Boots of this pattern are being made extensively, the gallant patentee granting gratuitous licences to makers for the use of his capital idea.

FREEZING MACHINE AND WINE COOLER.

MR. SIMPSON, of Oxford Street, shows, in the Western Annex, an ingenious apparatus, invented by Mr. Ash, for producing, with or without ice, several kinds of dessert ices, ready moulded for the table, and blocks of pure ice, for cooling wines, &c. The operation of the machine is very simple. The article to be iced being placed in the receptacle containing the freezing mixture, the piston is worked up and down till the desired effect is produced. For warm climates and domestic use, this is the simplest and best refrigerator we have seen.

ICE-MAKING MACHINE.

revolution before the twenty-four hour clock-face in that time. Every hour is divided into twelve parts, of five minutes each; the quarters and halves being more distinctly marked. The several portions of the day are also inscribed and coloured thereon, and the cardinal points given. In a right line with the pointer, a black meridian line passes over whatever place on the globe the time may be set for, showing the hour, not only there, but at all other places under the same meridian. On turning a button, which projects through the circular opening of the glass cover, it will cause the white meridian, attached to the south pole of the globe, to move over any place at which the time is required to be known; and the index fixed thereto, on passing before the hour-circle on the clock-face, will show

ASTRONOMICAL CLOCK. T. SHERRATT.

the time at that and all other places under such meridian. The inventor anticipates that when the elementary astronomical and geographical advantages possessed by these time-globes are taken into consideration, combined as they are with usefulness and cheapness—for the price of this ingenious instrument does exceed that of ordinary good clocks—they will be the means of stimulating inquiry and encouraging thought; in short, that they may of such things make

"Those think who never thought before :
And those who have thought, make them think the more."

Fine Arts in the Exhibition.—Sculpture.

WHEN the Exhibition doors are closed, and the crowd has departed; when the prize holders have all settled down into a belief that the jurors did the best they could in making their several awards; when the World's Show of 1862 is but a memory, what will be the chief objects that remain impressed on the minds of the vast majority of the visitors? Not, perhaps, the jewels and plate; for gold, and silver, and diamonds, flash and sparkle as they may, appeal but to a very limited class of minds; not the furniture and the clothing, for they are too familiar to our every day experience to make any very great impression; not the pottery or the paper, the horology, or the glass; the "substances used as food," or the "animal and vegetable substances used in manufactures;" not even the great fountain under the eastern dome, the Colebrookdale gates, or the King of Prussia's Berlin porcelain —but certainly the machinery and the Fine Arts department. As the machines in motion are a wonder and an attraction to the uninitiated in practical mechanics, so the pictures and the sculptures are never failing sources of delight to the visitors of educated taste. We say educated taste, for it is admitted that the pleasure arising from viewing a fine landscape or a cleverly-sculptured group is entirely a matter of education and association. Of the sculpture in the Exhibition, two figures stand out beyond the rest, and occupy considerable public attention—we mean Signor Magni's "Reading Girl" and Gibson's "Tinted Venus." Of the last we have already spoken briefly. "If," says a public writer, "the practice of tinting statues to admitted, then the 'Venus' of Mr. Gibson seems to go too far in one sense, and not enough so in another. If the characteristic chastity of sculpture is to be retained, the pure lucent marble is preferable, because it displays in its native texture, softly sparkling like the subdued light round a pearl, the most delicate finish of the artist's work. If discreet imitation is the aim of art, then the example goes not far enough. To stain pure marble of a pale buff colour does not add to its pictorial merit per se, and gives a sensuous, if not a sensual suggestiveness, which art should never render. Accepting the canon of the colourists, this statue is out of keeping with it wherever the uniform low key is violated, as in the strong vermilion of the lips and blue of the irises.

Penciling the eyelashes is another meretricious excess." In spite, however, of this opinion, it must be confessed that the figure is one of the most graceful and beautiful in the building. The same praise may be honestly bestowed upon the "Reading Girl," which is now the property of Mr. Nottage, the manager of the London Stereoscopic Company.

The easy grace and beauty observable in the pose of the "Reading Girl" are to be commended and imitated by young sculptors. Nothing so fine, so natural, and so complete, except perhaps the "Venus" of Gibson, appears in the Exhibition. It is understood that at the close of the season at South Kensington, this statue will be publicly exhibited by its purchasers.

The "Reading Girl" was exhibited at Florence in 1861, and was then the great centre of attraction. It was purchased by the Italian Government, who have lately transferred it to Mr. Nottage. The girl herself is popularly believed to be the daughter of Garibaldi, whose portrait is sculptured on the locket she wears on her breast. The lines she is supposed to be reading are by the Florentine poet Niccolini, whose theme is Garibaldi's valour and patriotism. The following lines, suggested by Magni's statue, have lately appeared:—

"Read on! read on! I will not try
   To rouse thee from thy theme;
   Thy rush-made chair, thy robe thrown by,
   Too real for sculpture seem!

"I take thee for some living maid,
   Enthralled by magic art,
   And hither, o'er the sea, conveyed,
   To play a subtle part.

"Ambitious of a prize beyond
   All other wonders shown,
   The enchanter waved his mystic wand,
   And turned thee into stone."

THE READING GIRL. SIGNOR MAGNI.

British Sculpture, since it has adopted the classic rule, has never been so fairly represented as in these Galleries. A national call alone could get together so many such valuable and such ponderous works, which, issuing originally from the studios of Banks, Nollekens, or Flaxman, almost a hundred years ago, here meet those of Chantrey, Westmacott, Wyatt, of the dead, and Messrs. Baily, Cardwell, Foley, Gibson, and Macdowell, the living representatives of their common art. There is need of originality, of knowledge, of true Art-feeling, and even self-respect amongst British Sculptors as represented here. It seems strange that Painting should progress from a few stars to a brilliant galaxy, and Architecture revive in two manifestations, the vitality of both being indicated by the vigour of their mutual combat, while Sculpture, which has certainly *not* lacked encouragement amongst us, considering how little it has produced to command admiration, contents itself, for the most part, with a revival of the antique, so unwisely directed as to have adopted the worst models of the very unequal, diverse, and even contradictory schools of Rome and Greece. On going from statue to statue, the fact that this contentment and servility have led to the present state of things strikes every one. Here are produced the forms, and even the *poses*, of mediocre or bad works, and, with a few noble exceptions, small signs of direct and personal study from nature. Mr. Lough, for example, reproduces the Apollo Belvidere whole, so to say, in his "Comus," with so little feeling for the original that the flesh is divested of the antique *morbidezza* and the face reduced to babyishness. Mr. Gibson, whose detailed execution is fair enough, painfully labours to galvanise the spirit of an epoch which must be for ever dead to us, and is rather curious than important to modern minds. It would be difficult to deny a palm to Baron Marochetti for his "Sir Jamsetjee Jeejeebhoy," sitting, beneath the eastern dome, so excellent are its simplicity and picturesque character. The last and most prominent element of this work is not, however, a noble one in sculpture. Here, then, the artist departs from the rigid rule of Art exactly at that point where his work is most popularly seductive; hence the critic conceives the aim of such a design to be popular and temporary rather than sound and high in motive.

We have seen in the many works where the sculptor is a slave of antique art, or of the romantic and sentimental taste which is its antithesis. These are the leading causes of failure in British sculpture, one springing from a dull spirit of imitation, the other little else than trifling with the intellectual spirit of art, travestying Apollo into Comus, as Mr. Lough did when he produced the statue bearing the last name. A third source of failure lies in the sheer want of ability on the part of the artist to feel, in any sense, what art should be. Of this a long list of examples might be furnished from those before us: its extent must have amazed our Continental visitors. If we turn to detailed criticism, it will be to point out a few works only. Mr. Thrupp's "Boys struggling for Grapes" is a tame, disproportioned revival of an old design. We place Mr. Adams in the above third class of incompetent sculptors on account of his "Massacre of the Innocents;" on stronger grounds still for the figure, designed from a German toy, styled "St. John," which is tame, feelingless, and merely a boy with a feeble face looking upwards. This gentleman's busts of "Sir W. Napier" and "Sir F. Burdett" differ in smoothness and ~~finish~~ but are equally meanly conceived. Mr. Earle's "Hyacinthus" with the disk is prettily designed and well executed. Mr. Foley's "Caractacus," a noble chief speaking to his people, has life in every limb, that seems to transport us with the sound of an imagined voice from the deep chest; he raises one hand, the palm flat to the sky, high above his head, grasping an axe in the other. "Egeria," by the same, a figure of large style, draws backward her heavy hair in masses,

Compare this with Mr. Wyon's "Britomart," to which it is placed pendent, a stage-struck damsel with a sword; or compare "Caractacus" with "The Bard," by Mr. Theed, as having a similar motive, but legs so short that one wonders how he will surmount the rock whereon the wind is to blow his "beard and hoary hair." It will be seen that this figure does not grasp the harp and stride—neither speaks nor sings, though his mouth is open. His business seems to be scowling, which he does plentifully. Mr. Weeke's "Sardanapalus" is better executed than "The Bard," but is merely a naked man demonstratively drinking. Mr. W. C. Marshall's "Sabrina" is but a young lady, naked; his "Ophelia" has better design, sitting, clasping her knee and singing. At the turn to Mr. Macdowell's "Psyche," the face reveals faults rife amongst British sculptors, timidity and feebleness of purpose.

And so we might go on, till we had exhausted the list of British sculptures. Turn for a while to the foreign examples.

There is greater variety of system discernible in French art than is to be found amongst ourselves, as indicated in "Agrippina and Caligula," by M. Maillet, really good Roman art. One would be readily induced to consider "Theseus subduing the Centaur," by M. Barye, to be a genuine bronze of the same date as the famous Townley Hercules, being as bold, broad, and square in form. The hero has mounted the double creature and bends him back, grasping the throat with terrible force: the character of energy imparted to both these figures is sustained in every limb. The execution is rough-hammered, but as faithful as can be required. How the French sculptors understand what we call *finish*, a nobler quality in their art than it is in painting, we may see from the delicate modelling of M. de Bay's "Bashfulness yielding to Love," and in more than one other example. We must not always take this extreme finish for granted as an exposition of subtle thought in design. The student will do well to look heedfully at a whole figure before he allows himself to be carried away by admiration of its details. M. D. D'Angers "Death of Barra" offers this point distinctly for consideration.

German sculpture is incompletely represented. "A Horseman fighting with a Lion," by M. Wolff (Prussia), is amongst the best from that country, but compares disadvantageously with the French work, "Theseus subduing Biénor," a like theme, in its lean and meagre forms. As a design, this is not without spirit, yet falls far short of the felicitous adaptation, or harsh repetition, of the antique seen in French Art. In the little figure "Mignon," M. Cauer (Prussia), a child looking up with a natural smile, there is some prettiness; there is broad simplicity in the "Young Italian Girl," by M. Sussman, who binds the long plaits of her hair. We find M. Rauch represented only by a "Model of the Monument to Frederick the Great," a splendid work with which the English public are familiar through the full-sized cast at the Crystal Palace. This composition offers a valuable opportunity for comparison with Baron Marochetti's unsatisfactory monumental group placed in the Horticultural Gardens. The "Charles Albert" is but a waisted-belted dandy at a review; the "Frederick," a conqueror and a king, who rides in front of his armies, and leads a nation on its course.

GIBSON'S TINTED VENUS.

Swedish sculptural art finds so noble a representative in the group clumsily styled "The Grapplers," by M. Molin, that it held the place possessed by Kiss's "Amazon" in 1851, in critical opinions. We have an illustration of this fine work on page 108.

Holland sends no sculpture, while Norway contributes but a few carvings. Belgium, on the contrary, is well and honourably represented, both in painting and the sister art; while Spain has, at least, one group characteristic enough of the gloomy and prosaic nature of her art, a "Dead Christ," by M. Bellver. A beautiful group in the Nave, however, the "Venus and Adonis" of M. Morlus, quite redeems the gravity of the last subject.

Italian sculpture has scarcely the invention, the dignity, or the elevation of motive we could have wished; exception, of course, being made in favour of two or three great works, like those of Signor Magni and Signor P. Costa, whose "Indian" is well composed and modelled. But we have already (p. 113) spoken at some length of Italian sculpture. We may conclude by saying that, in the opinion of those who claim to possess judgment and capacity, the present Exhibition is far superior to any other in excellence in the Fine Art Departments. High places are taken in sculpture by Foley, Baily, Bell, Lough, Woolner, and Gibson, among British artists; while such men as M. Molin, of Sweden, and M. Rauch, in Prussia, have secured to themselves world - wide reputations. The French, indeed, excel us in diversity of expression and variety of form; but, for pure sculptural dignity and grave integrity of purpose, the artists we have named stand at the head of their profession.

THE BRITISH GALLERIES.

The Galleries on the British side of the building, which may be said generally to run round the walls, and round the open or Glass Courts, like balconies, without any communication with each other across the Nave, are filled with specimens of art and manufactures. The Galleries round the South Courts, on the British side, are given up to textile fabrics. Beginning along the Nave side, with woollen and mixed goods, we pass round the corner, along the edge of the Middle Avenue into cotton, and from cotton into lace; then, turning the next corner, against the Picture Galleries, and, running through silk and velvet, into flax and hemp, we turn the next angle, along the west side of the South-east Transept, and run again into woollen and mixed fabrics. The Gallery opposite this, on the east side of the South-east Transept, is filled with clothing of all kinds, from hats to boots. All these

classes are under the management of Mr. George Wallis. The show here, in every corner, is worthy of the most careful inspection; the woollen fabrics of Yorkshire, the West of England, and Scotland being specially excellent. The Scotch hose, which has been gradually growing in popularity in England, is largely represented. The various clans represented are the Forbes, the Athole, Shepherd Tartan Gordon, McBain, Hunting Stewart, Rob Roy, Davidson, and Victoria. As a matter of curiosity it may be mentioned that in one of the pairs of hose—the McLauchlan—there are no less than one thousand and sixty diamonds, and in the manufacture of them no fewer than forty-two threads have been used. The result is the most perfect piece of this kind of manufacture that can well be imagined.

The lace and tapestry are very fine; Nottingham, London, and Dublin being well represented. Manchester and Glasgow show well in cotton manufactures; Rochdale and Witney in blankets; London, Macclesfield, Coventry, Leeds, and Derby in silks and ribbons; and Ireland in linens. The chintzes, particularly, are distinguished for great beauty in design and colour; many exhibitors having prepared an elaborate display of these elegant fabrics. Messrs. Clarke and Co., of [...] full assortment of [...] knitwear [...] [...] Exhibition [...] [...] Indian Departments. Although the extent of space occupied by lace manufacturers is a small one compared with that devoted to some other classes, there is no part of the Exhibition which will better repay careful examination. The lightness and elegance of the material, the varied display of its designs, and the vast amount of ingenuity displayed in their production are highly creditable alike to those engaged in the humbler class of life produced by hand, and to the manufacturers who by the use of machinery produce it in large quantity, and at such greatly reduced cost. The lace exhibited may be conveniently divided into two classes of real and imitation—the latter occupying, as might be expected, a very much larger amount of space than that which is the result of hand labour.

The display of the manufactures of Buckingham, Bedford, and Northampton shires far exceeds that shown by these counties in the Exhibition of 1851, not only in style, but also in variety of articles exhibited. Of the real old make (pound ground) scarcely anything is shown, the favourite samples being of a class called Maltese lace, which

PATTERN OF HANDKERCHIEF.

has been much in vogue since 1851. The specimens now exhibited are very beautiful, and evidence great art and skill in design and work. Some laces, the design composed of fern leaves, are well worthy of attention, and do great credit to the poor cottagers by whom they are made. They are, we believe, the first attempt in the style of lace exhibited. A child's frock of Bedfordshire lace, a collar and cuffs, in imitation of antique Saxony, and some wide black laces and black veils, speak highly in favour of the lacemakers of this county. Some collars and cuffs made from thread, so finely spun as to be of the enormous cost of 110s. per lb., and some well-executed laces, together with a magnificent lappet, maintain the reputation that Northamptonshire has always had for this branch of industry. This description of lace, which is made in the agricultural counties, employs a very large number of women and children, and,

before the increased consumption of machine-made lace, was productive of good wages to the makers; of late years, however, the pay of these poor people has been hardly sufficient to induce them to continue their efforts to produce high-class articles like those now exhibited. The condition of the lacemakers of the midland counties should induce our fair readers to give to this beautiful fabric an increased share of their patronage.

The gallery running round the British open courts on the north side of the Nave is devoted along the North-east Transept to India; and along the nave side to printing, paper and stationery, horology, surgical instruments, and philosophical instruments. Here Dr. Forbes Watson, Mr. Leighton, Mr. Trace, and Mr. Weld reign supreme over one of the most valuable and interesting divisions of the building.

Kamptulicon.

At page 72 we gave an illustration of the material which bears the odd-sounding title of Kamptulicon. We now insert engravings of two other specimens taken from the case of Messrs. Tayler, Harry, and Co., of Gutter Lane, Cheapside. Kamptulicon is a felted article, composed of india-rubber, gutta-percha, and cork, ground into fine particles, and then intimately mixed and subjected to great pressure. Messrs. Tayler, Harry, and Co., of Gutter Lane, Cheapside, are the principal manufacturers of it; and their establishment at Deptford, where the manufacture is carried on, is on a large scale. In the Great Exhibition they have deposited many examples of its various applications, and they have a case in the Eastern Annexe, in which they exhibit the materials employed and the stages of the manufacture. All the materials are well-known substances; but with respect to the cork it may be mentioned that it is the refuse of the cork cutters which is employed. Formerly, this refuse was thrown away as useless, but now a great demand has sprung up for it, so that the price has gradually advanced until it is now £7 10s. a ton. About three hundred tons a year are purchased for this manufacture, and the supply is not equal to the demand. The entire

manufacture, from the treatment of the native gums to the completion of the finished material by the application of oil colours, is conducted at Deptford, and we are informed that the entire process does not occupy more than ten hours. A considerable time, however, is required for seasoning it before it is fit to use as a floor-cloth. There has been a very extensive call for the manufactured article to be laid down on floors, where it wears very well, and gives back no noise to the step. It has been laid down in the Houses of Parliament, in many public offices, churches, hotels, and club-houses. For this purpose, it has been ornamented with various patterns. Several ornamental designs may be seen in the Exhibition. The designs are such as will leave the original surface as much as possible exposed. It then affords a degree of warmth intermediate between an oil-cloth and a carpet. The advantages derived from its use are, that it is a non-conductor of heat, and is a deadener of sound.

PATTERN OF KAMPTULICON.
(Prize Medal.)

It has also come into use for the cells of lunatics; the walls and floors being covered with kamptulicon, of from half an inch to one inch in thickness. The resilience of the material prevents the inmates doing themselves any personal injury; while, from its being a non-conductor of heat, it conduces to the maintenance of an equable temperature. It has been adopted for many years at Bethlehem Hospital and some other asylums. It is also of great service for lining the boxes or covering the backs of the stalls of kicking horses. By deadening the sounds of the blows, it has a great tendency to cure this vicious habit; while, by its elasticity, it prevents injury to the horse itself. It is used in the Royal stables and elsewhere. It also makes a good floor for riding schools, preventing noise, lessening the shock in the case of a fall, and preserving the feet of the horses from the concussion of hard pavement. Another of its manifold uses is as a covering for knife-cleaners, for which it possesses all the advantages of leather, at about one-fourth the cost. It is estimated that from forty to fifty thousand of these knife-boards are made and sold per annum.

Enamelled Tiles, &c.

AMONG the building contrivances in the South-West court (Class X.), there is an interesting series of architectural productions, illustrative of the clay manufactures of the Shropshire coal field. They are classified and arranged by George Maw, F.S.A., on behalf of the following exhibitors:—Messrs. John and Edward Burton, Ironbridge; Colebrookdale Company, Lightmoor Works, Colebrookdale; Messrs. George Davis and Co., Broseley; Mr. Doughty, Mr Robert Evans, Mr. William Exley, and Mr. G. W. Lewis, Jackfield, near Broseley; Madeley Wood Company, Madeley Wood Fire Brick Works; Messrs. Maw and Co., Benthall Works, Broseley; Messrs. W. B. Simpson and Sons, 456, West Strand, London Agents for Maw and Co.; Mrs. Thorn, Broseley. This classification is most exact, and at the same time interesting. All the objects appear in one or other of the following divisions:—Roofing materials, paving materials, draining materials, fire bricks, furnace materials, stove fittings, &c.; bricks, and the materials used in the construction of walls; accessories to the decoration of buildings, and various articles not included in the other divisions; and raw materials.

In the first division we have common, plain, and ornamental roofing tiles—glazed, unglazed, and enamelled—of various patterns and designs; the arrangements of this section being conducted by Mr. Digby Wyatt. There are also roof-crestings, gutter-tiles, fixed and loose ornaments, &c. Among the paving materials we find all kinds of tiles and paving-stones, with some very handsome designs for mosaic and encaustic tile pavements. The next division includes common fire-bricks, of various forms. Bricks, terra cotta, and blocks for gables, chimneys, arches, &c., are found in the next section; while among the accessories to decoration are found various terra cotta architectural decorations, including pillar-caps, chimney-tops, round columns, arch-bricks, &c.; examples of terra cotta balustrades;

terra cotta chimney-tops; flower-borders, edgings, tiles, and returns; hot-house and vinery squares and channels; sundry terra cotta vases, flower-pots, stands and pedestals, orchid pots, minionette, flower, and orange-tree boxes, the latter having a space between the slate lining and tiles to keep the soil cool, composed of majolica tiles, set in electro-bronzed framing, manufactured by Maw and Co., from designs by Mr. M. Digby Wyatt. But the most striking object in this section is the Chimney-piece shown in our engraving. It is composed of enamelled tiles and stone, and was manufactured by Messrs. Maw and Co., from a design by Digby Wyatt; the stone-work being executed by Mr. Yates, builder, of Shifnal. This is really a very elegant object, well suited for a library or other decorated room. It is, we hear, capable of being manufactured at a comparatively cheap rate.

Ireland's Contributions to the World's Fair.

If any enthusiastic Celt were to go to the Exhibition with a fixed determination of examining and admiring all the contributions from the sister kingdom, he would speedily find himself puzzled; for the varied and excellent collection from Ireland is distributed throughout most of the classes, and with the exception of the Belfast Linen

Taking the classification of the Royal Commissioners, we find Ireland represented in Class 1. (Mining, Quarrying, Metallurgy, and Mineral Products), Eastern Annexe, by various interesting products. The coal and mineral productions of County Donegal are shown in great variety. We have condensed peat, and peat charcoal; specimens

IRISH LINEN TROPHY. CENTRAL AVENUE.

Trophy, in the Central Avenue, no very prominent display is made of Irish produce and manufactures.

But it must by no means be supposed that Ireland is behindhand in the gallant show of 1862, or that her advance in social and commercial prosperity is not proportionally as great as it was in 1851. Ireland's place in the Exhibition is an honourable one; not separate from England, Scotland, and Wales, but taking part with them in all that tends to our national advantage, well-being, and glory.

of large quartz crystals, called "Irish diamonds;" polished marbles, from Galway; zinc ores, spelter, fire-clays, ochres, &c., from Tipperary, exhibited by the General Mining Company of Ireland; fossils and rocks, ores and sulphates, green and black marbles, from Connemara; magnetic ironstone, from Limerick; and various stone and other building materials. In Class 2 (Chemical Substances, &c.), Ireland is not particularly prominent, but there are still several objects worthy attentive examination. Especially interesting are the chemicals,

25.

principally fluid magnesia, camphor, and aërated extract of bark, shown by Sir J. Murray, of the Anatomy Office, Dublin; while pharmaceutical preparations from Ireland are shown, in more than one instance, by London agents and dealers. Among the Substances used for Food (Class 3, Eastern Annexe), there are some fine specimens of wheat and oats, shown by Mr. Cahill, of Kilkenny; while Mr. Irwin, of Boyle, shows black oats, and other cereals. In Class 4 (Animal and Vegetable Substances used in Manufactures), Messrs. Tucker and Co., of Belfast, show a quantity of good starch and glue; while Mr. C. Goggin, of Nassau Street, Dublin, has a handsome case of ornamental articles, manufactured of bog oak, in all degrees of colour, from a delicate mahogany to an ebony blackness, polished, and shining as only bog oak can. In the next class—Railway Plant, including Locomotives and Engines—Mr. H. L. Corlett, of Dublin, has some wellmade rails, brackets, joint-chairs, buffing-springs, &c.; while Mr. H. Shaw, of the same city, shows a railway-break of novel construction, by which, as the exhibitor declares, a long train may be brought to rest within a distance of sixty yards. In the Carriage Department (Class 6) are a variety of elegant vehicles. The visitor will especially notice a round-fronted brougham and Irish jaunting-car, by Messrs. J. Hutton and Sons, of Summer Hill, Dublin, which, for elegance of finish, convenience, and general appearance, is equal to any carriage in the South-east Court. The car is particularly light and springy; in fact, just the model of such a vehicle.

In the Machinery Annexe, Messrs. J. Combe and Co., of Belfast, have a fine series of machines for the preparation of flax; while Messrs. J. Rowan and Sons, of Belfast, have a scutching machine of improved construction. In the Processes Court, Messrs. Kennan and Sons, of Dublin, show a highly ingenious sculpturing machine, with lathes for amateurs. This sculpturing machine is capable of copying works of art from the round or flat, upon any scale, in ivory, wood, alabaster, &c. It is easily worked by one person, and the movement for copying proportional straight lines, &c., is novel. The cutting is performed by a revolving tool mounted on a bar, with universal centre, and guided by a brace, applied to the original work. It is capable of copying most intricate forms, and differs in many respects from any machine of the kind hitherto exhibited. Beside it are various specimens of carvings and turnings, showing the capabilities of both the machine and the lathes. The former is frequently to be seen in operation, surrounded by a curious and inquiring group.

Among the larger pieces of machinery in the Eastern Annexe (Class 9), the visitor will not have failed to notice the agricultural machinery shown by Messrs. Gray and Sons, of Belfast, which, with the log saws, root blasters, lawn mowers, and iron fences of Messrs. Kennan and Sons, of Dublin; the iron stalls for cattle, of Messrs. Musgrave Brothers, of Ann Street, Belfast, and the ingenious apparatus for separating grass-seeds, and the machine for bearding and dressing carrots, &c., of Mr. T. Scott, of Newcastle, County Down, make up a very respectable contribution towards Ireland's share in the agricultural implements of 1862.

In civil engineering, architectural, and building contrivances, Ireland does not show strongly; but the articles she does show are interesting as evidence of the advance to which we have already alluded. Messrs. J. Edmundson and Co., of Dublin, exhibit a portable gas apparatus for cooking, &c., which is exceedingly ingenious, and well manufactured. Sir J. Macneill has a fine model of the bridge over the river Boyne, at Drogheda; and Messrs. Turner and Gibson, of Dublin, show models of their balance rolling bridges for railways over water and public roads, &c.—highly useful contrivances. In the next class—Military Engineering, Armour, Accoutrements, and Small Arms—Mr. Rigby, and Messrs. Trulock and Harris, of Dublin, have some capital rifles, breech-loaders, muzzle-loaders, sporting guns, cannon, &c. In Naval Architecture and Ships' Tackle (Class 12), the Commissioners of Irish Lights show models of the Fastnet Rock Lighthouse, off Cape Clear; and the Port of Dublin Corporation show models of various lighthouses on improved principles.

Among the Philosophical Instruments (Class 13), Mr. Hogg, of Dublin, exhibits a curious and ingenious instrument, which he calls a "nephelescope," for viewing the upper series of clouds. Mr. Grubb, of Dublin, has a great equatorial achromatic, with an aperture of twelve inches, equipoised throughout, and manufactured on an improved and almost perfect system. Mr. J. Lewis, of the same city, has an automaton register and pentograph, applicable for photo-printing, and printing purposes generally. Mr. Minchin has an ingenious instrument for measuring the transparency of milk, which he calls a "galactoscope;" and Messrs. Yeates and Son, of Grafton Street, Dublin, have various astronomical, meteorological, philosophical, and mathematical instruments, of admirable workmanship. They consist mainly of two equatorially-mounted telescopes, on iron columns, the mounting possessing many improvements in detail. The clamping circles are quite independent of the divided circle, and at the opposite ends of their respective axes, that of the polar axis being directly under the northern pivot, and that of the declination axis close to the telescope. The clamping arrangement also differs from that in present use, being more effective, and perfectly free from strain or torsion. The smaller stand is particularly adapted for those who have no convenient space on which to erect an observatory. The iron column may be permanently fixed in the open air: the equatorial arrangement packs in a small box, from which it can be lifted into its place on the top of the column in a few moments, and may be thus placed and re-placed at the observer's pleasure, without its adjustments being materially affected. Equally good is Messrs. Yeates' new ellitograph. This instrument differs in three essential points from all elliptographs hitherto constructed. First, there is no limit whatever to the variation in the proportions of the ellipse formed by it; secondly, the facility of setting it to draw any ellipse whose major and minor axes are known; and, thirdly, the accuracy of the figure formed by it in all proportions. The same exhibitors also show a large public barometer (dial 3 feet in diameter).

Dr. Hemphill, of Clonmel, shows, in the next class, some exquisite photographs of antiquities, and views in Cashel and Cahir, County Tipperary; but among the horological instruments we do not find a single Irish exhibitor of clocks or watches; nor do we notice, in the Music Court, a solitary Irish bagpipe, to represent the musical genius of a country famous for national song and minstrelsy. In Surgery (Class 17), but two represent the sister country: Mr. Coghlan, of Wexford, who shows a probe-pointed knife, for obstetric purposes, and a drill carrier, for the use of dentists; and Mr. Tufnell, of Dublin, who has some highly useful surgical appliances.

In cotton Ireland is not represented; but in the national manufacture of flax she comes out very strongly. In the passage leading from the nave towards the entrance to the Royal Horticultural Gardens is the Belfast Linen Trophy, shown in our engraving. It contains specimens of the manufacture in all its stages, from the rough flax to cambric as fine as gossamer. The goods have been contributed by a great number of firms, who have not affixed their names to the articles fabricated by them, nobly co-operating, without a trace of jealousy, in affording an illustration of all that is achieved in this important department of Irish industry. Belfast may well be proud of the fabrics exhibited, which are all of admirable quality; and many interesting and profitable reflections will be suggested by comparing the raw material with the progressive series of forms, of constantly increasing delicacy, into which it is fashioned by human skill. In addition to this united display, flax, yarns, linens, drills, handkerchiefs, canvas, towellings, dresses, cambrics, sheetings, table-linen, diapers, &c., are shown by Messrs. Barbour, of Lisburn; Bell and Co., Brown and Liddell, Connor and Co., Charley and Co., Dunbar, Dickson, and Co., Fenton and Co., Jaffe Brothers, Johnston and Carlisle, M'Intyre and Patterson, Matier and Co., Moore and Weinberg, Richardson, Sons, and Owden, Girdwood and Co., and Preston, Smyth, and Co., all of Belfast; in addition to the display of Messrs. Clibborn, Hill, and Co., of Banbridge, County Down; and Messrs. J. N. Russell and Son, of Lansdowne Mills, Limerick, who show some fine specimens of Munster flax, linens, &c. In fact, the linen trade of Ireland is fully, completely, and excellently represented.

In poplins and friezes Messrs. Comyns, Son, and Co., of Dublin, and Messrs. F. Hinds and Son, of Norwich, make a good display; but, as might be expected, the grand show in poplins is made by Messrs. Pim Brothers, of Dublin, who, as in 1851, bear away the palm for excellence and thorough completeness in this excellent material for ladies' dresses.

In lace, tapestry, &c., again Ireland is pre-eminent. Messrs. Allen and Co., Messrs. J. Chambers and Co., and Messrs. Forrest and Son, all of Dublin, show beautiful specimens of silk embroidery on muslin cloth, handkerchiefs and sewed muslins, Irish point lace in tunics, and other articles. A large industry is now established in Ireland in connection with the manufacture of lace. For this much credit is due to Mr. Goblet, of Milk Street, London. Previous to 1850, an inferior kind of pillow-lace was produced, but it was thought that it would be possible to introduce the making of Valenciennes into the country—the grievous famine which had then recently occurred rendering it desirable that some new mode of employment for the people should, if possible, be introduced. Lord Clarendon and Sir William Somerville gave a ready and valuable support to the proposals of Mr. Goblet, and the result was the establishment of lace schools in many parts of Ireland. Mr. Goblet shows some very interesting specimens of lace produced in these schools, and by the peasantry on the estate of Sir William Somerville. Some works in crochet are also shown for the purpose of illustrating its applicability to various purposes. Among these examples may be mentioned a bishop's rochet. The design is made up of corn, and the part of the vine emblematic of the Holy Sacrament. "Tatting" also is a description of work extensively carried on in Ireland. A prejudice has existed for some years against its use, on the erroneous ground that it could not be washed. This, however, is now found to have been a mistake, and its use is now much more general than was formerly the case. A half-shawl, to be seen in this case, is probably the largest, as it is the finest specimen of this class of work ever produced. Mr. Manly, of New Finchley Road, is also an exhibitor of some very beautiful specimens of Irish point lace. A flounce and shawl, copied from old point lace, can with difficulty be distinguished from old point, and is remarkable for its finish and excellent effect. There is also some point lace, made from fine linen thread, which is remarkable not less for its admirable finish than for the extreme durability which it must possess. Some pearl tatting is shown by Mr. Manly, who was one of the most active in introducing the making of the point lace into Ireland.

The Misses Doherty, of Sligo, exhibit in Class 25—Skin, Feathers, and Hair, Transept of South Court—a good collection of horsehair ornaments made by the peasant girls in the neighbourhood; and in the same court, Mr. Hastings, of Limerick, shows a large number of brushes used for various purposes, the backs of which are made from oak taken from the old cathedral of Limerick, after being upwards of 700 years in use as part of the sacred building.

In hosiery Messrs. Wilson and Armstrong, of Nassau Street, Dublin, have a capital show of the famous Balbriggan stockings and gloves; and, among the boots and shoes, Messrs. Hook and Knowles show brogues and overshoes, of Irish design and manufacture.

In the Gallery of the North Court Mr. Ward, of Belfast, has some superior specimens of bookbinding—illuminated covers for table-books, and strong calf and sheep-skin for ledgers and accounts. He is the only Irish exhibitor in Class 28 (Paper, Stationery, Printing, and Bookbinding); but he fully and efficiently represents the industry of this country in this particular department.

In the Furniture Court Mr. Crimmin, of Killarney, has some exceedingly good and pretty articles in bog oak, well carved and otherwise designed, in excellent taste. Messrs. Strahan and Co., and Messrs. Ross and Co., of Dublin, make also a good show; the latter of portable furniture, for use on shipboard, and for travellers; the former, a carved cabinet of admirable workmanship, which has elicited a considerable degree of attention.

In Iron and General Hardware, Mr. Francis, of Camden Place,

Dublin, shows specimens of horse-shoes adapted for animals with faulty or diseased feet, shod hoofs, &c. This exhibitor holds the appointment of farrier to her Majesty, the Lord-Lieutenant, and officers of the staff at Dublin Castle, the Metropolitan police, &c.; and has obtained medals and honorary certificates from the Royal Dublin Society. He is the only Irishman we remark as exhibiting in Class 31.

Bog oak ornaments, set in silver and gold, are shown in the Precious Metals Court by Mr. Johnson, of Dublin; while Mr. Nolis, of Omagh, shows several fine pearls, found in the river Strule. Many of these are tastefully set. In the cases of both these exhibitors will be found specimens of the national brooch, in the shape of circles, half circles, harps, &c., jewelled and exquisitely engraved.

Glass and Pottery do not seem to be shown by any Irish exhibitor, though it is known that the sister island contains several manufactories of both these wares. But the national taste is represented by Messrs. O'Connor, of Berners Street, Oxford Street, who have obtained a Prize Medal for their stained and painted glass windows. Especially commendable is the west window for Aylesbury Parish Church, which probably dates from about 1420. This fine window is designed to illustrate three great epochs—viz., "The Fall of Man," "The Means of Grace," and "The Restoration of Man." This is carried out with two subjects from the Old Testament for each epoch, thus:—for "The Fall"—1. Adam and Eve eat the forbidden fruit; 2. Adam and Eve are expelled from Paradise. For "The Means of Grace"—1. The Passage of the Red Sea (type of Baptism); 2. Abraham offering Isaac (type of Holy Communion). For the "Restoration of Man"—1. The Feast of the Passover; 2. The Lifting up of the Brazen Serpent. The tracery (for a great number of openings) has, in the lower series of lights, figures of the twelve minor Prophets; above these are figures of the four major Prophets, over which again are figures of Noah, Abraham, Moses, and David. Surrounding these figures are cherubim, while in the seven centre lights of the tracery are represented the seven gifts of the Holy Spirit. The same exhibitors also show a compartment of the west window of St. Matthias' Church, Stoke Newington, designed and executed in the manner of the early glass-stainers, with figures of Isaiah, David, and Noah.

The portmanteaus, trunks, bags, imperials, and travelling requisites (Class 36) exhibited by Mr. G. Kane, of Dame Street, Dublin, complete the list of Irish goods shown in the World's Fair of 1862; at least, as far as a hasty glance through the industrial portion of the building allowed us to perceive. In the Fine Arts Department, the genius and skill of old Ireland are admirably set forth; for are there not the exquisite pictures of Mulready and Maclise among the paintings, and Lough and Foley among the sculptures? In all that appeals to poetry and imagination, in all that needs activity and bravery, the Celtic nations are particularly prominent. We cannot visit the International Exhibition without acknowledging the rapid industrial progress made by Ireland during the last quarter of a century. Mutual forbearance and chivalric feeling may enter as easily into the breasts of merchants and artisans as into those of warriors and statesmen; and we hail the vigorous attempts which Irishmen have lately made to rid themselves of the old prejudices against them, as so many hopeful pledges of successful enterprise and active business habits. Writing in the ILLUSTRATED EXHIBITOR of 1851, we said, looking at the Irish contributions to the International Bazaar in Hyde Park, "There is hope for Ireland! strong, vigorous, lively hope! Hope in the warm, generous, kindly hearts of her people; hope in the industry of hard hands, and the energy of thoughtful minds; hope in the clearer day dawning upon her green valleys, and shining out above the sterile mountain tops that overlook them; hope in the evidences of enterprise and skill exhibited in every object she has placed in the Glass Palace!"

If these words were true then, they are truer and more prophetic now; for the same hands and the same hearts that helped to win back India for England, and won the fight against the foe at Alma and Inkermann, and alike drove down cuirassier and charger on the field of Waterloo, are nerved for Ireland's right place and position among the nations.

Messrs. Chance's Contributions.

THE ROBIN HOOD WINDOW.

HAVING already at some length described the manufacture of stained glass windows, we need only to introduce the fine specimen shown in our engraving. This beautiful window, from the design of Sebastian Evans, M.A., manager of the ornamental department of Messrs. Chance's great establishment at Birmingham, is exhibited, together

Robin Hood's last shot.

MESSRS. CHANCE BROTHERS, BIRMINGHAM.

with another stained window, having for its subject the "Madonna and Child accompanied by the Four Archangels," in the North Gallery of the East Transept.

The design of the Robin Hood Window is taken from the following verses of the famous ballad, the legend being inscribed beneath the picture:—

ROBIN HOOD'S LAST SHOT.

" Yet he was beguiled, I wis,
　By a wicked woman,
The Prioress of Kirkleys,
　That nigh was of his kin,
For the love of a knight,
Sir Roger of Doncaster,
That was her own special,
Full evil may they fare !
　*　　*　　*
"'Give me my bent bow in
　my hand,
And a broad arrow I'll
　let flee,
And where this arrow is
　taken up,
There shall my grave
　digged be.
Lay me a green sod under
　my head,
And another at my feet;
And lay my bent bow at my
　side,
Which was my music
　sweet;
And make my grave of
　gravel and green,
As is most right and
　meet.'"

For boldness of design and originality of treatment, " Robin Hood's Last Shot" is unsurpassed in this particular department of art-manufacture. See how the murdered outlaw is gathering up his strength for a last dying effort; see how Little John stands by, indignant at the treachery of his master's kinswoman and her accomplice, and sorrowful at the thought of the rapidly-coming parting. Notice how all the details are made to accord with the general sentiment of the design; observe how delicately the warm and brilliant colours blend one with another, and how every inch of the space is made subservient to the one predominant purpose of the picture; and then say whether anything finer, out of the pale of ecclesiastical subjects, has ever been

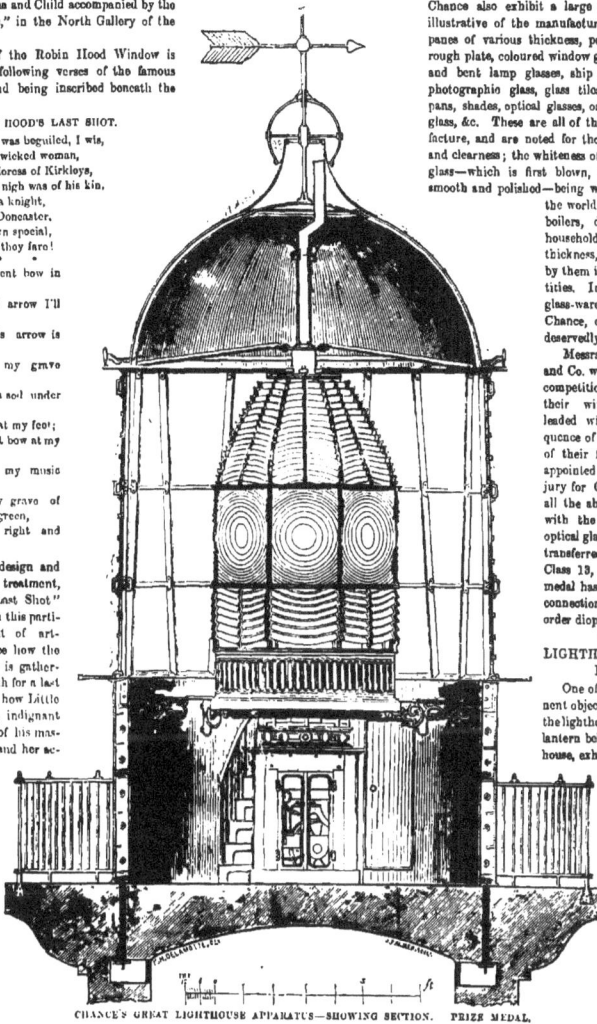

CHANCE'S GREAT LIGHTHOUSE APPARATUS—SHOWING SECTION.　PRIZE MEDAL.

accomplished in stained glass windows! Messrs. Chance also exhibit a large variety of objects illustrative of the manufacture of glass; sample panes of various thickness, patent plate, rolled rough plate, coloured window glass, hollow lenses, and bent lamp glasses, ship and signal lights, photographic glass, glass tiles, slates and milk pans, shades, optical glasses, ornamental window glass, &c. These are all of the very best manufacture, and are noted for their peculiar purity and clearness; the whiteness of their patent plate glass—which is first blown, and then ground smooth and polished—being well known all over the world. Tubes for steam boilers, deck lights, and household glass of superior thickness, are also produced by them in very large quantities. In all descriptions of glass-ware the name of Chance, of Birmingham, is deservedly celebrated.

Messrs. Chance Brothers and Co. were excluded from competition for a medal for their window glass and leaded windows, in consequence of the senior partner of their firm having been appointed a member of the jury for Class 34, to which all the above glass belongs, with the exception of the optical glass, which has been transferred by the jury to Class 19, and to which a medal has been awarded in connection with the first-order dioptric light.

LIGHTHOUSE APPARATUS.

One of the most prominent objects in the Nave is the lighthouse, or, rather, the lantern belonging to a lighthouse, exhibited by Messrs. Chance. This noble work is technically described as a "dioptric revolving apparatus of the first order, constructed according to Mr. Thomas Stevenson's holophotal improvement of the system of Augustin Fresnel." This apparatus is formed of an eight-sided frame, in the centre of which the flame is placed. Each side comprises a compound lens, and a series of totally reflecting prisms both above and below the lens; all these prisms, as well as the rings of the compound lens, being concentric, round a horizontal axis passing through the centre of the lens. The result is, to condense the light proceeding from the central flame into eight beams of parallel rays, without the aid of unnecessary reflections or refractions, so as to produce the maximum effect at sea.

The light-room is made of cast-iron; it is 7 feet high, being cylindrical within, and having externally sixteen sides, which are alternately large and small, to suit the lantern which it supports. It is provided, *outside*, just beneath the lantern, with a gallery or balcony, on which the keepers can stand to clean the lantern-panes; and also with an *inside* gallery, for the service of the apparatus. The inside of this light-room is lined with mahogany. The lantern is formed, first, of sixteen standards, alternately inclined to the right and left—they are made of wrought-iron, covered with gun-metal facings, by which combination the greatest strength and the least interception of light are obtained, together with the usual protection from the sea air; second, of gun-metal astragals, in two tiers, and of gun-metal sole-plates and sills; third, of a double copper dome, supported on iron rafters. The whole is surmounted by a revolving copper ball, carrying a wind-vane. The panes of the lantern are purposely omitted, to facilitate the inspection of the apparatus.

A square cast-iron pedestal, with glazed doors, contains the clock-work for imparting rotatory motion to the apparatus. By a contrivance communicated to the manufacturers by Professor Airy, and for the first time used in lighthouse machinery, the winder is so constructed as to maintain an uniform speed of rotation, without any check during the winding-up. In other particulars, the plan of the pedestal and of the clockwork is in accordance with the Scotch system. A revolving carriage, being an arrangement of rollers and guide-rollers, gives the least possible amount of friction, whilst it maintains the perfectly vertical position of the apparatus. There is a fixed cast-iron table, on which the oil-lamp is placed, and on which the keeper stands for the service of the lamp. The oil-lamp is a novel kind of "pressure-lamp," and consists of a turned gun-metal cylinder, in which the piston that forces the oil into the burner is worked by a weight placed outside the cylinder, instead of inside, as hitherto. Each of the four concentric wicks of the burner is supplied with oil by two independent feed-tubes communicating with the main pipe.

The dioptric or lenticular system of lighthouse illumination is distinguished for its superiority to the catoptric or reflector system in the essential qualities of powers, simplicity, durability, and economy. The whole of the optical apparatus, lamp, rotatory machine, lantern, and light-room, has been constructed by Chance Brothers and Co., at their glass works, near Birmingham. These exhibitors are the only manufacturers in Great Britain of dioptric lighthouse apparatus. They have constructed, within the few years during which they have pursued this branch of business, eighty-eight complete lights, of which thirty-nine are of the first and second orders; also thirty-four lanterns. These have been supplied to the lighthouse boards of Great Britain, and of the other principal maritime countries of the world. Their lights embrace all the successive improvements introduced by themselves or by others, and are testified to be excellent in design, material, and workmanship. Perfect optical adjustment of the lenses and prisms, in accordance with the local *data* of each lighthouse, is applied to all the apparatus of their construction.

Philosophical Instruments.

In the North Gallery are shown various optical, magnetic, surveying, and electric instruments, with telegraph appliances, models of engines, microscopes, and a beautiful series of instruments for the automatic registration of the variations of magnetometers, contributed by the managers of the Kew Observatory, under the direction of a committee of the British Association for the Advancement of Science. These present some convenient and important modifications of Mr. Brooke's ingenious instruments as employed in the Greenwich and Paris Observatories.

In this class (13) there are 140 exhibitors on the British side of the building, and several trophies in the shape of large telescopes and lighthouse lanterns, one of which, that of Messrs. Chance, we have just examined.

It can scarcely be expected that we should illustrate this class to any great extent; we select, however, two excellent instruments, contributed by F. Pastorelli and Co., of Cross Street, Hatton Garden, who show a large variety of very ingenious and admirably manufactured objects, useful in meteorological, optical, and mathematical science.

The instrument shown in the first engraving is known as

METFORD'S TRAVERSING THEODOLITE.

It is constructed with all the important improvements introduced by Mr. W. E. Metford, C.E., the results of actual practice in the field. The levelling gear consists of three inverted screws, having good seats fitted closely to their beds, and effectually shielded from dust by caps. To prevent the screws becoming loose, the arms that inclose them are made with sufficient spring to admit of their being slightly tightened.

The object of the traversing stage is to enable the observer to shift his instrument over the exact centre, after having set it up firmly, nearly level, and approximately over the point required. The main hollow centre of the instrument carries a circular foot, which is able to travel in any direction.

The check telescope, though not necessary in five-inch instruments, or for ordinary work, is of great importance in larger ones. It lies between the traversing stage and the horizontal limb, where it can generally be used without taking advantage of its capability of sliding out; but, by sliding it out, a total horizontal and vertical range of range is obtained. The sliding horizontal and vertical motions are all fixed by one screw. Sliding the telescope out was suggested by Mr. Newnham, C.E., of the Scinde Railway.

The horizontal limb, vernier circle, &c. This limb is arranged to take the compass, a level with a circular bubble, and two memorandum slates, on which constant errors, &c., may be recorded. The vernier plate is carried on four arms, and a diagonal brace—preventing twist in the arm—to which the tangent motion is attached. The horizontal limb has openings which enable the observer to take vertical angles to 70° in depression. Securely attached to the pivot, is an arm to take the lower tangent apparatus. The brace system of tangents is adopted, to prevent the loss of time occasioned by the wear of common tangents. All the pivots have broad bearing flanges, and the pivots themselves and the bearing flanges are in one casting, thus conducing greatly to the rigidity of the whole instrument. The conical pivots fit in their sockets throughout their whole length, and not at the ends only.

The circular bubble was first used by Troughton, for the purpose of obtaining an artificial horizon, but was adapted to the theodolite by Mr. Metford. Its great advantage is, that it shows exactly the direction in which the level has been departed from, and it is thus a great aid in setting up the instrument before adjusting the traverser. To the side of the main pivot is attached a strong curved bracket, divided at the top into two arms. This bracket has a T section throughout and on the ends, and at the junction of the arms is fixed the vertical circle. The improvement is unquestionably an important one, since by it the suspension of the telescope over the axis is permitted. The so-called curved bracket is not attended by weakness, for this bracket is exceedingly stiff. It has been used by Mr. Metford for eight years with perfect success. The microscopes hang on the head of the casting, and travel far more conveniently than in the common instrument

The telescope is a "dumpy," care being taken to have the object-glass of first-rate defining power. The eye-end passes clear over the axis, and by this means the instrument may be used as a transit. By this capability of turning over, it is of immense service in ranging railway curves, as regards accuracy in laying the tangent, and as regards time. It is also necessary in tunnelling, and in all altitude and azimuth observations, to which the instrument is perfectly adapted. A rectangular eye-piece is added to the telescope; it is taken out when the other eye-piece is used, and a stopper is inserted in its place; it is not, however, necessary to remove it entirely. The rays are turned with a prism, so that the loss of light is trifling. Each diaphragm consists of two independent discs; and each takes one cobweb, and is so constructed that each web can be placed vertically or hori-

beyond the brass cell. By this means rain and dust can be wiped off in the shortest time, and with the least amount of scratching, without any of the difficulty attending the same process in the case of the common deep-seated glasses. The eye-piece block—that which stops

IMPROVED LEVEL. F. PASTORELLI AND CO.

the end of the telescope barrel—pulls out, and the cobwebs and diaphragms are thus exposed.

This theodolite is stated by good judges to possess many important advantages—especially as regards steadiness and saving of time, from the use of the traversing stage. It is also very cheap—no small benefit to scientific observers—the high price of first-rate instruments being certainly a bar to their more general use. The other instrument shown in our engraving is

PASTORELLI'S IMPROVED LEVEL.

This instrument combines several improved arrangements, giving increased facility in use, greater steadiness and freedom from vibration, more accurate adjustment, with scarcely a possibility of deranging them. The stability of the tripod is of the utmost importance. The ordinary staff-head is defective, from the impossibility of properly tightening the joint pivots as they become worn. The new staff-head—an adoption of a plan of W. Froude, Esq., C.E.—has the cheeks cast on to a circular plate, the leg-joints being similar to an inverted mortar, with strong trunnions, which can be tightened in their bisected cylindrical bearings by means of capstan-headed screws.

The ball-joint is substituted for the ordinary parallel plates, which are limited in their action, compelling the staff-head to be placed within 3 deg. or 4 deg. from a horizontal plane, making the tripod subservient to the level.

In Messrs. Pastorelli's case will also be found a patent measuring level; improved prismatic compasses; various mathematical drawing instruments, after the patterns approved and brought into vogue by Mr. Froude; barometers, thermometers, hygrometers, a sympiesometer for taking altitudes—light, portable, and highly suitable for travellers; with several admirable instruments the use of which would not be understood by our readers without the aid of diagrams. It is needless to say that Messrs. Pastorelli have received at the hands of the jurors the Prize Medal, and high commendation.

TRAVERSING THEODOLITE. F. PASTORELLI AND CO.

zontally, as they come to be, and in the axis of the telescope also, independently of the other. This fine instrument is provided with improved illuminating apparatus and object-glass; which latter is placed within a cell backward, so as to allow the glass surface to project

Water Meters

EXHIBITED BY THE MANCHESTER WATER-METER COMPANY, ARDWICK, MANCHESTER.

FORTUNATELY, we have in this country water in abundance. But to bring it to our doors, and to convey it into our dwellings, it has frequently to be carried underground through miles of costly iron piping. This involves great expense; and the water so lavishly bestowed by Nature, and which seems almost as common as the sunshine, or the air we breathe, thus becomes an article of great momentary value, dearer in price than the gas which illuminates alike the mansion and the cottage. If, therefore, water be an article of such value, both as a necessity of life and as a marketable commodity, and if it is bought and sold at a higher rate per thousand feet than gas, surely there can be but one just method of buying and selling it — that of measurement. A housekeeper who, according to the present system of charging for water, pays in proportion to his rent, and not in proportion to the quantity he uses, has no inducement to guard against waste. He may, and in many cases does, waste many thousands of gallons in a year. But in gas we find nothing of the kind. And

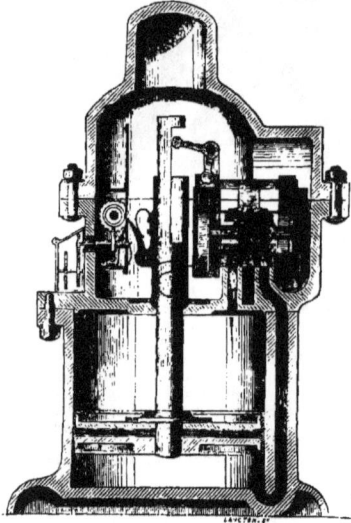

OFFICE AND TRADE WATER METER.

why? Because the person using it pays only for the quantity he consumes, and finds it to his advantage to guard against waste. And is it not reasonable to believe this would be the case with the consumers of water if they were allowed to buy it by measure?

This company exhibits three different water-meters—first, a water-meter for general and trade purposes (Chadwick Frost's patent); second, a small meter, for dwelling-houses, offices, &c.; and, third, a meter for measuring the water evaporated by steam-boilers, both H. Frost's patent.

The meter for general and trade purposes is constructed, as will be seen from the illustration, showing the interior view, on the principle of the piston and cylinder, the piston having a reciprocating action.

Its chief novelty is in the valve, which is actuated by the fluid, and reverses the course of the water in process of measurement.

The small meter for dwelling-houses is made also on the piston and cylinder principle, though it differs somewhat in arrangement

WATER METER FOR STEAM BOILERS.

from the meter already noticed. The interior illustration exhibits two measuring chambers. These chambers are fitted with pistons, packed with cupped leathers, and a valve of a peculiar and novel construction, arranged simply and with few parts, changes the inlet and outlet ports. The fluid acting against the rib or midfeather, on the back of the valve-plate, changes the position of the valve, and reverses the course of the fluid being measured.

On the termination of each stroke of the piston, and not till then, this change is completely effected, and accuracy of measurement is thus insured.

This object is effected without concussion, or stoppage in the flow. Except with the aid of tumbling weights, or springs, this has never before been accomplished in any high-pressure meter, with a single cylinder and piston.

The lower portion of this meter is an iron cylinder or measuring chamber, lined with brass, which is smoothly bored out. In the cylinder works a piston, which is packed with cupped leathers, similar to those used in hydraulic presses, and which divides the incoming from the outflowing water. In the upper part of the meter are the compound valve and the wheelwork of the index, which, being made of brass, are not liable to injury from the effects of water. No oiling or attention is required to any of the

SMALL WATER METER. OUTSIDE VIEW.

meters made by this company, as the working parts are made self-adjusting, and are lubricated by the water.

This meter has been thoroughly and practically tested for three

SMALL WATER METER. INSIDE VIEW.

and a half years, and it is now being used by a great many public and private water companies at home and abroad.

To water companies who desire to economise their water by preventing waste, and to deal equally towards all their customers, this meter will prove of inestimable use; while to small consumers it will afford the means of guaranteeing a supply of water at a fixed rate per thousand gallons, and remove the sense of injustice now experienced, in consequence of the charges for water being arbitrarily fixed, without reference to the quantity used.

In addition to their ordinary cold water meters, the exhibitors show a steam-boiler meter, for measuring hot water, the first and only one ever constructed entirely of metal, without packing or flexible material of any kind. As shown in the engraving of the interior of this meter, there are two square metal chambers, in which the water is measured as it flows through the meter. These chambers fit fluid-tight, in annular metal troughs, in which, by the action of the fluid in process of measurement against the fixed pistons or division-plates,

new invention of Mr. Frost, of the Manchester Water-meter Company, it is not unlikely that steam-ship owners, engineers, and other employers of steam-power, will avail themselves of what has, to them, so long been a desideratum. By using this meter the employer of steam-power is able to ascertain the relative value of different kinds of coal, or other fuel, consumed for the purpose of raising steam; the steam-producing power of differently constructed boilers; the value of various sorts of fire-bars and furnaces, and of the different modes of

THE RUSSIAN COURT.

they are made to reciprocate. Each of the two measuring chambers is accompanied with a valve, which admits the fluid to be measured through diagonally arranged water-ways, leading from the valves to the chambers. By means of cranks and connecting rods, the two measuring chambers give motion to a shaft, from which is communicated motion to the index above.

The great difficulty in constructing a meter to successfully resist the action of hot water, has prevented an extensive application of meters to steam-boilers. That difficulty being now removed by the

26.

fixing boilers, as well as other arrangements for economising fuel. It need hardly be said that the Manchester Water Meter Company, which exhibits the greatest variety of instruments of this kind, and the only steam-boiler meter in the Exhibition, have been awarded a Prize Medal " for originality of design and practical success in water-meters." This decision of the jury of Class 8 contrasts strongly with that of the jury on civil engineering, &c., at the Exhibition of 1851, who decided that they had " found no water-meters so far perfected as to satisfy the conditions of a good meter. '

Contributions of Russia to the International Exhibition.

RUSSIA in the Exhibition partakes very much of the character of Russia in the world—political, moral, and geographical. She is situated between Sweden, Norway, and Denmark on the one side, and Turkey and Greece on the other. She occupies considerable space, which is only partially filled. She abounds in contradictions, the acme of luxury and magnificence being divided from the depths of meanness and poverty by the very narrowest of lines, civilisation and refinement rubbing shoulders, and owning not merely acquaintance but relationship with squalor and barbarism—learning and science removed from ignorance and semi-slavery by scarcely a step—imperial magnificence and splendour contrasting oddly, yet naturally, with an aspect of society which, while yet in its pupilage, assumes the airs and dons the garb of the politest nation in the world !

Russia is represented by nearly seven hundred exhibitors from all parts of her great empire, and including branches of industry peculiar to her varied peoples. In a word, she seems to have tried hard and most successfully to make her exhibition a fair representation of her various thriving industries and immense natural resources. The position of Russia in the Exhibition will be understood by the following diagram :—

ENGLISH REFRESHMENT SALOONS.

ST. NICHOLAS.
Mineral Products

Silver Works

Porcelains

Embroidery.

Furs and Skins.

SWEDEN AND NORWAY.

Cotton.   Hemp & Flax.   Siberian Products.   Furniture.   Ebony Cabinets.   Fossils, &c.   Mosaics.

Woollen Cloths, &c.   Leather.   Tapestry.   Vases.   Iron & Copper.   Raw Materials.   Carpets.

GREECE.

TURKEY.

THE NAVE—NORTH SIDE.
Trophy of Jasper Vases, Porphyry, &c.

The Russian Court is an exceedingly fine one—containing a great number of very interesting objects, especially some fine works in green jasper and violet porphyry in the frontage facing the nave. One of these is a magnificent vase, five feet in diameter, with the handles richly ornamented with the most delicately sculptured faces; another is a candelabrum, seventeen feet high. The materials for these fine trophies, which bring to mind the laboriously minute carvings of the mediæval ages, are found in Siberia, where they are wrought to perfection entirely by hand labour—the toil of years. The porphyry vase, for instance, has a Russian inscription upon it, stating that it was commenced in 1856, and only finished at the close of last year, though this, in comparison with other works of the same kind, was speedily accomplished; for in the Hermitage at St. Petersburg is one magnificent vase of jasper, which it took no fewer than twenty-five years of uninterrupted hand labour to carve and polish. Near these trophies in the nave is a candelabrum, carved out of blocks of that handsomest of all minerals, lapis lazuli, which has lately been found in comparatively large quantities in Eastern Siberia. There is also a Siberian trophy, consisting of large blocks of blacklead, and other mineral products of that little known region. Russia does not, as in 1851, show any of those grand ornaments in malachite which formed so great an attraction in the Hyde Park Exhibition. There are only a few large lumps of it in its natural state, but polished on the surface and sides. The exhibitors, most probably, dislike repeating themselves on this occasion ; and they certainly make up, in the richness and variety of their collection, for the costly palace doors and malachite vases which were the wonder of all beholders. There is a very fine collection of works in silver in cups and statuettes, representing episodes in Russian life; bronzes, including a colossal statue of Catherine II.; ornamental china and glass work from the Imperial factory; and Florentine and Roman mosaics.

The empire of Russia is well represented in all kinds of cereals, and in a fine collection of minerals sent by one of the public administrations of the country. Among various curiosities is a valuable seal-skin carpet. Many exhibitors show in the wine and food class, and in the class for animal and vegetable substances used in manufactures. Under machinery Russia has a good display of carriages, and its strong numerical point in manufactures will be found in the skins, furs, feathers, leather, and articles of clothing. The visitor will also notice a valuable collection of works in mosaic, marble, " pietra-dura," paintings on china from the Imperial factory, on glass—plain, coloured, and jewelled. Most of the articles are luxurious and ornamental rather than useful, but they are of rare execution, value, and beauty. Two colossal china vases form part of the collection, on which have been copied, in a large size, a picture of Inigo Jones, from the original picture by Vandyke, and a picture of John Locke, from the original painting by Kneller. After the Exhibition, it is understood to be the intention of the Emperor to present these vases to the Royal Society and also to present a collection of precious marbles to the Geological Society. Tobacco and maize, silk and corn, wheat from the plains of the Volga and the Don, furs and skins from Siberia, hemp, flax, leather, oils, tallow, with various descriptions of precious stones—and many that are not precious, but very useful—all these go to make up a gallant show.

At the back of the court is a gigantic statue, twenty feet or more in height, representing St. Nicholas, the patron saint of the Russian people. It is said to weigh seven tons ; but, notwithstanding its colossal dimensions, the expression of benevolence and goodness on the face is remarkably well kept. Silk, spun and woven ; velvets, cottons, and linens; woollen goods, porcelain, and carpets, are all here in profusion. One coverlid especially attracts attention, not from the fact that it is well made or beautiful—for it is of cloth mosaic, a sort of ingenious patchwork—but because it bears an inscription in English, which runs as follows : —"£50 pounds stirling reward who kann make tablecover like this in four months' time. It will be paid by cloth mosike manufactur, Saint Petersberg." A carpet made by hand, representing various phases of Russian peasant life, is also interesting ; but the exhibitor asks £150 for it, which is about ten times the sum for which it might be produced by machine labour at Axminster or Kidderminster. Altogether, an hour may be very profitably spent in examining the various interesting objects in the industrial display made by the representatives of Russia's eighty millions of inhabitants. In the Fine Arts Department Russia has some good pictures and sculptures; but of these we have already spoken.

THE PRINCE OF WALES AND THE EXHIBITION.—The following very gratifying announcement has been issued by the Royal Commissioners :—His Royal Highness the Prince of Wales, being anxious to mark the deep interest in the success of the International Exhibition, an enterprise which owed its origin to his beloved father, has, with the approbation of her Majesty, graciously undertaken to distribute the medals and certificates of honourable mention at a state ceremonial early in the year 1863, after the building has been cleared. This gracious act will commend itself to all classes of the community. It is generally understood that the closing ceremonial will take place early in January, 1863, though no details of the important pageant are made public.

Glass for Domestic Purposes.

IS Glass "for Decorative and Household Purposes," the South Courts of the Exhibition are deservedly attractive. But in the Foreign Courts these manufactures are no less to be admired. In the South Court will be found stained glass and glass for buildings and decorations, glass for household use and fancy purposes, including chandeliers, lustres, girandoles, and candelabra; specimens of gilding on glass, medical glass, glass surgical instruments and chemical apparatus, and globes; and some samples of the material in the different stages of manufacture.

Having already noticed at some length the stained and painted glass in the Exhibition, we may now examine the chandeliers and candelabra. The crystal triumphs of Copeland, Dobson and Pearce, Green, Hodgetts, Lloyd and Summerfield, Moore, Naylor, Osler, Pearce, Phillips, Pellatt, Spiers and Son, and Wood are in themselves worth a visit to the Exhibition to behold. From the brave show we make one or two selections. Especially deserving of notice are the works of Messrs. Defries and Sons, of Houndsditch.

The magnitude, beauty, and originality of the great art show made by this firm entitle the Messrs. Defries to the highest credit as manufacturers. In some of their handsome cases are to be seen—what we believe to be a novelty in the manufacture — specimens of cut-glass jugs, decanters, tankards, and other vessels of the most beautiful forms, the ornamental treatment of which has been singularly successful. Free-handed but highly effective designs, made expressly with a view to the Exhibition, including wreaths of flowers and fruit, blending most harmo-

GLASS CHANDELIER FOR GAS.   MESSRS. DEFRIES AND SONS.   PRIZE MEDAL.

niously with the figures of the vessels, and the uses to which they are applied in the apparatus of the dessert-table, are beautifully etched upon them, and the general effect is charming in the extreme.

But the greatest curiosity in Messrs. Defries' show—and, indeed, in the Glass Court itself—is the Prismatic Mirror, one of eight designed and manufactured for the Sultan of Turkey, to adorn two of the principal saloons of the Imperial Palace on the Bosphorus. The apartments in question are called the Saloon Mehbeu and the Saloon Zwihlbech, the walls of which, on the side overlooking the Bosphorus, are of circular form. Both are furnished in the European style, with stoves and lofty mantelpieces; but a great difficulty arose in fitting the curved space over the fire-place with mirrors, as it was impossible to make mirrors of such a form and of the immense size required. To overcome this difficulty, which for a time was considered almost insurmountable, Messrs. Defries and Sons designed the prismatic mirrors, one of which is here shown. Each of the Sultan's saloons is to be decorated with four of these mirrors, fifteen feet high by eight broad, and containing 1,000 prisms. All the prisms join each other at the sides, so as to form almost one piece, and at the ends are dovetailed together, and hold into the frame by a system of copper rods, which fit into grooves cast in the glass. By this means the mirror is made concave, to suit the form of the wall. The weight of pure crystal glass in each mirror is one ton, and the weight of the metal back is one ton more. They will of course, be dispatched to the Bosphorus in pieces, and on arrival at their destination the backs of the prisms will be silvered, and all put together—each mirror in a gilt Turkish frame of great breadth and richness. To show the effect, one has been silvered and put together at Messrs. Defries' warehouse; and the play of colour and brilliancy of light reflected upon the whole mass of prisms is something inconceivably beautiful. In the palace, the mirrors will be

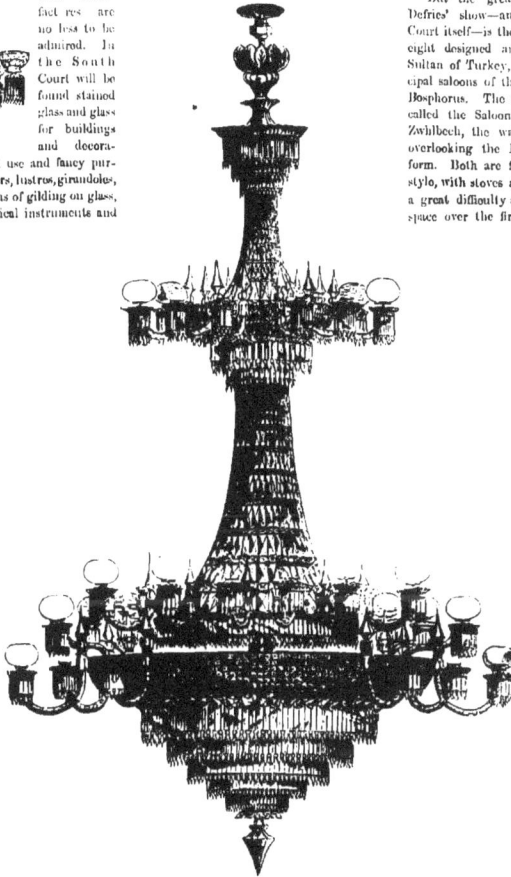

placed opposite each other, with a hundred-branched light before each—an arrangement, of course, that cannot be attempted in the Exhibition—so that the dazzling effect of the whole will only be fully seen at the great entertainments of the Sultan which follow the Ramazan. The whole design, arrangement, and manufacture of the mirrors reflect the very highest credit upon the enterprise and skill of Messrs. Defries; and from the interest which has been evinced in them since their exhibition, there seems little doubt that, in spite of their great cost, they will soon become fashionable enrichments in the palaces of the wealthy. The specimen of this new combination of prisms with a reflecting surface is certainly very effective, though it could not possibly be seen to greater disadvantage in the position which has been assigned to it in the building, the surrounding objects representing anything but the splendid entourage of the real ones in the Sultan's Palace. The prismatic mirror shown in the Exhibition contains 1,500 silvered prisms, and it is evident that, under favourable circumstances, and with an adequate source of light in a good position these mirrors may be made to produce a most dazzling effect. They can be made of any size, to fill up recesses in drawing-

rooms; and, indeed, their properties only require to be known to attract very general attention.

In the collection of the same firm, and constituting one of the most striking among the many beautiful objects comprised in Class 34, is a Monster Crystal Chandelier. There is a long series of drawing-room chandeliers, in glass, bronze, and ormolu, besides "star-lights," and many novelties in brass and ormolu gas-fittings; but this particular chandelier is so colossal in its magnitude, so elaborate in its design and construction, and so unique in its general effect, as to call for a slight description. The "dome" of the chandelier is surmounted by a Prince of Wales' coronet and plume, all of elaborately cut glass, and supported by eight diamond-cut pillars resting on a vase formed of prisms. Between these pillars is a glass tent comprised of cut diamond spangles. The centre, also, is supported by eight diamond-cut pillars terminating in graceful spires, which also rest on a vase of prisms. From the upper part of this vase springs the upper tier, containing alone 56 lights. This tier of lights is similarly supported, and each of its supporting pillars is surmounted by four smaller ones, all of them diamond-cut, each diamond being

GROUP OF GLASS. MESSRS. APSLEY PELLATT & CO. PRIZE MEDAL.

UPERGNES WITH GLASS STEMS, WITH MR. MARCH'S DESIGNS FOR FLOWER AND FRUIT DECORATIONS. MESSRS. DODSON AND PEARCE, ST. JAMES'S STREET. PRIZE MEDAL.

cut an inch and a half deep. Immediately below this, and supporting the columns just spoken of, comes the main body of the chandelier. From this spring 112 lights. The main body of the chandelier consists of richly-cut prisms, or rather truncated pyramids, each 3 feet 6 inches in length—a size, we believe, not before attained in this species of ornamentation. This arrangement produces a most elegant effect when viewed from below—that of one large prismatic dish, under which two other dishes are formed in a similar way; the whole being terminated with a richly-cut spire. The prismatic vase occupying the centre of the lower columns constitutes a singularly beautiful object in the whole composition, although all the component parts of it are kept in judicious subordination to one another. A bouquet of crystal flowers springs from this vase, an effect of no small difficulty to render faithfully, but which has been

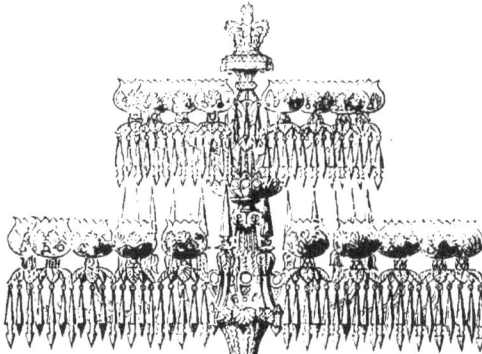

very cleverly managed. We may congratulate the firm on the very satisfactory execution of this fine work, every portion of which has been done upon their own premises. In good taste it is beyond all criticism. We are glad to observe that this and other firms do not perpetuate the error observable in the glass exhibition of 1851, of making chandeliers of coloured glass; for nothing can surpass the iridescent lustre of pure colourless flint glass. This beautiful object, then, displays 168 lights, arranged in two tiers. It is 14 feet in diameter, and 23 feet high, and the glass and metal of which it is composed weigh nearly three tons.

There has been lately placed in the Glass Court the handsome candelabrum here shown. This work is of magnificent proportions, and is really the finest object of the kind in the Exhibition. The base of the entire structure is sexagonal, the angles being occupied by six cut-glass pillars, the central cylinder

GRAND GLASS CANDELABRUM. MESSRS. DEFRIES AND SONS. HOUN DITCH.

of which is formed of one piece, fluted and cut in raised diamonds. This rests on a substratum, also cut and fluted. The six pillars terminate in large, solid pieces, "pineapple cut," and finishing with a large spire.

The main part of the base is 3ft. 6in. in diameter, and is formed of cut prisms, which meet a ring, of the same diameter as the base itself, from which the candelabrum diminishes towards the top. At this ring six large glass shields are let into six richly-cut panels, each 18in. by 17in., while the pyramidal abutments between the shields form supports the basis of the upper tier of pillars, which stand out in relief from the main stem. In the centre of the upper tier of pillars is a large tulip-shaped disc—a very beautiful specimen of cut glass; this rests upon a hexagonal plate, from which rises the large fluted and diamond-cut cylinder. The bowl supporting the first tier of lights is thirty inches in diameter, and is formed of large pieces of glass separately bent and cut, and afterwards fitted together. The upper bowl, from which the higher tier of lights springs, is, however, in one piece. The royal crown, which forms the summit of the candelabrum, is the first of its kind attempted in crystal glass, and may be considered eminently successful. The cushion is one solid piece of diamond-cut crystal. The whole structure contains so much rich and elaborate cutting, that its appearance when lighted up must be extremely brilliant, while the crowning ornament is so constructed as to intensify the general effect. Messrs. Defries are the manufacturers of the chandelier at the Royal Italian Opera, and at most of the principal theatres and music halls. They employ a vast number of persons, both at their warehouses in Houndsditch and at their works in Staffordshire, not only in producing all kinds of articles in crystal, but also in manufacturing various beautiful objects in porcelain, of which they are also large importers. Many of the most exquisite pieces of glass at the Exhibition have been purchased by the Queen, Prince Alfred, the Viceroy of Egypt, and other high and noble personages; but it is not alone for the wealthy that this eminent firm produces articles of luxury. They have, so to speak, brought chandeliers within the reach of the million; for some beautiful articles of this character are made by them at prices which, a few years since, would have been utterly impossible.

We have also introduced a couple of illustrations from the works on glass of other eminent manufacturers—a group from the case of Messrs. Apsley Pellatt and Co., to which our engraving does but scant justice, so exquisite are the cutting and engraving on some of the goblets, decanters, &c.—and specimens of the epergnes invented by

GLASS CHANDELIER. MESSRS. DEFRIES & SONS.

Mr. March, and shown by Messrs. Dobson and Pearce, of Piccadilly. These exquisite drawing-room decorations have been pronounced to be "unique and extraordinary," and they well deserve the praise thus bestowed; for nothing more graceful or more fitting the dessert-table has hitherto been produced. For fine art work, both in form and perfection of engraving, the collection shown by Dobson and Pearce stands almost unrivalled. One of the great gems in this collection—an engraved glass tazza, 12 inches high—was purchased almost the first day it was shown, for two hundred and fifty guineas, of a single small piece of modern glass. The exquisite engraving and design of this little bijou is something marvellous; the panels in the cup, with their fine cut designs, as delicately marked as steel engravings and as deep as intaglios (all cut with the wheel, even to the minutest chasing of its flower scroll work) make it one of the most extraordinary specimens of art manufacture of its kind in the Exhibition.

In Messrs. Dobson and Pearce's case will be noticed a beautiful claret jug, one side of which is deeply cut with a grotesque Raffaelesque design. The foliage scrollwork—apes, dragons, and other monsters which are, as it were, led into the design—is a perfect chapter on the weird combinations of Raffaelesque ornament. In this collection are also shown those cheapest, simplest, and best kinds of glass for domestic purpose; which, equally with the displays made by Pellatt, Phillips, Defries, Copeland, Green, Hodgetts, Naylor, Powell, and, in short, all the great glass manufacturers and glass dealers in England, merit and obtain a degree of attention from visitors as deserving as flattering.

The glass collection in the present Exhibition is certainly one of its most attractive features. Here are such triumphs of the engraver's art as Venice never knew. Here are small glass tazzas, which have been sold for 250 guineas; here are goblets which find eager competitors to purchase them for 50 guineas each; many claret jugs worth 100 guineas, and wineglasses that fetch as much as six and seven pounds a-piece. There are lustres and chandeliers, too, of all descriptions and almost every grade of excellence, from simple, classic designs up to the gorgeous crystal temple of Defries, which has cost over £3,000 to manufacture. The exquisite brilliancy of the works here on a sunny day, when their masses sparkle with a positive flood of light, is a sight wonderful to behold, and worth remembering as long as we live. Probably there is no other section, not even in machinery, in the whole building, where our superiority over foreign competition is more marked—certainly none where it has been more frankly and cordially acknowledged.

PARIAN STATUETTES, &c.

IN this page we introduce a group of statuettes, &c., in parian and other ceramic materials, from the exhibits of Mr. William Henry Goss, of Stoke-upon-Trent. It is only necessary to glance at our engraving to perceive with what exquisite taste this manufacturer has which not only form and outline are to be admired, but in which colour goes far to produce the beautiful effect observable in all the efforts of the potter's art. Few displays of porcelain are to be seen in the Exhibition which excel those made by Mr. Goss.

The great difficulty in producing good statuettes in parian,

GROUP OF STATUETTES—VASES, TAZZI, ETC. MR. W. H. GOSS. PRIZE MEDAL.

worked out the several designs he has produced in fictile wares. Here classic forms blend harmoniously with the more ordinary shapes in use in our domestic life. But to fully comprehend the charm which belongs to these and like objects, they must be examined in the material of which they are composed. Wood-engraving, after all, presents but a very faint and imperfect picture of articles like these, in arises from the fact that the fictile material is apt to shrink unequally in baking. Thus it may happen that one portion of a vase or figure is perfect, while another is defective, which fact would render the whole object unfit for sale. But in the parian statuettes, &c., under notice, the perfection of art-manufacture seems certainly to have been reached.

Musical Instruments in the Exhibition.

THE display of musical instruments on the British side of the building is very complete. Having already referred to these, however, we now and the second shows a patent concert grand, with all the modern improvements. This is enclosed in a case of admirable workmanship—

COTTAGE GRAND PIANOFORTE. MESSRS. HOPKINSON. PRIZE MEDAL.

PATENT CONCERT GRAND PIANOFORTE. MESSRS. HOPKINSON. PRIZE MEDAL.

merely introduce representations of two fine pianos, manufactured by Messrs. John and James Hopkinson, of Regent Street. The first engraving is of a cottage grand, with carvings in the Italian style; walnut, inlaid with ivory, tulip, box, and king woods, exquisitely carved. But it is not to their cases that pianos owe their chief excellence. Without the interior mechanism be of the first class, all the decoration in the world would render them but boxes of worthless discord. In the pianos of Messrs. Hopkinson—who has not heard them at the Exhibition discoursing "most excellent music," under the guidance of highly-educated fingers?—the outside ornament forms but the least part of their value. True, they are fine pieces of furniture; but they possess a far higher value, for they are famous musical instruments. To hear them well played is a treat for a professor, much less a mere musical amateur like the writer. In tone, touch, and all the requisites of first-rate pianos, they are perfect—fitted alike for the concert-room or the cottage parlour—brilliant, full, and at the same time delicate, and calculated in every respect to sustain the high reputation their makers have so long had with the musical world. The valuable improvements in the manufacture of pianofortes lately introduced have all been taken advantage of by the Messrs. Hopkinson, the resources of whose establishment enable them to compete, not only in excel-

THE ORCHESTRION.

ONE of the most ingenious and well constructed of the self-acting musical instruments in the Exhibition is the Orchestrion of Messrs. Imhof and Mukle, of Oxford Street. This grand instrument stands in the centre of the north court, and is so built as to be able to stand any variety of climate. It is thus equally fitted for use in St. Petersburg and Calcutta. It has been constructed for the International Exhibition of 1862, and is in itself a striking example of the capabilities of mechanism for producing perfect music. On this instrument hundreds of different effects, variations, and delicate shades of tone can be produced. The mechanism is so perfect that its action is instantaneous, and free from noise and inconvenience to the person working it. The great simplicity of its construction renders the Orchestrion a most durable instrument. As the two barrels can be conveniently removed from the front, the Orchestrion does not require more space

THE ORCHESTRION, OR SELF-ACTING ORGAN. MESSRS. IMHOF AND MUKLE. PRIZE MEDAL.

lence, but also in economy of production, with the best makers in the trade. To go to the Exhibition on a Saturday, and to hear a fantasia on one of these instruments, is a treat indeed; and when we come to consider what a complicated piece of work is the interior of a piano—the strings stretched to a tension equal to a pressure of several tons, and yet one faulty wire yet put manufactured whole machine out of order—when we think what ingenious appliances are necessary before these strings can answer to the light touch of a woman's finger—when we see that all the ends for which such an instrument are fully answered, and we find the English piano a highly-finished and complete box of harmony, our wonder and admiration may well be excited. To say that these instruments are as perfect as they can be made, is to say all that can be said of any piano yet manufactured; to compare them with the instruments of other eminent makers is simply futile. Among the best there can be no better.

27.

than its width. The deepest notes are placed in the centre of the instrument, so that the tuner can tune each and every pipe easily from the sides without removing anything. By the application of an additional fly, the speed can be regulated to the greatest nicety, so as to give detailed effects to the music in performing. In this and many other respects the Orchestrion is different and superior to other self-acting musical instruments. The exhibitors also show various kinds of musical instruments, especially an apparatus called the Flutonichorde, which can be attached to a piano, and add to it a prolonged flute-like note; musical clocks, boxes, hand organs, euterpeons, &c., the prices of which vary from five to a thousand guineas, the cost of the grand Orchestrion. In our engraving the method of working the instrument is seen, the front board being removed in order to show the interior. Altogether, this may be pronounced the most important and perfect self-acting organ produced since the last Exhibition.

Machinery in the Exhibition.—III.

SINCE 1851 there have been few actual new inventions in machinery, though there have been vast improvements on the machine-tools then in active operation. Great Britain must always be first in the production of the larger and more ponderous kinds of machinery, from

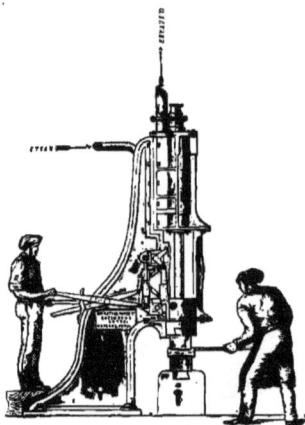

NAYLOR'S STEAM-HAMMER.

the fact of our almost boundless resources in coal and iron; but in the more delicate implements, and especially in cotton, silk, and flax machinery, we need fear no rival. The workmanship of ponderous masses of material into forms capable of exercising movement and developing force, is of the highest order; for an error of adjustment would be fatal to the operation of these mighty engines; and the difficulty attending accurate adjustment will be easily understood by even the non-mechanical reader, especially when large pieces of work are needed.

In no part of the manufacture of machine-tools is this fact so apparent as in the operation of steam-hammers. To these we have already referred (ante, p. 119); but we now introduce figures of the actual instruments, as they appear in the Western Annexe.

In this page are shown representations of Naylor's Patent Single and Double-action Steam-hammer, as exhibited by the

KIRKSTALL FORGE COMPANY,

Leeds, and Parliament Street, London. The valuable improvements developed in these hammers, also the advantages and capabilities they possess, are thus stated by the exhibitors:—

"Steam-hammers which have hitherto been constructed involve the same general principle of being lifted by steam pressure, and falling by gravity, the effect of the blow being dependent on the weight of the hammer, multiplied by the height of its fall. The greater the distance it falls, consequently the greater the force of the blow, the slower is the speed of working. The great practical drawback to the more extended application of steam-hammers, has been the impossibility of obtaining sufficient speed or quickness of stroke.

"The advantages of the double-action steam-hammer for forging are its being capable of working up to 200 strokes per minute (when required), which is from three to four times faster than any steam-

hammer hitherto constructed. The power can also be more than doubled, instantaneously, and as rapidly altered. The adjusting valve gearing also allows of instantly changing the length of stroke, and force of blow, by altering the position of the sliding wedges. It is completely under the control of the hand gear, which is easy to work in any position. The rapidity of the stroke obtained by it is particularly advantageous for forgings requiring a great number of blows by finishing the work at one heat, and saving both the fuel required for the second heat and the deterioration and waste of the iron. This principle of hammer is also adapted for riveting wrought-iron bridges, girders, ship-building, &c."

We have next illustrations of the

STEAM-HAMMERS EXHIBITED BY MESSRS. THWAITES AND CARBUTT,

of the Vulcan Iron Works, Bradford, Yorkshire. These being drawn on a larger scale than those of the Kirkstall Forge Company, would appear to be more important instruments; but in point of size they are really much the same. These hammers are made of a variety of constructions, consisting of three sizes—the smaller size from 2 cwt. up to 10 cwt.; the next size, from 7 cwt. to 3 tons; and the largest size, from 15 cwt. to 20 tons.

The smaller hammer is of double action, having the steam on the top and bottom of the piston. It is also adapted for hand motion, and is designed for general smithing purposes, allowing a long shaft to be pieced up, without the inconvenience which would be experienced by working it at a double standard hammer.

The next size is constructed so as to be worked either single or double action, and is made with a patent variable cut-off for the steam and exhaust, so that the intensity or softness of the blow may be regulated at any desired part of the stroke at pleasure, and is entirely under the control of the attendant.

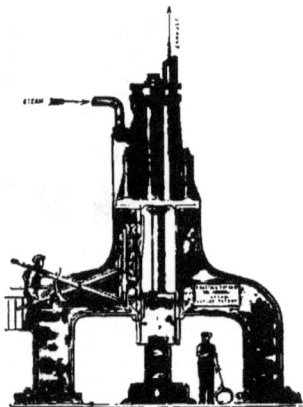

NAYLOR'S STEAM-HAMMER.

These are the kind of hammers shown by the exhibitors in the International Exhibition, and there are large numbers of their manufacture working in some of the principal engineering and iron and steel works in the kingdom.

The largest size steam-hammer is constructed so as to be worked single actioned, the steam merely lifting the tup, and, being exhausted, allowing the tup to fall and thus give the blow. Many of these have been made by Messrs. Thwaites and Carbutt, and for some purposes they are preferred, being hand-geared, and easily under the control of the attendant, having only two handles to actuate all the movements of the hammer, and on this account less liable to get out of order.

This firm are understood to have orders on hand for this description of hammer of various sizes up to 12 tons—no small proof of the just appreciation they hold in the favour of those most likely to estimate the merits of such machinery.

LOCOMOTIVES IN THE EXHIBITION.

OUR large engraving presents an accurate view of the locomotives in the Western Annexe. We are now so accustomed to the extraordinary capabilities of the steam-engine, that it has not only ceased to cause surprise, but, under ordinary circumstances, it scarcely arrests attention; it is worthy of deep consideration, nevertheless. It has changed man from

that which is at present in use. So admirable, indeed, were Newcomen's inventions, that what he introduced has been rather improved than discarded—an assertion that can be made regarding no other of the many who have laboured in the same field, not even of the illustrious Watt himself. Yet how different was Newcomen engine from the magnificent specimens to be seen in the Western Annexe. He applied steam only indirectly, and as a means of obtaining a vacuum, after which atmospheric pressure did the work; and hence, while he could obtain a motive power equal, even theoretically, to but fifteen pounds to the square inch, there is no limit to the pressure we can produce but the strength of the materials we employ. His cylinders were very roughly bored, and Watt himself found it very difficult to obtain anything like an accurately fitting piston; but the necessity for any species of machinery always leads to its invention; and hence, so admirable is the apparatus at present employed, that the largest cylinder is now bored with the utmost precision, and the various parts are fitted together with unerring accuracy. Newcomen's piston was

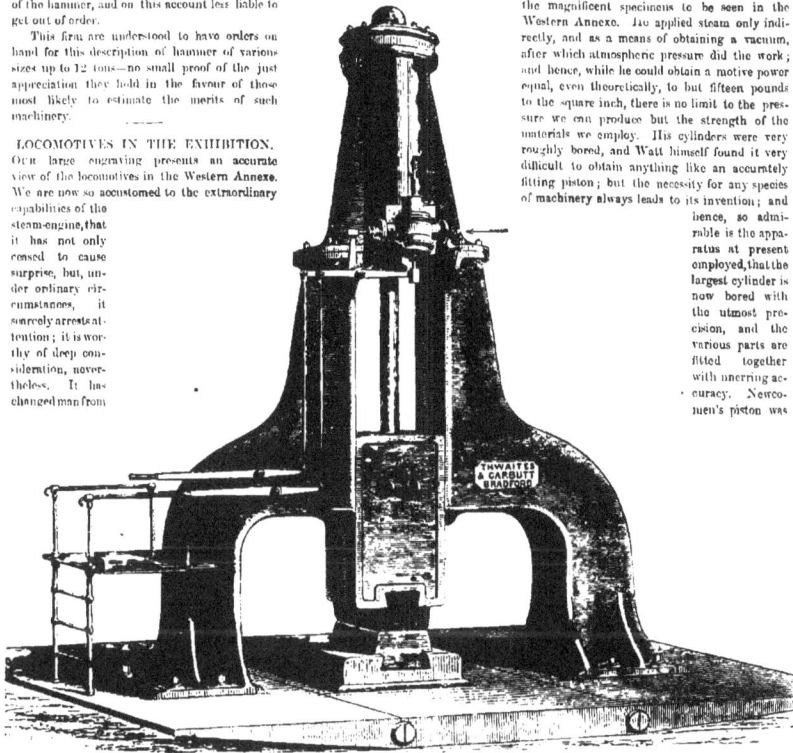

STEAM-HAMMER. MESSRS. THWAITES AND CARBUTT.

a pigmy to a giant. It not only enables him to spin a thread which almost rivals that of the silkworm in fineness, but gives him power to wield the most ponderous mass as if it were without weight, and to mould the hardest material as if it offered no resistance to his efforts. A century and a half has not elapsed since the first practical application of steam; for though the principles on which the steam-engine is founded were known for many ages, and steam had for some time been applied to the draining of the mines in Devonshire, it cannot be considered to have become, even indirectly, a motive power, until Newcomen, in 1705, gave to the world an engine that differed but little in its form and principal details from

packed with leather—a perishable substance, particularly when acted upon by steam. Watt's hemp-packing, though a great improvement, was still very imperfect, since its adjustment or renewal required the stoppage of the engine, and the displacement of more or less of its parts, not to speak of the leakage which occurred before it was considered sufficiently out of order to require attention. The metallic packing now universally adopted is free from these defects; it leaves little to be desired, for if properly made it causes hardly any friction, and the longer it works the better it acts. Newcomen used water to render his pistons air and steam-tight; and this, with the rush of cold air into the cylinder at every stroke, produced a serious waste of heat, [illegible] Purchase of [illegible]. Newcomen's engine [illegible], however, in a [illegible] form, [illegible] and it [illegible] to be used from [illegible] 1749 to 1770, with [illegible] improvements [illegible] by Smeaton, who [illegible] in [illegible] of his [illegible]. Among the alterations suggested by Smeaton was the shortening of the stroke, a principle which, as we shall find, has been carried very far indeed by modern engineers in the application of steam to navigation. Among its other advantages, it diminishes friction, for since the friction increases only in the same proportion as the circumference of the piston, while the surface of the latter increases as the square of its circumference, the friction and [illegible] of the piston are far from increasing to the same extent. Newcomen's engine having been long since superseded by a more perfect machine, the reader will find no example of it in the International Exhibition. Yet it is well worthy of remembrance [illegible] the germ of the present noble [illegible]; and its piston, beam, cylinder, and valves have been retained with [illegible] that have by no means destroyed their identity.

The history of the steam-engine in reality begins from 17[illegible], when Watt commenced his experiments. All his efforts were directed to the economisation of heat. Hence, to prevent the rush of cold air into the cylinder, he covered it, and moved the piston by the pressure of steam, instead of that of the atmosphere. To prevent the cooling of the cylinder internally, by the water which condensed the steam, he effected the condensation in a separate vessel, called the "condenser;" to prevent the cooling of the cylinder externally, by radiation, he surrounded it with a steam-jacket, and avoided radiation from that by a covering of wood, &c. He endeavoured to condense the steam without bringing it into contact with the condensing water, but did not obtain satisfactory results; this method has, however, been tried

VIEW IN THE WESTERN ANNEXE—LOCOMOTIVE AND MARINE ENGINES.

again of late, and surface condensation is used in several of the engines we shall notice. Where water is very impure, as at sea, it has great advantages, if the [illegible] can be rendered sufficiently [illegible] [illegible] is [illegible]. In 1769 Watt introduced the principle of expansion, [illegible] with [illegible] being cut off at some part of the stroke, after which, [illegible], the power [illegible] from the [illegible] [illegible] and therefore [illegible] expenditure of fuel. This principle is now [illegible], though in various ways, and it is carried to such perfection that in the best engines the steam may, by a very simple [illegible], be cut off at any part of the stroke. When we [illegible] it is frequently cut off at [illegible], and even less, [illegible]. Before Watt began his [illegible], motion could be obtained from steam only in right lines; but, by applying to it the crank, he caused it to produce a rotary motion, and thus rendered it applicable to every possible purpose. Watt [illegible] the "hotwell"—that is, a vessel into which the condensed steam [illegible] water are thrown by the air-pump [illegible] the condenser. This had the effect of cooling the water which was to supply the boiler, and of heating the water which was to keep the condenser cool. In the one case heat was wasted, and in the other perfect condensation was impeded; and, therefore, modern engineers have given it a different position, and the form of the condenser itself has been greatly altered.

When the steam-engine had been perfected by the ingenuity and perseverance of the great Watt, its subjugation to the purposes of locomotion soon suggested itself to clever and enterprising men. Thus we find that, in 1804, Trevithick constructed and patented the first locomotive engine. In its form [illegible] was ch-

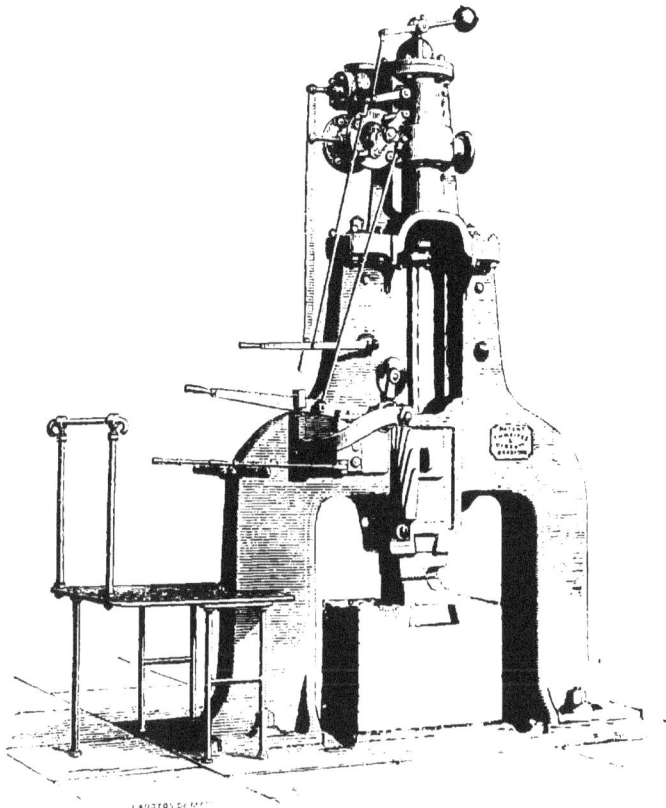

LANSTON CO M

distance, the driving wheels are sometimes made of very considerable size: those of the "Liverpool" were 8 feet in diameter; those of the Caledonian Railway Company's locomotive in the present Exhibition are still larger. When the crank is not truly balanced, the smaller the wheels the greater the tendency to jump at high velocities. There are many locomotives to which we shall direct attention; but for the present, as in other cases, we shall notice merely a number sufficient to illustrate the most important principles connected with them.

Sir W. Armstrong's locomotive is of great size: without the tender it weighs, when the boiler is charged, about 30 tons. The cylinders are 15½ inches in diameter, and the stroke is 22 inches. The six wheels are coupled, and there is a donkey-engine to supply the boiler with water when the engine is at rest; but the pumps may be worked by hand if the steam is not up. The "Manchester," a coal-burning engine, by Sharp, Stewart, and Co., is another powerful engine. When the boiler is charged it weighs 23 tons, but the weight is well distributed on the wheels. Pumps are not used, the boilers being fed by Giffard's injectors, and hence a donkey-engine is not required. It is provided with an oscillating solid door, which may be tilted so as to allow the clinkers to be pushed out and got rid of when the engine is at full speed, no stoppage being required. The fire-box contains 185 square feet of heating surface from the furnace, and there are about 1,200 tubes in the boiler. The driver and stoker are covered in from the weather, but so as not to prevent them from having easy access to every part of the machinery. American engines are never without this useful addition; and it seems an unnecessary cruelty to expose men whose duties are so important and laborious to rain, snow, and wind, from which they may be so easily protected without diminishing their efficiency.

In comparing foreign locomotives with those made in this country, the superior finish of the latter is sufficiently obvious. Some of the former are indeed extremely rude in appearance; thus the "Garigliano," from Pietrarsa Royal Works at Portici. Yet it must be viewed with pleasure, as it indicates the beginning of progress in a part of Italy which, under the late dynasty, was behind almost all other countries. It appears, moreover, that it was constructed in circumstances by no means favourable to accuracy or high finish, being, it is said, made during the late revolution. Austria has sent two locomotives, which,

though not very splendid in appearance, have been carefully put together, and exhibit features that are well worthy of being noticed; both were made in the workshops of the State Railway Company, and under the superintendence of the director of the establishment. In both of them cast steel is freely used in the cranks and other important parts, which allows them to be extremely light—a point very important for several reasons. One of them, the "Duplex," intended for very high velocities, has four cylinders, two at each side; those at the same side being connected with the same crank, but in such a way that their mechanical effects are always in exactly opposite phases. This arrangement is considered to render the action so uniform, that jumping would not occur even with small wheels; and with a speed of eighty-four miles an hour the motion was perfectly smooth and safe. The "Steyerdorf" is intended for steep gradients and very sharp curves. It is said to have drawn upwards of 200 tons up an incline of one in forty, and along a curve of 400 feet radius, in both cases with a speed of ten miles an hour. Great adhesive power is given by the coupling of its ten wheels; the couplings are so arranged that they become longer on the outside, and shorter in the inside of a curve; and the axles are allowed a play in the axle-boxes, that everything adjusting itself to circumstances, all kinds of strain may be avoided. Both these engines have run for three months; and it is stated that they have been sent to the Exhibition, not as specimens of finished workmanship, but as illustrations of what are believed to be useful principles not generally known; and hence our engineers would do well to examine them carefully; some hints may be occasionally furnished to them by those even who are less skilful than themselves.

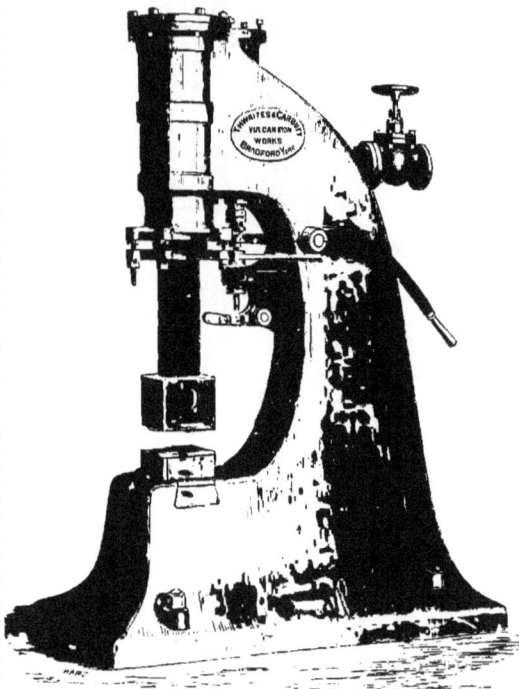

STEAM HAMMER. MESSRS. THWAITES AND CARBUTT.

MARINE ENGINES.

ALTHOUGH the adaptation of steam to navigation is practically of recent date, it is, in reality, one of the oldest applications of steam as a moving power. So early as 1543, Blasco de Garay impelled a boat at Barcelona solely by a large kettle of boiling water; but the way in which this effect was produced can now only be conjectured. Savary, Papin, and others proposed to propel vessels by steam; and in 1736 Jonathan Hulls drove a paddle-wheel, which was placed at the stern of a boat, by two atmospheric engines; steam navigation, therefore, is, in some respects, older than the steam-engine itself. But when Watt brought the steam-engine to perfection, the idea assumed a more thoroughly practical form; and in 1788 William Symington, a Scotch engineer, ran a boat on the Clyde Canal by steam, with a speed of seven miles an hour. Fulton, an American, having had an opportunity of carefully and fully examining one of Symington's boats, introduced the principle into America as his own invention, and in 1807 made his first trip by steam on the Hudson. Stephens immediately afterwards made a sea voyage by steam from the Hudson to Delaware, but his success did not encourage others; and the experiment was not repeated until long after. Thirty years elapsed before it was considered possible to cross the ocean by steam. Though steam continued to be used on the American rivers, and various improvements were made, it was totally neglected in this country. The first river steamer, which ran on the Clyde, did not appear until 1812, nor

When steam was applied to the purposes of navigation, the "beam," which in the engines of Newcomen and Watt was placed above, was greatly modified, to meet the altered circumstances, being changed by Napier into what are called "side-levers." These, in reality, are two smaller beams, placed low down, one at each side of the cylinder, and they are connected so as to produce the effect of but one. When it was necessary to elevate the crank-axle on account of the position of the paddles, this arrangement answered extremely well; but when a screw propeller is employed, the crank-axle must be lowered; and if the engines put it in motion, as is now invariably the case, without the multiplying effect of a wheel and pinion, &c., their velocity must be much greater than formerly. These considerations have caused a serious modification of the marine engine, but it has been changed still more by the extraordinary efforts made to diminish the space it occupies—a matter of great moment, both as giving more

LUSTRING MACHINE, FOR GIVING A GLOSS TO DYED SILK. MESSRS. LEVINSTEIN AND CO., MILAN. PRIZE MEDAL.

the first sea-boat until 1815; and not until one hundred years after Hulls had established the possibility of applying steam to navigation, and fifty years after Symington's experiments, was the Great Western, the first steamer expressly built for crossing the Atlantic, even commenced—so slow is the march of improvement at certain periods in the history of mankind. The use of paddle-wheels was at first universal, but they have been almost superseded by propellers, particularly in ships of war; and there can be no doubt that, after a time, paddles will be seen no more. In 1845, experiments made with the screw propeller were so successful, that the Admiralty ordered it to be fitted to several ships of war. These were at first intended only for harbour service; but a speed so unexpectedly great was attained by them, that the screw propeller was applied to general purposes. In 1845, only from 6½ to 7½ knots an hour were obtained with it; but this velocity has long since been far exceeded. Almost all the marine engines now exhibited have been made for screw propellers.

room in the vessel, and as increasing the strength of the engine itself. Various methods have been adopted to attain this object. The beam has in every case been got rid of by the use of direct action engines, and other means have been used which we shall mention and illustrate. Thus the piston and connecting-rods are made to occupy the space of only one of them, by using two piston-rods with each cylinder, and causing the connecting-rod to play between them. Again, the piston-rod is sometimes enlarged and made hollow, so that the connecting-rod which is attached to the middle of its interior may play freely, in accordance with the motion of the crank. Guides are dispensed with, as the stuffing boxes through which the hollow piston, termed a "trunk," passes, during the performance of its reciprocating motion, answer instead of them. It is clear that, when a trunk is used, the piston is in reality annular. Again, the cylinders are sometimes inverted, so that the engine used with paddles is, as it were, turned upside down, to accord with the reversed position of the crank-

29

VIEW IN THE WESTERN ANNEXE.   MACHINERY IN MOTION.

axle, when a propeller is employed. And finally, the connecting-rod is dispensed with by using oscillating engines, the piston-rods of which act directly on the cranks; and even one of the cranks may be rendered unnecessary by placing one cylinder at each side of the crank-axle, and causing both to make a certain angle with the horizon, so that the rods may work on the same crank-pin, and in such a way that the phases of their mechanical efficacy may always be in opposite states. Each of these arrangements has its advantages and disadvantages. Thus, when trunk-engines are used, the heat is wasted by the cold air rushing into the trunk, and the great diameter of the trunk, as compared with the ordinary.piston-rod, must seriously increase the friction, even with all the improvements that have been introduced; and since the packing boxes serve as guides, their wear must be very unequal. Inverted cylinders raise the centre of gravity to a great height, which is unfavourable to the steadiness of the vessel. When oscillating engines are used, large masses of matter are not only to be kept in motion, but the direction of their motion must be constantly changed, which, besides other inconveniences, cannot but absorb a large quantity of power. We shall direct the reader's attention to the most interesting examples of these various modifications of the steam-engine, as exemplified in the present Exhibition.

Maudslay and Field's horizontal marine propeller engines have been built for the "Valiant," an iron-plated ship. They are, together, of 800 horse-power. The steam is used expansively, and can be cut off at any part of the stroke. Double-ported slide valves are employed; two valves being attached to each cylinder, the ports are smaller, and less traverse is required. The cylinders, which are steam-cased, are 82 inches in diameter, and the stroke is 4 feet. Each piston has two rods, and the connecting-rod works between them. The two nuts of each gland of the cylinder cover are screwed up at the same time by an ingenious contrivance, which is easily accessible and free from danger to the engineer, even when the engines are in motion. The condenser is of the common kind; but the valves of the air-pumps are arranged in a somewhat novel and very convenient way. These engines are considered capable of making sixty strokes a minute. The same manufacturers exhibit one of the connecting-rods and crossheads belonging to engines which are to be placed in the "Prince Consort," and which, together, are of 1,350 horse-power. The connecting-rod, including the brasses, weighs about four tons; and the cross-head is of proportionate size. They also exhibit some very beautiful models, which are kept in motion by bands that are not at once perceived, and therefore they seem to be moved by steam.

Penn and Sons' horizontal marine trunk engines have been built for the Spanish Government, and are exhibited by permission. They are, together, of 600 horse-power; the cylinders are 78 inches in diameter, and the stroke is 3 feet 6 inches. The observer cannot fail to admire the beautiful finish of these engines. The same firm exhibit the crank-axle and one of the cylinders intended for the Achilles. The cylinder, a single casting, weighs about 18 tons; it is bored to an internal diameter of 112 inches, and a stroke of 4 feet. The weight of the axle, in its present finished state, and without counterpoises to the cranks, or any other adjuncts, is 18 tons 9 cwt.; in its rough state it was, of course, very much heavier; and it affords an excellent example of the enormous masses which the perfection and power of modern machinery enables the manufacturer to forge and finish with ease. The cylinder is a striking illustration of the great tendency of modern engineers to shorten the stroke in marine engines; cylinders were formerly very different in their proportions.

Rennie and Sons' horizontal marine propeller engines are intended for the "Reindeer," and they are of 200 horse-power. The arrangement of the parts is different from that of the trunk engine just examined—a cylinder and air-pump being placed at each side, which distributes the weight more uniformly; the crank of one engine drives the air-pump of the other; trunk air-pumps are used, and the feed and bilge-pumps are driven by the cross-heads of the air-pumps. The steam is used expansively, and the arrangement of the link motion, &c., is very convenient.

Tod and M'Gregor's inverted cylinder engines are of 60 horsepower. The diameter of the cylinders is 30 inches, and the length of the stroke is 1 foot 10 inches. Surface condensation is used; water is driven through the tubes of the condenser, the steam being condensed on their surfaces; and the air and feed-pumps are moved horizontally by concentrics on the crank-axle. The steam is worked expansively, and may be cut off at from 8 to 18 inches of the stroke. These engines are very compact, and occupy but small space, except, perhaps, as to height. They are expected to make about 170 revolutions in a minute. The centre of gravity is raised considerably by the great height at which the cylinders are placed ; but then the other arrangements tend to give it a very low position.

We have an opportunity of comparing a large French marine engine with those of British manufacture. The marine engines (1,195), intended for a screw-propeller, were made at the Forges et Chantiers de la Méditerranée, Marseilles, and are of 400 horse-power. The diameter of the cylinders is near 60 inches, and the stroke is 2 feet 10 inches. Not only do the connecting-rods work between the double piston-rods, but, for still greater economisation of space, they move also within the condensers, which act as guides for the cross-heads—an arrangement which seems likewise to secure great strength. The eccentrics are on a separate axle, being driven from the crank-axle by strong wheel-work. This arrangement has been considered convenient on account of the position of the valves, which are on the upper parts of the cylinders, and from the ease with which the starting, reversing, &c., is effected; and the eccentrics being smaller than if they were placed on the crank-axle, the amount of friction is diminished. The use of a separate axle is, however, of doubtful advantage. These engines may be considered a favourable specimen of foreign workmanship. A screw-propeller is attached, and the whole is put in motion, on the present occasion, by a small subsidiary engine. This enables the observer to examine the mode in which the large engines act, without steam being turned on them; but it must be admitted that the small engine seems to many, particularly without some degree of attention, to be meant as a help to the larger ones, and thus some confusion of ideas is produced.

LEVINSTEIN'S LUSTRING MACHINE.

On page 216 will be found an illustration of a very ingenious machine, with its attendant, whose face and figure are doubtless familiar to visitors to the Italian Court. The inventors of this machine have discovered and applied, by means of it, quite a new method of lustring silk. The steam being thrown directly upon it, a perfect lustre and a sensible extension of the silk are secured ; while, by the old system, in which the steam was introduced within the cylinders, not only was the lustre imperfect, but the original length of the silk was not in the smallest degree increased. This machine, so valuable on account of its simplicity, is capable of lustring 200 kilogrammes of sewing silk, and 130 of organzine and tramo daily. To all who feel an interest in the matter, this machine presents a very interesting subject for study. In the Italian Silk Department are to be seen silk of every colour and quality, the results of the application of the new invention. During the whole Exhibition the machine was to be seen at work during several days in the week. It has deservedly obtained the distinction of a Prize Medal.

HARRISON'S COTTON MACHINERY.

A VERY excellent series of machines for "winding, warping, sizing, and weaving cotton and linens," is exhibited by Messrs. Harrison and Sons, of Blackburn, Lancashire. An attentive study of the action of the several machines shown by this firm will explain to the uninitiated how cotton cloth is produced from the raw material. Our illustrations give a general view of the machines as they stand side by side in the Western Annexe; but perhaps the following verbal description may not be uninteresting:—

THE WINDING MACHINE (FIRST PROCESS).—This Machine is for winding yarn from the cop on to spools or bobbins ("warpers' bobbins"), for the purpose of warping or beaming by the succeeding process. Its movements are simple but interesting. They unwind the threads from the cop or spool, and direct them through minute interstices in what are termed "feathered guides," and through brushes (to intercept dirt and thick parts of each thread) on to the larger or 'warper's' bobbin, preventing carelessness on the part of the winder, and conducing to the comfort of the weaver and to the value of the cloth. It will be seen that the machine fills the bobbins in a uniformly regular manner, and that it has an arrangement on one side for winding cotton or linen yarn from "throstle bobbins" on to warpers' bobbins. It can be made of any number of spindles. The spindle rails are so arranged that the spindles can always be adjusted on a level with each other, after the displacement to which they are subjected by the operative in putting on the bobbins. The motion for shaping the bobbin is a very simple eccentric or "heart," by means of which the bobbin can be filled up in any form. Machines of the above description can be made for 450 or 500 spindles.

THE WARPING MACHINE (SECOND PROCESS) to wind the yarn from the warpers' bobbins on to beams for the sizing or dressing machine. This machine is made on an entirely new principle; the rollers run on an improved bearing, thereby greatly diminishing the tension on the yarn, and in a very great measure obviating breakages, the production being increased in the same ratio as the breakages are lessened. It is also supplied with a letting-back motion, whereby, when a thread is broken, the motion of the beam or roller is reversed, and by the aid of a simple mechanical arrangement the thread may easily be found and re-united. There is also a self-acting measuring and stopping motion, by means of which the machine is immediately stopped when the required length of yarn is wound on the beam. The drum or cylinder on which the beam revolves is made in such a manner that it may be expanded or contracted according to the width of beam required to be used. Among other improved appliances is an expanding and contracting comb. This improved machine is capable of working Surat and other low cottons, more delicate yarns, and yarns of lower qualities, than machines of the old principle, and will in this respect effect a considerable saving. It is also very applicable to silk.

THE SIZING MACHINE (THIRD PROCESS) commonly called "Slasher," for sizing or dressing, and afterwards drying the warp preparatory to being woven. In this machine the yarn is brought from the warpers' beams through boiling size, and over drying cylinders, after which it is wound on the weavers' beam. The yarn placed on the warper's beams by the last mentioned process is adjusted on a creel or stand. This stand can be made wider or narrower by adjusting screws, and the flanges can be so adjusted thereby that they can always be kept in a line with each other. The flanges are of tinned iron, light, but strong. They are convex on the inner side, to admit of the yarn coming off freely from the beam. The yarn passes through the boiling size contained in a box. This is lined with copper, to prevent oxidation, and to preserve the body of the box. The rollers in the size-box are hooped at the ends with brass, which run upon brass pulleys, rendering the motion smooth, and preventing the roller-ends from injury by the size. The size roller is of heavy copper, without a seam, being cast solid, and then bored out and expanded on a mandril to the required diameter. These rollers being made heavy, i.e., of good thickness, do not require renewal so often as rollers of less weight and thickness, and, being heavy, perform the process of squeezing much better. By being made without seam, the acid in the size does not affect any brazed part, as is common in seamed or brazed rollers. The use of the heald and reed is dispensed with, thus facilitating the management of the machine, and causing a saving of between 40 and 50 per cent. in the cost of labour. It is an arrangement for working the machine by friction, and a side-shaft motion, for preventing any tension being put upon the yarn whilst in a wet state. The elasticity is thus retained, and breakages in weaving almost altogether prevented, causing considerable increase in the production. By these arrangements coarse and fine yarns can be sized with equal facility, as also yarns of medium and low qualities. There are syphon boxes,

for the purpose of condensing the steam as it comes from the drying cylinders; or they can be connected with the size-box by means of steam-pipes, and the exhaust steam from the cylinders introduced into the size box for the purpose of boiling the size. In this manner no steam is wasted. There is also a patent Self-acting Pressure Diminishing Apparatus, perfectly certain in its action, to regulate the pressure of the steam, previous to its passing into the drying cylinders, and only admitting a sufficient quantity of steam for drying purposes. When the machine is stopped no steam is allowed to pass; thus at no time, whether at work or otherwise, is the steam wasted. There is an arrangement for letting out any water that may accumulate in the cylinders. The cylinders themselves are made on an improved principle, with an aperture or man-hole in the end of each, covered by movable plates, which can easily be removed, to allow the cylinders to be cleaned out or repaired, and can with equal facility be replaced. The joints of these plates are perfectly steam-tight, and the manner of their application rather adds to than detracts from the strength of the cylinders. The machine gives notice, by ringing a bell, when any desired length of yarn or "cut" is finished, and it at the same time marks it by a self-acting movement. There is an expanding comb, for guiding the threads on to the beam for the succeeding process of weaving by the power-loom; and this apparatus will likewise fill up the beam above the diameter of the flanges, by contracting the threads when level with the beam flanges, and thus beams do not require filling so often as ordinarily. Another arrangement of very great importance is that by means of which, simultaneously with the stoppage of the machine at any time, the steam is shut off from the cylinders. Perhaps in no other machine used in the cotton manufacture have there been so great advances in improvements as in the sizing machine. In 1851 there was a machine of this kind exhibited, which supplied one hundred and twenty looms, and required an attendant operative, whose wages were about £3 per week. That machine displaced six of the kind of machines previously in use, and as many attendants, whose united wages were about £18 per week, or £900 per year. But the production of the machine exhibited in the present Exhibition is about 100,000 yards of warp per week, or *sufficient to supply at least three hundred looms*; and this needs an operative who, being little more than a common labouring man, requires *only about twenty-six shillings per week wages*. Thus the production which previous to 1851 would have cost £18 *per week*, or £900 *per year*, in *wages*, and which was effected in 1851 for £3 *per week*, or £150 *per year*, is now done *for less than fourteen shillings a week*, or £35 *per year*; and as the machine does so much more work, it follows that fewer machines are needed, consequently *space and power are economised as well as wages*. Moreover, the machine is now worked with ease and safety, which could not be done in 1851. The machine can be made to dress warps suitable for any width of cloth.

WEAVING (FOURTH PROCESS).—Power-loom for weaving calicoes, shirtings, and printing cloths, also cambrics, jaconets, &c., with self-acting temple to keep the cloth stretched to its full width whilst being woven. Self-acting positive taking-up motion for receiving or rolling up the cloth. The taking-up roller in this loom is composed of sheet-iron covered with composition. This roller always presents a perfectly level surface to the cloth, being on this account much superior to the ordinary wooden roller covered with emery, the disadvantage of which is that it changes with the temperature—in damp weather becoming swollen, and in dry weather warped or crooked, causing great irregularity in the cloth. The improved roller always remains at one diameter. The picking tappets are provided with teeth on their inner surfaces, so that when bolted together they cannot break loose. There is an arrangement by which the driving-wheels are kept in proper gear, and which prevents damage to the yarn and machinery. This loom is also supplied with the weft-stopping motion, causing an instantaneous stoppage of the loom when the weft or shoot breaks or is absent; also with metallic picking motion for propelling the shuttle, the advantages of which are greater durability and precision. It is likewise supplied with a treading motion, by means of which a saving

quick speeds are not recommended for general use. The loom can also be arranged to weave twilled and fancy cloths.

The same exhibitors also show a power-loom for weaving heavy domestics, twilled goods, and strong drills and tweeds. This loom is on the fast reed principle. It combines all the advantages of the first-mentioned loom, together with modifications and arrangements necessary for weaving strong goods. It has a cast-iron taking-up roller, fluted and chased, and a patent break; also an improved appliance for preventing strain on the warp threads when the weft is being "beaten up." Messrs. Harrison are makers of looms on the principle of Mr. W. E. Taylor.

POWER-LOOM TO WEAVE LINENS.—This loom comprises many important improvements. It is also supplied with self-acting positive letting-off motion, which delivers the warp as required by the taking-up motion for the cloth, which motion is also positive. These two motions work in concert, and with such precision that the warp is delivered from the yarn beam with the same regularity as on the loom is almost empty as when it is full. The taking-up roller of this loom is covered with patent surfacing instead of emery. It is also supplied with the weft-stopping motion, and other important appliances. In all the above looms the cranks are made of one piece of iron, and bent by graduated pressure. The fibre of the iron by this process remains undisturbed, and renders the crank much stronger than when welded in the usual manner. The bend of the crank, which has heretofore been the weakest part, is now as strong as any other part of it. The yarns woven in this loom are spun by Messrs. Johnston and Carlisle, of Belfast.

In addition to the previous machines, J. Harrison and Sons are makers of knitting machines on an improved principle, for knitting heads or heddles by power, by means of which a superior quality of heald is produced, with none of the irregularity which occurs in hand-made healds—another important advantage in this a fine being a saving of 50 per cent. in the cost of products of this, for plaiting and measuring machines by power, for measuring the cloth, and laying it in folds, after it comes from the loom, and previous to being put in bales or bundles; cloth presses to press the cloth after it has been put into bundles; drum winding machines, to wind a portion or two of yarns from the hank on to the warpers' beams or warpers' machines, specially adapted for linen yarns with weft motion and presser; dressing machines; and various kinds of other machinery necessary for the production of cotton, linen, silk, and worsted goods.

AERO-HYDROSTATICAL HOISTING APPARATUS

IN the Western Annexe are to be seen two models, illustrating an ingenious apparatus for hoisting and lowering heavy weights, such as railway trains, from one level to another. The apparatus is termed an Aëro-hydrostatical Balance. The inventor states that the model has only lately been placed in the building; therefore the jurors could make no mention of it in their report. The principle of the apparatus is based upon the displacement of water and of air, two columns of air, in communication with each other by a tube, and set in motion by a surplus weight, which consists, generally, of a volume of water. When ponderous bodies are to be alternately and intermittently raised and lowered to or from great or small vertical heights, such as, for instance, a whole railway train, there needs but a surplus weight of from three to ten per cent. (according to the desired speed) of the whole weight to be hoisted or lowered, to enable that same weight to ascend or descend, whatever may be the space of time between each train.

The surplus weight necessary to lower the balance may, in most cases, be procured from an approximate or distant rivulet or stream, made to accumulate its water in a reservoir; no matter whether it be at a much lower level than the ground on which the apparatus stands.

The models represent a bridge, upon which stands a railway train,

of upwards of 25 per cent. in wear and tear of "healds" or "heddles" is effected, and which conserves in a superior degree the nap or cover of the cloth. This loom is on the loose reed principle, and capable of being worked at a speed of about 300 "picks" per minute; but these to be raised to a height of 115 feet in less than fifteen minutes, and is made to work by means of a tube 100 feet in length, leading from an air-holder.

In full size it would consist of two cylindrical air chambers or holders, eleven yards in diameter, having together a surface of 180 square yards, upon which rests a bridge bearing a train which, with the weight of the immersed air-holders, weigh 550 tons. A three-feet diameter tube, provided with a stop-cock or valve, puts them in communication with a *main acting chamber* or motor of an equal surface, 180 square yards, on the top of which is fixed a tank, made to contain sufficient water to equilibrate the 550 tons weight of the train. This acting chamber may be placed anywhere, at any distance where water can be had, and stands between two reservoirs, easily formed one above the other, from which water is procured for adding to the different loads of the train a surplus weight which enables them to be hoisted or lowered.

The inventor has also designed an aëro-hydrostatical apparatus, for instantly raising out of water any floating dock containing ships of any size to be repaired; it will practically be effective, simple, handy, and cheap, because no foundation or masonry of any kind will be required to erect it. Being movable, and floating on air, it can be towed anywhere in a dock, river, or the open sea. The inventor has entered into a contract with some first-rate engine and iron bridge builders in France for the construction of his apparatus, and also wishes to find an opportunity to apply it in England, being fully satisfied that it may render valuable services.

With respect to the steam-engines in the present Exhibition as compared with those of 1851, it may be observed—say the jurors in their report of Class 8—that "they show an increased employment of high pressure, great expansion, and super-heating, an increased use of surface condensation (generally effected by means of a great number of small horizontal tubes), a tendency towards simplicity in the framing and main moving parts, a general abandonment of devices that are more curious than useful, and a higher perfection of workmanship and finish; all of which improvements combine to produce greater economy of fuel, power, and repairs.

"Setting aside merit of a kind that does not require special explanation, such as simplicity, good workmanship, practical success, &c., the following remarks may be made as to those engines which present new and unusual features:—

"When the machinery of the present Exhibition is compared with that of 1851, it is found to be marked less by originality of invention, or the introduction of new principles, than by improvement in details, workmanship, and material; and that with respect to material in particular, the most striking improvements are those which consist in the greatly extended use of steel, and of iron approaching to steel in its properties."

With these remarks all practical men will coincide; it being doubtless a fact, that while we have made vast advances in machinery, these advances have all been in the right direction—the obtaining an increase of power with an increase of simplicity of manufacture. Instead of a multiplicity of wheels, and a confused assemblage of cranks, condensers, &c., as in the original steam-engine, we have now engines which appear to consist simply of piston, driving-wheel, and governor; but which, in fact, are far more powerful, and infinitely more useful, than their progenitors. This is also observable in the cotton machinery, of which Messrs. Harrison make so excellent a show.

Although the greater portion of the machinery is to be found in the Western Annexe, the Eastern Annexe is not deficient of similar attractions. At the very threshold may be seen a model to which the frequent accounts we read of terrible accidents in coal mines give far more than a passing interest. The model represents the mode of ventilation actually adopted in Hetton Colliery, and is exhibited by Messrs. Wood and Dalglish. It is very compact and easily under-

stood, and shows not only the mode of ventilation, but also the manner in which the coal is brought from the face of the workings. As Hetton Colliery has fortunately been seldom visited by accident,

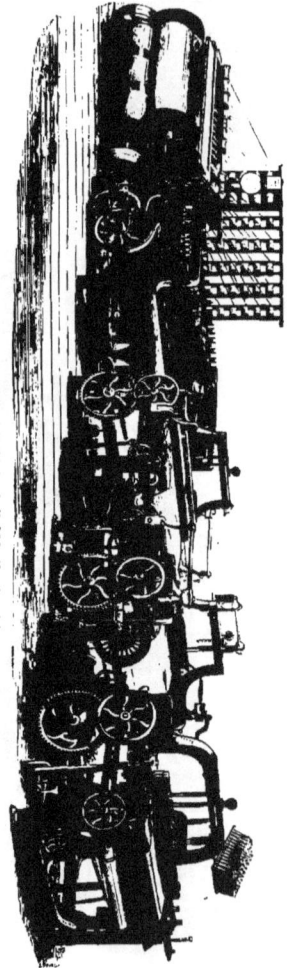

COTTON MACHINERY, J. HARRISON AND SONS.

it is but fair to believe that the comparative immunity it enjoys may, by the employment of the same skilful means, be extended to other collieries.

BOBBINS. MESSRS. DIXON AND SONS, LEEDS.

insufficient quantum of space awarded by the Commissioners to this influential firm, Mr. Thomas Ogden Dixon has managed remarkably well.

It is these illustrations of the manufacturing processes made use of in the northern division of this island that are so interesting and novel to us southerners, few of whom ever have the chance of seeing a cotton or worsted mill. Commending, therefore, this collection to our readers' attention, we may remark that Messrs. Dixon and Sons supply the principal mills in this country, France, Belgium, &c., through their resident agents, with the specialities for which they deservedly enjoy so high a reputation. We understand that Mr. T. O. Dixon is a member of the Society of Arts, and is proposed as a member of the Inventors' Society.

Messrs. Dixon are also the inventors of a series of improved knobs fastening. Messrs. Dixon are also patentees of an excellent and economic gas-burner, which has been somewhat extensively used in Yorkshire and Lancashire, and really deserves very wide publicity. Its claims to notice are thus stated by the manager of the Skipton Gas Works :—"Its economy ; its durability ; the iron burner requiring repeated change, the parent one being as good the second season as the first ; its incorrosive property, never stopping up from that cause like the ordinary burner. The small amount of heat evolved greatly diminishes the breakage of glass, and its anti-pressure property more completely secures the consumption of the gas, thus preventing to a large extent the deposition of soot on the surface of the glass." The purity of light produced by this burner, and the higher illuminating power of the gas passing through it, are great recommendations to its extensive employment for public and private lights.

MRS. DANIEL JONES'S MINIATURE PRINTING PRESS AND TYPES.

AMONG the vast efforts and many successful displays of taste, skill, and beautiful adaptations of industry and refinement which this great Exhibition presents there is one which, in a most singularly unaffected and perfect manner, appears to carry out and concentrate the early purposes of the departed and greatly regretted originator of the scheme for bringing together from all climes and peoples their intelligence and power in combination.

In the Processes Court, No. 1,691, Class 7 b, we find an undertaking for educational and devotional purposes, which, though occupying a space of only four feet square, is so managed as to be complete in itself.

Mrs. Daniel Jones announces in the "Illustrated Catalogue" a "Miniature Albion Printing Press," professing to be an appeal chiefly to ladies to turn their attention to a private study to produce gems of thought, in elegancies of well-assorted type, and clever arrangement, so as to relieve the fingers from the ornamental intricate worsted work and crochet labyrinthical pattern, and exert the same patience and perseverance in leisure hours to the cultivation of private circulation of new ideas, which would soon grow into a pleasure in the doing, and a necessity for fireside entertainment.

Mrs. Daniel Jones gives us head, hand, and heart work, and presents to us examples of what can be done by individual enterprise, in octavo pages, consisting of specimens of her printing, in about forty-six different languages, each in their national character. The Indian pages are especially well done, and interesting as a literary curiosity. The English page gives the key to the whole, and presents a prayer for universal peace, which, if accepted by all nations, would dull the edge of war, and would fully carry out the ideas of the late Prince Consort, and accord with the motto work exhibited about the building from his dictation.

This task has been great, but the excellent style of each printed page gives a stamp to the genius of the press; and the singular stillness and plain dealing, without any needless attempt to produce effect, keeps up our interest, and the attention is not drawn aside from the one desired object—universal peace.

MINIATURE ALBION PRINTING PRESS. MRS. DANIEL JONES.

In speaking of the merits of this undertaking as a whole, we see a useful, neat, powerful printing press, suited to the library, the merchant's office, the schoolmaster, and the boudoir of the lady, whose ingenuity and reflective habits would be greatly assisted could she, in her leisure hours, be enabled to print many beautiful passing thoughts, which otherwise float away, and have no means of being retained in the private manner which her judgment and sympathies would suggest.

However, as it is, that peace and war are yet in disputation around us, we must wait events, and in the meantime lend our assistance to point to efforts which, in our opinion, are most likely to be a good way towards a good end :

"Arms yield to arts, the
    sword unto the tongue,
Then give the glorie to
    the learned throng."

This ancient couplet, it is to be hoped, will be fully carried out in the great effort to bring assembled nations under one roof for industrial purposes.

Yet, when we see the triumph of the gigantic powers of the Armstrong gun over the iron sheets, and the intense interest that warlike inventions absorb from millions of visitors, we turn with doubt to the fairylike forms of the beautiful designs in fragile glass textures, standing side by side. They look to us as so many would-be pleaders for peace.

Having given this general description of this miniature printing press, we advise inspection, and heartily wish the originator the success which, in offering this powerful prayer in so many languages, she earnestly desires, and certainly appears fully to deserve.

Our illustration gives a good notion of the general appearance of Mrs. Jones's Miniature Printing Press. It is accompanied by cases of types, furniture (the pieces of wood necessary to enclose the page of metal types within the iron border or frame, called the chase), and all the necessary adjuncts of a small printing office. There is a well-known anecdote of a clergyman who, being unable to bear the expense of printing a volume of sermons, purchased types and a press, turned printer himself, and produced the book a page at a time. With Mrs. Daniel Jones's press, such a feat is rendered easy to all who are anxious to see their names in print; and that, too, at a very cheap rate. We understand that the exhibitor undertakes to give instruction to ladies in the mysteries of 'he compositor's and pressman's art.

MESSRS. BROWN-WESTHEAD'S POTTERY.

IN the South Court will be found, among a variety of works in parian, china, earthenware, and other fictile materials, the originals of executed in parian; and the last, also in parian, is the " Kneeling Venus," from the antique. It is about two feet in height, and is perfect in all that renders parian statuettes so valuable and so ornamental—namely, smoothness of surface, equality of shrinkage, and grace of outline. The same exhibitors also show busts of the Queen after Durham ; the Prince Consort, after Marochetti, and the

BACCHANTE VASE.

BUST OF APOLLO.

the engravings here introduced. The first figure represents a vase in china, copied from a Bacchante vase in the British Museum ; its height is a little over three feet, and in point of execution does great credit to the firm of Messrs. Brown-Westhead, Moore, and Co. of world-known " Venus and Cupid " of Gibson. These figures stand in their case amidst exquisite dinner, tea, dessert, and toilet services in china, earthenware, &c. The show made by this firm may be pronounced choice, well selected, and entirely successful. The orna-

MICHAEL ANGELO'S CUPID.

THE KNEELING (OR CROUCHING) VENUS.

Hanley, Staffordshire, the exhibitors. The second figure is in parian, and represents the "Apollo" from the original life-sized bust. The third is the Michael Angelo "Cupid," three feet in height, admirably mentation of ceramic ware is, of course, important ; but the forms to which such ornamentation is applied must, after all, be the grand distinction between the beautiful and the commonplace.

Mosaic Wall Pictures,

FOR DECORATING THE BUILDINGS ERECTED FOR INTERNATIONAL EXHIBITIONS.

It is proposed to raise sufficient funds to execute two large mosaic pictures, 23 feet high by 13 feet wide, as experiments for decorating the panels of the outside walls of the permanent picture galleries for International Exhibitions, in Cromwell Road, South Kensington. The mosaics will be made of pottery, in geometric forms, by the pressure of dry powder. Various experiments in laying the mosaics have been made by Messrs. Minton (Stoke-upon-Trent), with mosaics of their own manufacture, and by Messrs. W. B. Simpson and Sons, of West Strand, with mosaics manufactured by Messrs. Maw, whose works in terra cotta and mosaics we have already noticed. The experiments are very promising, and they prove that mosaic pictures may be as easily worked and used in England as in ancient Greece and Rome, or Mediæval Italy. They will be as imperishable as the hardest and most perfect terra cottas. They will create a new branch of industry, which may be worked in any locality, and probably by women as well as men. The designs will illustrate Industry, Science, and Art. Some cartoons have been already prepared by Mr. Cope, R.A., Mr. J. C. Hook, R.A., Mr. Godfrey Sykes, and Mr. Townroe; two of these

have been executed in mosaics, and placed in recesses of the wall in the Cromwell Road.

The ornamental borders will be designed, and the mosaics worked out, under the superintendence of Mr. Godfrey Sykes and his assistants. When all the necessary arrangements have been made after the close of the Exhibition of 1862, for filling the others, designs for other subjects will be sought from the artists named below.

The following are the principal subjects which, at present, it is proposed should be executed, and the artists named are those who have already kindly consented to undertake to make designs for them, when the proper period arrives :—

I.—SUBJECTS ILLUSTRATING THE PRODUCTION OF RAW MATERIALS.—1. Agriculture, Holman Hunt ; 2. Chemistry, W. Cave Thomas ; 3. Fishing, J. C. Hook, R.A.; 4. Hunting, Frederick Leighton ; 5. Metallurgy, Eyre Crowe; 6. Mining, F. Barwell ; 7. Planting, &c., Michael Mulready; 8. Quarrying, G. F. Watts; 9. Sheep Shearing, C. W. Cope, R.A.; 10. Vintage, F. R. Pickersgill, R.A.

II.—SUBJECTS ILLUSTRATING MACHINERY.—1. Astronomy, S. Hart, R.A. ; 2. Engineering; 3. Horology ; 4. Mechanics; 5. Navigation, J. E. Millais, A.R.A. ; 6. Railways, R. Townroe.

THE DEATH OF MARMION.

PIECES FROM THE DESSERT SERVICE.   SIR JAMES DUKE AND NEPHEWS.

III.—SUBJECTS ILLUSTRATING MANUFACTURES AND HAND LABOUR.—1. Bricklaying, D. Maclise, R.A.; 2. Carpentry, R. Burchett; 3. China Painting, H. A. Bowler; 4. Glass Blowing; 5. Iron Forging, Godfrey Sykes; 6. Jewellery, D. G. Rossetti; 7. Lace Making, R. Redgrave, R.A.; 8. Metal Casting, A. Elmore, R.A.; 9. Printing, R. Redgrave, R.A.; 10. Straw Plaiting, C. W. Cope, R.A.; 11. Weaving, Octavius Hudson; 12. Pottery, Godfrey Sykes.

IV.—SUBJECTS ILLUSTRATING FINE ARTS.—1. Architecture, W. Mulready, R.A.; 2. Painting, W. Mulready, R.A.; 3. Sculpture, W. Mulready, R.A.; 4. Music, J. C. Horsley, A.R.A.

The designs before they are executed will be approved by a committee of the artists; the Marquess of Salisbury, K.G., Mr. Layard, M.P., and Mr. Cole, C.B., act as a committee of management for carrying out the experiments.

Pottery.—III.

HAVING already referred to the wonderful show of porcelain and ceramic ware in the International Exhibition, we now introduce a few more illustrations. The pictures here introduced are taken from objects exhibited by Sir James Duke and Nephews, of the Hill Pottery, Burslem, Staffordshire; from the case of Messrs. Minton and Co., of Stoke-upon-Trent, and Messrs. Wedgwood and Sons, of Etruria.

The celebrated establishment which formerly belonged to Messrs.

decorated in a novel style, with birds spiritedly painted upon a delicate green or celeste ground; likewise a series of enamels, in the ancient Limoges style, and a pair of terra cotta wine-coolers, ornamented with Etruscan subjects in coloured enamels. At either end, and at the back of this case, there are well-executed subjects in Parian statuary marble, designed and modelled by W. C. Marshall, R.A., Bailey, and Geefs. These are the largest specimens we have seen of works in this fine

VASES AND STATUETTES.   SIR JAMES DUKE AND NEPHEWS.

Alcock and Co. having recently passed into the hands of Sir James Duke and Nephews, it was to be expected that the show made by these gentlemen would be unique and excellent. Nor has this expectation been disappointed; for among the various cases in the Pottery Court, those from which we have selected our illustrations certainly rank with the first in attraction and value.

The chief object exhibited by Sir J. Duke and Nephews is a dessert service, designed and executed under the superintendence of George Eyre, the head artist of the establishment. The principal pieces for the centre of the table are intricately perforated baskets of exquisitely painted and elegantly decorated porcelain, supported by Parian groups, representing the Grecian attendants upon Marriage—Peace, Commerce, and Industry; and a group of boys bird-nesting. The plates pertaining to this set have painted landscapes, illustrative of "The Task" of Cowper. In the same case as the above are several vases,

material. The greatest speciality of this firm, however, consists in their numerous and faithful copies of antique Etruscan and Grecian vases; and under this head is to be noticed a very novel and striking mode of decorating black vases, by giving to the whole ground of the vase an oxidised appearance, and placing the figures in high relief, by means of their being highly glazed. The china dinner, dessert, and tea-service patterns, also, are very numerous, and many of them evince much originality. Especially graceful is the "Marmion" group, illustrative of that well-known passage from Sir Walter Scott's celebrated poem :—

" With dying hand above his head
He shook the fragment of his blade,
And shouted, ' Victory !' "

Mr. Bayley's idea has been very faithfully rendered.

In the large group, "Cupid Captive," by W. Calder Marshall;

equally with the "Innocence Protected," by Beattie; the busts of
"Modesty," and "Vanity," by Mélé; the "Listening Venus," a

From the beautiful collection of Messrs. Josiah Wedgwood
and Sons, the successors of the celebrated potter of the Etruria

VASE IN PORCELAIN   MESSRS. WEDGWOOD AND CO., ETRURIA POTTERIES.

charming nude figure, holding a shell to her ear; and the Elcho
statuette, the casting is exquisitely pure· indeed, the whole collection

Works, in Staffordshire, we here introduce a single specimen; but
that is sufficient to evince the excellence of the workmanship,

VASES AND ORNAMENTS.   SIR JAMES DUKE AND NEPHEWS.

may be said to reflect the highest credit on the firm of Sir James
Duke and Nephews, of the celebrated Hill Pottery.

and the graceful fancy which presides over their production.
The statuettes, "Spring" and "Autumn," from the large and

Works of Art in Precious Metals,

EXHIBITED BY MESSRS. HOWELL AND JAMES.

THE present Exhibition was intended by its founder, the late lamented Prince Consort, to illustrate the progress made since 1851 in the application of the arts and sciences to manufactures and the wants of society. In selecting various works from their large and valuable stock for exhibition in the World's Show of 1862, Messrs. Howell and

James, the eminent gold and silversmiths, jewellers, and manufacturers of bronzes and English ormolu, of Regent Street, have studiously kept in mind the important object its promoters had in view—the giving a true test and picture of the point of development to which we have now arrived.

"If," they say in their public announcement, "there is one fact or

TIARA IN THE ETRUSCAN STYLE.

ONYX AND PEARL LOCKET IN THE SAXON STYLE.

DIAMOND AND ENAMEL BROOCH.

CARBUNCLE AND EMERALD LOCKET AND BROOCH IN THE HOLBEIN STYLE.

ALHAMBRESQUE HAIR PIN.

TURQUOISE AND ENAMEL BRACELET IN THE CELTIC STYLE.

SHAWL PIN OF CORAL AND PEARLS.

CARBUNCLE AND DIAMOND HOLBEIN LOCKET.

ART JEWELLERY. MESSRS. HOWELL AND JAMES.

lesson which, more than another, the Great Exhibition of 1851 was the means of impressing upon the minds of thoughtful and educated people, it was that the English artists and manufacturers were, to a great extent, deficient in their treatment of the precious metals as a medium of art. Elegance of form and propriety of ornament were, in the great majority of cases, in 1851, sacrificed to a profuse display of

and sold by the ton, rather than by the ounce. Quantity of metal, not quality of workmanship, nor beauty of design, was the first consideration with too many of the manufacturers of that day, who, in this respect, reflected but too faithfully the general taste of the public. Our experience during the last ten years has taught us that a great and salutary change has been effected in this respect, and that the true

EMERALD AND ENAMEL PENDANT IN THE CELLINI STYLE.

GOTHIC BRACELET OF CRYSTAL AND CORAL.

DIAMOND AND ENAMEL LOCKET IN THE ETRUSCAN STYLE.

ENAMELLED EAR-RING.

DIAMOND AND ENAMELLED LOCKET.

CORAL AND LIMOGES LOCKET.

GOTHIC EAR-RING.

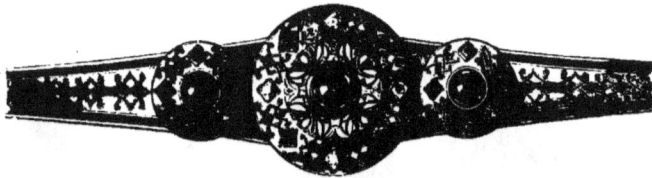

BRACELET OF CARBUNCLES, EMERALDS, AND DIAMONDS, IN THE HOLBEIN STYLE.

ART JEWELLERY.   MESSRS. HOWELL AND JAMES.

the metal. Like some of the native princes of the East, exhibitors seemed to revel in the store of gold and silver with which they could dazzle the eye and excite the cupidity and wonder of the spectator; and gold and silver seemed as though they were metals to be bought

principles of art and fitting forms of beauty are much more generally appreciated than they formerly were. It has been our object to encourage, and, as far as lay in our power, to lead this improved taste; and we may appeal to the judgment of all unbiassed minds whether the great bulk of the works in precious metals which we exhibit do not successfully illustrate the application of some of the highest principles of art to their production. We have endeavoured to show rich and costly metals as the vehicle for the display of the tasteful fancies of artists of acknowledged eminence in their profession ; and it is satisfactory to know that those efforts have been rewarded with a success much greater than, a few years since, we could have ventured to anticipate."

The illustrations we now introduce will, in the absence of the original works, afford evidence of the earnestness with which the exhibitors have striven to give a high character to the works that they have produced in jewellery and in the precious metals.

To describe each separate object thus introduced would occupy more space than we can afford. It will, therefore, be sufficient to say that the whole collection is unsurpassed in grace of design, beauty of form, and finish of workmanship.

Messrs. Howell and James are also makers and large importers of clocks, watches, and works in ormolu, as well as presentation-pieces in silver, &c. They are also producing a vast quantity of real lace, with the value of which, as an adjunct to female costume, every lady is acquainted. In ornaments for the toilet, and compagnons de voyage, they are likewise pre-eminent. The

SILVER CANDELABRUM.

elegant piece of plate we have introduced was designed by Professor Miller, of the South Kensington Museum, and is adapted for a candelabrum or centre piece. It is in the Renaissance style, and consists of a beautifully-proportioned pillar, supporting three branches for six lights, from which are suspended engraved silver dishes for fruit, the whole being surmounted by a silver basket for flowers.

The "Raffles Jubilee Testimonial," consisting of a solid silver casket, was presented to the Rev. Dr. Raffles, of Great George Street, Liverpool, by numerous friends and members of his congregation, to celebrate the anniversary of his fiftieth year among them, and also his retirement from the ministry. It is a most perfect specimen of fine art, and every detail has some special and direct significance and meaning in the design. On the centre of the lid, and surmounting all, stands the figure of Religion, pointing to the Bible as the way of life, and trampling on the serpent or evil spirit of the world ; the figure is clothed with the sacred emblems, " the helmet of Salvation, the breastplate of Righteousness, and the shield of Faith." Religion is supported on either side by figures of Faith and Hope (with their usual attributes, the cross and anchor), Charity being represented by the four panels round the body of the casket, which illustrate the acts a clergyman would be called upon to perform in the pursuance of his duties.

THE RAFFLES JUBILEE TESTIMONIAL. DESIGNED AND MODELLED BY FELIX M. MILLER.

The Contributions of Turkey.

THE Turkish trophy faces the nave, and is appropriately surmounted by the Crescent. The trophy itself is an object of considerable interest, being made up of richly brocaded silks and various pieces of metalwork, the brazier with which the Ottomans warm their houses in winter being particularly conspicuous. Behind, in the Turkish Court, are various curious objects; among which are numerous examples of fruits, woods, cereals, wools, silkworms' eggs, silver filigree work, cotton, maize, rice, an alarm clock, which rings a bell when the key is as their decorated pipes and smoking requisites, their delicate coffee-cups, and various articles in pottery, all evidence the national taste for the beautiful in form and colour. Especially interesting are the Damascus sword-blades and curious fire-arms. Among the weapons are to be seen the remarkable arm-rests used by the Dervishes. They contain a number of small steel blades, which enter the flesh when the arm rests upon them, and thus, by causing pain, remind the devotees of the necessity of action, and the sinfulness of unnecessary

THE TURKISH COURT.

inserted, travelling bags, carpets, rugs, Cashmere shawls, tobacco pipes, and a national jest book! The exquisite loveliness of the muslins and Broussa silks, embroidered in gold and colours, attracted great attention during the entire Exhibition season.

The prices fixed to the goods are nearly all in the Turkish cipher, or in the few instances where it is translated, the sum total is given in piastres, which is equally unintelligible to the mass of visitors.

The military dresses and trappings, the horse furniture, the sashes, embroidered shirts, and various weapons used by the Turks, as well rest and delay during their pilgrimages! The Turkish collection is principally due to the Government of the Sultan and Sir Hyde Clarke, who, at the suggestion of the Ministry of Commerce, gathered together a large number of representative objects. The Governor-General of Turkey and a few private exhibitors also make a very characteristic show. In the Fine Art Department Turkey is not altogether unrepresented; though the exhibition by the Ottomans of works of a high class, in either painting or sculpture, is certainly neither large nor important.

30.

Carriages in the Exhibition.

In the South-eastern Court are to be found the "Carriages not connected with rail or tramroads," shown by British exhibitors; while those contributed by foreigners appear in their several courts. Almost every kind of carriage and cart used at home and abroad is shown here by some one or two examples. Among them are improved landaus, sociables, and wagonettes; an improved and enlarged Hansom cab; Noculer's broughams, on indiarubber bearings; an improved

Among the provincial towns, Edinburgh, Dublin, Derby, Bristol, Liverpool, Manchester, Nottingham, Southampton, Glasgow, and Newcastle-on-Tyne produce largely for the home and export trade. On the continent of Europe, Paris holds the highest place, as regards the excellence and the extent of its carriage-building trade, which, of late years, has much increased, as well as improved in the style, workmanship, and durability of its productions. The French export of

THE "AMEMPTON" AS AN OPEN CARRIAGE. MR. EDWIN KESTERTON.

omnibus, with vis-à-vis seats, and access to the outside seats from the interior; various descriptions of improved phaetons; cart, to form cart or sleigh, for home or colonial use; perambulators, &c.; wheels with weldless steel tyres, light hickory wheels, and wheels with chain tyres; velocipedes; Bath chairs; improved and enlarged dog-carts; light carts for trade purposes; close and open family carriages, &c. More than a hundred different descriptions of vehicles are shown in this class.

carriages has also greatly increased of late years. A large trade is also carried on at Brussels, Hamburg, Vienna, Aix-la-Chapelle, Offenbach, Milan, Rome, the Hague, St. Petersburg, and other cities and towns. America, which only contributes to the Exhibition two very light carriages, has rapidly risen to a great producing country for carriages. Its productions are of a type quite original, and peculiar to the country; and in some points have acquired a singular excellence, as regards lightness, combined with comparative durability. To

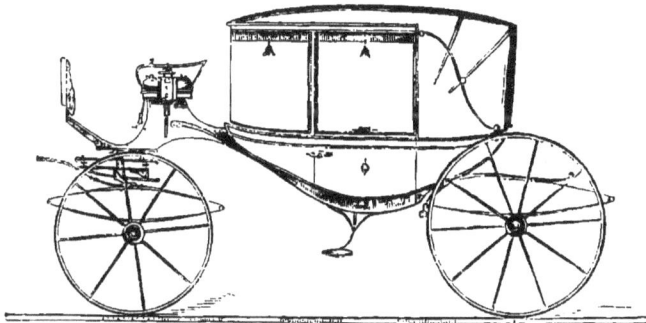

THE "AMEMPTON" AS A CLOSE CARRIAGE. MR. EDWIN KESTERTON.

The following graphic account of the British and foreign carriages in the Exhibition is condensed from the able "Jury Report" of Mr. G. N. Hooper, and issued by the Society of Arts:—As might be expected, the English carriages far outnumber the combined productions from all foreign countries, and those from London outnumber the examples from the provincial towns. London may indeed be said to be the chief seat of the carriage manufacture, both from the general excellence of the carriages built, and from the extent of the trade.

Europeans these light carriages have a very singular appearance; they, however, probably meet the wants of the American public, from their light draught. The bodies are small; there is difficulty of getting into the carriage; and the quantity of mud thrown by the very high wheels must be somewhat alarming. There exists an imperial manufactory for carriages at St. Petersburg, directed by an Englishman; it is well organised, and adapted for producing the private carriages used by the Russian Court. The various processes are there carried on, even to the weaving of the lace, and the production of the ornamental metal chasings. This manufactory has probably had a good effect in improving carriage-building in Russia, the contributions from which country are not only numerous, but show points of careful consideration in the construction and design. The Russian nobility, fond of having their equipages well turned out, import many carriages from England, France, and Germany. The carriages in Russia, and those sent there,

as regards the manufacture of private travelling carriages in England, it is now evidently a thing of the past, probably soon to pass out of mind, or only to be remembered by the older masters and craftsmen. An important omission may here be mentioned as regards public carriages for the streets of cities and towns. Was London, at last, really ashamed of its dirty and rickety cabs? As regards its street cabs, London is worse supplied than many European cities—with the

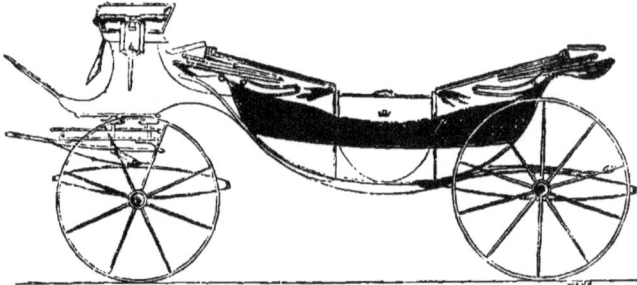

SOCIABLE LANDAU, OPEN. MESSRS. PEARCE AND COUNTZE.

must necessarily be strongly built, as the thaw in spring, after the winter frosts, so breaks up the road or paving, that a light or weak carriage must soon give way. Unlike these must be the carriages for the Australian markets, where, in consequence of the taste for light carriages built on the American system, much of the trade has fallen into the hands of the coach-builders of the United States. The tastes and requirements for private carriages have evidently of late years taken a great change. The English Department does not contain a

exception of a few clean and well turned-out Hansoms—and far worse than most of the English provincial towns. There is no necessity to vary the size and build of such vehicles, as they exist here in only two types: the "Hansom," as an open one; the "four-wheeler," as the close one. They might be produced in great numbers by machinery; all the parts might be duplicates one of another; the wheels, axles, springs, bodies, seats, &c., might all be made of one size and gauge, to interchange; the rapidity of manufacture, facility of repair, and

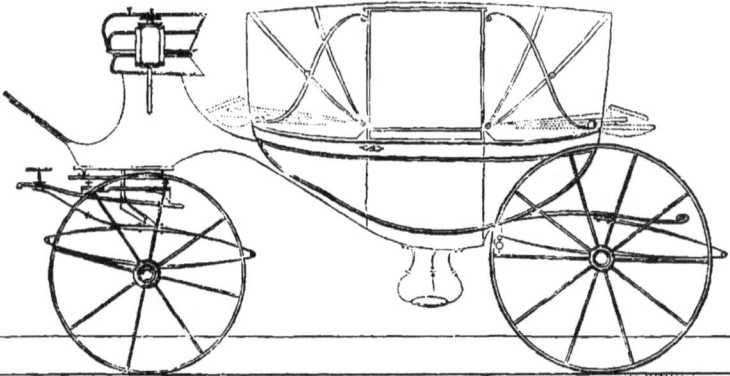

SOCIABLE LANDAU, CLOSED. MESSRS. PEARCE AND COUNTZE.

single carriage fitted with a hammer-cloth, though such carriages are still used by our aristocracy during the London season; nor is there one travelling carriage. We may now, perhaps, feel assured that the railway has the entire monopoly of transporting travellers on long journeys throughout Western Europe. There are still links missing in Spain, Italy, Sweden, Russia, and a few other states of Europe: but,

general economy of production would appear to be advantageous to all parties; and those of the public who cannot afford to keep carriages of their own might be carried in vehicles that should be at least clean, safe, and comfortable; and, with a little more care in warehousing they might be brought into use without that very pungent smell of the stable, that is, probably, disagreeable to every one, except the owner and the genuine London cabman. Woods are shown in such great quantities, and of such excellent quality, by many of the English colonies, that it will be strange if the colonies do not open a trade with the coach-builders of Europe. The only new woods recently adopted

working; then if they are adapted to the variations of our climate, and what effect a hot sun in summer, or a continuance of wet in winter, has upon them. The black walnut has been adopted by many of the principal upholsterers and pianoforte manufacturers, for th i?

BAROUCHE LANDAU.   MR. ISAAC ADELBERT.

by the English coach-builders are the Canadian black walnut and American hickory. The former grows to a great size, and is advantageously cut into panels, which are free from figured grain, and, for many purposes, are an excellent substitute for Honduras mahogany.

internal fittings. The hickory is a most valuable wood for the spokes of light wheels. The Americans seem to have been most successful in the making of wheels by machinery. A trade has now sprung up in the importation of wheels to England, for broughams and other light

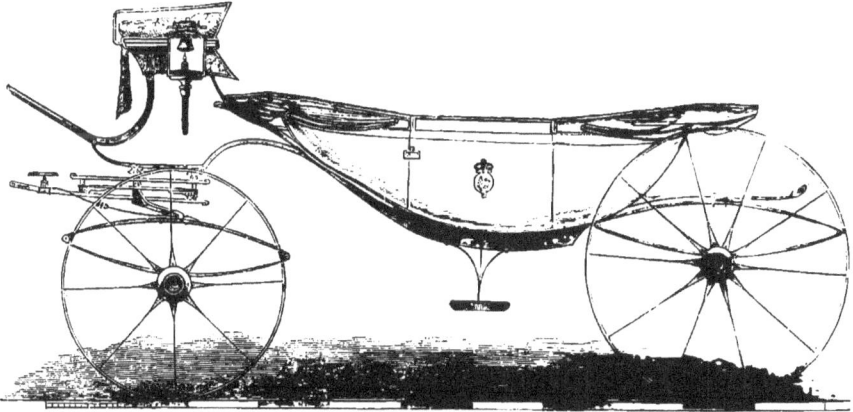

LANDAU.   MESSRS. WYBURN AND CO.

It must, however, be recollected that it requires time and great care to introduce new woods into a manufacture like that of carriages. They must first be thoroughly seasoned; it must then be ascertained by experiment if they require any peculiarity of treatment, or care in

carriages. A self-acting double-fold step, of very ingenious construction, is sent from the Duchy of Hesse. On a brougham sent from Russia is an ingenious double action spring door-lock, so that the inside and outside door-handles act independently, thus reducing the friction and wearing of the spindles. The same manufacturer shows an excellent droski, the national carriage of Russia. As such vehicles are the most numerous and the most popular in Russia, this deserves notice, especially as its construction is so totally different to any English carriage. The mode of attaching the shafts to the horse and of harnessing him merit inspection, as it is said that horses harnessed on the Russian plan rarely fall—in fact, are much supported by the way they are put to their work. The lightness and strength of Russian harness particularly merit attention, the leather part being so light as to appear unsafe to English eyes. This, however, is due to their peculiarly prepared harness leather, which is marvellously strong. As the Russians are almost as great in their way at driving as the English in theirs, their harness and methods of attaching horses to their work are worth attention. Many and very considerable changes have taken

a point that can hardly be too strongly insisted on : there are, however, a few rather glaring departures from the general care shown on this point. Not less so is the still prevalent practice with some coach-builders of overloading with superfluous ornaments carriages which, from their construction, are evidently intended for ordinary every-day use.

Another improvement, very recent among the British coach-builders is the use of tough steel, instead of iron, for carriages that are required to be built very light. This material might perhaps be more accurately described as a very dense, hard, and tough iron, that is capable of welding, but which requires more than ordinary care to work. The manufacture of fancy wood panels, imitating interlaced basket-work, is now established in England. This very ingenious invention is due to France, where it was first made by a retired soldier

BERLIN D'ORSAY. MESSRS. MOINGEARD BRO., PARIS

place in the manufacture of carriages since 1851, mainly in consequence of a smaller breed of horses being used, so that a demand has arisen for smaller and lighter carriages. In point of weight there is a remarkable difference in the carriages of this Exhibition and that of 1851. It is probable that there is an average diminution of about one-fourth in the weight of all the carriages shown in the British department. Added to this, manufacturers have endeavoured to combine greater elegance of general design with reduction of weight. Several manufacturers have combined the attributes of comfort, lightness, and elegance with great success. In the combination of colours the British department also shows progress, many of the carriages being painted and lined in excellent taste, the selection of colours showing attention to a point on which much of the appearance of a good equipage depends. As the best design, workmanship, and material may be entirely neutralised in appearance by a bad selection of colours, this is

of the Empire, named Fort, who not only produced large quantities for the French coach-builders, but for some time exported a considerable quantity to this country. By improved machinery, it is now made in England more accurately, and in a greater variety of patterns than in France. It is much used to give a light appearance to small carriages, principally for country use. It forms a neat and durable substitute for the real wicker-work formerly used, but which rapidly deteriorates by mud and moisture.

Among other changes is the increased use of the lever-break for carriages principally used in hilly parts of the country. Since their first introduction they have been much improved in simplicity, efficiency, and economy. Many of the British carriages are fitted in this manner. The break not only increases the safety of a carriage, but dispenses with the necessity of taking a second servant to put on and remove the common drag-shoe. A mode of applying pressure to both

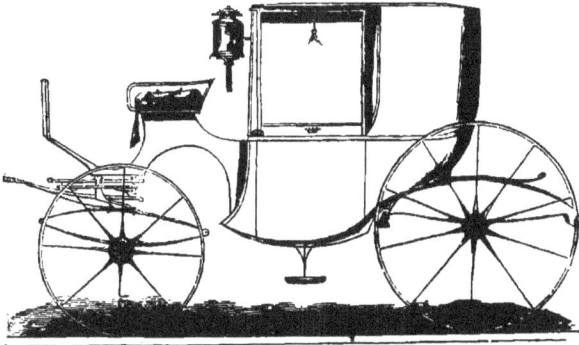

DROUGHAM.   MESSRS. WYBURN AND CO.

suited to the variable climate of the British isles, as they can be readily changed from an open to a close carriage, and *vice versa.* They do not, however, admit of that beauty of outline that is capable of being given to an entirely open or entirely close carriage; but from the amount of care and contrivance displayed—as evinced in many of those shown—they have such qualities as render them very convenient and desirable family carriages, either for London or pro-

suggested by the Prince, with whom and her Majesty it always remained a favourite carriage for country excursions. There are so many varieties of carriages of this type, and so much ingenuity has been bestowed on them, that it can hardly excite surprise that they are much appreciated by those who use carriages, especially in hilly parts of the country, where a compact, serviceable, and economical carriage is indispensable. A revival of an almost obsolete carriage, " the four-

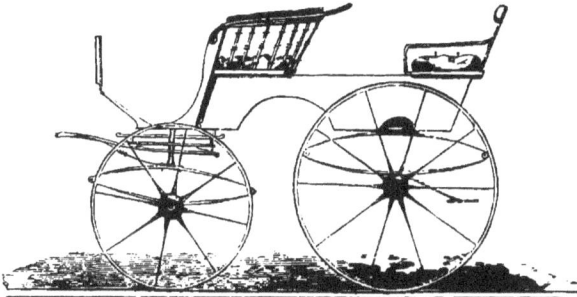

PHAETON.   MESSRS. WYBURN AND CO.

vincial use. There are shown several ingenious plans for enabling the heads of landaus to fall flatter than has been hitherto considered practicable. They have the advantage of converting the landau into a more open carriage than formerly, besides preventing an obstruction to the view. Most of these carriages are hung at such a very moderate distance from the ground, and with covered steps, that it is optional whether one or two servants shall accompany them.

Carriages of the wagonette type, where the sitters in the back

in-hand coach," has taken place within a few years. They are generally built on the model of the best mail and stage coaches of former times, but with a much higher degree of finish. It may appear very easy to the uninitiated to build such a carriage merely on the lines of former days, but in fact they require such careful and accurate planning of the several parts, individually and combined, that only those who have given much attention to them, and have to a certain extent been tutored by gentlemen who drive them, have been successful in turning out carriages of the kind that in most points meet their requirements. One of these carriages (Mr. Peters' drag) is the trophy of the British coach-builders, and occupied a conspicuous position in the nave of the Exhibition building. The revival of a taste for such carriages is worthy of remark, as the management of a "team" not only requires great bodily strength, good nerve, and a quick eye, but being an expensive amusement, is mostly confined to the aristocracy and persons of wealth, with whose habits it is principally associated, and indicates something of that vigour of body which generally distinguishes the British gentry.

The principle of suspending carriages on a single wrought-iron perch, first prominently introduced at the Exhibition of 1851, has produced a great change in the construction of nearly all C spring carriages now built, and has many advantages for small carriages hung low. It is, however, beyond a doubt that for carriages hung high, and requiring double folding steps, the perch of wood and iron combined, has the great recommendation of increased safety, as three iron plates and the wood must break before an accident can happen; whereas the solid iron perch depends for its safety on the soundness of a single weld.

In the French department in the main building are shown two photographs of a state railway carriage recently built for the Pope; its design and decoration are so far in advance of anything yet executed in England, that these photographs well deserve to be examined and placed in a more prominent position. The omnibus (usually drawn in Paris with two powerful, but slow horses) shown by France, for the traffic of the Paris streets, deserves careful examination. These carriages are all made on one model by machinery; and the parts interchange, so that repairs are very expeditiously executed. Although much too heavy for the London traffic with a pair of light horses, and too cumbersome for the crowded traffic of the streets in the city of London, they are comfortable, easy, and safe. The plan of suspending on three springs, both in front and behind, gives greater ease than the short elliptic springs common to the London vehicles. Were such carriages copied, but made shorter and lighter, and were the front box seats (to carry four) added, such carriages would be a great addition to the comfort of many thousands of Londoners, who have to make two journeys daily in the stuffy and ill-ventilated London omnibuses, which, by the recent innovation of roof seats, are so constantly overloaded as to strain and wear out the horses very rapidly, besides cruelly taxing them beyond their strength.

Since the opening of the Exhibition there have appeared in London a number of large, commodious, and well-ventilated omnibuses, even somewhat larger than the Paris omnibuses, drawn by three horses abreast. In the first place, the increased comfort to the public is undoubted; the horses seem to work with less strain on their muscles; the omnibuses having a larger base are steadier and safer, and having longer springs they are easier, and being fitted with pressure or lever breaks to the hind wheels, they can be stopped with greater facility. The cost of building the carriages larger somewhat increases the expense, as does also the addition of a third horse; however, to set against these charges are the increased number of passengers carried (about one-third), with the same number of attendants (driver and conductor), nearly equal expense of repair, and the saving in the wear and duration of the horses, so that the question of working them profitably in London may be considered almost certain. They might not be available for narrow streets, but many lines of omnibuses scarcely approach the narrow and crowded City streets.

Although the application of machinery to the construction of private carriages has progressed, aided by a well-known firm in Derby, which has for some years devoted attention to the subject, many reasons prevent its general application to private coach-building purposes. Some of these are, the great variety of carriages built by each manufacturer, the desire on the part of purchasers to have carriages made to dimensions of their own choice, and the variations of pattern, as fashion indicates the lines most favoured by those who lead in such matters. These continued changes, in some cases tending to improve-

ment, complicate the details of construction, already sufficiently intricate: whereas it may be cited as a general rule, that the most profitable and advantageous application of machinery is in the production of articles in great quantities as nearly as possible identical, such as the Enfield rifles, Armstrong guns, railway bars, axles, and wheels, &c. In conclusion, it may be remarked, that the British show of carriages (with some exceptions) sustains the reputation of the manufacture as to design, comfort, soundness, and good finish, as regards the type of carriages at present in most general demand. France comes next, with a small display of soundly built carriages; then follow Belgium, Germany, Russia, and Holland, each with a proportion of sound and genuine workmanship.

In illustration of these terse and valuable remarks, we introduce pictures of some of the most noteworthy of the carriages in the Exhibition. It is unnecessary to do more than direct attention to their several excellences. From Long Acre, the great mart of the London coachmakers, we have chosen a few of what we may call representative carriages. The Amemapton of Mr. Kesterton is adapted for use equally as an open or closed sociable. It is roomy, light, and elegant.—A similar vehicle is that of Messrs. Pearce and Countze, who exhibit their fine vehicle "in the wood"—that is to say, just as it comes from the body and carriage-makers' benches, and without a particle of paint, lining, or varnish. This is the only carriage in the Exhibition so shown; and, strange to say, that although exhibited expressly to show the construction of such a carriage, and the excellence of its workmanship, the jurors have accorded to it simply "honourable mention;" though, in their Report, this plan of exhibiting carriages is certainly highly commended.

M. Isaac Adelbert shows an elegant barouche landau, constructed with steel, instead of iron, and fitted with the noiseless spring patented by the exhibitor. Great lightness and elegance characterise this vehicle.

Messrs. Wyburn and Co. show a beautifully built landau and a brougham, than which nothing more perfect or complete are to be found in the Exhibition.

The landau, for which the prize model has been awarded, is of the extreme "clipper" shape, combining great lightness with ample room in the interior for four persons. The head is made to open so as to fall perfectly flat, both in front and behind, and thus to avoid all those projections and angles, which are so detrimental to the appearance of those carriages, as generally constructed.

When open, it is as roomy and elegant in appearance as the modern barouches, and may, in a few minutes, be converted into one of the lightest, strongest, and most commodious of close carriages.

The brougham, weighing rather under 6¾ cwt., is one of the lightest and most compact ever made, being suited for a horse of fifteen hands, and yet the interior affords comfortable room for two persons. From the graceful harmony of its hues, and the good taste displayed in its finish, it has been pronounced one of the neatest and most correct broughams ever turned out.

The French carriage shown in our engraving is built upon a very effective plan, while great taste is displayed in its fittings and appointments. It is called a Berlin D'Orsay, and is fitted for either town use or light travelling.

Other exhibitors show a variety of landaus, sociables, broughams, &c.; and one enterprising coachmaker actually sends a very good specimen carriage all the way from Melbourne, Australia. Carriages for riders of all classes are here—from the town chariot, prodigal of silk and heraldic painting, to the new omnibus by Shillibeer, and the "double-bodied basket-trap," fitted for a lady to drive through a country lane. Most of them, we are informed, are sold; and many of the most eminent makers have received from the visitors to the Exhibition orders enough to keep them at work for the next twelve-month.

Fire Engines and Fire Escapes.

In Class 8 are shown several of those very important and valuable machines, Fire Engines. Messrs. Merryweather and Son, of Long Acre; Messrs. Shand and Mason, of Blackfriars Road, and Mr. William Roberts, of Millwall, Poplar, are the principal exhibitors of Fire Engines; and from the excellent engines shown by the first firm we select a few illustrative examples.

MERRYWEATHER AND SON'S BRIGADE FIRE ENGINES.

Tho exhibitors show two sizes of their famous Brigade Fire Engines, one for thirty men, for use in cities and towns, and a smaller one for twenty men, for towns and country use. These, as well as the other fire engines by the same firm, have been placed in various parts of the Exhibition, by order of her Majesty's Commissioners, for service in case of fire. One of each size were placed in the Cromwell Road entrance. This class of engine, which has gained Messrs. Merryweather and Son world-wide celebrity, has never been surpassed for workmanship or performance. The larger sized engine, for thirty men, is well known as the "Prince Albert" of the Great Exhibition of 1851, and subsequently as "l'Empereur" of the Paris Exhibition, 1855; the smaller engine, for twenty men, as the "Paxton" of 1851. At both of these Exhibitions prize medals were awarded to Messrs. Merryweather and Son.

These Fire Engines are constructed with patent metallic valves, in valve chambers with covers, so that they are easily accessible. They are proof against injury by neglect, are not in any way affected by working foul or gritty water,

and retain their power unimpaired in all climates. They are made so as to discharge one or two streams of water at the same time, if occasion requires, are mounted on strong wheels, springs, axles, and wrought iron forecarriage for rapid travelling; they have also every convenience for carrying firemen, hose, suction-pipes, and tools; the working handles are made to fall over, so as when folded to be snug for travelling, and when extended, to provide sufficient room for the number of men required to work them. Messrs. Merryweather and Son's Brigade Fire Engines are extensively used by the London fire engine establishments, her Majesty's and several foreign governments, in the several provincial cities and towns, docks, railways, and in all parts of the civilized world. The larger engine is capable of discharging a powerful jet of water to a height of 130 feet, and the smaller engine to a height of 120 feet.

MERRYWEATHER'S IMPROVED FIRE ESCAPE.

These very valuable machines seem now to have received the approbation, through the increasing and praiseworthy endeavours of the Royal Society for the Protection of Life from Fire who have now upwards of seventy stationed each night in the metropolis. They are also used extensively in provincial towns, both at home and abroad. Messrs. Merryweather make large numbers of fire escapes, with all the newest improvements.

MERRYWEATHER AND SON'S PATENT STEAM FIRE ENGINE, "THE DELUGE."

We have here an engraving of one of the most novel and useful machines we have had occasion to notice in this work. Messrs. Merryweather are the makers and exhibitors of this the most powerful steam fire engine for land service, and the only one of the kind of British manufacture shown in the Exhibition.

Perceiving the necessity for more power to cope with the great conflagrations that so frequently occur, Messrs. Merryweather and Son, with their experience in making hand-worked and steam floating fire engines, have succeeded in producing a first-rate steam fire engine, which travels as easily from place to place as an ordinary hand-worked engine. The one here shown stood in the Cromwell Road entrance of the Exhibition.

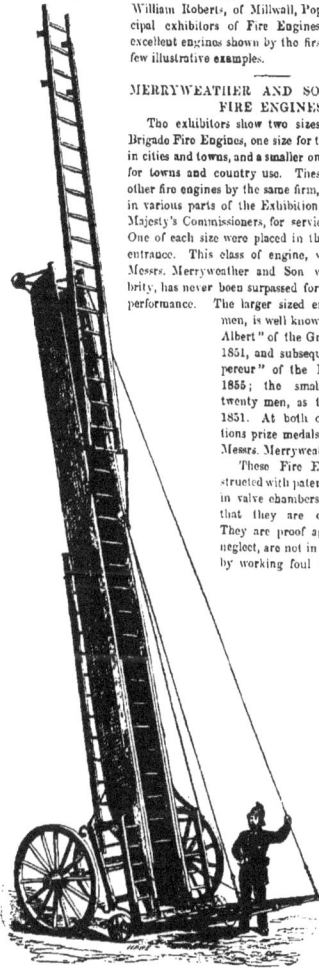

MERRYWEATHER'S IMPROVED FIRE ESCAPE.

MERRYWEATHER'S BRIGADE FIRE ENGINE.

and during the entire season attracted considerable attention from all classes of visitors. The boiler, which is of the most durable kind, is of the vertical order; it is constructed of steel, with copper tubes, to secure a large heating surface. The peculiar arrangement of the tubes entirely obviates priming, an inconvenience so great in many vertical boilers. The rapidity with which steam has been frequently raised by it has been greatly admired by all who have witnessed it. This is the most important feature in a steam fire engine, as the best chance of success in subduing a fire lays in attacking it in its early stage. At the several trials made with this engine, steam has been frequently raised from perfectly cold water to a pressure of 40lbs. per square inch in ten minutes from lighting the fire; a pressure of 100lbs. per square inch has been obtained in 11 minutes 50 seconds from applying the match.

very requisite in cold climates; it is provided with a simple means of making the piston self-lubricating, and is surmounted by a capacious air vessel, in the form of a sphere; beneath all are two delivery ways, for attaching hoses, and provided with stop valves. When starting the engine, nothing more is required than to open the steam valve, when the engine will run at any speed, according to the quantity of water required to be delivered, from 1 to 150 or 160 double strokes per minute. It discharges, when working at full speed, 500 gallons per minute.

No wood is used in the construction of the engine, except in the wheels. The engine is fitted with water tank and coal bunkers, has a box for carrying hose, suction pipes, tools, &c., which forms a seat for six men. The height and distance to which water can be projected has been tried against the lofty shaft at Messrs. Hodges' distillery.

MERRYWEATHER AND SON'S PATENT STEAM FIRE ENGINE, "THE DELUGE."

The engine, which is mounted on a strong wrought-iron frame, secured to the boiler, and mounted on high wheels and springs, for rapid travelling, consists of a steam cylinder 9 inches diameter, having direct action with one of Merryweather and Son's Patent Double Acting Fire Pumps, of 6½ inches diameter; the stroke of both is 15 inches, and they are tied together by strong guide rods. There is a very ingenious arrangement for working the slide valve, so as to dispense with a crank fly-wheel, &c., and to have as few working parts as possible. The working parts are strong and simple, and this arrangement produces a uniform speed of pistons throughout their stroke, which causes the engine to deliver an unusually steady column of water. The double acting pump before spoken of is in one casting, all gun metal, with large valves and water-ways, and has a great advantage in its construction, that no gritty or foul water can injure it—as all is ejected at each stroke—and that no water can possibly remain in it when at rest, so as to guard against accidents from frost,

A 1¼-in. jet was discharged 150 feet vertically, and a 1¼-in. jet 170 feet vertically. Horizontal distance, a 1¼-in. jet, 202 feet, a 1¼-in. jet 215 feet. At one trial the engine drew water vertically 14 feet, and then discharged it through a 1¼-in. nozzle clear over a building 60 feet high, to a distance of 210 feet. Messrs. Merryweather and Son are, we understand, now constructing smaller steam fire engines. Besides those here described, the exhibitors also show several of smaller size for railways, factories, mansions, farmers, &c. They are also the manufacturers of the splendid and elaborately ornamented fire engine justly presented to Mr. Frederick Hodges, the distiller, for his well-known exertions in the cause of humanity at numerous conflagrations. In addition to the prize medals received by Messrs. Merryweather and Son, at the Great Exhibition of 1851, and at Paris in 1855, they have had awarded to them by the jurors of the International Exhibition a Prize Medal for "improvements in design of fire engines," coupled with "good workmanship and performance."

31.

Cutlery, Iron, and General Hardware.

UNDER this title is comprised all the various articles exhibited in Classes 31 and 32, on both sides of the building. On the British side we have seen metal works produced in Birmingham, Sheffield, Wolverhampton, Rotherham, London, and other towns; whilst on the foreign side are seen the chef-d'œuvres of Paris, Lille, Rouen, and other places in France—principally bronzes and ornamental works in cast iron; Liège, Brussels, &c., in Belgium, with fine specimens of castings in iron and bronze; Posen, Dantzig, Frankfort, Cologne, and other places in Prussia, in many shapes both useful and ornamental; bronzes from Petersburg; tin and iron in several forms from Barcelona and Valencia in Spain; many excellent specimens from Stockholm, Eskilstuna in Sweden; lanterns and lamps, copper wares, &c., from Constantinople, and several capital castings from Canada and our other principal colonies; with lesser shows from other places all over the world. The advance made on every side in the design and finish of manufactures in the various metals is apparent to the most careless observer. We no longer see clumsy masses of metal badly constructed, but finished productions of the hammer, harmonious in design, colour, and general utility.

The Birmingham contribution to this collection contains a very complete representation of the various articles in metal for which the town and district has so long been celebrated. The general hardware court contains the productions of more than one hundred exhibitors. At its entrance will be found a display of metallic bedsteads, raw materials of every kind for the use of brass-founders, also gas-fittings of all kinds, and stamped and general brass-foundry. Tin-plate working and japan wares, wire-drawing, fire irons, stoves, and grates, iron-safes, hollow wares in copper and iron, tinned and enamelled, tubing of all kinds, scales and weighing-machines, medals and dies, hooks and eyes, pins, steel-pens, locks and general hardware, knife-cleaning machines, steel toys, metal mountings for the use of bookbinders, fire-guards, coffin furniture, saddlers' ironmongery, ornamental panels of various kinds, screws, nails, hinges, &c., are also exhibited; and, in fact, as far as Birmingham is concerned, all its leading branches of industry are fully represented by the chief manufacturers.

Iron is shown in the Birmingham Court from the Earl of Dudley's works at Round Oak, including several specimens of 3-inch, 2-inch, and 1-inch rods, twisted into the shape of a Stafford-shire knot whilst cold; a 27-feet rail, similar to those used by the London and North-Western Railway, twisted whilst cold in corkscrew form; an 8-feet rail, similarly twisted, the twist being about six inches; boiler-plates, capable of standing a pressure of 613 tons to the square inch. Various specimens of cold blast puddled steel, and other varieties of iron have also been contributed. Messrs. Hill and Smith, of Hart's Hill, send some specimens of self-acting iron gates, and ordinary gates and hurdles. Messrs. Wakins and Keep, of Stourbridge, supply anvils, ploughshares, spades, and other edge tools. Messrs. Cochrane, of Woodside Iron Works, contribute various specimens of iron work; Messrs. Tinsley and Wright, of Tipton, anchors and chains; and Mr. R. P. Parkes, of Tipton, chains.

In the Wolverhampton Court, Messrs. T. and C. Clark and Co. have a fine collection of hollow manufactures. A prominent feature in the display is a set of stable fittings in enamelled iron, consisting of manger, rack, water trough, stall, post, &c. All descriptions of tin and enamelled iron hollow ware, adapted to culinary and sanitary purposes, are here shown.

The Great Exhibition contained many specimens of metal work, not a few of them distinguished for various excellences. Every visitor must remember the excellent show made by Messrs. Hart, Feetham, and Hardman's exquisite collections, the trophies of Messrs. Bessemer, Warner, Dent, the Coal-brook Dale Company, and others. Among the most remarkable contributions, English or foreign, are the fine art works of the Messrs. Elkington. In the range of their works, as well as in design and in manufacture, there is an immense advance on the contributions by which the firm was distinguished in the Hyde Park Exhibition. Some of the specimens of chasing and enamelling, the former especially, were not equalled by anything of the kind in the building.

One of the most interesting articles in the Wolverhampton Court is a small aluminium casket, about twelve and a half inches long, nine inches wide, and eight inches deep. The casket is worth about £150,

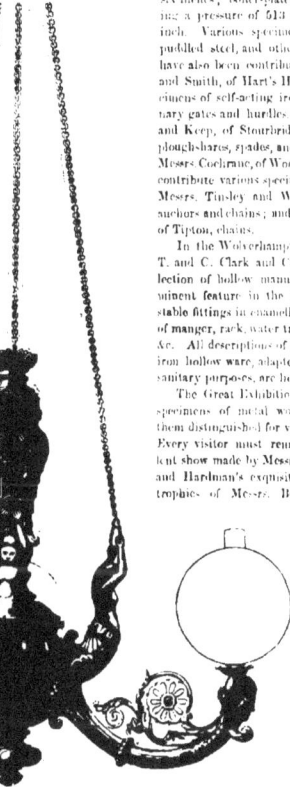

GAS CHANDELIER.   MR. JOSEPH HILL, BIRMINGHAM.

and was made, we believe, for Miss Burdett Coutts, in the Italian style of ornamentation.

In the Walsall division of the court, and in the hardware department generally, there was a large and splendid collection of lamps, chandeliers, bedsteads, gas and steam fittings, tubes, &c., of nearly all descriptions. All kinds of builders' ironmongery, taking in what is also known as "odd work," are represented. A number of samples of buckles, slides, and other of the lighter articles made of cast iron, are shown, prominence being given to many of those goods which are chiefly required for foreign markets. In this excellent collection of the really useful manufactures are some fine specimens of bronzing, and also samples of polished cast-iron goods.

The collections in the Sheffield and Rotherham Court comprise stove grates, fenders, fire-irons, hot-air stoves, kitchen ranges, ornamental iron-work, consisting of hat-stands, balusters, &c., manufactured by most of the firms who exhibited in the Exhibition of 1851. A portion of this court is occupied by Britannia metal goods, brass goods, consisting of high-pressure taps, cocks, hydrants, &c. Adjoining are exhibited, in cases round the walls, edge tools, joiners' tools, files, steel table-knives, scissors, sheep shears; and above, in vertical cases, saws, scythes, sickles, &c., and the general class of Sheffield manufactures.

On one block are exhibited goods of a similar character to those on the counters round the walls, but including steel springs, &c. Two other blocks are occupied by goods of a new class of manufacture, consisting of heavy castings of steel, crank axles for locomotives, driving wheels, axles, tyres, points for crossings, bells, railway - carriage springs, buffers, &c. &c. The counter under the gallery is covered with cases filled with fine cutlery—scissors, tailors' shears, table-knives, small edge-tools, bowie-knives, hatchets, &c., being samples of goods for which Sheffield holds so high a position.

The prominent features in Classes 31 and 32—placed in the south end of the South-eastern Transept—are the screen for Hereford Cathedral, already noticed; Bessemer's specimens of his patent steel (a new product since 1851); a new peal of bells, which are so made that they may be chimed by a child ignorant of music; and a large glass trophy, to which two firms have contributed elaborate specimens of ornamental metal-work, and two others equally elaborate specimens of mediæval work.

From this rich and varied display we make a few selections. The gas chandeliers of Mr. Joseph Hill, of Birmingham, are bold in style

and excellent in workmanship. The same exhibitor shows a variety of ornamental stampings for lamps, chandeliers, and general gas-fittings; husks and vases for metallic bedsteads, and ceiling roses, finished in white, gold, and colours, of various styles.

Messrs. D. Hulett and Co., of High Holborn, have a large variety of gaseliers, hall-lanterns, &c., in glass, ormolu, and bronze. The gaselier shown in our engraving is a gem in this kind of work. It is in the Renaissance style, after the manner of Owen Jones, and has been designed and modelled by the exhibitors with great skill. Purity of taste and excellence of workmanship are its leading features, and there is, besides, a certain fitness and appropriateness in the entire object which recommend it to admiration. Messrs. Hulett deserve especial mention for the care and skill they display in the getting up of this kind of domestic decoration, so superior to anything of the kind hitherto attempted in metal work adapted for chandeliers. The same firm also exhibit various gas-meters, gas-regulators, reflectors, ventilators, and other descriptions of gas and steam fittings. We are glad to observe that, though unnoticed by the jurors in their award, Mr. Waring, in his great work, has selected their mediæval gaselier as one of the gems of the International Exhibition.

On page 218 we have a group of wrought-iron, tinned and japanned ware, from the case of Messrs. Griffith and Browett, of Birmingham and London. The group consists of papier-maché trays, in the Moresque and Indian styles; patent raised hot water dishes and covers; soup and vegetable dishes, and soup tureens; patent tea and coffee-pot, sugar-basins, and cream-jugs; papier-maché folios, elegantly ornamented by a patent process; toilet sets, grocers' furniture, a Persian coal-vase, and a variety of curious and novel specimens of wrought iron raised from flat sheets of metal, without seam or brazing. Altogether, the show made by this firm is one of the most attractive in the Hardware Court.

GASELIER IN THE RENAISSANCE STYLE. MESSRS. HULETT AND CO.

WARNER'S BELLS AND CHIMING APPARATUS.

IN many of our towns and villages we try on a Sunday to make the church bells chime out sweet music for the holy day. But, to confess the truth, there is mostly very little music in it. The chimers very generally do not attempt more than a few "changes," which are too often spoiled by unequal time, or by one bell being made to sound louder than the rest—"sweet bells jangled out of tune." It is a very rare thing, indeed, either in town or country, to hear a set of chimes evenly and truly rung: where it is heard, it is a very great treat indeed. Well, this treat is now put within easy reach of every village—which has the good fortune to be possessed, in the first instance, of a good peal of bells—by the machine for whose invention Messrs. Warner and Sons, the well-known bell-founders, have received one of the medals of the International Exhibition. The apparatus, with a peal of eight bells, was placed in the South-east Transept, and there, three times a day, the machine was set to work, and the pleasant sounds from the sonorous and harmonious metal were familiar to visitors during the whole six months the Exhibition was open. The peal of bells themselves—cast by the founders of Big Ben of Westminster — were well worthy notice. They consist of a full peal of eight, tenor note E, weighing nineteen hundred weight, mounted on a strong frame, with all the fittings necessary for ringing—in short, they were placed here just as they will, in a few months' time, be mounted in the tower of Auckland Cathedral, at the Antipodes.

Beneath the floor a pit was sunk, in which was placed the apparatus in question. It consists of a large drum, made of wrought iron bars, about a quarter of an inch apart, between which are fixed a number of teeth. We give an engraving of the whole apparatus, in order to make our description clearer. This drum being made to revolve by means of a handle, the teeth catch the eight levers in connection with the hammers fixed on the bell-frame above. The lever being drawn down, the hammer is elevated; when the tooth releases the lever, the hammer falls and strikes a note. The principle is that of the barrel-organ, or musical snuff-box; and by this ingenious adaptation of it, one man can chime as many changes or as many tunes as are set upon the drum. The experienced campanologist will notice, too, in the woodcut that the hammers

PEAL OF EIGHT BELLS WORKED BY MACHINERY.
MESSRS. WARNER AND SONS. PRIZE MEDAL.

which chime are so set that they do not at all interfere with the ordinary ringing of the bells. Why should not every village, then, which has a peal of bells, have its chimes also? The machinery is not very costly, and the parish sexton or the vicar's footboy can work it.

This machine, however, is no substitute for ringers; the hammer thus falling by its own weight will never produce the volume of swelling sound which the swinging bell floats out of the weather-boarded belfry windows over moorland and lea. But the machine will certainly tend to encourage ringing, by promoting a taste for the music of the bells, rather than discourage its cultivation. Where, however, the ringers are troublesome fellows—and that fact does occur sometimes—the acquisition of one of Messrs. Warner and Son's machines will make the clergyman so independent of their services that he will be in a much better position for keeping them under control.

Messrs. Warner likewise exhibited a set of musical hand-bells, tuned to the chromatic scale, and various bells for domestic use. The bells in connection with Mr. Dent's large clock under the Eastern Dome were also cast by this firm.

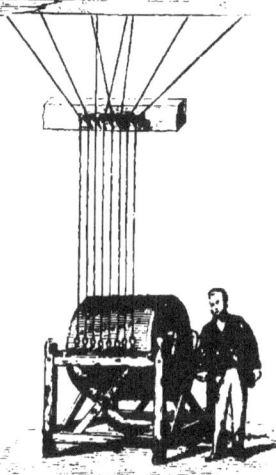

MESSRS. NAYLOR & VICKERS' CAST STEEL BELLS.

In the South Eastern Transept was placed the peal of cast steel bells, to which we alluded at page 22, and which, in their gothic tower, attracted such general attention. The bells themselves were painted blue, in order to avoid the deleterious effect of the atmosphere. They are very remarkable specimens of casting, and Messrs. Naylor and Vickers, of Sheffield, may well be proud of the distinction conferred on them by the award of a prize medal.

Cast steel bells are considered much stronger and more durable than bells made of bronze, while their weight and cost is diminished by nearly two-thirds. Thus, the peal of eight bells shown in our engraving costs about £300, with a tenor of 54 inches in diameter, tuned to E. The weight of the whole is not more than 8,000 lbs. The largest bell exhibited by Messrs. Naylor and Vickers is 7 feet 6 inches in diameter, and weighs 9,000 lbs. This also is priced at only £300.

It is not surprising that the bells in the Exhibition—and that there were a large number was evident from the clang every evening's "ringing out" caused—were viewed with great interest by all sorts of visitors, for bells are associated with our earliest recollections. Their music is of a very old fashion indeed, for it formed part of the ceremonial law of the Jews in the time of Moses. Egypt, Greece, Italy, China, Russia, England, have all been bell-loving countries, for, as Longfellow has it—

" The bells are the best preachers;
Their brazen lips are learned teachers,
From their pulpits of stone, in the upper air,
Sounding aloft, without crack or flaw,
Shriller than trumpets under the law,
Now a sermon and now a prayer,
The clamorous hammer is the tongue,
This way, that way, beaten and swung,

" The mellow wedding-bells—golden bells!
What a world of happiness their harmony foretells!
Through the balmy air of night,
How they ring out their delight;
From the molten-golden notes,
And all in tune,
What a liquid ditty floats
To the dove that listens, while she gloats

NAYLOR AND VICKERS' BELL TROPHY.   PRIZE MEDAL.

From mouth of brass, as from mouth of gold,
May be taught the Testaments, New and Old."

The bells, indeed, have voices that all o, us recognise and love.
Their brazen tongues speak, to our sympathies, and form part of our
dearest associations. They ring for births, weddings, and funerals;
alike for joys and sorrows their lusty peal clangs out upon the air.
Hear how a poet catches the very music of their chimes :—

On the moon !
Oh ! from out the sounding cells
What a gush of euphony voluminously wells !
How it swells ! How it dwells
On the future ! how it tells of the rapture that impels
To the swinging and the ringing
Of the bells, bells, bells,
To the rhyming and the chiming of the bells !"

LOCKS.

THE London Hardware Court in the Exhibition was adorned with a splendid and various collection of locks and keys, the principal exhibitors being Messrs. Chubb and Son, and Messrs. Hobbs and Co.

CHUBBS' BANK LOCK, FOR SPECIAL SECURITY OF IRON SAFES AND DOORS. PRIZE MEDAL.

Messrs. Chubbs' collection was got up in Wolverhampton, and was on view there during two days, attracting thousands of visitors of all grades, and exciting admiration from no one so much as from the locksmiths of the town, who expressed a universal regret that the collection was not destined for its natural position—the Wolverhampton Court. There were about 300 locks exhibited, varying between a gigantic rim lock weighing more than 2 cwt., and as finely finished as a lady's watch, and an elegant little gold lock, with four tumblers, set in a finger ring, and weighing 16 grains! All are made by hand! A "grand ornamental lock," 20 by 14½ inches, is a magnificent piece of workmanship. Some fifty keys are shown with elaborate bows, three so much so, that, although small, they are valued at upwards of a hundred guineas, the bow of each being composed of minute particles of steel, all separately riveted, and resembling so many brilliants. Messrs. Chubb made all the locks for the external doors. The master key to the whole is, as might be expected, a very handsome implement. Within the bow are the royal cypher, V.R., elegantly combined, and the date of the year, 1862, in gothic figures, surmounted by a crown. The design, we understand, was furnished by the Commissioners, and the whole of the filing and chiselling has been done by hand. The key was used by His Royal Highness the Duke of Cambridge, as First Commissioner, at the formal opening of the building.

In addition to locks and keys, Messrs. Chubb show a number of strong room doors and safes. Among the latter is the Jewel Safe, with ornamental sides and door, on each side a panel of Italian design, as shown in our engraving. The door is executed in a similar style, but in a mixture of dead and burnished steel, inlaid gilt scrolls, and ormolu mountings. The interior is fitted up in ornamental wood for the reception of jewellery. The door is secured by Chubbs' patent wheel lock throwing bolts all round. There is a second jewel safe with folding doors of dead steel, with inlaid gilt scrolls and ormolu mouldings. Also a very large banker's safe, weighing about four tons, the interior fitted with drawers, cupboards, and partitions for books. The outer folding-doors are made of wrought iron plates and hardened steel, combined in the most effective manner into a solid mass or plate 1½ inch in thickness. The doors are secured by two gunpowder-proof wheel locks,

throwing thirty-one bolts all round. There is a second banker's safe, having the same system of combined iron and hard steel applied throughout the entire casing of body, as well as the door.

The peculiarity of the locks exhibited by Messrs. Hobbs and Co.— the great rivals of our London lock-makers—is, that they are principally made by machinery. We have here several engravings of the locks themselves, and the implements employed in their manufacture.

The Bank Lock—our first engraving—is deemed unapproachable as a security of the repositories of treasure, and impregnable against every practicable method of picking, fraud, or violence. The "bits" or steps on the "web" of the key, that act on the levers inside the lock, are separate, instead of being, as in other keys, cut in the solid metal. These movable bits are fastened by a small screw on the end of the shank of the key, when it has the appearance of any other lever-lock key. There are, besides, spare "bits" to change, when desirable. The lock has three sets of levers, and is so constructed that, whatever arrangement the bits on the key may have when acting on the lock, the latter immediately adapts itself to the same arrangement, and it will lock and unlock with perfect facility; but it cannot be unlocked by any formation of the "bits" except that which locked it. By the self-changing principle of the lock, it assumes the new form of the key, and will work with it as readily and securely as it did before. The same results can be obtained by any and every permutation of the number of "bits" of which the key is composed, until millions, nay, thousands of millions of changes are worked, every change virtually converting the lock into a fresh lock, by this simple transposition of the key. Hence its name of "Parautoptic," or changeable.

The illustration represents a view of the lock, the key, and the spare "bits." To give an idea of the number of times this lock can be transposed, it may be mentioned, that a key of only six bits can be

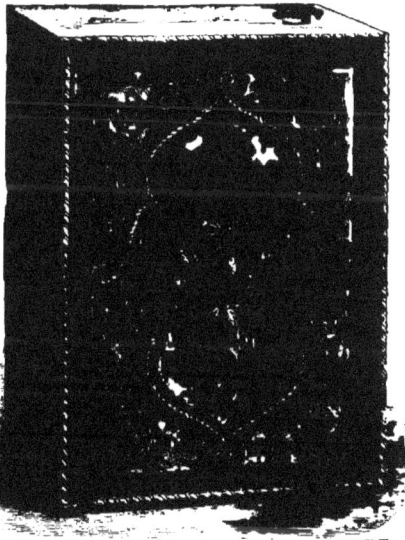

CHUBBS' PATENT JEWEL SAFE. PRIZE MEDAL.

altered seven hundred and twenty times; and, if two sets of bits are used, the transpositions extend to many thousand.

Hobbs' Patent Lock Indicator. This is a method of locking the doors of iron safes, strong rooms, custom stores, bonded vaults, prison cells, corridors, &c., by means of the handle, without a key, and showing to what extent the bolt has been shot. It may consist of the upper half of a dial, upon which are the words, "Open," "Shut," "Locked." When the door stands merely closed to, the index finger

unlocking, takes the index finger back to "Open," re-setting it again. The advantages of this index in dockyards, shipbuilders' stores, dock warehouses, prisons, &c., where certain officers are limited to departments of the premises by day or night, must be of the highest importance. This arrangement was first shown on the door of the iron safe exhibited by Messrs. Hobbs. This the jurors especially mentioned in their award.

Next we have illustrations of the cutters and dies wherewith these

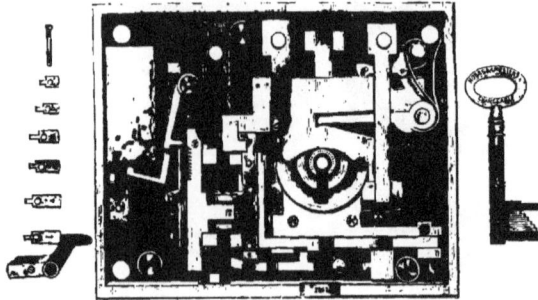

PATENT PARAUTOPTIC, OR BANK LOCK, WITH KEY AND BITS.

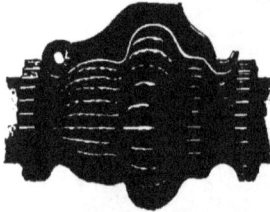

THE LOCK INDICATOR.

HOBBS' PATENT LOCK.

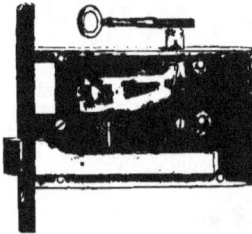

MORTISE LOCK.

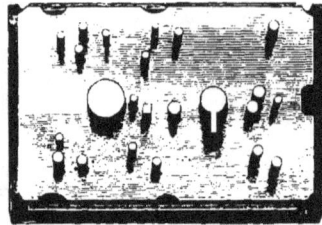

THE LOCK DIES.

MESSRS. HOBBS' LOCKS.   PRIZE MEDAL.

rests on "Open." This finger is fixed to the handle that works the lock, and, therefore, whichever way the handle moves, the finger must move with it. Turn the handle, and fasten the door by the first movement of the bolt, the finger will point to "Shut." A second motion of the handle, and the bolt shoots out beyond its reach, the finger, at the same moment, resting on "Locked." The lock can only be opened by the key, because, at the second turn, the handle loses its control of the bolt. The action of the bolt returning into the lock, or

locks are manufactured, as well as engravings of Hobbs' Mortise Lock, and the Patent Machine-made Lock. The application of machinery to the manufacture of locks dates from 1851, when the celebrated "Lock Controversy" took place. The identical lock which formerly sold for two guineas can now be purchased for eight shillings—a very important proof of the advantage of competition and machinery. Messrs. Hobbs offer a reward of £300 to any person who can pick their large lock; giving seven days for the examination of the lock, and thirty days to pick it—the only lock in the Exhibition for which a prize has been offered for picking.

Other exhibitors—Messrs. Bramah, Messrs. Hamilton, Messrs. Tucker and Reeves, all of London ; Messrs. Price, of Wolverhampton, &c.—make a good show of locks, and well sustain their old reputation; but there is no denying the fact that Messrs. Chubb and Son and Messrs. Hobbs and Co. stand at the head of the trade, for superiority of manufacture, and safety from the attacks of burglars, fire, or

require to be set to a given time before the lock can be opened, comprise no fewer than three thousand changes, and defy all attempts at opening by those who do not know the time at which the dials were set. Another description of detector lock contains a small gong, which rings out when the key is turned, like a lock in the Turkish collection. The contrast in the size of the padlocks is very striking, some being as small as the stone of a ring, and others as large as a cheese-plate, but all finished with the utmost nicety. Some of the

GROUP OF WROUGHT-IRON, BRONZED, AND JAPANNED GOODS.   MESSRS. GRIFFITH AND BROWETT.

gunpowder. The display of locks in the Exhibition was indeed surprising, revealing, as it did, the perfection of mechanism, with elaborate and artistic finish. There were all kinds of locks for chest, trunk, drawer, wardrobe, carpet-bag, portfolio, ledger, and till ; and padlocks, many of which are a combination of patents, and are perfectly unpickable. Two specimens of detector locks, with outer dials, which

folio locks are also so minute that a dozen of them might be sent by post for two stamps. The locks are all supplied with keys, and the inner sides of the case are hung round with keys and small padlocks. The keys are quite equal to the locks in finish and ornamentation, the design of the bows being very elaborate. Wolverhampton is the great seat of the lock manufacture in England, and it is admirably represented.

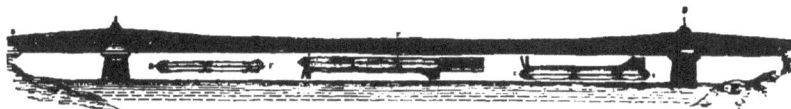

MR. SEDLEY'S PATENT BRIDGE.

A BRIDGE ON A NEW PRINCIPLE.

VISITORS to the Exhibition will remember the models of a bridge constructed on an entirely new principle, the invention of Mr. Angelo Sedley, engineer, of Great St. Helen's, Bishopsgate. This bridge is a combination of the tubular, girder, and suspension principles, and combines great simplicity and easy and economical construction; and the combination differs entirely from any employed up to the present time. No intermediate piers or subaqueous works are necessary. The bridge may be built as easily at a height of 500 feet above the level of the river or valley, as at a height of 25 feet ; and wood, iron, and steel may be used in combination ; or, in large spans, iron and steel only.

The models are built up of veneer, deal, and tape; weigh about 25lbs. each ; are on a scale of 60 feet to 1 foot, representing bridges 1,050 feet long, at a height of 40 and 80 feet from level of water ; and may be seen at the Museum of Patents, South Kensington, and the Crystal Palace, Sydenham.

The model of this bridge was tested and broken on Friday, Oct. 31st, by permission of the Commissioners, in the open area of the Eastern Annexe of the International Exhibition of 1862, when it bore a pressure of 503lbs. before it finally gave way; thus proving the excellence of the principle of construction proposed by Mr. Sedley.

Horology in the Great Exhibition.

WHEN it is remembered that, in addition to the whole of the watches and clocks annually produced in England, we are under the necessity of importing for home consumption watches from Switzerland, and clocks from France and America, of more than £1,000,000 worth per annum, the importance of the Horological Department of the Great Exhibition will be manifest.

For this reason, and from the fact that, as the foreign manufacturers increased in amount of late years, the quantity manufactured at home has fallen off more than one-third since the year 1855, this year's display of the respective rivals was regarded with much interest on all sides; it is, therefore, satisfactory to know that, both in quantity and quality, the English manufacturer maintained a most creditable position. Indeed, several of the most eminent houses have produced chronometers, duplex and lever watches of the highest quality for scientific construction and for precision of performance; while as to the

external form and decoration, it was clear that the application of art to this branch of manufacture has made considerable advance in the last ten years.

In clocks of a scientific construction the English have always been pre-eminent. As far back as 1715, the astronomical regulator was brought to absolute perfection by George Graham, whose escapement and pendulum are those still used for the most precise astronomical purposes at the present day; and it is equally true that in clocks chiming the quarters, suitable for the baronial hall, no foreign manufacturer has ventured to compete with this specialty of English workmanship. Fine specimens in the three points, for the use of the navigator, for the astronomer, and the nobleman, were displayed by such houses as Hislop, Delolme, Blackie, Frodsham, and Bennett—the highest class of instruments, in virtue of their extreme simplicity, in which respect the English regulator and chronometer have long left no room for improvement;

32

while in the more complex and intricate combination of mechanical contrivance, the Swiss produce specimens which to the English workman is felt to be forbidden ground; so also, whenever the clock is made an article of ornament for the mantelpiece, the machine is held to be of more importance as an object of art and beauty in design, than as a scientific instrument. The Frenchman is known to excel wherever the mind and delicate touch of the artist is required to produce a thing of beauty and elegance, and there France fairly merited the place of honour. In the midst of so much variety and extent of horological products, it would only create confusion to give a particular catalogue, specifying every peculiarity of its form and construction. We may take one example, the most prominent in the English department, that of Mr. Bennett, Cheapside. As president of his class, he felt bound to occupy such a position as would have every principal branch of horology fully represented in his case. It is a remarkable fact,

tation; while the huge time-ball descended with undeviating regularity, detached at every hour by the electric current from the Royal Observatory at Greenwich. Thus, so far as perfect precision can go, nothing more exact can be required. The lesson taught by this international display proved to the English workman that his best energies must be steadily directed to external elegance, to the higher cultivation of the fine arts as applicable to his mechanical production, and, above all, by a better system, and perhaps, by enlisting the valuable assistance of the female hand, to insure a mode of manufacture which shall cheapen the cost of production. The English must produce a watch good enough and cheap enough for the million; they must give the maximum of quality at the minimum of cost, and then it will be admitted that this great concourse of manufacturing ingenuity has not been organised in vain, and that the beneficial effect in this, as well as in many other departments, will be tended alike to the

GROUP IN PARIAN—FAITH, HOPE, AND CHARITY. FROM THE COLLECTION OF MESSRS. J. WEDGWOOD AND SONS, ETHRURIA, STAFFORDSHIRE.

demonstrating the absolute perfection of horological science, that Mr. Bennett produced and exhibited a chronometer, a regulator, and the time ball, the results of which in action were absolutely coincident for days and weeks together. This is the more striking, since these three very remarkable instruments were totally distinct in their organisation, their arrangements, and their motive and controlling powers—the chronometer moved with its mainspring and its balance; the regulator by its mercurial pendulum, and its weight, and the law of gravi-

advantage of the consumer and the producer. The manufacturer will flourish, the workman will enjoy the remuneration he so richly deserves, and will find the means of attaining a higher and more honourable social position; while among the whole world of watch-wearers the next generation may hope to see, in days of more strict punctuality and more swift locomotion, that it will become for every man and every woman as much the custom to wear an elegant watch as to possess an enlightened head.

Works in Terra Cotta,

EXHIBITED BY MARK H. BLANCHARD AND CO.

AMONG the "objects shown for architectural beauty"—Class 10, Sub-Class C—were various fine works in cast iron, zinc, lead, papier-maché, carton-pierre, wood, serpentine and other marbles, mosaic and other decorative applications of marbles, slate, &c., enamelled wares, scagliola, majolica, parian, earthenware, baked clay, terra cotta, &c.—taking

shape as fountains, chimney-pieces, cheap statuary columns, vases, tiles, bricks, carvings for building, and various other forms of decoration. In this sub-class, Prize Medals were obtained by twenty-two exhibitors on the British side; while honourable mention is made of eight others. Among the names of the British prizeholders, we find several of the more prominent exhibitors in the South Court.

Exhibitors from Austria, Belgium, Denmark, France, Greece, Italy, the Netherlands, Prussia, Russia, are also similarly distinguished. Of the works thus shown, we select a few examples from the objects exhibited by Mark H. Blanchard and Co., of the Blackfriars Road, who are rewarded with a Prize Medal for "articles in terra cotta applicable to architectural and decorative purposes."

"It is rather remarkable," says the writer of a paper read at the Royal Institute of British Architects, "that the revival of the manufacture of terra cotta, or, more properly, vitrified stone, in England, should have been effected by a lady, about eighty years ago. Miss Coade, from Lyme Regis, possessing a large share of scientific knowledge and energy, embarked in a small manufactory of terra cotta, or vitrified stone, in Lambeth, which, by her perseverance and good management, eventually attained a considerable degree of celebrity. To this original establishment in Lambeth the merit is due of greatly improving the

GARDEN VASE FOR FLOWERS.

composition of the material, and the processes by which its permanent character was attained. The proprietor had also sufficient enterprise and discrimination to avail herself of the talents of some distinguished artists, and thus produced works of a superior character, which may fairly vie with those of the chisel. The bas-relief in the pediment over the western portico at Greenwich Hospital,

representing the death of Nelson, was designed by West, and executed by Bacon and Panzetta, who also modelled many other distinguished works. The rood screen, or loft at St. George's Chapel, Windsor, was executed in the same material.

"With respect to modern instances of its use, St. Pancras Church may be considered as one of the most important, the greater part of the ornamental details being formed of this material, at the large outlay of £5,400. The work was executed by Mr. Rossi, from the designs of Mr. Inwood, the architect, and, according to present appearances, the material promises to be very durable. About the same time, extensive bas-reliefs, colossal figures, and other decorations executed in the same material, were placed on the front of the Custom House, London; but these specimens have been removed. The statue of Britannia, made of terra cotta, which crowns the Nelson Monument at Yarmouth, remains uninjured by the exposure to which the stone work seems yielding. The Bau Schule, in Berlin, by Schinkel, is a remarkable example of the modern adaptation of moulded brick and terra cotta, of which every part, even the face of the walls, is most carefully wrought and finished. The ancient examples are evidently formed simply of fine clay, or brick earth, carefully prepared and well burnt, and they are therefore precisely of the same nature as coarse pottery ware, and are correctly

VASE FROM THE ANTIQUE.

VASE FROM THE ANTIQUE.

designated terra cotta. But the modern terra cotta, or vitrified stone, is a very different substance, and greatly superior to them in hardness, texture, and colour. Its durability, if properly manufactured, may be deemed almost unlimited; and its economy, if judiciously applied, is a further recommendation; but this involves many important considerations for the judgment and discretion of the architect."

Mr. Blanchard obtained the Prize Medal in 1851; and in the report of the jurors of the Great Exhibition we learn that "several objects exhibited by him, including part of a gothic pinnacle, a capital, and some smaller articles, are of a very excellent colour, and the details of construction admirable. The tint is that of the material as it leaves the kiln, without artificial colour, stopping, wash, or paint, and is extremely hard and uniform; it does not alter on exposure. The works of this establishment have stood the test of time."

Messrs. Blanchard are the successors of Miss Coade; and in the present Exhibition they show a large variety of useful and ornamental

Terra cotta is a substance requiring but little care for its preservation, and is, next to glass, the most indestructible of all bodies used in the arts. It appears, indeed, that the less valuable material a work of art is executed in, the greater is its chance of preservation; and in all probability, had the ancient tombs of Greece contained vases of metal, they would have been disturbed centuries before the thirst of antiquities led us to explore their remains. Experience has proved that the only lasting material next to glass is highly-vitrified terra cotta.

One great recommendation of terra cotta is its comparatively small cost; another is the facility with which the material may be moulded into any architectural or decorative form; while a third, as already stated, is its nearly indestructible nature. To notice the principal works executed and shown by this firm would occupy too much of our space; but we may mention that, while the beautiful is judiciously selected, the useful has by no means been neglected. Thus, while we

GROUP OF OBJECTS IN TERRA COTTA. MESSRS. BLANCHARD AND CO. THREE SHOWN.

articles in this material, the forms of some of which are shown in our engravings. Many of these are from ancient examples, carefully remodelled from casts, and from original drawings made from private collections. Others are designed by the exhibitor and artists whom he has employed. The vases shown are of the embossed or sculptural class. Very few embossed vases of ancient workmanship are to be found in this material, compared with the great number found with plain outline and painted ornament. At the era of the fabrication of the best works in terra cotta, which is generally considered to be about 500 years before Christ, it was common with the Etruscans to adorn many parts of their temples with terra cotta; and it is remarkable that while nearly all the great works of architecture and art generally have either fallen to decay or suffered violent violence, these fragile memorials should have been preserved to our time with all the sharpness and freshness they possessed 2,500 years since. They convey to us a more intimate knowledge of the durability of the material, and the manners and customs of their authors, than the more costly monuments of antiquity.

have reproductions in this cheap material of Gibson's "Venus," Westmacott's "Psyche," Baily's "Flora," Thorwaldsen's "Venus," and various well-known examples of figures, groups, busts, statuettes, pedestals, &c., numerous examples of gables, terminals, tracery bosses, finials, balustrades for parapets, chimney shafts and pots, and garden borderings, &c., are manufactured in elegant forms. The garden bordering, or edging, we may state, is both useful and ornamental; for, while it adds to the neatness of the flower-beds, in preventing the mould from washing over the paths, stopping the drains, &c., it possesses the one great advantage over box edging that it never needs renewal, and can be removed and re-fixed at any time, when alteration in the forms of the parterre are desirable. In objects also for the conservatory, grounds, or garden, Messrs. Blanchard show a large and interesting variety. For fencing and telegraph posts, fireproof stairs, tessellated tiles, &c., terra cotta has been shown to be a most suitable material, combining beauty of design with amazing strength and durability. The columns in the Horticultural Gardens have been tested to a pressure of twenty tons!

Great Guns and Small Arms.

An engraving of the Small Arms Trophy in the nave will be found at page 57, followed by some description of the Armstrong Trophy now illustrated, and a general account of the ordnance, &c., shown in the Exhibition; and at page 128 we have an engraving of the Blakely cannon. Moreover, on pages 182 and 183 will be found an account of the manufacture of the Armstrong gun, with some reference to its

> "Brought iron under every day,
> Blown from over every main,
> And mixt, as life is mixt with pain,
> The works of peace with works of war."

Muskets, rifles, swords, sabres, and other military appliances have, of course, many attractive features; but other weapons used for less

THE ARMSTRONG GUN TROPHY.

introduction. But so important, in these times, is the manufacture of firearms, that we are induced again to refer to the subject.

Notwithstanding the dreams of universal peace and brotherhood indulged in by so many amiable enthusiasts, it is true that, in these days of artistic and industrial progress, arts and arms indeed go hand in hand. The Exhibition is an epitome of the world; and, as the Poet Laureate has it, all the evidences of the industry and skill of mankind, ranged under some few general heads, are here exhibited:—

harmful purposes also claim recognition. Sporting guns are shown in great variety, many of them being novel in their construction and elegant in their workmanship. Of all the sporting guns and rifles which the Exhibition of 1862 has brought into use, none are so important as "Daw's Patent Central Fire Breech-Loader." This valuable gun has been patented by Mr. G. H. Daw, of Threadneedle Street, and promises to become the sportsman's weapon par excellence. Mr. Daw's system of breech-loading is cortainly superior to any other yet brought forward, being at once correct in its principle, simple in its application, certain in its purpose, and apparently incapable of getting out of order. The principle is applicable to every description of fire-arm; while the several parts being manufactured by patent machinery, insure greater accuracy,

instead of the barrels falling over, as in other breech-loaders, in the new gun the stock is lowered by pressing the lever, the barrels remaining horizontal in the left hand, and held in the same place as when the gun is discharged. The cartridge is placed ready for discharge, as quickly as a copper cap can be placed on the nipple of an ordinary muzzle-load-

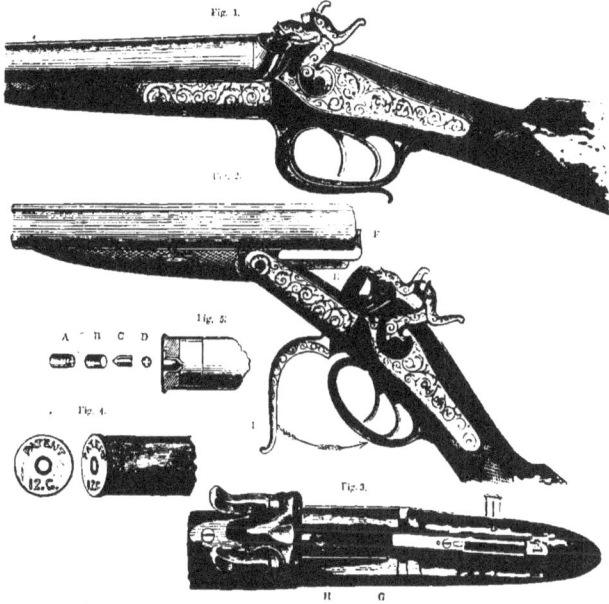

Fig. 1.

Fig. 2.

Fig. 5.

Fig. 4.

Fig. 3.

DAW'S PATENT CENTRAL-FIRE BREECH-LOADING GUN AND CARTRIDGE. PRIZE MEDAL.

and a more perfect gun, at a reasonable price, than was ever before introduced. Some guns used with the brass pin cartridge can be converted on the new patent principle at a trifling cost. Patents have, we understand, been secured in this and foreign countries.

ing gun; it has few pieces, is very substantial, is not affected by cold, rust, or wear, and is not likely to get out of order. It can be rapidly loaded or unloaded with the hammers down at half or full cock, with the greatest safety. The cartridges are exploded by an ordinary

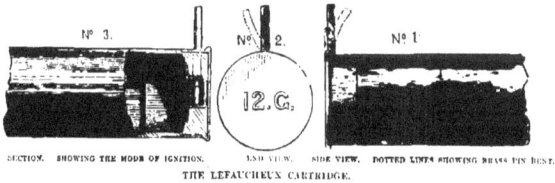

Nº 3. Nº 2. Nº 1.

SECTION. SHOWING THE MODE OF IGNITION. END VIEW. SIDE VIEW. DOTTED LINES SHOWING BRASS PIN BENT.

THE LEFAUCHEUX CARTRIDGE.

Daw's breech-loader resembles the ordinary muzzle-loader in appearance, while its lightness, elegance, simplicity, and superior shooting qualities cannot fail to be appreciated by all sportsmen. In opening or closing the breech, there is but one simple movement;

copper cap, in the centre of the cartridge, which is effected by a stroke from a strong steel piston; and, being central-fire, miss-fires are almost impossible. The cartridges having no brass pegs or dangerous projections, can be carried in the pocket with perfect safety; and the cartridge cases, after explosion, can never stick in the barrel. There is a strong, simple, steel slide, self-acting (without any spring or screws) to force out the cartridge case, and the improvement in the uniformity and hard shooting is extraordinary. The principle has been severely tested by some of the best sportsmen of the day, who have unhesitatingly pronounced the gun and cartridge the "acme of perfection." The ammunition is waterproof, moderate in price, and, by re-capping, can be used several times. Let us now endeavour to describe this admirable weapon by means of diagrams:—Fig. 1 shows gun complete; fig. 2, gun opened ready for loading; fig. 3, part of stock, with hinged fore-part, showing connection for barrels; fig. 4, form of cartridge, with cap in the centre, and below the surface; fig. 5, section of cartridge, showing brass cup, with communication hole in the centre, and direct into the charge.

A, percussion cap, with brass anvil inside, ready to be placed in brass cup, as seen in fig. 4; B, percussion cap; C, brass anvil, with grooves for communicating the flame into the powder. The conical end is placed towards the fulminate, and receives the blow of the piston from the fall of the hammer; D, bottom of anvil, showing the grooves and front part, which rests against the shoulder inside the cup, for resisting the blow of the piston; E, piston points, for exploding percussion caps; F, self-acting steel slide, for drawing out exploded cartridge cases; G (fig. 3), socket for receiving and fixing steel bolt on the barrel lump at breech end of barrels; H (fig. 3), steel bolt for locking and fastening the barrels; I (fig. 2), lever connected with steel bolt for opening or closing the breech.

In order to show in what manner the cartridge of the Daw gun

paper; blowing out of the pin; escape of gas through the pin-hole; difficulty in re-capping, &c.; brass pin soon widening hole in the chamber of barrels.

These objections are remedied in Mr. Daw's central-fire cartridges. Sportsmen will, therefore, understand and appreciate the use of a gun with cartridge which is entirely safe and certain to ignite,

SPORTING GUN. W. R. PAPE. HONOURABLE MENTION.

and which has the further advantage of being extremely moderate in price. The method of detonation is far superior to that of the Lefaucheux breech-loader, while in the several plans of locking and detaching the barrels, extracting the cartridge-cases, and re-capping them, such great simplicity has never before been attained. "I have," says a practical sportsman, "fired this gun in the dark without de-

WHITWORTH PROJECTILE.   WHITWORTH PROJECTILE.

THE WHITWORTH GUN. PRIZE MEDAL.

is superior to that of the breech-loaders in general use, we give a drawing of the ordinary "Lefaucheux" cartridge, hitherto in use. The principal objections to the above principle are—danger of explosion from the pin being forced on to the fulminate; liability to miss fire, from the brass pin getting bent; sticking in the barrel, requiring a rod to force it out from the muzzle; frequent separation of metal from the

tecting the slightest escape of gas. I therefore do not imagine that there will be the slightest tendency in the gun to get out of order. As far as I have been able to try it, I have the highest opinion of its merits." Testimonials from many of our best-known sportsmen are to the same effect; and, as it seems to us, there is little doubt of the Daw breech-loader becoming not only popular, but universally adopted by all who value

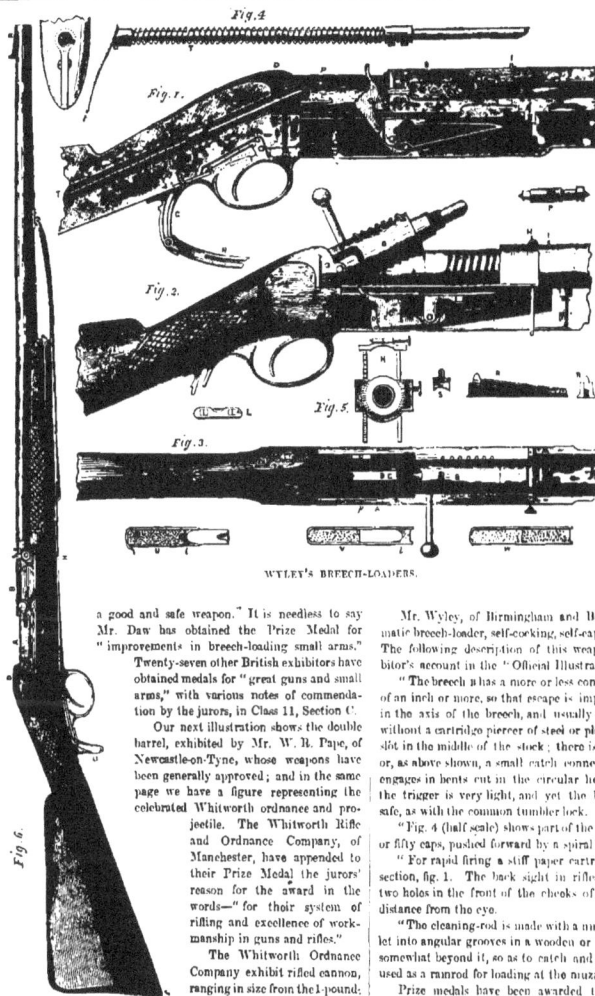

WYLEY'S BREECH-LOADERS.

a good and safe weapon." It is needless to say Mr. Daw has obtained the Prize Medal for "improvements in breech-loading small arms." Twenty-seven other British exhibitors have obtained medals for "great guns and small arms," with various notes of commendation by the jurors, in Class 11, Section C.

Our next illustration shows the double barrel, exhibited by Mr. W. R. Pape, of Newcastle-on-Tyne, whose weapons have been generally approved; and in the same page we have a figure representing the celebrated Whitworth ordnance and projectile. The Whitworth Rifle and Ordnance Company, of Manchester, have appended to their Prize Medal the jurors' reason for the award in the words—" for their system of rifling and excellence of workmanship in guns and rifles."

The Whitworth Ordnance Company exhibit rifled cannon, ranging in size from the 1-pound-er to the 70-pounder gun. These are all rifled, and are constructed of steel, iron, brass, wrought and cast-iron, the preference being given to the two first-mentioned metals. The shape of the solid projectile is seen in the smaller engravings. They are first cast and then planed. Hollow shot are similarly treated, and then filled in the same manner as the ordinary spherical shells. No special fuse is required, as the flash of the explosion ignites a fuse in the front, placed and used like the ordinary time-fuse. These cannon have a very long range, with a comparatively small charge of powder. The ranges of a 12-pounder rifled cannon, with a 12lb. shot, and 1½lb. of powder, are point blank, 350 yards; 1 degree of elevation, 900 yards; 5 degrees, 2,600 yards; 10 degrees, 4,500 yards; 20 degrees, 7,000 yards; and 35 degrees, 10,000 yards, or nearly six miles! The projectile penetrates iron armour-plates most effectually, especially when hard metal flat-fronted shot have been used. Lately there has been some little discussion as to the comparative merits of the Armstrong and the Whitworth guns. We do not presume to offer an opinion on the point in dispute. A case of the Whitworth rifles, manufactured by the same company, is also exhibited, containing military and sporting rifles of various weights and lengths.

Mr. Wyley, of Birmingham and Belfast, shows a "patent automatic breech-loader, self-cocking, self-capping, using any ammunition." The following description of this weapon is reduced from the exhibitor's account in the "Official Illustrated Catalogue":—

"The breech n has a more or less conical lip entering three quarters of an inch or more, so that escape is impossible. The nipple is placed in the axis of the breech, and usually screwed from inside, with or without a cartridge piercer of steel or platinum. The cock works in a slot in the middle of the stock; there is no tumbler; and the trigger, or, as above shown, a small catch connected to the trigger by a link engages in bents cut in the circular head of the cock. The pull of the trigger is very light, and yet the bents as deep, and the gun as safe, as with the common tumbler lock.

"Fig. 4 (half scale) shows part of the priming-tube, containing forty or fifty caps, pushed forward by a spiral spring outside.

"For rapid firing a stiff paper cartridge is used, as shown in the section, fig. 1. The back sight in rifles, H, fig. 5, slides vertically in two holes in the front of the cheeks of the breech-case, at the usual distance from the eye.

"The cleaning-rod is made with a number of india-rubber washers, let into angular grooves in a wooden or metallic head, and projecting somewhat beyond it, so as to catch and retain the fouling. It can be used as a ramrod for loading at the muzzle."

Prize medals have been awarded to several foreign exhibitors, especially to the French, who show some admirable weapons. Mr. Colt, of the United States, also obtains a medal for his well-known revolver; but for perfection of manufacture, truth of principle, and simplicity of design, the Daw Breech-loader is admitted to be the most valuable weapon shown in the International Exhibition of 1862.

The American Court.

THE show made by about seventy exhibitors from the United States was not certainly very extensive, but it was very interesting and highly suggestive, though occupying but a corner of the South Eastern transept at the British end of the building. The deplorable civil war in the United States has caused the American exhibition to be both small and incomplete. Nevertheless, we have numerous indications of the old "go-ahead" genius of the people who invented the reaping-

in the ordinary mode of manufacture. This is even a more important machine than that invented by Mr. Bigelow, for the weaving of Brussels carpets by steam, introduced in 1851, and now in 1862 shown by Messrs. Jackson and Graham in operation in the Western Annexe.

Sewing-machines, boot and shoemaking-machines, and other clever "notions" will also be remembered by the visitor as having excited his curiosity in the American Court. A machine for picking cotton in the

THE AMERICAN COURT.

machine, the sewing-machine, and a score of other useful appliances for the saving of labour in a country where labour is scarce and dear.

On entering the American Court, the visitor is struck with the sight of the reaping-machine of Mr. M'Cormick, and other implements familiar to the public in the Exhibition of 1851. Mr. Smith, of West Farms, in the State of New York, shows a power-loom for weaving the kind of carpet known among us as the "Axminster tufted pile." By this machine, an entire row of above a hundred tufts is placed at one operation, and in less time than a single tuft can be made by hand

field, to supersede manual labour, is also shown, as well as a fine caloric engine, a Californian pump, a printing press, a model for a water-wheel, a steam-pump and pumping-engines, and a flax-fibre dressing-machine. These were shown in the Western Annexe: but in the court itself there were a variety of labour-saving implements well worthy examination. Then, besides, there were a phaeton and buggy, with light hickory spokes, and a wagon for common roads, with an excellent collection of axes and other farming and engineering implements.

33.

Dr. Feuchtwanger, of New York, sent a capital and complete museum of minerals; and various exhibitors displayed specimens of the rock oil called petroleum. This extraordinary product of Nature

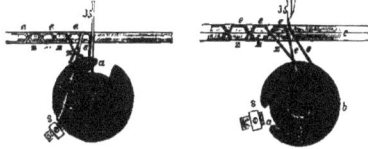

FIG. 1.—ROTATING HOOK.   FIG. 2.—BOBBIN, SHOWING FORMA-
                            TION OF STITCHES.

has been largely introduced into this country, and considerably improved by our manufacturers. The most useful and pure of the rock oils of America is that known as Cazeline. It is imported from Pennsylvania, the great emporium of petroleum, and, by means of chemical agencies, entirely deprived of its explosive qualities, and its naturally ungracious odour. It is useful for a large variety of purposes, such as the lubrication of machinery, &c.; but as a lamp-oil it is particularly valuable, as it gives a pure, soft, brilliant, white light, more than equal to coal gas in its intensity, and superior to it in the coolness with which it burns in common atmospheres. We understand that a company has been formed for the purification and sale of Cazeline in England, and that a very extensive demand has arisen for this admirable

FIG. 3.—LOCK-STITCH.

production of Nature. Having witnessed the burning of this oil, we can unhesitatingly declare that it is superior, in all respects, to any of the rock oils now in use.

Notice just inside the Court a frame of United States bank-notes, including not a few of the so-called skin-plasters of different States of the Union. Many of them are, however, excellent specimens of engraving. A revolving apparatus, for the exhibition of stereoscopic pictures, also struck us as novel; as also a collection of the headings of the various newspapers and political caricatures published in the States.

We have already noticed Mr. Cropsey's fine painting, "Autumn on the Hudson," which presents a faithful picture of the peculiar

SEWING MACHINE. MR. LUKE M'KERNAN.

atmospheric effect of what is known as the Indian summer, and the rich foliage of the forest on the banks of the noble river. There are also exhibited pianos, and various musical instruments; among others,

one called a "Toilodian." But the speciality of the American Court certainly lies in the variety and usefulness of the many

LABOUR-SAVING MACHINES,

some of which we now proceed to notice; merely premising that, for the sake of uniformity, we have here introduced some that belong not only to the United States, but also to England. These latter will be specified in the course of our remarks.

THE SEWING-MACHINE.

This useful invention owes its introduction to Mr. Howe, of the United States, where it is very largely employed. Mr. Howe commenced his invention in 1841, since which time it has been greatly improved. In the Processes' Court, as well as in the American Court, were to be seen at work at various stages of the sewing-machine, the

CORDING MACHINE—SHOWING METHOD OF WORKING.

general principles of which are now tolerably well understood. A description of one is a description of nearly all. Messrs. Wheeler and Wilson, of 139, Regent Street, had several of their

SEWING MACHINE. MESSRS. WHEELER AND WILSON.

improved sewing-machines in the Exhibition. The great peculiarity of their instrument is the possession of an apparatus for making what is called the "lock-stitch," which, when first introduced, was made with a shuttle—the use of which was attended with noise and necessitated rather heavy machinery. In forming the lock-stitch with Messrs. Wheeler and Wilson's machine, the loop of the upper thread, upon being thrust through the fabric, is seized by a rotating hook, as shown in fig. 1, and carried around the bobbin containing the lower thread (fig. 2), thereby interlocking the two threads. The point of interlocking being drawn into the fabric, the stitch is complete. There is no jerking motion; the succession of stitches form a direct line, and the thread is laid into the fabric evenly and firmly. This stitch (fig. 3), in formation, closely resembles the interlocking of threads in weaving, and, indeed, the seam is an additional interweaving of two threads with the fabric sewed. When properly formed, it is as firm and elastic as the fabric sewed, whether subject to lateral or longitudinal pressure, while it is buried so far below the surface of the fabric sewed that it is not affected by the action of the smoothing-iron in the laundry, or other wearing surfaces. Great gain has been achieved in substituting the rotating hook for the reciprocating shuttle. Power is economised, noisy and cumbersome gearing avoided, and the machine is adapted to the use of the finest thread. The mechanism is remarkable for its simplicity, and consequent freedom from derangement and need of repairs. It is recommended for beauty and excellence of stitch, *alike* upon *both sides* of the fabric sewed; strength, firmness, and durability of seam that will not rip or ravel, and made with economy of thread; its attachment and range of application to purposes and materials; compactness and elegance of model and finish; simplicity and thoroughness of construction; speed, ease of operation and management, and quietness of movement. It hems, fells, and gathers. Upwards of 80,000 of these machines have been sold, and in Canada and the United States it is generally preferred. It

set in motion by a gentle pressure of the foot upon the sandals. The motion is communicated directly by a band to the mandril, which drives the whole machinery. The needle, with the thread passing through the eye near the point from left to right, descends through the thread forming a loop, which is gently taken from the right of the needle by the rotating hook (fig. 1, preceding page). The rotating hook, in its revolution, enlarges the loop of the thread, and at the same time carries it around the bobbin containing the under thread (fig. 2), which is inclosed by the rotating hook, and confined in its place by a simple slide ring. By this method the upper and under threads are locked together, when the rise of the needle-arm draws up both, making in the centre of the fabric a firm "lock-stitch," presenting the same smooth appearance on both sides, and forming a seam much stronger

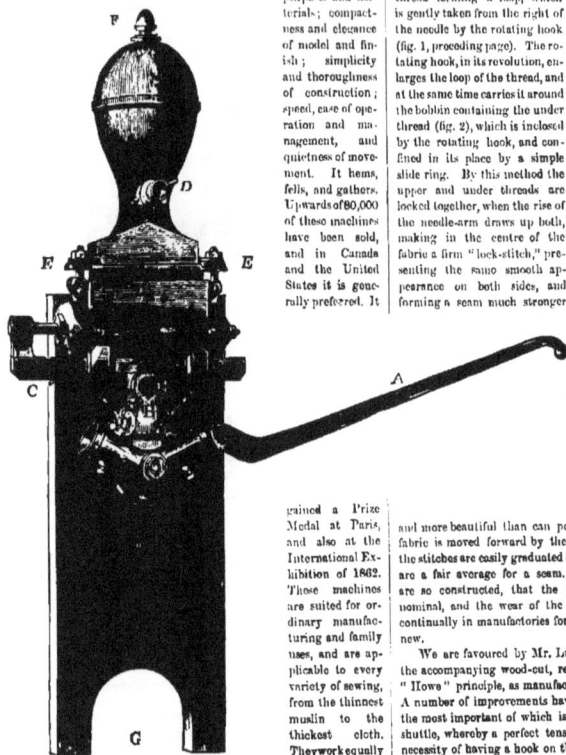

HANSBROW'S CALIFORNIA PUMP.

gained a Prize Medal at Paris, and also at the International Exhibition of 1862. These machines are suited for ordinary manufacturing and family uses, and are applicable to every variety of sewing, from the thinnest muslin to the thickest cloth. They work equally well upon silk, linen, woollen and cotton goods —

and more beautiful than can possibly be made by hand-sewing. The fabric is moved forward by the "feed" under the "cloth-plate," and the stitches are easily graduated by the operator. Three yards of thread are a fair average for a seam. The bearings and friction surfaces are so constructed, that the propelling power required is merely nominal, and the wear of the parts so trifling, that machines used continually in manufactories for five or six years are nearly as good as new.

We are favoured by Mr. Luke M'Kernon, of 98, Cheapside, with the accompanying wood-cut, representing a sewing machine on the "Howe" principle, as manufactured and sold by him in this country. A number of improvements have been added by him to this machine, the most important of which is a new arrangement for carrying the shuttle, whereby a perfect tension on the thread is obtained, and the necessity of having a hook on the heel of the shuttle entirely avoided, thus doing away with what was the cause of considerable inconvenience to the operator; the hook aforesaid being liable to break, and after wear not to be depended on.

An arrangement has also been added, whereby, according to the kind of work to be done, a greater or lesser degree of pressure on the pressing-pad or foot can be had at will by simply turning a thumb-screw in or out as desired.

The manner of placing the spool has also been altered from a perpendicular to a horizontal position; thus preventing the thread from

HANSBROW'S CALIFORNIA PUMP.

seaming, quilting, gathering, hemming, and felling—performing every species of sewing, except making button-holes and sewing on buttons. To work the machine, an operative seats herself at a small table on which the machine is placed, with her feet upon the sandals, by which it is driven. The fabric to be sewed is placed upon the cloth, plate beneath the needle, to pass from left to right. The machine is then at any time twisting round the spindle. The Howe Sewing Machine is the oldest patent sewing machine extant, the first machine being made in 1845.

Our large engraving on this page shows the sewing machines of Messrs. Simpson and Co., of 116, Cheapside, as they were at work at the Exhibition. By a most ingenious contrivance the edge of the material is folded by a gauge attached to the table of the machine at the time that the hemming is going on; while "sewing on" and either large or small "gatherings" are also effected by a simultaneous operation. The arrangement of the shuttle and the fly or frame which carries it is so perfect, and the method of regulating the tension of the thread so simple, that an even lock-stitch can be procured on both sides

Messrs. Simpson and Co. have prepared for this consummation in two respects—first, by producing their new invention at a lower price than that at which such machines are usually offered; and, secondly, by the very elegant form of their "Davenport" sewing machine, which combines a davenport (as its name implies), a lady's writing-desk, and the machine itself, in one elegant piece of furniture.

We have said that there are two means by which these machines will become popular, but there are really three, the last, but not the least, being the case with which the treadle is worked by a very slight pressure of the foot alone—an advantage in which most sewing machines are deficient.

That the sewing machine will come more and more into common

MESSRS. R. E. SIMPSON AND CO.'S SEWING MACHINES, AS SEEN IN THE PROCESS'S COURT.

without any liability to ravel or to rip out of the fabric. The various kinds of work simply require a change of needle and thread; and in the case of hem-folding, binding, and embroidery, the application of a gauge, which is fastened without difficulty. The operation of embroidery is one of the most extraordinary, and caused no little surprise amongst the visitors to the Great Exhibition. To see the piece of black cloth, upon which the pattern has been marked in a fine line of French chalk, come from under the needle converted in a few minutes into a gorgeous and elaborate slipper, dressing-gown, front, or child's frock, covered with crimson or gold arabesques, is a more marvellous feat than any of Messrs. Robin or Frickel's tricks of legerdemain; and to this display of the extraordinary facilities possessed by the new machine was doubtless owing the large number sold during the past three months.

family use in this country there seems little doubt; but what is to become of the needle-women if its use should be universal? Mr. Howitt answers the question for us. Writing in February, this talented lady says:—"Be not alarmed, kind-hearted philanthropists; for that which is in itself good can never ultimately produce evil. It is the sewing machine which will compel our senators and philanthropists to consider seriously the case of our sisters of the needle, and to legislate wisely for them. It is the sewing machine which will, in the end, emancipate miserable women from the slavery of 'gusset and band;' which will open to them wise and safe paths of emigration; which will convey away thousands of blameless, suffering women into new lands and for new homes of peace and plenty, where woman's time will be valuable, and where, consequently, the sewing machine will be again a household blessing—a household necessity.'"

We must hasten on to notice other ingenious implements. We have next several capital appliances shown in the American Court, and now supplied to the public through the agency of Messrs. Sanborn and Co., of 90, Cheapside.

Our engravings of

THE CALIFORNIAN PUMP

almost explain themselves. It combines the advantages of being

it, by giving motion to the rocking arm B, which moves the sliding bar c, attached to and under the barrel of the pump, through which bar the piston of the pump receives its motion. The inlet pipe to the pump passes up at o, at the back of the board. By loosening the nuts on the swinging bolts E E, the air chamber can be taken off, and the four valves removed for cleaning or repairing. D is the outlet for the water from the air chamber, and to which hose are attached when the

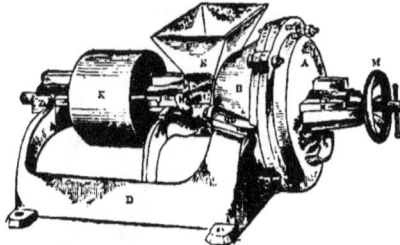

CONICAL BURR-STONE MILL.

WORKING SECTION OF THE SAME.

capable of doing all kinds of work in the way of a lifting, forcing, and fire-engine pump, and is alike adapted for the farm, the railway, the mine, the manufactory, the mill, the brewery, the garden, and various domestic uses. The following are some of the advantages claimed for it:—It is cheaper and more durable in all its parts than any other of an equal capacity. The valves are of the most simple construction, are readily accessible without removing a bolt or nut, not liable to get out of order, and can at all times be replaced without the necessity of calling in skilled labour. It is worked with less friction, and consequently requires less power, than any other double acting pump of

COW-MILKING MACHINE.

pump is used for a fire-engine. When only used for ordinary lifting purposes, the screw-plug F is taken out of the top of the air chamber to prevent the too violent ejection of water from it. The pump can be attached to a wall or post, and both inlet and outlet pipes can be brought out of the front or back when desired.

This pump is the invention of Mr. Hansbrow, who used it extensively in California. It deservedly obtained the Prize Medal at the Exhibition.

Messrs. Sanborn are also the importers of and agents for

THE CONICAL BURR-STONE MILL,

shown in our engravings. This mill is of light weight, but great power, and is useful to farmers, emigrants, and others.

Its construction will be understood by reference to the engraving : —a represents the running stone, which is a solid block of French burr, firmly secured to the spindle ; b b, segments of burr-stone, fitted in a cast-iron shell ; c c, the spindle or shaft ; d, the driving pulley, which may be either single or double with one loose ; e, the hopper ; f f f, the journal boxes, or bearings, which are filled with composition metal, and are very durable ; g, the jam-wheel, which prevents the set-screw from turning after the stone is adjusted ; h, the set-screw

CASK-CLEANSING MACHINE. W. ROBINSON, BRIDGEWATER. PRIZE MEDAL.

equal capacity. Owing to the arrangements of the valves with the barrel of the pump, it always remains primed, though not used for weeks at a time; and the valves do not become dry. The engraving represents the pump mounted on a board : A is the lever for working

which adjusts the stone ; i, the spout, or point of discharge l l, the cast-iron frame upon which the whole rests ; m, the feed regulator.

As the grinding surfaces are exactly fitted together, and ground to a perfect face, they grind even, and as fine or coarse as may be desired.

so that this mill will grind all kinds of grain, paints, colours, coffee, spices, drugs, &c., in a superior manner. As a portable mill this is a very valuable invention. The same exhibitors also show the now world-famed COW-MILKING MACHINE. By this curious machine the four teats of a cow are milked at the same time. No dirt can get into the milk; the machine, therefore, insures clean milking. The machine (including pail) weighs six pounds, and is as simple in its operation as a common hand - bellows, and is worked similarly, requiring no skill to operate it, and is as readily cleansed in all its parts as an ordinary milk-pail. Two years' practical use in the United States, and many trials in England, have proved this machine to be just what is needed by every country gentleman, farmer, and dairyman. Those who saw the Mechanical Cow-milker at work at the Exhibition will fully understand the interest excited by its appearance in this country. Experiments show that it is equally applicable to its destined use in England as in America. Having previously drawn attention to this ingenious apparatus, we pass on to

THE CLOTHES WRINGER AND STARCHER.

By the use of this machine, the applicability of which will at once be seen by referring to the drawing (p. 263), much labour is saved, while economy of time and labour are equally effected. Every housewife is aware that the twisting or wringing of clothes stretches and breaks the fibres, but this machine presses them so evenly that a newspaper, thoroughly soaked, can be wrung without breaking it, and it works so easy, that a child can operate it without trouble. Hot water does not injure the rollers; and woollen goods can be wrung out of boiling water, to prevent fulling, which cannot be done by hand. In starching it is valuable, especially on large articles, as it leaves the starch in the clothes perfectly even. The clothes go through straight and even without twist or strain, and will dry at half the time usually required. The cow exhibitors show a highly useful instrument, called

THE CLOTHES-DRYER.

This simple machine consists of an upright standard, with a double pulley on the top, through which a cord passes, and by means of which the clothes-line, are elevated and expanded, or lowered, as may be desired. The dryer is maintained at the proper height by the elevating cord passing under a self-acting cam, which holds it at any point. When not in use, it folds compactly together, like an umbrella, and can easily be removed under cover.

Every one knows the miseries of washing-day, when the house is full of steam, and the garden crowded with wet "things." By the use of the Wringer and the Clothes Dryer, all these miseries may be materially lessened, if not altogether avoided. The Clothes Dryer is emphatically one of the most useful of the American inventions yet introduced; it is, moreover, so cheap as to be within the means of every household.

Messrs. Sanborn are also agents for a number of useful

STEVENS'S PATENT BREAD-MAKING MACHINE.

BOX-CHURN.

BREAD-CUTTING MACHINE.

COMPOUND OVAL CHURN.

EGG-WHISK, OR WHIPPING-CAN.

machines for bookbinders. In our engraving is shown a board-cutter of improved construction. This, with "backing" machines, sewing machines, a grinding machine, piercing machines, and a standing-press, will be found to be highly useful to bookbinders, being, indeed, great improvements on the instruments in present use.

The patent Spinning and Rope-making Machines, again, are both

SANBORN'S CLOTHES WRINGER AND STARCHER.

novel and important, and, moreover, occupy so little space as to be capable of being worked in a back kitchen.

The advantages of the Spinning Machine are, that the yarn spun by it possesses the strength of the best quality spun by hand, with the smoothness and regularity of that spun by machinery. It makes 120 lbs. average size Manilla yarn per day, or 150 lbs. of green hemp, at a cost of 1s. 6d. for labour, requiring so little skill to operate it that girls are competent, and in a few days become expert hands. It is also well adapted for fine spinning. Yarns for twine and other purposes are made from this machine, of an excellent quality and great strength, and the manufacturer is enabled by the use of it to make yarn of first-rate quality for about half the usual cost.

The Rope Machine forms the strand and lays the rope in one operation. Its simplicity of construction removes all liability of its getting out of order, and renders it capable of being run at a higher rate of speed than many other machines of the same nature. It requires but little attention; two boys can attend to six machines. It is capable of making either large or small rope, and will "lay" equally well all kinds of material, whether hemp, Manilla, cotton, or jute.

PERRY'S PATENT PEN-HOLDER.

CLOTHES DRYER—CLOSED. In the next page we have an engraving of an improved pen-holder, admirably adapted for teaching youth to properly hold a pen, it being impossible to write with it if not held between the fingers in a correct position, as indicated by the three little plates for the thumb and forefingers. The only possible objection to be urged against this useful invention is its name, which is derived from two Greek words—*orthos*, upright; an *daktula*, fingers—the position of the fingers.

LABOUR-SAVING MACHINES SHOWN BY MR. BRADFORD.

The various instruments shown by Mr. Thomas Bradford, of 63, Fleet Street, attracted much attention, from their excellence and variety. Though not shown in the American Court, they are many of them of American-like simplicity and utility. The combined Washing, Wringing, and Mangling Machine, seen in our engraving, has

obtained the prize at more than a dozen agricultural meetings, as well as the Prize Medal at the International Exhibition. By a simple arrangement of rollers, &c., it will wash, wring, and mangle all kinds of articles, from a lady's lace collar to a blanket.

In another page we have

BRADFORD'S BREAD-CUTTING MACHINE,

a very capital contrivance for schools, hotels, public institutions, and

BRADFORD'S COMBINED WASHING, WRINGING, AND MANGLING MACHINE.

families. It cuts with ease, without crushing or tearing the bread; the slices can be varied in thickness, by regulating the guide, and are uniform throughout. The engraving will show the character of this useful implement.

THE BOX CHURN.

The dasher of this churn is of the best construction to create agitation, and carry down the air amongst the cream during the process of churning, producing butter quickly, and of better quality than any other box churn. A great advantage of this churn is, that the butter need not be touched with the hand, as it is made, washed, and salted in the churn; the liability of its turning rancid thus being entirely avoided. These ingeniously-contrived machines,

THE EGG WHISK AND WHISK CHURN,

are so simple in their construction and adaptation as to need no further description than is conveyed by the drawings. The egg whisk is one of the most simple yet effective articles ever constructed. It is admirably adapted for beating eggs, which can be done so quickly, and wrought to such a degree of lightness, as to be quite unattainable by the ordinary process. For puddings, whipt cream, cakes, sauces, &c. &c., it will be found unsurpassed, and will save both time and labour

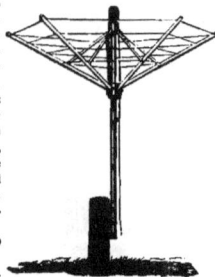

CLOTHES DRYER—READY FOR USE.

past. Little or no ceremony was observed at the official closing; beyond the singing of the National Anthem, no formality was observed. Nearly 40,000 visitors were present. As the clock struck four the well-known words of our national hymn were chanted by the members of

and, finally, "Rule Britannia" and "Auld Lang Syne." Visitors promenaded about the nave and transepts till dusk, unwilling to depart from the scene of so many pleasant meetings; and at last, when darkness had really over-shadowed the trophies and filled the courts and

MECHANICAL CONJURING TABLE, WITH APPARATUS. MR. NOVRA, REGENT STREET

the Sacred Harmonic Society, accompanied by a full swell of harmony from the many fine organs exhibited by Messrs. Walker and Hedgland, Messrs. Bevington, Mr. H. Willis, and Messrs. Foster and Andrews; afterwards, the French national air, "Partant pour la Syrie," was sung;

galleries, the palace was gradually deserted, and given over to the charge of the officials and the police.

And now, too, our pleasant labours draw to an end, and the last pages of the ILLUSTRATED EXHIBITOR warn us that there are yet a few items of information to record. First, as to the Exhibition itself. We may well compare it with its great predecessor of 1851. The following figures refer to the comparative extent of the two palaces:—

	1852 Building. Feet.	1851 Building. Feet.
Width of Nave and Transepts	85	72
Height of Nave and Transepts	100	64
Length of Transepts	692	155

	Tons.
Cast Iron	4,000
	No.
Columns, 25 feet in height (4 miles in length)	820
Girders (6 miles in length)	1,266
	s. d.
Cost of the Building (per cubic foot)	0 2
As compared with—	
Warehouses .	0 6
Dwelling Houses	0 9

CONCERT GRAND PIANOFORTE. MESSRS. KIRKMAN AND SON. PRIZE MEDAL.

The details of the International Exhibition building are as follows:—

	Feet.
Length of Annex (Agricultural Implements)	975
Height of ditto	45
Width of ditto	200
Length of Picture Gallery	1,152
Width of ditto	50
Height of ditto	38
Ditto to Tie-bar of Principals	43
Length of Auxiliary Picture Galleries	1,200
Width of Nave Galleries	50
Ditto of Central Entrance	150
Height of ditto	50

	Cubic Ft.
Scaffold for Erection of Domes contains	40,672
Ditto for Rib Transepts	30,396
Ditto for Nave Principals (weighing 57 tons, yet easily moved by four men)	4,740
Iron Girders to Floor of Picture Gallery (12 feet apart)	13½ by 12
Joists thereto (2 feet apart)	11 by 2½

	Lbs.
Floor proved to the foot	140

	Sq. Ft.
Felt for Roofs (11 Acres)	486,386
Glazing (247 Tons, or 1¾ Acres)	553,000
Bricks used	7,000,000

Ordinary Buildings	1 0
First-class Dwelling Houses	1 4
Houses of Parliament	3 0

And then as to the cost. The beautiful, fairy-like palace at Hyde Park cost, on the whole, less than £150,000. The contract with Messrs. Fox and Henderson for the building was only £79,800; but the purchase of the materials by the company formed for that purpose brought the total amount up to £142,780. Those among our readers who were not fortunate enough to visit the Industrial Palace in Hyde Park, may judge what was its charm by looking at the Crystal Palace at Sydenham—the same materials improved in the mode of construction.

The contractors' charge for the present structure, also inclusive of the purchase of materials, is £430,000, in addition to some items not yet made public.

The success of the present Exhibition is assured; though, as compared with that of 1851, such success is only partial. The Crystal Palace in Hyde Park was open during five and a half months, and was attended by 6,039,135 visitors, as estimated daily by the police. The total amount paid at the doors was £356,800. The produce of the sale of season tickets amounted to £67,600, and the gross total received from all sources was £505,107 5s. 7d., including the £67,400 which was subscribed before the undertaking commenced, and which was afterwards carried to the capital account, and made to swell the gross total. The actual money taken from all sources, less this subscription, was therefore £438,000.

The Paxton Temple of Glass received within its doors from 50,000 to 70,000 persons daily during the time of shilling entrances; and these numbers rose to nearly 110,000 at the last shilling days in October. After all was paid, and the accounts were finally made up, there remained a surplus of £186,436 18s. 6d. If from that we deduct the £67,400 subscribed by the public, we have a net profit of £119,036 18s. 6d. With this money, aided by a Government grant, the Com-

tion of space within the building was ill-contrived and indifferent; the facilities afforded to the Press were none at the commencement, and but grudgingly accorded when it was found that the fact was made public; the official catalogues were comparatively

it a short-lived and undeserved popularity. And yet, in spite and defiance of these short-comings, the Exhibition of 1862 has proved to be a limited success; proof this, if proof were needed, of the vital principle inherent in International Exhibitions of Art and Industry. Our readers would hardly have thanked us had we refrained from this expression of opinion—an opinion, be it remembered, shared by

THE PIPING BULLFINCH.

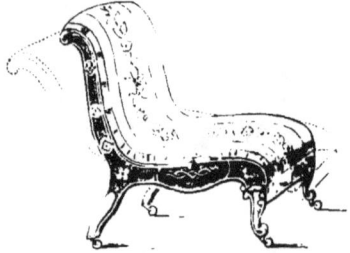

MR. SEDLEY'S EQUILIBRIUM CHAIR.

useless as works of reference, especially the so-called Illustrated Catalogue; the arrangements for the examination of goods by the jurors were incomplete and unsatisfactory; so much so, indeed, as to lead in many cases to most ridiculous and contradictory awards: in short, there has been displayed throughout a general want of good management and good taste. In our judgment, too, the very last act of the Royal Commissioners—the delaying the public distribution of the prizes by the Prince of Wales till January or February, 1863, when the building will be empty, cold, damp, and mildewed— is an inexcusable error. Great efforts will doubtless be made to render the ceremonial brilliant or imposing; but the public excitement and enthusiasm will have partially died out. The foreigners who came to the summer display of 1862 will hardly re-visit us in the middle of the dull English winter of 1863; and the monstrous structure of Captain Fowke will stand out in all its want of proportion and beauty, when deprived of that wonderful collection of artistic and industrial treasures which gave to

all whose opinions are worthy respect and record. That the managers of another experiment of the kind will profit by the example set them by the Exhibition of 1862, is as certain as that the Royal Commissioners almost ignored the principles which rendered the Exhibition of 1851 a splendid and unexampled triumph of executive skill and public appreciation.

MISCELLANEOUS OBJECTS.

To gather up the strings of a discourse, and to read a lesson from examples plentifully distributed is, at best, a difficult task. But yet the task must be attempted. Of course, it will be understood by our readers that the ILLUSTRATED EXHIBITOR is by no means a Catalogue of the objects shown at the International Exhibition; but that all we have endeavoured to do has been to direct attention to the more prominent and noteworthy of the articles which attracted public attention during the six months of the World's Show. We present a few more pictures, and make a few more remarks, and then close our labours. From the

MESSRS. ATKINS AND SON'S GLASS FOUNTAIN AND CAMDEN FILTERS.

beautiful show of MEDIÆVAL MANUFACTURES of Messrs. Hardman, of Birmingham, we select a group. In the centre is a grand eagle lectern, of polished brass, with open tracery panels surrounding the shaft. On either side are various articles of plate for ecclesiastical and domestic purposes; comprising chalices, flagons, lamps, alms-dishes, tea and coffee service, claret-jug, grace cup, &c. &c. These articles are of silver, most of them being enriched with gilding, enamels, and jewels. The back-ground of the engraving is composed of a pair of gates, of elaborate design, executed entirely of wrought-iron of the most exquisite finish. These gates were remarked as being perhaps the finest example of wrought-iron work in the Exhibition.

In the EDUCATIONAL DEPARTMENT (Class 29) were a variety of maps, mathematical apparatus, books, natural history collections, drawings and drawing materials, models, toys, &c. Among the prizes awarded by the jurors was one to Messrs. Cassell, Petter, and Galpin, for "the merit of their educational works." Among these works, so commended, the "Popular Educator" holds a prominent position, as one which has attained an almost world-wide reputation. Amid the many aids to education, toys cannot certainly be omitted; and of all descriptions of toys, those which excite wonder and surprise—which instruct while they amuse—which, from their very nature, are not apt to pall from too much familiarity—the toys, in fact, that continually present new features of attraction, are those most popular with all inquiring boys and girls.

Magic and mystery, parlour conjuring and legerdemain, present endless sources of pleasure for young people; and of all the stalls in the Educational Department that of Mr. Henry Novra was generally the most crowded. Our illustration presents some idea of what this exhibitor's stand contained. It shows a series of apparatus displayed upon a mechanical conjuring-table, with the legendary old wizard, in his old attitude, holding sway over the world of magic tricks, conjurations, and puzzling mysteries. By aid of these, any young gentleman or young lady can perform the wondrous feats of magic and prestidigitation which, in the hands of a Houdin, a Jacobs, or an Anderson, always excite the open-eyed wonder of audiences, both young and old. Mr. Novra is the manufacturer and exhibitor of a vast variety of magical apparatus, especially suitable for the amateur juvenile and drawing-room entertainment. He has devoted an earnest and inquiring mind to the perfection of mechanical toys, and, though by no means a public performer, has done much to familiarise the rising generation with such tricks as not only require ingenious concealment of their mechanism, but a certain aptitude in the performance. The marvellous effects produced by public performers are mainly due to the excellence of the mechanism provided for them; but so admirably are Mr. Novra's tricks adapted to the capacities of their performers, that while some are so complicated as to be successfully used only by a "Wizard of the North," others are simple enough to amuse a child.

Messrs. Mead and Powell, of the "Old Mansion House," Cheapside, exhibited a large variety of perambulators, baby-jumpers, rocking-horses, nursery yachts, &c.; together with a large variety of toys and games, all of which are manufactured in the very best style. The rocking-horse is arranged so as to swing without noise, by means of a bar of metal or wood, and kept in position by india-rubber straps, governed by a check strap. This arrangement insures perfect safety and freedom of action.

ORNAMENTAL GATE AND RAILING: MESSRS. R. W. KENNARD AND CO. PRIZE MEDAL.

Having already referred generally to the musical instruments in the Exhibition, it is not necessary to dilate upon the excellence of the pianos exhibited by Messrs. Kirkman and Son, of Soho Square; we introduce an illustration in order to show the beauty of the case merely—its exquisite tone is well known to all who had the pleasure of hearing it played upon. The Oblique Grand was exhibited in the Indian Department. It was seven octaves, from A to A, with under-dampers, repetition action, and all the latest improvements. The rosewood case of this fine instrument was elaborately carved at Madras. The designs and working drawings were sent from England by J. Kirkman and Son; the case was made, and the carvings executed, by the native workmen in the most correct manner. As a specimen of the native Indian skilled labour it is interesting, as showing the ready capability of the native carvers to apply the art in which they excel to any purpose that may be required. The top of this pianoforte is made out of a solid piece of rosewood, without a joint; it is five feet wide, and even in India it is rare to meet with rosewood of such large dimensions.

The automaton singing bird exhibited in the Swiss Court, and known as the PIPING BULLFINCH, is familiar to all frequenters of the Exhibition. Having already mentioned this specimen of ingenious workmanship, we now present his portrait.

The Mechanical Easy Chair, called the EQUILIBRIUM, exhibited by Mr. Sedley, of Regent Street, will commend itself to all who value a comfortable and easily-adjustible seat. This chair was exhibited in Class 30, manufactured in silver, and also in a variety of woods, as well as in iron and brass, and attracted considerable attention. This chair is fully described at page 47.

In the Processes Court few objects were more admired than the GLASS CIRCULATING FOUNTAINS and MOULDED CARBON FILTERS, exhibited by Messrs. T. Atkins and Son, of 62, Fleet Street. These fountains are constructed of glass tubes, and are so arranged that, by a very simple contrivance, water is made to circulate through them in a never-ceasing stream, and in an endless variety of pleasing forms. A novel and wide field for the development and adoption of these newly-invented fountains may, we think, be anticipated. As drawing-room and conservatory ornaments they are unequalled. But they would soon get out of order, and their glass tubes become discoloured and opaque, if the water were not rendered

perfectly free from animal, vegetable, or mineral deposits. This can only be perfectly accomplished, so far as we have seen, by means of the Filters of Moulded Carbon, patented and manufactured by Messrs. Atkins. These filters are superior to any yet introduced; but, like other excellent things in the Exhibition, they were not noticed by the jurors. Our engraving gives a good idea of the general appearance of the Fount in and its surroundings. From the main structure proceeded outlet pipes, from which flowed filtered aerated water for the use of visitors; this water had previously traversed through the glass architecture of the fountain. In glass bottles were displayed various depositions of earth, &c., the residue of filtration; and there were also shown Carbon Filters of many designs and sizes. Altogether, Atkins' Filter Fountain was one of the most original objects in the building.

Next we have an engraving of the beautiful ORNAMENTAL ENTRANCE GATES AND RAILINGS of cast-iron exhibited by Messrs. Kennard and Co., of the Falkirk Iron Works. They were especially manufactured for the Vista Alegre Palace, lately purchased by his Excellency Don José de Salmanca, for her Majesty the Queen of Spain. As a specimen of exquisite casting, nothing finer appeared in Class 31. The same exhibitors also showed verandahs, vases, and other ornaments in cast-iron, as well as drawings of various bridges erected by them in Spain, Italy, and India, and also of the celebrated viaduct at Cremelin, Monmouthshire.

Our last engraving is a VASE OF FLOWERS IN HUMAN HAIR, executed by Mr. I. Wall, of Upper Arcade, Bristol. Of all the objects exhibited in Sub-class C, Class 25, this is the most beautiful and artistic, especially considering the difficulty of working in such a material.

Having arrived thus far in our description of the International Exhibition, nothing now remains but to bring the work to a legitimate conclusion, by the addition to the text of appropriate Indexes, &c. The next number will therefore consist of a beautifully-engraved Frontispiece, a Title, Preface, Index, and List of Illustrations, with a portion of our List of British Prizeholders. This list—which cannot but prove interesting to exhibitors and the public, and greatly enhance the value of the work—will be completed in the following and concluding number of the ILLUSTRATED EXHIBITOR; and thus will our present labours have come to an end.

VASE OF FLOWERS IN HUMAN HAIR.   MR. I. WALL.

www.ingramcontent.com/pod-product-compliance
Lightning Source LLC
Chambersburg PA
CBHW030344270326
41926CB00009B/958